Principles of Small Business Management

Principles of Small Business Management

FIFTH EDITION

TIMOTHY S. HATTEN

Mesa State College

SOUTH-WESTERN
CENGAGE Learning

Australia • Brazil • Japan • Korea • Mexico • Singapore • Spain • United Kingdom • United States

Principles of Small Business Management,
Fifth Edition

Timothy S. Hatten

Vice President of Editorial, Business:
  Jack W. Calhoun

Editor-in-Chief: Melissa Acuña

Senior Acquisitions Editor:
  Michele Rhoades

Developmental Editor: Joanne Dauksewicz

Senior Editorial Assistant: Ruth Belanger

Marketing Director: Keri L. Witman

Senior Marketing Communications
  Manager: Jim Overly

Director, Content and Media Production:
  Barbara Fuller Jacobsen

Content Project Manager: Emily Nesheim

Associate Media Editor: Danny Bolan

Frontlist Buyer, Manufacturing:
  Arethea Thomas

Production Service: Knowledgeworks
  Global Limited

Senior Art Director: Tippy McIntosh

Cover Designer: Patti Hudepohl

Internal Designer: c miller design

Cover Photo Credits:

  B/W Image: iStockphoto

  Color Image: Shutterstock Images / maga

Rights Acquisitions Director:
  Audrey Pettengill

Rights Acquisitions Specialist: John Hill

Cengage Learning WebTutor™ is a trademark of Cengage Learning.

Library of Congress Control Number: 2010940544

International Edition:
ISBN-13: 978-1-111-52522-4
ISBN-10: 1-111-52522-6

Cengage Learning International Offices

Asia
www.cengageasia.com
tel: (65) 6410 1200

Australia/New Zealand
www.cengage.com.au
tel: (61) 3 9685 4111

Brazil
www.cengage.com.br
tel: (55) 11 3665 9900

India
www.cengage.co.in
tel: (91) 11 4364 1111

Latin America
www.cengage.com.mx
tel: (52) 55 1500 6000

UK/Europe/Middle East/Africa
www.cengage.co.uk
tel: (44) 0 1264 332 424

**Represented in Canada by
Nelson Education, Ltd.**
www.nelson.com
tel: (416) 752 9100 / (800) 668 0671

Cengage Learning is a leading provider of customized learning solutions with office locations around the globe, including Singapore, the United Kingdom, Australia, Mexico, Brazil, and Japan. Locate your local office at: **www.cengage.com/global**

For product information: **www.cengage.com/international**
Visit your local office: **www.cengage.com/global**
Visit our corporate website: **www.cengage.com**

Printed in China by China Translation & Printing Services Limited
1 2 3 4 5 6 7 14 13 12 11

To: Jill, Paige, Brittany, and Taylor

Brief Contents

Contents

PART 3   Financial and Legal Management 171

PART 4 **Marketing 251**

PART 5   Management 355

CHAPTER 15

Preface

Are you thinking about starting your own business some day? For many students, preparation for small business ownership begins with a course in small business management. My goal as a teacher (and the purpose of this text) is to help students fulfill their dreams of becoming entrepreneurs and achieving the independence that comes with small business success.

The theme of this book revolves around creating and maintaining a *sustainable competitive advantage* in a small business. Running a small business is difficult in today's rapidly evolving environment. At no other time has it been so important for businesses to hold a competitive advantage. Every chapter in this book can be used to create your competitive advantage—whether it be your idea, your product, your location, or your marketing plan. Running a small business is like being in a race with no finish line. You must continually strive to satisfy the changing wants and needs of your customers. This book can help you run your best race.

The writing style is personal and conversational. I have tried to avoid excessive use of jargon by explaining topics in simple, understandable language. The book is written in the first person, present tense, because I, the author, am speaking directly to you, the student. I believe that a good example can help make even the most complex concept more understandable and interesting to read. To strengthen the flow of the material and reinforce important points, examples have been carefully selected from the business press and small business owners I have known.

New to This Edition

In preparing this fifth edition, I incorporated suggestions from teachers and students who used the previous edition. In addition, an advisory board of educators from around the country helped me determine the best ways to meet the needs of students in this course. Here are some of the changes that have been made in this edition:

- Since small business management courses are so application oriented, special attention has been paid to the cases in the appendix to this text—15 of which are brand new. The actual small business owner's decision and expert commentary are included in the instructor material.
- Topics critical to small business have been added or updated. For example, since the economic recession has lingered like an unwanted houseguest, multiple boxes and examples have been included on running a small business in times of economic downturn.
- Speaking of highlight boxes, they are great for focusing attention, but we understand that there should not be too many of them, nor should they be too long. The best examples of small business practices have been presented in chapter-opening vignettes and feature boxes, then discussed further in the body of the text. Of the 68 highlight boxes, 57 are brand new, and the 11 others have been updated. Of the 18 chapter openers, all 18 are brand new.
- Every effort has been made to prevent "new edition bloat." Attention has been paid to items to delete and not just to add in order to stay current and streamlined.

Highlight Feature Boxes

To highlight important issues in small business management, four types of boxed features are used: *Entrepreneurial Snapshot*, *Manager's Notes*, *Reality Check*, and *Competitive Advantage: Innovation and Sustainability*. In this edition, the number of boxes was reduced to avoid reader confusion, and the length of boxes was shortened to hold the reader's attention. (Believe it or not, a rumor exists that some students actually skip reading these highlight boxes. Of course, you would never do this, as you would miss some of the juiciest stories.) Here are some examples of each type of highlight box:

Entrepreneurial Snapshot New to this fifth edition, these boxes reveal fascinating behind-the-scenes stories of people who have created some very interesting businesses. Examples include:

- Kevin Plank, creator of Under Armour
- Tom Szaky, founder of TerraCycle
- Thomas Edison, über inventor
- Norm Brodsky, entrepreneur of multiple businesses and *Inc.* magazine columnist
- Eliot and Barry Tattleman, of Jordan's Furniture
- Chuck & C. J. Buck, of Buck Knives
- Lorena Garcia, Big Chef Little Chef

Competitive Advantage: Innovation and Sustainability One of the most important (if not *the* most important) things you create in your small business is your competitive advantage—the factor that you manage better than everyone else. There are many ways to create a competitive advantage, and these boxes point out some of the most interesting:

- Competitive Intelligence
- Creative Release
- Negotiation Fine Points
- Economic Action Downturn
- Guppy in a Shark Tank: Small Business, Big Trade Shows
- Perks That Small Businesses Can Afford

Manager's Notes These features include specific tips, tactics, and actions used by successful small business owners:

- Small Business Readiness Assessment
- Business Plan Competition Tips
- Franchise Facts
- Business Valuation
- Letter of Confidentiality
- Small Business Dashboards—Computerized Accounting Packages
- Ask Your Banker
- Keep Your Trademark in Shape
- Making Decisions with GIS
- Sixty-Second Guide to Hiring
- Firing an Employee

Reality Check These real-world stories come from streetwise business practitioners who know how it's done and are willing to share the secrets of their success:

- College Students as Entrepreneurs
- Green Is Gold
- Feasibility Study

- Do You Have a Business or Hobby?
- Open-Book Management
- Urban Survival Shoes
- Recession Proof Your Small Business
- Slotting Fees: Unfair for Small Businesses?
- Credit Card Startup Funding
- Incubation Innovation
- Search Engine Optimization
- Even in a Recession—Don't Give Away the Farm
- China—Here We Come … or Not
- Working with Gen Yers

Effective Pedagogical Aids

The pedagogical features of this book are designed to complement, supplement, and reinforce material from the body of the text. The following features enhance critical thinking and show practical small business applications:

- *Chapter opening vignettes*, *Reality Checks*, and extensive use of examples throughout the book show you what *real* small businesses are doing.
- Each chapter begins with *Learning Objectives*, which directly correlate to the chapter topic headings and coverage. These same objectives are then revisited and identified in each *Chapter Summary*.
- A *running glossary* in the margin brings attention to important terms as they appear in the text.
- *Questions for Review and Discussion* allow you to assess your retention and comprehension of the chapter concepts.
- *Questions for Critical Thinking* prompt you to apply what you have learned to realistic situations.
- End-of-chapter *What Would You Do?* exercises are included to stimulate effective problem solving and classroom discussion.
- *Chapter Cases* (found in the text appendix) present actual business scenarios, allowing you to think critically about the management challenges presented and to further apply chapter concepts.

Complete Package of Support Materials

This edition of *Principles of Small Business Management* provides a support package that will encourage student success and increase instructor effectiveness.

Instructor's Resource Website This instructor's website, www.cengage.com/international, provides a variety of teaching resources in electronic format, allowing for easy customization to meet specific instructional needs. Files include Lecture PowerPoint® slides, PDF files from the Instructor's Manual, and the Test Bank Word files, along with ExamView, the computerized version of the Test Bank.

The comprehensive *Instructor's Resource Manual* includes teaching tips for each chapter, additional activities and supplemental content, lecture outlines with special teaching notes, suggested answers to end-of-chapter Questions for Review and Discussion and Questions for Critical Thinking, and comments on the What Would You Do? exercises and the chapter case and case questions (found in the text appendix). A Video Guide is also included at the end of the manual.

The *Test Bank* provides true/false, multiple-choice, mini-case, and essay questions, along with an answer key that includes the learning objective covered. *ExamView*, a computerized version of the Test Bank, provides instructors with all the tools they need to create, author/edit, customize, and deliver multiple types of tests. Instructors can import questions directly from the test bank, create their own questions, or edit existing questions.

CourseMate This new and unique online Web site makes course concepts come alive with interactive learning, study, and exam preparation tools supporting the printed text. CourseMate delivers what students need, including an interactive eBook, dynamic flashcards, interactive quizzes and video exercises, student PowerPoints, and games that test knowledge in a fun way.

- **Engagement Tracker**, a first-of-its-kind tool, monitors individual or group student engagement, progress, and comprehension in your course.
- **Interactive video exercises** allow students to relate the real-world events and issues shown in the chapter videos to specific in-text concepts.
- **Interactive quizzes** reinforce the text with rejoinders that refer back to the section of the chapter where the concept is discussed.

Instructor Companion Site The Instructor Companion Site can be found at www.cengage.com/international. It includes a complete Instructor Manual, Word files from both the Instructor Manual and Test Bank, and PowerPoint slides for easy downloading.

Student Companion Site The Student Companion Site includes interactive quizzes, a glossary, crossword puzzles, and sample student business plans. It can be found at www.cengagebrain.com. At the home page, students can use the search box at the top of the page to insert the ISBN of the title (from the back cover of their book). This will take them to the product page, where free companion resources can be found.

DVD This diverse collection of professionally produced videos can help instructors bring lectures to life by providing thought-provoking insights into real-world companies, products, and issues.

Acknowledgments

There are so many people to thank—some who made this book possible, some who made it better. Projects of this magnitude do not happen in a vacuum. Even though my name is on the cover, a lot of talented people contributed their knowledge and skills.

George Hoffman, Lynn Guza, Natalie Anderson, and Ellin Derrick all played key roles in the book's history. Michele Rhoades has been visionary and insightful as the acquisitions editor in bringing this book into the Cengage list. I am so fortunate to have been reunited with Joanne Dauksewicz as my patient, nurturing development editor—she is fabulous. Emily Nesheim, content project manager, and Devanand Srinivasan, senior project manager, were wonderful in coordinating the production process. There are many other people whose names I unfortunately do not know who worked their magic in helping to make the beautiful book you hold in your hands, and I sincerely thank them all. Of course, the entire group of Cengage sales reps will have a major impact on the success of this book. I appreciate all of their efforts. Thanks to Morgan Bridge and other faculty contributors.

I am especially grateful to Professor Amit Shah, Frostburg State University, for his help with the electronic ancillary program. I would also like to thank the many colleagues who have reviewed this text and provided feedback concerning their needs and their students' needs:

Tim Allwine, *Lower Columbia College*

Allen C. Amason, *University of Georgia*

Godwin Ariguzo, *University of Massachusetts–Dartmouth*

Walter H. Beck Sr., *Reinhardt College*

Joseph Bell, *University of Arkansas at Little Rock*

Rudy Butler, *Trenton State College*

J. Stephen Childers Jr., *Radford University*

Michael Cicero, *Highline Community College*

John Cipolla, *Lynn University*

Richard Cuba, *University of Baltimore*

Gary M. Donnelly, *Casper College*

Peter Eimer, *D'Youville College*

Vena Garrett, *Orange Coast College*

Arlen Gastinau, *Valencia Community College West*

Caroline Glackin, *Delaware State University*

Doug Hamilton, *Berkeley College of Business*

Gerald Hollier, *University of Texas at Brownsville*

David Hudson, *Spalding University*

Philip G. Kearney, *Niagara County Community College*

Paul Keaton, *University of Wisconsin–La Crosse*

Mary Beth Klinger, *College of Southern Maryland*

Paul Lamberson, *University of Southern Mississippi–Hattiesburg*

MaryLou Lockerby, *College of Dupage–Glen Ellyn*

Anthony S. Marshall, *Columbia College*

Carl McClain, *Palomar College*

Norman D. McElvany, *Johnson State College*

Milton Miller, *Carteret Community College–Morehead City*

Bill Motz, *Lansing Community College*

Suzy Murray, *Piedmont Technical College*

James C. Nicholas, *University of Bridgeport*

Grantley E. Nurse, *Raritan Valley Community College*

Cliff Olson, *Southern Adventist University*

Roger A. Pae, *Cuyahoga Community College*

Nancy Payne, *College of Dupage–Glen Ellyn*

Michael Pitts, *Virginia Commonwealth University*

Julia Truitt Poynter, *Transylvania University*

George B. Roorbach, *Lyndon State College*

Marty St. John, *Westmoreland County College*

Joe Salamone, *SUNY Buffalo*

Tom Sgritta, *University of North Carolina, Charlotte*

Gary Shields, *Wayne State University*

Pradip Shukla, *Chapman University*

Joseph Simon, *Caspar College*

Bernard Skown, *Stevens Institute of Technology*

William Soukoup, *University of San Diego*

David Steck, *Hillsborough Community College*

Jim Steele, *Chattanooga State Technical Community College*

Ray Sumners, *Westwood College of Technology*

Sharon A. Taylor, *Colorado Community Colleges Online*

Charles Tofloy, *George Washington University*

Jon Tomlinson, *University of Northwestern Ohio*

Barrry Van Hook, *Arizona State University*

Mike Wakefield, *Colorado State University–Pueblo*

Warren Weber, *California Polytechnic State University*

John Withey, *Indiana University*

Alan Zieber, *Portland State University*

Finally, my family: Saying thanks and giving acknowledgment to my family members is not enough, given the patience, sacrifice, and inspiration they have provided. My wife, Jill; daughters, Paige and Brittany; and son, Taylor, are the best. The perseverance and work ethic needed for a job of this magnitude were instilled in me by my father, Drexel, and mother, Marjorie—now gone but never forgotten.

Timothy S. Hatten

About the Author

Timothy S. Hatten is a professor at Mesa State College in Grand Junction, Colorado, where he has served as the chair of business administration and director of the MBA

Courtesy of Tim Hatten

program. He is currently codirector of the Entrepreneurial Business Institute. He received his PhD from the University of Missouri–Columbia, his MS from Central Missouri State University, and his BA from Western State College in Gunnison, Colorado. He is a Fulbright Scholar. He taught small business management and entrepreneurship at Reykjavik University in Iceland and business planning at the Russian-American Business Center in Magadan, Russia.

Dr. Hatten has been passionate about small and family businesses his whole life. He grew up with the family-owned International Harvester farm equipment dealership in Bethany, Missouri, which his father started. Later, he owned and managed a Chevrolet/Buick/Cadillac dealership with his father, Drexel, and brother, Gary.

Since entering academia, Dr. Hatten has actively brought students and small businesses together through the Small Business Institute program. He counsels and leads small business seminars through the Business Incubation Center in Grand Junction, Colorado. He approached writing this textbook as if it were a small business. His intent was to make a product (in this case, a book) that would benefit his customers (students and faculty).

Dr. Hatten is fortunate to live on the Western Slope of Colorado, where he has the opportunity to share his love of the mountains with his family.

Please send questions, comments, and suggestions to thatten@mesastate.edu.

## PART 1

Introduction to Small Business Management

Chapter 1
An Overview of Small Business

Chapter 2
Management, Entrepreneurship, and Ownership

When most people think of American business, corporate giants like General Motors, IBM, and Walmart generally come to mind first. There is no question that the companies that make up the *Fortune 500* control vast resources, products, and services that set world standards and employ many people. But as you will discover in these first two chapters, small businesses and the entrepreneurs who start them play a vital role in the American economy. **Chapter 1** illustrates the economic and social impact of small businesses. **Chapter 2** discusses the process and factors related to entrepreneurship.

1

An Overview of Small Business

CHAPTER LEARNING OUTCOMES

After reading this chapter, you should be able to:

1. Describe the characteristics of small business.

2. Recognize the role of small business in the U.S. economy.

3. Understand the importance of diversity in the marketplace and the workplace.

4. Identify some of the opportunities available to small businesses.

5. Suggest ways to court success in a small business venture.

6. Name the most common causes of small business failure.

E ntrepreneurs are people who often think big...they occasionally end up making a change in the world...and they usually have a lot of confidence. Elon Musk is a guy who does all of the above—and he's still in his thirties.

Musk is co-founder and chairman of Tesla Motors, maker of the world's only pure electric, high-performance cars. Most alternative fuel vehicles are thought of as being both style and performance challenged. Not the Tesla. The initial model, a two-seater road-ster, goes from zero to 60 miles per hour in a screaming 3.7 seconds while producing zero emissions. It also sports a very cool carbon-fiber body and will travel over 300 miles between charges. The four-door family-oriented model still goes from zero to 60 in 5.7 seconds. Not bad for a grocery hauler.

In addition to Tesla Motors, Musk is chief technology officer for SpaceX, one of the most advanced private companies building rockets for space transportation—ultimately aiming to establish a colony on Mars. The U.S. government takes Musk seriously: as the National Aeronautics and Space Administration (NASA) phases out the space shuttle program, it awarded SpaceX a $1.6 billion contract to haul cargo to the space station. Oh, and by the way, Musk is also building professionalism and efficiency into the home solar energy systems with his company SolarCity.

How does a person accomplish so much so young? Musk has always been an entrepreneur. At 12 years of age, growing up in South Africa, Elon created a video game titled Blaster and sold it to a computer magazine for the unheard of sum of $500. Later in life, after graduating with bachelor degrees in finance and physics, he was headed for grad school at Stanford with $2,000, a car, a computer, and no friends in the Bay Area. Instead of getting his PhD, he founded a company called Zip2, which he sold two years later for $307 million in cash to Compaq. Rather than living easy and large on the $22 million in his pocket, Musk looked at the problem of getting paid for transactions online. He created the company PayPal, changing the

© AFP PHOTO/Robyn BECK/Newscom

way we pay for stuff for Internet purchases, and sold it to eBay a couple of years later for $1.5 billion.

Elon Musk is a shining example of a serial entrepreneur (starting business after business) who builds innovative businesses which begin small, grow in size and impact, create much-needed jobs, and change the way we live. His accomplishments earned him the title Automotive Executive of the Year Innovator Award for 2010.

Sources: Lee Hawkins, "Tesla's Long Haul," *The Wall Street Journal*, January 12, 2010; Ben Oliver, "CAR Meets the World's Coolest Geek" *CAR*, March 5, 2010, 113; John O'Dell, "Tesla Roadster Logs New Record," *www.edmunds.com*, October 27, 2009; Max Chafkin, "Entrepreneur of the Year—Elon Musk," *Inc.*, December 2007, 115–125; Michael Copeland, "Tesla's Wild Ride," *Fortune*, July 21, 2008, 82–94; Ronald Grover, "To the Moon: Elon Musk's High-Power Visions," *BusinessWeek Online*, October 14, 2009, 18; and Dave Guilford, "Tesla's Tiny—But CEO Is Full of Confidence," *Automotive News*, October 21, 2009, 38.

What Is Small Business?

As the driver of the free enterprise system, small business generates a great deal of energy, innovation, and profit for millions of Americans. While the names of huge *Fortune* 500 corporations may be household words pumped into our lives via a multitude of media, small businesses have always been a central part of American life. In his 1835 book *Democracy in America*, Alexis de Tocqueville commented, "What astonishes me in the United States is not so much the marvellous grandeur of some undertakings as the innumerable multitude of small ones." If de Tocqueville were alive today, aside from being more than 200 years old, he would probably still be amazed at the contributions made by small businesses.

The U.S. Small Business Administration (SBA) Office of Advocacy estimates that there were 26.8 million businesses in the United States in 2006. Census data show that 22 percent of those 26.8 million businesses have employees, and 78 percent do not.[1] The IRS estimate may be overstated because one business can own other businesses, but all of the businesses are nevertheless counted separately. What a great time to be in (and be studying) small business! Check out the following facts. Did you realize that small businesses:

- Represent more than 99.7 percent of *all* employers?
- Employ more than half of all private sector employees?
- Pay 44 percent of total U.S. private payroll?
- Created 64 percent of net new jobs over the past 15 years?
- Represented 97.3 percent of all identified exporters and produced 30.2 percent of the known export value in FY 2007?
- Produce 13 times more patents per employee than large firms?
- Create more than 50 percent of private gross domestic product (GDP)?
- Hire 40 percent of high-tech workers (such as scientists, engineers, and computer programmers)?
- Are 52 percent home based and 2 percent franchises?[2]

Small businesses include everything from the stay-at-home parent who provides day care for other children, to the factory worker who makes after-hours deliveries, to the owner of a chain of fast-food restaurants. The 26.8 million businesses identified by the SBA included more than 9 million Americans who operate "sideline" businesses, part-time enterprises that supplement the owner's income.[3] Another 12 million people make owning and operating a small business their primary occupation. Seven million of these business owners employ only themselves—as carpenters, independent sales representatives, freelance writers, and other types of single-person businesses. The U.S. Census Bureau tracks firms by number of employees. These data show that approximately 5.9 million firms hire employees, and 19.5 million firms exist with no employees.[4] The firms included in the census figures are those that have a tangible location and claim income on a tax return. Figure 1.1 shows that 61 percent of employer firms (established firms with employees) have fewer than 5 employees. Slightly more than 100,000 businesses have 100 employees or more. Most people are surprised to learn that of the millions of businesses in the United States, only approximately 17,000 businesses have 500 or more workers on their payroll.

small business

A business is generally considered small if it is independently owned, operated, and financed; has fewer than 100 employees; and has relatively little impact on its industry.

Size Definitions

The definition of **small business** depends on the criteria for determining what is "small" and what qualifies as a "business." The most common criterion used to distinguish

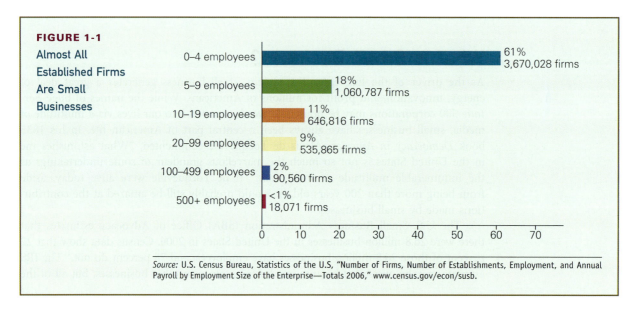

FIGURE 1-1

Almost All Established Firms Are Small Businesses

Employees	Percent / Firms
0–4 employees	61% / 3,670,028 firms
5–9 employees	18% / 1,060,787 firms
10–19 employees	11% / 646,816 firms
20–99 employees	9% / 535,865 firms
100–499 employees	2% / 90,560 firms
500+ employees	<1% / 18,071 firms

Source: U.S. Census Bureau, Statistics of the U.S, "Number of Firms, Number of Establishments, Employment, and Annual Payroll by Employment Size of the Enterprise—Totals 2006," www.census.gov/econ/susb.

between large and small businesses is the number of employees. Other criteria include sales revenue, the total value of assets, and the value of owners' equity. The SBA, a federally funded agency that provides loans and assistance to small businesses, has established definitions of business size that vary by industry. These definitions are based on annual sales revenues or number of employees, and they vary by industry codes assigned by the North American Industrial Classification System (NAICS).

The SBA's Size Policy Board makes recommendations of business size eligibility based on economic studies. In establishing and reviewing business size standards, it considers the following factors:

- Industry structure analysis
- Degree of competition
- Average firm size
- Start-up cost
- Entry barriers, distribution of sales, and employment by firm size
- Effects of different size standard levels on the objectives of SBA programs
- Comments from the public on notices of proposed rule making[5]

Small business size standards vary by the industry within which the business operates: construction, manufacturing, mining, transportation, wholesale trade, retail trade, and service. In general, manufacturers with fewer than 500 employees are classified

TABLE 1-1 Small Business Size Standards	RANGE OF SIZE STANDARDS BY INDUSTRY
	Construction: General building and heavy construction contractors have a size standard of $31 million in average annual receipts. Special trade construction contractors have a size standard of $13 million.
	Manufacturing: For approximately 75 percent of the manufacturing industries, the size standard is 500 employees. A small number have a 1,500-employee size standard, and the balance have a size standard of either 750 or 1,000 employees.
	Mining: All mining industries, except mining services, have a size standard of 500 employees.
	Retail Trade: Most retail trade industries have a size standard of $6.5 million in average annual receipts. A few, such as grocery stores, department stores, motor vehicle dealers, and electrical appliance dealers, have higher size standards. None exceed $26.5 million in annual receipts.
	Services: For the service industries, the most common size standard is $6.5 million in average annual receipts. Computer programming, data processing, and systems design have a size standard of $23 million. Engineering and architectural services have different size standards, as do a few other service industries. The highest annual receipts size standard in any service industry is $32.5 million. Research and development and environmental remediation services are the only service industries with size standards stated in number of employees.
	Wholesale Trade: For all wholesale trade industries, a size standard of 100 employees is applicable for loans and other financial programs. When acting as a dealer on federal contracts set aside for small business or issued under the *8(a) program,* the size standard is 500 employees, and the firm must deliver the product of a small domestic manufacturer.
	Other Industries: Other industry divisions include agriculture; transportation, communications, electric, gas, and sanitary services; finance; insurance; and real estate. Because of wide variations in the structures of the industries in these divisions, there is no common pattern of size standards. For specific size standards, refer to the size regulations in 13 CFR § 121.201 or the table of small business size standards.

Source: Small Business Administration, "Guide to SBA's Definitions of Small Business—Summary of Size Standards by Industry Division," www.sba.gov/size/indexguide.html.

as small, as are wholesalers with fewer than 100 employees, and retailers or services with less than $6 million in annual revenue. Table 1.1 details more specific size standards.

Why is it important to classify businesses as big or small? Aside from facilitating academic discussion of the contributions made by these businesses, the classifications are important in that they determine whether a business may qualify for SBA assistance and for government set-aside programs, which require a percentage of each government agency's purchases to be made from small businesses.

Types of Industries

Some industries lend themselves to small business operation more than others do. In construction, for instance, 90 percent of companies in the industry are classified as small by the SBA. Manufacturing and mining industries have long been associated with mass employment, as well as mass production, yet SBA data show that 30 percent of manufacturers and mining companies are classified as small. More than 64 percent of all retail businesses are small, employing about 15 million people in selling goods to their ultimate consumers. More than three out of every four arts, entertainment, and recreational service businesses are small.[6]

The industry that employs the largest number of people in small business, however, is services. Seventy-one percent of all service businesses are small. More than 28 million people are employed by small businesses that provide a broad range of services from restaurants to lawn care to telecommunications. As indicated by industry percentages and by sheer numbers of employees, small businesses are important to every industry sector (see Figure 1.2).

For purposes of discussion in this book, we will consider a business to be small if it meets the following criteria:

- *It is independently owned, operated, and financed.* One or very few people run the business.

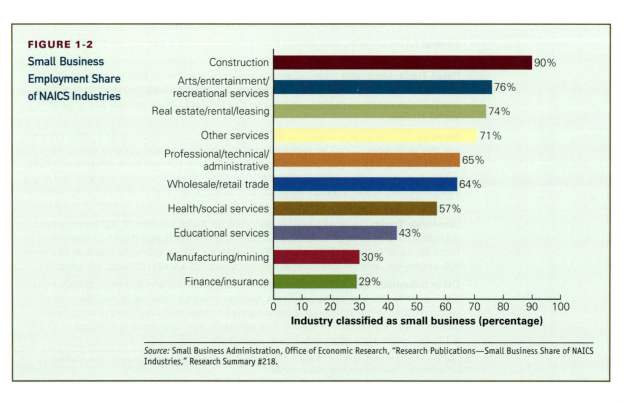

FIGURE 1-2

Small Business Employment Share of NAICS Industries

Industry classified as small business (percentage)

Industry	Percentage
Construction	90%
Arts/entertainment/recreational services	76%
Real estate/rental/leasing	74%
Other services	71%
Professional/technical/administrative	65%
Wholesale/retail trade	64%
Health/social services	57%
Educational services	43%
Manufacturing/mining	30%
Finance/insurance	29%

Source: Small Business Administration, Office of Economic Research, "Research Publications—Small Business Share of NAICS Industries," Research Summary #218.

- *It has fewer than 100 employees.* Although SBA standards allow 500 or more employees for some types of businesses to qualify as "small," the most common limit is 100.
- *It has relatively little impact on its industry.* Tesla Motors, described in the chapter opener, had annual revenue of $200 million for 2009. Although this is an impressive figure, the firm is still classified as a small business because it has little influence on Toyota or General Motors, which had 2009 sales of $211 billion and $149 billion, respectively.[7]

Small Businesses in the U.S. Economy

Until the early 1800s, all businesses were small in the way just described. Most goods were produced one at a time by workers in their cottages or in small artisan studios. Much of the U.S. economy was based on agriculture. With the Industrial Revolution, however, mass production became possible. Innovations such as Samuel Slater's textile machinery, Eli Whitney's cotton gin, and Samuel Colt's use of interchangeable parts in producing firearms changed the way business was conducted. Factories brought people, raw materials, and machinery together to produce large quantities of goods.

Although the early manufacturers were small, by the late 1800s businesses were able to grow rapidly in industries that relied on economies of scale for their profitability. *Economy of scale* is the lowering of costs through production of larger quantities: The more units you make, the less each costs. During this time, for example, Andrew Carnegie founded U.S. Steel, Henry Ford introduced the assembly line for manufacturing automobiles, and Cornelius Vanderbilt speculated in steamships and railroads. Although these individuals had begun as entrepreneurs, their companies eventually came to dominate their respective industries. The costs of competing with them became prohibitively high as the masses of capital they had accumulated formed a barrier to entry for newcomers to the industry. The subsequent industrialization of America decreased the impact of new entrepreneurs over the first half of the twentieth century.[8] Small businesses still existed during this period, of course, but the economic momentum that large businesses had gathered kept small businesses in minor roles.

The decades following World War II also favored big business over small business. Industrial giants like General Motors and IBM, and retailers like Sears, Roebuck and Co., flourished during this period by tapping into the expanding consumer economy.

In the late 1950s and early 1960s, another economic change began. Businesses began paying more attention to consumer wants and needs, rather than focusing solely on production. This paradigm shift was called the **marketing concept**—finding out what people want and then producing that good or service, rather than making products and then trying to convince people to buy them. With this shift came an increased importance ascribed to the service economy. The emphasis on customer service by businesses adopting the marketing concept started to provide more opportunities for small business. Today, the **service sector** of our economy makes up about 60 percent of total U.S. jobs, producing services for customers rather than tangible products. The growth of this sector is important to small businesses because they can compete effectively in it.

By the early 1970s, corporate profits had begun to decline, while these large firms' costs increased. Entrepreneurs such as Steve Jobs of Apple Computer and Bill Gates of Microsoft started small businesses and created entirely new industries that had never before existed. Managers began to realize that bigger is not necessarily better and that economy of scale does not guarantee lower costs. Other start-ups, such as Walmart and The Limited, both of which were founded in the 1960s, dealt serious blows to retail giants like Sears in the 1970s. Because their organizational structures were flatter, the newer companies could respond more quickly to customers' changing desires, and they were more flexible in changing their products and services.

"Managers began to realize that bigger is not necessarily better and that economy of scale does not guarantee lower costs."

marketing concept
The business philosophy of discovering what consumers want and then providing the good or service that will satisfy their needs.

service sector
Businesses that provide services, rather than tangible goods.

A new term entered the business vocabulary during the 1990s that continues to affect the business world today—**downsizing**. Downsizing can involve the reduction of a business's workforce to shore up dwindling profits. It can also stem from a business's decision to concentrate on what it does best. Any segment of a business in which its owner does not have special skills can be put up for sale, eliminated, or sent out for someone else to do (*outsourced*). The effects of downsizing and outsourcing on small business are twofold. First, many people who lose their jobs with large businesses start small businesses of their own. Second, these new businesses often do the work that large businesses no longer perform themselves—temporary employment, cleaning services, and independent contracting, for example. While downsizing and outsourcing are often painful to the displaced individuals, they ultimately enhance the productivity and competitiveness of companies.[9]

The global economic crisis that began in 2007–2010 has had a tremendous impact on small business. Disruption of small business financing is significant due to the close connection between the business and owner—including home second mortgages and lines of credit, putting the small business owner's home in play in case of loan default. Tactics for small business owners to deal with the credit squeeze revolve primarily around protecting cash flow to decrease dependence on external funding. As of mid-2010, small business funding has not eased.[10] Tactics for small businesses to weather the economic storm will be found in several chapters of this new edition, including:

- Finding opportunities that are recession resistant
- Jettisoning the bottom 10 percent of problem customers
- Protecting cash—in multiple ways
- Enhancing small business image
- Building and enhancing relationships
- Cross-training employees
- Getting pricing correct

Increased Business Start-ups   Indeed, the rate of small business growth has more than doubled in the last 30 years. In 1970, 264,000 new businesses were started.[11] In 1980, that figure had grown to 532,000; it reached 585,000 in 1990, 574,000 in 2000, and 670,100 in 2006.[12] Although a lot of attention tends to be paid to the failure rate of small businesses, many people continue going into business for themselves. New businesses compared with closures are consistently close in number. For example, in 2005 there were 670,100 new starts and 599,300 closures—each representing about 10 percent of the total.[13]

Increasing Interest at Colleges and Universities   The growing economic importance of small business has not escaped notice on college and university campuses. In 1971, only 16 schools in the United States offered courses in entrepreneurship. By 2010 that number had grown to 2,000.[14] Other evidence of increased interest in entrepreneurship education at U.S. colleges and universities and those in other countries is the proliferation of centers for entrepreneurship, student-run business incubators, and endowed faculty entrepreneurship positions—406 in the United States and 563 worldwide.[15]

"In 1971, only 16 schools in the United States offered courses in entrepreneurship. By 2010 that number had grown to 2,000."

What can explain this phenomenal growth of interest in small business at educational institutions? For one thing, it parallels the explosion in small business formation. For another thing, since mistakes made in running a small business are expensive in terms of both time and money, many prospective business owners attend school in order to make those mistakes on paper and not in reality.

Some students don't wait for graduation to take advantage of hot college trends—such as Ryan Dickerson, a junior at Syracuse University, who found his dorm room to be more than a little cramped. But the son of an interior designer knew he just needed a little creativity in optimizing the space. Dickerson created the "bed transforming pillow" to

© Image copyright mangostock 2010. Used under license from Shutterstock.com

Small business ownership provides satisfaction and pride of ownership regardless of background.

convert his single bed into a couch during the day. Thus, Rylaxing was born in 2009. Both the three-foot-long halfback and the six-foot fullback come in a variety of colors (including cheetah print). After a year selling on his own campus, Ryan plans to sell at colleges across the country.[16]

Workforce Diversity and Small Business Ownership

Data from the Census Bureau Survey of Business Owners (SBO) and Bureau of Labor Statistics show that self-employment rose 12.2 percent from 1995 to 2004. Women's self-employment increased 20 percent over the same period. The trend toward self-employment is reflected in all nonwhite categories by large percentage gains, although in 2004, white Americans still constituted most of the self-employed—88.3 percent.[17] Trends of an aging population, increasing birthrate of minority groups, more attention to the needs and abilities of people with handicaps, and more women entering the workforce are changing the way our nation and our businesses operate. The intent of most civil rights laws (see Chapter 10) is to ensure that all groups are represented and that discrimination is not tolerated. Wheels of change tend to move slowly, and inequities persist for all groups of people, but progress is being made, especially among the self-employed.

Within the SBA's Office of Advocacy, the Office of Economic Research produces reports on the economic activity of small minority- and women-owned firms and assesses the effects of regulation on them. Its report "Dynamics of Minority-Owned Employer Establishments, 1997–2001" (see this report and "Women in Business, 2006" at www.sba.gov/advo/stats) reviewed the most recent available statistical information on minority-owned firms, their composition, industrial distribution, legal forms of ownership, growth, and turnover. It also looked at socioeconomic characteristics of minority business owners. The report suggested that although minority-owned businesses are vital to the growth of the U.S. economy, significant issues continue to hamper their growth. Some statistics from the report follow:

- The number of minority-owned firms and their annual revenues were as follows:[18]

    - Asian-owned firms totalled 1,103,587 and generated $326.7 billion annual revenue.
    - Black-owned firms totalled 1,197,567 and generated $88.6 billion annual revenue.
    - Hispanic-owned businesses totalled 1,573,464 and generated $222 billion annual revenue.
    - American Indian/Alaska Native-owned firms totalled 201,387 and generated $26.9 billion annual revenue.
    - Native Hawaiian- and other Pacific Islander-owned firms totalled 28,948 and generated $4.3 billion annual revenue.

- Of all U.S. businesses, 5.8 percent were owned by Hispanic Americans, 4.4 percent by Asian Americans, 4.0 percent by African Americans, and 0.9 percent by American Indians.

- Of minority-owned businesses, 39.5 percent were Hispanic owned, 30.0 percent Asian owned, 27.1 percent African American owned, and 6.5 percent American Indian owned.
- *Business density*—the number of individuals in the population divided by the number of businesses in the population, with the lower the number indicating the higher the density—was 10.1 for nonminorities, 11.7 for Asians and Pacific Islanders, 12.6 for American Indians and Alaska Natives, 29.4 for Hispanics, and 42.1 for African Americans. Among Asians, Koreans had the highest business density, and "other Pacific Islanders" had the lowest. Among Hispanics, Spaniards had the highest, and Puerto Ricans the lowest.
- During 1997–2001, 27.4 percent of nonwhite businesses expanded their operations, compared with 34 percent of Hispanic-owned employer establishments, 32.1 percent of Asian/Pacific Islander-owned businesses, 27.8 percent of American Indian/Alaska Native-owned establishments, and 25.7 percent of African American-owned businesses.
- SBA data show that the four-year survival rate for nonminority-owned businesses was 72.6 percent between 1997 and 2001. Those for minority-owned businesses were 72.1 percent for Asian/Pacific Islander-owned businesses, 68.6 percent for Hispanic-owned businesses, 67 percent for American Indian/Native Alaskan-owned businesses, and 61 percent for African American-owned businesses.[19]

Now consider some of the findings of businesses owned by women, summarized in several SBA Office of Advocacy reports:

- Various measures of the number of women-owned businesses exist, including measures of self-employment and business tax returns. Women owned more than 50 percent of 5.4 million businesses in 2001.
- The 6.5 million women-owned businesses generated $940.8 billion in revenues in 2002, employed more than 7.1 million workers, and had nearly $173.7 billion in payroll in 2002.
- In addition, another 2.7 million firms are owned equally by both women and men; these firms add another $731.4 billion in revenues and employ another 5.7 million workers.
- Women-owned businesses represented 28.2 percent of all nonfarm businesses in the United States.
- In 1998, of all U.S. sole proprietorships, 37 percent were operated by women. Women-operated businesses generated 18 percent of total business receipts and 22 percent of net income.
- Women-owned businesses were concentrated in the wholesale and retail trade and manufacturing industries.
- Women's share of total self-employment increased from 22 percent in 1976 to 33.6 percent in 2004.
- Compared with non-Hispanic white business owners, of whom 28 percent were women, minority groups in the United States had larger shares of women business owners, ranging from 31 percent of Asian American to 46 percent of African American business owners.[20]

"These data show that when faced with the choice of working for someone else or working for themselves, people from widely varied backgrounds choose the latter."

These data show that when faced with the choice of working for someone else or working for themselves, people from widely varied backgrounds choose the latter.

Resources exist to specifically assist women- and minority-owned businesses. The SBA 8(a) federal certification program promotes access for entrepreneurs who are socially or economically disadvantaged to federal contracts. SBA 8(a) certification provides women and minority business owners preference in bidding on federal and some state contracts. Professional organizations such as the National Association of Women Business Owners (nawbo.org) and Women's Business Enterprise National Council (wbenc.org) provide networking, educational, and corporate contract information.[21]

The Value of Diversity to Business

Considering the number of problems that most small business owners face, perhaps more of them will make the same discovery that Ernest Drew did in the following story: Diversity in the workplace can provide creative problem-solving ideas.

Ernest Drew, CEO of chemical producer Hoechst Celanese, learned the value of diversity during a company conference. A group of 125 top company officials, primarily white men, was separated into groups with 50 women and minority employees. Some of the groups comprised a variety of races and genders; others were composed of white men only. The groups were asked to analyze a problem concerning corporate culture and suggest ways to change it. According to Drew, the more diverse teams produced the broadest solutions. "They had ideas I hadn't even thought of," he recalled. "For the first time, we realized that diversity is a strength as it relates to problem solving."[22] Drew's conclusion that a varied workforce is needed at every level of an organization can be applied to businesses of any size.

Secrets of Small Business Success

When large and small businesses compete directly against one another, it might seem that large businesses would always have a better chance of winning. In reality, small businesses have certain inherent factors that work in their favor. You will improve your chances of achieving success in running a small business if you identify your competitive advantage, remain flexible and innovative, cultivate a close relationship with your customers, and strive for quality.

It may come as a surprise, but big businesses need small businesses—a symbiotic relationship exists between them. For instance, John Deere relies on hundreds of vendors, many of which are small, to produce component parts for its farm equipment. Deere's extensive network of 3,400 independent dealers comprising small businesses provides sales and service for its equipment. These relationships enable Deere, the world's largest manufacturer of farm equipment, to focus on what it does best, while at the same time creating economic opportunity for hundreds of individual entrepreneurs.

Small businesses perform more efficiently than larger ones in several areas. For example, although large manufacturers tend to enjoy a higher profit margin due to their economies of scale, small businesses are often better at distribution. Most wholesale and retail businesses are small, which serves to link large manufacturers more efficiently with the millions of consumers spread all over the world.

"It may come as a surprise, but big businesses need small businesses—a symbiotic relationship exists between them."

Competitive Advantage

To be successful in business, you have to offer your customers more value than your competitors do. That value gives the business its ***competitive advantage***. For example, suppose you are a printer whose competitors offer only black-and-white printing. An investment in color printing equipment would give your business a competitive advantage, at least until your competitors purchased similar equipment. The stronger and more sustainable your competitive advantage, the better your chances are of winning and keeping customers. You must have a product or service that your business provides better than

competitive advantage
The facet of a business that is better than the competition's. A competitive advantage can be built from many different factors.

the competition, or the pressures of the marketplace may make your business obsolete (see Chapter 3).

Flexibility To take advantage of economies of scale, large businesses usually seek to devote resources to produce large quantities of products over long periods of time. This commitment of resources limits their ability to react to new and quickly changing markets as small businesses do. Imagine the difference between making a sharp turn in a loaded 18-wheel tractor trailer and a small pickup truck. Now apply the analogy to large and small businesses turning in new directions. The big truck has a lot more capacity, but the pickup has more maneuverability in reaching customers.

Innovation Real innovation has come most often from independent inventors and small businesses. The reason? The research and development departments of most large businesses tend to concentrate on the improvement of the products their companies already make. This practice makes sense for companies trying to profit from their large investments in plant and equipment. At the same time, it tends to discourage the development of totally new ideas and products. For example, telecommunications giant AT&T has an incentive to improve its existing line of telephones and services to better serve its customers. In contrast, the idea of inventing a product that would make telephones obsolete would threaten its investment.

Small businesses have contributed many inventions that we use daily. The long list would include zippers, air conditioners, helicopters, computers, instant cameras, audiotape recorders, double-knit fabric, fiber-optic examining equipment, heart valves, optical scanners, soft contact lenses, airplanes, and automobiles, most of which were later produced by large manufacturers. In fact, many say that the greatest value of entrepreneurial companies is the way they force larger competitors to respond to innovation. Small businesses innovate by introducing new technology and markets, creating new markets, developing new products, and nurturing new ideas—actions that larger businesses have to compete with, thereby requiring the larger businesses to change.

Manager's Notes

Straight from the Source

Rieva Lesonsky, editorial director of *Entrepreneur* magazine, shares a few of her favorite inspirational quotes for entrepreneurs and small business owners:

- Only those who dare to fail miserably can achieve greatly—Robert Kennedy.
- Even if you're on the right track, you'll get run over if you just sit there—Will Rogers.
- If everything seems under control, you're just not going fast enough—Mario Andretti.
- Creativity is allowing yourself to make mistakes. Art is knowing which ones to keep—Scott Adams.
- People are always blaming their circumstances for what they are. I don't believe in circumstances. The people who succeed are the people who look for circumstances they want. And if they can't find them, they make them—George Bernard Shaw.

What famous quotations can you find that relate to self-employment?

Source: Rieva Lesonsky, "Words to Live By," *Entrepreneur,* March 2007, 10.

creative destruction
The replacement of existing products, processes, ideas, and businesses with new and better ones.

"Small businesses are the driving force of change that leads to creative destruction, especially in the development of new technology."

Economist Joseph Schumpeter called the replacement of existing products, processes, ideas, and businesses with new and better ones *creative destruction*. It is not an easy process. Yet, although change can be threatening, it is vitally necessary in a capitalist system.[23] Small businesses are the driving force of change that leads to creative destruction, especially in the development of new technology.[24]

Small businesses play a major role in creating the innovation that Schumpeter discussed. Four types of innovation that small businesses are most likely to produce include:

- *Product innovation:* Developing a new or improved product.
- *Service innovation:* Offering a new or altered service for sale.
- *Process innovation:* Inventing a new way to organize physical inputs to produce a product or service.
- *Management innovation:* Creating a new way to organize a business's resources.

The most common types of innovation relate to services and products. Thirty-eight percent of all innovations are service related, and 32 percent are product related. Interestingly, the SBA found that the majority of innovations originate from the smallest businesses, those with 1 to 19 employees. More than three-fourths of service innovations are generated by very small businesses, which also generate 65 percent of both product and process innovations.[25] Recent research reported to the SBA's Office of Advocacy showed that small patenting firms produce 13 to 14 times more patents per employee as large patenting firms.[26]

The process of creative destruction is not limited to high-technology businesses or to the largest companies. A small business owner who does not keep up with market innovations risks being left behind. Creative destruction occurs in mundane as well as exotic industries, such as chains of beauty salons replacing barber shops. Knowledge is the key to innovation and advancement. For this reason, it is important for you to keep current with business literature by reading periodicals such as *Inc.*, *Fast Company*, or *Fortune Small Business* that cover small business topics and any specialized trade journals that exist for your type of business. Many business schools also have executive education programs, which range from two days to a year or longer, specifically designed for small business owners.

Close Relationship to Customers Small business owners get to know their customers and neighborhood on a personal level. This closeness allows them to provide individualized service and gives them firsthand knowledge of customer wants and needs. By contrast, large businesses get to "know" their customers only through limited samples of marketing research (which may be misleading). Knowing customers personally can allow small businesses to build a competitive advantage based on specialty products, personalized service, and quality, which enables them to compete with the bigger businesses' lower prices gained through mass production. For this reason, you should always remember that the rapport you build with your customers is of vital importance—it is what makes them come back again and again.

Getting Started on the Right Foot

Before starting your own business, you will want to make sure that you have the right tools to succeed. Look for a market large enough to generate a profit, sufficient capital, skilled employees, and accurate information.

Market Size and Definition Who will buy your product or service? Marketing techniques help you find out what consumers want and in what quantity. Armed with this information, you can make an informed decision about the profitability of offering a particular good or service. Once you conclude that a market is large enough to support your business, you will want to learn what your customers have in common and how their likes and dislikes will affect your market, so as to serve them better and remain competitive.

Gathering Sufficient Capital   All too often, entrepreneurs try to start a business without obtaining sufficient start-up capital. The lifeblood of any young business is cash; starting on a financial shoestring hurts your chances of success. Profit is the ultimate goal, but inadequate cash flow cuts off the blood supply (see Chapter 8).

You may need to be creative in finding start-up capital. A second mortgage, loans from friends or relatives, a line of credit from a bank or credit union, or a combination of sources may be sufficient. Thorough planning will give you the best estimate of how much money you will need. Once you have made your best estimate, double it—or at least get access to more capital. You'll probably need it.

Finding and Keeping Effective Employees   Maintaining a capable workforce is a never-ending task for small businesses. Frequently, small business owners get caught up in the urgency to "fill positions with warm bodies" without spending enough time on the selection process. You should hire, train, and motivate your employees before opening for business (see Chapter 17).

Once established, you must understand that your most valuable assets walk out the door at closing time. In other words, your employees are your most valuable assets. It is their skill, knowledge, and information that make your business successful. These intangible assets are called **intellectual capital**.

intellectual capital
The valuable skills and knowledge that employees of a business possess.

Getting Accurate Information   Managers at any organization will tell you how difficult it is to make a decision before acquiring all the relevant information. This difficulty is compounded for the aspiring small business owner, who does not yet possess the expertise or experience needed to oversee every functional area of the business, from accounting to sales. Consult a variety of sources of information, from self-help books in your local library to experts in your nearest Small Business Development Center. A more accurate picture can be drawn if you consider several vantage points.

Understanding the Risks of Small Business Ownership

The decision to start your own business should be made with a full understanding of the risks involved. If you go in with both eyes open, you will be able to anticipate problems, reduce the possibility of loss, and increase your chances of success. The prospect of failure should serve as a warning to you. Many new businesses do not get past their second or third years. Running a small business involves much more than simply getting an idea, hanging out a sign, and opening for business the next day. You need a vision, resources, and a plan to take advantage of the opportunity that exists.

"Running a small business involves much more than simply getting an idea, hanging out a sign, and opening for business the next day."

What Is Business Failure?

Even though business owners launch their ventures with the best of intentions and work long, hard hours, some businesses inevitably fail. Dun & Bradstreet, a financial research firm, defines a *business failure* as a business that closes as a result of either (1) actions such as bankruptcy, foreclosure, or voluntary withdrawal from the business *with a financial loss to a creditor*; or (2) a court action such as receivership (taken over involuntarily) or reorganization (receiving protection from creditors).[27]

How long do start-up businesses typically last? A recent study on business longevity by the National Federation of Independent Business (NFIB), titled "Business Starts and

ENTREPRENEURIAL SNAPSHOT

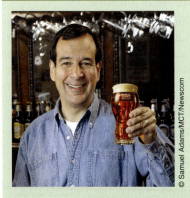

© Samuel Adams/MCT/Newscom

Beer Entrepreneur

On Patriot's Day 1985, Jim Koch (pronounced "cook") started Boston Beer Company. Koch brewed his beer, called Samuel Adams, according to a family recipe dating from the 1870s. Although he had never been in the beer business before, he became at age 37 a sixth-generation brewer. Intending to compete directly with the best imports, Koch advertised his beer with patriotic slogans like "Declare your independence from foreign beer." The namesake of the beer was a revolutionary war hero who had helped organize the Boston Tea Party.

Like many entrepreneurs, Koch started his business on a shoestring: $100,000 from personal savings and $250,000 borrowed from family and friends—a small amount for a brewery. To reduce overhead expenses, he arranged to use the excess capacity of a brewery in Pittsburgh. For the first several years, Koch was the company's only salesperson, traveling from bar to bar enticing bartenders to taste samples of Samuel Adams that he carried in his briefcase. Sometimes as many as 15 calls were needed before he eventually won the sale.

Samuel Adams was not made for the mass market. At first it was brewed in batches of only 6,500 cases each. Koch marketed the beer as being geared toward people who were tired of drinking "ordinary" beer and were willing to pay for premium quality. Koch enjoyed saying that major breweries spill more beer in a minute than he made in a year. Quality was his focus, not quantity.

The company that started with one person and one recipe has grown to have more than 250 employees and 17 different styles of beer that have won more than 650 brewing awards—more than any other beer in

history has won. Koch was honored with the Beverage Forum 2008 Lifetime Achievement Award. Koch has never been satisfied to make the same beer as others. He has even created a new category he calls "extreme beer." These new niche beers, like Triple Bock, Millennium Ale, and Utopia, are very strong and compete with the finest cognac, port, or sherry in blind taste tests. For example, Utopia is about 25 percent alcohol and sells for about $100 per 25-ounce bottle. Such beverages are a product of Koch's passion for quality. Appropriately, Boston Beer Company's ads stress product and process—not image—by not featuring musclebound men or bikini-clad women. Because Samuel Adams was the first beer to have a freshness date stamped on its label, Koch wrote a radio ad touting that fact: "Maybe other beer commercials want you to think that if you drink their beer, you'll get lucky. But I can guarantee with Samuel Adams, you'll always get a date." Anheuser-Busch later mimicked the practice.

The company was the first to enter the chasm between *micro* brewery and *major* brewery. Boston Beer has about a 0.6 percent share of the U.S. market (that is about 1 of every 200 beers consumed). Its incredible growth and success have come from its fanatical attention to quality, its use of marketing tools that no other microbrewery had used—advertising, merchandising, and hard selling—and the perseverance of its founder, Jim Koch, an entrepreneur with a vision. "Just like baby boomers adopted wine, their kids are adopting beer, and the parallels are extraordinary and enormous," he says; "people want a better experience with their beer."

Sources: Adapted from "The World of Beer," www.samueladams.com; John Holl, "Make Your Beer and Drink It, Too," *New York Times*, February 28, 2010, 8; Julie Sloane, "How We Got Started," *Fortune Small Business*, September 2004; Jenny McCune, "Brewing Up Profits," *Management Review*, April 1994, 16–20; James Koch, "Portrait of the CEO as Salesman," *Inc.*, March 1988, 44–46; Mike Beirne, "Brewer Goes to Extremes to Elevate Beer Segment," *Brandweek*, August 8, 2005; and Adrienne Carter "Beer Takes Its Place at the Table," *BusinessWeek*, June 19, 2006.

Stops," found that slightly more than 10 percent of businesses ceased operations in less than one year. Twenty-five percent stopped business between one and two years, while another 20 percent closed their doors between their third and fifth anniversaries. Only 13 percent lasted longer than 21 years.

"May I be excused? I've got to start up my own company."

Causes of Business Failure

The rates of business failure vary greatly by industry and are affected by factors such as type of ownership, size of the business, and expertise of the owner. The causes of business failure are many and complex; however, the most common causes are inadequate management and financing (see Figure 1.3).

Although financial problems are listed as the most common cause of business failure, consider management's role in controlling them. Could business failure due to industry weakness be linked to poor management? Yes, if the owner tried to enter an industry or market with no room for another competitor or responded only slowly to industry changes. High operating expenses and insufficient profit margins also reflect ineffective management. Finally, business failure due to insufficient capital suggests inexperienced management.

Inadequate Management *Business management* is the efficient and effective use of resources. For small business owners, management skills are especially desirable—and often especially difficult to obtain. Lack of experience is one of their most pressing problems. Small business owners must be generalists; they do not have the luxury of specialized management. On the one hand, they may not be able to afford to hire the full-time experts who could help avert costly mistakes. On the other hand, their limited resources will not permit them to make many mistakes and stay in business. As a small

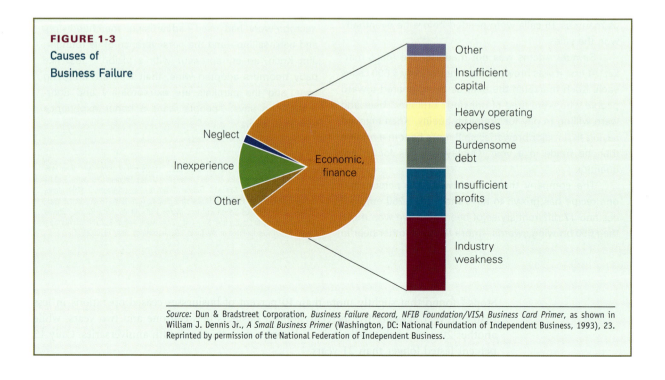

FIGURE 1-3

Causes of Business Failure

Neglect
Inexperience
Other
Economic, finance

Other
Insufficient capital
Heavy operating expenses
Burdensome debt
Insufficient profits
Industry weakness

Source: Dun & Bradstreet Corporation, *Business Failure Record, NFIB Foundation/VISA Business Card Primer*, as shown in William J. Dennis Jr., *A Small Business Primer* (Washington, DC: National Foundation of Independent Business, 1993), 23. Reprinted by permission of the National Federation of Independent Business.

business manager, you will probably have to make decisions in areas in which you have little expertise.

Entrepreneurs are generally correct in pointing to internal factors as the reason for the failure of their businesses; these factors are the cause of 89 percent of such failures.[28] Internal problems are those more directly under the control of the manager, such as adequate capital, cash flow, facilities/equipment inventory control, human resources, leadership, organizational structure, and accounting systems.

The manager of a small business must be a leader, a planner, and a worker. You may be a "top gun" in sales, but that skill could work against you. You might be tempted to concentrate on sales while ignoring other equally important areas of the business, such as record keeping, inventory, and customer service.

Inadequate Financing Business failure due to inadequate financing can be caused by improper managerial control as well as shortage of capital. On the one hand, if you don't have adequate funds to begin with, you will not be able to afford the facilities or personnel you need to start up the business correctly. On the other hand, if you do possess adequate capital but do not manage your resources wisely, you may be unable to maintain adequate inventory or keep the balance needed to run the business.

There are a lot of ways to fail in business. You can extend too much credit. You can fail to plan for the future or not have strategic direction. You can overinvest in fixed assets or hire the wrong people. Identifying mistakes that can be made is merely one component of the problem. Figuring out how to avoid them is the hard part.[29]

Business Termination versus Failure

business termination
When a business ceases operation for any reason.

business failure
When a business closes with a financial loss to a creditor.

There is a difference between a **business termination** and a **business failure**. A *termination* occurs when a business no longer exists for any reason. A *failure* occurs when a business closes with a financial loss to a creditor. Reasons for a termination abound. The owner may have an opportunity to sell her business to someone else for a healthy profit, or be ready to move on to a new business or to retire, or she may have simply lost interest in the business. The market for the business's product may have changed or become saturated. Perhaps the owner has decided it would be more appealing to work for someone else. In other cases, businesses may change form. A partnership may be restructured as a corporation, or a business may move to a new location. Businesses that undergo such changes are considered terminated even though they continue in another form.

Mistakes Leading to Business Failure

No one likes to think about failing, yet many small business owners invite failure by ignoring basic rules for success. One of the most common mistakes is to neglect to plan for the future because planning seems too hard or time-consuming. Planning what you want to do with your business, where you want it to go, and how you're going to get there are prerequisites for a sound business. Of course, that doesn't mean you can't change your plans as circumstances dictate. Your plan should provide a road map for your business, showing you both the expressways and the scenic routes—and the detours.

Another common mistake is failing to understand the commitment and hard work that are required for turning a business into a success. Having to work long hours and do things you don't enjoy because no one else is available to do them are part and parcel of owning a small business. Yet, when you have the freedom of being your own boss, the hard work and long hours often don't seem so demanding!

Still another mistake that small business owners make, particularly with rapidly growing businesses, is not hiring additional employees soon enough or not using existing employees effectively. There comes a point in the growth of a business when it is no longer possible for the manager to do it all, but she resists delegation in the belief that it means she is giving up control. It is important to recognize that delegating tasks to others isn't giving up control—it's giving up the execution of details.

The last type of mistake discussed here involves finances. Inaccurate estimates of cash flow and capital requirements can swamp a business quickly. Figuring the correct amount of money needed for starting a business is a tough balancing act: Asking for too little may hinder growth and actually jeopardize survival, whereas asking for too much might cause lenders or investors to hesitate. An important rule to remember in terms of arranging financing or calculating cash-flow projections is to figure the unexpected into your financial plans. In this way, you can have more of a cushion to fall back on if things don't go exactly according to plan. After all, without the right amount of capital, it's impossible to succeed.[30]

Business failure, then, is a serious reality. How can a small business owner avoid it? Difficult changes may be needed, and change requires leaders to overcome all sorts of human dynamics, like inertia, tradition, and head-in-the-sand hoping that things will get better. Strategic moments require courage, or at least a lack of sentimentality, which is rare. It is in these moments that the best leaders find a mirror and ask themselves the defining question that the late, great Peter Drucker posed nearly 40 years ago: "If you weren't already in your business, would you enter it today?" If the answer is no, Drucker said, you need to face a second tough question: "What are you going to do about it?" Every leader should heed this good advice and, if need be, follow it through to its conclusion, whether that will be to fix, sell, or close the business.[31]

> *"Inaccurate estimates of cash flow and capital requirements can swamp a business quickly."*

Failure Rate Controversy

Almost everyone has heard the story about the supposedly high rate of failure for small businesses. "Did you know that 90 percent of all new businesses fail within one year?" the story usually begins, as if to confirm one's worst fears about business ownership. For educators and business people, this piece of modern folklore is known as "the myth that would not die." Actually, only about 18 percent of all new businesses are forced to close their doors with a loss to creditors.[32] The rest either close voluntarily or are still in business. Over the past several decades, the number of new businesses that have opened has approached or exceeded the number that have closed. Table 1.2 shows a net increase in business formations (more businesses were started than stopped operations).

Sometimes researchers include business terminations in their failure-rate calculations, resulting in an artificially high number of failures. Economic consultant David Birch describes the misinterpretation of economic data as "like being at the end

TABLE 1-2 U.S. Business Start-Ups, Closures, and Bankruptcies		NEW	CLOSURES	BANKRUPTCIES
	2008	627,200	595,600	43,546
	2005	644,122	565,745	39,201
	2003	612,296	540,658	35,037
	2000	574,300	542,831	35,472
	1995	594,369	497,246	50,516
	1990	584,892	531,892	63,912

Source: Small Business Administration, Office of Advocacy, "Frequently Asked Questions," www.sba.gov/advo, March 2010.

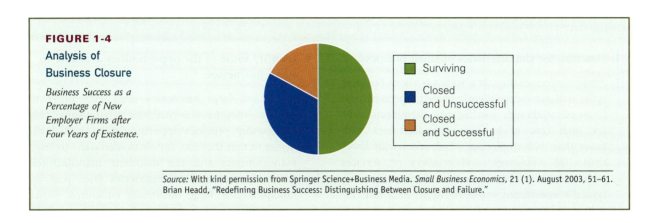

FIGURE 1-4

Analysis of
Business Closure

*Business Success as a
Percentage of New
Employer Firms after
Four Years of Existence.*

- Surviving
- Closed and Unsuccessful
- Closed and Successful

Source: With kind permission from Springer Science+Business Media. *Small Business Economics*, 21 (1). August 2003, 51–61. Brian Headd, "Redefining Business Success: Distinguishing Between Closure and Failure."

of a whisper chain. It's a myth everyone agrees to."[33] Fortunately for small business owners, this high number of failures is indeed a myth, not a fact.

Analysis of business closure data as part of the recent U.S. Census Bureau's Characteristics of Business Owners (CBO) reveals some interesting findings—including the finding that about one-third of closed businesses were successful at the time of their closure. The study represented a universe of about 17 million businesses with a sample of 78,147 businesses. It was one of the first major studies to include "closing while successful" as a possible outcome (see Figure 1.4). That option could well challenge the failure myth, or the view that business closure is always negative. Entrepreneurs certainly devise exit strategies to close or sell a business before losses accumulate or to move on to other opportunities.[34]

Starting a business does involve risk, but the assumption of risk is part of life. In 2007, the divorce rate was 3.7 per 1,000.[35] Of every 10,000 students who start college, about 52 percent fail to graduate.[36] Would you decide not to get married because the divorce rate is too high? Were you afraid to go to college because of the dropout rate? The point to remember is that if you have a clear vision, know your product and your market, and devote the time and effort needed, your small business, like many others, can succeed.

Is Government Intervention the Answer?

With the U.S. unemployment rate above 10 percent and parts of Europe pushing 20 percent, policymakers around the world are looking to promote entrepreneurship. Governments can play an integral role in private job creation—specifically, creating infrastructure like utilities, transportation, and higher education. But when it comes to specifics like becoming venture capitalists and deciding which companies survive or die, government intervention has a much poorer track record,[37] for example Dubai's entrepreneurial hub floating in red ink and the European Union's European Investment Fund's failure to turn 2 billion euros ($1.8 billion at the time) in 2001 into businesses.

Two recent books shed light upon what governments have done well and what they can do better in supporting entrepreneurship: Josh Lerner, *Boulevard of Broken Dreams: Why Public Efforts to Boost Entrepreneurship and Venture Capital Have Failed—and What to Do about It*; and Dan Senor and Saul Singer, *Start-Up Nation: The Story of Israel's Economic Miracle*. These authors point to factors such as ignoring competitive advantages of countries and the temptation to spread wealth to every region rather than let entrepreneurial clusters develop.

Summary

1. Describe the characteristics of small business.

Small businesses include a wide variety of business types that are independently owned, operated, and financed. Although specific size definitions exist for each type of business, manufacturers with fewer than 500 employees, wholesalers with fewer than 100 employees, and retailers or services with annual revenues less than $3.5 million are typically considered small. By itself, each individual small business has relatively little impact in its industry.

2. Recognize the role of small business in the U.S. economy.

Small businesses provided the economic foundation on which the U.S. economy was built. Today these businesses are creating new jobs even as large businesses continue eliminating jobs. Small businesses are more flexible than large ones in the products and services they offer. Most real product innovations come from small businesses.

3. Understand the importance of diversity in the marketplace and the workplace.

As the population becomes more diverse, the owners and employees of small businesses are likewise becoming more diverse. Businesses owned by women and minorities are growing at a faster rate than the overall rate of business growth. Diversity is important in small business because a wide range of viewpoints and personal backgrounds can improve problem solving.

4. Identify some of the opportunities available to small businesses.

Small and large businesses need each other to survive—they have a symbiotic relationship. This relationship provides opportunities to small businesses in that they can supply needed parts to large manufacturers and can distribute manufactured goods. Moreover, small businesses often pick up functions that large businesses outsource. Other opportunities exist for small businesses where they enjoy the advantage of being able to profitably serve smaller niches than can their larger counterparts. For all these reasons, small businesses are rapidly becoming important players in international trade.

5. Suggest ways to court success in a small business venture.

To prevent your small business from becoming another casualty noted in business failure statistics, you must begin with a clearly defined competitive advantage. You must offer a product or service that people want and are willing to buy. You must do something substantially better than your competition does it. You must remain flexible and innovative, stay close to your customers, and strive for quality.

6. Name the most common causes of small business failure.

Ineffective and inefficient management, which shows up in many ways, is the number one cause of business failure. Inadequate financing, industry weakness, inexperience, and neglect are other major causes.

Questions for Review and Discussion

1. How would you define *small business*?
2. Name a company that seems large but might be classified as small because it has relatively little impact on its industry.
3. Large businesses depend on small businesses. Why?
4. Define *outsourcing*, and describe its impact on small business.
5. Why are small businesses more likely than large businesses to be innovative?
6. Explain the term *creative destruction*.
7. How can being close to your customers give you a competitive advantage?
8. How would you show that small business is becoming a more important part of the economy?
9. The text compares the failure rate for small businesses with the divorce rate in marriage and the student failure rate in college. Are these fair comparisons?

10. Describe four causes of small business failure. How does the quality of management relate to each of these causes?
11. Describe the techniques that a business with which you are familiar has used to prevent its failure.
12. How would the computer industry be different today if there were no businesses with fewer than 500 employees? Would personal computers exist?
13. Predict the future of small business. In what industries will it be most involved? What trends do you foresee? Will the failure rate go up or down? Will the importance of small business increase or decrease by the year 2020?

Questions for Critical Thinking

1. This chapter discussed the evolution of small business in the U.S. economy. On the heels of the rapid growth in the popularity of Internet businesses in the late 1990s and the ensuing bust in 2000, what will be the next stage in small business's evolution? Is the Internet just another business tool, or will it re-create the way business is done?
2. Is *creative destruction* just another economic theory for the foundation of capitalism? Build a case supporting your answer.

What Would You Do?

Everyone likes to eat…you love food…why not open a restaurant? It may not be *quite* that easy. Kenny Lao, 30, knew he better be unique when he started his New York City Rickshaw Dumpling Bar in 2006. But Lao says, "If you have a strong concept and have your execution and operation strategies down pat, any time is a good time to open a restaurant—even now." Lao built his dumpling empire on six varieties of dumplings (including a chocolate dessert dumpling) and simple add-ons like Asian salad, noodle soup, and green-tea milkshakes. It takes approximately 2.5 minutes from order to delivery. Rickshaw sells about 1.4 million dumplings per year for $1.3 million in revenue.

Source: Eileen Figure Sandlin, "The Main Ingredients," *Entrepreneur*, March 2007, 100–108.

Questions

1. Evaluate the business idea of Kenny Lao's business. Dumplings are his signature menu item on his cool website www.rickshawdumplings.com. If you were to venture into the restaurant business, what would be your signature item? What would be your competitive advantage?
2. Look at Figure 1.4, "Causes of Business Failure." If a restaurant business goes under, what do you think are the most likely reasons?

2

Management, Entrepreneurship, and Ownership

CHAPTER LEARNING OUTCOMES

After reading this chapter, you should be able to:

1. **Articulate the differences between the small business manager and the entrepreneur.**

2. **Discuss the steps in preparing for small business ownership.**

3. **Enumerate the advantages and disadvantages of self-employment.**

4. **Describe the three main forms of ownership—sole proprietorship, partnership, and corporation—and their unique features.**

When John Goscha was a freshman at Babson College, he lived in a dorm for student entrepreneurs. He and his friends would brainstorm ideas for businesses and products—like many of you do right now. Goscha and crew would hang big sheets of paper on the walls to track their idea maps. They loved the idea of being able to write all over the walls, but putting up that much whiteboard wasn't practical.

The entrepreneurial gears started grinding in John's head, leading him to the concept of IdeaPaint—paint that could be applied to any surface to turn it into a whiteboard that you can write on with any dry erase marker. Paint for creating chalkboards existed, but for whiteboard did not. Finding the paint formula that would do what the team wanted proved problematic. Goscha, Morgen Newman, and Jeff Avallon spent three years in development with paint and chemical coating laboratories. Two labs said it was impossible because whiteboards were cured in high-intensity ovens. Applying this type of coating with a single roller was not going to happen.

Then they found CAS-MI labs in Ypsilanti, Michigan, with scientists willing to give it the old college try. Pitching investors without a finished product is no easy task, but they raised enough between family, two professors, a College Board member, friends, and a few angel investors to finally get it right.

Once they had a working product, the challenge was not over. By this time, century-old paint manufacturer Rust-Oleum had its own dry-erase paint on the shelves of Target and on Amazon.com. The payoff came when IdeaPaint was launched in 2008 at an architectural show by painting 3,000 square feet of the Chicago Merchandise Mart and hiring artists to draw murals with markers. It got attention. Phil Maguire, senior category manager for Akzo Nobel (the largest paint and coating company in the world), which distributes IdeaPaint, says, "a growing number of architects and painters view it as breakthrough technology." Not bad for a college project.

Of course, as good entrepreneurs, the founders now use IdeaPaint to brainstorm new products for mainstream consumers and businesses.

Sources: Joel Holland, "Waaaay Outside the Lines," *Entrepreneur*, March 2010, 76; "Who's Next—Stroke of Genius," *Inc.*, October 2009, 74; "Transform Any Space with IdeaPaint," *Buildings*, January 1, 2009, 84; and Jennifer Alsever, "IdeaPaint All Over Your Office Walls," *CNNMoney.com*, March 8, 2010.

The Entrepreneur-Manager Relationship

What is the difference between a small business manager and an entrepreneur? Aren't all small business owners also entrepreneurs? Don't all entrepreneurs start as small business owners? The terms are often used interchangeably, and although some overlap exists between them, there are enough differences to warrant studying them separately.

In fact, entrepreneurship and small business management are both *processes*, not isolated incidents. **Entrepreneurship** is the process of identifying opportunities for which marketable needs exist and assuming the risk of creating an organization to satisfy them. An entrepreneur needs the vision to spot opportunities and the ability to capitalize on them. **Small business management**, by contrast, is the ongoing process of owning and operating an established business. A small business manager must be able to deal with all the challenges of moving the business forward—hiring and retaining good employees, reacting to changing customer wants and needs, making sales, and keeping cash flow positive, for example.

The processes of entrepreneurship and small business management both present challenges and rewards as the business progresses through different stages.

What Is an Entrepreneur?

An entrepreneur is a person who sees an opportunity or has an idea and assumes the risk of starting a business to take advantage of that opportunity or idea. The risks that go with creating an organization can be financial, material, and psychological. The term *entrepreneur*, a French word that dates from the seventeenth century, translates literally as "between-taker" or "go-between."[1] It originally referred to men who organized and managed exploration expeditions and military maneuvers. The term has evolved over the years to have a multitude of definitions, but most include the following behaviors:

- *Creation.* A new business is started.
- *Innovation.* The business involves a new product, process, market, material, or organization.

entrepreneurship
The process of identifying opportunities for which marketable needs exist and assuming the risk of creating an organization to satisfy them.

small business management
The ongoing process of owning and operating an established business.

- *Risk assumption.* The owner of the business bears the risk of potential loss or failure of the business.
- *General management.* The owner of the business guides the business and allocates the business's resources.
- *Performance intention.* High levels of growth and/or profit are expected.[2]

All new businesses require a certain amount of entrepreneurial skill. The degree of entrepreneurship involved depends on the amount of each of these behaviors that is needed. Current academic research in the field of entrepreneurship emphasizes opportunity recognition, social capital, and trust. For an interesting article reviewing the scholarly development of entrepreneurship topics, see "Is There Conceptual Convergence in Entrepreneurship Research?"[3]

Entrepreneurship and the Small Business Manager

Entrepreneurship involves the start-up process. Small business management focuses on running a business over a long period of time and may or may not involve the start-up process. Although you cannot study one without considering the other, they are different. In managing a small business, most of the "entrepreneuring" was done a long time ago. Of course, a good manager is always looking for new ways to please customers, but the original innovation and the triggering event that launched the business make way for more stability in the maturity stage of the business.

The manager of a small business needs perseverance, patience, and critical-thinking skills to deal with the day-to-day challenges that arise in running a business over a long period of time.

Manager's Notes

Are You Ready?

Becoming an entrepreneur is not for everyone. In business, there are no guarantees. There is simply no way to eliminate all of the risks. It takes a special person with a strong commitment and specific skills to be successful as an entrepreneur.

Are you ready to start your own business? Use the following assessment questions to better understand how prepared you are. This guide is designed to help you better understand your readiness for starting a small business. It is not a scientific assessment tool. Rather, it is a tool that will prompt you with questions and assist you in evaluating your skills, characteristics, and experience as they relate to your readiness for starting a business.

General

1. Do you think you are ready to start a business?
2. Do you have support for your business from family and friends?
3. Have you ever worked in a business similar to what you are starting?
4. Would people who know you say you are entrepreneurial?
5. Have you ever taken a small business course or seminar?

Personal Characteristics

6. Are you a leader?
7. Do you like to make your own decisions?
8. Do others turn to you for help in making decisions?
9. Do you enjoy competition?

10. Do you have willpower and self-discipline?
11. Do you plan ahead?
12. Do you like people?
13. Do you get along well with others?
14. Would people who know you say you are outgoing?

Personal Conditions

15. Are you aware that running your own business may require working more than 12 hours a day, 6 days a week, and maybe Sundays and holidays?
16. Do you have the physical stamina to handle a "self-employed" workload and schedule?
17. Do you have the emotional strength to deal effectively with pressure?
18. Are you prepared, if needed, to temporarily lower your standard of living until your business is firmly established?
19. Are you prepared to lose a portion of your savings?

Skills and Experience

20. Do you know what basic skills you will need in order to have a successful business?
21. Do you possess those skills?
22. Do you feel comfortable using a computer?
23. Have you ever worked in a managerial or supervisory capacity?
24. Do you think you can be comfortable hiring, disciplining, and delegating tasks to employees?
25. If you discover you do not have the basic skills needed for your business, will you be willing to delay your plans until you have acquired the necessary skills?

Source: Online Training—Small Business Primer, www.sba.gov/services/training/onlinecourses/index.html.

A Model of the Start-Up Process

entrepreneurship process
The stage of a business's life that involves innovation, a triggering event, and implementation of the business.

The processes of entrepreneurship and small business management can be thought of as making up a spectrum that includes six distinct stages (see Figure 2.1).[4] The stages of the entrepreneurship process are innovation, a triggering event, and implementation. The stages of the small business management process are growth, maturity, and harvest.

The ***entrepreneurship process*** begins with an *innovative idea* for a new product, process, or service, which is refined as you think it through. You may tell your idea to family

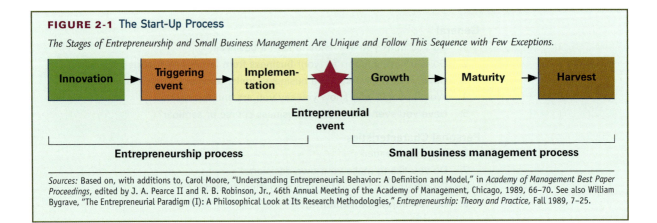

FIGURE 2-1 The Start-Up Process

The Stages of Entrepreneurship and Small Business Management Are Unique and Follow This Sequence with Few Exceptions.

Innovation → Triggering event → Implementation → ★ → Growth → Maturity → Harvest

Entrepreneurial event

Entrepreneurship process | Small business management process

Sources: Based on, with additions to, Carol Moore, "Understanding Entrepreneurial Behavior: A Definition and Model," in *Academy of Management Best Paper Proceedings*, edited by J. A. Pearce II and R. B. Robinson, Jr., 46th Annual Meeting of the Academy of Management, Chicago, 1989, 66–70. See also William Bygrave, "The Entrepreneurial Paradigm (I): A Philosophical Look at Its Research Methodologies," *Entrepreneurship: Theory and Practice,* Fall 1989, 7–25.

members or close friends to get their feedback as you develop and cultivate it. You may visit a consultant at a local small business development center for more outside suggestions for your innovative business idea. Perhaps you even wake up late at night thinking of a new facet of your idea. That is your brain working through the creative process subconsciously. The time span for the innovation stage may be months or even years before the potential entrepreneur moves on to the next stage. Usually a specific event or occurrence sparks the entrepreneur to proceed from thinking to doing—a *triggering event*.

When a triggering event occurs in the entrepreneur's life, he or she begins bringing the organization to life. This event could be the loss of a job, the successful gathering of resources to support the organization, or some other factor that sets the wheels in motion.

Implementation is the stage of the entrepreneurial process in which the organization is formed. It can also be called the *entrepreneurial event*.[5] Risk increases at this stage of the entrepreneurial process because a business is now formed. The innovation goes from being just an idea in your head to committing resources to bring it to reality. The commitment needed to bring an idea to life is a key element in entrepreneurial behavior. Implementation involves one of the following: (1) introducing new products, (2) introducing new methods of production, (3) opening new markets, (4) opening new supply sources, or (5) industrial reorganization.[6]

Entrepreneurship is, in essence, the creation of a new organization.[7] By defining entrepreneurship in terms of the organization rather than the person involved, we can say that entrepreneurship ends when the creation stage of the organization ends. This is the point where the ***small business management process*** begins. The rest of this book will concentrate on the process of managing a small business from growth through harvest.

The small business manager guides and nurtures the business through the desired level of ***growth***. The growth stage does not mean that every small business manager is attempting to get his or her business to *Fortune* 500 size. A common goal for growth of small businesses is to reach a critical mass, a point at which an adequate living is provided for the owner and family, with enough growth remaining to keep the business going.

The ***maturity*** stage of the organization is reached when the business is considered well established. The survival of the business seems fairly well assured, although the small business manager will still face many other problems and challenges. Many pure entrepreneurs do not stay with the business until this stage. They have usually moved on to other new opportunities before this point is reached. Small business managers, by contrast, are more committed to the long haul.

This stage could be as short as a few months (in the case of a fad product) or as long as decades. Maturity in organizations can be similar to maturity in people and in nature. It is characterized by more stability than that of the growth and implementation stages. Of course, organizations should not become too complacent or stop looking for new ways to evolve and grow, just as people should continue learning and growing throughout their lives.

In the ***harvest*** stage, the owner removes him or herself from the business. Harvesting a business can be thought of as picking the fruit after years of labor. In his book *The Seven Habits of Highly Effective People*, Steven Covey says that one of the keys of being effective in life is "beginning with the end in mind."[8] This advice applies to effectively harvesting a business also. Therefore, it is a time that should be planned for carefully.

The harvest can take many forms. For example, the business might be sold to another individual who will step into the position of manager. Ownership of the business could be transferred to its employees via an *employee stock ownership plan (ESOP)*. It could be sold to the public through an *initial public offering (IPO)*. The business could merge with another existing business to form an entirely new business. Finally, the harvest could be prompted by failure, in which case the doors are closed, the creditors paid,

triggering event
A specific event or occurrence that sparks the entrepreneur to proceed from thinking to doing.

implementation
The part of the entrepreneurial process that occurs when the organization is formed.

small business management process
The stage of a business's life that involves growth, maturity, and harvest.

growth
Achievement of a critical mass in the business, a point at which an adequate living is provided for the owner and family, with enough growth remaining to keep the business going.

maturity
The stage of the organization when the business is considered well established.

harvest
The stage when the owner removes him or herself from the business. Harvesting a business can be thought of as picking the fruit after years of labor.

and the assets liquidated. Although made in a different context, George Bernard Shaw's statement, "Any darned fool can start a love affair, but it takes a real genius to end one successfully," can also apply to harvesting a business.

Not every business reaches all of these stages. Maturity cannot occur unless the idea is implemented. A business cannot be harvested unless it has grown.

environmental factors
Forces that occur outside of the business that affect the business and its owner.

Figure 2.2 adds **environmental factors** to our model to show what is going on outside the business at each stage of development. Management guru Peter Drucker points out that innovation occurs as a response to opportunities within several environments.[9] For example, other entrepreneurs might serve as role models when we are in the innovation and triggering-event stages. Businesses in the implementation and growth stages must respond to competitive forces, consumer desires, capabilities of suppliers, legal regulations, and other forces. The environmental factors that affect the way in which a business must operate change from one stage to the next.

The personal characteristics of the entrepreneur or the small business manager that are most significant in running a business will vary from one stage to the next. As you will see in the next section, personal characteristics or traits are not useful in predicting who will be a successful entrepreneur or small business manager, but they do affect the motivations, actions, and effectiveness of those running a small business (see Figure 2.3). For example, in the innovation and triggering-event stages, a high tolerance for ambiguity, a strong need to achieve, and a willingness to accept risk are important for entrepreneurs. In the growth and maturity stages, the personal characteristics needed to be a successful small business manager are different from those needed to be a successful entrepreneur. In these stages the small business manager needs to be persevering, committed to the long run of the business, a motivator of others, and a leader.

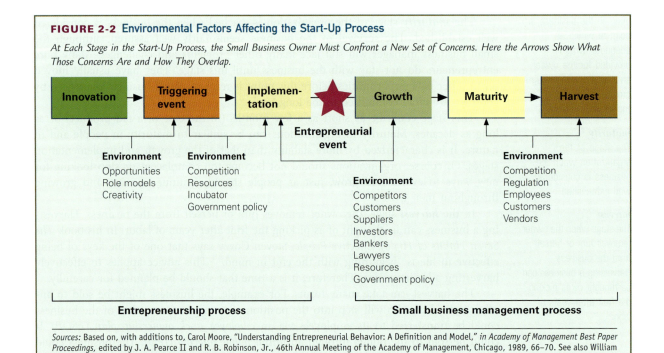

FIGURE 2-2 Environmental Factors Affecting the Start-Up Process

At Each Stage in the Start-Up Process, the Small Business Owner Must Confront a New Set of Concerns. Here the Arrows Show What Those Concerns Are and How They Overlap.

Innovation → Triggering event → Implementation → ★ Entrepreneurial event → Growth → Maturity → Harvest

Environment
Opportunities
Role models
Creativity

Environment
Competition
Resources
Incubator
Government policy

Environment
Competitors
Customers
Suppliers
Investors
Bankers
Lawyers
Resources
Government policy

Environment
Competition
Regulation
Employees
Customers
Vendors

Entrepreneurship process   **Small business management process**

Sources: Based on, with additions to, Carol Moore, "Understanding Entrepreneurial Behavior: A Definition and Model," *in Academy of Management Best Paper Proceedings,* edited by J. A. Pearce II and R. B. Robinson, Jr., 46th Annual Meeting of the Academy of Management, Chicago, 1989, 66–70. See also William Bygrave, "The Entrepreneurial Paradigm (I): A Philosophical Look at Its Research Methodologies," *Entrepreneurship: Theory and Practice,* Fall 1989, 7–25.

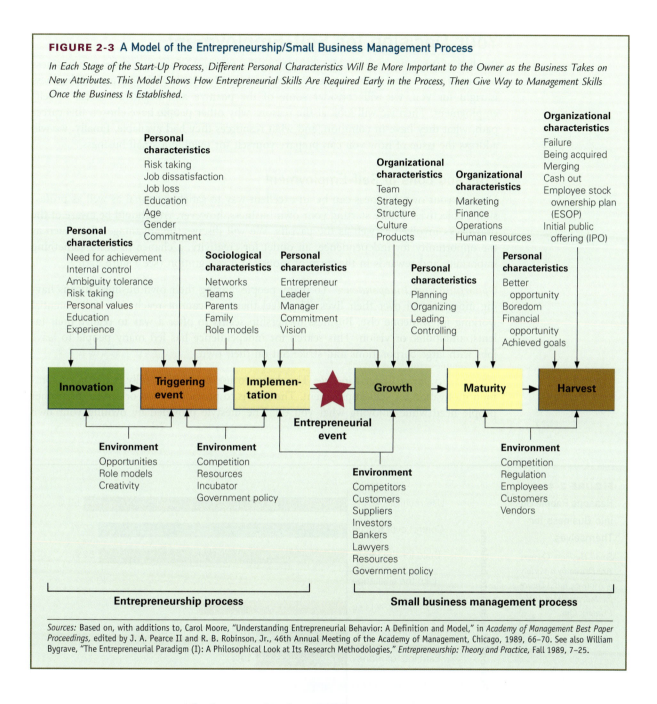

FIGURE 2-3 A Model of the Entrepreneurship/Small Business Management Process

In Each Stage of the Start-Up Process, Different Personal Characteristics Will Be More Important to the Owner as the Business Takes on New Attributes. This Model Shows How Entrepreneurial Skills Are Required Early in the Process, Then Give Way to Management Skills Once the Business Is Established.

Personal characteristics
Risk taking
Job dissatisfaction
Job loss
Education
Age
Gender
Commitment

Personal characteristics
Need for achievement
Internal control
Ambiguity tolerance
Risk taking
Personal values
Education
Experience

Sociological characteristics
Networks
Teams
Parents
Family
Role models

Personal characteristics
Entrepreneur
Leader
Manager
Commitment
Vision

Organizational characteristics
Team
Strategy
Structure
Culture
Products

Organizational characteristics
Marketing
Finance
Operations
Human resources

Organizational characteristics
Failure
Being acquired
Merging
Cash out
Employee stock
ownership plan
(ESOP)
Initial public
offering (IPO)

Personal characteristics
Planning
Organizing
Leading
Controlling

Personal characteristics
Better
opportunity
Boredom
Financial
opportunity
Achieved goals

| Innovation | Triggering event | Implemen-tation | ★ | Growth | Maturity | Harvest |

Entrepreneurial event

Environment
Opportunities
Role models
Creativity

Environment
Competition
Resources
Incubator
Government policy

Environment
Competitors
Customers
Suppliers
Investors
Bankers
Lawyers
Resources
Government policy

Environment
Competition
Regulation
Employees
Customers
Vendors

Entrepreneurship process   **Small business management process**

Sources: Based on, with additions to, Carol Moore, "Understanding Entrepreneurial Behavior: A Definition and Model," in *Academy of Management Best Paper Proceedings*, edited by J. A. Pearce II and R. B. Robinson, Jr., 46th Annual Meeting of the Academy of Management, Chicago, 1989, 66–70. See also William Bygrave, "The Entrepreneurial Paradigm (I): A Philosophical Look at Its Research Methodologies," *Entrepreneurship: Theory and Practice*, Fall 1989, 7–25.

The business also changes as it matures. In the growth stage, attention is placed on team building, setting strategies, and creating the structure and culture of the business. In the maturity stage, more attention can be directed to specific functions of the business. The people within the business gravitate toward, specialize in, and concentrate on what they do best, be it marketing, finance, or managing human resources.

The purpose of the entrepreneurship and small business management model is to illustrate the stages of both processes and factors that are significant in each. The purpose of this book is to assist you as you proceed from the innovation stage through the management of your successful business to a satisfying harvest.

Your Decision for Self-Employment

Readers of this text are probably considering the prospect of starting their own business now or at some time in the future. To help you decide whether owning a small business is right for you, we will consider some of the positive and negative aspects of self-employment. Then we will look at the reasons why other people have chosen this career path, what they have in common, and what resources they had available. Finally, we will address the issue of how you can prepare yourself for owning a small business.

Pros and Cons of Self-Employment

Owning your own business can be an excellent way to satisfy personal as well as professional objectives. Before starting your own business, however, you should be aware of the drawbacks involved as well as the payoffs. We will discuss the advantages first, such as the opportunity for independence, an outlet for creativity, a chance to build something important, and rewards in the form of money and recognition (see Figure 2.4).

Opportunity for Independence   To many people, having their own business means having more control over their lives. They feel that they cannot reach their full potential working for someone else. Business ownership seems to offer a way to realize their talents, ambitions, or vision. This search for independence has led many people to leave jobs with large corporations and strike out on their own.

Opportunity for a Better Lifestyle   The desire to use one's skills fully is the most common motivation for self-employment. The idea is to provide a good or service that other people need while enjoying what you do. The lifestyle provided by owning your own

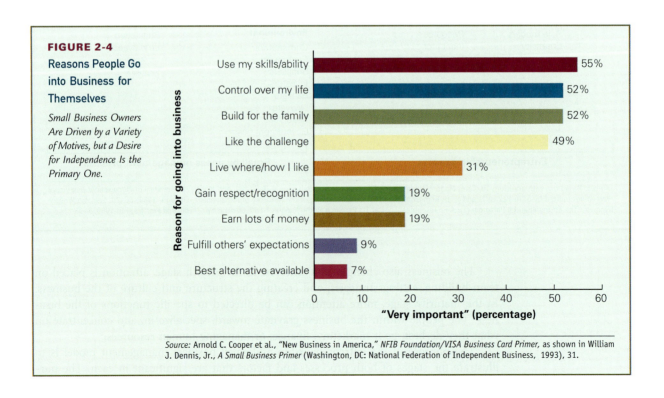

FIGURE 2-4

Reasons People Go into Business for Themselves

Small Business Owners Are Driven by a Variety of Motives, but a Desire for Independence Is the Primary One.

Reason for going into business:
- Use my skills/ability — 55%
- Control over my life — 52%
- Build for the family — 52%
- Like the challenge — 49%
- Live where/how I like — 31%
- Gain respect/recognition — 19%
- Earn lots of money — 19%
- Fulfill others' expectations — 9%
- Best alternative available — 7%

"Very important" (percentage)

Source: Arnold C. Cooper et al., "New Business in America," *NFIB Foundation/VISA Business Card Primer,* as shown in William J. Dennis, Jr., *A Small Business Primer* (Washington, DC: National Federation of Independent Business, 1993), 31.

business can make going to work fun. Working becomes a creative outlet that gives you the opportunity to use a combination of your previously untapped talents.

Also attractive to most entrepreneurs is the challenge presented by running their own business. Such people are often bored working for someone else. As a business owner, the only limitations you face arise from a challenge to your own perseverance and creativity, not from barriers placed before you by other people or the constraints of an organization.

About half of small business owners are motivated by familial concerns (refer again to Figure 2.4). They may feel not only that self-employment is the best way to provide for their children now, but also that their business is a legacy for their children. Children, in turn, may enter the family business out of self-interest or to help ease their parents' burden.

Opportunity for Profit Less than 20 percent of small business owners express a desire to earn lots of money. Most people do not start businesses to get rich, but rather to earn an honest living. Nonetheless, the direct correlation between effort and compensation is a powerful motivation to work hard. The fact that you can keep all the money you earn is a strong incentive for many entrepreneurs.

Risks of Self-Employment Small business ownership offers ample opportunities to satisfy your material and psychological needs, but it also poses certain risks of which you should be aware. Personal liability, uncertain income, long working hours, and frequently limited compensation while the business grows are some of the disadvantages of self-employment. Moreover, not having anyone looking over your shoulder may leave you with fewer places to turn for advice when the going gets tough. And even though you are your own boss, you are still answerable to many masters: You must respond to customer demands and complaints, keep your employees happy, obey government regulations, and grapple with competitive pressures.

The uncertainty of your income is one of the most challenging aspects of starting a business. There is no guaranteed paycheck at the end of the pay period, as exists when you are working for someone else. Your young business will require you to pump any revenue generated back into it. As the owner, you will be the last person to be paid, and you will probably have to live on your savings for a while. Going through the first year of business without collecting a salary is common for entrepreneurs.

> "A small business manager needs perseverance, patience, and intelligence to meet the ongoing challenges of keeping a company vibrant."

The reliable, if dull, nine-to-five work schedule is another luxury that small business owners must do without. To get your business off the ground during the critical start-up phase, you may find yourself being the company president during the day and its janitor at night. Owning and running a business require a tremendous commitment of time and effort. You must be willing to make sure that everything that must be done actually gets done. In a recent study conducted by the Families and Work Institute, among the 3,500 small business respondents, 43 percent worked more than 50 hours per week, while 38 percent worked between 35 and 50 hours per week. (The same study also showed those same small business owners earned an average of $112,800 per year—so there *is* a payoff!)[10]

When you own a business, it becomes an extension of your personality. Unfortunately, it can also take over your life, especially at the beginning. Families, friends, and other commitments must sometimes take a backseat to the business. This problem is complicated by the fact that people often start businesses in their child-rearing years. Married couples going into business together face a volatile mix of business and marital pressures that do not always lead to happy endings.

Reality Check

Small Biz on Campus

As many of you reading this textbook already realize, now is a great time to be studying entrepreneurship and small business management. But not all of you are waiting until graduation to launch your ventures.

- Ryan Allis and Aaron Houghton formed iContact after meeting at University of North Carolina at Chapel Hill. iContact is a Web-based e-mail management that the partners use to make more than profits. Their social-responsibility policy is called the "4 - 1s," meaning: (1) 1 percent of employee time can be used to volunteer with a nonprofit group, (2) 1 percent of the product is donated to qualified organizations, (3) 1 percent of payroll is given to 501(c)(3) nonprofits, and (4) 1 percent of equity in the company is committed to iContact Foundation. Oh, and their 1 percents are no small potatoes—revenue has grown from $300,000 in 2004 to $26.4 million in 2009.
- As previous generations bought old cars to rebuild and customize, Brian Laoruangroch is this generation's equivalent of a grease monkey. At University of Missouri-Columbia, Brian started buying old cell phones and refurbishing and selling them on eBay as a hobby. He eventually opened a kiosk in a local mall and scored a $50,000 SBA-backed bank loan—a coup for an undergrad business. The recession accelerated his sales, explained by his slogan, "Change your phone, not your plan." Running a $500,000 business before graduating is a challenge, but makes him pay more attention in class. Brian says, "I was learning important business concepts while I was using them in my own business. I was genuinely more interested in what they were teaching."
- Whitney Williams founded Tramonti as a senior at Texas Christian University. Inspired by artisans she met on a trip to Italy, Williams started making custom jewelry (Tramonti means "sunset" in Italian). She started by selling through trunk shows, selling pieces ranging from $30 to $300—before setting up a Web site last year (tramontibywhitney.com). Upon graduation, plans include expanding her line to shoes, clothing, and accessories.

Sources: Joel Holland "Save the World, Make a Million," *Entrepreneur*, April 2010, 76; Jacob Stokes, "The Coolest College Start-Ups," *Inc.*, March 2009, 82; and Josh Spiro, "Cool College Start-Ups 2010," *Inc.*, March 2010, 91.

Traits of Successful Entrepreneurs

"Virtually every successful entrepreneur possesses these four characteristics of passion, determination, trustworthiness, and knowledge."

Since the early 1960s, researchers have tried to identify the personal characteristics that will predict those people who will be successful entrepreneurs. The conclusion of more than 30 years of research is that successful entrepreneurs cannot be predicted. They come in every shape, size, and color, and from all backgrounds. Still, in this section we will briefly examine some characteristics seen among individuals who tend to rise to the top of any profession. The point to remember when you are considering starting a business is that no particular combination of characteristics guarantees success. People possessing all the positive traits discussed here have experienced business failure. However, certain qualities seem to be prerequisites of success.

First, you need to have a *passion* for what you are doing. Caring very deeply about what you are trying to accomplish through your business is imperative. If you go into business with a take-it-or-leave-it, it-will-go-or-it-won't attitude, you are probably wasting your time and money. *Determination* is also critical. You must realize that you have choices and are not a victim of fate. You need to believe that you can succeed if you work long enough and hard enough. *Trustworthiness* is important to entrepreneurs because of their many interpersonal, institutional, or organizational relationships (often

© Deb McGwin Photo & Design

Joanna Alberti demonstrates traits of a successful entrepreneur by turning a folder of doodles and quotable quotes into a successful greeting-card business revolving around a fictional woman named Sophie. Alberti competes against greeting-card giants such as Hallmark at www .sophiesphilosophies.com.

need to achieve
The personal quality, linked to entrepreneurship, of being motivated to excel and choose situations in which success is likely.

locus of control
A person's belief concerning the degree to which internal or external forces control his or her future.

untested) under conditions of uncertainty.[11] Finally, you need a deep *knowledge* of the area in which you are working. Your customers should see you as a reliable source in solving their wants and needs. Virtually every successful entrepreneur possesses these four characteristics of passion, determination, trustworthiness, and knowledge.[12] In other words, perseverance, the technical skills to run a business, belief in yourself, and the ability to inspire others to trust you are all important for success.

A pioneer in entrepreneurial research, David McClelland identified entrepreneurs as people with a higher **need to achieve** than nonentrepreneurs.[13] People with a high need to achieve are attracted to jobs that challenge their skills and problem-solving abilities, yet offer a good chance of success. They equally avoid goals that seem almost impossible to achieve and those that pose no challenge. They prefer tasks in which the outcome depends on their individual effort.

Locus of control is a term used to explain how people view their ability to determine their own fate. Entrepreneurs tend to have a stronger internal locus of control than people in the general population.[14] People with a high internal locus of control believe that the outcome of an event is determined by their own actions. Luck, chance, fate, or the control of other people (external factors) are less important than one's own efforts.[15] When faced with a problem or a difficult situation, internals look within themselves for solutions. Internal locus of control is the force that compels many people to start their own businesses in an effort to gain independence, autonomy, and freedom.

Successful entrepreneurs and small business owners are innovative and creative. *Innovation* results from the ability to conceive of and create new and unique products, processes, or services. Entrepreneurs see opportunities in the marketplace and visualize creative new ways to take advantage of them.

How do entrepreneurs tend to view *risk taking*? A myth about entrepreneurs is that they are wild-eyed, risk-seeking, financial daredevils. While acceptance of financial risk is necessary to start a business, the prototypical entrepreneur tends to accept moderate risk only after careful examination of what she is about to get into.

Consider the case of Scott Schmidt, the entrepreneurial athlete who started what has become known as "extreme skiing." Basically, he jumps from 60-foot cliffs on skis for a living. Ski equipment companies sponsor him for endorsements and video production. If you saw him from the ski lift, you would say, "That guy is a maniac for taking that risk." The same is often said of other entrepreneurs by people looking in from outside the situation. Actually, Schmidt very carefully charts his takeoff and landing points, and he does not see himself as reckless. An analogy can be drawn between Schmidt's adventurous style of skiing and the risks of starting a new business.

Entrepreneurs carefully plan their next moves in their business plans. Once they are in the air, entrepreneurs must trust their remarkable talent to help them react to what comes their way as they fall. Entrepreneurs don't risk life and limb because they look for ways to minimize their risks by careful observation and planning, just as Schmidt precisely plans his moves. They commonly do not see unknown situations as risky, because they know their strengths and talents, are confident of success, and have analyzed the playing field. In similar fashion, Scott Schmidt doesn't consider himself reckless. He considers himself very good at what he does.[16] That is a typical entrepreneurial attitude.

"If one characteristic of successful entrepreneurs stands out above all others across all types of businesses, however, it would have to be their incredible tenacity."

Other traits that are useful in owning your own business are a high level of energy, confidence, an orientation toward the future, optimism, a desire for feedback, a high tolerance for ambiguity, flexibility/adaptability, and commitment. If one characteristic of successful entrepreneurs stands out above all others across all types of businesses, however, it would have to be their *incredible tenacity*.

Preparing Yourself for Business Ownership

How do you prepare for an undertaking like owning your own business? Do you need experience? Do you need education? The answer to the latter two questions is always "yes." But what kind? And how much? These questions are tougher to answer because their answers depend on the type of business you plan to enter. The experience you would need to open a franchised bookstore differs from that needed for an upscale restaurant.

Entrepreneurs and small business owners typically have higher education levels than the general public. About 60 percent of new business owners have had at least some college education (see Figure 2.5).[17] Exceptions do exist, however—people have dropped out of school and gone on to start successful businesses—so it is difficult to generalize. Even so, in a majority of cases we can conclude that more education increases the chances of success. Note should be taken that, for the most successful small businesses, the CEOs of *Inc.* 500 companies have significantly higher education levels (refer again to Figure 2.5).

Entrepreneurship and small business management are the fastest-growing classes in business schools across the country.[18] In 1971, Karl Vesper of the University of Washington found that 16 U.S. schools offered a course in entrepreneurship. In his 1993 update of that study, that number had grown to 370. By 2010, 2,000 institutions offered courses in entrepreneurship.[19] Some of the nation's top business schools, such as Babson, University of Houston, University of Arizona, Baylor, and Temple (ranked as the top five Best Undergrad Programs for Entrepreneurs by *Entrepreneur* magazine in 2009), as well

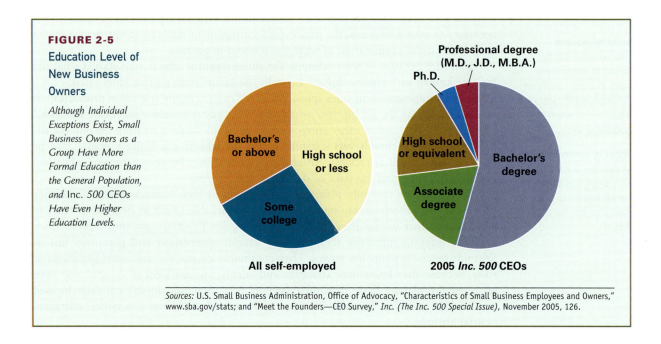

FIGURE 2-5

Education Level of New Business Owners

Although Individual Exceptions Exist, Small Business Owners as a Group Have More Formal Education than the General Population, and Inc. 500 CEOs Have Even Higher Education Levels.

Sources: U.S. Small Business Administration, Office of Advocacy, "Characteristics of Small Business Employees and Owners," www.sba.gov/stats; and "Meet the Founders—CEO Survey," *Inc. (The Inc. 500 Special Issue)*, November 2005, 126.

as many other four-year colleges and community colleges, are offering degrees in entrepreneurship and small business management.[20] Until very recently, the leaders of most business schools argued that entrepreneurship could not be taught. Now, however, the increased academic attention is constructing a body of knowledge on the processes of starting and running small businesses, which proves that entrepreneurial processes can be and are being learned.

The SBA and other nonacademic agencies offer start-your-own-business seminars to prospective entrepreneurs. Executive education programs offered through college extension departments are providing curricula specifically designed for entrepreneurs and small business owners. These one-day to one-year programs provide valuable skills without a degree.

Obtaining practical experience in your type of business is an important part of your education. You can learn valuable skills from various jobs that will prepare you for owning your own business. For example, working in a restaurant, in retail sales, or in a customer service department can hone your customer relations skills, which are crucial in running your own business but difficult to learn in a classroom.

The analytical and relational skills that you learn in formal educational settings are important, but remember that your future development depends on lifelong learning. (*Commencement*, after all, means "beginning"—the beginning of your business career!) Finally, don't overlook hobbies and other interests in preparing for self-employment. Participating in team sports and student organizations, for instance, can cultivate your team spirit and facility in working with others. Your marketing skills can be improved through knowledge of languages or fine art. Sometimes an avocation can turn into a vocation. For example, more than one weekend gardener has become a successful greenhouse owner.

Of course, no amount of experience or education can completely prepare you for owning your own business. Because every person, situation, and business is different, you are certainly going to encounter situations for which you could not have possibly prepared. Get as much experience and education as you can, but at some point you must "take off and hang on." You have to find a way to make your business go.

Forms of Business Organization

One of the first decisions you will need to make in starting a business is choosing a form of ownership. This section will lead you through your options and present the advantages and disadvantages of each.

Several issues should be considered when making this decision. To what extent do you want to be personally liable for financial and legal risk? Who will have controlling interest of the business? How will the business be financed? The three basic legal structures you can choose for your firm are sole proprietorship, partnership, or corporation, with specialized options of partnerships and corporations available.

About 72 percent of all businesses that exist in the United States are sole proprietorships, making this the most common form of ownership (see Figures 2.6, 2.7, and 2.8). Yet, sole proprietorships account for only 4 percent of the total revenue generated by businesses and only 18 percent of the net profits earned. By comparison, corporations bring in 84 percent of business-generated revenue and 59 percent of the net income earned, even though they account for only 20 percent of the total number of businesses. Partnerships are also in the minority, with 9 percent of the total number of businesses, 12 percent of the revenue, and 23 percent of the net income earned.

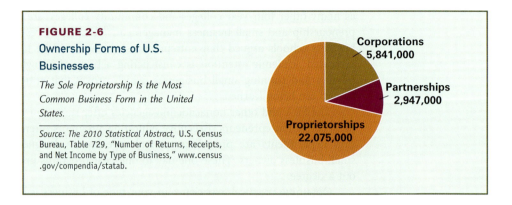

FIGURE 2-6

Ownership Forms of U.S. Businesses

The Sole Proprietorship Is the Most Common Business Form in the United States.

Source: The 2010 Statistical Abstract, U.S. Census Bureau, Table 729, "Number of Returns, Receipts, and Net Income by Type of Business," www.census .gov/compendia/statab.

Corporations
5,841,000

Partnerships
2,947,000

Proprietorships
22,075,000

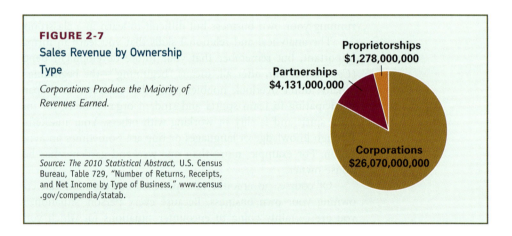

FIGURE 2-7

Sales Revenue by Ownership Type

Corporations Produce the Majority of Revenues Earned.

Source: The 2010 Statistical Abstract, U.S. Census Bureau, Table 729, "Number of Returns, Receipts, and Net Income by Type of Business," www.census .gov/compendia/statab.

Proprietorships
$1,278,000,000

Partnerships
$4,131,000,000

Corporations
$26,070,000,000

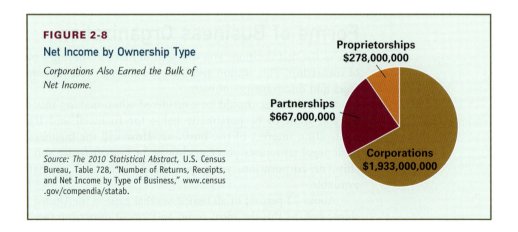

FIGURE 2-8

Net Income by Ownership Type

Corporations Also Earned the Bulk of Net Income.

Source: The 2010 Statistical Abstract, U.S. Census Bureau, Table 728, "Number of Returns, Receipts, and Net Income by Type of Business," www.census .gov/compendia/statab.

Proprietorships
$278,000,000

Partnerships
$667,000,000

Corporations
$1,933,000,000

Figure 2.9 shows that proprietorships increased in number and as a percentage of the total of the 27 million small businesses that existed in the United States from 1980 to 2003. This trend illustrates the rise of very small businesses. The number of corporations grew gradually, whereas the number of partnerships remained relatively constant. Changes in tax laws have an effect on the number of businesses of each type that are formed.

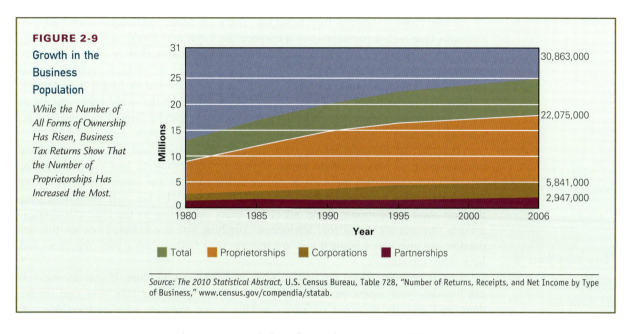

FIGURE 2-9

Growth in the Business Population

While the Number of All Forms of Ownership Has Risen, Business Tax Returns Show That the Number of Proprietorships Has Increased the Most.

Source: *The 2010 Statistical Abstract,* U.S. Census Bureau, Table 728, "Number of Returns, Receipts, and Net Income by Type of Business," www.census.gov/compendia/statab.

There is no single best form of organization. The choice depends on your short- and long-term needs, your tax situation, and your personal preferences, abilities, and resources. Don't confuse legal form of ownership with the size of the business. When you walk into a small neighborhood business, can you assume that it is a sole proprietorship? Not necessarily. A one-person flower shop may be a corporation, or a multimillion-dollar factory could be a sole proprietorship.

Sole Proprietorship

sole proprietorship
A business owned and operated by one person.

A *sole proprietorship* is a business that is owned and operated by one person. There are no legal requirements to establish a sole proprietorship. In most states, if you are operating under a name other than your full first and last legal names, you must register the business as a trade name with the state department of revenue (see Table 2.1).

Advantages As the owner of a sole proprietorship, you have complete control of the business. The sole proprietorship is well suited to the aspiring entrepreneur's desire for independence. You don't have to consult with any partners, stockholders, or boards of directors. As a result of this independence, you are free to respond quickly to new market needs. Because you make all the decisions and bear all the responsibility, you do not have to share profits with anyone. You may have a smaller pie, but it's all *your* pie. As Mel Brooks in the movie *History of the World, Part I,* said, "It's good to be the king." No one else in the business tells you what to do, criticizes your mistakes, or second-guesses your decisions.

TABLE 2-1

Balancing the Advantages and Disadvantages of Sole Proprietorships

ADVANTAGES	DISADVANTAGES
Independence	Unlimited liability
Easy to set up	Limited resources
Easy to close	Limited skills
Tax benefits	Lack of continuity

A sole proprietorship is easy to set up. There are fewer legal requirements and restrictions than with a partnership or a corporation. Legal and license costs are at a minimum. An inexpensive business license from the city or county clerk is all that is usually required—and sometimes not even that—unless your type of business requires special permits. For example, businesses selling food must be inspected by health departments. Otherwise, you need only hang your sign on the door and let the world know you are in business. The fast, simple way in which a proprietorship can be formed reduces start-up costs and stress.

The Internal Revenue Service (IRS) regards the business and the owner in a sole proprietorship as being a single entity. If your business shows a loss the first year or two (which is common), those losses can be deducted from any other income you have for the year. This tax advantage is short-lived, however. The tax code states that your business must make money three out of five years. According to the IRS, only money-making ventures are considered businesses. Anything else is a hobby. Even so, this deduction can give you a boost if you are starting your business on a part-time basis and have other income.

Just as proprietorships are easy to open, they are easy to close. If you choose, you can liquidate your assets, pay your bills, turn off the lights, and take your sign off the door, and you are then out of business. This is not the case with partnerships and corporations.

"You may have a smaller pie, but it's all your pie."

unlimited liability
The potential for an owner to lose more than has been invested in a business.

Disadvantages The biggest disadvantage of a sole proprietorship is its *unlimited liability*. As a sole proprietor, you are personally liable for all debts incurred by the business. If the business should fail, you could lose more than you invested in it. Personal assets, such as your home and car, might have to be liquidated to cover the business debt. Thus, although there are few caps on the potential for return with a sole proprietorship, there are similarly few caps on the amount you could lose.

The sole proprietorship is the most difficult form of business for which to raise capital from outside sources. As one individual, you have access to fewer financial resources than a group of people could gather. Lenders believe that their chances of seeing a return on their investment are reduced in a sole proprietorship and therefore are not as likely to loan money to this type of business.

The total responsibility of running a sole proprietorship may mean independence, but it can also be a disadvantage. Just as you are limited to the amount of capital you can raise, so you are limited to and by your own skills and capabilities. You may be an expert in some areas of running a business but be deficient in others.

Total responsibility can also mean a lack of continuity in the business. If you should become unable to work through illness, disability, or death, the business will cease to exist. Long vacations can become virtually impossible to take.

Partnership

partnership
An association of two or more persons to carry on as co-owners of a business for profit.

If two or more people are going into business together, they have two choices: form a partnership or form a corporation. A *partnership* is defined as an association of two or more persons to carry on as co-owners of a business for profit. Legally you can have a partnership without a written agreement (although it is not recommended), so the paperwork requirements for starting a partnership are about the same as those for a proprietorship.

When you form a partnership with friends, family, or associates, you may not think it is necessary to have a written agreement because you are so familiar with each other. You do. Problems are inevitable for every partnership, and the human memory is far too

The biggest advantage of a partnership is that you can pool your talents and resources.

© Walter Hodges/Jupiter Images

frail to depend upon in times of business difficulty. An agreement that is well thought out when the partnership is formed can save the business—and a friendship—later. Without a written agreement, a partnership operates according to the rules of the state under the Uniform Partnership Act (UPA). The intent of the UPA is to settle problems between partners. For example, without a written agreement that states otherwise, each partner shares equally in the profit and management of the business. The UPA is discussed in more detail later in this chapter.

Partners should bring complementary skills and resources to the alliance to give it a better chance of success. For instance, if one partner has creative abilities, the other partner should have a good business (financial) sense. Partners may also complement each other by providing different business contacts or amounts of capital. Think of the relationship this way: if both partners possess the same qualities, one of them probably isn't needed.

There are two types of partnerships: general and limited. Most of this discussion will focus on the **general partnership**, which is more common. In a general partnership, each partner faces the same personal liability as a sole proprietor. In a limited partnership, at least one of the partners has limited liability. This section will concentrate on general partnerships, with limited partnerships being discussed at the end of the section.

general partnership
A business structure in which the business owners share the management and risk of the business.

Advantages The biggest advantage of partnerships should be the pooling of managerial talent and capital to create a product or service that is better than what any of the partners could have created individually (see Table 2.2).

Access to additional capital is an advantage of partnerships. Partners can pool their money. Moreover, credit is easier to obtain than for a proprietor. The reason is that the

TABLE 2-2 Balancing the Advantages and Disadvantages of Partnerships	**ADVANTAGES**	**DISADVANTAGES**
	Pooled talent	Unlimited liability
	Pooled resources	Potential for management conflict
	Easy to form	Less independence than proprietorships
	Tax benefits	Continuity or transfer of ownership

"An agreement that is well thought out when the partnership is formed can save the business—and a friendship—later."

creditor can collect the debt from any one or all of the partners. Partnerships can also benefit from more management expertise in decision making. With more partners involved, there is a higher chance of someone knowing what to do or having prior experience in any given situation.

Partnerships, like proprietorships, have a tax advantage in that the owners pay taxes as individuals. Therefore, profits are taxed only once on each partner's share of the income. The partnership must file an informational return that reports how much money it earned or lost during the tax year and what share of the income or loss belongs to each partner.

Partnerships are easy to create. All you need are the appropriate business licenses and a tax number, and you're in business—for better or for worse.

Disadvantages As with sole proprietorships, a disadvantage of partnerships is that the general partners carry the burden of unlimited liability. Each general partner's liability is not limited to the amount of his or her investment but rather extends to that partner's personal property as well. Even if the partnership agreement specifies a defined split in profits, each partner is 100 percent responsible for all liabilities.

In a partnership, you can be held liable for the negligence of your partners. A great deal of trust, a comprehensive agreement, and a good lawyer are, therefore, needed before opening such a business. Similarly, each partner can act as an agent of the partnership. In other words, any partner can enter into a contract for the partnership, incurring debt or other responsibilities, or selling assets, unless limited by the *articles of partnership*, discussed in detail later in this chapter. The choice of a business partner is much like choosing a partner for marriage. You need to know and be able to live with the other person's character, work habits, and values to make sure you are compatible.

The potential for managerial conflict within the partnership is one of the most serious problems that can threaten its viability. If partners disagree on matters that involve core issues, such as a future direction for the business, the partnership could literally split at the seams.

If a common reason to go into small business is independence, entering into a partnership limits that independence. For example, what happens if you want to reinvest profits in the business, but your partner wants to start holding your business meetings in Hawaii and have the company buy each of you new cars? Some resolution must be found, or the entire business could be in jeopardy. Being a partner requires compromise and cooperation.

Although the ability to raise capital is better with a partnership than with a proprietorship, a partnership still cannot usually gather as many resources as a corporation.

Another financial problem could occur when the partnership decides to retain some of its income and reinvest it in the business. All partners must pay income tax on their share of the partnership's income, even if they do not receive those funds. This requirement could prove financially difficult for some partners.

Continuity can also be a problem for partnerships. Difficulties may arise if a partner wants to withdraw from the partnership, dies, or becomes unable to continue in the business. Even if the partnership agreement identifies the value of each owner's share, the remaining partners may not have the financial resources to buy out the one who wants to leave. If a partner leaves, the partnership is dissolved. The remaining partners must find a new partner to bring in, contribute additional capital themselves, or terminate the business. This problem can be avoided in advance by including a *buy-sell agreement* in the *articles of partnership*, which will be discussed in detail later in this chapter.

The buy-sell agreement spells out what will happen if one of the partners wants to leave voluntarily, becomes disabled, or dies. A sensible solution is a "right of first refusal" clause, which requires the selling partner to give the remaining partners the first chance to buy the exiting partner's share. This proactive solution is highly recommended for all partnerships and corporations.

limited partnership
A business structure in which one or more of the owners may be granted limited liability as long as one partner is designated as a general partner with unlimited liability.

Limited Partnership The **limited partnership** was created to avoid some of the problems of a general partnership while retaining its basic benefits. A limited partnership must have at least one general partner who retains unlimited liability and all of the other responsibilities discussed in the general partnership section. In addition, any number of limited partners with limited liability is allowed. Limited partners are usually passive investors. All they can lose is the amount they invest in the business. With very few exceptions, limited partners cannot participate in the management of the business without losing their liability protection. Limited partnerships are a good way for the general partners to acquire capital—from the limited partners—without giving up control, taking on debt, or going through the process of forming a corporation.

The cost and complication of organizing a limited partnership can be as high as those for forming a corporation. A document called a *limited partnership agreement* is required in most states. This agreement identifies each partner's potential liability and the amount of capital each partner supplies. Most limited partnerships are formed for real estate investment because of the tax advantages to the limited partners, who can write off depreciation and other deductions from their personal taxes.[21]

Uniform Partnership Act Signed in 1917 and revised in 1994, the Uniform Partnership Act (UPA) covers most legal issues concerning partnerships and has been adopted by every state in the union except Louisiana. The intent of the UPA is to settle problems that arise between partners. The best way for partners to protect their individual interests and the interests of the business is to draft their own articles of partnership (discussed later). Because partnerships can be formed by two people simply verbally agreeing start a business, however, not all of them write such articles. Even if the partners do not draw up a written agreement, the UPA provides some measure of protection and regulation for them, including the following provisions:

- All partners must agree to any assignment of partnership property.
- Each partner has one vote, no matter what percentage of the partnership she owns, unless a written agreement states otherwise.
- Accurate bookkeeping records are required, and all partners have the right to examine them.
- Each partner owes loyalty to the partnership by not doing anything that would intentionally harm the partnership or the other partners.
- Partners may draw on their share of the profits. This ability provides partners with access to their own capital.
- Salaries must be part of a written agreement. If a loss is incurred, partners must pay their share.

State-specific revisions to this act primarily involve the way in which a general partnership can become a *limited-liability partnership (LLP),*[22] which is very similar to a *limited-liability company (LLC),* which is discussed in detail later in this chapter.

articles of partnership
The contract between partners of a business that defines obligations and responsibilities of the business owners.

Articles of Partnership The formal contract between the principals, or people forming a partnership, is called the **articles of partnership**. The purpose of this contract is to outline the partners' obligations and responsibilities. As a legal document, it helps to prevent problems from arising between partners and provides a mechanism for solving any problems that do arise. A partnership agreement can save your business and your friendship. Articles of partnership usually specify the following items:

- *The name, location, and purpose of the partnership.* States the name of the partnership, where it is located, and why it exists.
- *The contribution of each partner in cash, services, or property.* Describes what each partner brings to the company.
- *The authority of each partner and the need for consensual decision making.* Specifies, for example, that large purchases (say, over $5,000) or contracts require the approval of a majority (or both) of the partners.
- *The management responsibilities of each partner.* Specifies, for example, that all partners must be actively involved and participate equally in the management and the operation of the business.
- *The duration of the partnership.* States whether the partnership is created to last indefinitely or for a specific period of time or for a specific project, such as building a new shopping center. The latter type of partnership is called a *joint venture*.
- *The division of profits and losses.* Specifies the distribution of profits or losses, which does not have to be exactly equal. The distribution could be allocated according to the same percentages that the partners contributed to the partnership. If not exactly equal, the division must be clearly stated.
- *The salaries and draws of partners.* States how the partners will be compensated, a decision that is made after the decision about how to divide profits and losses at the end of the accounting period. A *draw* is the removal of expected profits by a partner.
- *The procedure for dispute settlement or arbitration.* Describes a procedure for mediation or arbitration to solve serious disagreements, thus saving a costly trip to court.
- *The procedure for sale of partnership interest.* Provides veto power to partners in case one partner tries to sell his or her interest in the business.
- *The procedure for addition of a new partner.* States whether the vote for adding a new partner can be a simple majority or must be unanimous.
- *The procedure for absence or disability of a partner.* Describes the procedure for dealing with an accident, illness, or death of a partner.
- *The procedure and conditions for dissolving the partnership.* Describes what will happen if and when the partnership ends.

joint venture
A partnership that is created to complete a specified purpose and is limited in duration.

Corporation

The **corporation** is the most complicated business structure to form. In the eyes of the law, a corporation is an autonomous entity that has the legal rights of a person, including the ability to sue and be sued, to own property, and to engage in business transactions. A corporation must act in accordance with its charter and the laws of the state in which it exists. These laws vary by state.

This section is concerned with the type of corporation most common among small businesses—a **closely held corporation**. With this type of business, relatively few people (usually fewer than ten) own stock. Most owners participate in the firm's management, and those who don't are usually family or friends. By contrast, corporations that sell shares of stock to the public and are listed on a stock exchange are called **public corporations**. Public corporations must comply with more detailed and rigorous federal, state, and Securities and Exchange Commission (SEC) regulations, such as disclosing financial information in the company's annual report. These are different animals from the closely held corporations of small businesses.

corporation
A business structure that creates an entity separate from its owners and managers.

closely held corporation
A corporation owned by a limited group of people. Its stock is not traded publicly.

public corporations
A corporation that sells shares of stock to the public and is listed on a stock exchange.

C corporation

A separate legal entity that reports its income and expenses on a corporate income tax return and is taxed on its profits at corporate income tax rates.

This discussion will begin with the regular, or *C*, corporation. Later we will look at variations called the *S corporation* and the *limited-liability company (LLC)*. The **C corporation** is a separate legal entity that reports its income and expenses on a corporate income tax return and is taxed on its profits at corporate income tax rates.

Advantages   By far the biggest advantage of forming a corporation is the limited liability it offers its owners. In a corporation, the most you stand to lose is the amount you have invested in it. If the business fails or if it is sued, your personal property remains protected from creditors (see Table 2.3).

As an example of how limited liability can be an advantage to a small business, consider the case of Kathy, owner of a local pub. Kathy is worried that one of her employees might inadvertently or intentionally serve alcohol to a minor or to an intoxicated person. If the intoxicated person were to get into an automobile accident, Kathy could be sued. In addition to buying liability insurance, Kathy has also incorporated her business so her personal assets will be protected in the event of a lawsuit.

Corporations generally have easier access to financing, because bankers, venture capitalists, and other lending institutions tend to regard them as being more stable than proprietorships or partnerships. Corporations have proven to be the best way to accumulate large pools of capital.

Corporations can also take advantage of the skills of several people and draw on their increased human and managerial resources. Boards of directors can bring valuable expertise and advice to small corporations. Also, because a corporation has a life of its own, it continues to operate even if its stockholders change. Transfer of ownership can be completed through the sale of the stock.

Disadvantages   Complying with requirements of the state corporate code poses challenges that are not faced by proprietorships or partnerships. Even the smallest corporation must file *articles of incorporation* (described later in this chapter) with the secretary of state, adopt bylaws, and keep records from annual stockholder and director meetings. Directors must meet to show that they are setting policy and are actively involved in running the corporation. Fulfilling these requirements is necessary to prevent the IRS, creditors, or lawsuits from removing the limited-liability protection of a corporation. If a business does not meet these requirements, it is not considered to be operating as a corporation, and therefore forfeits the limited-liability protection of its directors and stockholders, leaving them personally responsible for liabilities. The process of denying limited-liability protection is referred to as "piercing the corporate veil."[23]

The legal and administrative costs incurred in starting a corporation can be a sizable disadvantage. *Self-incorporation kits* exist, but be careful about going through the incorporation process without the aid of an attorney. The cost of incorporating can easily reach $1,000 before the business is even open.

TABLE 2-3

Balancing the Advantages and Disadvantages of Corporations

ADVANTAGES	DISADVANTAGES
Limited liability	Expensive to start
Increased access to resources	Complex to maintain
Transfer of ownership	Double taxation*

*C corporation only.

Corporate profits face double taxation in that the profits are taxed at the corporate level first and can be taxed again once the profits are distributed to stockholders. If a stockholder also works in the corporation, she is considered to be an employee and must be paid a "reasonable wage," which is subject to state and federal payroll taxes.

Even the limited liability that incorporation affords may not completely protect your personal property. If you use debt financing or borrow money, lenders will probably expect you to secure the loan with your personal property. Therefore, if the business must be liquidated, your personal property can be attached.

If you sell stock in your corporation, you inevitably give up some control of your business. The more capital you need to raise, the more control you must relinquish. If large blocks of stock are sold, you may end up as a minority stockholder of what used to be your own business. Raising capital in this way may be necessary for growth, but you lose some measure of control in the process.

articles of incorporation
A document describing the business that is filed with the state in which a business is formed.

Forming a Corporation   The process of incorporating your business includes the following steps: First, you must prepare **articles of incorporation** and file them with the secretary of state where you are incorporating. You must choose a board of directors, adopt bylaws, elect officers, and issue stock. At the time you incorporate, you must also decide whether to form a C corporation, an S corporation, or a limited-liability company (LLC), all of which will be described in this chapter.

You are not required to use an attorney to file articles of incorporation, but attempting the process and making a mistake could end up costing you more than an attorney would have charged for the job. Although states vary in their requirements, articles of incorporation usually include the following items:

- *The name of your company.* The name you choose must be registered with the state in which it will operate. This registration prevents companies from operating under the same name, which could create confusion for the consumer. Your corporation's name must not be deceptive about its type of business.
- *The purpose of your corporation.* You must state the intended nature of your business. Being specific about your purpose will give financial institutions a better idea of what you do. Incorporating in a state that permits very general information in this section allows you to change the nature of your business without reincorporating.
- *The names and addresses of the incorporators.* Some states require at least one incorporator to reside in that state.
- *The names and addresses of the corporation's initial officers and directors.*
- *The address of the corporation's home office.* You must establish headquarters in the state from which you receive your charter or register as an out-of-state corporation in your own state.
- *The amount of capital required at time of incorporation.* The proposed capital structure includes the amount and type of capital stock you issue at the time of incorporation.
- *Capital stock to be authorized.* In this section, you specify the types of stock and the number of shares that the corporation will issue.
- *Bylaws of the corporation.* A corporation's bylaws are the rules and regulations by which it agrees to operate. Bylaws must stipulate the rights and powers of shareholders, directors, and officers; the time and place for the annual shareholder meeting and the number needed for a quorum (the number needed to transact business); how the board of directors is to be elected and compensated; the dates of the corporation's fiscal year; and who within the corporation is authorized to sign contracts.

- *Length of time the corporation will operate.* Most corporations are established with the intention that they will operate in perpetuity. However, you may specify a duration for the corporation's existence.

Some small business owners minimize the legal costs of forming a corporation by doing much of the background work themselves. Several software companies have jumped on this do-it-yourself bandwagon. For instance, the PC Law Library, published by Cosmi Corporation of Rancho Dominguez, California, contains more than 200 legal documents for both business and personal situations. Nolo Press of Berkeley, California, a publisher of legal reference books, has developed Nolo's Partnership Maker and Incorporator Pro. These software packages provide standard and alternative clauses that can be included in partnership agreements and articles of incorporation.

If you decide to use such software, it is highly advisable that you have an attorney who is familiar with your state's incorporation or partnership laws review your papers to make sure that all the required information has been covered.

Specialized Forms of Corporations

You have two other options to consider in addition to the C corporation. S corporations and limited-liability companies are corporations that are granted special tax status by the Internal Revenue Service. A competent tax advisor can assist you to determine whether one of these options could provide a tax advantage for your business.

S corporation
A special type of corporation in which the owners are taxed as partners.

S Corporation An **S corporation** provides you with the limited-liability protection of a corporation while allowing the tax advantages of a partnership. It avoids the double-taxation disadvantage of regular corporations and lets you offset losses of the business against your personal income tax. The S corporation files an informational tax return to report its income and expenses but it is not taxed separately. Income and expenses of the S corporation "flow through" to the shareholders in proportion to the number of shares they own. Profits are taxed to shareholders at their individual income tax rate.

To qualify as an S corporation, a business must meet the following requirements:

- Shareholders must be individuals, estates, or trusts—not other corporations.
- Nonresident aliens cannot be shareholders.
- Only one class of outstanding common stock can be issued.
- All shareholders must consent to the election of the S corporation.
- State regulations specify the portion of revenue that must be derived from business activity, not from passive investments.
- There can be no more than 100 shareholders.[24]

limited-liability company (LLC)
A relatively new type of corporation that taxes the owners as partners yet provides a more flexible structure than an S corporation.

Limited-Liability Company A relatively new form of ownership, the **limited-liability company (LLC)**, is quickly becoming the "hot" business form on its way to becoming the entity of choice for the future. First recognized by the IRS in 1988, LLCs offer the limited-liability protection of a corporation and the tax advantages of a partnership without the restrictions of an S corporation. The LLC is still evolving, so it is wise to keep a watchful eye on its development. For example, although the LLC is provided pass-through treatment of revenue for federal taxation purposes, individual states may tax it differently. Most states tax it as a partnership, but some, such as Florida, tax it as a corporation.[25] Check with your tax accountant to see how LLCs are taxed in your state. Furthermore, some states allow the formation of an LLC by a single individual, in which case the IRS will treat it as a sole proprietorship.

The owners of an LLC are called *members*. Unlike the situation for C and S corporations, shares of stock do not represent ownership by the members. Rather, the rights and responsibilities of members are specified by the operating agreement of the LLC, which is like a combination of the bylaws and a shareholder agreement in other corporations. LLCs offer small business owners greater flexibility than either C or S corporations in that they can write the operating agreement to contain any provision desired regarding the LLC's internal structure and operations. In particular, LLCs are not constrained by the regulations imposed on C and S corporations dictating who can and cannot participate in them, what they can or cannot own, or how profits and losses will be allocated to members. For example, the owners of an LLC can allocate 50 percent of the business's profits to a person who owns 30 percent of the company. This distribution is not allowable in C or S corporations.

Although the requirements and rules that govern LLCs vary from state to state, there is some consistency. For example, almost every state requires an LLC designator (such as LLC, L.C., Limited Company, or Ltd.) in the business name. Still, it is a good idea to check your local regulations when starting an LLC.

You should seriously consider forming an LLC if you need flexibility in the legal structure of your business, desire limited liability, and prefer to be taxed as a partnership rather than as a corporation.

nonprofit corporation
A tax-exempt corporation that exists for a purpose other than making a profit.

Nonprofit Corporation   The **nonprofit corporation** is a tax-exempt organization formed for religious, charitable, literary, artistic, scientific, or educational purposes. Nonprofit corporations depend largely on grants from private foundations and public donations to meet their expenses. People or organizations that contribute to a nonprofit can deduct their contributions from their own taxes.

Assets dedicated to nonprofit purposes cannot be reclassified. If its directors decide to terminate the corporation, its assets must go to another nonprofit organization.[26] The details of forming and running a nonprofit corporation are beyond the interest of most readers of this book. To learn more about this business form, consult the sources listed in the endnotes.

Summary

1. Articulate the differences between the small business manager and the entrepreneur.

An entrepreneur is a person who takes advantage of an opportunity and assumes the risk involved in creating a business for the purpose of making a profit. A small business manager is involved in the day-to-day operation of an established business. Each faces significant challenges, but they are at different stages of development in the entrepreneurship/small business management model.

2. Discuss the steps in preparing for small business ownership.

The entrepreneurship process involves an *innovative* idea for a new product, process, or service. A *triggering event* is something that happens to the entrepreneur that causes him to begin bringing the idea to reality. *Implementation* is the stage at which the entrepreneur forms a business based on her idea. The first stage of the small business management process is *growth*, which usually means the business is becoming large enough to generate

enough profit to support itself and its owner. The *maturity* stage is reached when the business is stable and well established. The *harvest* stage occurs when the small business manager leaves the business because of its sale, merger, or failure.

3. Enumerate the advantages and disadvantages of self-employment.

The advantages of self-employment include the opportunity for independence, the chance for a better lifestyle, and the potential for significant profit. The disadvantages include the personal liability you would face should the business fail, the uncertainty of an income, and the long working hours.

4. Describe the three main forms of ownership—sole proprietorship, partnership, and corporation—and their unique features.

There are several choices for the form of ownership of your small business. The most common is the sole proprietorship. If you choose a partnership, you have the choice of a general partnership, in which all partners are fully liable for the business, or a limited partnership, in which at least one partner retains unlimited liability. A corporation offers its owners limited liability. In forming a corporation, you are creating a legal entity that has the same rights as a person. Variations of corporations include S corporations, limited-liability companies, and nonprofit corporations.

Questions for Review and Discussion

1. What do entrepreneurs do that distinguishes them from other persons involved in business?
2. Why might personality characteristics be good predictors of who will be a successful entrepreneur?
3. If a friend told you that entrepreneurs are high-risk takers, how would you set the story straight?
4. Describe the significance of triggering events in entrepreneurship. Give examples.
5. How is small business management different from entrepreneurship?
6. Why would an entrepreneur be concerned about harvesting a business that has not yet been started?
7. Explain why people who own a small business may not enjoy pure independence.
8. If personal characteristics or personality traits do not predict who will be a successful entrepreneur, why are they significant to the study of entrepreneurship or small business management? Which characteristics do you think are most important?
9. Sole proprietorships account for 76 percent of all U.S. businesses and generate 6 percent of all business revenue. Only 18 percent of all sole proprietorships are incorporated, but they generate 90 percent of all revenue. What do these statistics tell you about the two forms of ownership?
10. Under what conditions would you consider joining a partnership? Why would you avoid becoming a partner?
11. When would forming a limited-liability company be more advantageous than creating a C corporation or a partnership?

Questions for Critical Thinking

1. Think of an activity that you love to do; it could be a personal interest or a hobby. How could you turn your passion for this activity into a business? What questions would you have to answer for yourself before you took this step? What triggering events in your personal life would it take for you to start this business?
2. Imagine that the principal from the high school you attended (and graduated from) called to invite you to make a presentation to a newly founded entrepreneurship club at the school. What would you tell this group of high school students about owning their own business as a career option?

What Would You Do?

"Gardeners love this crap." That's the slogan for Pierce Ledbetter's Memphis, Tennessee–based company, Zoo Doo. In 1990, while still a student at Cornell University, Ledbetter returned home to Memphis and talked the managers at the local zoo into selling him composted animal manure from the enormous amounts produced by the zoo's animals daily. Why would any sane individual want animal manure? Well, it's extremely rich in soil nutrients. Wanting to cash in on the gardening craze just beginning to sweep across the United States, Ledbetter saw a marketing opportunity. He began selling his "Zoo Doo" in attractively designed pails. He even had the unique idea of having the manure compressed into various animal-shaped sculptures that gardeners could place in their gardens to decompose naturally and organically. His designs caught the eye of garden centers and mass merchandisers across the United States. Ledbetter's Zoo Doo now claims sales of about $1.5 million.

But having a great product and a great slogan isn't enough to make any small business a success. It's important to choose a form of business ownership that best meets your individual needs, goals, and constraints.

Factors such as availability of adequate funding, amount of management expertise, product liability possibilities, and willingness to share decision making can influence which form of ownership is most appropriate.

Source: Cyndee Miller, "Entrepreneur Steps Firmly into the Field of Manure," *Marketing News,* June 22, 1992, 15, 18.

Questions

1. Put yourself in Pierce Ledbetter's shoes (and watch where you step!). Discuss the advantages and disadvantages of organizing Zoo Doo as a sole proprietorship, a partnership, or a corporation. Think of all the possible factors that might influence your choice.

2. Now that you've looked at the various ways to organize Zoo Doo, it's time to convince your management professor at Cornell University of your decision. Write a letter describing the approach you've decided to take in organizing your Zoo Doo business and why.

PART 2

Small Business Planning

Getting a small business started and keeping it successful will not happen by accident. Planning is required to gather the resources needed and to allocate them wisely. Although some successful businesses have been established without a formal plan, none was created without planning. The most important thing about business planning is not the written plan that is produced, but rather the strategic thinking that goes into the writing. The next two chapters will take you through several facets of business planning. **Chapter 3** discusses social responsibility and strategic planning. **Chapter 4** concentrates on the operational side of business planning.

A small business owner has three primary options for getting into business: A franchise can be purchased, an existing business can be bought, or a new venture can be created. Each strategy has its advantages and disadvantages, but which one is right for your business? Circumstances may mean that only one or two of these options are available to you. The correct path depends on several factors that will be explored as you make your early decisions. **Chapter 5** introduces us to franchising, **Chapter 6** covers the purchase of an existing business, and **Chapter 7** focuses on the excitement and risks of starting from scratch.

3

Focusing on Ethical Issues and Strategy

CHAPTER LEARNING OUTCOMES

After reading this chapter, you should be able to:

1. **Explain the relationship between social responsibility, ethics, and strategic planning.**

2. **Name the levels of social responsibility.**

3. **Discuss how to establish a code of ethics for your business.**

4. **Describe each step in the strategic planning process, and explain the importance of competitive advantage.**

D o socially responsible products come from government mandates? How about from demands of environmental groups? Once again, entrepreneurs are the true answer. While motorcycles are a common commuting tool in Asian and European countries, Americans purchase about 1 million motorcycles each year—and only about 10 percent of those are for commuting to school and work. Craig Bramscher intends to change that.

Bramscher is founder and CEO of Brammo motorcycles. Brammos could be called the cycles of "no," as in no noise, no smell, no clutch, no gears, no shifting, no emissions. The 100-percent electric cycles can travel 50 miles at 60 miles per hour and take about

three hours to recharge when plugged into a regular household outlet. Brammos cycles are green by several definitions—besides producing no emissions, their shells are made from recycled water bottles. Prices hover about $8,000 before the deduction of a federal income tax credit.

Brammos cycles are manufactured in a 21,000 square-foot plant in Ashland, Oregon, where Bramscher plans to build 10,000 cycles per year. When demand increases in Europe and Asia, production facilities will be built in late 2010 to bump capacity to 100,000 units. Once produced, the bikes are sold exclusively through Best Buy (six on the West Coast

so far) and serviced by the Geek Squad. Bramscher calls his product "electronics that you ride."

Bramscher sees "a hunger and interest" for his bikes globally. His vision for the future comes from a combination of his technical background and entrepreneurial spirit. After graduating from Harvard, he ran several computer companies including DreamMedia—the sale of which generated about $10 million for seed money that sprouted into e-motorcycles.

As innovative as Brammos cycles are, they are not alone in the market. Mission One, from Mission Motors, set a land-speed record for an electric motorcycle by hitting 150 miles per hour on the Bonneville Salt Flats. That'll break the image of cycles that don't roar as being dorky!

Sources: Susan Carpenter, "(batteries included)", *Entrepreneur,* April 2010, 24–36; Lynne D. Johnson, "Worldwide Debut of Brammo Enertia Electric Motorcycle," *Fast Company,* June 9, 2009, www.fastcompany.com; and www.brammo.com.

Relationship between Social Responsibility, Ethics, and Strategic Planning

What do concepts like social responsibility and ethics have to do with strategic planning in business? They are rarely covered together in textbooks, but the connection between them is especially strong in small businesses because of the inseparability of the owner and the business. The direction in which the business is heading is the same direction in which the owner is going. What is important to the business is what is important to the owner. In many cases, a small business is an extension of the owner's life and personality.

Strategic planning is the guiding process used to identify the direction for your business. It spells out a long-term game plan for operating your business. *Social responsibilities* are the obligations of a business to maximize the positive effects it has on society and minimize the negative effects. *Ethics* are the rules of moral values that guide decision making—your understanding of the difference between right and wrong.

> *"In many cases, a small business is an extension of the owner's life and personality."*

Let's look at the relationship between social responsibility, ethics, and strategic planning in the following way: When you assess your company's external environment for opportunities and threats, you identify what you might do. When you look at your internal strengths and weaknesses, you see what you can do and cannot do. Your personal values are ingrained in the business; they are what you want to do. Your ethical standards will determine what is right for you to do. Finally, in responding to everyone who could be affected by your business, social responsibility guides what you should do.

The connection between social responsibility, ethics, and strategic planning is especially strong in small business. In fact, at a very fundamental level, they are more difficult to separate than to connect.

Social Responsibilities of Small Business

social responsibility
The obligation of a business to have a positive effect on society on four levels—economic, legal, ethical, and philanthropic.

Social responsibility means different things to different people. In this chapter, we will define it as the managerial obligation to take action to protect and improve society as a whole, while achieving the goals of the business.[1] The manager of a socially responsible business should attempt to make a profit, obey the law, act ethically, and be a good corporate citizen.

Your level of commitment to these responsibilities and the strategic planning process you conduct form the heart of your business—the foundation and philosophy on which the business rests. Knowing what is important to yourself, your business, and everyone affected by its actions (social responsibility) is significant in deciding where you want to go and how to get there (strategic planning). The business you start or operate takes on a *culture*, or a set of shared beliefs, of its own. When you create a business, *your* values have a strong influence on the culture of the business you create. The values and culture of your business are demonstrated by your socially responsible (or irresponsible) actions.

As noted earlier, social responsibilities are the obligations of a business to maximize the positive effects it has on society and minimize the negative effects. There are four levels of social responsibility: economic, legal, ethical, and philanthropic (see Figure 3.1).[2] Although the primary responsibility of a business is economic, our legal system also enforces what we, as a collective group or society, consider proper behavior for a business. In addition, the firm itself decides what is ethical behavior, or what is right beyond legal requirements. Finally, a business is expected to act like a good citizen and help improve the quality of life for everyone—a philanthropic obligation. Although all four of these obligations have always existed, ethical and philanthropic issues have received considerable attention recently.

Economic Responsibility

As a businessperson in a free enterprise system, you have not only the fundamental right but also the responsibility to make a profit. You are in business because you are providing a good or a service that is needed. If you do not make a profit, how can you stay in business? If you don't stay in business, how can you provide that good or service to people who need it?

Historically, the primary role for business has been economic. When entrepreneurs assume the risk of going into business, profit is their incentive. If you don't attend to the economics of your business, you can't take care of anything else. Therefore, the economic responsibilities of your business include a commitment to being as profitable as possible; to making sure employees, creditors, and suppliers are paid; to maintaining a strong competitive position; and to maintaining efficient operation of your business.

"If you don't attend to the economics of your business, you can't take care of anything else."

FIGURE 3-1
Pyramid of Social Responsibility

Businesses Are Expected to Act in a Responsible Manner in Four Interconnected Areas.

Philanthropic Goodwill — Be a good corporate citizen. Contribute resources to the community; improve quality of life.

Ethical Responsibility — Be ethical. Obligation to do what is right, just, and fair. Avoid harm.

Legal Obligations — Obey the law. Law is society's codification of right and wrong. Play by the rules of the game.

Economic Responsibility — Be profitable. The foundation on which all other levels rest.

Source: Reprinted from *Business Horizons*, July–August 1991. "The Pyramid of Corporate Social Responsibility: Toward the Moral Management of Organizational Stakeholders," by Archie B. Carroll. Copyright © 1991 with permission from Elsevier.

Economist Milton Friedman emphasizes the economic side of social responsibility. Friedman contends that business owners should not be expected to know what social problems should receive priority or how many resources should be dedicated to solving them. He states, "There is one and only one social responsibility of business: to use its resources and energy in activities designed to increase its profits so long as it stays within the rules of the game ... [and] engages in open and free competition, without deception and fraud."[3] His point of view is that business revenues that are diverted to outside causes raise prices to consumers, decrease employee pay, and may support issues with which some of the business's stakeholders do not agree. Friedman quotes another believer in free enterprise, Adam Smith, who in 1776 said, "I have never known much good done by those who profess to trade for the public good."[4] Basically, Friedman's argument is that businesses should produce goods and services and let concerned individuals and government agencies solve social problems.

Legal Obligations

Above making a profit, each of us is expected to comply with the federal, state, and local laws that lay out the ground rules for operation. Laws can be seen as society's codes of right and wrong; in other words, laws exist to ensure that individuals and businesses do what is considered right by society as a whole. These codes change continually, as laws are added, repealed, or amended in an attempt to match changes in public sentiment. Laws regulating business activity generally involve four areas: (1) consumers, (2) the competition, (3) the environment, and (4) employees.

Consumer Protection Laws geared toward consumer protection became popular when Ralph Nader started the *consumer protection movement* in the early 1960s. Beginning with his safety campaign in the automotive industry, Nader and the consumer activist group he formed, Nader's Raiders, have fought to protect the safety and rights of consumers. Consumer activism has taken the form of letter-writing campaigns, lobbying of government agencies, and boycotting of companies that are perceived to be irresponsible.

Of course, consumer protection did not start in the 1960s. Laws protecting consumers from unsafe business practices date back to 1906, when the Pure Food and Drug Act was passed, largely in response to Upton Sinclair's 1905 book about the meatpacking industry, *The Jungle*. Today, government agencies such as the Consumer Product Safety Commission and the Food and Drug Administration (FDA) set safety standards and regulations for consumer products, food, and drugs.

Trade Protection Laws that protect competition date back to the Sherman Antitrust Act of 1890, which prohibits monopolies. These laws see competition and unrestrained trade as creating a series of checks and balances on businesses, prompting them to provide quality products and services at reasonable prices. The Federal Trade Commission (FTC) enforces many of these laws.

Environmental Protection Laws protecting the environment were passed beginning in the 1960s to set minimum standards for business practices concerning air, water, and noise. The Environmental Protection Agency (EPA) was created to enforce many of these laws.

Employee Protection The 1960s saw the passage of legislation regarding equality in the workplace. The Civil Rights Act of 1964 prohibits discrimination in employment on the basis of race, color, sex, religion, or national origin. The Equal Employment Opportunity

Commission (EEOC) enforces these laws in addition to the Age Discrimination in Employment Act (ADEA) and the Equal Pay Act (EPA).[5] Although the Americans with Disabilities Act (ADA) of 1990, equal employment opportunity (EEO), and affirmative action regulate diversity in the workplace (see Chapter 10 for more details on these issues), a small business owner must keep the big picture in mind. The key to managing diversity is to see people as individuals with strengths and weaknesses and to create a climate where all can contribute.[6]

Consequences for Small Business Some laws have unexpected consequences that place a heavier burden on small business than on large ones. For example, the intent of the Sarbanes-Oxley Act was to make publicly traded firms more trustworthy, but instead it has prevented many successful small businesses from making initial public offerings of their stock. Initial compliance for firms covered by the legislation may cost as much as several hundred thousand dollars, and maintaining that compliance may add another $50,000 per year in accounting and legal fees.[7] Because of this legal burden, and the auditing requirements of Section 404 that can be crushing for small businesses, many entrepreneurs who would like to go public have decided against taking that step—at least for now.[8]

Sexual harassment is an ongoing problem in small businesses, although it generally doesn't receive as much public attention as multimillion-dollar corporate settlements of sexual harassment lawsuits. Sexual harassment can damage a person's dignity, productivity, and eagerness to come to work, which is costly both to that person and to the business.[9] EEOC guidelines define sexual harassment as unwelcome sexual advances, requests for sexual favors, and other verbal or physical conduct of a sexual nature when (1) sexual activity is required to get or keep a job or (2) a hostile environment is created in which work is unreasonably difficult.[10] To help keep your small business free of harassment, the American Management Association recommends that you take the following steps:

- Have a clear written policy prohibiting sexual harassment.
- Hold mandatory supervisory training programs on policies and prevention of harassment.
- Ensure that the workplace is free of offensive materials.
- Implement a program for steps to take when a complaint of harassment is received.
- Keep informed of all complaints and steps taken.
- Make sure the commitment against harassment exists at every level.[11]

Public attitudes ebb and flow on many subjects. Society's attitude toward office romances (not including extramarital affairs and boss-employee relations) is swinging toward greater tolerance and away from the dictum to "keep it professional." In a recent survey by the American Management Association, two-thirds of the managers questioned said that it is acceptable to date a colleague.[12] The Society of Human Resource Management, however, reports that most businesses ban fraternization between people in the same chain of command.

How do you, as a small business owner, allow love to bloom in the workplace and still guard against sexual harassment lawsuits? Some employers ask coworkers who are dating to sign a "love contract," or *consensual-relationship agreement*, in which both parties acknowledge that they are willing participants.[13]

Ethical Responsibility

Although economic and legal responsibilities are shown in Figure 3.1 as separate levels of obligation, they actually coexist because together they represent the minimum threshold of socially acceptable business behavior. *Ethics* are the rules of moral values that guide decision making by groups and individuals. They represent a person's fundamental orientation toward life—what he or she sees as right and wrong. Ethical responsibilities of a business encompass how the organization's decisions and actions show concern for what its stakeholders (employees, customers, stockholders, and the community) consider fair and just.

The literature of business ethics identifies four dominant ethical perspectives:

- *Idealism* includes religious and other beliefs and principles.
- *Utilitarianism* deals with the consequences of one's own actions.
- *Deontology* is a rule-based, or duty-based, principle.
- *Virtue ethics* is concerned with the character of an individual.[14]

As individuals, we resolve ethical issues by being guided by one of these perspectives. Research has shown that no single ethical perspective dominates among small business owners. Rather, they consider ethical considerations in general to be very important in the way they conduct their businesses, no matter which principle actually influences their individual behavior at a given time.

Changes in ethical standards and values usually precede changes in laws. As described in the previous section on legal obligations, society's expectations changed dramatically in the 1960s, which led to the passage of new laws. Changing values cause constant interaction between the legal and ethical levels of social responsibility. Even businesses that set high ethical standards and try to operate well above legal standards, however, may have difficulty keeping up with expectations that perpetually rise.

Philanthropic Goodwill

Philanthropy is the highest level illustrated on the social responsibility pyramid of Figure 3.1. It includes businesses participating in programs that improve the quality of life, raise the standard of living, and promote goodwill. The difference between ethical responsibility and ***philanthropic goodwill*** is that the latter is seen not so much as an obligation but rather as a contribution to society to make it a better place. Businesses that do not participate in these activities are not seen as unethical, but those that do tend to be seen in a more positive light.

philanthropic goodwill
The level of social responsibility in which a business does good without the expectation of anything in return.

Philanthropic activity is not limited to the wealthy or to large corporations writing seven-figure donation checks. Average citizens and small businesses can be and are philanthropic. A small business can sponsor a local Special Olympics meet, contribute to a Habitat for Humanity project, lead a community United Way campaign, or sponsor a Little League baseball team. Albert Vasquez allows a church group to convert his Tucson, Arizona, El Saguarito Mexican food restaurant into a center of worship on Sunday mornings. Kerry Stratford, co-owner of Boelts Bros. Associates, and his partners have donated more than 500 hours in their studios creating designs and advertising for nonprofit groups.[15]

One small business owner can make a difference. Over the past few years, the term *social entrepreneur* has emerged as a way to describe the use of business skills to marshal resources, create organizations that operate efficiently and effectively, and aspire to change society. In 2004, *Fast Company* created the Social Capitalist Awards to recognize new companies created to accomplish missions such as reinventing public education, employing homeless people, and building libraries in Nepal. For example, New Leaf develops and sells eco-friendly paper—40 million pounds of it annually. In an industry notorious for both severe environmental impact and resistance to change, New Leaf says it saved 183,796 trees, nearly 40 million gallons of water, and 14.8 million pounds of greenhouse gases in 2010. Its growth (25 percent in 2010) has helped spark new eco-conscious product innovation from larger competitors.[16] The award for the top change-making organization is based on five major criteria:

- *Entrepreneurship*: the ability to do a lot with a little, gather needed resources, and build an organization
- *Innovation*: a "big idea" that represents a dramatic leap from any solution that has existed previously
- *Social impact*: pure and simple results
- *Aspiration*: lofty goals that are in line with resources available
- *Sustainability*: the ability to last and produce results into the future

Ethics and Business Strategy

business ethics
The rules of moral values that guide decision making—your understanding of the difference between right and wrong.

Business ethics means more than simply passing moral judgment on what should and should not be done in a particular situation. It is part of the conscious decisions you make about the direction you want your business to take. It is a link between morality, responsibility, and decision making within the organization.[17]

The 2009 Ethics Resource Center (ERC) conducted its National Business Ethics Survey and found some interesting results regarding small businesses. Eighty percent of U.S. small business respondents considered their top managers ethical; 49 percent of employees had ever observed misconduct at work, and 63 percent of them reported it. Only 58 percent had written codes of ethics; 41 percent offered ethical training.[18]

A poll by RISE business published in *BusinessWeek* magazine asked people who run small and large businesses whether they found certain business practices to be acceptable or unacceptable. A greater percentage of those who ran small businesses, called "entrepreneurs" in this study, disapproved of questionable business practices than did managers of large businesses. Compare their responses to your own (see Figure 3.2).

Codes of Ethics

code of ethics
The tool with which the owner of a business communicates ethical expectations to everyone associated with the business.

A *code of ethics* is a formal statement of what your business expects in the way of ethical behavior. It can serve as a guide for employee conduct to help employees determine what behaviors are acceptable. Because the purpose of a code of ethics is to let everyone know what is expected and what is considered right, it should be included in an employee handbook (see Chapter 17 on human resource management).

Your code of ethics should reflect *your* ethical ideals, be concise so that it can be easily remembered, be written clearly, and apply equally to all employees, regardless of level of authority.[19] Your expectations and the consequences of breaking the code should be communicated to all employees. Small businesses, especially in fast-paced, high-tech industries, often ignore formal codes of conduct because of their push for rapid growth. This mistake can cause expensive legal problems later.

An explicit code of ethics and the expectation that employees must adhere to it can reap many benefits for your small business, including the following:

- Obtaining high standards of performance at all levels of your workforce
- Reducing anxiety and confusion over what is considered acceptable employee conduct
- Allowing employees to operate as freely as possible within a defined range of behavior
- Avoiding double standards that undermine employee morale and productivity
- Developing a public presence and image that are consistent with your organization's ideals[20]

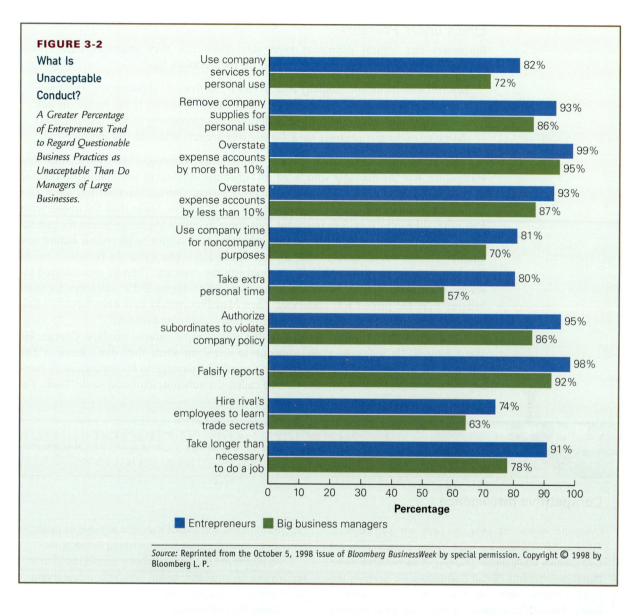

FIGURE 3-2

What Is Unacceptable Conduct?

A Greater Percentage of Entrepreneurs Tend to Regard Questionable Business Practices as Unacceptable Than Do Managers of Large Businesses.

Use company services for personal use — 82% / 72%

Remove company supplies for personal use — 93% / 86%

Overstate expense accounts by more than 10% — 99% / 95%

Overstate expense accounts by less than 10% — 93% / 87%

Use company time for noncompany purposes — 81% / 70%

Take extra personal time — 80% / 57%

Authorize subordinates to violate company policy — 95% / 86%

Falsify reports — 98% / 92%

Hire rival's employees to learn trade secrets — 74% / 63%

Take longer than necessary to do a job — 91% / 78%

Percentage

■ Entrepreneurs ■ Big business managers

Source: Reprinted from the October 5, 1998 issue of *Bloomberg BusinessWeek* by special permission. Copyright © 1998 by Bloomberg L. P.

If you want to maintain and encourage ethical behavior in your business, it must be part of your company's goals. By establishing ethical policies, rules, and standards in your code of ethics, you can treat them like any other company goal, such as increasing profit or market share. Establishing ethical goals allows you to take corrective action by punishing employees who do not comply with company standards and by rewarding those who do. If your code of ethics is supported and strictly enforced by you and your management team, it will become part of your company's culture and will improve ethical behavior. Conversely, if your managers and employees see your code of ethics as a window-dressing facade, it will accomplish nothing. Don't just take a "three Ps" approach—print it, post it, and pray they read it. Instead, talk about your code when it is implemented, review it annually, and use employee suggestions to improve it.[21]

Another recommendation is to include a *frequently asked questions (FAQs)* section in the code of ethics section of your employee handbook. Have these FAQs relate specifically to your industry, because many of your new employees will have the same questions.[22]

Ethics under Pressure

Businesses face ethical dilemmas every day. How can they maintain high ethical standards when the effects of doing so will hit their bottom line?

You run a construction company and receive a bid from a subcontractor. You know a mistake was made; the bid is accidentally 20 percent too low. If you accept the bid, it could put the subcontractor out of business. But accepting it will improve your chance of winning a contract for a big housing project. What do you do?[23]

Robert George, CEO of Medallion Construction Company of Merrimack, New Hampshire, was the manager who faced this dilemma. Medallion was bidding to become the general contractor for a $2.5 million public housing contract. An electrical contractor from the area submitted a bid that was $30,000, or 20 percent, lower than the quotes from four other subcontractors. Subcontractor bids come in only a few hours before the general contractors must deliver their bids so that subcontractors cannot be played off against one another. George was tempted to take the bid that he knew was a mistake because it would have almost guaranteed that Medallion would win the contract. Then he reconsidered for several reasons. Accepting the bid could have caused problems if the subcontractor went belly-up once the project was underway. Then Medallion would have been forced to find a replacement, which might have caused time delays and cost overruns.

Aside from the pragmatic problems, the ethical ramifications troubled George. He asked himself, "Is it fair to allow someone to screw up when they don't know it and you do?" He decided that the money wasn't worth the damage to his reputation of ruining a fellow small businessperson. George called the subcontractor and said, "Look, I'm

Competitive Advantage
INNOVATION AND SUSTAINABILITY

Competitive Intelligence

Everyone needs to keep an eye on competitors. *Fortune 500* companies have entire departments for Competitive intelligence (CI), and CI consultants serve those departments. Small businesses are seen as too busy minding their own business to mind anyone else's. Actually, they need to keep closer track because the impact of competitive moves are felt quicker and deeper.

Determine who matters – Competitive intelligence does not have to take a lot of time or money, spies, or subterfuge. Focus on four or five competitors (more is overwhelming for small businesses).

Focus on what matters – When watching a competitor, what are you looking for? In CI jargon, you are tracking the Four Corners: (1) its goals or drivers (revenue or profit generators), (2) its management's assumptions about the market you compete within,

(3) the strategies and tactics it uses to achieve its goals, and (4) its capabilities in accomplishing those goals.

Formulize the process – Create a simple repository for anyone on your staff to file information found and to be available to anyone who could benefit from it.

Gathering intelligence – First stop: Google. But not just the search engine, set up e-mail alerts about search terms (like competitor business name, owner name, or other unique key words) on news.google.com. When your carefully selected terms appear anywhere online, you are notified. Also check your competitor's Web site; dissect it using Fagen Finder (www.fagenfinder.com/urlinfo) to learn what sites it is linked to and what directories it is listed in. Finally, many libraries subscribe to ReferenceUSA, offering detailed company information, including financials.

Source: "How To: Keep Tabs on the Competition," *Inc. Guidebook*, April 2010, 53–56.

not going to tell you what your competitors bid, but your number is very low—in my opinion, too low." The subcontractor withdrew his bid. Medallion still won the contract.

A year later, the same subcontractor submitted another low bid on a different project. This time the low bid was intentional. The subcontractor offered a 2 percent discount because he remembered how honestly George had treated him earlier. Sometimes high ethics can have material rewards. Having a reputation for high ethical standards can give you an "ethical edge," a competitive advantage for your business. Being known for doing what is right can help you attract talented people, win loyal customers, forge relationships with suppliers, and earn the public's trust.

> *You spend months trying to negotiate a deal to sell your equipment in Japan. You deliver your product as agreed, but the Japanese distributor tells you it is not what the customer expected. The distributor wants you to reengineer the equipment even though it clearly meets the written specifications. What do you do?*

David Lincoln is president of Lincoln Laser Company, a manufacturer located in Phoenix, Arizona. Lincoln thought he had a done deal with a distributor from Japan that had spent months scrutinizing Lincoln's $300,000 machine that scans printed circuit-board wiring for very small cracks or breaks. The distributor finally ordered eight machines. Unfortunately, the Japanese client wasn't happy after delivery. Lincoln said, "They thought it should inspect *every type* of printed circuit board, even though we explained repeatedly that it was suitable only for a certain class of boards." To change the machine so that it could inspect every type of circuit board would require Lincoln to have the software rewritten, pull engineers from another project, and borrow funds to pay for the additional work.

Lincoln's first instinct was to say, "This is what you agreed to; we supplied what we said we would. You bought it, so now pay up." He could have said "no" and been acting ethically according to common business practices in the United States. Instead, he decided to go beyond his basic obligation and do what he felt was the right thing under the circumstances. As Lincoln reflected on the differences between American and Japanese customers, he realized that he had expected Japanese customers to act like American clients without taking into account the differences in adaptation levels between the two groups. In other words, he hadn't taken the time to become sensitive to cultural differences. Fortunately, Lincoln was able to secure financing to accommodate its customers—keeping the ethical principles, credibility, and Japanese market for his company intact.

Here are some more ethical situations to consider:

- Your company, a maker of data storage products, has just released a new external hard drive with special padding to reduce damage if dropped. You discover that the new hard drive includes an unintentional little bonus: a software worm that will turn every customer's PC into a spam distributor. What do you do?[24]
- You own a high-tech business in a very competitive industry. You find out that a competitor has developed a scientific discovery that will give it a significant competitive advantage. Your profits will be severely cut, but not eliminated, for at least a year. If you had some hope of hiring one of your competitor's employees who knows the details of its secret, would you hire him or her?
- A high-ranking government official from a country where payments regularly lubricate decision-making processes asks you for a $200,000 consulting fee. For this fee, he promises to help you obtain a $100 million contract that will produce at least $5 million of profit for your company. What do you do?

Green Can Be Gold

Efforts of businesses to act in a socially responsible manner toward the environment are usually called  *green marketing*. Small businesses can show concern for the environment (and cut costs at the same time) by recycling paper products and office supplies, purchasing environmentally benign products, and using environmentally safe product packaging. Each business must decide how it can have the greatest positive environmental impact. Not every business can affect issues such as vehicle-related air pollution or ozone depletion, of course, but every business should recognize the power of the green movement and the rise in environmental consciousness.

Ira Ehrenpreis, of the National Venture Capital Association, says that "cleantech is the greatest economic opportunity of the twenty-first century. The green of the environment and the green of economic and financial returns go hand in hand." Venture capitalists invested $4.9 billion into 356 alternative energy deals for 2009 (and that was in a recession).

Here are some guidelines for incorporating a green marketing program into your business:

- Environmentalism is not a passing fad—it is strongly supported—so pay attention to what your target market supports and buys.
- Get an energy audit. Most local utilities offer businesses free consultations on how businesses can reduce usage and save money.
- Green marketing can be a sustainable competitive advantage leading to long-term profit.
- Tell suppliers that you're interested in sustainable products, and set specific goals for buying recycled, refurbished, or used products. Make the environment, and not just price, a factor in your purchasing decisions.
- Green marketing involves the actual production of your product, raw material procurement, and disposal.
- A successful green-marketing strategy depends on effective communication with customers and suppliers about your efforts.
- Green marketing needs to be integrated into the strategic planning process.
- Don't limit your vision with thoughts like "SUV owners are not green consumers." Just look at the SUVs parked at any suburban Whole Foods Market.

Sources: Julie Bennett, "Are We Headed Toward a Green Bubble?", *Entrepreneur,* April 2010, 50–54; "How to Make *Your* Business Greener," *Inc.,* November 2006, 103; and Cait Murphy, "The Next Big Thing," *Fortune Small Business,* June 2003, 64.

- You recently hired a manager who is having a problem with sexual harassment from another manager. She informs you, as the business owner, what is happening and tells you she is considering legal action. Unfortunately, you have been so busy dealing with incredible growth that you haven't had a chance to write formal policies. What do you do?
- An advertising agency has created and released a marketing and advertising campaign for your consumer product. The campaign has proven to be offensive to some minority groups (who do not buy your product), and those parties have expressed their objections. Sales for your product have increased by 45 percent since the campaign started. What do you do?[25]

strategic plan
A long-term planning tool used for viewing a business and the environments in which it operates in broadest terms.

Strategic Planning

Recall from Chapter 1 that poor management is the major cause of business failure. Since the first function of good management is good planning, a good **strategic plan** is a priority for the small business owner. Strategic planning is a long-range management tool that helps small businesses be proactive in the way they respond to environmental changes. The process of strategic planning provides an overview of your business and all the factors that may affect it in the next three to five years. It will help you formulate goals for your business so as to take advantage of opportunities and avoid threats. From your goals, you can determine the most appropriate steps you need to take to accomplish them—an *action plan.*

At the beginning of this chapter, the question was posed about the connection between social responsibility, ethics, and strategic planning. If the intent of the strategic planning process is to produce a working document for your business to follow, the relationship can be seen in this way: When you assess your company's external environment for opportunities and threats, you identify what you *might do.* When you look at the internal strengths and weaknesses, you see what you *can do* and *cannot do.* Your personal values are ingrained into the business; they are what you *want to do.* Your ethical standards will determine what is *right for you to do.* Finally, in responding to everyone who could be affected by your business, social responsibility guides what you *should do.* When viewed in this manner, social responsibility, ethics, and strategic planning are not only connected but also impossible to separate.

Writing a strategic plan generally involves a six-step process, as shown in Figure 3.3: (1) formulating your mission statement, (2) completing an environmental analysis, (3) performing a competitive analysis, (4) analyzing your strategic alternatives, (5) setting your goals and strategies, and (6) setting up a control system.

Yogi Berra once said, "You've got to be very careful if you don't know where you're going, because you might not get there."[26] Strategic planning is how entrepreneurs determine how to "get there."

Mission Statement

mission statement
A description of the reason why an organization exists.

A **mission statement** provides direction for the company by answering a simple question: What business are we really in? The mission statement should be specific enough to tell the reader something about what the business is and how it operates, but it should *not* be a long, elaborate document detailing all of your business philosophies.

By accurately describing the purpose, scope, and direction of your business, your mission statement communicates what you want your business to do and to be. It is the foundation on which all other goals and strategies are based. Without a

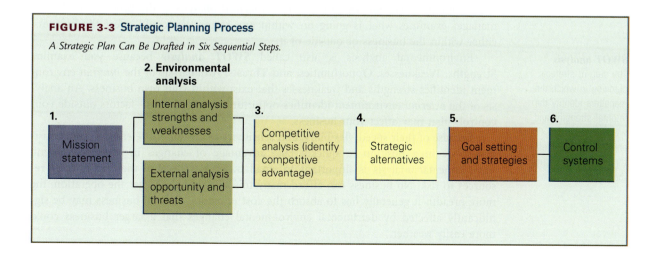

FIGURE 3-3 Strategic Planning Process

A Strategic Plan Can Be Drafted in Six Sequential Steps.

1. Mission statement

2. Environmental analysis
Internal analysis strengths and weaknesses
External analysis opportunity and threats

3. Competitive analysis (identify competitive advantage)

4. Strategic alternatives

5. Goal setting and strategies

6. Control systems

concrete statement of organizational mission, the values and beliefs of a small business must be interpreted from the actions and decisions of individual managers.[27] The result may not be what you, as the owner, desire. Another value of a mission statement derives from the commitment you make by printing and publicizing your strategy and philosophy. You have more incentive to stick to your ideas and expect others to follow them if they are written down and shared than if you keep them to yourself.

Management consultant and author Tom Peters writes that a company's mission statement should be 25 words or less in length.[28] This brevity will allow everyone in the organization to understand and articulate it. Great Harvest Bakery's mission statement is a good example of a brief but heartfelt statement of values:

- Be loose and have fun.
- Bake phenomenal bread.
- Run fast to help customers.
- Create strong, exciting bakeries.
- Give generously to others.

Good mission statements, like Great Harvest's, maintain a balance between ideas and reality. From Great Harvest's statement, you can tell what the company wants to achieve and how. It says what the business is and, by implication, what it is not. Does Great Harvest intend to diversify into wedding cakes and frozen pies to become a major force in the baking industry? No, the company intends to focus on making and selling the best bread possible.

Because the mission statement lies at the heart of the strategic planning process, you can see in Great Harvest's statement and principles the connection between strategic planning and social responsibility. You can even see evidence of the pyramid of social responsibility in its stated principles. The importance of making a profit corresponds with the economic responsibility level of the pyramid. The principle of treating one another with respect and dignity incorporates ethics into its strategic plan. The company's principle of contributing positively to the community and the environment shows ethics and philanthropy.

Environmental Analysis

Large and small businesses alike must operate in constantly changing environments. The ability to adapt to change is a major determinant of success or failure for any business in a free enterprise system. Essentially, *environmental analysis* is the process in which a manager examines what is going on within any sector that could affect the business, either within the business or outside of it.

SWOT analysis
The step of strategic planning in which the managers identify the internal strengths and weaknesses of a business and the opportunities and threats that exist outside the business.

Environmental analysis is also called **SWOT analysis** because you examine **S**trengths, **W**eaknesses, **O**pportunities, and **T**hreats. An analysis of the *internal* environment identifies strengths and weaknesses that exist within your own business. An analysis of the *external* environment identifies opportunities and threats—factors outside your control—that may affect your business.

Because of their speed, flexibility, and sensitivity to customer preferences, small businesses are in a position to quickly take advantage of changes in the environment. Environmental analysis is important to small businesses because they have fewer resources to risk. No business can afford many mistakes, but the larger the operation, the more breadth it generally has to absorb the cost of errors. A small business may be significantly affected by detrimental environmental changes that a larger business could more easily weather.

External Analysis *Opportunities* are positive alternatives that you may choose to help attain your company's mission. Although you should always be scanning for opportunities, you cannot pursue every one. Your strategic plan will help you identify those that are right for your business.

Threats are obstacles to achieving your mission or goals. They are generally events or factors over which you have no control: a change in interest rates, new government regulations, or a competitor's new product. Although you cannot control these threats, you can prepare for them or take positive action to cope with them. Threats and opportunities can be found by scanning developments in the following environments:

- *Economic.* Much of the economic data readily available on the international and national levels are very valuable to small businesses operating in smaller, more isolated markets. As a small business owner, you need to be aware of economic conditions that affect your target markets, such as unemployment rates, interest rates, total sales, and tax rates within your community.
- *Legal/regulatory.* Some factors can affect small businesses in more than one environment. For example, the passage of the North American Free Trade Agreement (NAFTA) changed both regulations and the competitive environment. With regulations altered to encourage trade between the United States, Canada, and Mexico, many small businesses have found a wealth of new opportunity in new markets. Other businesses have seen the changes as a threat because they brought new competition.
- *Sociocultural.* What members of society value and desire as they pass from one life stage to another has an effect on what they purchase. For example, the increased popularity of tattoos among teens and twenty-somethings means opportunity for skin artists who are able to provide this service in a small business. Will the next opportunity for an entrepreneur be an innovative new process for removing those tattoos?
- *Technological.* Technology is the application of scientific knowledge for practical purposes. Few environmental forces have caused as much excitement in the business community as the emergence of the Internet. Entrepreneurs are scrambling to find ways to take advantage of the opportunities of e-business.
- *Competitive.* Actions of your competitors are considered forces within your competitive environment. You face a difficult task in not only tracking what your competitors are currently doing, but also predicting their reactions to your moves. If you drop the price of your product to gain more market share, will competing business managers react by holding their prices constant or by cutting their prices below yours? This situation could escalate into an expensive price war.

Are opportunities and threats easy to identify? No, and they never have been. Writer Mark Twain once said, "I was seldom able to see an opportunity until it had ceased to be one."

Internal Analysis An *internal analysis* assesses the strengths and weaknesses of your company. It identifies what it is that your company does well and what it could do better. Internal analysis is important for two reasons. First, since your personal opinion of your own business is sure to be biased (we tend to look at ourselves through the proverbial rose-colored glasses), you need an objective analysis of the capacity and potential of your business. Second, an internal analysis can help you match the strengths of your business with the opportunities that exist. The idea is to put together a realistic profile of your business to determine whether you can take advantage of opportunities and react to the threats identified in the environmental analysis. This isn't as easy as it sounds,

"Are opportunities and threats easy to identify? No, and they never have been. Writer Mark Twain once said, 'I was seldom able to see an opportunity until it had ceased to be one.'"

because you have to view your environments not as if they are snapshots, but rather as several videos playing simultaneously. The key is to match opportunities that are still unfolding with resources that are still being acquired.

Although most of us have no problem identifying our strengths, some of us may need help realizing our weaknesses. The following diagnostic tests can help you evaluate your business realistically:

- Visit your newest, lowest-level employee. Can he or she tell you why the business exists? Name major competitors? Say what you do well? List major customers? If not, your vision isn't coming across.
- Can that same employee describe what he or she is doing to contribute to your competitive advantage?
- Ask a long-term employee how things went yesterday. If you get answers like "Okay" or "Fine … just fine," you may have a potential problem. If you hear specifics, consider it a good sign.
- Observe what the business looks like after hours. Is the place neat and orderly, or does it look like a tornado struck? Although neatness doesn't guarantee success, you should be able to find the checkbook, phone book, and most of the furniture.
- Observe your business during work hours. Invent a reason to be where you can watch and hear what goes on. What impression do you get of the business?
- Select a few customers at random to call or visit. Ask them how they were treated the last time they were in your business, and emphasize that you would like an *honest* answer.
- Call your business during the busiest part of the day. How quickly is the phone answered? Is the response efficient, friendly, surly, or overly chatty?
- Ask a friend to visit your business as a mystery shopper. Would he or she come back again?[29]

Competitive Analysis

competitive advantage
The facet of a business that it does better than all of its competitors.

If you were forced to condense the description of your business down to the one factor that makes you successful and sets your business apart from all other similar businesses, you would recognize your **competitive advantage**, which is found by means of a *competitive analysis*. The heart of your company's strategy and reason for being in business is your competitive advantage. You must do *something* better than everyone else; otherwise, your business isn't needed. Furthermore, your competitive advantage must be sustainable over time to remain a benefit to you. If it can be easily copied by competitors, you have to find a new way to stay ahead.

Without analysis, competition will likely be viewed with bias. Competitors are rarely as slow, backward, and inferior in all areas as we would like to believe they are. Competition should be viewed as formidable and serious. In competitive analysis, you are trying to identify *competitive weaknesses*. In what areas is the competition truly weak and therefore vulnerable? Some bias may be removed if you are as specific as possible in writing your competitive analysis. For example, instead of saying that your competitors offer poor service, qualify your remarks with references to return policies, delivery, schedules, or fees.

How can you analyze the competition? The process of gathering competitive intelligence doesn't have to be prohibitively expensive. A little effort and creativity combined with keeping your eyes open can yield a lot of information. Here are common ways that can help small business owners gather information for compiling their competitive analyses:

- Read articles in trade publications. A proliferation of specialized publications in every industry makes your gathering easier—for example, read *Progressive Grocer* if you are selling food products, or *Lodging Hospitality* if you are interested in travel accommodations.

- Listen to what your customers and salespeople say about competitors. These groups make the most frequent comparisons of you and the competition.
- Keep a file on key competitors. Information is useless unless you can access it easily. Include published information, notes of conversations, and competitors' sales, product, or service brochures. These readily available sources of information can help you determine how your competitors position themselves.
- Establish a regular time, perhaps a monthly meeting, to meet with key employees to evaluate the information in these competitive information files.
- Attend industry trade shows, exhibits, and conferences. A lot can be learned from competitors' booths and through the networking (or socializing) that goes on at such events.
- Buy competitors' products and take them apart to determine their quality and other advantages. Consider incorporating the best elements of competing products into your own products. This process is called *reverse engineering* and is part of a process of establishing comparison standards called *benchmarking*.
- Consult published credit reports on your competitors. Companies like Dun & Bradstreet (D&B) make standard credit reports available. See what D&B says about the competition.[30]

For a practical application of competitive analysis that small business owners can use, try this: Rank your business and four competitors you have identified in each of the following areas. Using Figure 3.4 as a guide, rank each business from 1 to 5, with 5 being the lowest and 1 the highest. Assign only one 1 per area, one 2, and so on. No ties are allowed, so you will end up with a ranked list of the five companies. This exercise

FIGURE 3-4
Competitive
Analysis

Areas of Comparison	Your Business	Competitor A	Competitor B	Competitor C	Competitor D
1. Image	_____	_____	_____	_____	_____
2. Location	_____	_____	_____	_____	_____
3. Layout	_____	_____	_____	_____	_____
4. Atmosphere	_____	_____	_____	_____	_____
5. Products	_____	_____	_____	_____	_____
6. Services	_____	_____	_____	_____	_____
7. Pricing	_____	_____	_____	_____	_____
8. Advertising	_____	_____	_____	_____	_____
9. Sales methods	_____	_____	_____	_____	_____
TOTALS	_____	_____	_____	_____	_____

will help you improve your competitive position and possibly point out new areas in which your business might enjoy a competitive advantage.

Areas of Comparison (For example only; add or delete areas that most apply to your business.)

1. *Image.* How do consumers perceive the reputation and the physical appearance of the business?
2. *Location.* Is the business convenient to customers in terms of distance, parking, traffic, and visibility?
3. *Layout.* Are customers well served with the physical layout of the business?
4. *Atmosphere.* When customers enter the business, do they get a feeling that it is appropriate for your type of business?
5. *Products.* Can customers find the products they expect from your type of business?
6. *Services.* Do customers receive the quantity and quality of services they expect?
7. *Pricing.* Do customers perceive the prices charged to be appropriate given the quality of the products sold? Do they receive the value they expect?
8. *Advertising.* Does the advertising of the business reach its target market?
9. *Sales methods.* Are customers comfortable with the methods the business uses to sell products?

Defining Your Competitive Advantage Your strategic plan helps you define a competitive advantage by analyzing different environments, studying your competition, and choosing appropriate strategies. Advantages you have over your competitors could include price, product features and functions, time of delivery (if speed is important to customers), place of business (if being located near customers is needed), and public perception (the positive image your business projects). Remember, a competitive advantage must be sustainable. If competitors can easily copy it, then it is not a true competitive advantage.

Three core ideas are valuable in defining your competitive advantage. First, keep in mind that any advantage is relative, not absolute. What matters in customers' minds is not the absolute performance of your product or service, but its performance compared with that of other products. For example, no toothpaste can make teeth turn pure white, but you could build an advantage if you developed a toothpaste that gets teeth noticeably whiter than competing toothpastes do.

Second, you should strive for multiple types of competitive advantage. Doing more than one thing better than other businesses will increase the chances that you can maintain an advantage over a longer period of time.

Third, remember that areas of competition change over time. Customers' tastes and priorities change as products and the processes for making them evolve, as the availability of substitute products changes, and for a variety of other reasons that can affect your competitive advantage. For example, in the past consumers compared watches based on their ability to keep time accurately. The introduction of the quartz watch, however, changed customer priorities. The cheapest quartz watch in the display case kept time more accurately than the most expensive mechanical watch, so the differentiating factors for watches became styles (types of watch faces) and features (built-in calculators, stopwatches, and television remote controls).[31]

Five Basic Forces of Competition One of the leading researchers and writers on the topic of competitive advantage is Michael Porter, a professor at Harvard Business School. Porter has identified five basic forces of competition that exist within every industry. Analyzing these forces for your chosen industry can help you determine the attractiveness of the industry and the prospects for earning a return on your investment (see Figure 3.5).

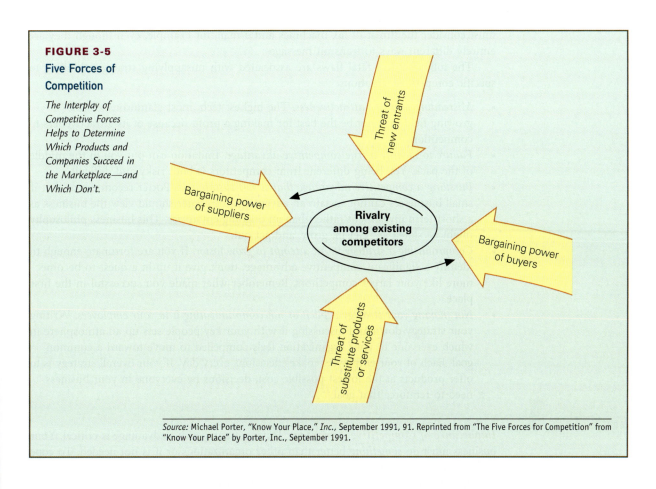

FIGURE 3-5

Five Forces of Competition

The Interplay of Competitive Forces Helps to Determine Which Products and Companies Succeed in the Marketplace—and Which Don't.

Threat of new entrants

Bargaining power of suppliers

Rivalry among existing competitors

Bargaining power of buyers

Threat of substitute products or services

Source: Michael Porter, "Know Your Place," *Inc.,* September 1991, 91. Reprinted from "The Five Forces for Competition" from "Know Your Place" by Porter, Inc., September 1991.

The degree of "rivalry among existing competitors" in Figure 3.5 refers to how passively or aggressively the businesses within an industry compete. If they consistently attack one another, the attractiveness of the industry is reduced because the potential to make a profit is decreased. For example, compare the airline industry, where strong rivalries produce low profits, with the packaged consumer goods industry, where companies try to attract different groups of customers.

The "threat of new entrants" in the figure is a function of how easily other businesses can enter your market, which keeps prices and profits down. If a certain type of food, such as Cajun bagels, becomes popular, very little prevents new bakeries from opening or converting to produce this popular item. Low barriers to entry reduce profitability for incumbents.

The "bargaining power of suppliers" affects the price you will have to pay to produce your goods. If the supplies in question are commodities carried by several companies, suppliers will have little power to raise the prices they charge. By contrast, if you have only one or two choices of vendors, or if you require very specialized goods, you may have to pay what the suppliers ask.

The "bargaining power of buyers" affects how much latitude you have in changing your prices. The more potential substitutes your buyers have, the more power they have to influence your prices or the extent of services you must provide to keep their business.

The "threat of substitute products or services" is determined by the options your customers have when buying your product or service. The greater the number of substitutes available, the more your profit margin can be squeezed. Overnight delivery services must consider the threat of fax machines and e-mail, for example, even though they are entirely different ways to transmit messages.

The following five fatal flaws are associated with misapplying strategic thinking to specific competitive situations:

- *Misreading industry attractiveness.* The highest-tech, most glamorous, fastest-growing field may not be the best for making a profit because of its attractiveness to competition.
- *Failure to identify a true competitive advantage.* Imitation can put you in the middle of the pack. Yet, being different from competitors is both risky and difficult.
- *Pursuing a competitive advantage that is not sustainable.* Porter recommends that if small businesses cannot sustain an advantage, the owner should view the business as a short-term investment rather than an ongoing enterprise. This business philosophy might be stated as "Get in, grow, and get out."
- *Compromising a strategy in an attempt to grow faster.* If you are fortunate enough to identify a significant competitive advantage, don't give it up in a quest to become more like your larger competitors. Remember what made you successful in the first place.
- *Not making your strategy explicit or not communicating it to your employees.* Writing your strategy down and discussing it with your key people sets up an atmosphere in which everyone in your organization feels compelled to move toward a common goal. Each of your employees makes decisions every day. If your overall strategy is to offer products at the lowest possible cost, decisions by everyone in your business need to reinforce that goal.[32]

Importance of Competitive Advantage Having a competitive advantage is critical. Your business must do *something* better than other organizations or it is not needed. To cope with a quickly changing competitive environment, small businesses need to be market driven.[33] Part of becoming market driven includes closely monitoring changing customer wants and needs, determining how those changes will affect customer satisfaction, and developing strategies to gain an edge. Small businesses cannot rely on the inertia of the marketplace for their survival.[34] When running a small business, you cannot solve problems simply by throwing money at them. Instead, you need to see your competitive environment with crystal clarity, then identify and secure a position you can defend.

In developing your competitive advantage, you will inevitably make decisions under conditions of uncertainty. This is the art, rather than the science, of marketing-related decision making. In his book *Marketing Mistakes*, Robert Hartley notes that we can seldom predict with any exactitude the reactions of consumers or the countermoves and retaliations of competitors.[35] Although it may be easy to play Monday-morning quarterback, viewing mistakes with 20-20 hindsight, we will do better to decide to learn from others' mistakes, especially when looking for a competitive advantage. Of course, no one ever deliberately set out to design a bad product or start a business that would fail. Nevertheless, what seems to be a good idea for achieving a competitive advantage often may not be, for one reason or another.

The lack, or loss, of competitive advantage exists in every size of business. Apple Computer, which began small, has fought to maintain the competitive advantage of ease of use. In 1983, Apple tried to break into the business market for personal computers with the Lisa. Although that computer was easy to use and had nice graphics, its advantages were not noticed by the business community because of its limited software and expensive price tag ($10,000).[36] Similar problems (performance below customer expectations and high price) plagued Apple's Newton MessagePad when it came out in

1993—many of the features of the Newton were found in the PalmPilot that launched PDAs (personal digital assistants). Timing is everything. Occasionally, competitive advantages are gained well after a product is introduced. For instance, the unsuccessful Lisa evolved into the Macintosh, one of the world's most popular models.

The list of products and businesses that have failed to gain a competitive advantage is long and distinguished. Entrants include Ford's Edsel (a car with lots of innovations— and lots more problems), To-Fitness Tofu Pasta, Gerber Singles (adult-targeted baby foods that looked like dog food), Cucumber Antiperspirant Spray, and R.J. Reynolds' Premier (cigarettes that didn't burn or smoke). Premier appealed to nonsmokers … but nonsmokers don't buy cigarettes, and even Reynolds' president admitted that they "tasted like crap."[37] As you see, there are many lessons to learn from others' mistakes.

Benefits of Competitive Advantage Gaining a sustainable competitive advantage can help you establish a self-sustaining position in the marketplace. Whether your edge comes from external factors, such as luck or the failure of a competitor, or internal factors, such as exceptional skills or superior resources, it can set up a cycle of success (see Figure 3.6).[38]

Because of your competitive advantage, your customers will be more satisfied with your business than with your competitors' businesses. You will, in turn, gain market share. Increased market share translates into larger sales and profits, which in turn give you more resources for improving your products, facilities, and human resources—all of which allow you to improve your competitive advantage. As additional resources come into the business from outside the company, they can be used to build and fortify operational sources of advantage.[39] Businesses that don't gain competitive advantage, therefore, lose out in this cycle. Their customers receive less value and are less satisfied. Their market share, sales volume, and profit fall. Without profits, they have fewer resources to reinvest in the business, so positioning is difficult to maintain. The gap between follower and leader grows wider.

© AP Photo/Richard Vogel, File

Some products fail while being hugely popular. YouTube lost $174 million in 2009, capturing lots of eyes but few advertising dollars or pay per view. Google purchased YouTube for $1.65 billion.

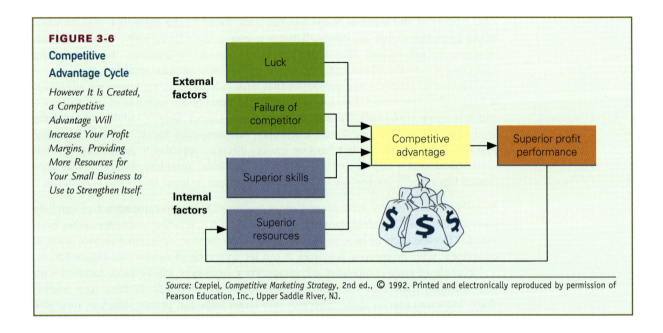

FIGURE 3-6

Competitive Advantage Cycle

However It Is Created, a Competitive Advantage Will Increase Your Profit Margins, Providing More Resources for Your Small Business to Use to Strengthen Itself.

Source: Czepiel, *Competitive Marketing Strategy*, 2nd ed., © 1992. Printed and electronically reproduced by permission of Pearson Education, Inc., Upper Saddle River, NJ.

How to Create Competitive Advantage Three generic competitive strategies exist through which a business can gain a competitive advantage: lower cost, differentiation, and focus strategies.[40] Using *focus strategies* means aiming at a narrow segment of a market. By definition, all small businesses target niches or narrow market segments, so let's concentrate on the first two strategies.

You must find a way to lower your costs if you intend to compete primarily on price. If you try to compete on price without obtaining a cost advantage, your business is headed for trouble. Such an advantage can come from reduced labor costs, less expensive raw materials or supplies, more efficient distribution, or any number of other factors.

A competitive advantage based on *differentiation* means that your product or service is different from those offered by your competitors. Its value comes from the fact that you can show customers why your difference is better, not just cheaper. In this way, differentiation can effectively remove direct competition. For example, when a mass merchandiser such as Walmart or Target enters a town, small retailers are not necessarily run out of business. Studies that measured the impact of Walmart's entrance on local retailers in Iowa have shown that as long as the small retail stores stock different merchandise than Walmart, they actually benefit due to the increased number of shoppers coming into town. Small stores should differentiate rather than try to compete head-to-head with the giants.[41] Walmart pushes its manufacturing clients (70 percent of its inventory comes from China) to make more, faster, in order to keep shelves full of homogenous items. Small manufacturers and retailers can compete via different product design, service, and quality.[42]

An advantage does not have to involve features of the product. It can come from anything your business does—including quality, customer service, and distribution. Research shows that competitive advantage has four key components: the competitor identification process, the sources of the advantage, the positions of the advantage, and the performance outcomes achieved.[43]

To create a sustainable competitive advantage, your strategy must incorporate a combination of methods to continuously differentiate your product and to improve it in areas that make a meaningful difference to your customers.[44] But how can you keep up with the ever-changing tastes and preferences of your customers? There are so many questions about your customers you must try to answer. The products and services that people like and dislike at any particular time are shaped by hundreds of influences, many of which can't be identified. Nevertheless, you need to gather as many facts as possible about your markets in an objective and orderly manner. *Market research* offers a way to answer at least some questions about your customers' changing wants and needs, to help you create and hold on to your competitive advantage.

Strategic Alternatives

The process of defining *strategic alternatives* begins by identifying problems based on information gained in earlier steps. Next is the drafting of a list of alternatives. Thus, in this two-step process, you identify what is wrong and then determine what you can do about it.

Problem identification is the most difficult part of strategic planning. It takes thorough SWOT and competitive analyses and a lot of analytical thinking to pinpoint problems like a current strategy that no longer suits your environment or a mismatch between your strengths and an opportunity that you have discerned. Bracing up one of your weaknesses and preparing for an upcoming threat are tasks that demand your attention. If completion of your SWOT and competitive analyses identifies no major problems or new strategies needed, don't fix anything. Always look to be proactive, but don't ignore the possibility that keeping to the status quo might be the best choice.

Few problems can be solved with a single solution or with the first idea that comes to mind. Therefore, you should try to generate as many potential solutions as possible. Don't evaluate ideas as you generate them, as criticism stifles creativity. Only after you've exhausted the possibilities should you evaluate whether each alternative would solve your particular problem or work in your company. Once your list of alternative strategies is compiled, you need to consider its potential effects on your company's resources, environment, and people.

Although there is a strong temptation to list strategic alternatives informally in one's mind, research has shown that putting ideas down on paper leads to a wider range of alternatives and stimulates the creativity and insightful thinking that are the bases for good strategic change.[45]

Goal Setting and Strategies

Your mission statement sets the broadest direction for your business. SWOT and competitive analyses help you refine or change that direction, but the goals that you set must stem from your mission statement. Obviously, goals are needed before you can build

Manager's Notes

Playing Hardball

Winners in business often play rough and do not apologize for it. Toyota, Dell, and Walmart don't pull any punches when going head-to-head with their competitors. They play hardball. They exemplify single-minded pursuit of a competitive advantage and all the benefits that accompany it.

Playing hardball means working with intensity. It makes your company strong and vibrant, which results in more affordable products for satisfied customers. To use a baseball analogy, if an aggressive batter (competitor) is crowding the plate, a hardball player (a successful entrepreneur) will throw a hard, inside, brush-back pitch to establish strength. Hardball players play tough, but stay within the rules—they don't cheat.

Stalk and Lachenauer described their Hardball Manifesto in a recent *Harvard Business Review* article. The manifesto includes five key points:

- *Focus relentlessly on competitive advantage. Always try to widen the gap* with competitors. Don't be satisfied with today's competitive advantage—go for tomorrow's also.
- *Strive for "extreme" competitive advantage*. Try to develop a facet that puts your advantage out of the reach of competitors.
- *Avoid attacking directly.* Hardball players tend to prefer the economies of force gained by an indirect attack over direct confrontation.
- *Exploit people's will to win.* Hardball entrepreneurs understand that people have a natural desire to win, and they build upon that desire in their employees.
- *Know the caution zone.* Hardball players know where the boundaries of legal and social conventions are; they may play close to those lines, but don't cross them.

Sources: George Stalk, Jr., and Rob Lachenauer, "Hard Ball," *Harvard Business Review,* April 2004, 62; Rick Whiting, "Competitive Hardball," *CRN,* April 28, 2008, 11; and Adam Gaumont, "How to Play Hardball," *BC Business,* July 2009, 33.

a set of strategies. As the cliché goes, "If you don't put up a target, you won't hit anything." Goals need to be

- *Written in terms of outcomes rather than actions.* A good goal states where you want to be, not how you want to get there. For example, a goal should focus on increasing sales rather than on your intention to send one of your brochures to every address in town.
- *Measurable.* In order to tell whether you have accomplished a goal, you must be able to measure the outcome.
- *Challenging, yet attainable.* Goals that are too easy to accomplish are not motivating. Goals that are not likely to be accomplished are self-defeating and decrease motivation.
- *Communicated to everyone in the company.* A team effort is difficult to produce if some of your players don't know the goals.
- *Written with a time frame for achievement.* Performance and motivation increase when people have goals accompanied by a time frame as compared with open-ended goals.

Writing usable goals isn't easy at first. If you state that your goal is to be "successful," is that a good goal? It sounds positive; it sounds nice. But is it measurable? No. How can you tell whether you have achieved a goal such as this? You can't, because there is no defined outcome. There is also no time frame. Do you intend to be successful this year? By the time you are 90? Goals need the characteristics listed previously to be useful.

Although you will have only one mission statement, you will have several business-level goals that apply to your entire organization. Each functional area of your business (for example, marketing, finance, human resources, and production) will have its own set of specific goals that relate directly to achieving your business-level goals (see Figure 3.7). Even if you are the only person performing marketing, finance, human resource management, and production duties, these areas of your small business must still be addressed individually.

- Your *mission statement* describes who you are, what your business is, and why it exists.
- A *business-level goal* describes what you want your overall business to accomplish to achieve your company mission.
- A *function-level goal* describes the performance desired of specific departments (or functional areas, such as marketing, production, and so on) to achieve your business-level goals.
- A *strategy* is a plan of action that details how you will attain your function-level goals.

In the final stage of goal setting, specific strategies are developed to accomplish your goals. For example, a *marketing strategy* might be to hire Jerry Seinfeld to be spokesperson for your new stand-up comedy computer program. This strategy should help you attain your *function-level marketing goal* of capturing 20 percent market share of the total comedy software market. Your marketing goal should help you attain your *business-level goal* of increasing third-quarter profits by 8 percent, which in turn ensures that you accomplish your company *mission* of satisfying the entertainment needs of lonely computer operators and thereby earn a profit.

Function-level goals and strategies must coordinate with one another and with business-level goals for the business to run smoothly. For example, the marketing department may develop a strategy of advertising on the Internet that will bring in orders from all over the globe. This result is great as long as the production department can increase capacity, the human resource department can hire and train enough new employees, and all other areas of the business are prepared. Each functional area must see itself as an integral part of the entire business and act accordingly.

Control Systems

Planning for the future is an inexact science. Very rarely do the actual outcomes of your plans exactly match what you anticipated. When things don't turn out as you planned,

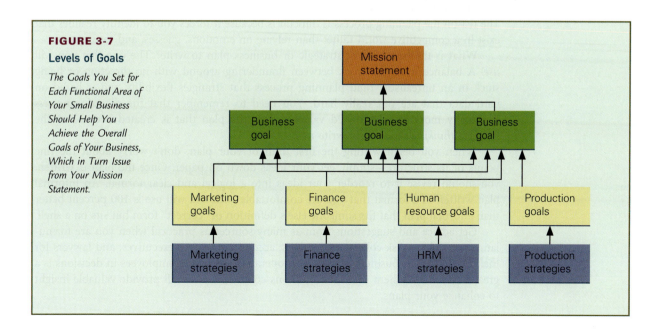

FIGURE 3-7

Levels of Goals

The Goals You Set for Each Functional Area of Your Small Business Should Help You Achieve the Overall Goals of Your Business, Which in Turn Issue from Your Mission Statement.

you must ask, "Why was there a deviation?" Having a control process built into the strategic planning process will help answer this question.

Your strategic plan, including all of its separate parts, sets a standard of comparison for your business's actual performance. The purpose of control systems is to provide you with information to start the planning process all over again. After checking your controls, you either readjust the standards of your plan or create new goals for your plan, and off you go for another planning period. This is why goals must be (1) written in terms of outcomes rather than actions; (2) measurable; (3) challenging, yet attainable; (4) communicated; and (5) written with a time frame for achievement. You need to collect accurate data about what you have done so you can compare this information with your planned standards. Control systems don't need to be expensive and elaborate. They should be simple enough to become a natural part of your management process.

Strategic Planning in Action

Strategic plans are different from *business plans* (see Chapter 4). Business plans and strategic plans support each other and overlap to some degree, but they seek to accomplish different purposes. Business plans are written primarily to test the feasibility of a business idea, acquire financing, and coordinate the start-up phase. Strategic plans are needed both before the business is started and continuously while it is in operation to match the direction of the business with changes that occur within its environments.

Strategic planning addresses strategic growth—where you are going. Business planning addresses operational growth—how you will get there. Strategic planning looks outward from the business at the long-term prospects for your products, your markets, your competition, and so on. Business planning, or organizational growth, focuses on the internal concerns of your business, such as capital, personnel, and marketing. Eventually, the two plans will converge, as your long-term strategic goals will be strongly influenced by operational decisions made when the business was started.[46] Strategic planning requires you to broaden your thinking and forces you to look at general issues over the next three to five years—countering the realities of the competitive world with concrete plans instead of wishful thinking. Most sections of a strategic plan will not be extremely detailed but will provide outlines for direction. A business plan, by comparison, needs to be as detailed as possible.

Planning is difficult; consequently, many small business owners would like to ignore it. The reason the planning process is difficult is because it forces you to identify realities that exist in a competitive world rather than relying on emotions, guesses, and assumptions.

What is the best kind of strategic or business plan to write? The one that you will *use*! A balance must be struck between floundering around with no direction or being stuck in an unrealistic, rigid planning process that strangles flexibility and is based on hard data that are not really hard. You need to remember that the *planning process* is actually more important and valuable than the plan that is created because of the *strategic thinking* required to write it.

When you begin writing the first draft of your plan, don't worry about the fine points of its structure—simply get your ideas down on paper. Once the plan is written, you should revise it to reorder your ideas into a logical and clear format. An informal plan written in a format that you are comfortable with and will use is 100 percent better than a formal plan that fits someone else's definition of "correct" form but sits on a shelf.

Get advice and suggestions from as many sources as practical when you are formulating your plans. Ask colleagues, bankers, accountants, other executives, and lawyers for their input. If your business is already in operation, including employees in decisions is a great way to show them that their opinions count. They can all provide valuable insight to enhance your plans.

Summary

1. Explain the relationship between social responsibility, ethics, and strategic planning.

The social responsibility and ethics of your business are the commitments you make to doing what is right. Strategic planning is the process of deciding where you want your business to go and how it will get there. All three concepts work together to form the foundation on which your entire business rests.

2. Name the levels of social responsibility.

You have an economic responsibility to make your business profitable. Without profit, your business cannot contribute anything to society. Your legal obligation to obey the law describes the minimal behavior expected for your firm to be part of society. Your ethical responsibility covers your obligation to do what is right. Philanthropic goodwill is contributing to others without expecting anything in return.

3. Discuss how to establish a code of ethics for your business.

Business ethics encompasses more than deciding what should and should not be done in a particular situation. It supplies the fundamental basis for the course you want your business to take. A code of ethics offers a way for you to communicate your ethical expectations to everyone involved in your business. The code should represent your ethical ideals, be concise enough to be remembered, be written clearly, and apply to everyone in the organization.

4. Describe each step in the strategic planning process, and explain the importance of competitive advantage.

The strategic planning process includes defining your mission statement, conducting an environmental analysis (internal and external, or SWOT, analysis), analyzing the competition and defining your competitive advantage, identifying strategic alternatives, setting goals, and establishing systems to measure effectiveness. A competitive advantage is the facet of your business that gives your company an edge over the competition. The strategic plan helps you to identify and establish competitive advantage by analyzing the environment and the competitive landscape.

Questions for Review and Discussion

1. Write a brief summary of the connection between social responsibility, ethics, and strategic planning in a small business setting.
2. Discuss the four groups of laws that generally regulate business activity in this country, and give some historical background on the major laws that affect all entrepreneurs today.
3. Define the purpose of a code of ethics, and write a brief code that would be suitable for a small business.
4. Although a certain practice may be widely accepted in the business community and be perfectly legal, does that necessarily mean it is always moral? Qualify your answer with examples.
5. Write a mission statement for a small business that not only functions as a strategic planning guide but also incorporates the company's philosophy of social responsibility and ethical standards.
6. Explain how cultural differences between countries can have either a positive or a negative effect on an entrepreneur who is pursuing a contract either outside the United States or with persons of different ethnic backgrounds in the United States.
7. Why is environmental analysis more crucial to the small business owner than to larger corporations?
8. You are an entrepreneur and wish to perform a self-evaluation of your business environment. How would you go about this task? Be specific about what you hope to discover through the evaluation of your employees, product, management, and so on.
9. What is the value of competitive analysis to the small business owner? What sorts of things

should you know about your competition, and what analytical methods can you use to find out this information?

10. Goal setting is a major part of the entrepreneur's business plan. Outline specific methods for setting goals that are realistic, fit into the overall mission of the company, and can be related to the strategic planning process that is in place at the organization.

Questions for Critical Thinking

1. How can a small business show that it is socially responsible? Think of evidence of social responsibility (like sponsoring a Little League team) that a small business can demonstrate.

2. What does strategic planning mean to the small business owner? How does the size of the organization affect the strategic planning process, and how much input should be sought from outside sources while outlining the strategic plan?

What Would You Do?

Some small businesses, by the very nature of what they produce or market, find it difficult to clarify how they plan to fulfill the four levels of social responsibility (economic, legal, ethical, and philanthropic). Through strategic planning, even companies in somewhat controversial and questionable industries can define how they will be socially responsible. Consider Grand Casinos of Minneapolis. As more and more states have legalized gambling in selected locations, Lyle Berman, CEO of Grand Casinos, has been there to develop and manage the casinos. His company has proved so successful that it ranked first on *Fortune*'s list of America's 100 fastest-growing companies. Yet Grand Casinos' business—gambling—tends to arouse considerable controversy. Obviously, Berman could use strategic planning to help identify areas in which his company could fulfill its social responsibilities.

Questions

1. You are in charge of strategic planning for Grand Casinos. The company wants to open and manage a casino in rural Iowa. Community residents have asked you and your strategic planning team to attend a town meeting to discuss the casino. You will need to prepare a description of how your company is fulfilling its social responsibility. (Use Figure 3.1 as a guide.) Other members of the class will act as community residents. As a resident, prepare your questions and concerns for confronting the Grand Casinos team.

4

Creating the Business Plan

CHAPTER LEARNING OUTCOMES

After reading this chapter, you should be able to:

1. **Explain the purpose and importance of the business plan.**

2. **Describe the components of a business plan.**

3. **Recognize the importance of reviewing your business plan.**

Entrepreneurs solve problems by creating businesses. A common problem that many people face is finding just the right gift for a special someone—whether the occasion is a twenty-first birthday or a fiftieth anniversary. The problem is complicated further when a group is sharing in the gift giving.

Enter Eden Clark, president of eDivvy, which allows groups from office parties or weddings to select gifts from retailers like Target or Macy's and invite others to contribute to the price. Rather than each person in a group getting someone a $50 gift, they go in together on the gift and get a $200 to $300 treasure to be long remembered. eDivvy provides a list of recommendations and popular gifts, collects money, and pays the retailer when the cost is covered. Recommended birthday gifts include a Garmin Colorado GPS system ($100 each when split six ways), a 17-inch car video roof-mount monitor ($33.33 when split six ways), or a LCD digital picture frame ($17 when split six ways).

Launched in spring 2009, the 11-person firm generated $52,000 in less than a full year. Projected 2010 revenue is just over $1 million on 35,000 group gift purchases. Retailers benefit by receiving traffic from each member of the group and are able to advertise on the site.

eDivvy receives 4 percent of every group purchase and 5 to 15 percent of each group purchase from the retailer. The company is seeking $1.5 million in outside funding to expand. What would you, as a potential investor, want to see in a business plan for eDivvy before investing?

Sources: April Joyner, "Elevator Pitch: eDivvy Helps People Buy Group Gifts Online," *Inc.*, March 2010, 105; Reuters press release, June 24, 2009; and "An Interview with Edin Jarrin, eDivvy," June 1, 2009, www.socaltech.com.

Every Business Needs a Plan

Successful small business owners know where they want to go and find a way to get there. To see their dreams of owning a profitable business become a reality, they know they must plan each step along the way. Starting a business is like going on vacation—you don't reach your destination by accident. Whether you want to hike through Denali National Park in Alaska or sell frozen yogurt to tourists in Miami, you need a map and adequate provisions.

business plan

A document describing a business that is used to test the feasibility of a business idea, to raise capital, and to serve as a road map for future operations.

A *business plan* is a written document that demonstrates persuasively that enough products or services can be sold at a profit for your firm to become a viable business. Planning is an essential ingredient for any successful business. Although we all create mental plans, those thoughts need to be committed to writing before starting a business.[1] A written plan can help us find omissions and flaws in our ideas by allowing other people to critically review and analyze them.

A business plan tells the reader what your business objectives are; *when, where, why,* and *how* your business will accomplish its objectives; and *who* will be involved in running the business. When planning, you must define the goals of your business, determine the actions that need to be taken to accomplish them, gather and commit the necessary resources, and aim for well-defined targets. A business plan can mean the difference between running a business proactively and reactively. When NASA launched *Apollo 7,* the first manned spacecraft to land on the moon, it didn't aim at the moon. Instead, NASA pointed the rocket to the point in space where the moon would be, factoring in the time needed to get there. Similarly, a business plan should aim at the point where you want your business to be in the future.

© Mike Baldwin / Cornered

LOANS

Apparently, wild hopes and dreams, re-enacted by Barbie and Ken, are no substitute for a solid business plan.

© www.cartoonstock.com

The Purpose

The three primary reasons for writing business plans are (1) to help you determine the feasibility of your business idea, (2) to attract capital for starting up the business, and (3) to provide direction for your business after it is in operation.

Proving Feasibility Writing a business plan is one of the best ways to prevent costly oversights. Committing your ideas to paper forces you to look critically at your means, goals, and expectations. Many people thinking of starting a small business get caught up in the excitement and emotions of the process. It is truly an exciting time! Unfortunately, business decisions based purely on emotion are often not the best long-term choices.

Wanting to have a business does not automatically mean that a market exists to support your desire. You may love boats and want to build a business around them, but if you live 100 miles from the nearest body of water and are unwilling to move, it is unlikely that you can create a viable boat business. Norm Brodsky is a successful entrepreneur who writes a column in *Inc.* magazine titled "Street Smarts." Brodsky states, "The initial goal of every business is to survive long enough to see whether or not the business is viable—no matter what type of business, or how much capital you have. You never know for sure if a business is viable until you do it in the real world."[2] Writing your plan can help remove strong personal emotions from the decision-making process. You need to be passionate about the business you are in, but emotion must be balanced and tempered with logic and rationality.

Attracting Capital   Almost all start-ups must secure capital from bankers or investors. One of the first questions a banker or investor will ask when approached about participating in a business is "Where is your plan?" You need to appreciate the bankers' position. They have to be accountable to depositors for the money entrusted to their care. Bankers in general are financially conservative, so before they risk their capital, they will want assurances that you are knowledgeable and realistic in your projections. Therefore, a complete business plan is needed before you can raise any significant capital. Your business plan will show that you know what you are doing and have thought through the problems and opportunities. Potential investors will also have questions about your plan. They will want to know when your business will break even, when it will be profitable, and if your numbers are real.[3]

Providing Direction   Business plans should provide a road map for future operation. "Can't see the forest for the trees" and "It's difficult to remember that your initial objective was to drain the swamp when you're up to your hips in alligators" are clichés that well apply to starting a small business in that so much of your time can be consumed by handling immediate problems ("management by spot fire" or paying attention to the latest dilemma to flare up) that you have trouble concentrating on the overall needs of the business. By having a road map to guide you over the long term, you are more likely to stay on course. Free or inexpensive business-planning assistance is available to entrepreneurs from such sources as Small Business Development Centers.

"Free or inexpensive business-planning assistance is available to entrepreneurs from such sources as Small Business Development Centers."

Don't misunderstand—providing direction does not mean that directions (and plans) don't change. Craig Knouf understands that point very well. He calculates that he has revised his original business plan more than 120 times since he first wrote it in 1997 for Associated Business Systems, an office equipment supplier in Portland, Oregon. Knouf meets with his seven vice presidents to take a look at the 30-page document every month to review current goals and every quarter for three-month goals, and he holds a two-day meeting to discuss annual long-term objectives. Knouf says, "If you only looked at the plan every quarter, by the time you realize the mistake, you're five months off. You're done. You're not going to get back on track."[4]

The Practice: Guidelines for Writing a Business Plan

No rigid formula for writing business plans exists that would fit every new business. Plans are unique to each business situation. Even so, some general guidelines should be followed.

Consider Your Audience   You need to show the benefit of your business to your reader. Investors want their money to go into market-driven businesses, which satisfy the wants and needs of customers, rather than technology-driven ones, which focus more on the product or service being offered than on what people want.[5]

Keep It Brief   Your business plan should be long enough to cover all the major issues facing the business, yet not look like a copy of *War and Peace*. Your final plan should be complete, yet concise. Including financial projections and appendices, it should be less than 40 pages long. Your first draft will probably be longer, but you can sharpen your ideas by editing the final document to 40 or fewer pages.

Point of View   Try to write your business plan in the third person (do not use *I* or *we*). This approach helps maintain objectivity by removing your personal emotions from the writing process.

Create a Professional Image   The overall appearance of your business plan should be professional and attractive, but not extravagant. Having your document laser printed on white paper, with a colored-stock cover, dividers, and spiral binding, is perfectly acceptable. Think of the message your business plan will send to bankers and investors. For example, having it bound in leather with gold leaf–trimmed pages is not a good sign. Does the plan's appearance suggest that you really need the money or will spend it wisely? Conversely, what might potential investors think of a business plan scratched out on a Big Chief tablet with a crayon? Would it look as if you were really serious about your business?

As you write the first draft of your plan, have several people who are not involved in your business read your work to get their initial reactions. Do they quickly grasp the essence of your proposal? Are they excited about your idea? Do they exclaim, "Wow!"? Getting feedback while you are still writing the plan can help you refine your work and get the reader to say, "Wow!"

Manager's Notes

Good, Bad, and Ugly Business Plans

In their jobs, loan officers at a bank and small business consultants are constantly examining business plans. A discussion with them about good and poor business plans reveals that they've seen the gamut from excellent to just plain awful. Let's look at selected pages from two specific examples of business plans—one well written and one that needs a lot of revision. (Needless to say, the poorly written business plan has been altered to protect the identity of the guilty writer.)

Company A   The business plan for Cameo's Fine Jewelry & Timepieces was written as a class project by an undergraduate business student. Although the student chose to take a different career direction, the plan summary in Figure 4.1a and the full plan in the appendix to this book are solid and fundable.

Company B   Jay's Quarterback Club was the idea for a sports bar and restaurant in Norcross, Georgia. When Jay M. went looking for financing for his idea, however, he found that potential investors and lenders were reluctant to loan him the start-up capital. A close look at his business plan reveals mistakes that might explain their reluctance. Selected pages from that plan follow in Figure 4.1b.

FIGURE 4-1A
Example of a Good Business Plan

A Professional-Looking Report, with Sound Financial Projections, Is Essential to Prospective Business Owners. Of the Hundreds of Loan Proposals That an Investor or Banker Must Sort through Each Year, Only a Fraction Will Be Funded.

Cameo's Fine Jewelry & Timepieces Executive Summary

Cameo's Fine Jewelry & Timepieces is designed to be the Western Slope of Colorado's finest, most exquisite jewelry store available. Located in the heart of Grand Junction, Cameo's will offer jewelry and watches from world-renowned artists and designers from countries known for their quality such as Switzerland, Germany, Italy, and the U.S. Galleries will feature the work of Cartier, Rolex, Pippo Italia, Hearts on Fire, Paul Klecka, and many more.

The experience our customers receive through our atmosphere and customer service will be as fine as the jewelry itself. Our retail format will take on the elements of both a gallery and a lounge. Saltwater fish tanks will enhance the environment, and a wine and cocktail bar will be available to our customers. The sales staff and on-duty gemologist will be able to assist in finding that perfect piece of jewelry, and if it's not available, they will be able to order it or create a custom piece. Socials will invite the community to come enjoy the galleries and become more educated on the different qualities of jewelry.

Location and Target Market   Grand Junction serves as an ideal location, being that it is the largest city on the Western Slope of Colorado and acts as a retail hub for the surrounding communities. Since Cameo's will be the only jewelry store on the Western Slope that offers this level of quality, it will draw from a four-county region including Mesa, Garfield, Delta, and Montrose counties, which have a total population of 254,666. After taking into account age, percent of population who purchase jewelry, yearly weddings, and salary, there are 101,096 jewelry consumers within this geographic market. My goal is to obtain a 1 percent market share during the first year of business, which would provide 1,011 customers.

With this market penetration, and an average jewelry purchase of $2,000, Cameo's would sell $2,022,000 worth of products in the first fiscal year. The cash position at the end of the first fiscal year will equal $460,052, making this a very attractive and profitable venture to pursue.

Competitive Advantage   Cameo's defining strengths will be that of location and facility as well as inventory. Cameo's will be housed in a 6,850 square foot renovated building on 4th and Main in Grand Junction. Being downtown means that Cameo's will fall under the guidance of the Downtown Partnership. The purpose of the Downtown Partnership is to oversee the promotion of the downtown area and provide community-benefiting events. Some events held downtown include an October fest, a farmer's market, a parade of lights, and an art hop.

Cameo's exclusive inventory will also set it apart from other jewelry stores. Many pieces in inventory will be rare or hard to find and certainly the only one available within this geographic market.

There are several things that make the jewelry industry as a whole very attractive, including strong growth, a stable position, and new product creation, innovation, and trends. Currently the jewelry industry is growing annually at a rate of 9 percent, allowing for more retail outlets in one geographic region.

Jewelry is very stable because it is never going away, nor is it a fad item. Jewelry is often considered a necessity in times of marriage and anniversary, and is often used as a gift. There are many new jewelry products entering the market all the time that are technologically, fashion, and trend driven, which creates an increase in demand.

Management   My passion for watches, and the jewelry industry, combined with previous work experience will enable me to make this business a success. Previous employment has provided me with experience in the necessary functions of this business, including management, marketing, event planning, and financials.

My skills in marketing and event planning will prove most beneficial to the startup of this business. The product costs in this industry are very high, and general knowledge is

FIGURE 4-1A
(Continued)

low; therefore, providing information and educating the consumer are crucial. Special events will draw consumers into the store in order to show them what it has to offer.

Finances   Financial projections show that equipment, supplies, fixtures, and leasehold improvements totaling $111,000 are needed, along with a beginning inventory of $513,500 and operating expenses of just over $90,000, which all together will create total initial capitalization costs of $730,000. The owner brings $73,000 of equity and seeks a bank loan of $657,000 at competitive terms.

Cash flow projections show positive cash flow in year 1, totaling approximately $380,000.

FIGURE 4-1B

Example of a Poor Business Plan

A Sloppy Appearance Can Hurt the Chances of Your Plan Being Taken Seriously by Lenders and Investors.

JAY'S QUARTERBACK ~~CULB~~ CLUB

Proposed Business

My idea is to open a bar/restaurant that have a sports theme. Sports are big business right now and the timing is perfect. I think that people are really interested in sports and will be willing to pay good money for this type of dining experience. People eat out a lot and my business will give them another place to spend their money.

Marketing Research and Marketing Plan

I've done some research in the community and haven't seen any restaurant or bar like Jay's Quarterback Club. Since there's nobody else doing this type of business, I won't have no direct competition. So marketing expenses will be minimal. Perhaps I'll run some newspaper advertisements and put out coupons iif I need to when sales aren't enough to help me pay the expenses.

Operations Plan

As soon as I get word on my financing, I'll start looking for an appropriate location for my business. If I can't find something that fits my needs, I'll just build one. I've been checking into suppliers for food and other materials I'll need. I feel confident that I can dedvelop good contacts and have reliable sources.

As far as employees goes, with the level of business that I know we can accomplish in the first few months of operations, I will be hiring 4 additional employees: cook, bartender, and 2 waitpersons. This will leave me free to do the scheduling, ordering, and managing.

Sales Projections

I've worked in restaurants in the past and have a lot of experience there so I believe that my bar/restaurant can make lots of money. I believe that my first year's sales will be $500,000 and expenses will be $410,000. That means I'll make $90,000. I intend to have several cost controls but, still it's really hard to tell exactly what my expenses will be, though. In the second year, because we'll be familiar to the customer, I know we can increase sales by 20% for total revenue of $510,000. I think I can hold my expenses constant at $90,000.

Conclusion

Since I've had a lot of experience working in restaurants, I am positive that I can make this venture work. The theme will be unique and there's not anyone else doing this, so there shouldn't be any problem attracting paying customers. If you'd like more information, I'd be happy to share my idea for Jay's Quaterback Club with you in person. Just call me at my home number. Thanks for your consideration.

Where to Get Help Who should write the business plan for your proposed venture? You should! The person who is best qualified and who receives the most benefit from the planning process is the person who is going to implement the plan. It is *your* business, after all, and it needs to be *your* plan. With that stated, can you get aid in writing the plan? Of course you can, and you should seek such help if you need it. Here are some sources:

- The Small Business Administration home page at www.sba.gov
- Your local Small Business Development Center
- A local SCORE (Service Corp of Retired Executives) chapter
- Your local Chamber of Commerce
- A nearby college or university
- One of the many paperback guides written on business plans available at any bookstore

Computer software is available to perform many functions of our daily lives. We can balance our checkbook or design our dream house using software, for example. Although software packages can make our lives easier, you need to be careful not to use one to generate a "cookie-cutter" business plan. Filling in a few blanks on a master document does not produce a workable business plan any more than a paint-by-numbers kit produces valuable art. Because your business will be different from others, you need to emphasize your competitive advantage and show your objectives.

This is not to imply that you should not use word-processing, spreadsheet, or graphics packages to produce your plan. You should, because they can be extremely helpful. Instead, this caveat applies to "canned" business plans. If you wish to investigate business-planning software, check out JIAN's BizPlanBuilder Interactive and Palo Alto Software's Business Plan Pro, but remember that writing a business plan is as much an art as it is a science.[6]

Business Plan Contents

A business plan should be tailored to fit your particular business. Write the plan yourself, even if you seek assistance from lawyers, accountants, or consultants. In 40 or fewer pages, the plan should present your strengths clearly and in a logical order.

Although a plan's contents will vary from business to business, its structure is fairly standardized. Your plan should contain as many of the following sections as appropriate for your type of venture.[7] Not every business will require every one of these sections. For example, if your business is a start-up, it won't have a history section, but you can describe your management experience.

Cover Page

The cover page should include the name of the business, its address and phone number, and the date the plan was issued. If this information is overlooked, you have a problem if a potential investor tries to reach you to ask additional questions (or send a check).

Table of Contents

You want the business plan to be as easy to read as possible. An orderly table of contents will allow the reader to turn directly to the sections desired.

executive summary
A condensed abstract of a business plan used to spark the reader's interest in the business and to highlight crucial information.

Executive Summary

The *executive summary* gives a one- to two-page overview of your entire plan. It is the most important section of the plan because readers do not want to wade through 35 to 40 pages to get the essential facts. If you do not capture the reader's attention here, he or she is not likely to read the rest of the plan.

The executive summary should include the following components:

- *Company information*—what product or service you provide, your competitive advantage, when the company was formed, your company objectives, and the background of you and your management team.
- *Market opportunity*—the expected size and growth rate of your market, your expected market share, and any relevant industry trends.
- *Financial data*—financial forecasts for the first three years of operations, equity investment desired, and long-term loans that will be needed.

The information in the preceding list is a lot to condense into two pages, but all of it is important, and if you truly understand what you are writing about, you will find that you can explain it simply and succinctly. A first-rate executive summary provides you with a two-sentence "elevator pitch," so named in case you would ever find yourself contained in an elevator with a venture capitalist and need to explain your business concept quickly.[8]

Although the executive summary is the first section of the plan, it should be written last. You are condensing what you have already written into the summary, not expanding the summary to fill the plan. Here's a hint for writing the executive summary: As you compose all the other sections of the plan, highlight a few key sentences that are important enough to include in your executive summary. To see examples of executive summaries, refer to the complete plan included in Appendix A and the sample plans on this book's Web site.

> *"A first-rate executive summary provides you with a two-sentence 'elevator pitch,' so named in case you would ever find yourself contained in an elevator with a venture capitalist and need to explain your business concept quickly."*

Company Information

In this section, you should describe the background of your company, your choice of legal business form, and the reasons for the company's establishment. How did your company get to the point where it is today? Give the company's history by describing in some detail what your business does and how it satisfies customers' needs. How did you choose and develop your products or services to be sold? Don't be afraid to describe any setbacks or missteps you have taken along the way to forming your business. They represent reality, and leaving them out could make your plan and projections look "too good to be true" to lenders or investors.

Environmental and Industry Analysis

In the section on environmental and industry analysis, you have an opportunity to show how your business fits into larger contexts. An *environmental analysis* shows identified trends and changes that are happening at the national and international levels that may influence the future of your small business. Introduce environmental categories such as economic, competitive, legal, political, cultural, and technological arenas that affect and are affected by your business. Discuss the future outlook and trends within these categories. For example, a cultural trend of "Buy American" might create a competitive advantage for your small manufacturing business. Changes in the legal or political arena can provide opportunities as well. Suppose the Environmental Protection Agency (EPA) banned lead fishing sinkers because of possible contamination of water supplies. What if you had just created a line of fishing sinkers produced from some material other than lead?

While you generally cannot control such external environments, you can describe the opportunities that changes in them present in your business plan. As an entrepreneur, you have to understand the world in which you operate and how you can best assess the opportunities that arise there.

Opportunity can come from recycling, as seen with these circuit boards. Veolia Environmental Services has installed the first mechanized demolition and sorting unit for **WEEE** (Waste Electrical and Electronic Equipment) in Gonesse, France. This automatic process dismantles small household appliances with a recovery rate of up to 90%.

After completing the environmental analysis, you should do an *industry* analysis describing the industry within which your business operates. Here you will focus on specific industry trends. Describe industry demand—pertinent data will likely be readily available from industry trade publications or other published sources. How do you determine what other businesses or products should be included as part of your industry? One helpful way to draw the line between what and whom to include in your industry is to consider possible substitutes for your product. If you own a business that sells ice cream, do your customers view frozen yogurt or custard as a potential substitute for your frozen treats? If so, you should consider businesses that sell these products to be part of your industry. What competitive reactions and industry-wide trends can you identify? Who are the major players in your industry? Have any businesses recently entered or exited the field? Why did they leave? Is the industry growing or declining? Who are the new competitors in the industry?

Lenders want to see that you have a clear understanding of how your industry operates. Specifically, which of Porter's five forces (threat of new entrants, bargaining power of customers, threat of substitutes, bargaining power of suppliers, and rivalry among existing competitors; see Chapter 3) are rated as high or low for the industry you intend to enter?[9]

The environmental and industry analyses are tricky sections of your business plan to write. As stated earlier, your plan must be concise, but in this section especially you must cover huge, comprehensive issues and factors that could fill volumes. Feel like you are being pulled in several different directions at once? Good—now you are starting to realize the complexity of what you are getting into. Think of the environmental and industry analysis section in the following way: As a small business owner, you have to be knowledgeable about all current and potential factors that could affect your business. Of course, the business plan is not the place to describe every possible development in detail. Instead, treat this section as if you are showing only the tip of the iceberg that represents your accumulated knowledge, and make it clear that you are prepared to answer questions relating to less critical factors that you chose not to include in your business plan.

Products or Services

In this section, you can go into detail describing your product or service. How is your product or service different from those currently on the market? Are there any other uses for it that could increase current sales? Include drawings or photos if appropriate. Describe any patents or trademarks that you hold, as these give you a proprietary position that can be defended. Describe your competitive advantage. What sets your product or service apart as better than the competition's?

What is your product's potential for growth? How do you intend to manage your product or service through the product life cycle? Can you expand the product line or develop related products? In this section of your business plan, you can discuss potential product lines as well as current ones.

Marketing Research and Evaluation

You need to present evidence that a market exists for your business. A section on marketing research and evaluation, presenting the facts you have gathered on the size and nature of your markets, will tell investors if a large enough market exists and if you can be competitive in that market. State the market size in dollars and units. Give your sales forecast by estimating from your marketing research how many units and dollars worth of your product you expect to sell in a given time period. That sales forecast becomes the basis for projecting many of your financial statements. Indicate your primary and secondary sources of data, and the methods you used to estimate total market size and your market share.

Target Markets and Market Segmentation You must identify your target markets and then concentrate your marketing efforts on these key areas. These markets must share some identifiable need that you can satisfy. What do the people who buy your product have in common with one another? To segment your markets, you could use a demographic characteristic (for example, 18- to 25-year-old females), a psychographic variable (similar lifestyles, usage rate of product, or degree of loyalty), a geographic variable (anyone who lives within a five-mile radius of your business), or another variable. Describe actual customers who have expressed a desire to buy your product. What trends do you expect will affect your markets?

"A danger of segmentation and target marketing is that it encourages the belief that those segments and markets will stay the same—they won't."

Market Trends Markets and consumer tastes change, so you will need to explain how you will assess your customers' needs over time. A danger of segmentation and target marketing is that it encourages the belief that those segments and markets will stay the same—they won't. Specify how you will continue to evaluate consumer needs so you can identify market trends and, based on that information, improve your market lines and aid new product development.

Competition Among three or four primary competitors, identify the price leader, the quality leader, and the service leader. Realistically discuss the strengths and weaknesses of each. Compare your products or services with those of competitors on the basis of price, product performance, and other attributes.

This section offers a good opportunity to include the SWOT analysis you completed in the strategic planning chapter (Chapter 3). Identify the strengths and weaknesses of your business and the opportunities and threats that exist outside your business.

Market Share Because you have identified the size of your market and your competitors, you can estimate the *market share* you intend to gain—that is, the percentage of total industry sales. Market share can effectively be shown and explained using a pie chart.

Your job in writing the marketing-research section of your business plan is to convince the reader that a large enough market exists for your product for you to achieve your projected sales forecasts.

Marketing Plan Your *marketing plan* shows how you intend to achieve your sales forecast. You should start by explaining your overall marketing strategy, identifying your potential markets, and explaining what you have decided is the best way to reach them. Include your *marketing objectives* (what you want to achieve) and the strategies you will use to accomplish these objectives.

Pricing as Part of Marketing Plan Your pricing policy is one of the most important decisions you will have to make. The price must be "right" to penetrate the market, to maintain your market position, and especially to make profits. Compare your pricing policies with those of the competitors you identified earlier. Explain how your gross margin will allow you to make a profit after covering all expenses. Many people go into business with the intent of charging lower prices than the competition. If this is your goal, explain how you can follow this strategy and still make a profit—through greater efficiency in manufacturing or distribution of the product, lower labor costs, lower overhead, or whatever else allows you to undercut the competition's price.

You should discuss the relationship between your price, your market share, and your profits. For example, by charging a higher price than the competition, you may reduce your sales volume but realize a higher gross margin and increase your business's bottom line.

Promotion as Part of Marketing Plan How will you attract the attention of and communicate with your potential customers? For industrial products, you might use trade shows and advertise in trade magazines, via direct mail, or through promotional brochures. For consumer products, you should describe your plans for advertising and promotional campaigns. You should also give the advertising schedule and costs involved. Examples of advertising or brochures may be included in the appendix of the business plan.

Place as Part of Marketing Plan Describe how you intend to sell and distribute your products. Will you use your own sales force or independent sales representatives or distributors? If you will hire your own sales force, describe how it will be structured, the sales expected per salesperson per year, and the pay structure. Your own sales force will concentrate more on your products because it will sell them exclusively. If you will use sales representatives, describe how those individuals will be selected, the territories they will cover, and the rates they will charge. Independent sales representatives may also handle products and lines other than yours, but they are much less expensive for you because they are not your employees. Your place strategy should describe the level of coverage (local, regional, or national) you will use initially and as your business grows. It should include the channels of distribution you will use to get and to sell products.

Service Policies as Part of Marketing Plan If you sell a product that may require service, such as cameras, copy machines, or bicycles, describe your service and warranty policies. These policies can be important in the customer's decision-making process. How will you handle customer service problems? Describe the terms and types of warranties offered. Explain whether you will provide service via your own service department, subcontract out the service work, or return products to the factory. Also state whether service is intended to be a profit center or a break-even operation.

Personalized customer service is a competitive advantage for many small businesses.

Manufacturing and Operations Plan

The manufacturing and operations plan will stress elements related to your business's production. It will outline your needs in terms of facilities, location, space requirements, capital equipment, labor force, inventory control, and purchasing. Stress the areas most relevant to your type of business. For instance, if you are starting a manufacturing business, outline the production processes and your control systems for inventory, purchasing, and production. The business plan for a service business should focus on your location, overhead, and labor force productivity.

Geographic Location Describe your planned geographic location and its advantages and disadvantages in terms of wage rates, unionization, labor pool, proximity to customers and suppliers, types of transportation available, tax rates, utility costs, and zoning. Again, you should stress the features most relevant to your business. Proximity to customers is especially important to a service business, whereas access to transportation will be of greater concern to a manufacturing business.

Facilities What kind of facilities does your business need? Discuss your requirements for floor space (including offices, sales room, manufacturing plant space, and storage areas), parking, loading areas, and special equipment. Will you rent, lease, or purchase these facilities? How long will they remain adequate: One year? Three years? Is expansion possible?

Make-or-Buy Policy In a manufacturing business, you must decide what you will produce and what you will purchase as components to be assembled into the finished product. This is called the *make-or-buy decision*. Many factors go into this decision (see Chapter 12). In your business plan, you should justify the advantages of your policy. Describe potential subcontractors and suppliers.

Control Systems What is your approach to controlling quality, inventory, and production? How will you measure your progress toward the goals you have set for your business?

Labor Force At the location you have selected, is there a sufficient quantity of adequately skilled people in the local labor force to meet your needs? What kinds of training will you need to provide? Can you afford to offer this training and still remain competitive? Training can be a hidden cost that can turn a profit into a loss.

> *"Training can be a hidden cost that can turn a profit into a loss."*

Management Team

A good management team is the key to transforming your vision into a successful business. Show how your team is balanced in terms of technical skills (possessing the knowledge specific to your type of business), business skills (the ability to successfully run a business), and experience. As when building any other kind of team, the skills and talents of your management team need to complement one another. Include a job description for each management position, and specify the key people who will fill these slots. Can you show how their skills complement one another? Have these individuals worked together before? An *organization chart* can be included in the appendix of your plan to graphically show how these positions fit together. Résumés for each key manager should be included in the appendix.

State how your key managers will be compensated. Your chances of obtaining financing are very slim unless the managers are willing to accept substantially less than their market value for salary while the business is getting started. Managers must be committed to putting as many proceeds as possible back into the business.

Discuss the management training your key people have had and may still need. Be as specific as possible on the cost, type, and availability of this management or technical training.

Like your managers, you may need professional assistance at times. Identify other people with whom you will work, including a lawyer, a certified public accountant, an insurance agent, and a banker. Identify contacts you have supporting you in these areas.

Anyone who is considering putting money into your business will scrutinize this section thoroughly. Therefore, your plan must answer the following questions about the management team members, which were first posed by Harvard professor William Sahlman:

- Where are the founders from?
- Where have they been educated?
- Where have they worked, and for whom?
- What have they accomplished—professionally and personally—in the past?
- What is their reputation within the *business* community?
- What experience do they have that is directly relevant to the opportunity they are pursuing?
- What skills, abilities, and knowledge do they have?
- How realistic are they about the venture's chances for success and the tribulations it will face?
- Who else needs to be on the team?
- Are they prepared to recruit high-quality people?
- How will they respond to adversity?
- Do they have the mettle to make the inevitable hard choices?
- How committed are they to this venture?
- What are their motivations?[10]

Timeline

Create a timeline outlining the interrelationships and timing of the major events planned for your venture. In addition to helping you calculate your business needs and minimize risk, the timeline is an indicator to investors that you have thoroughly researched potential problems and are aware of deadlines. Keep in mind that people tend to underestimate the time needed to complete projects. Your schedule should be realistic and attainable.

Critical Risks and Assumptions

All business plans contain implicit assumptions, such as how your business will operate, what economic conditions will be, and how you will react in different situations. Identification and discussion of any potential major trends, problems, or risks that you think you may encounter will show the reader that you are in touch with reality. These risks and assumptions could relate to your industry, markets, company, or personnel.

This section gives you a place to establish alternate plans in case the unexpected happens. If potential investors discover unstated negative factors after the fact, they may quickly question the credibility of both you and the business. Too many businesses are started with only a plan A and no thought about what will happen if X, Y, or Z occurs.[11] Possible contingencies that you should anticipate include the following scenarios:

- *Unreliable sales forecasts.* What will you do if your market does not develop as quickly as you predicted or, conversely, if your market develops too quickly? Each of these situations creates its own problems. Sales that are too low may cause serious financial problems. Sales that are too high may cause bottlenecks in production, difficulties in purchasing enough products from vendors or suppliers, trouble hiring and scheduling employees, or dissatisfied customers who must wait longer than they expected for your product or service.
- *Competitors' ability to underprice or to make your product obsolete.*
- *Unfavorable industry-wide trends.* Not long ago, businesses that produced asbestos made up a thriving industry supplying products for automotive and building construction firms. Then reports linking asbestos with cancer drastically affected the demand for that product and virtually eliminated the industry.
- *Appropriately trained workers not as available as predicted.*
- *Erratic supply of products or raw materials.*
- *Any one of the 10,000 other things you didn't expect.*

Benefits to the Community

Your new business will affect the lives of many other people besides yourself. Describe the potential benefits to the community that the formation of your business could provide.

- *Economic development*—number of jobs created (total and skilled), purchase of supplies from local businesses, and the multiplier effect (which shows the number of hands that new dollars brought into the community pass through before exiting).
- *Community development*—providing needed goods or services, improving physical assets or the appearance of the community, and contributing to a community's standard of living.
- *Human development*—providing new technical skills or other training, creating opportunities for career advancement, developing management or leadership skills, offering attractive wages, and providing other types of individual growth.

Competitive Advantage
INNOVATION AND SUSTAINABILITY

Bring It On

You're in this class, and maybe you've even finished writing your assigned business plan. How about entering it into a collegiate business plan competition? There are a lot of them around now—nearly 3,500 students competed in some 70 contests at the regional, national, and international levels. The prizes can include hundreds of thousands of dollars plus access to venture capital. The Carrot Capital Venture Bowl offers a top prize of $750,000; however, most B-school competitions generally offer less than $100,000.

Matt Ferris and Bruce Black wrote a business plan for KidSmart Vocal Smoke Detector while in the University of Georgia's MBA program. KidSmart includes a personalized message in a parent's own voice giving instructions to children in case of fire. Ferris and Black's plan won second place in the Carrot Capital Venture Bowl, but the pair turned down the $750,000 prize because they felt the offer was too restrictive. They went on to win

Moot Corp.'s prize and bagged $100,000, without having to give up as much company ownership as the other competition required. That $100,000 will come in handy as the alarms go on sale on QVC television shopping channel and in catalogs like those produced by Sharper Image, Hammacher Schlemmer, and SkyMall.

And here is another college-student success story: Medical students Jon Mathy, Eshan Alipour, Eric Allison, and Amita Shukla created a device that bypasses an artery blockage the way water in a river flows around a big boulder and eliminates the need for surgery. They identified a huge market and wrote a business plan that won Stanford University's business plan annual competition. And so VisiVas was born.

Sources: Jennifer Merritt, "Will Your Plan Win a Prize?" *BusinessWeek,* March 15, 2004, 108; Elaine Pofeldt et al., "Here Comes the Competition," *Fortune Small Business,* November 2003, 38; and Carolina Braunschweig, "No Business Plans, Please," *Venture Capital Journal,* August 2003, 24–31.

© Image Source/Getty Images

Exit Strategy

Every business will benefit by devoting some attention to a succession plan. Before you begin your business is a good time to consider how you intend to get yourself (and your money) out of it. Do you intend to sell it in 20 years? Will your children take it over? How will you prepare them for ownership? Do you intend to grow the business to the point of an initial public offering? How will investors get their money back?

Financial Plan

Your financial plan is where you demonstrate that all the information from previous sections of your business plan, such as marketing, operations, sales, and strategies, can come together to form a viable, profitable business. Potential investors will closely scrutinize the financial section of your business plan to ensure that it is feasible before they become involved. Projections should be your best estimates of future operations. Your financial plan should include the following statements (existing businesses will need historical statements and pro forma projections, whereas start-ups will have only projections):

- Sources and uses of capital (initial and projected)
- Cash flow projections for three years
- Balance sheets for three years
- Profit-and-loss statements for three years
- Break-even analysis

We will discuss how to prepare these documents in later chapters. (See Chapter 8 for cash flow projections, balance sheets, and profit-and-loss statements, and Chapter 9 for sources and uses of capital.) With the financial statements, you need to show

sources and uses of funds
A financial document used by start-up businesses that shows where capital comes from and what it will be used for.

cash flow statement
A financial document that shows the amount of money a business has on hand at the beginning of a time period, receipts coming into the business, and money going out of the business during the same period.

balance sheet
A financial document that shows the assets, liabilities, and owner's equity for a business.

conclusions and important points, such as how much equity and how much debt are included, the highest amount of cash needed, and how long the payback period for loans is expected to be.

Sources and Uses of Funds The simple **sources and uses of funds** form shows where your money is coming from and how you are spending it (see Figure 4.2).

Cash Flow Statement The most important financial statement for a small business is the **cash flow statement**, because if you run out of cash, you're out of business. In a cash flow statement, working from your opening cash balance, you add all the money that comes into your business for a given time period (week, month, quarter), and then you subtract all the money you spend for the same time period. The result is your closing cash balance, which becomes your opening balance for the next time period (see Figure 4.3).

You should project a cash flow statement by month for the first year of operation and by quarter for the second and third years. *Cash flow* shows you what the highest amount of working capital will be. It can be especially critical if your sales are seasonal in nature or cyclical.

Balance Sheet The **balance sheet** shows all the assets *owned* by your business and the liabilities, or what is *owed* against those assets (see Figure 4.4). The difference between the two is what the company has *earned*, or the net worth of the business, which is also called *capital*. From the balance sheet, bankers and investors will calculate some key ratios, such as debt-to-equity and current ratio (see Chapter 8), to help determine the financial health of your business. You need to prepare balance sheets ending at each of the first three years of operation.

FIGURE 4-2

Sources and Uses of Funds Worksheet

A Sources and Uses of Funds Worksheet Shows Where Money Comes from and What It Is Used For.

Sources of Funds:

Debt:
Term loans $ _____
Refinancing of old debt   _____
Lines of credit   _____
Line 1   _____
Line 2   _____
Mortgage   _____

Equity:
Investments   _____

Total Sources: $ _____

Uses of Funds:
Property $ _____
Inventory   _____
Equipment (itemize)   _____
                                        _____
                                        _____
Working capital   _____
Cash reserve   _____
Total Uses: $ _____

FIGURE 4-3

Sample Components of a Cash Flow Statement

A Cash Flow Statement Shows How Money Enters and Exits Your Business.

Opening cash balance

Add:
- Cash receipts
- Collection of accounts receivable
- New loans or investment
- Other sources of cash
  - Total receipts

Less:
- Utilities
- Salaries
- Office supplies
- Accounts payable
- Leased equipment
- Sales expenses
- Loan payments
- General expenses
  - Total disbursements

Cash increase (or decrease)

Closing cash balance

FIGURE 4-4

Balance Sheet

A Balance Sheet Shows What You Own and Whom You Owe.

For year ended [month] [day], [year]

	Year 1	Year 2	Year 3
Current Assets			
Cash	$_____	$_____	$_____
Accounts Receivable	_____	_____	_____
Inventory	_____	_____	_____
Supplies	_____	_____	_____
Prepaid Expenses	_____	_____	_____
Fixed Assets			
Real Estate	_____	_____	_____
Equipment	_____	_____	_____
Fixtures and Leasehold Improvements	_____	_____	_____
Vehicles	_____	_____	_____
Other Assets			
License	_____	_____	_____
Goodwill	_____	_____	_____
TOTAL ASSETS	$_____	$_____	$_____
Current Liabilities			
Accounts Payable	_____	_____	_____
Notes Payable (due within 1 year)	_____	_____	_____
Accrued Expenses	_____	_____	_____
Taxes Owed	_____	_____	_____
Long-Term Liabilities			
Notes Payable (due after 1 year)	_____	_____	_____
Bank Loans	_____	_____	_____
TOTAL LIABILITIES	$_____	$_____	$_____
NET WORTH (assets minus liabilities)	$_____	$_____	$_____

Profit-and-Loss Statement Don't expect the pro forma for your business plan to be a finely honed, 100 percent accurate projection of the future. With a ***profit-and-loss statement***, your objective is to come up with as close an approximation as possible of what your sales revenues and expenses will be. In making your projections, it is helpful to break sales down by product line (or types of services) and then determine a best-case scenario, a worst-case scenario, and a most-likely scenario somewhere between the two extremes for each category. This practice helps create realistic projections. Remember that lenders and investors (especially venture capitalists) are professionals at picking apart business plans.[12]

Start preparing this statement in the left-hand column to show what your sales and expenses would be under the worst conditions (see Figure 4.5). Assume that you have difficulty getting products, that the weather is terrible, that your salespeople are out spending all their time playing golf instead of selling, and that the state highway

FIGURE 4-5
**Profit-and-Loss
Statement**

*Projecting the Best and the
Worst That Could Happen
Helps You Calculate What
Your Profits or Losses Are
Likely to Be.*

	Low	Most Likely	High
SALES:			
Product/service line 1	$ _____	$ _____	$ _____
Product/service line 2	_____	_____	_____
Product/service line 3	_____	_____	_____
Product/service line 4	_____	_____	_____
TOTAL SALES REVENUE			
Cost of Goods Sold:			
Product/service line 1	_____	_____	_____
Product/service line 2	_____	_____	_____
Product/service line 3	_____	_____	_____
Product/service line 4	_____	_____	_____
TOTAL COST OF GOODS SOLD	$ _____	$ _____	$ _____
GROSS PROFIT	$ _____	$ _____	$ _____
EXPENSES:			
Variable:			
Payroll	$ _____	$ _____	$ _____
Sales commission	_____	_____	_____
Freight and delivery	_____	_____	_____
Travel and entertainment	_____	_____	_____
Semivariable:			
Advertising/promotion	_____	_____	_____
FICA/payroll tax	_____	_____	_____
Supplies	_____	_____	_____
Telephone	_____	_____	_____
Fixed:			
Rent	_____	_____	_____
Utilities	_____	_____	_____
Property taxes	_____	_____	_____
Dues and subscriptions	_____	_____	_____
TOTAL EXPENSES	_____	_____	_____
Profit before depreciation	_____	_____	_____
Depreciation	_____	_____	_____
NET PROFIT	$ _____	$ _____	$ _____

Note: Expense items for your business will vary from these three categories. For illustration purposes only.

department closes the road that runs in front of your only location for repairs. Imagine that anything bad that can happen will happen. Now, in the right-hand column, make projections assuming that everything goes exactly your way. What would your sales and expenses be if customers with cash in their hands are waiting in line outside your door every morning at opening time, if suppliers rearrange their schedules so that you never run out of stock, and if competitors all close their doors for a month of vacation just as you are beginning operations? This is a lot more fun, of course, but not any more likely to happen than the first scenario, although either could happen. Your most realistic estimate will fall between these two extremes in the center column.

Question and test your projections. Is there enough demand for you to reach your sales goal? Do you have enough space, equipment, and employees to reach your sales goal? Break your sales down into the number of units, then the number of units bought per customer, and then the number of units sold per day. When viewed this way, you may find that every person in town would have to buy eight bagels per day, 365 days per year, for you to achieve your sales projections for your proposed bagel shop. (Yes, real business plans get written with such projections.) Obviously, you would need to revise your goal, expand your menu, do more to control your expenses, or convince people to eat more bagels than is humanly possible for your business to succeed to meet such a projection.

break-even point
The point at which sales and costs are equal and a business is neither making nor losing money.

Break-even Analysis How many units (or dollars' worth) of your products or service will have to be sold to cover your costs? A *break-even analysis* will give you a sales projection of how many units or dollars need to be sold to reach your **break-even point**—that is, the point at which you are neither making nor losing money (see Figure 4.6; see also Chapter 14).

Reality Check

Feasible, Viable, Good Idea?

A full-blown business plan is not always needed. A feasibility study is an abbreviated planning process to determine whether to proceed with the next step in creating a new venture or launching a new product. The goal is to identify and "make or break" issues that would argue against an action or suggest whether a favorable outcome can be accomplished.

Step 1: SWOT Analysis

As covered in Chapter 3, begin by considering all strengths, weaknesses, opportunities, and threats for the purpose of positioning strengths with external opportunities and internal weaknesses away from threats.

Step 2: Financial Feasibility

Can you gather data that shows that the business or product generates more money than it will cost (in a reasonable time period)? If not, why investigate further?

Step 3: Marketing Feasibility

Can your business opportunity generate a high enough sales volume to justify all other necessary costs—and can the target market be reached so they will buy?

Test 4: Resource Feasibility

Even if your idea passes the previous tests, you still won't succeed if you cannot muster all resources (personnel, raw materials, money, etc.).

Test 5: Other Aspects

Finally, consider specific factors such as appropriate location for business, adequate suppliers and vendors, and costs versus benefits.

A feasibility study will indicate if it is possible to turn an idea into a business, but what you are REALLY looking for is if it will be *viable*. Viability means that something is not only possible but also profitable.

Sources: "Feasibility Study," www.inc.com/encyclopedia, April 27, 2010; Brad Sugars, "How to Research Your Market," Entrepreneur.com/startingabusiness, March 2, 2007; and Tamara Monosoff, "Get Your Product to Market in 6 Steps," *Entrepreneur*, May 7, 2009.

FIGURE 4-6

Break-even Analysis

At What Point Will You Make Money?

1. Total sales $ _____
2. Fixed costs $ _____
3. Gross margin $ _____
4. Gross margin as percentage of sales (line 3/line 1) %   _____ %
5. Breakeven sales (line 2/line 4) $ _____
6. Profit goal $ _____
7. Sales required to achieve profit goal [(line 2 + line 6)/line 4] $ _____

To reinforce your financial projections, you may want to compare them to industry averages for your chosen industry. *Robert Morris Associates Annual Statement* publishes an annual index showing industry averages of key manufacturing, wholesale, and retail business groups. Compare your projected financial ratios with industry averages to give the reader an established benchmark (see Chapter 8).

Appendix

Supplemental information and documents not crucial to the business plan, but of potential interest to the reader, are gathered in the appendix. Résumés of owners and principal managers, advertising samples, brochures, and any related information can be included. Different types of information, such as résumés, advertising samples, an organization chart, and a floor plan, should each be placed in a separate appendix and labeled with successive letters of the alphabet (Appendix A, Appendix B, and so on). Be sure to identify each appendix in your table of contents (for example, "Appendix A: Advertising Samples").

Review Process

Writing a business plan is a project that involves a long series of interrelated steps. Beginning with your idea for a business, you want to determine its feasibility through the creation of your business plan. The technique illustrated in Figure 4.7 will allow you to identify the steps you need to take in writing your plan. Steps connected by lines show that lower-numbered steps need to be completed before moving on to higher-numbered ones. Steps that are shown as being parallel take place simultaneously. For example, steps 6 through 10 can be completed at the same time, and all must be accomplished before you can estimate how much capital you need in step 11.

Like any project involving a number of complex steps and calculations, your business plan should be carefully reviewed and revised before you present it to potential investors. After you have written your plan, rate it yourself the way lenders and investors will evaluate it (see Manager's Notebook, "How Does Your Plan Rate?").

Business Plan Mistakes

Often we can learn from the mistakes of others. Writing business plans is no exception. Bankers and investors who assess hundreds of business plans each year look for reasons to reject the proposals. This practice helps them to weed out potentially unworthy investments and to identify the likely winners—the most organized, focused, and realistic proposals.

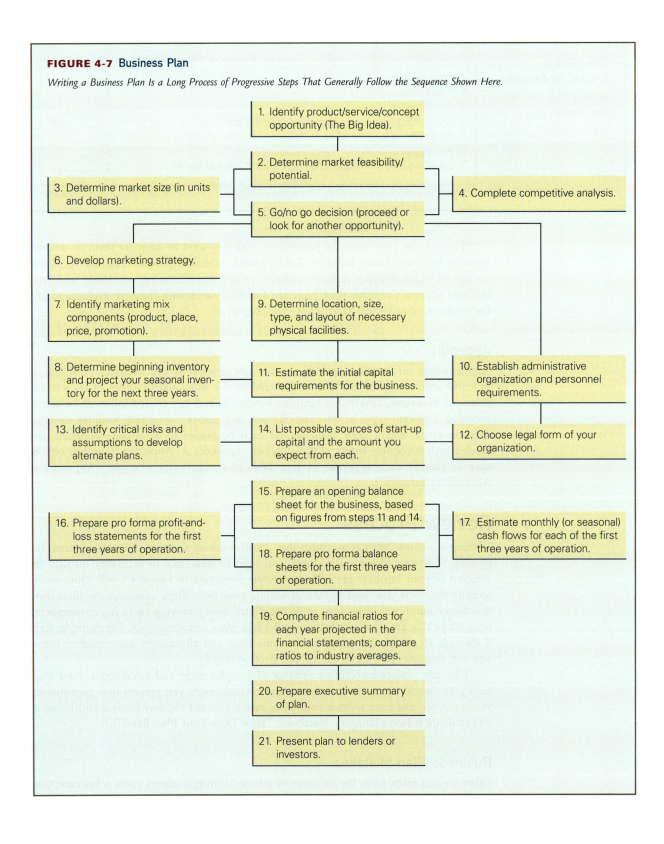

FIGURE 4-7 Business Plan

Writing a Business Plan Is a Long Process of Progressive Steps That Generally Follow the Sequence Shown Here.

Your business plan says a lot about your level of financial and professional knowledge. How can you keep investors focused on your ideas while keeping your plan out of the "reject" pile? It helps to avoid the most common errors.

- *Submitting a "rough copy."* Your plan should be a cleanly typed copy without coffee stains and scratched-out words. If you haven't worked your idea out completely enough to present a plan you're proud of, why should the investor take you seriously?
- *Depending on outdated financial information or industry comparisons.* It is important to be as current as possible to convince the investor that you are a realistic planner.
- *Trying to impress financiers with technojargon.* If you can't express yourself in common language in your business plan, how will you be able to market it?
- *Lacking marketing strategies.* Getting your product or business known by potential buyers is key. "We'll just depend on word-of-mouth advertising" won't cut it.
- *Making unsubstantiated assumptions.* Explain how and why you have reached your conclusions at any point in the plan. Don't assume that the competition will roll over without a fight or that phenomenal growth will begin the moment you get the money.
- *Being overly optimistic.* Too much "blue sky and rainbows" will lead the investor to wonder if your plan is realistic. Describe potential pitfalls and your strategies to cope with them.
- *Misunderstanding financial information.* Even if you get help from an accountant in preparing your financial documents, be sure you understand and can interpret what they say.
- *Ignoring the macroenvironment.* How will competitors react to your business? What other economic factors are likely to change? Considering the business climate and environment will help demonstrate the breadth of your understanding.
- *Avoiding or disguising potential negative aspects.* If you fail to mention possible problems, or misrepresent them, you will give the impression that you are either naive or devious, and lenders find neither trait especially charming.
- *Having no personal equity in the company.* If you aren't willing to risk your own money in the venture, why should the investor? A vested interest in the business will help to convince potential lenders that you will work as hard as possible to make the business succeed. Or, if you have invested only $1,000, is it reasonable to seek $20 million in capital?[13]

Manager's Notes

How Does Your Plan Rate?

On the following checklist, take the perspective of a potential lender or investor who is rating your business plan. Give each section a grade ranging from A to F, with A being the best grade. Would you want to invest your money in a business that doesn't earn an A in as many categories as possible? Use your rating to identify areas that can be improved.

GRADE	MODEL (A) PLAN
Business Description	
Company	Simply explained and feasible
Industry	Growing in market niches that are presently unsatisfied
Products	Proprietary position; quality exceeds customer's expectations
Services	Described clearly; service level exceeds customer expectations
Previous success	Business has past record of success
Competitive advantage	Identified and sustainable
Risks turned into opportunities	Risks identified; how to minimize risks is shown
Orientation of business	Market oriented, not product oriented
Marketing	
Target market(s)	Clearly identified
Size of target market(s)	Large enough to support viable business
User benefits identified	Benefit to customers clearly shown
Management Team	
Experience of team	Successful previous experience in similar business
Key managers identified	Managers with complementary skills on team
Financial Plan	
Projections	Realistic and supported
Rate of return	Exceptionally high; loans can be paid back in less than one year
Participation by owner	Owner has significant personal investment
Participation by others	Other investors already involved
Plan Packaging	
Appearance	Professional, laser-printed, bound, no spelling or grammatical errors
Executive summary	Concise description of business that prompts reader to say, "Wow!"
Body of plan	Sections of plan appropriate and complete
Appendices	Appropriate supporting documentation
Plan standardized or custom	Plan custom-written for specific business, not "canned"

Summary

1. Explain the purpose and importance of the business plan.

Business plans are important to (1) raise capital, (2) provide a road map for future operations, and (3) prevent omissions.

2. Describe the components of a business plan.

The major sections of a business plan include the cover page, table of contents, executive summary, company, environmental and industry analysis, products or services, marketing research and evaluation, manufacturing and operations plan, management team, timeline, critical risks and assumptions, benefits to the community, exit strategy, financial plan, and appendix.

3. Recognize the importance of reviewing your business plan.

Like any project involving a number of complex steps and calculations, your business plan should be carefully reviewed and revised before you present it to potential investors. After you have written your plan, evaluate it as you think lenders and investors will.

Questions for Review and Discussion

1. Why wouldn't a 100-page business plan be four times better than a 25-page business plan?
2. Should you write a business plan even if you do not need outside financing? Why or why not?
3. Who should write the business plan?
4. If successful companies like Pizza Hut have been started without a business plan, why does the author claim they are so important?
5. Why do entrepreneurs have trouble remaining objective when writing their business plans?
6. Why do some prospective business owners refuse to plan?
7. Why is the executive summary the most important section of the business plan?
8. Talk to the owner of a small business. Did he or she write a business plan? A strategic plan? If he or she received any assistance, where did it come from?

Questions for Critical Thinking

1. When you reach the point in your career where you are ready to start your own business (or your next one), will you write a business plan before beginning? Why or why not? If you would choose to start a business without a business plan, what would be an alternative for testing feasibility?
2. You are an investor in small businesses, and you have three business plans on your desk. Which of the following potential business owners do you think would be the best bet for an investment (if you could pick only one)?

a. A recent college grad, full of energy and ideas, but short on experience
b. A middle-management corporate refugee desiring a business of her own after experiencing frustration with bureaucratic red tape
c. A serial entrepreneur who has previously started seven businesses, three of which were huge successes and four of which failed, losing their entire investment

What Would You Do?

Your telephone rings early one morning. It is your small business/entrepreneurship professor, who tells you he just received notification that he has won the first Nobel Prize in Entrepreneurship. His plane leaves soon for Stockholm, where he will pick up the award, so he won't be in class today. Because you are one of the star students in this class, the professor asks you to conduct today's class, covering Chapter 4, "Creating the Business Plan." Write an outline of how you would teach this class and what you would cover to effectively teach this material. Would you lecture? How would you keep discussion going? Would you show business plan samples? Where would you find them? Would you show Web pages? Which ones? You can do anything (except cancel class!) that your professor would do, but *what would you do*?

5

Deciding to Franchise

CHAPTER LEARNING OUTCOMES

After reading this chapter, you should be able to:

1. **Explain what a franchise is and how it operates.**

2. **Articulate the difference between product-distribution franchises and business-format franchises.**

3. **Compare the advantages and disadvantages of franchising.**

4. **Explain how to evaluate a potential franchise.**

5. **Explore franchising in the international marketplace.**

When one peruses *Entrepreneur* magazine's Franchise 500 list, the name Subway pops up regularly, taking the top spot 16 times in the 29 times the list has been compiled—including 2010. Even in a recession, people love $5 Footlongs (an idea that came from a South Florida franchisee). Subway has been in business for four decades and has grown to over 32,000 franchises. That's 32,000 individual businesses! How big can one franchise system grow? The entrepreneur who started and oversaw the growth of this juggernaut, Fred DeLuca, thinks there is still a lot of room to grow.

In 1965, 17-year-old DeLuca was looking for a way to fund his college education. Family friend Pete Buck agreed to provide him with $1,000 on the condition that Fred would start a sandwich shop (operating under the principle that it is better to teach someone to fish than to give him a fish). Fred found a location in Bridgeport, Connecti-

cut; built a counter and did other remodeling himself; and got the place open. The requirement for a specialty $550 sink almost kept the whole empire from forming, but Pete came through with another thousand dollars.

Some lessons that Fred learned are ones that don't come from business school. He tells the story of what happened during Subway's first year of operation this way:

His car had broken down, and while he was walking, "this kid picked me up, we get to talking, and we passed by my store. He says to me, 'That is a great place to eat. They make terrific sandwiches, and you get all the soda you want for free.' I said, 'How does it work?' he said, 'You order some sandwiches, and when the kid'—he was referring to me—'when the kid turns around to make them, you just take a case of soda out of the cooler and sneak it out to your car.'" DeLuca and Subway have come far since those days.

Watch the video clip accompanying this chapter for more insight into entrepreneur Fred DeLuca's success in building a company that now receives more than 2,000 inquiries from potential franchisees each week. Subway's success can be tied to sticking to a proven concept, while staying open to innovation—more than 7,000 nontraditional Subways have popped up in convenience stores, department stores, racetracks, college dorms, and even one megachurch. But the most unique Subway location has to be the 36 shipping containers welded together, painted yellow, and lifted story by story by crane as the Manhattan Freedom Tower is constructed until it reaches the 105th floor. As the building progresses, it could take as long as 45 minutes for the 2,000 workers to ride elevators to the ground for lunch. To add variety and entice the workers to stay on top, this Subway is serving breakfast and snacks like hamburgers, hot dogs, and pretzels.

Sources: Jason Daley, "Year of the Sandwich," *Entrepreneur*, January 2010, 60; Jason Daley, "A Tall Order," *Entrepreneur*, April 2010, 124; "The Billionaire Bootstrapper," *Inc.*, July 2006, 108; and "Decisions: Fred DeLuca," *Management Today*, February 2009, 22.

About Franchising

franchise
A contractual license to operate an individually owned business as part of a larger chain.

franchisor
The parent company that develops a product or business process and sells the rights to franchisees.

franchisee
The small business-person who purchases the franchise so as to sell the product or service of the franchisor.

Over the past 50 years or so, franchising has become a very attractive means of starting and operating a small business. Some of the most familiar franchises are McDonald's, H&R Block, AAMCO Transmissions, GNC (General Nutrition Centers), and Dairy Queen. A *franchise* is an agreement that binds a *franchisor* (a parent company of the product, service, or method) with a *franchisee* (a small business that pays fees and royalties for exclusive rights to local distribution of the product or service). Through the franchise agreement, the franchisee gains the benefit of the parent company's expertise, experience, management systems, marketing, and financial help. Franchisors benefit because they can expand their operations by building a base of franchisees rather than by using their own capital and resources.

Background

Franchises have experienced considerable growth since the 1950s. However, contrary to popular belief, the concept did not originate with McDonald's. In fact, franchises have existed since the early 1800s.

In the 1830s, Cyrus McCormick was making reapers, and Isaac Singer began manufacturing sewing machines. As America's economic system began to shift from being based on agriculture and small business to being based on industry and big business, business methods needed to change as well. Early manufacturers also had to provide distribution of their products. To do so, they faced the choice of setting up a company-owned system or developing contracts with independent firms to represent them. The choice was not an easy one. Direct ownership guaranteed complete control and ensured quality levels of service. On the other hand, direct ownership was expensive

Manager's Notes

Just the Facts ...

The International Franchise Association Educational Foundation conducts and reports research studies to provide a statistical basis for answering key questions posed about franchising. Some interesting findings the IFA has uncovered include:

- The median initial franchise fee for standard franchises was $25,147.
- Franchises classified as Standard Programs—either stand-alone or in-line stores—totaled 93 percent.
- Franchises that were home based totaled 6 percent.
- Franchises that were vehicle or mobile based totaled 7 percent.
- Franchises that were started with an initial investment of $240,000 or less totaled 80 percent.
- Franchisors that had been in operation one year or less totaled 15 percent.
- The minimum total initial investment for a lodging franchise was reported as $4.1 million.
- Most franchise systems charged royalties based on a percentage of gross sales—the average was 6.7 percent.
- Companies offering an exclusive territory to franchisees totaled 73 percent.

Source: International Franchise Association Educational Foundation series, www.franchise.org/education.aspx, accessed May 2010.

and difficult to manage. McCormick and Singer were two of the first to use agents in building sales networks quickly, at little cost to themselves.[1] This use of exclusive agents laid the groundwork for today's franchising. The exclusive contractual agreement between franchisor and franchisee has evolved past agency, but it has become a viable business alternative.

Franchising Today

Today franchising is found in almost every industry (see Figure 5.1). More than 909,000 U.S. businesses are franchised. Interest in international franchising is also growing quickly. Franchised businesses generate annual sales of $2.31 trillion, or nearly 15.3 percent of the U.S. private sector economy and 40 percent of all retail sales![2] Franchised businesses directly produce almost 10 million jobs—roughly the same number of people employed by all manufacturers of durable goods.

A study titled "2010 Franchise Business Economic Outlook" for the International Franchise Association reported economic activity that happened (1) within franchised businesses and (2) because of franchised businesses. In total, franchised businesses supported more than 18 million jobs and had a payroll exceeding $500 billion.

"Franchised businesses directly produce almost 10 million jobs—roughly the same number of people employed by all manufacturers of durable goods."

Franchising Systems

There are two types of franchises: product-distribution franchises and business-format franchises. These two forms are used by producers, wholesalers, and retailers to distribute goods and services to consumers and other businesses.

FIGURE 5-1

Not All Franchises Sell French Fries

The Distribution of Franchises by Business Lines Shows a Wide Diversity of Products and Services.

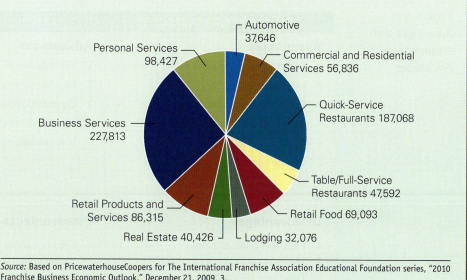

Automotive 37,646

Personal Services 98,427

Commercial and Residential Services 56,836

Quick-Service Restaurants 187,068

Business Services 227,813

Table/Full-Service Restaurants 47,592

Retail Products and Services 86,315

Retail Food 69,093

Real Estate 40,426

Lodging 32,076

Source: Based on PricewaterhouseCoopers for The International Franchise Association Educational Foundation series, "2010 Franchise Business Economic Outlook," December 21, 2009, 3.

Product-Distribution Franchising

product-distribution franchising
A type of franchising in which the franchisee agrees to purchase the products of the franchisor or to use the franchisor's name.

Product-distribution franchising allows the franchisee (or dealer) to buy products from the franchisor (or supplier) or to license the use of its trade name. This approach typically connects a single manufacturer with many dealers. The idea is to make products available to consumers in a specific geographic region through exclusive dealers. Soft-drink bottlers and gasoline stations, for example, use this type of franchising. Auto manufacturers also use this system to make their cars, service, and parts available. Your local Chevrolet dealer, for instance, has full use of the Chevrolet trade name, brand names (like Corvette), and logos (like the bow tie symbol) to promote the dealership in your area. Product franchisors regulate their franchisees' locations to avoid excessive competition between them. As a consequence, Chevrolet would not allow a new dealership that sells its products to set up across the street from your established local dealer.

Business-Format Franchising

business-format franchising
A type of franchising in which the franchisee adopts the franchisor's entire method of operation.

Business-format franchising is more of a *turnkey* approach to franchising. In other words, the franchisee purchases not only the franchisor's product to sell but also the entire way of doing business, including operation procedures, marketing packages, the physical building and equipment, and full business services. Business-format franchising is commonly used in quick-service restaurants (56.3 percent), lodging (18.2 percent), retail food (14.2 percent), and table/full-service restaurants (13.1 percent).

Why Open a Franchise?

If you are considering the purchase of a franchise, you should compare its advantages and disadvantages to those of starting a new business or buying an existing nonfranchised business (see Chapters 6 and 7). You should also determine whether the unique characteristics of franchising fit your personal needs and desires. Some small business owners would rather assume the risk and expense of starting an independent business than have to follow someone else's policies and procedures. Others prefer the advantages that a

TABLE 5-1 Advantages and Disadvantages of Franchising	FRANCHISEE'S PERSPECTIVE	FRANCHISOR'S PERSPECTIVE
	Advantages	**Advantages**
	1. Proven product or service	1. Expansion with limited capital
	2. Marketing expertise	2. Multiple sources of capital
	3. Financial assistance	3. Controlled expansion
	4. Technical and managerial assistance	4. Motivated franchisees
	5. Opportunity to learn business	5. Bulk-purchasing discounts
	6. Quality control standards	
	7. Efficiency	
	8. Opportunity for growth	
	Disadvantages	**Disadvantages**
	1. Fees and profit sharing	1. Loss of control
	2. Restrictions of freedom	2. Sharing profit with franchisees
	3. Overdependence or unsatisfied expectations	3. Potential for disputes with franchisees
	4. Risk of fraud or misunderstanding	
	5. Termination of the agreement	
	6. Performance of other franchisees	

franchise's proven system can provide. Sometimes it makes sense not to reinvent the wheel (see Table 5.1).

Advantages to Franchisee

For the franchisee, there are eight major advantages of franchising: proven product or service, marketing expertise, financial assistance, technical and managerial assistance, an opportunity to learn the business through professional guidance, quality control standards, efficiency, and opportunity for growth.[3]

Proven Product The most valuable advantage to a franchisee is that you are selling a proven product or service. Customers are aware of the product; they know the name, and they know what to expect. For example, travelers may not know anything about the Ramada Inn in Colorado Springs, but they know Ramada's reputation and are more likely to stay there than at some independent, unknown motel.

Marketing Expertise Franchisors spend millions of dollars on national or regional advertising to help build an image that independent businesses could not afford. Franchisors also develop print, broadcast, and point-of-purchase advertising. Local franchisees do share in these advertising costs, usually based on their gross revenues, but it is still a great advantage to have access to the marketing expertise of the franchisor at relatively low cost.

Financial Assistance Some franchisors provide financial assistance to new franchisees. This assistance typically comes in the form of trade credit on inventory or overhead reduction by the franchisor's choosing, purchasing, and owning buildings and real estate.

"The most valuable advantage to a franchisee is that you are selling a proven product or service."

Franchises have become a recognizable part of the business landscape.

© Richard Levine / Alamy

Professional Guidance A franchise can provide a source of managerial and technical assistance not available to an independent business. You can benefit from the accumulated years of experience and knowledge of the franchisor. Most franchisors provide training, both as preparation for running the business and as instruction after the business gets off the ground. This training can allow a person without prior experience to be successful in owning a franchise. A good franchisor is available to provide day-to-day assistance and professional guidance should a crisis arise. In addition, franchisees can receive a great deal of technical help regarding store layout and design, location, purchasing, and equipment.

Opportunity to Learn Although it is not usually advisable to go into a business in an unfamiliar field, franchising can provide an opportunity to become successful doing exactly that. Thus, franchising can be helpful for a midcareer change of direction. In fact, some franchisors prefer their franchisees not to have experience in that particular field. They prefer to train their business owners from scratch so there are no bad habits to break.

Recognized Standards Franchisors impose quality standards for franchisees to follow, a feature that might not seem advantageous at first glance—if independence is your motive for self-employment, why would you want to meet standards set by someone else? The benefit, though, is that the practice ensures consistency to customers. Consumers can walk into a McDonald's anywhere in the world and know what to expect. A franchisor's quality control regulations help franchisees to maintain high standards of cleanliness, service, and productivity. As a franchisee, you will benefit from standardized quality control, because if another franchisee in your organization provides inferior service, it will affect attitudes toward *your* business.

Efficiency Because of increased efficiency, a franchise can sometimes be started and operated with less capital than it takes to start an independent business. Franchisors have already been through the learning curve and worked most of the bugs out of the process. Inventory needs, such as what to stock and what will sell quickly, are known before you open the doors, so you won't waste money on equipment, inventory, or supplies that you don't need. Many franchisors often provide financial resources for start-up and working capital for inventory.

"As a franchisee, you have the chance to learn from someone else's mistakes."

Potential for Business Growth If you are successful with a franchise, you will often have the opportunity to multiply that success by expanding to other franchises in other locations. Most franchisors have provisions to open other territories.

These eight advantages share a common theme—the opportunity to benefit from someone else's experience. In other words, as a franchisee, you have the chance to learn from someone else's mistakes.

Disadvantages to Franchisee

Of course, franchising has its drawbacks, too. You must give up some control, some decision-making power, and some freedom. Other disadvantages to the franchisee include fees, problems caused by overdependence on the franchisor or by not receiving what was expected from the franchisor, the possibility of fraud or misunderstanding, termination of the agreement, and the potentially negative effect of poor performance of other franchisees.

Cost of Franchise The services, assistance, and assurance in buying a franchise come at a price. Every franchisor will charge a fee and/or a specified percentage of sales revenue (see Table 5.2). The disadvantage to the franchisees is that they are usually required to raise most of the capital before they begin operations. The total investment can range from $500 for a windshield repair franchise to $45 million for a Hilton Inn.

These fees and percentages may begin to seem excessive after you have been in business for a while and see how they affect your bottom line. It is not uncommon for franchisees to be grateful for the assistance that a franchisor provides in starting the business, only to become frustrated by the royalties that have to be paid a few years later.

Restrictions on Freedom or Creativity The restrictions placed on their freedom may be a problem for some franchisees. Most people open their own businesses because they have a desire for independence, but franchises have policies and procedures that must be followed to maintain the franchise agreement. Also, the size of your market will be limited by territorial restrictions. And although you may feel that some products, promotions, or policies are not appropriate for your area, you will have little recourse after the franchise agreement has been signed.

TABLE 5-2
Getting In

FRANCHISE	FRANCHISE FEE	START-UP COSTS	ROYALTY (PERCENTAGE)
Jiffy Lube	$10–35k	$229k–323k	4%
FastSigns	$27.5k	$170k–316k	6%
Jazzercise	$500–1k	$2.9k–75.5k	20%
Abrakadoodle	$39.5k–49.9k	$51k–75k	8%
Big Apple Bagels	$25,000	$254k–379k	5%
Rocky Mountain Chocolate Factory	$24,500	$158k–592k	5%
Bad Ass Coffee	$35,000	$225k	6%
MaggieMoo's	$5k–25k	$217k–335k	6%
Taco Time	$30,000	$145k–721k	6%
Subway	$15,000	$84k–258k	8%
Hawthorn Suites	$40,000	$6.9M–10.9M	5%
Merry Maids	$25k–59k	$24.8–59.5	5%–7%
Gold's Gym	$25k	$531k–3.9M	3%
McDonald's	$45,000	$996k–1.8M	10% or more
Cartridge World	$30,000	$120k–194k	6%
GarageTek	$25k–50k	$75k–255k	6%
Supercuts	$22.5k	$111k–240k	6%
Camp Bow-Wow	$25k–50k	$64k–738k	6%

Source: "Franchise 500," *Entrepreneur*, January 2010, 134–199, www.entrepreneur.com/franchise500.

Overdependence or Unsatisfied Expectations Even though a franchisee is bound by contractual agreement, overdependence on the franchisor can still pose a problem. Franchisors do not always know what is best for every set of local conditions. The franchisee must be willing and able to apply his or her own managerial decisions in running the business in the way best suited to the local market and avoid being overly dependent on the franchisor's guidance. The flip side of overdependence is dealing with a franchisor that does not provide all the assistance that the franchisee expected.

Risk of Fraud or Misunderstanding Less-than-scrupulous franchisors have been known to mislead potential franchisees by making promises that are not fulfilled. To avoid being taken in by a fraudulent franchise, consult an attorney and talk with as many current franchisees as possible. Do not think that because the agreement looks standard it is unnecessary for you to understand every section. Look especially at the fine print.

Problems of Termination or Transfer Difficulty in terminating the franchise agreement or having it terminated against your will can be a disadvantage to the franchisee. Before entering into the franchise, you should understand the section of the agreement that describes how you can get out of the deal. For instance, what if you want to transfer your rights to a family member, or sell the franchise to someone else, or otherwise terminate your agreement? What provisions does the contract make for you to renew the agreement? Most franchise agreements cover a specific period of time—typically 5–20 years. Some may be renewed in perpetuity if both parties agree. Otherwise, both sides must consider franchise renewal when the term of the agreement expires. Check the agreement to see whether the franchisee has a *right of first refusal*, which means that the franchisee must decline to continue the agreement before the franchisor can offer the franchise to someone else. Check whether the franchisor must provide *just cause* for termination or must give a definite reason why the agreement is not being continued. Remember that a franchise is a contract. Any questions regarding it should be directed to your legal counsel.

> *"Remember that a franchise is a contract. Any questions regarding it should be directed to your legal counsel."*

Poor Performance of Other Franchisees Poor performance on the part of other franchisees can lead to problems for you. If the franchisor tolerates substandard performance, a few franchisees can seriously affect the sales of many others. Customers view franchises as an entire unit, because the implicit message from franchises is that "we are all alike"— for good or ill. If customers are treated unsatisfactorily in one location, they are likely to believe the same treatment will occur elsewhere.

Advantages to Franchisor

Now let's look at franchising from the franchisor's perspective. First, we will consider the positive aspects: smaller capital investment required than if outlets were formed independently, multiple sources of capital coming into the business, expansion of the business happening much faster than if the franchisor were in business alone, synergy created by a group of motivated franchisees, and volume discounts for bulk purchasing.

Expansion with Smaller Capital Investment From the perspective of the franchisor, the biggest advantage of offering franchises is the expansion of its distribution sources with limited equity investments. The franchise fees from franchisees provide capital to the franchisor. The franchisor therefore does not have to borrow from lenders or attract outside investors. For a business with limited capital, franchising, in which franchisees share the financial burden, may be the only viable way to expand.

Multiple Sources of Revenue Franchisors often build several sources of revenue into their franchise agreements. These sources might include the franchise fee, which is paid when the agreement is signed; a percentage of the franchise's monthly gross operating revenues; and revenue from selling the necessary products and supplies to the franchisees. For example, a fast-food restaurant franchisee could have a franchise fee of up to $200,000; pay 3 to 8 percent of monthly gross sales as a royalty fee; and be required to purchase all food items (from hamburger to condiments), office supplies, and restaurant supplies (napkins, coffee filters, and paper cups) from the franchisor.

Controlled Expansion When compared with the expansion of a corporate chain, expanding via franchising can be accomplished with a simpler management structure. Very rapid growth of a corporation can be more of a problem than an opportunity, however, if the growth outpaces central management's capacity to control and monitor it. When this happens, problems with inconsistency, communications, and especially cash flow generally appear. Although franchisors still face these problems to some degree, the franchise network reduces them.

Motivated Franchisees Because franchisees own their own business, they are almost always more highly motivated to make it succeed than an employee working for someone else. Franchisees have a direct personal interest in the entire operation, so they are inspired to perform and thus create positive synergy within the franchise.

Bulk Purchasing Centralized purchasing of products and supplies allows franchisors to take advantage of volume discounts, because they are buying for all the franchise locations. This economy of scale can increase profit margins and hold down costs for franchisees.

> *"Franchisees have a direct personal interest in the entire operation, so they are inspired to perform and thus create positive synergy within the franchise."*

Disadvantages to Franchisor

Problems exist in every method of business operation, and franchising is no exception. Loss of control over the business is the biggest disadvantage faced by franchisors. Other potential problems relate to profit sharing and disputes with franchisees.

Loss of Control Franchisees who do not maintain their businesses reflect poorly not only on other franchisees, but also on the franchisor. Although the franchisor does control the organization to the limit specified by the franchise agreement, franchisees are still independent businesspeople. After the franchise agreement has been signed, the franchisor must get permission from franchisees before any products or services are changed, added, or eliminated. Permission is often negotiated individually. This system makes it difficult for the franchisor to adapt products to meet changing customer needs, especially if a wide variety of consumer tastes are being served over a large geographic area.

One way franchisors have dealt with this problem is by establishing some company-owned units. Because these sites are not independently owned businesses, the franchisor can test-market new products, services, and procedures in them. In this way, the franchisor can track and respond to changing customer needs, as well as use these units as examples when negotiating with franchisees.

Profit Sharing If franchisees are able to recover their initial investment within two or three years, they could enjoy a 30 to 50 percent return on investment. This return can provide motivation for the franchisees, but it represents profit that the franchisor is not making with a company-owned unit.

Franchisee Disputes Friction between franchisees and franchisors may arise over such issues as payment of fees, expansion, and hours of operation. These potential conflicts point to the importance of good communication between both sides and the need to have a clearly written franchise agreement.

Selecting a Franchise

Choosing the right franchise is a serious decision. Investing in a franchise represents a major commitment of time and money. Before taking the plunge into franchising, determine what you need in a business and evaluate what several different franchises can offer you and your customers.

Evaluate Your Needs

The choice of which franchise to buy is not an easy one. You need to find a franchise opportunity that matches your interests, skills, and needs. Ask yourself the following questions to determine whether franchising is the appropriate route to small business ownership for you:

- How much equity capital will you need to purchase the franchise and operate it until your income equals your expenses? Where are you going to get it?
- Are you prepared to give up some independence of action to secure the advantages offered by the franchise?
- Do you really believe you have the innate ability, training, and experience to work smoothly and profitably with the franchisor, your employees, and your customers?
- Are you ready to make a long-term commitment to working with this franchisor, offering its product or service to your public?[4]

Do Your Research

Inc., *Fortune Small Business*, the *Wall Street Journal*, and *Entrepreneur* are general business periodicals that contain advertising and articles related to franchising. Trade journals and magazines that specialize in franchising include *Franchise*, *Franchising Opportunities World*, and *Quarterly Franchising World*.

Trade associations can be valuable sources of information when you are investigating franchise opportunities. The major trade association of franchising is the International Franchise Association (IFA), which can be found at www.franchise.org. The IFA is a leading source of information for franchisors and franchisees alike, offering publications that contain industry-wide data as well as company-specific information. Also check *The Franchise Handbook*, which gives you an idea of the requirements, expectations, and assistance available for each franchise at www.franchise1.com. Figure 5.2 shows examples of the types of franchise descriptions you can find in this handbook.

Other Information Sources The American Franchisee Association (AFA), based in Chicago (www.franchisee.org), and the American Association of Franchisees and Dealers (AAFD), headquartered in San Diego (www.aafd.org), are trade associations that provide information and services, represent the interests of members, and were formed to help negotiate better terms and conditions from franchisors. The AAFD has developed a Franchisee Bill of Rights as a code of ethical business conduct for franchised businesses.

On Yahoo!, under the Business and Economy category, Small Business Information, you will find a link to another source of franchise information, called FranNet. FranNet (www.frannet.com) can provide you with the information needed to help you select the right franchise. Additional information on franchises can be found by using any of the popular search engines and doing a keyword search for "franchise." Better yet, go to a full-text online database like ABI-INFORM, Business Source Premier, or Lexis-Nexis to search for general and company-specific information on franchises.

"Before taking the plunge into franchising, determine what you need in a business and evaluate what several different franchises can offer you and your customers."

FIGURE 5-2
Franchise Information

Marble Slab Creamery
3100 S. Gessner, #305
Houston, TX 77063
www.marbleslab.com
Contact: marbleslab@marbleslab.com

Company Description: Marble Slab Creamery offers homemade, superpremium ice cream that is prepared to order on a marble slab. Customers can create their own ice cream concoctions by combining any flavor of ice cream with "mix-ins" such as fresh fruit, candy, cookies, or nuts. The ice cream and mix-ins are then folded together on a frozen marble slab and served on a freshly baked waffle cone. Other products include smoothies, shakes, sundaes, banana splits, ice cream pies/cakes, specialty coffees, and bakery items.

# of Franchised Units: 380 in 30 states in 2 countries
Company-Owned Units: 1
In Business Since: 1983
Franchising Since: 1984
Franchising Fee: $28,000
Royalties: 6%
Capital Requirements: $250,000 net worth, $60,000 liquid
Financing Options: None
Training and Support: Assistance is available on site selection, lease negotiation, architectural layout, and construction supervision. A ten-day training program in Houston, Texas, is required.

Play It Again Sports
Grow Biz International, Inc.
4200 Dalhberg Dr.
Minneapolis, MN 55422-4837
www.playitagainsports
Contact: mpeterson@growbiz.com

Company Description: Play It Again Sports buys and sells new and used sporting goods. Stores carry items such as golf clubs and bags, baseball bats and gloves, in-line skates, and fitness equipment. Play It Again Sports is owned by Grow Biz International, which also franchises Music Go Round, Once Upon a Child, Plato's Closet, and Re-Tool.

# of Franchised Units: 556
Company-Owned Units: 2
In Business Since: 1983
Franchising Since: 1988
Franchise Fee: $20,000
Capital Requirements: $153,000–$265,000 total investment, $50,000–$75,000 start-up cash
Financing Options: Assistance in preparation of a comprehensive business plan.

Training and Support: Training includes such topics as site selection, lease negotiations, store build-out, POS inventory management, business operating system, evaluating product, and local store marketing.

Subway
325 Bic Dr.
Milford, CT 06460
www.subway.com
Contact: franchise@subway.com

Company Description: Today, Subway is the world's largest and fastest-growing franchise. In 1965, 17-year-old Fred DeLuca and family friend Peter Buck started a tiny sandwich shop as a way for Fred to get through college. In 2004, *Entrepreneur* magazine chose Subway as the overall number one franchise in all categories for the twelfth time. More than 50% of franchises purchased are sold to existing owners who choose to reinvest.

# of Franchised Units: 17,500+ in 74 countries
Company-Owned Units: 1
In Business Since: 1965
Franchising Since: 1974
Franchise Fee: $15,000
Royalty Fee: 8%
Capital Requirements: $84,000–$258,000
Financing Options: Franchise fee financing, start-up financing, and equipment leasing are available.
Training and Support: Two weeks training with 50% in classroom and 50% hands-on. Follow-up support is given by field staff and headquarters' staff.

General Nutrition Centers
GNC Franchising
300 Sixth Ave.
Pittsburgh, PA 15222
www.gncfranchising.com

Company Description: In 1935 David Shakarian started a health food store in Pittsburgh called Lackzoom. It specialized in yogurt (which his father introduced to the United States) but also carried health food products such as honey and grains. Today, as the leading national specialty retailer of vitamins, minerals, herbs, and sports nutrition supplements, GNC capitalizes on the accelerating trend toward self-care. *Entrepreneur* magazine has ranked GNC as the industry's number one franchise for 14 consecutive years.

# of Franchised Units: 1,878 in 50 states in 28 countries

FIGURE 5-2
(Continued)

Company-Owned Units: 2,933
In Business Since: 1935
Franchising Since: 1988
Franchise Fee: $40,000
Royalty Fee: 6%
Capital Requirements: $132,681–$182,031
Financing Options: GNC offers direct company financing for start-up fees, equipment, inventory, and accounts receivable to qualified individuals.
Training and Support: New franchisees receive three weeks of initial training, including an intensive one-week training class at corporate headquarters. On-site assistance is provided prior to opening, with ongoing support. Franchisees benefit from GNC's multimillion-dollar national advertising program.

Merry Maids
P.O. Box 751017
Memphis, TN 38175-1017
www.merrymaids.com

Company Description: The world's largest residential cleaning service. *Entrepreneur* magazine ranked Merry Maids as number one in the industry for 10 consecutive years. Name recognition for the Merry Maids brand is very high. The company is committed to training and support, and it provides a comprehensive software and equipment/supply package. Products and supplies are available online. The company is a member of the ServiceMaster family of industry-leading brands.
# of Franchised Units: 1,399 in 48 states in 7 countries
Company-Owned Units: 143
Franchise Fee: $19,000–$27,000
Capital Requirements: $19,550–$26,950+. A larger investment is required to buy an existing franchise.

Financing Options: Up to 80% available toward franchise fee.
Training and Support: Includes an eight-day training session at headquarters, all start-up equipment and supplies for two teams, a Buddy Program, educational programs, a toll-free number for assistance; national TV ads, a free Web site for each franchise, a weekly intranet bulletin board, newsletters, regional meetings, a national convention, a proprietary intranet Web site, and 17 field regional coordinators.

Dunkin' Donuts
14 Pacella Park Dr.
Randolph, MA 02368
www.dunkindonuts.com

Company Description: In 1946, William Rosenberg founded Industrial Luncheon Services, a company that delivered meals and snacks to workers in the Boston area. That success led him to start the Open Kettle, a doughnut shop in Quincy, Massachusetts. Two years later he changed the name to Dunkin' Donuts. Today, the company sells doughnuts, muffins, bagels, coffee, and fruit drinks.
# of Franchised Units: 6,892 in 43 states in 20 countries
Company-Owned Units: 0
In Business Since: 1950
Franchising Since: 1955
Franchise Fee: $40,000–80,000
Capital Requirements: $600,000 in liquid assets, $1.2 million net worth
Financing Options: Yes
Training and Support: Yes

Sources: *Entrepreneur Franchise 500*, January 2007, 164–259, www.entrepreneur.com; www.franchisehandbook.com; and individual company Web pages.

You might also want to check out the Better Business Bureau's Web site (www.bbb .org/bbb). There you'll find a publications directory, membership list, and contact information for Better Business Bureaus nationwide. You can also access the bureau's newsletter, check the scam alerts, and even file a complaint online.

Still another source of franchise information is the Institute of Management and Administration's Web page (http://ioma.com/ioma), which provides links to hundreds of other business sites, including many industry-specific resources.

Questions to Ask When you have a general idea of the franchise you are interested in, contact the company and ask for a copy of its *disclosure statement* (discussed shortly). Before you sign the required contracts with a chosen franchisor, talk to current and former franchisees. They can provide priceless information that you could not learn anywhere else.

Reality Check

Go to the Source

A good place to get information about a particular franchise is from the people who are currently running one. Ask the following questions to get the real scoop:

- What does the business cost to operate on a monthly basis?
- How long did it take to break even?
- How profitable is the franchise?
- How much does the company charge for advertising fees? (Be careful if this number is more than 1–3 percent of gross sales.)
- Does the money go toward ads in the local market or mainly toward building the parent company's national image? (You should expect about 50 percent to benefit the franchisee.)
- How many units have failed?
- How rapid is unit turnover?
- How many stores does the parent company own? (About 25 percent is acceptable. Too

many could weaken franchisee bargaining power; too few could indicate a weak system.)

- Would you buy the franchise again? (The bottom line.)

Remember when you are talking with these current franchise owners that many of them are struggling to internally validate the decision they have made regarding this business. They will often tell you that things are going great, sales are up, and they would definitely do it all over again. They may be trying to convince themselves. To get a realistic picture of what you are facing, push them to tell you exactly how much profit they have made in each year of operation. Might you have to go two years without making a profit? Could you do that?

_____

Sources: Fran Finders, "Questions to Ask a Current Franchisee," www.fran finders.com/franchise-information; and Carrie Bach, "Ten Reasons to Buy a Franchise," _Entrepreneur_, October 2009, www.entrepreneur.com.

Once you have found a franchise you would consider buying (or possibly a few from which to choose), evaluate the opportunities represented by asking yourself the following questions:

- Did your lawyer approve the franchise contract you are considering after he or she studied it paragraph by paragraph?
- Does the franchise call on you to take any steps that are, according to your lawyer, unwise or illegal in your state, county, or city?
- Does the franchise give you an _exclusive territory_ (discussed later in this chapter) for the length of the franchise, or can the franchisor sell a second or third franchise in your territory?
- Is the franchisor connected in any way with any other franchise company handling similar merchandise or services? If so, what is your protection against this second franchisor organization?
- Under what circumstances can you terminate the franchise contract and at what cost to you, if you decide for any reason at all that you wish to cancel it?
- If you sell your franchise, will you be compensated for your goodwill, or will the goodwill you have built into the business be lost by you?

Evaluate what the franchisor will offer you and your customers by asking the following questions about the franchisor:

- How many years has the firm offering you a franchise been in operation?
- Does it have a reputation for honesty and fair dealing among the local firms holding its franchise?

- Has the franchisor shown you any certified figures indicating exact net profits of one or more going firms that you personally checked with the franchisee(s)?
- Will the firm assist you with

  A management training program?
  Capital?
  An employee training program?
  Credit?
  A public relations program?
  Merchandise ideas?

- Will the firm help you find a good location for your new business?
- Is the franchising firm adequately financed so that it can carry out its stated plan of financial assistance and expansion?
- Is the franchisor a one-person company or a corporation with experienced management trained in depth (so that there will always be an experienced person at its head)?
- Exactly what can the franchisor do for you that you cannot do for yourself?
- Has the franchisor investigated you carefully enough to assure itself that you can successfully operate one of its franchises at a profit to both of you?
- Does your state have a law regulating the sale of franchises, and has the franchisor complied with that law?

Analyze the Market

What do you know about your market—the people buying your product or service? In answering the following questions, you can determine whether a franchise is the best way to match what the franchisor has to offer with your skills and your customers' needs:

"Will the product or service you are considering be in greater demand, in about the same demand, or in less demand five years from now?"

1. Have you made any study to determine whether the product or service that you propose to sell under franchise has a market in your territory at the prices you will have to charge?
2. Will the population in your proposed territory increase, remain static, or decrease over the next five years?
3. Will the product or service you are considering be in greater demand, in about the same demand, or in less demand five years from now?
4. What competition already exists in your territory for the product or service you contemplate selling?
   a. Nonfranchise firms?
   b. Franchise firms?

Disclosure Statements

disclosure statements
Information that franchisors are required to provide to potential franchisees.

Franchisors are required by the Federal Trade Commission (FTC) to provide **disclosure statements** to prospective or actual franchisees. Comparing disclosure statements from each franchise you are considering will help you identify risks, fees, benefits, and restrictions involved. Figure 5.3 provides a sample table of contents for a disclosure statement. The entire document can be several hundred pages long. As a prospective franchisee, you would want to read the document carefully and consult a lawyer to review the franchise agreement. Disclosure statements identify and provide information on the following 20 items:

1. *The franchisor.* Information identifying the franchisor and its affiliates and describing their business experience.
2. *Business experience of the franchisor.* Information identifying and describing the business experience of each of the franchisor's officers, directors, and management

FIGURE 5-3
Franchise
Disclosure
Statement

Table of Contents

Section
1. Franchisor and Any Predecessors
2. Identity and Business Experience of Persons Affiliated with the Franchisor
3. Litigation
4. Bankruptcy
5. Developer's/Franchisee's Initial Franchise Fee or Other Initial Payment
6. Other Fees
7. Franchisee's Initial Investment
8. Obligation of Franchisee to Purchase or Lease from Designated Sources
9. Obligations of Franchisee to Purchase or Lease in Accordance with
   Specifications or from Approved Suppliers
10. Financing Arrangements
11. Obligations of the Franchisor: Other Supervision, Assistance, or Services
12. Exclusive Area or Territory
13. Trademarks, Trade Names, and Service Marks
14. Patent and Copyrights
15. Obligation of Franchisee to Participate in the Actual Operations of the
    Franchise
16. Restrictions on Goods and Services Offered by Developer/Franchise
17. Renewal, Termination, Repurchase, Modification, and Assignment of the
    Franchise Agreement and Related Information
18. Arrangements with Public Figures
19. Statement of per-Franchise Average Gross Sales and Ranges of Gross Sales for
    the Year Ended Month, Day, Year
20. Other Franchises of the Franchisor
21. Financial Statements
22. Contracts
EXHIBIT A   Franchise Agreement
EXHIBIT B   Area Development Agreement
EXHIBIT C   Preliminary Agreement
EXHIBIT D   Royalty Incentive Rider
EXHIBIT E   Disclosure Acknowledgment Statement
EXHIBIT F   List of Franchisees as of Month, Day, Year
EXHIBIT G   List of Franchisees Who Have Ceased Doing Business in the
                 One-Year Period Immediately Preceding Month, Day, Year
EXHIBIT H   Financial Statements of Franchisor

personnel responsible for franchise services, training, and other aspects of the franchises in the franchise program.
3. *Litigation.* A description of the lawsuits in which the franchisor and its officers, directors, and management personnel have been involved.
4. *Bankruptcy.* Information about any previous bankruptcies in which the franchisor and its officers, director, and management personnel have been involved in the past 15 years.
5. *Initial fee.* Information about the initial franchise fee and other initial payments that are required to obtain the franchise. The franchisor must also tell how your fee will be used and whether you must pay in one lump sum or can pay in installments. If every franchisee does not pay the same amount, the franchisor must describe the formula for calculating the initial fee.

6. *Other fees.* A description of the continuing payments that franchisees are required to make after the franchise opens, and the conditions for receiving refunds.

7. *Estimate of total initial investment.* The franchisor must provide a high-range and a low-range estimate of your start-up costs. Included expenses would cover real estate, equipment and other fixed assets, inventory, deposits, and working capital.

8. *Purchase obligations.* Information about any restrictions on the quality of goods and services used in the franchise and where they may be purchased, including restrictions requiring purchases from the franchisor or its affiliates.

9. *Financial assistance available.* Terms and conditions of any assistance available from the franchisor or its affiliates in financing the purchase of the franchise.

10. *Product or service restrictions.* A description of restrictions on the goods or services that franchisees are permitted to sell. This could include whether you are required to carry the franchisor's full line of products or if you can supplement them with other products.

11. *Exclusive territory.* A description of any territorial protection or restrictions on the customers with whom the franchisee may deal. Franchisees of Subway sandwich shops and other franchises have alleged that the franchisor has placed franchises too close together and overlapped territories. This practice cuts into the sales volume and market size of individual stores.

12. *Renewal, termination, or assignment of franchise agreement.* A description of the conditions under which the franchise may be repurchased or refused renewal by the franchisor, transferred to a third party by the franchisee, and terminated or modified by either party.

13. *Training provided.* A description of the training program provided to franchisees, including location, length and content of training, cost of program, who pays for travel and lodging, and any additional or refresher courses available.

14. *Public figure arrangements.* A disclosure of any involvement by celebrities or public figures in promoting the franchise. If celebrities are involved, you need to be told if they are involved in actual management and how they are being compensated.

15. *Site selection.* A description of any assistance in selecting a site for the franchise that will be provided by the franchisor. Some franchises, like McDonald's, complete all site analysis and make all location decisions without input from franchisees. Others give franchisees complete discretion in site selection.

16. *Information about franchisees.* You will receive information about the present number of franchises; the number of new franchises projected; and the number that have been terminated, chose not to renew, or were repurchased. Franchisors must give you the names, addresses, and phone numbers of all franchisees located in your state; contact several of them.

17. *Franchisor financial statements.* The audited financial statements of the franchisors are included to show you the financial condition of the company.

18. *Personal participation of franchisees.* A description of the extent to which franchisees must personally participate in the operation of the franchise. Some permit franchisees to own the franchise but hire a manager to run the day-to-day business. Others require franchisees to be personally involved.

19. *Earning capacity.* A complete statement of the basis for any earnings claims made to the franchisee, including the percentage of existing franchises that have actually achieved the results that are claimed. Franchisors do not have to make any projections of what a franchisee may earn, but if they do, they must also describe the basis and assumptions used to make claims.

20. *Use of intellectual property.* The franchisor must describe your use of its trademarks, trade names, logos, or other symbols. You should receive full use of them because they account for a great deal of the value of a franchise.[5]

"Don't assume that the disclosure statement tells you everything you need to know about the franchise."

The FTC has revised the *Uniform Franchise Offering Circular (UFOC)* several times in the past 25 years. The changes were intended to replace much of the "legalese" wording of disclosure statements with plain English and to provide more standardized information for comparing franchises. The UFOC still has a way to go before it qualifies as "easy reading," but stay with it. This is a very important document to understand.[6] Don't assume that the disclosure statement tells you everything you need to know about the franchise. It is a good start, but it does not constitute full due diligence.

When you receive a disclosure statement, you will be asked to sign and date a statement indicating that you received it. The franchisor may not accept any money from you for 10 working days from the time you sign the disclosure. This cooling-off period allows you the time to study, evaluate, and prepare your financing.[7]

The Franchise Agreement

franchise agreement
The legal contract that binds both parties involved in the franchise.

The **franchise agreement** is a document that spells out the rights and obligations of both parties in a franchise. This contract defines the precise, detailed conditions of the legal relationship between the franchisee and the franchisor. Its length, terms, and complexity will vary from one franchise and industry to another, so as to maintain the delicate balance of power between franchisees and franchisors.[8] It may or may not be possible for you to negotiate the contents of the contract, depending on how long the franchisor has been established and what the current market conditions are.

You should remember that the franchisor wrote the contract and that most of the conditions contained in it are weighted in the franchisor's favor. Read this document carefully yourself, but never sign a franchise agreement without getting your lawyer's opinion. Make sure your attorney and accountant have experience with franchising. Some of the most important topics that you should understand in franchise agreements are fees to be paid, ways in which the agreement can be terminated or renewed, and your rights to *exclusive territory* (discussed later in this chapter).

franchise fee
The one-time payment made to become a franchisee.

Franchise, Royalty, and Advertising Fees   The **franchise fee** is the amount of money you have to pay to become a franchisee. Some agreements require you to have a percentage of the total franchise fee from a nonborrowed source, meaning, obviously, that you can't borrow that amount. Agreements may or may not allow you to form a corporation to avoid personal liability.

royalty fees
The ongoing payments that franchisees pay to franchisors—usually a percentage of gross sales.

Royalty fees are usually a percentage of gross sales that you pay to the franchisor. Remember that royalties are calculated from gross sales, not from profits. If your business generates $350,000 of sales and the royalty fee is 8 percent, you have to pay $28,000 to the franchisor whether you make a profit or not. And you still have all your other operating expenses to cover.

When comparing two franchises, look at the combination of franchise fees and royalties. For example, suppose franchise X charges $25,000 for the franchise fee and a 10 percent royalty (not including advertising fees), and franchise Y charges a $37,500 franchise fee with a 5 percent royalty (no advertising fees, either). Assume that gross sales for each franchise would be $250,000 per year. The total fee you would pay for either would be $50,000 for the first year. But for each year after the first, you would pay $25,000 ($250,000 × 10%) with franchise X and only half that with franchise Y ($250,000 × 5%).

If the franchise agreement requires you to pay advertising fees, you want to be sure that a portion of your fee goes to local advertising in your area. If you operate a franchise on the outer geographic fringe of the franchise's operations, the franchisor could spend all of your advertising dollars where there is a greater concentration of other franchises, but none of *your* customers.

When it comes to total fees in franchising, you generally get what you pay for. If a deal looks too good to be true (unlimited potential earnings with no risk), it probably is.[9]

Competitive Advantage
INNOVATION AND SUSTAINABILITY

Franchise—*Failed!*

Many new ideas sound good. It's only when looking in retrospect that we say "Really, we wanted *that*?" Let's look at a few franchises that went both boom and bust:

- **eBay Stores.** Yep, stores that would list items for people who apparently thought it was too complicated. In 2005, there were over 7,000 such businesses across the country. iSold It was one of the leading franchisors, until 2007 when they issued a statement of concern regarding profits.
- **Meal preparation commercial kitchens.** Busy home cooks would prepare a week's worth of family meals using pre-chopped ingredients, pack them up, and take them home to cook later. Super Suppers and Dinners by Design had over 200 and 55 franchisees, respectively, in 2006—until the

economy started to soften, when people started making meals, at home.

- **Dating services.** Before match.com, eharmony.com, and craigslist, dating service franchises were hot stuff. Together Dating, The Right One, and It's Just Lunch peaked in the early 2000s. You gotta change with the times.
- **Frozen yogurt.** Tricky one—is it in or out? In the late 1980s and early 1990s, franchises like TCBY topped 3,000 outlets. Then they dropped to below 500 in 2002. Now, fro-yo is making a comeback. Pinkberry and Red Mango are making some serious growth in the premium treat category.

Source: Kara Ohngren, "Kaboom!" *Entrepreneur*, January 2010, 102–104.

© Image Source/Getty Images

Termination of the Franchise Agreement The agreement should state how you, as the franchisee, could lose your franchise rights. Also described should be the franchisee's obligations if you choose to terminate the agreement. Make sure the franchisor must show "good cause" to terminate the agreement—that is, there must be a good reason to discontinue the deal. Some states require a good-cause clause.

Terms and Renewal of Agreement The franchise contract includes a section that specifies how long the agreement will remain in effect and what renewal process will apply. Most franchise contracts run from 5 to 15 years. Will you have to pay a renewal fee or, possibly worse, negotiate a whole new franchise agreement? Because fees and royalties are generally higher for well-established franchises, your royalties and fees would probably increase if you have to sign a new agreement 10 years from now.

Exclusive Territory You need to know the geographic size of the territory and the exclusive rights the franchisee would have. Franchisors may identify how many franchises a territory can support without oversaturation and then issue that many, regardless of the businesses' specific locations. Rights of first refusal, advertising restrictions, and performance quotas for the territory are addressed in this section.[10]

This issue of *exclusive territory* is the subject of much controversy in the franchising world. Patrick Leddy Jr. had run a Baskin-Robbins franchise for 13 years when he learned that the franchisor was planning to open a new store less than two miles away from his site. He protested, but Baskin-Robbins opened the new store anyway. Leddy's sales plunged. When he tried to sell his store, he could not find a buyer because of his declining sales. Many franchisees cited examples like Leddy's case when they called for a federal law to prevent what they called widespread unfair treatment by franchisors.[11]

In reviewing the franchise opportunity, a potential franchisee should gather and verify the accuracy of the information included in the franchise agreement and all other information provided by the franchisor. This process is called **due diligence**. It means doing your homework and investigating the franchise on your own, rather than

due diligence
The process of thoroughly investigating the accuracy of information before signing a franchise (or any other) agreement.

"The cost of consulting professionals is small compared to the amount of time and money you will invest in a franchise."

accepting everything the franchisor says at face value. This is a big commitment, so you should investigate matters thoroughly. Some information you can find yourself; some you will need professional assistance to gather and interpret.

Get Professional Advice

Consult a lawyer and a CPA before you sign any franchise agreement. Ask your accountant to read the financial data in the company's disclosure statements to determine whether the franchisor would be able to meet its obligation to you if you buy a franchise. Then ask a lawyer who is familiar with franchise law to inform you of all your rights and obligations contained in the franchise agreement—it *is* negotiable, but you have to push. Query your lawyer about any state or local laws that would affect your franchise. The cost of consulting professionals is small compared to the amount of time and money you will invest in a franchise. Do not assume that the disclosure statement tells you everything you need to know about the franchise. That is not the intent of the document.

International Franchising

Overseas franchising has become a major activity for U.S. companies faced with constantly increasing levels of domestic competition. Some franchises are signing few new franchises domestically, but are still rapidly adding foreign operations. Carlos Poza, of the U.S. Commercial Service of the Department of Commerce, reminds us that "95 percent of the world's consumers live outside the U.S. Because the world's consumers know U.S. products are excellent, our companies enjoy a competitive advantage—which means big opportunities for U.S. franchisors."[12]

Ray Kroc, who built McDonald's into a franchise giant, once said, "Saturation is for sponges." What Kroc was saying is that by expanding less crowded or underserved markets, you can increase sales and profits.

Canada is an increasingly attractive market for U.S. franchises because it is close and its markets are similar. With the passage of the North American Free Trade Agreement (NAFTA), franchise opportunities south of the border have become a dominant force in both the retailing and restaurant sectors. For example, TCBY Enterprises is quickly opening stores in Mexico. Both Eastern and Western European and Pacific Rim countries (especially Taiwan, Thailand, Indonesia, and Singapore) are also attractive targets for franchise expansion. When expanding abroad, however, franchisors must be sensitive to the demographic, economic, cultural, and legal climates of the host country.

The success of U.S. franchises is spreading all over the globe. In response, many governments are enacting legislation to regulate franchise operations. Following are some highlights of franchise legislation from a variety of countries:

© Iain Masterton / Alamy

Franchises are finding growth opportunities in many countries—like this McDonald's in Tokyo, Japan.

- *United States.* This chapter has highlighted the federal laws covering disclosure statements, registration requirements, and restrictions on the sale and offering of franchises.

- *Canada.* Unlike the United States, Canada has no federal legislation uniquely directed toward franchising. Only the province of Alberta has a specific franchise law, which relates to timely disclosure of information.
- *France.* Although French law does not use the word *franchising*, disclosure documents are required to be received by franchisees 20 days prior to execution of the franchise agreement.
- *Mexico.* The Industrial Property Law calls for disclosure; however, the franchisor may, if desired, exclude any confidential information that would benefit a competing franchise system. This is probably the single best place for franchisors to test their international exposure. For example, Dairy Queen tripled its franchisees in Mexico between 2001 and 2004, from 13 to 50.[13]
- *Brazil.* Federal law does not seek to regulate the relationship between franchisor and franchisee, but the franchisee must receive full information at least 10 days before execution of the franchise agreement. Brazil is a strong marketplace that is worth the challenges.[14]
- *Spain.* In January 1996, the Spanish government enacted the Retail Trade Act, which requires franchisors to register their company name with the federal government and disclose full information in writing to potential franchisees.
- *Australia.* The Australian government enacted the Franchising Code of Conduct in 1998 to help franchisees make informed decisions.
- *Indonesia.* The government of Indonesia passed the Government Regulation on Franchising in 1997 to provide order in the business of franchising and protection to consumers.
- *Russia.* The Civil Code of Russia regulates the contractual agreement between franchisors and franchisees.
- *Republic of China.* Under legislation passed in 1997, it was required that prospective franchisees receive specific information at least 10 days before signing an agreement. China is McDonald's seventh-largest market by revenue, with 600 stores in 94 Chinese cities. KFC is the largest U.S. restaurant chain in China, with more than 900 locations.[15]

Summary

1. Explain what a franchise is and how it operates.

Franchising is a legal agreement that allows a franchisee to use a product, service, or method of the franchisor in exchange for fees and royalties. A franchisee is an independent businessperson who agrees to operate under the policies and procedures set up by the franchisor.

2. Articulate the difference between product-distribution franchises and business-format franchises.

Product-distribution franchises allow the franchisee to purchase the right to use the trade name of the manufacturer and to buy or sell the manufacturer's products. Business-format franchises allow the franchisee to duplicate the franchisor's way of doing business.

3. Compare the advantages and disadvantages of franchising.

There are eight major advantages of franchising from the franchisee's perspective: proven product or service, marketing expertise, financial assistance, technical and managerial assistance, opportunity to learn, quality control standards, efficiency, and opportunity for growth. The primary disadvantages to the franchisee include fees, restrictions on his or her freedom to operate the business, overdependence on the franchisor, unsatisfied expectations of the franchisor, termination of the agreement, and poor performance of other franchisees.

4. Explain how to evaluate a potential franchise.

To evaluate a franchise opportunity, you should send for a copy of the company's disclosure statement (the company is required to send it to you), research the company through business periodicals, talk to current and former franchisees, and check out the franchisor's reputation with the International Franchise Association.

5. Explore franchising in the international marketplace.

Franchises are rapidly exploring opportunities for international expansion when faced with saturated domestic markets. Foreign markets are often less crowded and more underserved.

Questions for Review and Discussion

1. What is the difference between a franchise, a franchisee, and a franchisor?
2. How would you explain the difference between franchises and other forms of business ownership?
3. Why would you prefer to buy a franchise than to start a new business or buy an existing business?
4. Why is franchising important in today's economy?
5. What is the difference between product-distribution franchises and business-format franchises? Give an example of each that has not been cited in the text.
6. What are the biggest advantage and the biggest disadvantage of franchising? Justify your answer.
7. What do you expect to get in return for paying a franchise fee?
8. What is a royalty fee?
9. Is the disclosure statement the *only* source of information you need to check out a potential franchise? Why or why not?
10. After reading about the topics included in a franchise agreement, who do you think controls most of the power in a franchise: the franchisee or the franchisor? Explain.
11. What are potential sources of conflict between franchisees and franchisors?
12. You are worried that someone else will buy a specific franchise in your area before you do. Would it be appropriate to sign the franchise agreement before talking to your lawyer or accountant if you intend to meet with them later? Explain.
13. If you are the franchisee of a bookstore and are offered twice the business's book value to sell it to a third party, should you or the franchisor collect the additional money? Take a position and justify it.
14. What do you think will be the growth areas (in products, services, and geographic areas) for franchises in the near future?

Questions for Critical Thinking

1. Explain how a franchise could be considered a partnership. What makes a franchise agreement simpler than a partnership that you would start with another individual?
2. After having read about entrepreneurship in Chapter 2, would you consider someone who buys a franchise to be an entrepreneur? Does franchising stifle entrepreneurship?

What Would You Do?

You're convinced that purchasing a franchise is your method of choice for becoming a small business owner. Before you jump in, though, you'd better do your homework. For this exercise, we'll first present some basic information about two possible franchise operations; then it's your turn.

Snip 'N Clip (SNC Franchise Corporation)

This franchisor began business in 1958 and started franchising in 1985. Its business is providing all kinds of hair care procedures. There are 84 locations throughout the United States, 43 of which are owned by franchisees. The initial franchise fee is $10,000, and total investment ranges from $50,950 to $58,450. The company doesn't offer financing.

Smoothie King

This smoothie company finished on top of the juice bar category in *Entrepreneur* magazine's 2007 Franchise 500 list (it finished as number 91 overall). Smoothie King began franchising in 1988, selling healthy snacks in Covington, Louisiana. There were 437 independent franchises in 2006. The franchise fee is $25,000, the royalty fee is 6 percent, and start-up costs range from $121,000 to $250,000. The company offers financing for the franchise fee, start-up costs, equipment, and inventory.

Questions

1. Choose one of the two franchises presented and draft a business plan outline.
2. Divide the class into teams to discuss the merits and potential drawbacks of each of these franchises.

© Image Source/Getty Images

6

Buying a Business

CHAPTER LEARNING OUTCOMES

After reading this chapter, you should be able to:

1. Compare the advantages and disadvantages of buying an existing business.

2. Propose ways of locating a suitable business for sale.

3. Explain how to measure the condition of a business and determine why it might be offered for sale.

4. Differentiate between tangible and intangible assets, and assess the value of each.

5. Calculate the price to pay for a business.

6. Understand factors that are important when finalizing the purchase of a business.

7. Describe what makes a family business different from other types of business.

© Craig Cameron Olsen

For Sale: California Ski Area … Rick Metcalf grew up skiing Mount Waterman, an 8,000-foot-high mountain about 45 miles northeast of Los Angeles in the San Gabriel Mountains with 235 skiable acres. After 60 years of operation, the ski area was no longer financially viable and closed in 2002. The forest service was going to remove all the equipment from the hill and restore this historic mountain back to the National Forest. Metcalf immediately contacted four Waterman enthusiasts, Craig Stewart, Brien Metcalf, Robin Hoffner, and Roberto Martinez. Metcalf had since become a mortgage broker in San Diego, but memories of days on those slopes led him to purchase it in 2006. He pumped $1 million into renovations over the next 18 months, including upgrades to three chairlifts and the lodge. Waterman reopened in February 2008. But after only two seasons of operation, Metcalf has decided the mountain needs more improvements than he is willing to fund—specifically, snowmaking equipment.

The first full season under Metcalf's ownership, the lifts operated only on weekends—a total of 23 ski days. An average of

125 customers per day generated about $143,000 in ticket sales and concessions. This summer, the chairlifts also opened for hikers and mountain bikers. Day passes cost $10 for hikers and $25 for bikers.

The mountain has 27 groomed trails with a thousand feet of vertical drop. Runs include blue, green, and black (beginner to expert). The three chairlifts are doubles. The 2,200-square-foot lodge includes a snack-bar-style restaurant with a bar and fireplace. A rental shop is also included to augment revenue. Metcalf is not happy about selling. "It's not a real difficult business model to operate," he says. "But it's definitely not a get-rich kind of thing."

Business at a glance:

- Year founded—1942 (lift ticket price of $2.50/day)
- Open season—mid-December/mid-March
- Annual snowfall—180 inches/average
- Elevation at summit—8,030 feet
- Vertical drop—1,030 feet
- Number of runs—27
- Number of lifts—3
- Lift ticket—$50/day
- 2008–2009 revenue—$143,493
- Operating profit—$90,411
- Selling price—$1.65 million

PRICE BASIS: The price is based on improvements plus potential for growth. Ski facilities historically sell for 6 to 10 times EBITDA (earnings before interest, taxes, depreciation, and amortization), says Michael Berry, president of the National Ski Areas Association. That makes Mount Waterman's price, at 18 times operating profit, seem high.

UP SIDES: Mount Waterman is about an hour's drive from Los Angeles County and its 10 million people. Stepped-up marketing could attract many more skiers. The mountain can handle 1,500 skiers a day (many more than the 125/day average).

DOWN SIDES: It would cost several million dollars to install snowmaking equipment, considered a must in today's industry. The small resort has not come close to its potential.

BOTTOM LINE: Mount Waterman is a turnkey ski mountain at an affordable price. To tap its full potential, though, a new owner should be prepared to invest in snowmaking and marketing.

Are you interested? Use the material in this chapter to help analyze what you would need to do to prepare to buy a business such as this one.

Sources: Darren Dahl, "Business for Sale: A California Ski Resort," *Inc.* October 1, 2009, 28; www.mtwaterman.org/who_we_are, accessed May 2010; "Mt. Waterman Ski Area, San Gabriel Mountains, California," www.gottagoitsnows.com/skiareas; Warren Miller, "WARREN'S WORLD: Mount Waterman," March 21, 2010, and Flathead Beacon, www.flatheadbeacon.com/articles/article/warrens_world_mount_waterman/16760.

Business-Buyout Alternative

Suppose you are a prospective small business owner. You possess the necessary personal qualities, managerial ability, and capital to run a business, but you haven't decided on the approach you should take to get into business. If you aren't inheriting a family business, then you have three choices for getting started:

- You may buy out an existing establishment.
- You may acquire a franchised business.
- You may start a new firm yourself.

This chapter discusses the many factors to be considered in buying an existing business and taking over a family business.

Advantages of Buying a Business

The opportunity to buy a firm already in operation is appealing for a number of reasons. Like franchising, it offers a way to avoid some beginners' hazards.[1] The existing firm is already functioning—maybe it is even a proven success. Many of the serious problems typically encountered by start-ups should have been either avoided or corrected by now. The ongoing business is analogous to a ship after its "shakedown cruise," a new automobile after the usual small adjustments have been made, or a computer program that has been "debugged." But remember one thing: Just as there are no perfect ships, cars, or software programs for sale out there, neither are there any perfect businesses on the market. You are searching for an opportunity, so *some* flaws in a business can make it more attractive. You just have to be able to correct them while keeping all the parts that work going strong.

Competitive Advantage
INNOVATION AND SUSTAINABILITY

In the Box – Negotiating Strategies

Even the best valuation tools for placing a value on a business for sale can only deliver two numbers—an asking price and an offering price. What's in between? Negotiation ... finding the amount that will make both parties get to "I accept."

- Stay rationally focused on the issue being negotiated. Don't try to sidestep issues to avoid telling the truth. Norm Brodsky advises, "The more forthright you are with the other party, the more likely you are to arrive at a satisfactory outcome."
- Exhaustive preparation is more important than aggressive argument. The more knowledge you have of a situation, the better you will be able to negotiate. The more you are able to demonstrate that you know what you are talking about and be reasonable, the more you will be able to set discussion parameters.
- Think through your alternatives. The more options you feel you have, the better a negotiating position you'll be in.
- Spend less time talking and more time listening and asking good questions. Sometimes silence is your best response.

- Embrace your fear. Bob Woolf, sports and entertainment attorney, stated that "95 percent of the folks you'll ever negotiate with feel just as nervous and, yes, as *scared* as you do."
- Let the other side make the first offer. If you're underestimating yourself, you might make a needlessly weak opening move.
- Have confidence. You probably underestimate your experience. We all negotiate every day—the skills you develop back-and-forth with spouses, colleagues, children, professors, and fellow airplane passengers all improve your business negotiation skills.

The magic number that you and the seller both agree upon may not exist for every deal. Be prepared to walk away from *every* deal, or you're not really negotiating.

———
Sources: Christine Lagoria, "7 Tips for Masterful Negotiating," *Inc.*, April 26, 2010, www.inc.com/guides/2010/04/tips-for-great-negotiating; Darren Dahl, "Coming to Terms," *Inc.*, March 2010, 114–115; and Theodore Guth, "Proactive Negotiation for Selling Your Business," *Entrepreneur*, October 5, 2009, www.entrepreneur.com/growyourbusiness/sellingyourbusiness.

"Existing businesses must be scrutinized carefully to determine whether they are a worthy investment of your time and money."

Buying an existing business is a popular way for would-be owners to acquire a small business. Of the 6 million U.S. businesses with 19 or fewer employees, at least 1 million are for sale at any given time.[2]

There are several advantages to buying an existing business as compared with the other methods of getting into business. Because customers are used to doing business with the company at its present address, they are likely to continue doing so once you take over. If the business has been making money, you will break even sooner than if you start your own business from the ground up. Your planning for an ongoing business can be based on actual historical figures, rather than relying on projections, as with a start-up. Your inventory, equipment, and suppliers are already in place, managed by employees who already know how to operate the business. Financing may be available from the owner. If the timing of the deal occurs when you are ready to buy a business and the owner needs to sell for a legitimate reason, you may get a bargain (see Table 6.1).

Disadvantages of Buying a Business

Could this business that you're considering buying be what is called in the used-car business a "lemon"? Most people don't sell their cars until they feel the vehicle needs considerable mechanical attention. Is the same true of selling businesses?

There are disadvantages to buying an existing business as a way to become your own boss (see Table 6.1 again). The image of the business already exists and may prove difficult to change should you desire to improve it. The employees who come with the

---

TABLE 6-1

Advantages and Disadvantages of Buying a Business

Advantages

1. Customer base is established.
2. Location is already familiar to customers.
3. Planning can be based on known historical data.
4. Supplier relationships are already in place.
5. Inventory and equipment are already in place.
6. Employees are experienced.
7. Possibility of owner financing exists.
8. Quick entry is available.
9. Control systems are already in place (e.g., accounting, inventory, and personnel controls).
10. Business image is already set in minds of customers.

Disadvantages

1. Business image may be difficult to change.
2. Employees may be ones you would not choose.
3. Business may not have operated the way you like and could be difficult to change.
4. Inventory or equipment may be obsolete.
5. Financing costs could drain your cash flow and threaten the business's survival.
6. Business's location may be undesirable, or a good location may be about to become not so good.
7. Potential liability exists for past business contracts.
8. Misrepresentation is possible (yes, the person selling the business may be lying).

business may not be the ones whom you would choose to hire. The previous owners may have established precedents that can be difficult to change. The way the business operates may be outmoded. The inventory or equipment may be outdated. The purchase price may create a burden on future cash flow and profitability. You may pay too much for the business due to misrepresentation or inaccurate appraisal. The business's facilities or location may not be the best. You may be held liable for contracts left over from previous owners.

How Do You Find a Business for Sale?

If you have decided that you're interested in purchasing an existing business and have narrowed your choices down to a few types of businesses, how do you locate one to buy? Perhaps you are currently employed by a small business. Is there a chance that it may be available for purchase sometime soon? Because you know the inner workings of the business, it might be a good place to start. Newspaper advertising is a traditional place for someone who is actively trying to sell a business to start marketing it. Don't stop your quest with the newspaper, however, because many good opportunities are never advertised. Word of mouth through friends and family may turn up businesses that don't appear to be available through formal channels.

People who counsel small businesses on a regular basis, such as bankers, lawyers, accountants, and Small Business Administration representatives, can be good sources for finding firms for sale. Real estate brokers often have listings for business opportunities, which include real estate and buildings. Trade associations generally have publications that list member businesses for sale.[3]

Don't overlook a direct approach to finding a business. If you have been a regular customer of an establishment and have an attraction to it, why not politely ask the owner if he or she has ever thought of selling it? The timing may be perfect if the owner is considering a move to another part of the country or is exploring another new business. Perhaps this is an unlikely way to find a business, but what do you have to lose by asking?

business brokers
A business intermediary that brings sellers of their businesses together with potential buyers.

Nearly every city has one or more **business brokers**. Most inspect and appraise a business establishment offered for sale before listing and advertising it. Some also assist a buyer in financing the purchase, but not all of them will provide you with the same level of service. A few will work very hard for you in trying to find a business that matches your talents and needs. Most will tell you what is available at the moment, but not much more than that. Some will do you more harm than good. Remember, business brokers normally receive their commission from the seller, so their loyalty is to the seller, not to you.

Unfortunately for prospective buyers, the market is rife with "business opportunity" scams. As with any scam, the individuals most likely to be targeted are those venturing into unknown territory and trusting the wrong people. The practice of selling unprofitable (and unfixable) businesses to unwary buyers has been around as long as business itself. The ruse is most common in the retail field, where a single business unit can wreck a dozen or more owners through successive sales and resales to a steady stream of newcomers, each confident that he or she can succeed where others have failed.

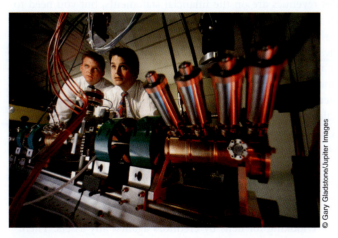

© Gary Gladstone/Jupiter Images

Discoveries in fields like life sciences, energy, and physics create business opportunities.

Naturally, the brokers who promote these sales make more in commissions the more frequently the business changes hands. Check for recommendations from bankers, accountants, and other businesspeople who have used the broker in the past. You need to be on guard to keep from being included among that group immortalized by the late P. T. Barnum, who allegedly said, "There's a sucker born every minute."

Brokers must take classes and pass examinations to become *certified business intermediaries* (CBIs). To find a reliable business broker, check the International Business Brokers Association at www.ibba.org.

What Do You Look for in a Business?

To successfully analyze the value of any business, you should have enough experience to recognize specific details that are most relevant in that type of business. You need enough knowledge to take the information provided by sales, personnel, or financial records and (1) evaluate the past performance of the business and (2) predict its probable future developments. You need objectivity to avoid excess enthusiasm that might blind you to the facts. *Don't let emotions cloud your business decisions.*

"Don't let emotions cloud your business decisions."

At a minimum, you should ask the following questions to gather information about the business you are considering buying:

- **History**—How long has the business existed? Who founded it? How many owners has it had? Why have others sold out?
- **Inventory**—What is the current status of all products and materials? What is present now? What existed at the end of the previous fiscal year? Have the inventory appraised, keeping in mind that you do not have to accept the value set by the seller. The saleability and value are major points of negotiation.
- **Tax returns for the past five years**—Investigate how comingled the seller's personal and business dealings had been—were business funds used to purchase personal items or trips? You and your accountant need to analyze returns to get an accurate financial net worth for the business.
- **Financial statements for the past five years**—Compare these with the seller's tax returns to determine the true earning power of the business. What is the profit record? Is profit increasing or decreasing? What are the true reasons for the increase or the decrease?
- **Sales records**—Yes, sales revenues are on the financial statements, but you need to evaluate sales by month for the past 48 months. Analyze by product line and by other factors such as cash sales versus credit. This will give you a picture of the seasonality of the business and trend lines. Do further analysis on the top 10 (or whatever break number makes sense) customers. It's fine if the seller does not want to identify them by name—a code is fine since you are more interested in trends.
- **Contracts and legal documents**—This would include all leases, purchase agreements with suppliers, sales contracts with customers, union contracts, and employment contracts. If the business involves intellectual property, such as patents, have those documents analyzed by a specialist. Real estate leases are especially sensitive since location can be a huge competitive advantage for your small business. What are the terms and length of the lease? Is it transferable? Does the landlord have the right of first refusal (i.e., does the landlord have to approve you?)? Can the lease be renewed?
- **List of liabilities**—You are looking for liens by creditors against any assets. There may by claims such as employee benefits or out-of-court settlements still being paid off that do not show up on financial statements that a savvy accountant can find.

- **List of accounts receivable**—While A/R are on the balance sheet, you need to see an aging schedule breaking them down by 30, 60, and 90+ days. The longer accounts are outstanding, the less value they have.
- **List of accounts payable**—You need to see a schedule just like accounts receivable because of the impact on cash flow.
- **Sales taxes**—When buying the assets of a business, you can avoid responsibility for the seller's debts and liabilities—except *sales taxes*. If the seller has been under-reporting (or not paying) sales taxes, the state can (and will) come after you for the entire amount owed. You can sue the seller and get a settlement, but if that person has skipped the country, you are stuck. Do not pay a cent for a business until you have a *clearance certificate* from the state tax authority (ask your lawyer).
- **Furniture, fixtures, and equipment**—ff&e is a standard comparison for what you are physically buying. As with inventory, valuation, condition, age, and whether equipment is purchased or leased have an impact on value.
- **Marketing**—How has the seller communicated with customers? Get copies of all advertising and sales literature. This will give you insight into the image of the business and how customers perceive it.
- **Suppliers**—Are there dependable sources of supply for all the inventory, supplies, or materials that the company needs? Evaluate current price lists and discount schedules.
- **Organizational chart of current employees**—Since employees are a valuable asset, you need to understand how they work together. You need to be especially careful to see if key people are willing to remain. Are any salaries inflated, or does the seller have a relative on the payroll who does not work for the business?
- **Industry and market region trends**—What about present and future competition? Are new competitors or substitute materials or methods visible on the horizon? What is the condition of the area around the business? Are traffic routes or parking regulations likely to change?
- **Key ties**—Does the present owner have family, religious, social, or political connections that have been important to the success of the business?
- **Seller's plans**—Why does the present owner want to sell? Where will the owner go? What is he or she going to do? What do people (customers, suppliers, local citizens) think of the present owner and of the business?
- **Buy or build**—How does this business, in its present condition, compare with one that you could start and develop yourself in a reasonable amount of time?[4]

Are you bored with the idea of shopping for a business the old-fashioned ways, such as through classified ads and business brokers? Then go online—specifically, go to www .bizbuysell.com, a very comprehensive site for buying or selling a business that offers a database of thousands of established businesses for sale. You begin by choosing where you want your business to be. All 50 states, plus Africa, Asia, Australia/New Zealand, Canada, the Caribbean, Central America, Europe, and South America, are represented. Next, you choose the type of business that interests you. You can choose all business categories or pick from retail, service, manufacturing, wholesale, construction, transportation, finance, and several other miscellaneous categories.

due diligence
The process of fact finding to determine the total condition of a business being considered for purchase.

Due Diligence

For the buyout entrepreneur, preparation is the key to a successful business purchase. You need to analyze your own skills, find good advisors, write a business plan, and, most importantly, do *due diligence*. Due diligence means the disclosure and assimilation of public and proprietary information relating to the business for sale. Many prospective buyers mistakenly view due diligence as a financial review, but in fact it goes far beyond the numbers. This step comprises a complete investigation and review of a business that begins the moment you become interested in a business.[5]

Due diligence begins by addressing the overall financial health of the company. What trends have occurred with revenues, expenses, and profit margins? Have they grown, stagnated, or declined? Will the products become obsolete in the foreseeable future? If a small business does not have audited financial statements signed by an accountant (and many don't), then insist on seeing the owner's tax returns (because it's more difficult to lie about those documents). Beyond inspecting the owner's financial documents, you should visit the local county courthouse to check for any existing or pending litigation or liens filed against the business or its owners. The Better Business Bureau can tell you about past or current complaints.

Although the financial scandals of the past few years have centered on large corporations, they have created a heightened level of skepticism about mergers and acquisitions of all sizes of businesses—and increased the emphasis placed on due diligence.[6] The Sarbanes-Oxley Act increases the extent to which executives are held responsible for the accuracy of their company's financial statements. Because business buyers may be liable for any financial-reporting discrepancies found after the business purchase, they have a strong incentive to be thoroughly knowledgeable about the firm's accounting practices.[7]

Since buying a business is risky no matter how much due diligence is performed, a new type of insurance has recently been developed to shift some risk to a third party. This insurance, consisting of *representations and warranties policies*, covers financial losses suffered if a seller makes false claims in the representations and warranties section of a sale contract.[8]

General Considerations

If you aspire to try entrepreneurship by buying an existing business, don't rush into a deal. Talk with the firm's banker and verify account balances with its major customers and creditors. Be sure you get any verbal understandings in writing from the seller.

Put the earnest money in escrow with a reputable third party. Before an agreement to purchase is signed, have all papers checked by your accountant and attorney.

If the business you are buying involves inventory, you need to be familiar with the *bulk-sales provisions* of the Uniform Commercial Code. Although the law varies from state to state, it generally requires a seller to provide a list of all business creditors and amounts due to each buyer. You, as the buyer, must then notify each creditor that the business is changing hands. This step protects you from claims against the merchandise previously purchased.

Why Is the Business Being Sold?

When the owner of a business decides to sell it, the reasons he gives to prospective buyers may be somewhat different from those known to the business community, and both of these explanations may be somewhat different from the actual facts. There are at least as many factors that could contribute to the sale of a business as there are reasons for business liquidations. Be careful. Business owners who are aware of future problems (such as a lost contract for a strong line of merchandise or a new law that will affect the business unfavorably) may not tell you everything they know. For a prospective buyer, a discussion with the firm's customers and suppliers is recommended. Check with city planners about proposed changes in streets or routing of transportation lines that might have a serious effect on the business in the near future.

Although anyone can be misled or defrauded, a savvy business buyer with good business sense will rely on his or her ability to analyze the market, judge the competitive situation, and estimate the profits that could be made from the business, rather than relying on the present owner's reasons for selling. These "reasons" are often too difficult to verify.

One point to consider as you search for a business is the list of alternatives in which you could invest your money, such as the stock market, money market funds, or even a savings account. By viewing the purchase of a business as an investment, you can compare alternatives on the same terms.

Financial Condition

A study of the financial statements of the business will reveal how consistently the business has rewarded its previous owner's efforts. As a prospective purchaser, you must decide if the income reported thus far would be satisfactory to you and your family. If it is not, could it be increased? You will want to compare the firm's operating ratios with industry averages to identify where costs could be reduced or more money is needed.

The seller's books alone should not be taken as proof of stated sales or profits. You should also inspect bank deposits for at least five years or for as long as the present owner has operated the business.

When analyzing the financial statements of the business, don't rely strictly on the most recent year of operation. Profits can be artificially pumped up and expenses cut temporarily for almost every business. Check whether the business employs the same number of people as in previous years; most businesses can operate shorthanded for a while to cut labor expenses. Maintenance on equipment, vehicles, or the building can be cut to increase short-term profit figures. Profits that appear on the books may also be overstated by insufficient write-offs of bad debts, inventory shortages and obsolescence, and underdepreciation of the firm's fixed assets.

Ask to see the owner's tax returns. This request shouldn't create a problem if everything is legitimate. Compare bills and receipts with sales tax receipts. Reconcile past purchases with the sales and markup claimed. Make certain that all back taxes have been paid. Make sure that interest payments and other current obligations are not in arrears.

Realize that the financial information you need in order to analyze the overall condition of the business is sensitive information to the seller, especially if the two of you don't know each other. You can decrease the seller's suspicions about your using this information to aid a competing business or for some other improper use by writing a *letter of confidentiality* (see the example of one in the Manager's Notes).

Independent Audit Before any serious discussion of purchasing a business takes place, an *independent audit* should be conducted. This exercise will identify the condition of the financial statements. You will want to know whether the business's accounting practices are legitimate and whether its valuation of inventory, equipment, and real estate is realistic.

Even audited statements need some subjective interpretation, however. For example, owners may underreport their income for tax reasons. A family member may be on the payroll and paid a salary although unneeded by the business. Business owners who use a company car or a credit card for nonbusiness purposes also misrepresent their business expenses.

Profit Trend The financial records of the business can tell you whether sales volume is increasing or decreasing. If it is going up, which departments or product lines account for the increased volume? Did the increased volume lead to increased profitability? In

Manager's Notes

Show and Don't Tell

Becky Homecki, CEO

Becky's TechnoWidgets, Inc.

Dear Ms. Homecki:

It was a pleasure to talk with you last week concerning the possible purchase of your business. Our conversation has brought my interest in your business to the point where I would like to examine your financial records for the past five years. Along with the company records I also wish to see tax returns filed for that period of time.

I realize that this information is confidential in nature and that you are concerned about improper use of these records. I assure you that I request this information strictly for the purpose of making a purchase decision regarding your business and the terms of the deal. The only persons to whom I will disclose this confidential information are my spouse, my attorney, and my accountant. I will obtain signed confidentiality statements from them before showing them your records.

I will return all of your records, including any copies made, within two weeks of their delivery to me. Thank you for your trust. I will not violate it, and I look forward to continuing our business transaction.

Sincerely,

Andre Preneur

other words, what is the *profit trend*? Many businesses have failed by concentrating on selling a high volume of goods at such low margins that making net profits proved impossible.

If the sales volume is decreasing, is it due to the business's failure to keep up with competition or its inability to adjust to changing times? Or is the decline simply due to a lack of effective marketing?

Interpret net profit of the business you are considering in terms of the amount of capital investment you will have to make in the business as well as sales volume. In other words, a $5,000 annual net profit from a business that requires a $10,000 investment and sales of $20,000 is much more attractive than a business that generates the same profit but requires a $100,000 investment and sales of $200,000.[9]

Expense Ratios Industry averages comparing expenses to sales exist for every size and type of business. Industry-wide *expense ratios* are calculated by most trade associations, many commercial banks, accounting firms, university bureaus of business research, and firms like Dun & Bradstreet and Robert Morris Associates (RMA).

For example, RMA publishes industry averages for 392 specific types of businesses in the manufacturing, wholesale, retail, and service sectors in *RMA Annual Statement Studies*.[10] Comparisons are made in terms of percentages of assets, liabilities, and income data. RMA also provides industry averages of 16 common financial ratios, such as current ratio, quick ratio, sales/working capital, and sales/receivables. (These and other financial ratios are explained further in Chapter 8.)

Imagine you are interested in buying a health club. The location is good, the advertising has caught your attention for several months, and the club boasts state-of-the-art equipment. You are very excited about the possibilities and are now looking over the financial statements. You divide the total current assets by the total current liabilities to calculate the club's *current ratio*, which shows the ability of a business to meet its current obligations. Let's suppose you get a current ratio of 0.5 for this business.

Now you want to get an idea of management performance, which is shown by the *operating ratio*, so you divide the profit before taxes by total assets and multiply by 100 (to convert to a percentage). This computation gives you 4.8 percent. You ask yourself, "Are a current ratio of 0.5 and an operating ratio of 4.8 percent good or bad for a health club?" They could be either. You need something to compare them with to tell you whether they are in line. You go to the library at a nearby university to compare your figures with RMA industry averages. You look in the RMA reports under "Service— Physical Fitness Facilities," where you find the median current ratio listed at 0.9 and the median percentage profit before taxes divided by total assets at 7.5 percent. Your figures are well below the industry averages, so you decide to dig deeper to find out why such large deviations exist between the business you are interested in buying and the average for other similar-sized businesses in the health club industry.

Expense ratios are standards or guides for comparison. Their effective use depends on your ability to identify existing problems and to change conditions that have caused any ratios to be appreciably lower than the standard.

Other Measures of Financial Health Profit ratios are excellent indicators of a business's worth, but you should also examine other aspects of its financial health. A complete financial health examination consists of the calculation and interpretation of a variety of other financial ratios in addition to those relating to profit. Of particular interest to you and your accountant will be the following factors:

1. The working capital and the cash flow of the business (is there enough of both to adequately keep the business going?)
2. The relationship between the firm's fixed assets and the owner's tangible net worth
3. The firm's debt load, or leverage

Another key factor in business valuation is what other companies in your industry have sold for. Each year, *Inc.* magazine, in partnership with Business Valuation Resources of Portland, Oregon, publishes an issue that contains a comprehensive business valuation guide with graphics and tables that illustrate different companies selling for a premium or below their annual revenue. For example, in 2007, companies in the life sciences, energy, financial services, and technology sectors boasted high sale prices and robust sale multiples.[11]

What Are You Buying?

When buying an existing business, you need to realize that the value of that business comes from what the business owns (its assets and what it earns), its cash flow, and the factors that make the business unique, such as the risk involved (see Figure 6.1).

Tangible Assets

tangible assets
Assets owned by a business that can be seen and examined.

The ***tangible assets*** of a business, such as inventory, equipment, and buildings, are generally easier to place a fair market value on than intangible assets, such as trade names,

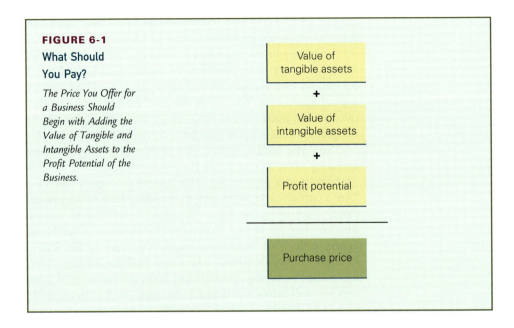

FIGURE 6-1

**What Should
You Pay?**

*The Price You Offer for
a Business Should
Begin with Adding the
Value of Tangible and
Intangible Assets to the
Profit Potential of the
Business.*

Value of
tangible assets

+

Value of
intangible assets

+

Profit potential

———————————————

Purchase price

customer lists, and goodwill. If the firm is selling its accounts receivable, you should determine how many of these accounts are collectible and discount them accordingly. Receivables that are 120 days or older are not worth as much as those less than 30 days old, because the odds are greater that you will not collect them. This process is called *aging accounts receivable*. Of the other tangible assets of a business that are up for sale, inventories and equipment should be examined the most closely, because they are most likely to be outdated and therefore worth less than what the seller is asking.

Inventory Inventory needs to be timely, fresh, and well balanced. One indication that the business has been well managed is an inventory of goods that people want; that are provided in the proper sizes, designs, and colors; and that are priced to fit local buying power and purchasing habits.

Your biggest concern about inventory should be that you aren't buying *dead stock* (merchandise that has no, or very little, value) that the seller has listed as being worth its original value. The loss in value of dead stock should be incurred by the original buyer, and you must ensure that the loss is not passed on to you as part of the sale.

Equipment It is important that a business be equipped with current, usable machines and equipment. *Book value* (discussed under "What Are the Tangible Assets Worth?" later in this chapter) of electronic office equipment, especially computers, becomes outdated quickly. A cash register designed for the bookkeeping requirements of a generation ago, for example, will not record the information now required for tax reporting or scan UPC codes for efficient inventory control.

Often the usefulness of the firm's equipment was outlived long ago and its value depreciated. The owner may have delayed so long in replacing equipment that it has no trade-in value, and without this discount the owner finds the price of new equipment to be exorbitant. This reason alone could lead to his or her decision to sell the business. Anything the owner makes on the fixtures and equipment is new, clear profit, an extra bonus on his or her period of operation.

Manager's Notes

What's It Really Worth?

Not all accounts receivable are created equal. Those that have been owed the longest are worth less because they are the least likely to be collected. In other words, the longer someone takes to pay his or her account, the more likely it is that this person will never pay the debt. Therefore, in valuing a business for sale, you need to reduce the cash value of long overdue accounts so as to reflect the odds that they will not be paid.

Determining how much to reduce the value of old accounts should be based on the debtor company's past payment trends. In the hypothetical example of a company we'll call Fabio's Floral Wholesalers, accounts receivable 30 days and younger have a 100 percent likelihood of being paid. Accounts 31 to 60 days old have historically had a 70 percent probability of being paid, those 61 to 90 days old have had a 50 percent probability of being paid, and those older than 90 days have had a 25 percent probability of being paid. These percentages were determined by looking at the company's accounts receivable history—a fair and logical request to make of the business owner.

Accounts Receivable	Probability Percentage	Book Value	Aged Value
30 days and younger	100	$ 75,000	$ 75,000
31 to 60 days	70	50,000	35,000
61 to 90 days	50	30,000	15,000
Over 90 days	25	30,000	7,500
Total Value		$185,000	$132,500

You can see that there's a significant difference in the aged value and the book value of the accounts receivable: $52,500! When you're buying an existing business, play it smart and be sure to value accounts receivable accurately.

Sources: Michelle Dunnis, "Strengthen Your Credit Policy Today," *Entrepreneur,* October 5, 2009, www.entrepreneur.com/money/paymentsandcollections; and Bridget McCrea and Alan Hughes, "Turning Receivables into Received," *Black Enterprise,* February 2004, 46.

Intangible Assets

intangible assets
Assets that have value to a business but are not visible.

Businesses are also made up of **intangible assets** that may have real value to the purchaser. Among these are goodwill; favorable leases and other advantageous contracts; and patents, copyrights, and trademarks.

goodwill
The intangible asset that allows businesses to earn a higher return than a comparable business with the same tangible assets might generate.

Goodwill **Goodwill** is an intangible asset that enables a business to earn a higher return than a comparable business with the same tangible assets might generate. Few businesses that are for sale have much goodwill value.

We all know businesses in existence for years that have not established enough goodwill for the average customer to see the business as being "special." If strong competition existed, such companies would have been driven out of business long ago. From a consumer-preference standpoint, they are at the bottom of the scale. This public attitude cannot be changed quickly. A good name can be ruined in far less time than it takes to improve a bad one.

A successful business has goodwill as an asset. Taking over a popular business brings with it public acceptance that has been built up over a period of many years, which is naturally valuable to the new owner. (Goodwill is discussed further later on in this chapter.)

Leases and Other Contracts   A lease on a favorable location is a valuable business asset. If the selling firm possesses a lease on its building, or if it has any unfulfilled sales contracts, you should determine whether the lease and other contracts are transferable to you or whether they must be renegotiated.

Patents, Copyrights, and Trademarks   *Intellectual property*—which includes patents, copyrights, and trademarks—can also be a valuable intangible asset. *Patent rights* give protection of your machine, your process, or a combination of the two against unauthorized use or infringement for only a limited period of time, after which they are open to use by others. Thus it is important for the prospective buyer of an existing business to determine precisely when the firm's patent rights expire and to value these rights based on the time remaining.

Copyrights offer the best protection for books, periodicals, materials prepared for oral presentation, advertising copy, pictorial illustrations, commercial prints or labels, and similar intellectual property. Unlike patent rights, copyrights are renewable.

Registered *trademarks* protect you against unauthorized use or infringement of a symbol, such as the Mercedes-Benz star or McDonald's arches, used in marketing goods. The function of trademarks is to identify specific products and to create and maintain a demand for those products. Because trademark protection lasts as long as the trademark is in continuous use, you should consider its value when purchasing a business that owns a trademark.

Personnel

When purchasing a business, you should regard the people working there as being equally important as profits and production. Retention of certain key people will keep a successful business going. New employees rarely come in as properly trained and steady workers. To help you estimate expenses related to finding, hiring, and training new employees, you will want to know if there are enough qualified people presently employed. Will any of these people depart with the previous owner? Are any key individuals unwilling or unable to continue working for you? The loss of a key person or two in a small business can have a serious impact on future earnings.

The Seller's Personal Plans

As a prospective purchaser of an existing business, you should not feel that all sellers of businesses have questionable ethical and moral principles. Nevertheless, you should remember that "*Caveat emptor*—Let the buyer beware" has been a reliable maxim for years. There are laws against fraud and misrepresentation, but intent to defraud is usually very difficult to prove in court.

You can reduce your risk by writing protective clauses into contracts of sale, such as a **noncompete clause**, in which the seller promises not to enter into the same kind of business as a competitor within a specified geographic area for a reasonable number of years. If the seller resists agreeing to such a clause, it may be a signal that he or she intends to enter into a similar business in the future.

For a noncompete clause to be legally enforced, it must be reasonable. For example, setting a 25-mile noncompete zone when selling a New York City business would take in a market of about 20 million people—probably an unreasonable restraint that might prevent the seller from earning a living in the future.

"This public attitude cannot be changed quickly. A good name can be ruined in far less time than it takes to improve a bad one."

noncompete clause
A provision often included in a contract to purchase a business that restricts the seller from entering the same type of business within a specified area for a certain amount of time.

An example of a noncompete clause would read as follows:

> *Seller shall not establish, engage in, or become interested in, directly or indirectly, as an employee, owner, partner, agent, shareholder, or otherwise, within a radius of ten miles from the city of _____, any business, trade, or occupation similar to the business covered by this sales agreement for a period of three years. At the closing, the seller agrees to sign an agreement on this subject in the form set forth in Exhibit _____.[12]*

How Much Should You Pay?

Even if you don't plan to buy an existing business, the methods of evaluating one are useful to know so that you can appraise the success of a firm. But if you are planning to buy a business, certain additional factors come into play. When you make a substantial financial investment in a business, you should expect to receive personal satisfaction as well as an adequate living. A business bought at the wrong price, at the wrong time, or in the wrong place can cost you and your family more than the dollars invested and lost. After you have thoroughly investigated the business, weighed the information collected, and decided that the business will satisfy your expectations, a price must be agreed on.

Determining the purchase price for a business involves analyzing several important factors: (1) valuation of the firm's tangible net assets; (2) valuation of the firm's intangible assets, especially any goodwill that has been built up; (3) expected future earnings; (4) market demand for the particular type of business; and (5) general condition of the business (including the completeness and accuracy of its records, employee esprit de corps, and physical condition of facilities).[13]

A beginning point (not a finely tuned ending point) for business valuation is the *multiple method*. This approach is based on a formula that applies a weighting factor to the owner-benefit figure of the previous year(s) so as to arrive at a possible purchase price. The *owner benefit* is a combination of several factors:

Pretax Profit + Owner's Salary + Additional Owner Perks + Interest + Depreciation

Most small businesses will sell for a one- to three-times multiple of this figure. Granted, this is a wide range, so how do you determine which multiple to apply? Use a multiple of 1 for those businesses where the seller is "the business"—such as consulting businesses, professional practices, and one-person businesses. Multiples of 3 are more appropriate for businesses that have been in existence for several years, have demonstrated sustainable growth, boast a solid base of clients, own assets that will not have to be replaced in the immediate future, and are involved in growth industries, among other things. A study of hundreds of businesses sold in a recent year in the state of Florida indicated that the average multiple was 2.1 times the owner benefit.[14]

balance-sheet methods of valuation
A method of determining the value of a business based on the worth of its assets.

income-statement methods of valuation
A method of determining the value of a business based on its profit potential.

Approaches to valuing a business that focus on the value of the business's assets are called **balance-sheet methods of valuation**. They are most appropriate for businesses that generate earnings primarily from their assets rather than from the contributions of their employees. Approaches that focus more on the profits or cash flow that a business generates are called **income-statement methods of valuation**. As a methodology, the *discounted cash flow* (an income-statement method) is often considered the preferred tool with which to value businesses. What sets this approach apart from the other approaches is that it is based on future operating results rather than on historical operating results. As a result, companies can be valued based on their future cash flows, which may be somewhat different than the historical results, especially if the buyer expects to operate some aspects of the business differently.

Discounted cash-flow analysis consists of projecting future cash flows (generally for five years) before debts are subtracted and after taxes are paid. A *discount rate* (expressed as a percentage that represents the risk associated with the investment) is then derived and applied to the future cash flows and *terminal value* (a current value for a company's long-term future cash flows). This detailed analysis depends on accurate financial projections and specific discount-rate assumptions.[15]

What Are the Tangible Assets Worth?

The worth of tangible assets is what the balance-sheet method of valuation seeks to establish. Their value is determined based on one of three factors:

- *Book value.* What the asset originally cost or what it is worth from an accounting viewpoint; the amount shown on the books as representing the asset's value as a part of the firm's worth.
- *Replacement value.* What it would cost to buy the same materials, merchandise, or machinery today; relative availability and desirability of new items must be considered.
- *Liquidation value.* How much the seller could get for this business, or any part of it, if it were placed on the open market.

There are significant differences in these three approaches to determining value. Book value may not hold up in the marketplace. Buildings and equipment may not be correctly depreciated, whereas land may have appreciated. Replacement value may not be a reliable figure because of opportunities to buy used equipment. It is significant as a measure of value only in comparison to what it would cost to start your own business. Liquidation value is the most realistic approach in determining the value of tangible assets to the buyer of a business. It may represent the lowest figure that the seller would be willing to accept.

You have to determine the value of the following physical assets before serious bargaining can begin:

1. Cost of the inventory adjusted for slow-moving or dead stock
2. Cost of the equipment less depreciation
3. Supplies
4. Accounts receivable less bad debts
5. Market value of the building

Don't make an offer for a business based on the seller's asking price. You may feel as if you got a real bargain if you talk the seller down to half of what he or she is asking—but half might still be twice as much as the business is worth.[16]

"Goodwill is the term used to describe the difference between the purchase price of a company and the net value of the tangible assets."

What Are the Intangible Assets Worth?

An established business may be worth more than the sum of its physical assets, and its owner may be unwilling to sell for liquidation value alone. The value of a business's intangible assets is difficult to determine. Intangible assets are the product of a firm's past earnings, and they are the basis on which its earnings are projected.

Goodwill is the term used to describe the difference between the purchase price of a company and the net value of the tangible assets. Goodwill is the most difficult asset to value at a price that the seller will think is fair. It includes intangible but very real assets with real value to the prospective purchaser. Goodwill can be regarded as (1) compensation to the owner for his or her losses on beginner's mistakes you might have made if you had started from scratch and (2) payment for the privilege of carrying on an established and profitable business.[17] It should be small enough to be made up from profits within a reasonably short period.

What is goodwill worth? To determine a company's goodwill, you can start by using the income-statement method of valuation. To do so, you should capitalize your projected future earnings at an assumed rate of interest that would be in excess of the "normal" return (earnings adjusted to remove any unusual occurrences like a lawsuit settlement or a one-time gain from the sale of real estate) in that type and size of business. The *capitalization rate* is a figure assigned to show the risk and expected growth rate associated with future earnings.

For example, suppose that the liquidation value of the firm's tangible net assets is $224,000 and that the normal before-tax rate of return on the owner's investment in this business is 15 percent, or $33,600 per year. We will assume that the actual profit during the past few years has averaged $83,600, exclusive of the present owner's salary (which may have been overstated or understated).

From the profit, we will deduct a reasonable salary for the owner or manager—what he or she might earn by managing this type of business for someone else. If we assume a going-rate annual salary of $40,000, then the excess profit to be capitalized (that is, the amount of profit based on goodwill) is $10,000 ($83,600 minus $40,000 salary minus a normal profit of $33,600).

The rate of capitalization is negotiated by the buyer and the seller of the business. It should be appropriate to the risk taken. The more certain you are of the estimated profits, the more you will pay for goodwill. The less certain you are (the higher you perceive your risk to be), the less you will pay.

If you assume a 25 percent rate of return on estimated earnings coming from goodwill, then the value of the intangible assets is $10,000/0.25, or $40,000. Usually this relationship is expressed as a ratio or multiplier of 4, "four times (excess) earnings." You would expect to recover the amount invested in goodwill in no more than four years. When you put these two figures together, you come up with an offering price of $264,000 for the business—net tangible assets of $224,000 at liquidation value plus goodwill valued at $40,000. The calculations for this price are shown in Table 6.2.

If the average annual net earnings of the business before subtracting the owner's salary (line 4) is $73,600 or less, then there is no goodwill value. Even though the business may have existed for a long time, the earnings would be less than you could earn through outside investment. In that case, your price would be determined by capitalizing

TABLE 6-2			
Calculating Purchase Price of Existing Business	1.	Adjusted value of tangible net worth	$224,000
	2.	Earning power at 15 percent	33,600
	3.	Reasonable salary for owner or manager	40,000
			73,600
	4.	Average annual net earnings before subtracting owner's salary	83,600
	5.	Extra earning power of business (line 4: total of lines 2 and 3)	10,000
	6.	Value of intangibles using four-year profit figure for moderately well-established firm in four years (line 5)	40,000
	7.	Offering price (line 1; line 6)	$264,000

the average annual profit (net earnings minus all expenses and owner's salary) by the normal or expected rate of return on investment in this business. For example,

$$\text{Profit} = \$73,600 - \$40,000 = \$33,600$$
$$\text{Offering Price} = \$33,600/0.15 = \$224,000$$

Valuing goodwill is a highly subjective process. The value of intangible assets comes down to what you think they are worth and what you are willing to pay. You will need to negotiate with the seller to reach a consensus.

Buying the Business

To complete the purchase of your business, you need to negotiate the terms of the deal and prepare for the closing.

Terms of Sale

After a price for the business has been agreed upon, the terms of sale need to be negotiated. Few buyers are able to raise the funds required to pay cash for a business. A lump-sum payment may be in neither the buyer's nor the seller's best interests for tax reasons, unless the seller intends to reinvest in another business. Paying in installments is often the most practical solution.

By building installment payments into your cash-flow projection, you should be assured that the business can be paid for out of earnings. Installments assure the seller that his investment in the business will be returned on a tax-deferred basis, as opposed to paying all taxes at one time with a lump-sum payment. With an installment sale, the seller has some motivation to help with the buyer's success.

A seller may need to take steps to make the business more affordable. One way to do so is by *thinning the assets*. That is, the seller can adjust the assets to be more manageable for the new owner in one or more of the following ways:

- Separate real estate ownership from business ownership. The new owner leases rather than purchases the building. The buyer has less to borrow, and the seller receives a steady rental income.
- Lease equipment and/or fixtures in the same manner as real estate.
- Sell off excess inventory.
- Factor accounts receivable or carry the old accounts.

"If you are buying the stock of a business rather than just the assets, you need protection from unknown tax liabilities."

If you are buying the stock of a business rather than just the assets, you need protection from unknown tax liabilities. The best way to accomplish this is to place part of the purchase price (anywhere from 5 percent to 30 percent) in an escrow account. This *holdback money* is earmarked to pay for any corporate liabilities, including taxes owed, that arise after the deal has closed.

Closing the Deal

When you and the seller have reached an agreement on the sale of the business, several conditions must be met to ensure a smooth, legal transaction. Closing can be handled by using either a settlement attorney or an escrow settlement.

A *settlement attorney* acts as a neutral party by drawing up the necessary documents and representing both the buyer and the seller. Both parties meet with the settlement attorney at the agreed-upon closing date to sign the papers after all the conditions of the sale have been met, such as financing being secured by the buyer and a search completed to determine whether any liens against the business's assets exist.

In an *escrow settlement*, the buyer deposits the money, and the seller provides the bill of sale and other documents to an escrow agent. You can find an escrow agent at most financial institutions, such as banks and trusts that have escrow departments, or through an escrow company. The escrow agent holds the funds and documents until proof is shown that all conditions of the sale have been satisfied. When these conditions are met, the escrow agent releases the funds and documents to the rightful owners.

Taking Over a Family Business

A fourth route into small business (besides starting from scratch, buying an existing business, or franchising) is taking over a family business. This alternative offers special opportunities and risks.

ENTREPRENEURIAL SNAPSHOT

Their Family Business Tree is a Sequoia

© Courtesy Avedis Zildjian Company

We discussed the failure rate of small businesses in Chapter 1, where it was pointed out that most businesses do not survive to see their twentieth birthday. Family-owned businesses are much hardier, but still not invincible. Fewer than 30 percent survive into the second generation, barely 10 percent make it into the third generation, and only about 4 percent last until the fourth generation. Thus one way to measure business success, beyond revenues generated, profits earned, or societal impact, would be longevity. Ever wonder what the oldest family business in the United States might be? Perhaps not, but it's an interesting question. Making the list of the top 100 are some household names like number 68, Levi Strauss (founded 1853), and number 88, Anheuser-Busch (founded 1860).

But the hands-down endurance award goes to a business that has lasted through *14 generations* and was started in 1623! Zildjian Cymbal Company of Norwell, Massachusetts, was founded in Constantinople by Avedis I, who discovered a metal alloy that created superior-sounding, more durable cymbals. The sultan named him "Zildjian," Armenian for "cymbalsmith."

The Zildjian family arrived in the United States in 1910, moving here to escape persecution of Christian Armenians in their native land. The company was brought here in 1929. It was good timing, as Avedis Zildjian III was able to supply his cymbals to the jazz drummers of the day. Those instruments have remained synonymous with hot drummers throughout the Jazz Age, the big band era, and today's rock and roll. Avedis's son Armand applied new technology to the company's traditional approach by creating a modern factory.

As you might have guessed, not all has gone smoothly over the past 385-plus years. When company leader Avedis died in 1979, his sons Robert and Armand locked horns in a nasty courtroom battle for control over the company (cymbaling rivalry?). Robert left Zildjian and set up a competing cymbal company, Sabian, in Canada. He was legally barred from referencing the family history or name in his business or even using the letter "Z" in his company name.

Today Armand's daughters Craigie (the company's CEO) and Debbie (vice president of human resources) are the first female chiefs in Zildjian's long history.

Since you are undoubtedly wondering, the oldest family business in the world is Kongo Gumi, founded in 578. For more than 1,400 years and 40 generations, the Kongo family has built and repaired religious temples from its base in Osaka, Japan.

Sources: Kathleen Martin, "Global Cymbals," *Marketing*, March 22, 2004, 13; "America's Oldest Family Companies," May 2004, www.familybusinessmagazine.com; and Paul I. Karofsky, "A Commitment to Passion: The Succession Story of the Avedis Zildjian Company," www.fambiz.com/articles.

What Is Different about Family Businesses?

"Family businesses account for nearly 50 percent of the U.S. GDP."

Family businesses are those in which two or more members of the same family control, are directly involved in, and own a majority of the business. Family businesses account for 80 percent of all businesses in the United States and are responsible for nearly 50 percent of the U.S. gross domestic product (GDP).[18] They are obviously an important part of our economy, but what makes them different from nonfamily businesses? Two critical factors are (1) the complex interrelationships of family members interacting with one another and interacting with the business, and (2) the intricate succession planning needed.

Complex Interrelationships

When you run a family business, you have three overlapping perspectives on its operation (see Figure 6.2).[19] For example, suppose a family member needs a job. From the family perspective, you would see the business as an opportunity to help one of your own. From the ownership perspective, you might be concerned about the effect of a new hire on profits. From a management perspective, you would be concerned about how this hire would affect nonfamily employees.

Everyone involved in a family business will have a different perspective, depending on each person's position within the business. The successful leader of this business must maintain all three perspectives simultaneously.

Planning Succession

Many entrepreneurs dream of the time when they will be able to "pass the torch" of their successful business on to their children. Unfortunately, many factors, such as jealousy, lack of interest, or ineptitude, can cause the flame to go out. Less than one-third of family businesses survive through the second generation, and fewer than one in ten makes it through the third generation.[20] The major cause of family business failure is lack of a

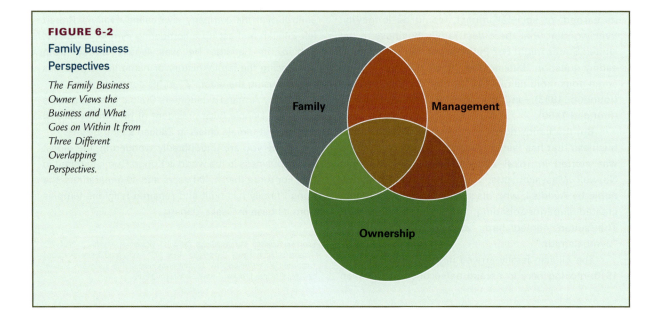

FIGURE 6-2
Family Business Perspectives

The Family Business Owner Views the Business and What Goes on Within It from Three Different Overlapping Perspectives.

Family

Management

Ownership

business succession plan. There appear to be four reasons for family inability to create such a document:

1. It is difficult for senior family members to address their own mortality.
2. Many senior family members are worried that the way younger family members run the business will not maintain its success. Only 20 percent are confident of the next generation's commitment to the business.[21]
3. Transfer of control is put off until too late because of seniors' concern for their personal long-term financial security.
4. Seniors (like most small business owners) are too personally tied to the business and lacking in outside interests to be attracted to retirement.[22]

If the potential successor wants to take over the family business, she must gain acceptance and trust within the organization (see Figure 6.3). When a family member enters the business, he is not usually immediately accepted by nonfamily employees. This skepticism increases when that person moves up to a leadership position within the business. The successor must earn credibility by showing that she is capable of running the business. Only after being accepted and earning credibility will the new manager have legitimate power and become successful as the new leader.[23]

General Family Business Policies

Because family businesses have situations and problems unique to them, they need a set of policies that are not needed in other types of businesses. Such a set of policies can help prevent problems such as animosity from nonfamily employees, which can decrease their motivation and productivity.[24]

- To be hired, family members must meet the same criteria as nonfamily employees.
- In performance reviews, family members must meet the same standards as nonfamily employees.

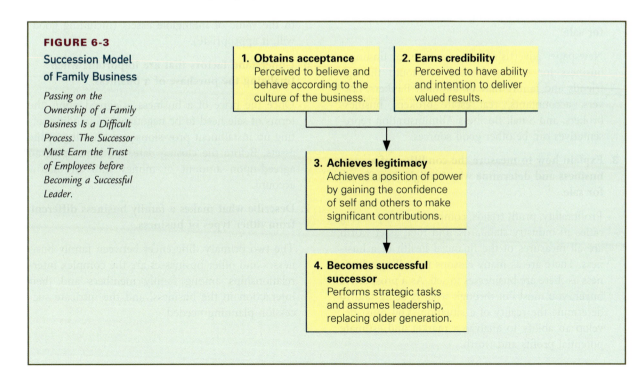

FIGURE 6-3

Succession Model of Family Business

Passing on the Ownership of a Family Business Is a Difficult Process. The Successor Must Earn the Trust of Employees before Becoming a Successful Leader.

1. Obtains acceptance
Perceived to believe and behave according to the culture of the business.

2. Earns credibility
Perceived to have ability and intention to deliver valued results.

3. Achieves legitimacy
Achieves a position of power by gaining the confidence of self and others to make significant contributions.

4. Becomes successful successor
Performs strategic tasks and assumes leadership, replacing older generation.

- Family members should be supervised by nonfamily employees when possible.
- If family members are younger than age 30, they are only eligible for "temporary" employment (less than one year).
- No family member can stay in an entry-level position permanently.
- All positions will be compensated at fair market value.
- For family members to seek permanent employment, they must have at least five years' experience outside the company. Family members must prove their worth to another employer to be useful here.[25]

Want more information about family businesses? Check out www.fambiz.com (more than 300 articles on family business issues and additional links) and www.familybusinessmagazine.com/index.html (*Family Business* magazine online).

Summary

1. Compare the advantages and disadvantages of buying an existing business.

The advantages of buying an existing business include the fact that it is an already functioning operation, customers are used to doing business with it, and you will break even sooner than if you started from the ground up. The disadvantages include the difficulty of changing the business's image or the way it does business, outdated inventory and equipment, too high a purchase price, poor location, and liabilities for previous contracts.

2. Propose ways of locating a suitable business for sale.

Newspaper advertising is one source for finding a business for sale, and word of mouth through friends and family may be another. Bankers, lawyers, accountants, real estate brokers, business brokers, and Small Business Administration representatives can be other good sources.

3. Explain how to measure the condition of a business and determine why it might be offered for sale.

Profitability, profit trends, comparison of operating ratios to industry standards, and total asset worth are all measures of the financial health of a business. There are as many reasons for selling a business as there are businesses to sell. As a prospective buyer, you must cut through what is being said to determine the reality of a situation. You must develop an ability to analyze a market and estimate potential profits and worth.

4. Differentiate between tangible and intangible assets, and assess the value of each.

Tangible assets are those that can be seen and examined. Real estate, inventory, and equipment are important tangible assets. Intangible assets, though unseen, are no less valuable. Goodwill; leases and contracts; and patents, copyrights, and trademarks are examples.

5. Calculate the price to pay for a business.

The offering price to pay for a business is calculated by adding the adjusted value of tangible assets to the value of intangible assets (including goodwill, if appropriate).

6. Understand factors that are important when finalizing the purchase of a business.

Once the price of a business is agreed upon, the terms of sale need to be negotiated—including setting up installment provisions and thinning of the assets. Before the closing date, the buyer puts an agreed-upon amount of money into an escrow account.

7. Describe what makes a family business different from other types of business.

The two primary differences between family businesses and other businesses are the complex interrelationships among family members and their interaction in the business, and the intricate succession planning needed.

Questions for Review and Discussion

1. What are some arguments for buying an established business rather than starting one yourself?
2. When buying an established business, what questions should you ask about it? From whom might you seek information about the business?
3. Which is more important in appraising a business: profitability or return on investment? Discuss.
4. Should one ever consider purchasing a presently unsuccessful business (that is, a business with relatively low or no profits)? Explain.
5. What factors warrant special attention in appraising a firm's (a) inventory, (b) equipment, and (c) accounts receivable?
6. What should a prospective buyer know about the seller's inventory sources and other resource contacts? How is this information obtained?
7. Does competition help or hurt the valuation of a business? Explain.
8. Discuss the ways in which the tangible assets of a business may be valued. What is the most realistic approach to determining a business's true value? Why?
9. What is goodwill, and how may its value be determined?
10. How can a buyer determine the rate of return to use in evaluating the worth of a business?
11. What is meant by "thinning the assets"? Cite examples.
12. Discuss the advantages of working through a business broker. What precautions should one take when dealing with a business broker?

Questions for Critical Thinking

1. You are analyzing the financial records of a business you have been thinking about buying. You discover that although the firm has excellent current and quick-asset ratios by industry standards (meaning its current assets are higher than its current liabilities), its cash is low, and it hasn't paid its bills on time. What might have caused this problem? Would it influence your decision to buy the business?
2. A mother believes that all of her family's children should have equal ownership of the family business regardless of their participation in the business. The father sees the situation completely differently; he believes that the children who are actively involved should receive more ownership. How can this dispute be resolved?

What Would You Do?

A family in the Pacific Northwest owns a retail clothing store. Two brothers work in the business, and their mother is president of the company. Sibling rivalry was a problem while the boys were growing up, and now that they are in the family business together, it is reappearing. In addition to her role as president, the mother often finds herself playing the role of referee and "chief emotional officer" when the young men fight. The continued rivalry between the brothers and the mother's need to intervene between them has interfered with a normally functional business. The family realizes that its business system is entangled with its family system, but they are not sure what to do about it.

Questions

1. What should the mother do to help her family (and her business) operate more normally?
2. Would bringing in a nonfamily manager with direct-line control over each brother help or cause more problems? How can they ever decide who will eventually take over control of the business?

7

Creating a Business

CHAPTER LEARNING OUTCOMES

After reading this chapter, you should be able to:

1. Discuss the advantages and disadvantages of starting a business from scratch.

2. Describe types of new businesses and discuss the characteristics commonly shared by fast-growth companies.

3. Evaluate potential start-ups and suggest sources of business ideas.

4. Explain the most important points to consider when starting a new business.

Derek Johnson is a 20-something problem solver. Solutions that have led him to become CEO of group SMS (Short Message Service, which makes texting possible) start-up Tatango and social media agency Derek Media.

While still enrolled at the University of Houston Entrepreneurial Program, Johnson heard from friends in sororities and fraternities about the problems they were having getting announcements out to their chapters. Facebook, e-mail, and message boards were not working. A little digging showed Derek that mass-texting services did not exist. Could there be a business opportunity lurking?

From his vision to provide groups a free, easy, and fast way to communicate with other group members via SMS, Derek Johnson founded Tatango.com in 2007. Tatango has grown from campus Greek connector to the leader in its industry. As CEO, Derek is primarily focused on how to best translate user needs into an always improving service while strategically steering the company toward its goals. Tango Voice allows group leaders to record and send voice messages to all mobile phones in their group, eliminating the need for complex

phone trees. Johnson says, "Text messaging is great for certain types of group messages, but sometimes a group needs a little more room to convey their message."

Derek raised half a million dollars in investments for the company from private investors and the Bellingham Angel Group. Tatango has done more than 50 million messages since its launch, servicing all types of groups such as college organizations, churches, athletic teams, political campaigns, and nonprofit groups. Revenue for 2010 is on track to hit $500k.

Johnson learned a lot about building a community of users and fans using social marketing networks the right way. With this expertise, Tatango began receiving requests from companies for tips and strategies. Derek received incredible feedback from presenting social media seminars for other businesses, leading him to launch Derek Media Agency. Clients range from publicly traded companies, to nonprofit foundations, to popular restaurants and bars. With social marketing gaining momentum each day, Derek Media is on the cutting edge of new approaches toward developing an invaluable online community for businesses and organizations of all kinds.

Even though Derek left college before graduating, he believes that college is a great time for a start-up business. He says, "In college you have time and resources to research and test potential business concepts. It's the best time to start a new business, because no matter what happens, you will still be able to eat and sleep with a roof over your head." His advice for starting a business while still in college:

- Identify a problem. "Ask people what keeps them up at night."
- Zero in and start small. "Pick a problem people will pay to fix with a product or service. Find something you can do with minimal capital and human resources and don't worry about getting big right away."
- Be the best. "If you struggle to come up with a simple, clear answer to the question of what you do best, you need to narrow your focus more."
- Do the research. "Fast-track product testing by surveying and selling to students and using college resources and faculty."
- Just do it. "The biggest hurdle is going forward with an idea. A lot of people stop at the idea point and think too hard about the product and say, 'I don't know.'"
- Be ready to sacrifice. "You are going to miss out on some of your social life, which isn't fun. But when you graduate, you will be doing something you love. I have worked my ass off to be where I am today and I realize it's going to take a lot more work to get where I want to go."

Sources: Joel Holland, "What's Your Problem?" *Entrepreneur*, May 2010, 70; "Interview with Derek Johnson," www.entrepreneurship-interviews.com, July 18, 2008; Don Reisinger, "Tatango Makes Sending Group Voice Messages Free," www.cnet.com, October 15, 2008; www.thederekjohnson.com, accessed June 15, 2010.

About Start-ups

Starting a business from the ground up is more difficult than buying an existing business or a franchise because nothing is in place. There is also more risk involved. However, to many people, the process of taking an idea through all the steps, time, money, and energy needed to become a viable business is the essence of entrepreneurship. The period in which you create a brand-new business is an *exciting* time.

During times of economic recession with the unemployment rate hovering around double digits, a term arises called *necessary entrepreneurship*—people starting businesses because other job opportunities evaporate. The Global Entrepreneurship Monitor longitudinal research project found that "necessary" was a factor for 24.7 percent of new U.S. ventures in 2009, compared with 16.3 in 2007.[1]

As we have seen in previous chapters, small business owners cross a wide spectrum of groups so there is no such thing as a "typical" owner or small business. But data from the Small Business Success Index provide some interesting insights:

- The median age for a U.S. small business owner is 49.5 years.
- 29 percent are female.
- Over half have a four-year college degree (51 percent), but 20 percent have no more than a high school diploma, and 28 percent attended trade school, only some college, or hold a two-year degree.
- 82 percent of owners started the business.
- 83 percent work in their business full-time.
- The average age of small businesses is 15 years.
- Small businesses have an average of 1.7 owners; 57 percent have a single owner, 34 percent have two owners, and 8 percent have three owners.
- The median annual revenue is $189,000.[2]

Would you prefer to be totally independent? Can you set up an accounting system that is readable to you and acceptable to your bank and the Internal Revenue Service? Can you come up with a promotional campaign that will get you noticed? Are you willing to devote the time and sources needed to succeed? Can you find sources of products, components, or distribution? Can you find employees with the skills your business will need? If so, you may be ready to start your own business.

Advantages of Starting from Scratch

When you begin a business from scratch, you have the freedom to mold your new creation into whatever you feel is appropriate. Other advantages of starting from scratch include the ability to create your own distinctive competitive advantage. Many entrepreneurs thrive on the challenge of beginning a new enterprise. You can feel pride when creating something that didn't exist before and in realizing your own goals. The fact that the business is all new can be an advantage in itself—there is no carryover baggage of someone else's mistakes, location, employees, or products. You establish your own image.

Disadvantages of Starting from Scratch

The risk of failure is higher with a start-up than with the purchase of an existing business or franchise. You may have trouble identifying market needs in your area that you are able to satisfy. You must make people aware that your business exists—it can be tough to get noticed. Also, you must deal with thousands of details that you didn't foresee, from how to choose the right vendors, to where to put the coffeepot, to where to find motivated employees.

Types of New Businesses

No matter what type of business you are starting, your most important resource is your time. Nothing happens until you make it happen. You have to create and build on the enthusiasm that will attract others to your idea and your business. In the beginning, the only thing you have is your vision, and only you will be responsible for its success.

As the service industry plays an ever greater role in the U.S. economy, start-up businesses are becoming increasingly popular. The reason? Service businesses tend to be

"The fact that the business is all new can be an advantage in itself— there is no carryover baggage of someone else's mistakes, location, employees, or products."

labor intensive
A business that is more dependent on the services of people than on money and equipment.

capital intensive
A business that depends greatly upon equipment and capital for its operations.

e-business
A business that shares information, maintains customer relationships, and conducts transactions by means of telecommunications networks.

more ***labor intensive***, or dependent on the services of people, as opposed to manufacturing businesses, which are more ***capital intensive***, or dependent on equipment and capital.

Start by finding out all you can about your industry and trade area from books, newsletters, trade publications, magazines, organizations, and people already in business. After all your questions are answered and your investigation is complete, if you are ready for the challenge, you will find several possible routes for starting your business.

Let's look at a few of those routes that people take, aside from seeking to achieve the typical goal of a low-growth, stable start-up that will provide the small business owner with a comfortable, modest living.

E-Businesses

Nothing has changed the small business landscape quite like the Internet. It is the ultimate in making one-to-one connections—which is where small businesses have always thrived. You can begin an ***e-business*** with relatively low overhead and potentially reach markets all over the world. But keep in mind that the Internet, though a powerful tool, doesn't make all other business metrics obsolete. You still have to make a profit, keep employees happy and motivated, provide customer service, and offer a product that inspires customers to turn over their hard-earned money to obtain it. Contrary to popular opinion at one time, electronic business is not all about "click here to buy." As the Internet has begun to mature, the e-business model has evolved into "click here to get more information," "click here to start the just-in-time inventory flow," or "click here to let a new employee go through the orientation process." In other words, e-business has evolved into part of a multichannel marketing strategy that benefits from traditional business models and lessons that don't have to be thrown out with the emergence of new media.[3]

Describing electronic business in a few paragraphs is a difficult task, because one simple model does not exist. Your e-biz may be something as simple as taking a current avocation (like tying flies for fishing or making custom pillows) and selling your concoctions on eBay or Etsy, business to consumer. You may not ever personally touch a product, but provide value by connecting other businesses, business to business. In these few paragraphs we won't get into the technical details of mips, megs, and browsers. You, as a webpreneur, will need an understanding of the leading edge of technology. Unfortunately (or fortunately), that edge moves so quickly that we can't do justice to it here. What we can cover here are basic characteristics that a successful Web business must possess.

- *It's not just retail.* E-commerce still accounts for only a modest 3.6 percent ($142 billion) of total retail sales. In 2008 (latest data available), business-to-business transactions accounted for 92 percent of all e-commerce.[4]
- *Have a sound business strategy, beginning with having a good reason to be online.* But how do you commit to long-term strategic planning in an economy that moves at the speed of the Internet? John Noble, vice president of corporate Internet strategy at Putnam Investments, suggests that you need to figure out which strategic moves you want to make first. Only then can you figure out how to use technology to accomplish your strategy. If you make decisions based strictly on what is technically possible today, you will be out of position in 6 to 12 months. Doing business on the Internet has become a two-pronged endeavor: You need both bright ideas and the capacity to execute them. As a consequence, Internet strategy has evolved into more of a team effort among people who provide an overarching vision and the *information technology (IT)* people who turn those visions into reality.[5]

- *Have a clear market analysis and create traffic coverage.* Believe it or not, not everyone is on the Web! Are your customers? If they aren't, why are you? The "if you build it, they will come" model seldom works.[6] As with brick-and-mortar businesses, you need to generate traffic into your site. Jonathan Wall of online IT reseller dabs.com says that IT skills such as Java and .NET programming are not difficult for him to source. The most complex and sophisticated part of his business is actually marketing.[7]
- *Logistics are huge.* When people buy online, something usually has to get shipped. As Wall notes, "It's not hard to build a Web site that takes orders 24/7. But being able to take an order at 9:30 p.m. and have it delivered by 10:00 a.m. the next day takes a massive investment and a lot of hard work."
- *Use the Internet to save money.* E-business is as much about reducing costs as it is about generating revenue. Creating value-chain efficiencies and meeting increasing customer expectations is what e-biz is about.
- *Build your competitive advantage.* E-business can be boiled down to four ideas: accelerating the *speed* of business, reducing *costs*, enhancing *customer* service, and improving the business *process*. The field is still wide open. Indeed, 78 percent of chief information officers report that they have not tapped the full competitive advantage of e-business.[8]

Home-Based Businesses

The fastest-growing segment of business start-ups comprises those operated out of people's homes. The number of people running businesses from home now tops 15 million.[9] Homepreneurs range from Alex Andon manufacturing jellyfish tanks in his house (he even raises jellyfish in one of his bathtubs) to Sheri Reingold teaching 90 students piano in her home (probably not all at once). Two points stand out as advantages for this type of business: schedule flexibility and low overhead.

The common perception of home businesses is that they are mere hobbies or sideline businesses of little economic consequence. But data from Network Solutions Small Business Success Index show that home businesses account for 34 percent of all small businesses that provide more than half of the owner's household income. The vast majority—75 percent—report that they work full-time in their home business. About 35 percent have revenues greater than $125,000 and 8.5 percent generate more than $500,000. Finally, median household income is substantially higher than it is for the population as a whole: roughly $75,000 for homepreneurs versus $50,233 for households in general.[10]

Kwame Tutuh used to teach second grade. Now he teaches child safety and runs an Ident-A-Kid business out of his Fulton County, Georgia, home. His business produces identification cards so parents can quickly provide the child's photograph, fingerprints, and description to authorities if a child is abducted or lost. He has exclusive territory to contract with schools and day care centers for access to photograph and gather data on children. At his home office, he uses a laptop, proprietary software, digital fingerprint scanner, and other minimal equipment to produce as many as 200 cards at a time. Generating $140,000 revenue in 2008, Tutuh states, "I'm in the perfect sector. The economy can be at its worst but we're still going to do whatever it takes to protect our children."[11]

Running a business out of your home can provide flexibility in your personal life, but it takes serious organization and self-discipline. Let's look at some of this approach's advantages and disadvantages.

Running a home-based business provides flexibility to also care for other important things.

home-based business
A popular type of business that operates from the owner's home, rather than from a separate location.

Advantages of a Home-Based Business Advantages of a **home-based business** include the following:

- Control over work hours
- Convenience
- Ability to care for domestic responsibilities (such as children, parents, or the household)
- Low overhead expenses
- Lack of workplace distractions (coworkers popping in, chatting around the coffee machine)
- Decreased commute time
- Tax advantages

Disadvantages of a Home-Based Business Disadvantages of a home-based business include the following:

- Difficulty setting aside long blocks of time
- Informal, cramped, insufficient workspace at home
- Demands on family members to cooperate
- Lack of respect (people may think you are unemployed or doing this as a hobby)
- Domestic interruptions (houses can get noisy and crowded)
- Lack of workplace camaraderie (houses can get quiet and lonely)
- Zoning issues[12]

What kind of businesses can you run from your home? Some possibilities include specialty travel tours planner, computer consultant, personal chef, concierge service, Web site consultant, event planner, cart or kiosk business, translation service, feng shui consultant, online auctioneer, and technology writer.[13]

Starting a Business on the Side

Many people start businesses while keeping their regular jobs. Although this approach is generally not recommended as a way to enter business, the Bureau of Labor Statistics estimates that more than 1.2 million people take this step each year.[14]

Sara Crevin started her side business when her son Jake was one year old. Like all toddlers, Jake would throw his sippy cup to the floor from his high chair, stroller, and car seat. Picking up dirty cups and looking for lost ones do not rank high on busy parents' lists of favorite things to do. Crevin created the SippiGrip strap that attaches to bottles, cups, or pacifiers. She ran her business as a sideline until 2007, when she formed BooginHead LLC and decided to turn it into a serious business. She has certainly done that as her company is on track to generate $1 million revenue in 2010.[15]

"Working a full-time job while getting a business off the ground may require superhuman organizational skills and discipline, yet it can offer some notable advantages."

Working a full-time job while getting a business off the ground may require superhuman organizational skills and discipline, yet it can offer some notable advantages. A transitional period can allow you to test the waters without pursuing complete immersion in the marketplace. You can also prepare yourself psychologically, experientially, and financially, so that when—or if—you leave your job, you will have a running start. Before taking this route, however, you should be absolutely clear about your company's moonlighting policy and avoid doing anything that might resemble a conflict of interest. Moonlighting policies could include not starting an identical business or not soliciting current customers.

Fast-Growth Start-ups

Not every new business can be or desires to be a hyper-growth company like, for example, the top company on the 2009 *Inc.* 500 list, Northern Capital Insurance, which had a three-year growth rate of 19,812 percent! It is informative to see what characteristics and patterns these fast-growth companies shared in *Inc.*'s database (see Figure 7.1).

1. *They rely on team effort.* In contrast to low-growth firms, most fast-growth companies are started by partnerships. In an increasingly complex and competitive environment, teams can deal with a much wider range of problems than can an individual operating alone. Fifty-six percent of the fast-growth CEOs started with partners or cofounders.
2. *They're headed by people who know their line of work.* A majority of the CEOs of high-growth companies had at least 10 years of experience in the industry. In contrast, owners of low-growth companies typically have just a few years of prior experience.
3. *They're headed by people who have started other businesses.* Research shows that 63 percent of the founders of high-growth companies had previously started other companies, and 23 percent had started three or more businesses. This compares to only 20 percent of all business owners who had been self-employed previously. Some 61 percent started in the founder's home.
4. *They're making big bucks.* The 445 men and 57 women who run *Inc.* 500 companies take risks and are handsomely rewarded for their derring-do. Average first-year compensation was $92,000. Forty percent take home more than $500,000 annually, and more than 20 percent have generated a net worth in excess of $7.5 million.
5. *They're high-tech.* Of the fast-growth companies, 41 percent use new technology to achieve a competitive advantage. Another 40 percent say that new technology gives them somewhat of an edge.
6. *They're better financed—but not by much.* This factor is more difficult to measure because of the subjectivity in determining what "well financed" means. Thirteen percent of *Inc.* 500 companies started with an investment of less than $1,000, and 23 percent began with between $1,000 and $10,000. Only 27 percent had initial start-up capital exceeding $100,000. Eighty-seven percent of *Inc.* 500 companies were self-funded.
7. *They have exit strategies.* The majority (66 percent) plan to sell their business to outside investors. Going public is the exit strategy for 28 percent, while 23 percent plan to sell out to partners. Seventeen percent plan to pass the business on to children, and 16 percent intend to transfer ownership to employees via ESOP.[16]

Evaluating Potential Start-ups

The first thing you need to start your own business is an idea. Of course, not every idea is automatically a viable business opportunity. You must be able to turn your idea into a profitable business. How do you tell when an idea is also an opportunity? Where do people come up with viable business ideas that are opportunities?

Business Ideas

Although there is no shortage of ideas for new and improved products and services, there is a difference between ideas and opportunities. Are all ideas business opportunities? No. A business opportunity is attractive, durable, timely, and anchored in a product or service that creates or adds value for its buyer or end user. Many ideas for new

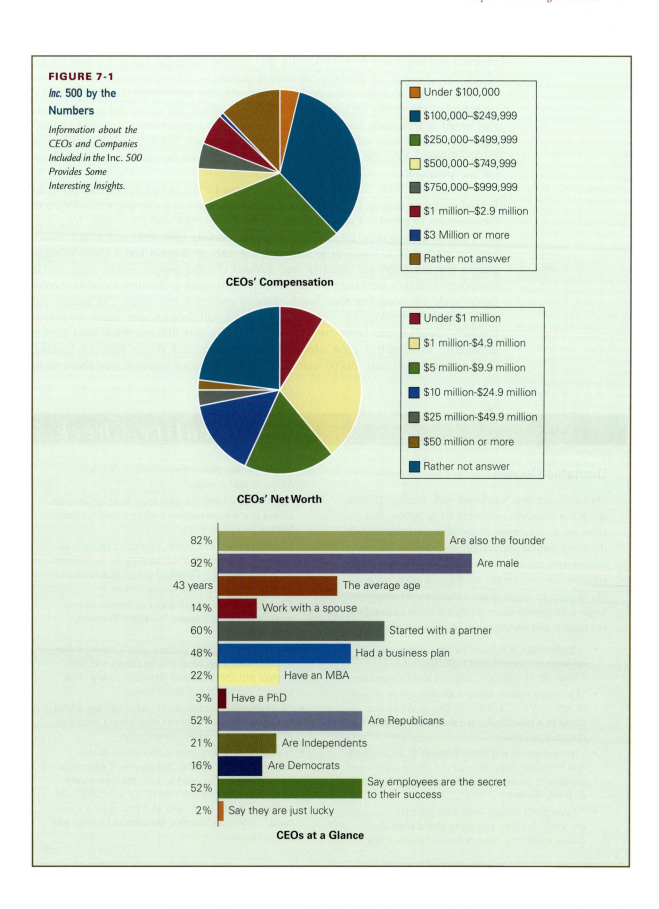

FIGURE 7-1

Inc. **500 by the Numbers**

Information about the CEOs and Companies Included in the Inc. 500 Provides Some Interesting Insights.

CEOs' Compensation

- Under $100,000
- $100,000–$249,999
- $250,000–$499,999
- $500,000–$749,999
- $750,000–$999,999
- $1 million–$2.9 million
- $3 Million or more
- Rather not answer

CEOs' Net Worth

- Under $1 million
- $1 million–$4.9 million
- $5 million–$9.9 million
- $10 million–$24.9 million
- $25 million–$49.9 million
- $50 million or more
- Rather not answer

CEOs at a Glance

- 82% Are also the founder
- 92% Are male
- 43 years The average age
- 14% Work with a spouse
- 60% Started with a partner
- 48% Had a business plan
- 22% Have an MBA
- 3% Have a PhD
- 52% Are Republicans
- 21% Are Independents
- 16% Are Democrats
- 52% Say employees are the secret to their success
- 2% Say they are just lucky

products and businesses do not add value for customers or users. Maybe the time for the idea has yet to come, or maybe it has already passed.

Consider the idea for a new device for removing the crown caps that were common on bottles of soft drinks for many years. You could concoct an exotic and ingenious tool that would be technically feasible to produce, but is there an opportunity to build a business from it? Not since soft drink and beer companies switched to resealable bottles and screw-off tops to solve the same consumer problem that your invention does. Good idea—but no opportunity.

An idea that is too far ahead of the market can be just as bad as one that is too far behind consumer desires. In 1987, Jerry Kaplan left his job as a software writer for Lotus Development to start Go Computers because he thought the world was ready for portable, pen-based computers. He had some big-time backing from IBM and AT&T, which together pitched in $75 million to help with the start-up. Kaplan had a vision of salespeople, lawyers, insurance adjusters, and millions of other people writing away on Go computers as if they were paper. Unfortunately, consumers at the time found that computers could not recognize their handwriting or convert it into print. The market was ready, but the technology was not. Now, two and a half decades later, many consumers regularly use iPads and tablet computers that are not that different from what Kaplan envisioned. Even with a great idea, a talented leader, and strong financial backing, Go Computers sold only 20,000 units and lasted only three years—it was ahead of its

---

Reality Check

Quotable Quotes

Entrepreneurs are fascinated with quotes. Quotes spark our creativity, motivate us to action, and inspire us to greatness. They offer us insights into the spirit behind innovation and genius. Inspiring quotes can come from authors, poets, inventors, scholars, and entrepreneurs. So here are some notable quotes to begin your collection, whether you begin jotting them down on Post-it notes or grabbing red lipstick and writing them across your mirrors.

- "Opportunity is missed by most because it is dressed in overalls and looks like work." – *Thomas Alva Edison, Inventor and Entrepreneur*
- "For every failure, there's an alternative course of action. You just have to find it. When you come to a roadblock, take a detour." – *Mary Kay Ash, Entrepreneur*
- "The young do not know enough to be prudent, and therefore they attempt the impossible—and achieve it, generation after generation." – *Pearl S. Buck, Author*
- "If you don't design your own life plan, chances are you'll fall into someone else's plan. And guess what they have planned for you? Not

much." – *Jim Rohn, Entrepreneur, Author, Motivational Speaker*
- "Do not go where the path may lead, go instead where there is no path and leave a trail." – *Ralph Waldo Emerson, Poet*
- "Watch, listen, and learn. You can't know it all yourself. Anyone who thinks they do is destined for mediocrity." – *Donald Trump, Business Mogul*
- "The only place where success comes before work is in the dictionary." – *Vidal Sassoon, Entrepreneur*
- "If you work just for money, you'll never make it, but if you love what you're doing and you always put the customer first, success will be yours." – *Ray Kroc, Entrepreneur*
- "A successful person is one who can lay a firm foundation with the bricks that others throw at him." – *David Brinkley, Newscaster*
- "I've missed more than 9,000 shots in my career. I've lost almost 300 games. Twenty-six times I've been trusted to take the game winning shot and missed. I've failed over and over and over again in my life and that is why I succeed." – *Michael Jordan, Basketball Legend and Entrepreneur*

market. When Go closed, Kaplan said that he believed that "a new class of computing devices will come into being … it's just a question of when."[17] He was right—just look around today at the success of handheld computers. But a start-up, even one with substantial resources, can't wait for technology or markets to catch up with an idea.

Harvard Business School professor Clayton M. Christiansen, in his book *The Innovator's Dilemma: When New Technologies Cause Great Firms to Fail*, discusses how some innovations *sustain* industries—offering better performance, more features, and everything that existing customers are seeking. Other innovations *disrupt* an industry—bringing out useful products that people have never seen before.[18]

You've probably heard of the term **window of opportunity**. These windows constantly open and close (sometimes rapidly) as the market for a particular product ("product" meaning either goods or services) or business changes. Products go through stages of introduction, growth, maturity, and decline in the **product life cycle**. During the introduction stage, the window of opportunity is wide open because little or no competition exists. As products progress through this cycle, competition increases, consumer expectations expand, and profit margins decline so that the window of opportunity is not open quite as wide (see Figure 7.2).

Optimally, you want to get through while the window is still opening—if the opportunity is the right one for you. To decide whether you should pursue an opportunity, ask yourself the following questions about your business idea:

- Does your idea solve a consumer want or need? This answer can give you insight into current and future demand.
- If there is a demand, are there enough people who will buy your product to support a business? How much competition for that demand exists?
- Can this idea be turned into a *profitable* business?
- Do you have the skills needed to take advantage of this opportunity?
- Why hasn't anyone else done it? If others have, what happened to them?

In the idea stage of your thinking (before you actually pursue an opportunity), you should discuss your idea with a wide variety of people to get feedback on it. Although praise may make you feel good at this stage, what you really need are people who can objectively look for possible flaws and point out the shortcomings of your idea.

"Opportunity is missed by most because it is dressed in overalls and looks like work." – Thomas Alva Edison, Inventor and Entrepreneur

window of opportunity
A period of time in which an opportunity is available.

product life cycle
Stages that products in a marketplace pass through over time.

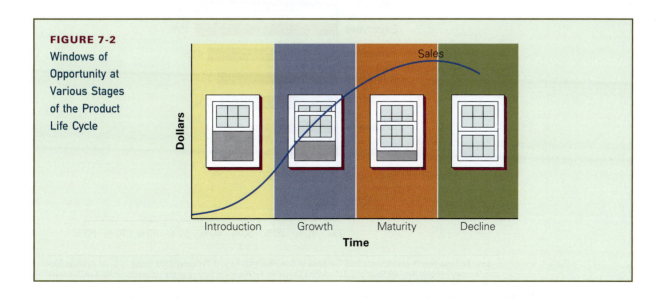

FIGURE 7-2
Windows of Opportunity at Various Stages of the Product Life Cycle

Your final decision as to whether your idea represents an opportunity that you should pursue will come from a combination of research and intuition. Both are valuable management tools, but don't rely exclusively on either. Although research has kept some good ideas from becoming products or businesses, it has kept many more bad ones from turning into losing propositions. Do your homework; thoroughly investigate your possibilities. At the same time, don't get "analysis paralysis," which prevents you from acting because you think you need more testing or questioning—while the window of opportunity closes. Managerial decision making is as much an art as it is a science. Sometimes you will have to make decisions without the benefit of having every last shred of evidence possible. Get all the information that is practical, but also listen to your gut instincts.

Where Business Ideas Come From

Creativity is important to small business success. The Network Solutions Small Business Success Index provides data on where owners get their ideas. Not surprisingly, customers provided business ideas for over two-thirds. Other sources included newspapers and trade journals, competitors, and employees[19] (see Figure 7.3).

Prior Work Experience Experience can be a wonderful teacher. Working for someone else in your area of interest can help you avoid many errors and begin to build competitive advantages. It gives you the chance to ask yourself, "What would I do differently, if I ran this business?"

corridor principle
The idea that opportunities become available to an entrepreneur only after the entrepreneur has started a business.

One start-up may even lead to another. Seeing opportunities for new ventures after starting the first business is known as the ***corridor principle***.[20] Entrepreneurs start second, third, and succeeding businesses as they move down new venture corridors that did not open to them until they got into business. As we saw with fast-growth start-ups, 63 percent of fast-growth CEOs had started other companies in the past, suggesting that one idea really does lead to another.

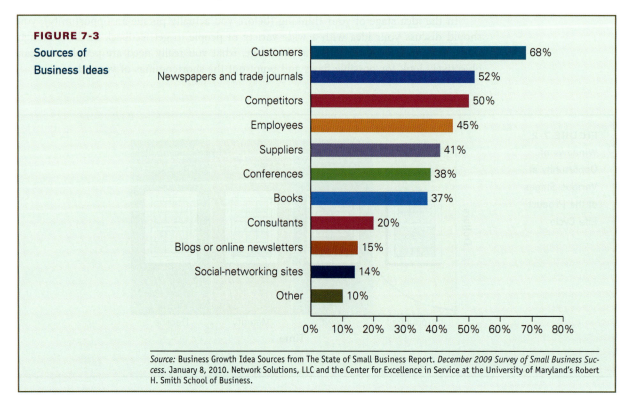

FIGURE 7-3

Sources of Business Ideas

Source	Percentage
Customers	68%
Newspapers and trade journals	52%
Competitors	50%
Employees	45%
Suppliers	41%
Conferences	38%
Books	37%
Consultants	20%
Blogs or online newsletters	15%
Social-networking sites	14%
Other	10%

Source: Business Growth Idea Sources from The State of Small Business Report. *December 2009 Survey of Small Business Success.* January 8, 2010. Network Solutions, LLC and the Center for Excellence in Service at the University of Maryland's Robert H. Smith School of Business.

Research shows that big ideas occur to small business owners almost twice as often after the business is already running as before it begins.[21] This trend illustrates that experience pays off whether you are working for someone else or for yourself.

Hobbies and Avocations Turning what you do for pleasure into a part-time or full-time business is a possibility that you should consider. It helps ensure that your business will be one that you enjoy and understand. If you enjoy fishing, could you potentially use your skills to become a guide? If you love pets, could you channel your affections into a dog-grooming or pet-sitting business?

Julian Bayley has turned an ice-carving hobby into a nice little business. When Elton John hosted his annual White Tie and Tiara charity gala at his mansion near Windsor Castle, ordinary dishes would not do. He called on Bayley's Canadian company, Ice Culture, to use its computer-aided machinery to mill caviar hors d'oeuvre trays for his 450 guests. Bayley has come a long way from his ice-carving hobby to designing and building a $45,000 computer-guided router modified for shaping crystal-clear ice. He also developed an ice lathe that can produce ice vases and oversized bottles—pretty cool.

Chance Happening (Serendipity) *Serendipity* means finding something valuable that you were not looking for. Sometimes business opportunities come to you unexpectedly. The ability to recognize them takes an open mind, flexibility, a sense of adventure, and good business sense.

Brother and sister Ethan and Abby Margalith had to borrow a truck in the summer of 1973 to move a few things to a local swap meet. Both were just out of high school and out of work. While driving the truck to the swap meet, the pair realized that moving could be their summer job. Their first truck was a 1944 weapons carrier that they got for free by rescuing it from a mudslide. Starving Students Movers, Inc. became the low-priced alternative to other movers that were characterized by full uniforms and high prices. The Margaliths used their sense of humor in their advertising—one ad stated that they offered "24-hour service for lease breakers." Even without knowing what they were doing, they had more business than they could handle. Ethan has stated that it wasn't until he got to law school that he realized he and his sister were really running a business. He finished law school but decided that the moving business is fun, exciting, and profitable, so he stayed in the field with his sister. Starving Students has locations from California to Virginia. The company has proudly moved families, companies, government agencies like the U.S. Secret Service and the FBI, and even celebrities like Cher, Jerry Seinfeld, and Tom Hanks—and it all started with digging a truck out of the mud![22]

Hung Van Thai has struggled to make his entrepreneurial ideas work in a very tough environment—communist Vietnam. Thai started his first two private businesses successfully, only to have the government take them away. The first was a soap-manufacturing operation that had sales of $5,000 per day, half of which was net profit. All too soon, however, government authorities shut down his operations because he was undercutting the state-owned soap producers. After that, Thai started his second business, making plastic slippers. Again, because of his success, he attracted government attention. But this time, Thai offered to turn his business into a state-owned facility if the government would leave him alone, and his offer was accepted. In the late 1980s, as the Vietnamese government began easing up on economic controls, Thai saw his chance to once again start his own private company. His third start-up, Hunsan Company, a manufacturer and retailer of sports shoes, has since thrived. Hunsan's sales have topped $12 million. Thai hopes to become a viable player in the intensely competitive global shoe industry. He's living proof that the corridor principle—whereby one business naturally leads to another—is alive and well in the global marketplace.[23]

"Sometimes business opportunities come to you unexpectedly. The ability to recognize them takes an open mind, flexibility, a sense of adventure, and good business sense."

Competitive Advantage
INNOVATION AND SUSTAINABILITY

Creative Release

Once you have your business up and going (because of your creativity), how do you keep yourself and others in your business creative? Creativity is a matter of providing the proper business environment—your key to sustaining a competitive advantage. Almost every business has a creative pool with potential that is greater than its performance. How do you provide a spark that keeps your company's employees motivated and competitive?

- *Engage employees from all departments in brainstorming sessions.* People from different backgrounds and functional areas do perceive things differently—exactly what you want for creativity.
- *Set aside time to deliberately evoke creativity.* Experiment with different ways to generate ideas.
- *Add a creative exercise to meeting agendas.* Build time into meeting agendas for a creative exercise to encourage people to think innovatively.
- *Study creativity.* There is no shortage of books and articles on the subject.

- *Encourage and enable employees to pursue outside interests.* New experiences will create different mental associations and connections.
- *Create inspiring work space.* Creative environments give employees an outlet to refresh their minds.
- *Fund extracurricular projects or classes.* For example, an employee taking an improv comedy class or joining a Toastmasters club can improve confidence. Confidence is a foundation for creativity.
- *Try to fail quickly.* Once you find a good idea, don't move halfheartedly. When Scott Anthony, who owns Innosight Ventures, assigns one employee to thoroughly examine a company idea, he states, "When we think of an idea, we don't ask for a person to spend 5 percent of his or her time on it. We say, 'This is your focus for three to six months.' If you're serious, you need to commit them to it."

Sources: Jennifer Alsever, "How to Innovate," *Fortune Small Business,* October 2009, 68–75; Sara Wilson, "5 Ways to Spur Employee Creativity," *Entrepreneur,* March 2009, www.entrepreneur.com; Kim Orr, "Creativity Counts," *Entrepreneur's Startups,* May 2008, www.entrepreneur.com; and Mark Hendricks, "Brain Drain," *Entrepreneur,* November 2007, www.entrepreneur.com.

© Image Source/Getty Images

Getting Started

Most of the topics involved in starting your own business are covered in detail in other sections or entire chapters of this book. Let's look at what else is needed to get a business off the ground.

What Do You Do First?

You must first decide that you want to work for yourself rather than for someone else. You need to generate a number of ideas for a new product or service, something that people will buy, until you come up with the right opportunity that matches your skills and interests.

Whether you are starting a business because you have a product or service that is new to the world or because it is not available locally, you must get past some basic questions: Is there a need for this business? Is this business needed here? Is it needed now? These questions address the most critical concern in getting a business off the ground—the feasibility of your idea. Owning a business is a dream of many Americans, but there is usually a gap between that dream and bringing it to reality. Careful planning is needed to bridge that gap.

Reality Check

Urban Survival Shoes

Senior New York University students Susie Levitt and Katie Shea learned a lot as summer interns on Wall Street—one lesson was term sheets, another was that walking long blocks in high heels killed their feet. The petite powerhouses needed "emergency footwear" flat shoes that would fit into small handbags.

What Levitt and Shea designed was a stylish, foldable black ballet flat with a rubber sole that splits in the middle to fold in half and tuck into a tiny zippered pouch. The pouch unfolds into a tote bag for carrying high heels home. They gave their sole product an attractive name and price: Citisole at $24.99.

The pair proceeded to write a business plan for a business course, set up an LLC named FUNK-

tional Enterprises, and protected their intellectual property through the help of another professor in a patent protection class. To hit their target retail price that had to cut costs as much as possible—eventually finding a contract manufacturer in Ningbo, China, to produce their initial 1,000 pairs. Channels of distribution include sororities and other student groups in return for 10 percent of the proceeds to donate to charity to help fulfill their community service requirements. Boutiques across the country and their Web site www.citisoles.com help make sure the new business is off and running.

Sources: Joel Holland, "Putting Your School to Work," *Entrepreneur*, December 2009, 78; Katie Shea and Susie Levitt, "Alibaba's Newpreneur of the Year Essay," www.inc.com/newpreneur; Lore Croghan, "Businesses Get the Old College Try," *New York Daily News*, June 1, 2009, 4; and Meghan Casserly, "For Commuters, Choice in Footwear," *Forbes*, June 1, 2009, www.forbes.com.

Susie Levitt and Katie Shea created Citisole shoes to relieve businesswomen from painful cross-town walks in high heels.

© David Lang

Importance of Planning to a Start-up

Before you launch your business, you should write a comprehensive *business plan* (see Chapter 4). A business plan not only helps you determine the direction of your business and keeps you on track after it opens, but also will be required if you need to borrow money to start your business. It shows your banker that you have seriously evaluated the business opportunity and considered how you will be able to pay back the loan.

In addition to writing your business plan, you need to decide and record other important steps in starting your business.

- *Market analysis.* For your small business to be successful, you must get to know your market by gathering and analyzing facts about your potential customers so as to determine the demand for your product. Market analysis takes time and effort, but it does not have to be statistically complex or expensive. Who will buy your product? What do your customers have in common with one another? Where do they live? How much will they spend?

- *Competitive analysis.* Your business needs a competitive advantage that separates it from your competitors. Before you can develop your own uniqueness, you need to know what other businesses do and how they are perceived. An exercise to help you remove some of the subjectivity of the competitive analysis process begins with you identifying four of your direct competitors and setting up a grid on which you will rank your business as it compares to those competitors.

- *Start-up costs.* How much money will you need to start your business? Before you can seek funding, you must itemize your expected expenses (see Figure 7.4). Although some of these expenses will be ongoing, others will be incurred only when you start the business. There will be many expenses that you do not expect; therefore, add 10 percent to your subtotal to help offset them.

- *Capital equipment assets.* Assets such as computers, office equipment, fixtures, and furniture—capital equipment assets—have a life of more than one year. List the equipment you need along with the rest of your start-up costs. Beware of the temptation to buy the newest, most expensive, or fastest equipment available before you open your doors. You don't have any revenue yet, and more small businesses have failed due to lack of sales than due to lack of expensive "goodies." Is good used equipment available? Should you lease rather than buy? If sales do materialize, you can replace used equipment with new items by paying for them from actual profits.

- *Legal form of business.* As discussed in Chapter 2, when starting a business you need to consider the appropriate legal form of business: sole proprietorship, partnership,

FIGURE 7-4

How Much Money Will You Need?

Initial Capital Item	Estimated Cost
Capital equipment	
	_____
	_____
	_____
Beginning inventory	_____
Legal fees	_____
Accounting fees	_____
Licenses and permits	_____
Remodeling and decorating	_____
Deposits (utilities, telephone)	_____
Advertising (preopening)	_____
Insurance	_____
Start-up supplies	_____
Cash reserve (petty cash, credit accounts)	_____
Other expenditures:	_____
	_____
	_____
Subtotal start-up expenses:	$ _____
Add 10% safety factor:	_____
TOTAL START-UP EXPENSES	$ _____

or corporation. Your decision will be based on tax considerations, personal liability, and cost and ease of organizing.

- *Location of business.* Consider how important the location of your business is to your customers (see Chapter 13). If customers come to your business, your location decision is critical. If your business comes to them, or if you don't meet with customers face to face, location is a less critical decision.
- *Marketing plan.* The marketing decisions you need to make before you open your business include who your customers are, how you will reach your potential customers, what you will sell them, where it will be available, and how much it will cost (see Chapter 11).

As you see, some important aspects of starting your business are not included in the business plan. Now let's look at what your business will focus on, how you will approach customer service, what licenses you will need to acquire, and what kinds of taxes you must withhold to begin business.

operational excellence
Creates a competitive advantage by holding down costs to provide customers with the lowest-priced products.

product leaders
A business that creates a competitive advantage based on providing the highest-quality products possible.

How Will You Compete?

Before you begin your small business, consider what you want to be known for. Because no business can be all things to all people, you need to determine what your customers value and then strive to exceed their expectations. For instance, if your customers value low prices, you must set up your business to cut costs wherever possible, so that you can keep your prices low. If your customers value convenience, you need to set up your business with a focus on providing speed and ease of use for them.

In providing value to your customers, we can identify three grounds on which companies compete: operational excellence, product leadership, and customer intimacy.[24] In choosing to focus on one of these disciplines, you are not abandoning the other two. Instead, you are defining your position in consumers' minds. Visualize your choice by picturing each discipline as a mountain on which you choose to compete by raising the expectation levels of customers in that area (see Figure 7.5). By becoming a leader in that discipline, you will be better able to defend against competing companies below you on that figurative mountain.

Companies that pursue **operational excellence** know that their customers value low price, so they concentrate on the efficiency of their operations in an effort to hold down costs. They don't have the very best products or cutting-edge innovations. Instead, they strive to offer good products at the lowest price possible. Dell Computer is an example of a company that competes on operational excellence.

Companies that are **product leaders** constantly innovate to make the best products available even better. This kind of commitment to quality is not inexpensive, but product leaders know that price is not the most important factor to their customers. New Balance athletic shoes are known for their technical excellence, not for their inexpensive price or their customer service.

"It used to be all about truth and justice. Now, mostly I fight for market share."

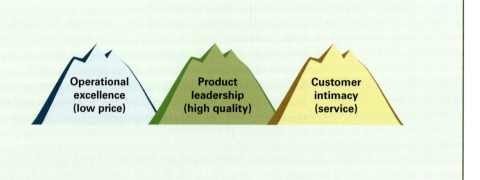

FIGURE 7-5

On Which Mountain Will You Compete?

When Setting up Your Small Business, You Must Decide How You Will Satisfy Your Customers. Do You Need to Offer Them the Best Product, the Best Price, or the Best Service?

Operational excellence (low price)

Product leadership (high quality)

Customer intimacy (service)

customer intimacy
Maintaining a long-term relationship with customers through superior service that results in a competitive advantage.

Companies that focus on developing ***customer intimacy*** are not looking for a one-time sale. Rather, they seek to build a long-term, close working relationship with their customers. Their customers want to be treated as if they are the company's only customer. The Lands' End operator you speak with on the telephone sees records of clothing sizes, styles, and colors from your previous orders as soon as you call. Customer-intimate companies offer specific rather than general solutions to their customers' problems.

ENTREPRENEURIAL SNAPSHOT

Über Inventor—Old School

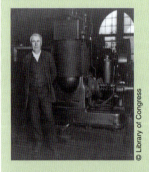
© Library of Congress

In a chapter on starting a business from scratch based on innovation, it seems appropriate to profile one of the greatest inventors of all time—Thomas Edison. Born in 1847, Edison had very little formal education. In fact, he was homeschooled by his mother.

The list of inventions and companies that Edison created is far too long to fully discuss here, but his 1,093 patents remain a record. Go to http://inventors.about.com/library/inventors for a description of all his patents.

Edison's first patent was for an "electrographic vote-recording machine" to be used in the House of Representatives to end long sessions of filibustering and expedite the political process. Members of Congress were amazed by the technology but ultimately rejected the invention. Edison then vowed to never again invent anything that was neither practical nor marketable. That approach made Edison more of an entrepreneur than an inventor—inventors are typically more interested in seeing what they can make rather than what will sell.

Contrary to popular belief, Edison did not "invent" the light bulb. Instead, he improved upon a 50-year-old idea to develop the first device that was even remotely practical for home use. Imagine the challenge he faced in bringing his works to market. To make money from incandescent lighting, for example, he had to first develop the following:

- The parallel circuit
- A durable light bulb
- An improved dynamo
- The underground conductor network
- Devices for maintaining constant voltage
- Safety fuses and insulating materials, and light sockets with on-off switches

Fortunately, Edison did consider the market value of his inventions. For example, he founded General Electric, he created the first motion pictures, and he made the first sound recording. Remember his many contributions as you listen to MP3s while on your way to see the latest action-adventure movie.

Sources: Daniel Wren and Ronald Greenwood, *Management Innovators: The People and Ideas That Have Shaped Modern Business* (New York: Oxford University Press, 1998), 16–24; and Mary Bellis, "The Inventions of Thomas Edison," www.inventors.about.com.

Customer Service

Your business relationship with your customers does not end with the sale of your product or service. Increasing your level of customer service and adopting professional standards in this area are critical endeavors, especially in an industry where all competitors appear to be the same. Satisfying the customer is not a means to achieve a goal—*it is the goal.* Customer service can be your competitive advantage.

The importance of a start-up business providing an emphasis on the highest-quality customer service cannot be overstated. Very often the difference between one business and another is the people in it—and the way they treat customers. What is really different between car rental companies? They have basically the same cars. The prices, contracts, and advertisements are all nearly identical. The difference appears when someone answers the telephone. How long does it take to answer? Is the person's voice pleasant and professional, or hostile and bored? Does he have quick access to the information that the customer called for, or does he offer to call back and never does? Does she take the time to understand the customer's needs and make truly helpful suggestions, or does she just try to push any car on the customer? Customer service can be a huge competitive advantage.[25]

> *"Very often the difference between one business and another is the people in it—and the way they treat customers"*

Licenses, Permits, and Regulations

If your business has no employees, you have fewer legal requirements to meet. First, let's look at the common requirements for all businesses. You need to file your business name with the secretary of state of the state in which you are forming your business. This step ensures that the name you have chosen for your business is not registered by another company. If it is, you will have to find another name for your business.

You must obtain the appropriate local licenses from the city hall and county clerk's office before you start your business. Find out if you can operate your business in the location you have picked by checking local zoning ordinances. You may need a special permit for certain types of businesses. For example, if your business handles processed food, it must pass a local health department inspection.

Most states collect sales tax on tangible property sold. If your state does, you must apply for a state sales-tax identification number to use when paying the sales taxes you collect. Contact the department of revenue in your state for information regarding your requirements. Many types of businesspeople, such as accountants, electricians, motor vehicle dealers, cosmetologists, and securities dealers, require specific licenses. These licenses are obtained from the state agency that oversees the particular type of business.

Very few small businesses are likely to need any type of federal permit or license to operate. If you will produce alcohol, firearms, tobacco products, or meat products, or give investment advice, contact an attorney regarding regulations.

Taxes

When your business begins operation, you must make advance payments of your estimated federal (and possibly state) income taxes. Individual tax payments are due in four quarterly installments—on the fifteenth day of April, June, September, and January. It is important that you remember to set money aside from your revenues so that it will be available when your quarterly taxes are due. The Internal Revenue Service is not known for its sense of humor if funds are not available.

If your business is a sole proprietorship, you report your self-employment income on IRS Form 1040 Schedule C or C-EZ, or Schedule F if your business is farming. A partnership reports partnership income on IRS Form 1065, and each partner reports her individual share of that income on Schedule SE and Schedule E. Corporations file tax returns on IRS Form 1120. Any payment in excess of $600 made for items like rent, interest, or services from independent contractors must be shown on Form 1096, and copies of Form 1099 must be sent to the people you paid.

When you begin employing other people, you become an agent of the U.S. government and must begin collecting income and Social Security taxes. You must get a federal employer identification number, which identifies your business for all tax purposes. Your local IRS office can supply you with a business tax kit that contains all of the necessary forms. You must withhold 7.51 percent of an employee's wages for Social Security tax, and you must pay a matching 7.51 percent employer's Social Security tax. You pay both halves of the tax on a quarterly basis when you submit your payroll tax return.

independent contractor
A person who is not employed by a business and, unlike employees, is not eligible for a benefit package.

If a person provides services to your business but is not an employee, he is considered to be an *independent contractor*. Because independent contractors are considered to be self-employed, you do not have to withhold Social Security taxes, federal or state income taxes, or unemployment taxes from their earnings—an obvious advantage to you. Because of the advantage of classifying a person as an independent contractor rather than an employee, the IRS imposes stiff penalties on businesses that improperly treat employees as independent contractors.

You must deposit a percentage of each employee's earnings for federal and state unemployment tax purposes with a federal tax deposit coupon. The federal unemployment tax rate is 6.2 percent of the first $7,000 per employee, but a credit of up to 5.4 percent is allowed for state unemployment tax. In reality, only 0.8 percent goes toward the federal tax. The state rate you pay depends on the amount of claims filed by former employees. The more claims, the higher your unemployment tax will be, within certain limits.

Summary

1. Discuss the advantages and disadvantages of starting a business from scratch.

When starting a business from scratch, the small business owner is free to establish a distinct competitive advantage. There are no negative images or prior mistakes to overcome, as may occur when purchasing an existing business. The creation of a new business builds pride of ownership. However, the risk of failure is higher for a start-up because there are more uncertainties regarding the size and existence of a market for the business.

2. Describe types of new businesses and discuss the characteristics commonly shared by fast-growth companies.

E-businesses have completely changed the small business landscape. Other types of new businesses include home-based businesses and part-time businesses. Some small businesses start with the intention of becoming hyper-growth companies. These companies are generally led by teams of people with prior experience in starting that type of business (usually high-tech manufacturing). They are well financed and constantly looking for opportunities to expand into new markets.

3. Evaluate potential start-ups and suggest sources of business ideas.

When a new product idea is introduced to the market, the window of opportunity is open the widest (assuming it is a product that people want and will buy), because little competition exists. As a product progresses through the product life cycle, the window of opportunity closes, as more competition enters the market and demand declines.

Most people get ideas for new businesses from their prior employment. Turning a hobby or outside interest into a business is also a common tactic. Ideas may come from other people's suggestions or spring from information gained while taking a class. Sometimes business ideas even occur by chance.

4. Explain the most important points to consider when starting a new business.

The entrepreneur needs to begin by questioning the feasibility of her idea. Then, to bridge the gap between dream and reality, careful planning is needed. Entrepreneurs need to carefully consider the costs of starting a new business, and they must analyze the market and competitive landscape to ensure that their competitive advantage really exists.

Providing customers with outstanding service during and after the sale of a product is of utmost importance in business start-ups. Customer service is the basis for establishing a long-term relationship with customers.

Start-ups also have legal requirements. Entrepreneurs must file the business name with the state of origin and obtain local business licenses and any industry-specific permits required. They must also apply for a tax identification number to collect and process sales taxes, if necessary.

Questions for Review and Discussion

1. Compare and contrast the advantages and disadvantages of starting a business from the ground up. Be sure to include the different types of businesses in your analysis.
2. Define *hyper-growth* companies, and evaluate the reasons for their phenomenal rate of growth. What are the most valid explanations for the rate of success found in these companies?
3. Explain the concept of *window of opportunity* as it relates to new start-ups, from idea conception through the final decision about whether to turn the idea into a reality.
4. Entrepreneurs get their ideas for business start-ups from various sources. Name these sources, and identify the ones most likely to lead to success.
5. Give some examples of things the new entrepreneur should immediately investigate to ensure to the maximum extent possible that the business will "get off the ground."
6. Is a business plan really necessary for a very small start-up business? How much market analysis and competitive analysis should the new entrepreneur conduct prior to start-up?
7. What are some of the tangible resources that the new entrepreneur might need in order to go into business? What are some options for obtaining capital for a business that is brand-new and therefore has no financial history?
8. After start-up, what is the *single* most important tool the small business owner has at his disposal to ensure the success of the business? Why is it so crucial?
9. What are some examples of consumer preferences and values? What are some examples of things the new business owner can do to ensure capturing some of the market for the good or service being produced?
10. Discuss the legal ramifications of starting your own business. Where should the new entrepreneur seek information and advice regarding laws that govern the type of business that is being promoted?

Questions for Critical Thinking

1. What criteria do you see as most critical in differentiating an idea from an opportunity?
2. Many entrepreneurs test the waters of a market by starting a sideline business. What are the advantages and disadvantages of selling items on Internet auctions like eBay? Is a person who regularly has 20 or 25 items for sale at any given time an entrepreneur? What types of products would be most appropriately sold in this manner?

What Would You Do?

Carrie Ann thinks she has identified a hot opportunity. She has watched the demand for tattoos and body art increase over the last several years. Carrie Ann believes that this trend is now leveling off and that in the near future many people who have gotten tattoos will want them removed. In anticipation, she has developed a nonsurgical approach to tattoo removal that consists of a cream applied to the tattoo. The area is then covered with gauze, and the cream must be reapplied every day for two weeks. At the end of two weeks, the tattoo is gone. A tube of Carrie Ann's cream will retail for about $50.

Questions

1. Carrie Ann is concerned about the timing of her product's introduction. She is not sure the window of opportunity is open wide enough at this time for her business to succeed, but she worries that if she waits for the opportunity to develop more fully, another product will beat her cream to market. How would you advise her in her opportunity analysis?

2. Carrie Ann's business could become a fast-growth player as described in this chapter. What would she need to do to become a fast-growth company?

Financial and Legal Management

As a small business owner, you will need to depend on the advice of several professionals—most significantly, accountants, lenders, and lawyers. To make the best decisions for your business based on their advice, however, you need a thorough understanding of accounting systems, financial management, and the law. You have to understand your own accounting system and financial statement analysis, ways to finance your business, and the laws and regulations that apply to your business. **Chapter 8** covers accounting systems and financial statements and their use, **Chapter 9** discusses small businesses' financial needs, and **Chapter 10** examines the legal environment of small business.

8

Accounting Basics

CHAPTER LEARNING OUTCOMES

After reading this chapter, you should be able to:

1. Discuss the importance and uses of financial records in a small business.

2. Itemize the accounting records needed for a small business.

3. Explain the 11 ratios used to analyze financial statements.

4. Illustrate the importance of and procedures for managing cash flow.

So why should a small business owner, busy with developing a product or service, marketing, hiring employees, and the host of other tasks necessary for the success of the company worry about the accounting records and review the financial statements? After all, isn't that what the accountant is hired to do? The accounting records that become the necessary information for the financial statements can provide important and timely information that small business owners need in order to make appropriate decisions. The information can also be used to do quick checks and make sure the

company is on track to make a profit. In fact, analyzing the financial statements can be a bit like playing detective.

For example, when Krispy Kreme Doughnuts was founded in 1937 by Vernon Rudolph in Winston-Salem, North Carolina, the doughnuts were produced to sell to local grocery stores. The doughnuts soon became so popular that Vernon cut a hole in the wall of the building where he was producing the doughnuts so he could sell directly to the customer—a doughnut drive-through. With the popularity of the doughnut, expansion soon occurred with the majority of the new stores started as franchises. Today, Krispy Kreme has 582 stores located in 18 countries around the world with the majority of those stores (499) franchise stores.

So if a prospective small business owner was considering opening a Krispy Kreme franchise, what pieces of financial detective work might they want to consider, particularly after seeing a 2008 headline in the *Wall Street Journal* stating that Krispy Kreme had posted profits but sales were down. How could this statement be true, and where could an answer to that question be found?

A company's financial statements can provide a prospective franchisee a wealth of information. Looking at the Annual Reports for Krispy Kreme located at www.sec.gov, some interesting pieces of information come to light. According to the 2010 Annual Report, the company counts as revenue four areas: company store sales, domestic franchise revenue, international franchise revenue, and KK supply chain revenue. Digging back a bit further, the 2007 *Annual Report* has a section that contains details on the KK Supply Chain, which includes the statement "KK Supply Chain produces doughnut mixes and manufactures our doughnut-making equipment, which all factory stores are required to purchase" (*Annual Report*, Form 10-K, pp. 4–5). Another statement is made that all franchisees are required to purchase the doughnut mix and doughnut-making machines from Krispy Kreme.

So now after performing a little financial detective digging and delving into some financial statements, could it be that as long as Krispy Kreme was opening new franchises and selling the required equipment to those franchises, revenues were increasing, even if the sales of doughnuts were dropping? Since the KK Supply Chain was counted as revenue, the dollars that franchises were spending were helping to increase revenues. However, a prospective franchisee would be more concerned about doughnut sales since that would be the profit producer for the small business owner. As Americans become more health conscious, doughnuts are certainly not on the menu and Krispy Kreme doughnut sales fell. This trend focused on more healthy food choices was further highlighted in early 2010 with First Lady Michelle Obama's "Let's Move" campaign. So, maybe with this new information provided by the financial statements, a prospective franchisee might want to more carefully consider this business opportunity.

Financial statements can provide a wealth of information for small business owners interested in franchising or small business owners as they compare their company to a much larger company. This process and these financial documents, as well as ratio analysis, will be further discussed in the chapter. Good luck playing financial detective.

Sources: *Annual Reports,* Form 10-K, Krispy Kreme found at www.sec.gov/edgar, http://www.krispykreme.com/history.html, http://investor .krispykreme.com/overview.cfm; Jennifer Hoyt, "Krispy Kreme Posts Profit, but Sales Keep Weakening," *Wall Street Journal*, June 10, 2008, http://online.wsj.com; and Janet Adamy, "First Lady Girds to Fight Fat," *Wall Street Journal*, February 9, 2010, http://online.wsj.com.

Small Business Accounting

Are you intimidated by the thought of accounting systems, with row after row and column after column of numbers? If you are, you aren't alone. But you shouldn't be frightened by or dread the numbers of your business, because accounting isn't about making rows and columns of numbers. Rather, it is about organizing and communicating what's going on in your business. Think of numbers as the language of business.

Computers help us take piles of raw *data* and turn them into usable *information* with which to make managerial decisions. For example, consider a marketing research project you have conducted. You have received thousands of completed questionnaires, each with 20 responses. You would have a very difficult time interpreting these thousands of pages because they contain raw, unprocessed data. If you were to enter all of these data into a statistical program on a computer, however, you could organize them into means, trends, and a few meaningful numbers—in other words, into *information* that would enable you to make marketing decisions.

Accounting systems accomplish a similar purpose. Think of the many piles of checks, receipts, invoices, and other papers your business generates in a month as data. Everything you need to know about the financial health of your business is contained in those piles, but it is not in an easily usable form. Accounting systems transform piles of data into smaller bites of usable information by first recording every transaction that occurs in your business in *journals*, then transferring (or posting) the entries into *ledgers* (both of which are described in this chapter). The process is basically the same whether you use pencil and paper or an accounting program on a personal computer. From the ledger you make *financial statements* like a balance sheet, income statement, and statement of cash flow. These statements communicate how your business is faring much better than the stacks of papers with which you started.

In the last step in the accounting process, you take certain numbers from your financial statements to compute key *ratios* that can be compared to industry averages or historical figures from your own business to help you make financial decisions. The intent of this chapter is not to turn you into an accountant, but rather to help you understand the communication process—or accounting language—better (see Figure 8.1). The accounting process helps you to translate numbers—the language of business—into plain English.

So how is a new entrepreneur supposed to get the accounting process started? How can you create an orderly system from nothing without having prior expertise in accounting? Many business owners start by purchasing a simple accounting software package (see Manager's Notes, "Small Business Dashboard"). Another stellar piece of advice is to pay an accounting firm that specializes in small businesses to set up your accounting system. You don't have to use the firm to handle all of your accounting needs like payroll preparation, tax form preparation, and creation of monthly financial statements, although you could. Money would be wisely spent getting a system that will work for your business from the very beginning—as opposed to throwing all receipts, invoices, and paperwork into a shoebox and panicking when the time comes to file quarterly taxes. Do yourself and your business a favor, and get started correctly by using the services of a professional.

Yet another reason why small businesses need the services of an accountant is that the Sarbanes-Oxley Act of 2002 set new financial reporting requirements for companies in an increased effort to prevent fraudulent reporting.[1] Section 404 of this act has specific implications for small businesses, which have been hit harder by these regulatory requirements due to the implementation costs involved. There was discussion as of spring 2010 to exempt smaller companies from these new requirements.[2] A recent survey of

accounting

The system within a business for converting raw data from source documents (like invoices, sales receipts, bills, and checks) into information that will help a manager make business decisions.

"The accounting process helps you to translate numbers—the language of business—into plain English."

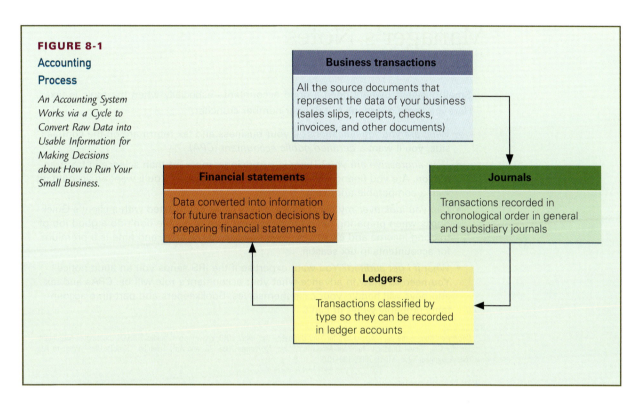

FIGURE 8-1

Accounting Process

An Accounting System Works via a Cycle to Convert Raw Data into Usable Information for Making Decisions about How to Run Your Small Business.

Business transactions

All the source documents that represent the data of your business (sales slips, receipts, checks, invoices, and other documents)

Journals

Transactions recorded in chronological order in general and subsidiary journals

Ledgers

Transactions classified by type so they can be recorded in ledger accounts

Financial statements

Data converted into information for future transaction decisions by preparing financial statements

small business owners by Intuit Professional Accounting Solutions revealed that tax advice is the primary service for which these businesspeople rely on their accountants. Financial statement preparation, bookkeeping, and payroll also rank highly as reasons to consult an accountant,[3] as well as assisting with other financial areas such as obtaining financing, cost controls, and financial decision making.[4]

How Important Are Financial Records?

Financial records are important to businesses for several reasons. Remember when we discussed common reasons for failure of small businesses in Chapter 1? Most of the mismanagement decisions that spell the doom of many small businesses are related to financial and accounting issues.

All too often, the last thing small business owners think of is careful accounting, but it should really be the first issue addressed. While you are plagued with a lot of worries—from making payroll to buying products to selling your services—you can put yourself at a competitive disadvantage by not being accounting oriented from the beginning. Many small business owners don't hire an accountant right away because they are afraid of the cost, but many accounting firms specialize in small businesses and are available at reasonable prices. It's like the advice you have probably heard your whole life: Getting things right the first time costs less than fixing mistakes the second or third time.

Accurate Information for Management

You need to have accurate financial information to know the financial health of your business. To make effective management decisions, you must know things like how much your accounts receivable are worth, how old each account is, how quickly your inventory is turning over, which items are not moving, how much your firm owes,

Manager's Notes

Ask ...

Small business owners need a good accountant—especially when the topic is taxes. Here are some questions to ask your number cruncher:

- *What are your qualifications?* If your business and tax return are on the complex side, you'll want a *certified public accountant (CPA)*.
- *How aggressive are you?* There is surprisingly more art than science in tax preparation. Are you financially conservative or aggressive? You'll want an accountant with a comparable approach.
- *Can you look over my QuickBooks?* Many CPAs get irritated with a client's QuickBooks when preparing tax returns because a lot of people don't do a good job of tracking income and expenses. Fixing messes takes time, and time is a premium for accountants in tax season.
- *What if I get audited?* You want expertise if the IRS sends you an audit notice. You need to know in advance what your accountant's role will be. CPAs and tax attorneys will handle your case themselves. Bookkeepers and part-time accountants probably won't or can't.

Sources: "Choose the Right Accountant for Your Business," *Inc.,* April 2010, www.inc.com/guides/2010/04/choosing-an-accountant; Jennifer Gill, "Smart Questions for Your Accountant," *Inc.,* November 2006, 36; and Amy Feldman, "SpecTaxUlar—What to Ask Your Accountant," *Inc.,* March 2006, 100–107.

when debts are due, and how much your business owes in taxes and FICA (Social Security taxes). Good records are needed to answer these and many other similar questions. Without good records, these questions are impossible to answer. Accurate financial records also allow you to identify problems and make needed changes before the problems become a threat to your business.

Banking and Tax Requirements

The information on your financial statements is needed to prepare your tax returns. If the Internal Revenue Service audits your business, you will be expected to produce the relevant accounting records and statements.

Bankers and investors use your financial statements to evaluate the condition of your business. If you need the services of either, you must not only produce statements, but also be ready to explain and defend their contents.

Small Business Accounting Basics

The accounting system provides you with information for making decisions about your small business. To access this information, you need to understand which entry systems you can use and how accounting equations work. Your accounting system should be easy to use, accurate, timely, consistent, understandable, dependable, and complete.

Double- and Single-Entry Systems

Accounting systems revolve around three elements: assets, liabilities, and owner's equity. *Assets* are what your business owns. *Liabilities* are what your business owes. *Owner's equity* is what you (the owner) have invested in the business (it can also be called *capital* or *net worth*).

assets
Any resource that a business owns and expects to use to its benefit.

liabilities
A debt owed by a business to another organization or individual.

owner's equity
The amount of money the owner of a business would receive if all of the assets were sold and all of the liabilities were paid.

double-entry accounting

An accounting system in which every business transaction is recorded in an asset account and a liability or owner's equity account so that the system will balance.

single-entry accounting

An accounting system in which the flow of income and expenses is recorded in a running log, basically like a checkbook.

As the name implies, with a **double-entry accounting** system, all transactions are recorded in two ways—once as a *debit* to one account and again as a *credit* to another account. Every "plus" must be balanced by a "minus." So, for example, a transaction shows how assets are affected on one side and how liabilities and owner's equity are affected on the other.

A double-entry accounting system increases the accuracy of your system and provides a self-checking audit. If you make a mistake in recording a transaction, your accounts will not balance, indicating that you need to go back over the books to find the error. Debits must always equal credits. To increase an asset, you debit the account. To increase a liability or equity, you credit the account.

A **single-entry accounting** system does exist and may be used by small sole proprietorships. With a single-entry system, you record the flow of income and expenses in a running log, basically like a checkbook. It allows you to produce a monthly statement but not to make a balance sheet, an income statement, or other financial records. The single-entry system is simple but not self-checking, as is a double-entry system.

Popular computer programs like Quicken employ a single-entry accounting system. These programs provide attractive features like the ability to track expense categories, post amounts to those accounts, and print reports, but they are still pretty much electronic check registers. Many small, one-person businesses begin with them because of their simplicity and then graduate to more powerful, full-feature systems like the Peachtree or Great Plains accounting programs. Other advantages include the ability to integrate your online bank account, create a tracking system of who has done what in record keeping, and also limit or provide access of information to specific employees or your accountant.[5] There is no one-size-fits-all computer accounting program that is suitable for all small businesses.[6] You may have to adjust your system as your business grows.

On the subject of beginning simply: *Always* use separate checkbooks for your business and your personal life. Avoid the temptation to combine the two by thinking that "the business money and personal money are all mine—I'll just keep them together." At some point you will need to separate them, which can be very difficult to do later. Also, write checks instead of paying for items with cash. They serve as an accurate form of record keeping. Finally, reconcile your bank accounts monthly, and make sure all errors are corrected.

Manager's Notes

Small Business Dashboard

Accounting systems of any type provide information for managers to make informed decisions. Think of driving a vehicle—your eyes are constantly moving from gauges to horizon to gauges to mirror. Right? Same thing in driving a business—eyes watching many things and directions at once, and accounting provides the dashboard.

Computerized accounting can save time in entering accounting data and generating accounting statements, can improve the traceability of income and expenses (which could prove important for audits), and can increase the timeliness and frequency of your accounting statements.

Selecting appropriate hardware and accounting software can pose a major challenge. To facilitate your decision making, let's examine some of the better-known accounting packages.

QuickBooks Pro (www.quickbooks.com).
America's #1 small business financial software helps make your business more profit-able. New features show you exactly where your business stands and saves you time to focus on your business: organize your finances all in one place; manage customer, vendor, and employee data; save money—track every dollar in and out; know where your business stands financially. A powerful feature of this package is the ability for multiple users to access files to increase collaboration and productivity stands with real-time reports.

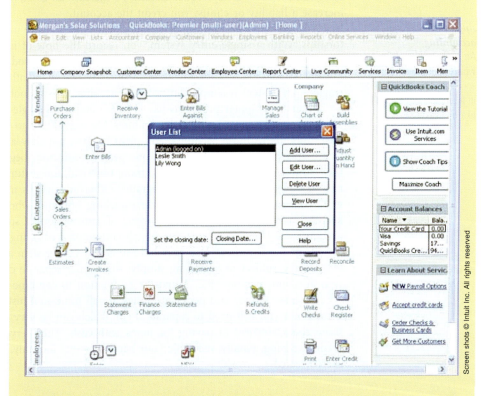

Sage Peachtree Complete Accounting (www.peachtree.com).
Peachtree Complete Accounting, a powerful, comprehensive accounting package, has added features like job costing, time and billing, in-depth inventory capabilities, and analysis tools. Its multi-user option helps improve productivity while providing screen-level security and a clear audit trail. Save time with simplified dashboards, management centers, integration with Microsoft Excel, and comparative budgeting. The Internal Accounting Review helps you track errors and deter fraud. Available with more than 100 customizable business reports and financial statements.

Keep in mind that your choice of an accounting software package depends on the size of your business and its accounting needs. Generally speaking, the more features and customization options provided in the package, the more expensive it will be and the more complex to install and use.

A new breed of online financial management software has emerged in the last few years that takes advantage of the growing confidence that businesses are devel-oping in the Web as a safe business environment. Web-hosted software is known as "software in the cloud."

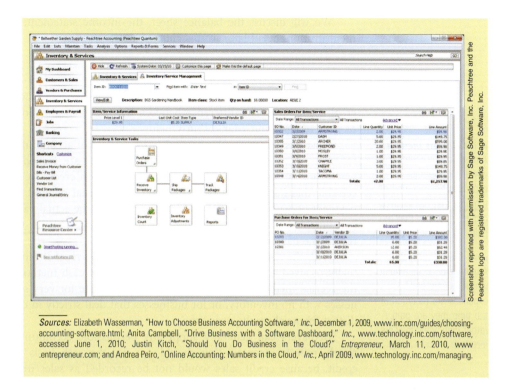

Sources: Elizabeth Wasserman, "How to Choose Business Accounting Software," *Inc.*, December 1, 2009, www.inc.com/guides/choosing-accounting-software.html; Anita Campbell, "Drive Business with a Software Dashboard," *Inc.*, www.technology.inc.com/software, accessed June 1, 2010; Justin Kitch, "Should You Do Business in the Cloud?" *Entrepreneur*, March 11, 2010, www.entrepreneur.com; and Andrea Peiro, "Online Accounting: Numbers in the Cloud," *Inc.*, April 2009, www.technology.inc.com/managing.

Accounting Equations

As stated earlier, numbers are the language of business. Three equations are the foundation of that language:

$$\text{Assets} = \text{Liabilities} + \text{Owner's equity}$$

$$\text{Profit} = \text{Revenue} - \text{Expenses}$$

$$\text{Cash flow} = \text{Receipts} - \text{Disbursements}$$

The first equation, Assets = Liabilities + Owner's equity, is the basis of the *balance sheet.* Any entry that you make on one side of the equation must also be entered on the other side to maintain a balance. For example, suppose you have a good month and decide to pay off a $2,000 note you took out at the bank six months ago. You would credit your cash account (an asset) by $2,000 and debit your notes payable account (a liability) by $2,000. Your balance sheet remains in equilibrium. Of course, any equation can be rearranged if you understand it. For example:

$$\text{Owner's equity} = \text{Assets} - \text{Liabilities}$$

You can also think of this equation as follows:

$$\text{What you have} = \text{What you own} - \text{What you owe}$$

The second equation, Profit = Revenue − Expenses, represents the activity described on the *income statement.* In other words, the money you get to keep equals the money your business brings in minus what you have to spend.

The third equation, Cash flow = Receipts − Disbursements, is the basis of the *cash-flow statement.* The money you have on hand at any given time equals the money you bring in minus what you have to pay out.

We will discuss the balance sheet, the income statement, and the cash-flow statement in more detail later in this chapter.

Cash and Accrual Methods of Accounting

One decision you need to make in your accounting system is whether to use cash or accrual accounting. The difference between the two relates to how each shows the timing of your receipts and your disbursements.

Most businesses use the **accrual-basis method** of accounting. With this method, you report your income and expenses at the time they are earned or incurred, rather than when they are collected or paid. Sales you make on credit are recorded as accounts receivable that have not yet been collected. The accrual method also allows you to record payment of expenses over a period of time, even if the actual payment is made in a single installment. For example, you may pay for insurance once or twice a year, but you can record the payments on a monthly basis.

With the **cash-basis method** of accounting, you record transactions when cash is actually received and expenses are actually paid. The cash method is simpler to keep than the accrual method. Although it may be appropriate for very small businesses, for businesses with no inventory, or for businesses that deal strictly in cash, the cash method can distort financial results over time.

Taxpayers can generally adopt any permissible accounting method, as long as it clearly reflects income.[7] You should not use the cash basis if your business extends credit, because credit sales would not be recorded as sales until you receive payment. Also, your accounts payable would not be recorded as an expense until the bill is paid.

What Accounting Records Do You Need?

To turn data into management information, you need to follow certain guidelines, or standards, called **generally accepted accounting principles (GAAP)**. The group that monitors the appropriateness of these principles is the Financial Accounting Standards Board (FASB).[8] The GAAP guidelines are intended to create financial statement formats that are uniform across industries. Because business is complex, flexibility in GAAP methods is acceptable as long as consistency is maintained within the business.

Journals and Ledgers Your accounting actually begins when you record your raw data, from sources such as sales slips, purchase invoices, and check stubs, in journals. A *journal* is simply a place to write down the date of your transactions, the amounts, and the accounts to be debited and credited. You will have several journals, such as sales, purchases, cash receipts, and cash disbursements journals.

At some regular time interval (daily, weekly, or monthly), you will post the transactions recorded in all your journals in a general ledger. A *general ledger* is a summary book for recording all transactions and account balances. One of the advantages of using a computerized accounting system is that it can perform the monotonous task of posting electronically. To speed the posting process and to facilitate access to accounts, each account is assigned a two-digit number. The first digit indicates the class of the account (1 for assets, 2 for liabilities, 3 for capital, 4 for income, and 5 for expenses). The second digit is assigned to each account within the class. For example, your cash account could be assigned account number 11. The first 1 shows that the account is an asset, whereas the second 1 means that it is your first asset listed. Your inventory could be assigned the account number 13, meaning that it is the third asset listed.

At the end of your accounting period or fiscal year, you will close and total each individual account in your general ledger. At this point, or at any time you wish if you

---

accrual-basis method
A method of accounting in which income and expenses are recorded at the time they are incurred rather than when they are paid.

cash-basis method
A method of accounting in which income and expenses are recorded at the time they are paid, rather than when they are incurred.

generally accepted accounting principles (GAAP)
Standards established so that all businesses produce comparable financial statements.

journal
A chronological record of all financial transactions of a business.

general ledger
A record of all financial transactions divided into accounts and usually compiled at the end of each month.

are using a computerized accounting package, you can prepare your financial statements to see where your business stands financially. The three most important statements for providing financial information about your business are the income statement, the balance sheet, and the statement of cash flow.

income statement
A financial statement that shows the revenue and expenses of a firm, allowing you to calculate the profit or loss produced in a specific period of time.

Income Statement The **income statement**, also called the *profit-and-loss (P&L) statement*, summarizes the income and expenses that your company has totaled over a period of time (see Figure 8.2). The income statement illustrates the accounting equation of Profit = Revenue − Expenses. This statement can generally be broken down into the following sections:

- Net sales
- Cost of goods sold

FIGURE 8-2
Stereo City Income Statement

Stereo City Income Statement for Year Ended, December 31, 2012

		Percentage of Sales
INCOME		
Net Sales	$450,000	100.00
Cost of Goods Sold	270,000	60.00
GROSS PROFIT ON SALES	$180,000	40.00
EXPENSES		
Selling Expense		
Advertising	$ 12,000	2.67
Delivery and Freight	10,000	2.22
Sales Salaries	25,000	5.56
Miscellaneous Selling Expenses	1,000	0.22
Administrative Expense		
Licenses	$150	0.03
Insurance	2,400	0.53
Nonsales Salaries	38,000	8.44
Payroll Taxes	6,300	1.40
Rent/Mortgage	12,400	2.76
Utilities	6,000	1.33
Legal Fees	1,500	0.33
Depreciation	42,000	9.33
Miscellaneous Administrative Expenses	500	0.11
TOTAL EXPENSES	$157,250	34.94
INCOME FROM OPERATIONS	$ 22,750	5.06
OTHER INCOME		
Interest Income	$300	0.07
OTHER EXPENSES		
Interest Expense	$ 15,000	3.33
NET PROFIT (LOSS) BEFORE TAXES	$ 8,050	1.79
INCOME TAXES	$ 3,220	0.72
NET PROFIT (LOSS) AFTER TAXES	$ 4,830	1.07
NOTE:		
Cash Flow from Operations Equals Net Profit or Loss after Taxes plus Depreciation	$ 46,830	

- Gross margin
- Expenses
- Operating Income
- Net income (or loss)

Not only does the income statement show an itemization of your sales, cost of goods sold, and expenses, but it also allows you to calculate the percentage relationship of each item of expense to sales. Including these percentages on your financial statements produces a **common-size financial statement**. Common-size financial statements are valuable tools for checking the efficiency trends of your business by measuring and controlling individual expense items.

Consider the example of Stereo City, a retail company that sells home electronic equipment. Stereo City's net sales for the accounting period covered by Figure 8.2 were $450,000. The business had a 40 percent gross profit (or margin), which means that, out of net sales, Stereo City acquired $180,000 with which to cover its operating expenses. Total expenses were $157,250 (34.94 percent of sales). After adding interest income and deducting interest expenses and taxes, the company's net profit—the bottom line—was $4,830.

common-size financial statement
A financial statement that includes a percentage breakdown of each item.

Balance Sheet While the income statement shows the financial condition of your business over time, the **balance sheet** provides an instant "snapshot" of your business at any given moment (usually at the end of the month, quarter, or fiscal year; see Figure 8.3). A balance sheet has two main sections—one showing the assets of the business and one showing the liabilities and owner's equity of the business. As explained previously under "Accounting Equations," these two sides must balance.

On Stereo City's sample balance sheet, you will see a column of percentages of total assets, liabilities, and owner's equity. As with the common-size income statement, these percentages on the common-size balance sheet can indicate accounts and areas that are out of line compared to industry averages, such as those published by Financial Research Associates, Robert Morris Associates, or trade associations.

balance sheet
A financial statement that shows a firm's assets, liabilities, and owner's equity.

Statement of Cash Flow The **statement of cash flow** highlights the cash coming into and going out of your business. It is summarized by the accounting equation of Cash flow = Receipts – Disbursements (see Figure 8.4). The importance of tracking and forecasting your cash flow is difficult to overstate because it is often more critical to survival of the business than profits. Many businesses show considerable profit but have problems paying their bills—meaning that they have a cash flow problem.

It is common for new businesses to experience a situation in which more cash goes out than comes in, which is called *negative cash flow*. This condition is not too alarming if it happens when the business is very young or if it happens only occasionally. However, if you experience negative cash flow regularly, you may be *undercapitalized*, which is a serious problem.[9] Managing your cash flow will be covered in more detail later in this chapter.

statement of cash flow
A financial statement that shows the cash inflows and outflows of a business.

What If You Are Starting a New Business? If you are starting a new business, you don't have historical data to compile in financial statements. Even so, you must estimate how much money you will need, what your expenses will be at different sales levels, and how much money you can expect to make. Financial planning and budgeting are important parts of the business-planning process. Making financial projections can reveal whether you should even start the business. Are the financial risks you are about to take worth the *realistic* return you can expect? Such projections are made in **pro forma financial statements**, which are either full or partial estimates, because you are

pro forma financial statements
Financial statements that project what a firm's financial condition will be in the future.

FIGURE 8-3

Stereo City Balance Sheet

Stereo City Balance Sheet December 31, 2012

Stereo City Balance Sheet

December 31, 2012

ASSETS		Percentage of Total Assets
Current Assets:		
Cash	$ 3,500	1.08
Accounts Receivable	12,000	3.71
Inventory	125,000	38.64
Prepaid Expenses	5,000	1.55
Short-Term Investments	10,000	3.09
Total Current Assets	$155,500	48.07
Fixed Assets:		
Building	$150,000	46.37
Equipment	25,000	7.73
Leasehold Improvements	20,000	6.18
Other Fixed Assets	15,000	4.64
Gross Fixed Assets	$210,000	64.91
Less: Accumulated Depreciation	42,000	12.98
Net Fixed Assets	$168,000	51.93
Total Assets	$323,500	100.00

LIABILITIES AND OWNERS' EQUITY		Percentage of Liability and Equity
Current Liabilities:		
Accounts Payable	$ 75,000	23.18
Accruals	7,500	2.32
Current Portion of Long-Term Debt	17,500	5.41
Other Current Liabilities	5,000	1.55
Total Current Liabilities	$105,000	32.46
Long-Term Liabilities:		
Mortgage Loan	$ 93,000	28.75
Term Loan	39,500	12.21
Total Long-Term Liabilities	$132,500	40.96
Total Liabilities	$237,500	73.42
Owners' Equity		
Paid-in Capital	$ 75,000	23.18
Retained Earnings	11,000	3.40
Total Owners' Equity	$ 86,000	26.58
Total Liabilities and Owners' Equity	$323,500	100.00

"Making financial projections can reveal whether you should even start the business. Are the financial risks you are about to take worth the realistic return you can expect?"

making projections rather than recording actual transactions. (*Pro forma* is Latin for "for the sake of form.") Because these statements help you determine your future cash needs and financial condition, a new business should prepare them at least every quarter, if not every month.

In preparing pro forma statements, you need to state the assumptions you are making for your projections. How did you come up with the numbers? Did you grab them out of the air? Did the owner of a similar (but noncompeting) business share his actual numbers for you to use as a base? Are they based on industry averages, such as *Robert Morris Associates' RMA Annual Statement Studies?* The closer the numbers are to what will really happen, the more useful the statements are for decision making.

FIGURE 8-4
Stereo City Cash Flow Statement

Stereo City Statement of Cash Flows for Year Ending, December 31, 2012

	October	November	December	January	February	March	April	May	June	July	August	September	Total
Cash Receipts:													
Retail Receipts (a)	$46,875	$46,875	$46,875	$28,125	$28,125	$28,125	$37,500	$37,500	$37,500	$37,500	$37,500	$37,500	$450,000
Interest Income				100				100				100	300
Total Cash Receipts	$46,875	$46,875	$46,875	$28,225	$28,125	$28,125	$37,500	$37,600	$37,500	$37,500	$37,500	$37,600	$450,300
Cash Disbursements:													
Cost of Goods Sold (b)	$28,125	$28,125	$28,125	$16,875	$16,875	$16,875	$22,500	$22,500	$22,500	$22,500	$22,500	$22,500	$270,000
Sales Expenses	2,403	2,403	2,403	1,562	1,562	1,562	2,083	2,083	2,083	2,083	2,083	2,090	25,000
Advertising	1,000	1,000	1,000	1,000	1,000	1,000	1,000	1,000	1,000	1,000	1,000	1,000	12,000
Insurance	0	400	0	0	400	0	0	400	0	0	400	0	2,400
Legal and Accounting	0	0	375	0	0	375	0	0	375	0	0	375	1,500
Delivery Expenses	1,042	1,042	1,042	625	625	625	833	833	833	833	833	834	10,000
**Fixed Cash Disbursements	4,328	4,328	4,328	4,328	4,328	4,328	4,328	4,328	4,328	4,328	4,328	4,328	51,930
Mortgage (c)	1,033	1,033	1,033	1,033	1,033	1,033	1,033	1,033	1,033	1,033	1,033	1,037	12,400
Term Loan (d)	1,466	1,466	1,466	1,466	1,466	1,466	1,466	1,466	1,466	1,466	1,466	1,466	17,592
Total Cash Disbursements	$39,596	$40,197	$39,972	$26,889	$27,489	$27,264	$33,243	$33,843	$33,618	$33,243	$33,843	$33,630	$402,822
Net Cash Flow	$ 7,279	$ 6,679	$ 6,904	$ 1,337	$ 637	$ 862	$ 4,258	$ 3,758	$ 3,883	$ 4,258	$ 3,658	$ 3,971	$ 47,478
Cumulative Cash Flow	$ 7,279	$13,957	$20,861	$22,197	$22,834	$23,695	$27,953	$31,710	$35,593	$39,850	$43,508	$47,478	
**FCD													
Fixed Cash Disbursements:													
Utilities	$ 6,000												
Non-sales Salaries	38,000												
Payroll Taxes and Benefits	6,300												
Licenses	150												
Misc. Selling Expenses	1,000												
Miscellaneous	480												
Total FCD	$51,930												
Avg FDC per month	$ 4,328												
Cash on Hand:													
Opening Balance	$ 3,500	$10,779	$17,457	$24,361	$25,697	$26,334	$27,195	$31,453	$35,210	$39,093	$43,350	$47,008	
- Cash Receipts	46,875	46,875	46,875	28,225	28,125	28,125	37,500	37,600	37,500	37,500	37,500	37,600	
- Cash Disbursements	(39,596)	(40,197)	(39,972)	(26,889)	(27,489)	(27,264)	(33,243)	(33,843)	(33,618)	(33,243)	(33,843)	(33,630)	
Total = New Cash Balance	$10,779	$17,457	$24,361	$25,697	$26,334	$27,195	$31,453	$35,210	$39,093	$43,350	$47,008	$50,978	

(a) This assumes that all sales are collected in the month the sale is made.

(b) This is just the Cost of Goods row from the monthly income projection worksheet. Cost of Goods is calculated as 40 percent of the estimated total sales for the month.

(c) The mortgage payments (including both principal and interest) are for a $93,000 15-year loan at 10.6 percent. You can use the spreadsheet function @PMT() to calculate this:

Payment = @PMT(loan amount, rate per month, number of months)

= @PMT ($93,000, .106/12, 15*12)

(d) The loan is $39,500 for 2 ½ years at 8.5 percent. The amount shown includes both principal and interest and is calculated as follows: Payment = @PMT (39,500, .085/12, 2.5*12)

(e) A typical strategy for established businesses with fairly predictable revenues and expenses is to open an account such as a "Money Market Deposit Account" with their bank. This account, which is interest earning, is used to store excess cash balances and cover cash shortages.

Financial statements provide information to make informed business decisions just like instruments in your car help you stay in control—and out of trouble.

Using Financial Statements to Run Your Small Business

Creating financial statements is one thing, but using them to make informed decisions to run your small business is another. Here's an analogy: When you are driving a vehicle, how do you know when something needs attention? By looking at the instruments on your dashboard. Think of financial statements as your instruments for running your business. Just as in driving, to make correct management decisions you need to know what to look at and when to check. Here's a *Financial Status Checklist* for checking the gauges:

DAILY

1. Check your cash balance on hand.
2. Check your bank balance.
3. Calculate daily summaries of sales and cash receipts.
4. Note any problems in your credit collections.
5. Record any money paid out.

WEEKLY

1. *Cash flow*. Update a spreadsheet of regular receipts and disbursement entries. The discipline required by this endeavor will help you see what is going on in your business and help you to plan for any cash deficiencies.
2. *Accounts receivable*. Note especially slow-paying accounts.
3. *Accounts payable*. Note discounts offered.
4. *Payroll*. Calculate the accumulation of hours worked and total payroll owed.
5. *Taxes*. Note when tax items are due and which reports are required.

MONTHLY

1. If you use an outside accounting service, provide records of your receipts, disbursements, bank accounts, and journals.
2. Review your income statement.
3. Review your balance sheet.
4. Reconcile your business checking account.
5. Balance your petty cash account.
6. Review federal tax requirements and make deposits.
7. Review and age your accounts receivable.

Analyzing Financial Statements

Your ability to make sound financial decisions will depend on how well you can understand, interpret, and use the information contained in your company's financial statements. This section gives an overview of the most common form of financial analysis: ratio analysis.

Reality Check

Do You Have a Business or a Hobby?

If your sideline business produces revenue but consistently loses money, be careful—the IRS could consider your writing, woodwork, artwork, or crafts to be a hobby. If your business is classified as a hobby, you can't deduct the related expenses. Business expenses are fully deductible on Schedule C of your tax return. If your direct costs exceed your business income, you can use that loss to offset your other income on Form 1040.

Hobby expenses can't be used to offset income or losses, even if they exceed the income from your hobby. How does the IRS determine whether you have a business or a hobby? The agency presumes that if you show a profit in three of the past five years, you have a business. If you fail the three-of-five-year test and can't demonstrate the following, you have a hobby. To classify your operation as a business, you have to prove a profit motive. You can do so by demonstrating that you:

- Conduct activity in a businesslike manner
- Devote a significant amount of time and effort to the activity
- Have expertise in the activity
- Had losses because of circumstances beyond your control
- Have tried to increase profitability by changing methods of operation
- Depend on income from the activity for your livelihood
- Have made a profit in the past
- Must engage in considerable activity that could not be considered "pleasurable" (such as cleaning animal stalls)

Source: Based on Janet Attard, "Don't Get Caught by the Hobby Trap," www .businessknowhow.com.

Ratio Analysis

Suppose that two entrepreneurs are comparing how well their respective businesses performed last year. The first entrepreneur, Ms. Alpha, determines that her store made 50 percent more profits last year than the store owned by the second entrepreneur, Mr. Beta. Should Ms. Alpha feel proud? To answer this question, we need more information.

The profit figures tell us only part of the story. Although generating 50 percent more profits *seems* good, we need to see how profit relates to other aspects of each business. For example, what if Ms. Alpha's store is four times the size of Mr. Beta's store? Or what if Ms. Alpha's store made three times as many sales as Mr. Beta's store? Now does 50 percent more profit seem as good?

The reality is that fair comparisons can be made only when we demonstrate the relationships between differing financial accounts of the businesses. The relationships that show the relative size of some financial quantity to another financial quantity of a firm are called *financial ratios*. Four important categories of financial ratios are the liquidity, activity, leverage, and profitability ratios.[10] It is important to use more than one ratio from each of the four categories of ratios and to use all categories when analyzing your company. Just like you check more than just the gas gauge on the car before a trip, each of the categories of ratios and the types of comparison provide differing insight into the financial workings of your business.

financial ratios
Calculations that compare important financial aspects of a business.

Using Financial Ratios

Financial ratios by themselves tell us very little. For purposes of analysis, ratios are useful only when compared to other ratios. Three types of ratio comparisons can be employed: benchmarking analysis, which compares firms to industry leaders; industry average analysis, which compares firms' financial ratios to the industry averages; and trend analysis, which compares a single firm's present performance with its own past performance, preferably for more than two years.

Benchmarking is taking an industry leader or major competitor, computing their ratios, and then comparing the small business to that firm. Since ratios take away the size differential, even a new start-up can compare itself to the best in the industry and set financial targets based upon industry leaders.

Industry average analysis is often done by comparing an individual firm's ratios against the standard ratios for the firm's industry. Such industry ratios may be found in resources available in most college or large public libraries. Look for Robert Morris Associates' *RMA Annual Statement Studies* or Dun & Bradstreet's *Industry Norms and Key Business Ratios*. Another good source is *Financial Studies of the Small Business* from Financial Research Associates.

Table 8.1 shows an example of the financial ratio information located in *Robert Morris Associates' RMA Annual Statement Studies*. At the top of the page are column headings showing the amount of sales for your company. Choose the column that matches the sales figure on your income statement. Looking down the column you will find three sets of numbers for each ratio listed. These three numbers provide a range so you can determine how close your company is to meeting the industry numbers. For example, the current ratio for the industry listed on the table shows .7, 1.5, and 3.9. If the current ratio for your company is 1.6, you are falling right in the middle of the numbers but are not anywhere close to the top or the best in the industry. Your company could easily use more liquidity. When using the RMA, make sure you calculate your ratios using the same formulas as the RMA. The formulas are listed on the page.

Trend analysis involves comparing your own numbers to your numbers from last year and the year before. Trends can be seen using this analysis that can show a small business owner where changes need to occur in order to keep the company profitable. If there is potential trouble in any of the four main areas of analysis (liquidity, activity, leverage, and profitability), managers will have time to correct these problems before the problems become overbearing. The key to potential solutions is found in the ratios themselves. For example, if the trend analysis shows that the firm's liquidity is diminishing, the managers will want to take action to enhance the firm's liquidity position.

---

benchmarking
A comparison of a firm's financial ratios to industry leaders.

industry average analysis
A comparison of a firm's financial ratios to the industry averages.

"The profit figures tell us only part of the story."

trend analysis
A comparison of a single firm's present performance with its own past performance, preferably for more than two years.

TABLE 8-1
Comparing Company and Industry Ratios

	STEREO CITY	INDUSTRY
Liquidity		
Current Ratio	1.48	1.60
Quick Ratio	0.29	0.50
Activity		
Average Collection	9.7	8.0
Total Asset Turnover	1.4	4.2
Leverage		
Debt Ratio	73.0	61.5
Times Interest Earned	1.5	6.1
Profitability		
Return on Assets*	1.49	6.2

*Uses pretax profit.
Source: Based on *RMA Annual Statement Studies* 2009, NAICS 443112 Retail Radio, Television, and Other Electronics Stores, 931.

Liquidity Ratios

liquidity ratios
Financial ratios used to measure a firm's ability to meet its short-term obligations to creditors as they come due.

Liquidity ratios are used to measure a firm's ability to meet its short-term obligations to creditors as they come due. *Liquidity* refers to how quickly an asset can be turned into the amount of cash it is actually currently worth —the more quickly it can become cash, the more liquid it is said to be. The financial data used to determine liquidity are the firm's current assets and current liabilities found on the balance sheet. There are two important liquidity ratios: the current ratio and the quick (or acid-test) ratio.

current ratio
A financial ratio that measures the number of times the firm can cover its current liabilities with its current assets.

Current Ratio The *current ratio* measures the number of times the firm can cover its current liabilities with its current assets. The current ratio assumes that both accounts receivable and inventory can be easily converted to cash. Current ratios of 1.0 or less are considered low and indicative of financial difficulties. Current ratios of more than 2.0 often suggest excessive liquidity that may be adverse to the firm's profitability.

$$\text{Current ratio} = \frac{\text{Current assets}}{\text{Current liabilities}}$$

Using Stereo City's balance sheet, we compute the company's current ratio as follows:

$$\frac{\$155,000}{\$105,000} = 1.48$$

Thus Stereo City can cover its current liabilities 1.48 times with its current assets. Another way of looking at this ratio is to recognize that the company has $1.48 of current assets for each $1.00 of current liabilities. When compared to the middle industry average number of 1.5 from the RMA Table, Stereo City is only off by two cents compared to the industry and far above the low number of 70 cents. So Stereo City is doing reasonably well in the area of liquidity, with some room for improvement, when including inventory in the calculation.

quick acid-test ratio
A financial ratio that measures the firm's ability to meet its current obligations with the most liquid of its current assets.

Quick Ratio The *quick (acid-test) ratio* measures the firm's ability to meet its current obligations with the most liquid of its current assets. The quick ratio is computed as follows:

$$\text{Quick ratio} = \frac{\text{Current assets} - \text{Inventory}}{\text{Current liabilities}}$$

Using the data from Stereo City's balance sheet, we compute the quick ratio as

$$\frac{\$155,000 - \$125,000}{\$105,000} = 0.29$$

Stereo City has only $0.29 in liquid assets for each $1.00 of current liabilities. The company obviously counts on making sales to pay its current obligations. When compared to the industry average of .60, Stereo City is much less liquid than other companies, and short-term creditors, like suppliers, may be concerned about the ability of Stereo City to pay its accounts payable on time.

activity ratios
Financial ratios that measure the speed with which various asset accounts are converted into sales or cash.

Activity Ratios

Activity ratios measure the speed with which various assets are converted into sales or cash. These ratios are often used to measure how efficiently a firm uses its assets. Four important activity ratios exist: inventory turnover, average collection period, fixed asset turnover, and total asset turnover.

inventory turnover
An activity ratio that measures the liquidity of the firm's inventory—how quickly goods are sold and replenished.

Inventory Turnover **Inventory turnover** measures the liquidity of the firm's inventory—how quickly goods are sold and replenished. The higher the inventory turnover, the more times the firm is selling, or "turning over," its inventory. A high inventory ratio generally implies efficient inventory management. Inventory turnover is computed as follows:

$$\text{Inventory turnover} = \frac{\text{Cost of goods sold}}{\text{Inventory}}$$

Using data from Stereo City's income statement and balance sheet, we compute the inventory turnover as

$$\frac{\$270{,}000}{\$125{,}000} = 2.16$$

Thus Stereo City restocked its inventory 2.16 times last year. When compared to the industry average turnover number of 8.7, Stereo City is not selling their products close to the number of times of the competition. Increasing sales should become a primary focus for the company.

average collection period
A measure of how long it takes a firm to convert a credit sale (internal store credit, not credit card sales) into a usable form (cash).

Average Collection Period The **average collection period** is a measure of how long it takes a firm to convert a credit sale (internal store credit, not credit card sales) into a usable form (cash). All firms that extend credit must compute this ratio to determine the effectiveness of their credit-granting and collection policies. High average collection periods usually indicate many uncollectible receivables, whereas low average collection periods may indicate overly restrictive credit-granting policies. The average collection period is computed as follows:

$$\text{Average collection period} = \frac{\text{Accounts receivable}}{\text{Average sales per day}}$$

Using the data from Stereo City's balance sheet and income statement, we compute the average collection period as

$$\frac{\$12{,}000}{\$450{,}000/365} = 9.93$$

Stereo City collects its receivables in fewer than 10 days. The industry average is 13.1 days, so it is taking Stereo City less time to collect credit sales than other companies in the industry, which should have a positive impact on cash flow.

fixed asset turnover
An activity ratio that measures how efficiently a firm is using its assets to generate sales.

Fixed Asset Turnover The **fixed asset turnover** ratio measures how efficiently the firm is using its assets to generate sales. This ratio is particularly important for businesses with a lot of equipment or buildings since it is measuring the effectiveness of these assets in generating sales. A low ratio can indicate that sales are off due perhaps to marketing efforts that are ineffective or that the equipment being used is older and requiring increasing downtime for maintenance. The fixed asset turnover ratio is calculated as follows:

$$\text{Fixed asset turnover} = \frac{\text{Sales}}{\text{Net fixed assets}}$$

Using the data from Stereo City's income statement and balance sheet, we compute the fixed asset turnover ratio as

$$\frac{\$450{,}000}{\$168{,}000} = 2.68$$

Stereo City turns over its net fixed assets 2.68 times per year, compared to the industry average of 33.5. This ratio shows that Stereo City is not using its fixed assets, property, plant, and equipment nearly as efficiently as the industry.

total asset turnover
An activity ratio that measures how efficiently the firm uses all of its assets to generate sales; a high ratio generally reflects good overall management.

Total Asset Turnover The **total asset turnover** ratio measures how efficiently the firm uses all of its assets to generate sales, so a high ratio generally reflects good overall management. A low ratio may indicate flaws in the firm's overall strategy, poor marketing efforts, or improper capital expenditures. Total asset turnover is calculated as follows:

$$\text{Total asset turnover} = \frac{\text{Sales}}{\text{Total assets}}$$

Using the data from Stereo City's income statement and balance sheet, we compute the total asset turnover as

$$\frac{\$450,000}{\$323,500} = 1.39$$

Stereo City turns its assets over 1.39 times per year, compared to the industry average of 3.5, which indicates that Stereo City has some major issues with the efficient use of its assets. If any of the other activity ratios are not on target, the total asset turnover ratio will be off also, so it is not surprising that this ratio confirms the activity problems Stereo City is currently experiencing.

Leverage Ratios

leverage ratios
Financial ratios that measure the extent to which a firm uses debt as a source of financing and its ability to service that debt.

Leverage ratios measure the extent to which a firm uses debt as a source of financing and its ability to service that debt. The term *leverage* refers to the magnification of risk and potential return that come with using other people's money to generate profits. Think of the increased power that is gained when a fulcrum is moved under a simple lever. The farther the fulcrum is from the point where you are pushing on the lever, the more weight you can lift. The more debt a firm uses, the more financial leverage it has. Two important leverage ratios are the debt ratio and the times-interest-earned ratio.

debt ratio
A leverage ratio that measures the proportion of a firm's total assets that is acquired with borrowed funds.

Debt Ratio The **debt ratio** measures the proportion of a firm's total assets that is acquired with borrowed funds. Total debt includes short-term debt, long-term debt, and long-term obligations such as leases. A high ratio indicates a more aggressive approach to financing and is evidence of a high-risk, high-expected-return strategy. A low ratio indicates a more conservative approach to financing. The debt ratio is calculated as follows:

$$\text{Debt ratio} = \frac{\text{Total debt}}{\text{Total assets}}$$

Using the data from Stereo City's balance sheet, we compute the debt ratio as

$$\frac{\$237,5000}{\$323,500} = 0.73$$

This ratio indicates that the company has financed 73 percent of its assets with borrowed funds. That is, $0.73 of every $1.00 of funding for Stereo City has come from debt.

times interest earned
A leverage ratio that calculates the firm's ability to meet its interest requirements.

Times-Interest-Earned Ratio **Times interest earned** calculates the firm's ability to meet its interest requirements. It shows how far operating income can decline before the firm will likely experience difficulties in servicing its debt obligations. A high ratio indicates a low-risk situation but may also suggest an inefficient use of leverage. A low ratio indicates that immediate action should be taken to ensure that no debt payments will go into default status. Times interest earned is computed as follows:

$$\text{Times interest earned} = \frac{\text{Operating income}}{\text{Interest expense}}$$

Using the data from Stereo City's income statement, we compute times interest earned as

$$\frac{\$22,750}{\$15,000} = 1.52$$

Thus the company has operating income 1.52 times its interest obligations compared to the industry average of 1.1 times. Stereo City can easily make its interest obligations compared to the industry, which will be viewed as a good sign by any potential lenders.

Profitability Ratios

profitability ratios
Financial ratios that are used to measure the ability of a company to turn sales into profits and to earn profits on assets and owner's equity committed.

Profitability ratios are used to measure the ability of a company to turn sales into profits and to earn profits on assets committed. Additionally, profitability ratios allow some insight into the overall effectiveness of the management team. There are three important profitability ratios: net profit margin, return on assets, and return on equity.

net profit margin
A profitability ratio that measures the percentage of each sales dollar that remains as profit after all expenses, including taxes, have been paid.

Net Profit Margin The **net profit margin** measures the percentage of each sales dollar that remains as profit after all expenses, including taxes, have been paid. This ratio is widely used as a gauge of management efficiency. Although net profit margins vary greatly by industry, a low ratio may indicate that expenses are too high relative to sales. Net profit margin can be obtained from a common-size income statement or computed with the following formula:

$$\text{Net profit} = \frac{\text{Net income}}{\text{sales}}$$

Using the data from Stereo City's income statement, we compute the net profit margin as

$$\frac{\$4,830}{\$450,000} = 0.0107$$

This company actually generates 1.07 cents of after-tax profit for each $1.00 of sales.

return on assets
A profitability ratio that indicates the firm's effectiveness in generating profits from its available assets; also known as *return on investment.*

Return on Assets Also known as *return on investment*, **return on assets** indicates the firm's effectiveness in generating profits from its available assets. The higher this ratio is, the better. A high ratio shows effective management and good chances for future growth. The return on assets is found with the following formula:

$$\text{Return on assets} = \frac{\text{Net profit after taxes}}{\text{Total assets}}$$

Using the data from Stereo City's income statement and balance sheet, we compute the return on assets as

$$\frac{\$4,830}{\$323,500} = 0.0149$$

This company generates approximately 1.5 cents of after-tax profit for each $1.00 of assets the company has at its disposal. The industry average is 2.5, again indicating that Stereo City may not effectively be using its assets compared to the industry.

return on equity

A profitability ratio that measures the return the firm earned on its owner's investment in the firm.

Return on Equity The **return on equity** measures the return the firm earned on its owner's investment in the firm. In general, the higher this ratio, the better off financially the owner will be. However, return on equity is highly affected by the amount of financial leverage (borrowed money) used by the firm and may not provide an accurate measure of management effectiveness. The return on equity is calculated as follows:

$$\text{Return on equity} = \frac{\text{Net profit after taxes}}{\text{Owner's equity}}$$

Using the data from Stereo City's income statement and balance sheet, we compute the return on equity as

$$\frac{\$4,830}{\$86,000} = 0.0562$$

This company generates a little more than 5.5 cents of after-tax profit for each $1.00 of owner's equity. This ratio tells a business owner if he or he is receiving enough return from invested money. Compared to the industry average of 41.8, Stereo City is not making a comparable return for its investors. In the Stereo City example, 5.5 percent return is not much for the risk involved. That $86,000 could be placed in a relatively safe investment like a corporate bond, where it could earn a much higher return with less risk. This kind of information can tell a business owner whether a business is a good investment compared with other alternative uses for her money.

After reviewing all the ratios, from the data we can conclude that Stereo City potentially has three major problems.

First, Stereo City's quick ratio is only about half the industry average. This could mean that the company has the possibility of liquidity issues if the inventory does not sell in a timely manner. Short-term creditors may be reluctant to extend credit for supplies being purchased, which would force Stereo City to a cash-only basis for purchases.

Second, Stereo City appears to have a problem with selling inventory. The company needs to focus on increasing sales and turning over their inventory. Increasing marketing efforts or training salespeople may both be options to fix this problem.

Third, Stereo City's total asset turnover, fixed asset turnover, and return on asset ratios are considerably below the industry averages. The likely cause is that the firm has insufficient sales to support the size of the business. The company must work harder to increase sales or more efficiently use its current assets. If the small business owner does not make productive changes soon, Stereo City may face serious financial difficulties and even closure of the business.

Because ratio analysis has revealed that Stereo City needs to increase its liquidity, increasing current assets (especially cash and short-term investments) and decreasing current liabilities are possible solutions. Any action that boosts the firm's liquidity helps to avoid the risk of Stereo City's becoming insolvent because of diminishing liquidity.

Reviewing financial ratios annually can help you circumvent difficult situations before they have the opportunity to occur. Thus ratio analysis allows small business owners and managers to become proactive directors of the financial aspects of their ventures.

If you find that you enjoy working with accounting information or creating accounting systems, you might even consider starting a small business to provide those services. Finding a unique accounting-services niche can be profitable. Consider, for instance, what Combined Resource Technology (CRT) of Baton Rouge, Louisiana, did. CRT started out as a real estate development company. However, when the oil and gas price crash battered Louisiana's economy, CRT found that it owed some $14 million to banks on loans it had taken out to buy a regional shopping center and several apartment buildings. To avoid failure of their business, CRT partners Darwyn Williams and Chris Moran had to do something quickly. Although their properties' values had plunged, the pair found that the tax assessor's property valuations hadn't changed. Out of desperation was born their new accounting-services business. In its new life, CRT peruses tax rolls to identify over-assessed properties and contacts the owners about getting the taxes reduced— for a fee, of course. CRT has since expanded its cost-reduction services beyond taxes, to include utilities, waste disposal, freight, leases, and any other areas where the firm can help business owners reduce costs. CRT provides a unique accounting service that others have been willing to pay for.[11]

Managing Cash Flow

Each business day, approximately a dozen U.S. small businesses declare bankruptcy. The majority of these business failures are caused by poor cash-flow management.[12] Companies from the smallest start-ups to the largest conglomerates all share the same need for positive cash flow. A company that does not effectively manage its cash flow is poised for collapse.

Cash Flow Defined

The accounting definition of **cash flow** is the sum of net income plus any noncash expenses, such as depreciation and amortization. This treatment of cash flow is largely misunderstood by many small business owners. A more "bottom-line" approach is to define cash flow as the difference between the actual amount of cash a company brings in and the actual amount of cash a company disburses in a given time period.

The most important aspects of this refined definition are the inclusion of the terms *actual cash* and *time period*. The goal of good cash flow management is to have enough cash on hand when you need it. It doesn't matter if your company will have a positive cash balance three months from now if your payroll, taxes, insurance, and suppliers all need to be paid today.

Cash flow management requires as much attention as developing new customers, perfecting products and services, and engaging in all other day-to-day operating activities. The basic strategy is to maximize your use of cash. This means not only ensuring consistent cash inflows, but also developing a disciplined approach to cash outflows.

Could your cash flow management system be computerized? As noted earlier in the chapter, single-entry general ledger accounting software packages are certainly easy to use. However, these packages can provide an unrealistic view of your business's cash flow. In a single-entry system, all cash coming into the business is put on the left-hand side of the ledger, and cash flowing out of the business appears on the right-hand side. However, if your business has accounts receivable or accounts payable, a single-entry system can fool you into thinking you have enough cash on hand to meet expenses or to pursue business expansion. Plante & Moran have an online tool available, their Liquidity Stress Test, located at http://stresstest.plantemoran.com. The results of this test can help a business to develop a plan for cash deficiencies, in order to more effectively manage cash flows.[13]

Cash Flow Fundamentals

The first step in cash-flow management is to understand the purpose and nature of cash flow. Why do you need cash flow? How is cash flow generated? How do firms become insolvent even though they are profitable? To answer these questions, we need to look at the motives for having cash, the cash-to-cash cycle, and the timing of cash inflows and outflows.

"A company that does not effectively manage its cash flow—by balancing its income and expenses on a day-to-day basis— is poised for collapse."

cash flow
The sum of net income plus any noncash expenses, such as depreciation and amortization, or the difference between the actual amount of cash a company brings in and the actual amount of cash a company disburses in a given time period.

Motives for Having Cash A firm needs cash for three reasons: (1) to make transactions, (2) to protect against unanticipated problems, and (3) to invest in opportunities as they arise. Of these, the primary motive is to make transactions—to pay the bills incurred by the business. If a business cannot meet its obligations, it is insolvent. Continued insolvency leads directly to bankruptcy.

Businesses, like individuals, occasionally run into unanticipated problems. Thefts, fires, floods, and other natural and human-made disasters affect businesses in the same way they affect individuals. Those businesses that have "saved for a rainy day" are able to withstand such setbacks. Those that have not planned ahead often suffer—and may even fail—as a result.

Finally, sometimes a business is presented with an opportunity to invest in a profitable venture. If the business has enough cash on hand to do so, it may reap significant rewards. If not, it has lost a chance to add to its cash flow in a way other than through normal operations.

Each of these three motives is important to understand, as they combine to create the proper mentality for the cash flow manager. If a firm does not proactively manage its cash flow, it will be exposed to many risks, any of which may spell disaster.

cash-to-cash cycle
The period of time from when money is spent on raw materials until it is collected on the sale of a finished good.

Cash-to-Cash Cycle The **cash-to-cash cycle** of the firm, sometimes known as the *operating cycle*, tracks the way cash flows through the business. It identifies how long it takes from the time a firm makes a cash outlay for raw materials or inventory until the cash is collected from the sale of the finished good. Figure 8.5 shows a typical cash-to-cash cycle.

The firm begins with cash that is used to purchase raw materials or inventory. It will normally take some time to manufacture or otherwise hold finished goods until they sell. As sales are made, cash is replenished immediately by cash sales, but accounts receivable are created by credit sales. The firm must then collect the receivables to secure cash.

The cash flow process is continuous, with all activities occurring simultaneously. When the process is operating smoothly, cash flow is easy to monitor and control. However, for most firms, it is often erratic and subject to many complications, which makes cash flow management a challenge.

Timing of Cash Flows The major complication of cash flow management is timing. While some cash inflows and outflows will transpire on a regular schedule (such as monthly interest income or payroll costs), other cash flows occur on no schedule whatsoever. For example, when a firm needs to make periodic purchases of capital equipment, which are not part of the daily cash-to-cash process, it will cause a major disruption in the firm's cash flow.

Even though a firm might send out all of its billings to credit customers at one time, you can be sure that these customers will not all pay at the same time. Uncollected

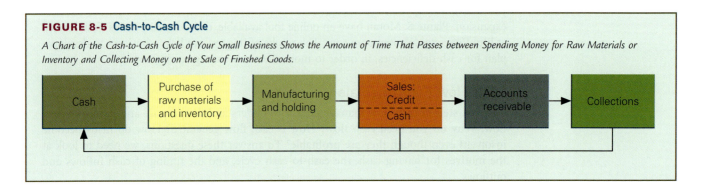

FIGURE 8-5 Cash-to-Cash Cycle

A Chart of the Cash-to-Cash Cycle of Your Small Business Shows the Amount of Time That Passes between Spending Money for Raw Materials or Inventory and Collecting Money on the Sale of Finished Goods.

Cash → Purchase of raw materials and inventory → Manufacturing and holding → Sales: Credit / Cash → Accounts receivable → Collections

receivables may count as revenue on an accrual-based income statement, but they are worthless from a cash flow standpoint until they turn into real money.

The small business owner needs to become well versed in the patterns of cash inflows and outflows of the firm. The nuances of timing become critical. A few tools are available that can assist in this process, which we will now discuss.

Cash Flow Management Tools

Once you have a good idea about the purpose and nature of cash flow, you are ready to take steps to manage it. Using cash budgets, aging schedules, and float to control the inflow and outflow of cash is paramount for effective management.

cash budgets
A plan for short-term uses and sources of cash.

Cash Budgets **Cash budgets** (also known as *cash forecasts*) allow the firm to plan its short-term cash needs, paying particular attention to periods of surplus and shortage. Whenever the firm is likely to experience a cash surplus, it can plan to make a short-term investment. When the firm is expected to experience a cash shortage, it can plan to arrange for a short-term loan.

Competitive Advantage
INNOVATION AND SUSTAINABILITY

Open-Book Management

Open-book management (OBM) is going strong, in spite of recessions and skeptics. Small businesses are finding that if employees have access to and understand financial statements, better decisions—from the kind of mechanic tape used to negotiating sales—can be made by employees. Once thought off-limits to all but owners, OBM encourages small business owners to share critical financial information with employees regularly, which then allows better decision making throughout the company. When employees know and understand the numbers, they can measure their contributions to the company's bottom line and assess how their performance can make a difference in those numbers.

One of the first proponents of OBM was Jack Stack, president and CEO of Springfield Remanufacturing Company. In *The Great Game of Business*, he stated that you need to teach employees the rules of the game, give them the information (the financials) they need to play the game, and make sure they share in the risks and rewards. A commercial aircraft supplier in Milwaukee, Tracer, found that by allowing employees access to financial information about the company, employees could make decisions even when the founder, Bill Morales, was not on site. It also helped the company to avoid layoffs in 2009 even when sales fell 30 percent. During that time,

employees found ways to cut costs, like lowering the utility bill from $5,000 a month to $900.

Employees at Texas Air Composites in Cedar Hill, Texas, found numerous ways to cut shop supplies, like finding tape that was $2.50 a roll instead of $15 that did the same job. Once employees became aware of the costs through OBM, they were willing to take steps to curtail costs. Even Tony Hsieh of Zappos.com fame has embraced OBM, sharing financial information not only with employees but also with suppliers. He feels that the more people looking over the financial information, the better.

OBM is all about giving employees not only access to financial information but also control and incentive to change that financial information to positively impact the company, which then also benefits the employee. According to the National Center for Employee Ownership, revenues for companies using OBM increased by 1.7 percent more each year. Over time, this makes a difference. So, small business owners, open up and let more eyes peruse those important financial numbers.

Sources: David Drickhamer, "Warehouse Software Firm Builds Open-Book Management Principles into Its Product," *Material Handling Management*, January 2006, 30–31; Jena McGregor, "Zappos' Secret: It's An Open Book," *BusinessWeek*, March 23, 2009, 62; Stan Luxenberg, "Open Those Books," *BusinessWeek*, Summer 2006 Small Biz Supplement, 32; and John Tozzi, "To Beat the Recession, Open Your Books," *BusinessWeek* Online, July 8, 2009, 13.

A cash budget typically covers a one-year period that is divided into smaller intervals. The number of intervals is dictated by the nature of the business. The more uncertain the firm's cash flows are, the more intervals are required. Using monthly intervals is common, but some firms require daily cash budgets.

The cash budget requires the small business owner to determine all the known cash inflows and outflows that will occur during the year. Both the amount of cash involved and the cycle's length of time must be disclosed. This information is then put into a format like that shown in Table 8.2. The table lists some of the most common types of cash inflows and outflows experienced by a typical small business. Its categories should be modified to fit the particulars of each individual business. The most important point is to include all relevant sources of and demands for cash.

TABLE 8-2
Cash Budget Format

	JANUARY	FEBRUARY	MARCH	APRIL	MAY
Beginning Cash					
Plus Receipts:					
Cash Sales					
Receivable Collections					
Interest					
Owner Contributions					
Other Receipts					
Total Receipts					
Minus Disbursements:					
Cash Purchases					
Payment of Accounts Payable					
Wages and Salaries					
Payroll Taxes					
Advertising					
Office Supplies					
Rent/Mortgage					
Utilities					
Telephone					
Insurance					
Legal/Accounting					
Taxes and Licenses					
Interest Payments					
Loan Principal Payments					
Dues and Subscriptions					
Travel					
Miscellaneous Disbursements					
Total Disbursements					
Ending Cash (Beginning Cash + Receipts − Disbursements)					

Many businesses find that adding a *reconciliation* component to the bottom of the cash budget is helpful. This reconciliation summarizes the total cash inflows and outflows for the period. When this summary is combined with the beginning cash balance, you have the current cash status of the firm. Because there will be some minimum cash balance required to begin the next period, the ending cash figure is compared to this minimum figure. If there is a positive difference (ending cash minus minimum cash balance), the firm has cash to invest. If there is a negative difference, the firm must arrange for financing before beginning the new cycle.

By forecasting the inflows and outflows of cash, the small business owner will have a picture of when the firm will have cash surpluses and cash shortages. This knowledge allows the cash flow to be managed proactively rather than reactively.

Cash budgeting is, however, not always easy to do. As noted earlier, there are always disruptions to the process. Unforeseen cash outflows and inconsistent cash inflows plague many small businesses.

aging schedules
A listing of a firm's accounts receivable according to the length of time they are outstanding.

macro-aging schedule
A list of accounts receivable by age category.

micro-aging schedule
A list of accounts receivable showing each customer, the amount that customer owes, and the amount that is past due.

Aging Schedules *Aging schedules* are listings of a firm's accounts receivable according to the length of time they are outstanding. A *macro-aging schedule* simply lists categories of outstanding accounts with the percentage of accounts that falls within each category (see Table 8.3). This schedule allows the small business owner to forecast the collection of receivables. Suppose that the firm made credit sales of $10,000 three months ago, $12,000 two months ago, and $5,000 last month, and that it predicts it will make credit sales of $7,500 this month. Expected receivables collections for this month will be: $(0.25 \times \$7,500) + (0.5 \times \$5,000) + (0.2 \times \$12,000) + (0.05 \times \$10,000) = \$7,275$. This is the amount the cash flow manager will place in the Receivables Collection slot of the cash budget for that month.

The *micro-aging schedule* offers another approach to showing receivables. This technique lists the status of each credit customer's account (usually in alphabetical order). It allows the small business owner to concentrate his collection efforts on the specific companies that are delinquent in their payments (see Table 8.4).

This aging schedule is invaluable for controlling receivables. Not only do you have the same information as shown in the macro-aging schedule, but you also have specific information on each credit customer that will enable you to make decisions about extending credit in the future.

Strategies for Cash Flow Management

Once the small business owner understands some of the basic tools of cash flow management, she should develop a strategy for the firm. Which accounts should be concentrated on? At what intervals are cash budgets needed? What information is available or needs to be made available to track cash flow? Is the firm's bank providing services to assist in cash flow management? The answers to these questions, among others, help shape cash flow strategy.

TABLE 8-3 Macro-Aging Schedule	AGE OF RECEIVABLES	PERCENTAGE
	0–30 days	25
	31–60 days	50
	61–90 days	20
	Over 90 days	5

TABLE 8-4 Micro-Aging Schedule				PAST-DUE DAYS			
CUSTOMER	**AMOUNT**	**CURRENT**	**1-30**	**31-60**	**61-90**	**+90**
Aardvark Supply	$1,500	$1,000	$200	$500	$2,250	
Beaver Trucking	2,250					
Canary Labs	1,000	500	500			
...						
Total	11,000	5,000	750	3,000	2,250	
Percentage	100	45	7	27	21	

Accounts Receivable The first place to look for ways to improve cash flow is in accounts receivable. The key to an effective cash flow management system is the ability to collect receivables quickly. If customers abuse your credit policies by paying slowly, any future sales to them will have to be COD (cash on delivery) until they prove that you will receive your money in a reasonable amount of time.

Receivables have inherent procedural problems in most small businesses. Information often gets lost or delayed between salespeople, shipping departments, and the accounting clerks who create the billing statements. Most firms bill only once a month and may delay that step if workers are busy with other activities.

Managing your accounts receivable is an important step in controlling your cash flow. You need a healthy stream of cash for your small business to succeed. The following tips can help you accelerate the flow:

- *Establish sound credit practices.* Never give credit until you are comfortable with a customer's ability to pay. You can get a credit report from Dun & Bradstreet to indicate a purchasing company's general financial health.
- *Process orders quickly.* Ensure that each order is handled on or before the date specified by the customer. Unnecessary delays can add days or weeks to customer payments.
- *Prepare the invoice the same day as the order is received.* Especially on large amounts, don't wait until some "billing date" just because that's when you normally do it.
- *Mail the invoice the same day it is prepared.* The sooner the bill is in the mail, the sooner it is likely to be paid. When possible, send the invoice with the order.
- *Offer discounts for prompt payment.* Give customers an incentive to pay sooner. Trade discounts typically amount to 1 to 2 percent if the bill is paid within 10 days.
- *Aggressively follow up on past-due accounts.* Call the customer as soon as a bill becomes past due, and ask when payment can be expected. Keep a record of customer responses and follow-up calls. For customers with genuine financial problems, try to get even a small amount each week.
- *Deposit payments promptly.* Accelerate receipt of checks by using a bank lockbox.
- *Negotiate better terms from suppliers and banks.* Improving cash flow also includes slowing the rate of money going out.
- *Keep a tight control on inventory.* Items sitting in inventory tie up money that could be used elsewhere. Be sure that deep discounts on volume purchases can financially justify the drain they will put on cash flow.
- *Review and reduce expenses.* Take a hard look at all expenses. What effect will an expense have on your bottom line?

© Polka Dot Images/Getty Images

Inventory in a warehouse is just like cash sitting on a shelf.

- *Pay bills on time, but not before they are due.* Unless you receive enough trade discount incentive to pay early, don't rush to send payments.
- *Be smart in designing your invoice.* Make sure that the amount due, due date, discount for early payment, and penalty for late payment are clearly laid out.[14]

Inventory Inventory is another area that can drain cash flow. According to James Howard, chairman of the board of Asset Growth Partners, Inc., a New York City financial consulting firm for small businesses, inventory costs are often overlooked or understated by many small businesses. "A typical manufacturing company pays 25 to 30 percent of the value of the inventory for the cost of borrowed money, warehouse space, materials handling, staff, lift-truck expenses, and fixed costs."[15]

Cash flow determines how much inventory can safely be carried by a firm while still allowing sufficient cash for other operations. The inventory-turnover ratio lends insight to this situation. If, for example, a firm has an inventory ratio of 12, it has to keep only one month's worth of projected sales in stock before enough cash returns to pay for the next month's worth of inventory. By comparison, if the firm has a ratio of 4, it must keep three months' worth of projected sales on the shelves. This system ties up cash for as much as 90 days. In this case the firm should try to find suppliers that have terms extending to 90 days. Otherwise, it may have to borrow to meet current cash needs. The cash flow management goal is to commit just enough cash to inventory to meet demand.

Accounts Payable Another cash flow management tool is trade terms. Under trade terms a small business owner works with his suppliers to establish when, how much, and under what conditions payments are made to suppliers. This allows small business owners to more effectively control cash outlays, since a major part of cash often goes to paying suppliers. Vendors, when approached up-front, are often more than willing to work out a payment schedule that benefits the small business owner if it also insures they get paid on a basis they can depend upon.[16]

Banks Ideally, your bank should be your partner in cash flow management. The small business owner should request the firm's bank to provide an *account analysis*. This analysis shows the banking services the business used during the month, the bank's charge for each service, the balances maintained in all accounts during the month, and the minimum balances required by the bank to pay for the services.

A review of the account analysis will indicate whether any excess account balances are on deposit. These should immediately be removed and invested. Also, your firm may be better off removing all account balances that are earning little or no interest and reinvesting them at higher rates, even if it means having to pay fees for bank services.

Finally, determine how quickly checks that your firm deposits in the bank become available as cash. Banks normally require delays of up to two business days. They should have an *availability schedule*, and the small business owner needs to request one from each bank in the area to determine whether his bank is competitive. Remember—the faster a deposited check becomes available as cash, the sooner your business has use of the money for other purposes.

Other Areas of Cash Flow Concern Although receivables, inventory, and bank services are the most likely places on which to concentrate cash flow management strategies, several other areas also deserve attention:

1. *Compensation.* Look for duplication of effort and lack of productivity within the firm's workforce. Cut personnel hours in those areas to save on wage and payroll tax costs.
2. *Supplies.* Review all petty cash accounts. Show employees the cost of supplies by marking the cost of each item, such as tablets, on the boxes.
3. *Deliveries.* Keep track of local delivery costs to the business. It may be cheaper to hire a part-time worker to pick up supplies than to pay other companies to deliver items.
4. *Insurance.* Ask insurance carriers about ways to reduce premiums. One independent grocery store reduced premiums for its stock personnel by 15 percent simply by requiring them to wear supports while working.
5. *Borrowing.* Take the cost of borrowing into account when determining operational expenses. Even short-term loans can have a large effect on profit and cash flow.

The process of cash flow management may seem confusing to you in the beginning, but you may find it relatively easy to monitor once everything is in place. Armed with a cash budget, aging schedules, and a set of feasible strategies, you can avoid cash flow problems and maximize your use of this precious resource.

Summary

1. Discuss the importance and uses of financial records in a small business.

You need financial records so you can make managerial decisions on topics concerning how much money is owed to your business, how much money you owe, and how to identify financial problems before they become serious dilemmas. Financial records are also needed to prepare your tax returns and to inform your banker and investors about your business's financial status. Without accurate financial records, you cannot exercise the kind of clear-sighted management control needed to survive in a competitive marketplace.

2. Itemize the accounting records needed for a small business.

The accounting records of your small business need to follow the standards of generally accepted accounting principles (GAAP). From your source documents, such as sales slips, purchase invoices, and check stubs, you should record all the transactions in journals. Information from your journals should then be posted in (transferred into) a general ledger. Financial statements like your balance sheet, income statement, and statement of cash flow are produced from the transactions in your general ledger.

3. **Explain the 11 ratios used to analyze financial statements.**

   Ratio analysis enables you to compare the financial condition of your business to its performance in previous time periods or to the performance of similarly sized businesses within your industry. Four important types of financial ratios discussed in this chapter are liquidity (current and quick, or acid-test, ratios), activity (inventory turnover, average collection period, fixed asset turnover, and total asset turnover), leverage (debt and times interest earned), and profitability ratios (net profit margin, return on assets, and return on equity).

4. **Illustrate the importance of and procedures for managing cash flow.**

   Cash flow is the difference between the amount of cash actually brought into your business and the amount paid out in a given period of time. Cash flow represents the lifeblood of your business because if you do not have enough money to pay for your operating expenses, you are out of business.

Questions for Review and Discussion

1. How can financial records allow you to identify problems in your business?
2. Assets = Liabilities + Owner's equity. How would you restate this equation if you wanted to know what your liabilities are? Your owner's equity?
3. What purpose do GAAP and FASB serve for a small business owner?
4. Explain the difference between cash and accrual accounting.
5. Define the term *leverage* as it applies to accounting.
6. How can profitability ratios allow insight into the effectiveness of management? Liquidity ratios? Activity ratios? Leverage ratios?
7. If you were setting up open-book management in your business, what would you teach employees to make it work?
8. Explain the difference between macro-aging and micro-aging accounts receivable schedules.
9. Cash flow has been described as the lifeblood of a business. How would you explain this description to someone who does not understand business finance?
10. The sales projection for your retail business is $650,000. The industry average for the asset turnover ratio is 5. How much inventory (total assets) should you plan to stock?

Questions for Critical Thinking

1. You need to write a business plan for a start-up business. How do you come up with the numbers for your pro forma financial statements? Do you just guess and make them up? (*Hint:* The process starts with a sales forecast.)
2. Cash flow is more important than profit for a small business. Why? If your income statement shows a profit at the end of the month, how can anything be more important than that?

What Would You Do?

The popularity of soccer as a participation sport attracted Leo Hernandez and Gil Ferguson to open an indoor soccer arena with retail shops selling soccer-related merchandise. Last year's financial statements for their business OnGoal are shown here. Leo and Gil are hoping to expand their business by opening another facility. However, before they approach banks or potential investors, they need to look closely at what the accounting statements show them.

Questions

1. Calculate liquidity, activity, leverage, and profitability ratios for OnGoal.
2. Pair off and compare your ratios. Discuss which of the ratios look weak and which look positive. Develop a one-page explanation of the company's ratios that you can show to potential lenders.

OnGoal
Balance Sheet
December 31, 20—

ASSETS

Current Assets:

Cash	$7,120	
Accounts Receivable	2,400	
Merchandise Inventory	18,200	
Prepaid Expenses	3,040	
Total Current Assets		$40,760

Fixed Assets:

Fixtures	$16,800	
Less Accumulated Depreciation	3,600	
Building	78,000	
Less Accumulated Depreciation	7,800	
Equipment	12,000	
Less Accumulated Depreciation	4,000	
Total Fixed Assets		$91,400
TOTAL ASSETS:		$132,160

LIABILITIES/EQUITY

Current Liabilities:

Accounts Payable	$6,000	
Notes Payable	4,000	
Contracts Payable	8,000	
Total Current Liabilities		$18,000

Fixed Liabilities:

Long-term Note Payable	$75,000	

Owners' Equity:

Shares Held by Hernandez and Ferguson	$39,160	
TOTAL LIABILITIES/EQUITY:		$132,160

OnGoal
Income Statement
Year Ended December 31, 20—

SALES			$178,000
Cost of Goods Sold:			
Beginning Inventory, January 1	$18,000		
Purchases During Year	22,000		
Less Ending Inventory, December 31	18,200		
Cost of Goods Sold		$21,800	
GROSS MARGIN			$156,200
Operating Expenses:			
Payment on Building Note	$34,000		
Salaries	68,000		
Supplies	7,460		
Advertising/Promotion	3,000		
Insurance Expense	18,000		
Utilities Expense	10,000		
Miscellaneous Expenses	4,000		
Total Operating Expenses		$144,460	
NET PROFIT FROM OPERATIONS:			$11,740

9
Financing Your Business

CHAPTER LEARNING OUTCOMES

After reading this chapter, you should be able to:

1. **Determine the financing needs of your business.**

2. **Define basic financing terminology.**

3. **Explain where to look for sources of funding.**

One of the most challenging aspects of a small business is acquiring the funding necessary to open your doors for the very first time and to keep your business running until you start to produce positive cash flow. Dollars needed by your new start-up range from rent, to equipment, to production of your product, to hiring employees, to paying for needed licenses and permits. Where does a budding entrepreneur look for the financing so desperately needed?

There are several sources of financing available for small business owners. The more exotic-sounding sources are called angels and venture capitalists. Both groups are willing

to loan dollars for great new ideas; however, both have requirements that must be met before the dollars are provided. Rosalind Resnick states in a *Wall Street Journal* article that most small business owners are unlikely to receive funding from these two groups; only one in 200 will receive money from angels and one in 500 from venture capitalists. Other sources of funding include banks and the Small Business Administration.

A source not necessarily discussed as much but used more frequently involves personal sources of funding like relatives, old employers, and even the people from whom supplies will be purchased. Relatives and a previous employer have the advantages of knowing you well and having a personal interest in your success. Providing financing may actually be something they see as an opportunity to be supportive of your new venture. Suppliers or a potential supplier may have a vested interest in that if your company does well, they too will have success as they provide products and services for your venture. Following are some examples:

Minami Satoh invested around $400,000 of his own dollars in his small business, Japan Traditional Foods, Inc. His company produces around 700 packages of natto a day with a monthly revenue stream of about $5,000. Natto is a fermented soybean common in Japanese diets but not so much in the United States. Mr. Satoh is betting on the health benefits as an antioxidant as the ticket to increase sales in the United States and move his company forward.

Zach Workman and his family put up $200,000 of seed money for his business Power Brands. Mr. Workman is a college student who decided to produce a healthy energy drink that didn't contain the usual sugars or preservatives found in other products. So with a family recipe and family dollars, his product was on track for $1 million in sales the first year.

When John Ruocco's uncle was killed by a drunk driver, Mr. Ruocco decided to try to prevent similar tragedies in the future. He developed a product, the Interceptor, that when installed in a car, tests the alcohol level of the person driving before they start the car and then while they drive. If the Interceptor detects a blood alcohol level that is too high, it sends a voice message to the driver asking them to pull the car over. If the driver ignores the request, the car's location is sent to a 911 dispatcher. Mr. Ruocco and his sister both invested their own money in the development of this technology.

As you can see, these entrepreneurs were so committed to the success of their small business that not only have they invested their time and effort, but also they and family members have invested money to get their new businesses up and going.

Sources: Deborah Cohen, "Inventor Puts the DUI Checkpoint on the Dash," www.msnbc.com, May 12, 2010, retrieved May 29, 2010; "In Tough Times, Students Start Businesses," *Inc.com*, March 2, 2009, retrieved from www.msnbc.com May 29, 2010; Yukari Kane, "Tempting U.S. Palates with Fermented Soy," *Wall Street Journal Online*, May 19, 2010; and Rosalind Resnick, "How to Find Your First Investors," *Wall Street Journal Online*, May 28, 2010.

Small Business Finance

Although some entrepreneurs are well versed in determining their need for capital and knowing where to find it, the failure of many businesses can be traced to undercapitalization, not having the funds available to get started and carry you through until your business starts to produce a positive cash flow. A common approach is "not to worry about it" until the situation gets out of hand. However, every small business owner should understand how to define the amount of funding required to efficiently operate his business. Furthermore, the ability to be a proactive manager of the financial aspects of a business is of paramount importance when the economy takes a downturn. As you've seen in earlier chapters, when circumstances change quickly, you must be prepared to adapt to the new milieu. According to a survey by American Express in April 2009, cash flow is a problem for 57 percent of the respondents, with 60 percent stating they are using personal finances in order to keep their company afloat.[1] This chapter covers issues of financing that every entrepreneur should understand before starting a business so that your company does not become a failed business statistic.

Because service businesses often require the purchase of fewer fixed assets at start-up than do retailers or manufacturers, they can offer a good route to self-employment. Providing outsourcing services for larger companies can be lucrative and can be anything from payroll to human resource management to information technology. The processes most often outsourced, according to an article in *Credit Management*, are "information technology, payroll, finance, personal assistants and receptionists."[2] For small business service firms this trend means new opportunities. How? It's a win-win situation for all parties involved. For the outsourcing firm, this approach offers a way to reduce operating costs, because providers of a single type of service have a lower cost structure resulting from economies of scale. For the small service business, it's a prime market to exploit.

Initial Capital Requirements

"Each business must have its assets in place—cash, inventory, patents, equipment, buildings, whatever it needs to operate—before it ever opens its doors."

The fundamental financial building blocks for an entrepreneur are recognizing (1) what assets are required to open the business; (2) what expenses will be required; (3) which expenses cannot be changed and must be paid, called fixed costs, and (4) knowing how these costs will be financed. This knowledge relates to the business's *initial capital requirements*. Recall from Chapter 8 the importance of the balance sheet. The balance sheet lists the investment decisions of the business owner in the asset column and the financing decisions in the liabilities and owner's equity columns. The financing necessary to acquire each asset required for the business must come from either owner-provided funds (equity) or borrowed funds (liabilities).

The process of determining initial capital requirements begins with identifying the short-term and long-term assets as well as the expenses, including fixed costs necessary to get the business started. Once you have this list, you must then determine how to pay these costs necessary to get your business up and running.[3]

Defining Required Assets

short-term assets
Assets that will be converted into cash within one year.

long-term assets
Assets that will not be converted into cash within one year.

Every business needs a set of short-term and long-term assets in place before the business ever opens its doors. Typical **short-term assets** include cash and inventory but may also include *prepaid expenses* (such as rent or insurance paid in advance) and a *working capital* (cash) reserve. Because many businesses are not profitable in the first year or so of operation, having a cash reserve with which to pay bills can help you avoid becoming insolvent.

The most common **long-term assets** are buildings and equipment, but these assets may also include land, leasehold improvements, patents, and a host of other items. Each of these assets must be in the business *before* the enterprise earns its first dollar of sales. This means you must carefully evaluate your situation to determine exactly what has to be in place for the business to operate effectively. A useful exercise to help accomplish this task is to prepare a list of the assets the business would have if money were no object. Next, review this "wish list" to determine the essential assets that are needed to operate the business on a "bare-bones" basis. Finally, estimate the cost of these assets under each scenario.

As an example, suppose you are an entrepreneur starting a restaurant and want seating for 100 people. If money were no object, you could choose brand-new oak dining sets at a cost of $1,200 per six-piece place setting. As a less expensive alternative, at an auction of restaurant supplies and equipment, you could purchase used pine dining sets at a cost of $200 per six-place setting. Either choice will allow the seating requirement to be met.

After carefully completing this exercise for all assets, you will end up with a list of assets with a minimum-dollar investment and another list of assets needed for the dream business. Often your actual business will wind up somewhere in the middle of those two lists as you make final decisions.

Expenses should be carefully evaluated, especially fixed costs. Fixed costs must be paid, even if the business has no revenue and can cause serious challenges for a small business owner. These costs are items like a five-year lease on the building you have just rented. That lease amount may have to be paid, depending upon the lease agreement, even if you shut your doors. Developing a plan to pay for these costs is important and a part of your initial capitalization requirements.

With the final list of required assets and fixed costs and corresponding dollar costs in hand, you can then determine your financing requirements. Remember that each dollar of assets must be supported by a dollar of equity or liability funds. Expenses must also be paid. How much equity can you contribute personally to the enterprise? Note that this contribution does not necessarily have to be all in the form of cash.

The market value of the owner's assets used in the business plus all cash contributions from the owner to purchase assets or set up cash reserves constitute the *owner's equity*. For example, if your business requires a delivery vehicle and you already own a van with a market value of $12,000 that would be suitable for deliveries, the asset will be listed as "Delivery Vehicle—$12,000," and the balancing entry would be $12,000 of owner's equity.

The final step in the process is to subtract the total dollar value of the owner's equity from the total dollar value of the required assets. Generally, this step yields the dollar amount that must come from other sources. Sometimes there will be more owner's equity than needed to finance the required assets. In this situation, the entrepreneur can afford to invest in more assets or in more expensive assets—such as the new oak dining sets rather than the used pine dining sets for the restaurant mentioned earlier. More commonly, however, businesses will need additional capital to finance the required assets. This additional capital will come from one or more sources, which are most likely external to the business.

It may not take as much start-up money as you might think to launch a new business. Of the 2004 *Inc.* 500 (the latest year that start-up money needed for the fastest-growing companies was provided), 36 percent needed less than $20,000 in capitalization (see Figure 9.1).

The Five "Cs" of Credit

When an entrepreneur decides to seek external financing, she must be able to prove creditworthiness to potential providers of funds. A traditional guideline used by many lenders is the *five "Cs" of credit*, where each "C" represents a critical qualifying element:

1. *Capacity.* Capacity refers to the applicant's ability to repay the loan. It is usually estimated by examining the amount of cash and marketable securities available, and both historical and projected cash flows of the business. The amount of debt you already have will also be considered.
2. *Capital.* Capital is a function of the applicant's personal financial strength. The net worth of a business—the value of its assets minus the value of its liabilities—determines its capital. The bank wants to know what you own outside of the business that might be an alternate repayment source.[4]

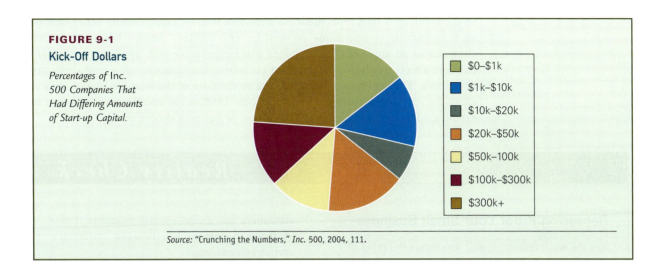

FIGURE 9-1

Kick-Off Dollars

Percentages of Inc. *500 Companies That Had Differing Amounts of Start-up Capital.*

Legend:
- $0–$1k
- $1k–$10k
- $10k–$20k
- $20k–$50k
- $50k–100k
- $100k–$300k
- $300k+

Source: "Crunching the Numbers," *Inc.* 500, 2004, 111.

3. *Collateral.* Assets owned by the applicant that can be pledged as security for the repayment of the loan constitute collateral. If the loan is not repaid, the lender can confiscate the pledged assets. The value of collateral is not based on the assets' market value, but rather is discounted to take into account the value that would be received if the assets had to be liquidated, which is frequently significantly less than market value (see Table 9.1).

4. *Character.* The applicant's character is considered important in that it indicates his apparent willingness to repay the loan. Character is judged primarily on the basis

TABLE 9-1

General Approximation of Different Forms of Collateral Valuations

COLLATERAL TYPE	BANK	SMALL BUSINESS ADMINISTRATION
House	(Market value × 0.75) – mortgage balance	(Market value × 0.80) – mortgage balance
Car	Nothing	Nothing
Truck and heavy equipment	Depreciated value × 0.50	Same
Office equipment	Nothing	Nothing
Furniture and fixtures	Depreciated value × 0.50	Same
Inventory: perishables	Nothing	Nothing
Jewelry	Nothing	Nothing
Other	10%–50%	10%–50%
Receivables	Under 90 days × 0.75	Under 90 days × 0.50
Stocks and bonds	50%–90%	50%–90%
Mutual funds	Nothing	Nothing
IRA	Nothing	Nothing
CD	100%	100%

Source: U.S. Small Business Administration, "Borrowing Money," www.sba.gov/smallbusinessplanner/start/financestartup/SERV_BORROW.html.

of the applicant's past repayment patterns, but lenders may consider other factors, such as marital status, home ownership, and military service when attributing character to an applicant. The lender's prior experience with applicant repayment patterns affects its choice of factors in evaluating the character of a new applicant.

5. *Conditions.* The general economic climate at the time of the loan application may affect the applicant's ability to repay the loan. Lenders are usually more reluctant to extend credit in times of economic recession or business downturns.

Reality Check

Recession Proof Your Small Business

Say the word *recession*, and fear enters the mind of any business owner, particularly the small business owner. With pockets that are not deep and little room for error, the small business owner has fewer resources at his disposal when customers start buying less. However, just because the economy is in a slump does not mean that your business has to follow. Here are some tips for surviving the economic downturn and avoiding the fear factor:

1. Make good business decisions all the time. Good business decisions work well during good times but are particularly important during economic downturns. If a decision will only work during periods when sales are high, reconsider the decision.

2. Focus on cash. You must have the cash on hand to pay current bills. If you cannot get the cash, cut spending until the money coming in is at least equal to the money going out.

3. Manage your current debt. With cash flow decreased, it may be necessary to again cut expenses in order to meet your interest and tax payments. This is not the time to miss a credit payment since that missed payment could put you into default, which means your entire loan is now due.

4. Cut excess expenses. Remember what it was like when you first opened your doors and you were scrimping on every penny. Reassess and cut those expenses that, while nice, may not be essential. Economic downturns are great opportunities to trim excesses that have built up over time.

5. Watch your customer base. While having fewer customers who place larger orders seems easier when times are good, having only a few large

customers can create serious problems if one of those customers has financial challenges and cannot pay you.

6. Is the industry you are in going to survive the downturn? Look at the economy and your competition. Then honestly evaluate where your business fits. Which of you will likely survive? These times provide opportunities to reassess the long-term financial viability of your business.

7. Keep a six-month reserve. Having a rainy-day fund can be key during down times. Make sure you keep enough cash on hand to pay all necessary bills six months out. This will provide some "wiggle room" and time for making changes if your sales fall off.

8. Keep your best employees if at all possible. Too frequently in a downturn, the highest-paid employees are let go, who frequently are also your best employees. If you plan on ramping up your business once the economy is moving forward, don't let one of your best assets—your employees—go. Cut other expenses first.

9. Are you still having fun? If not, this may be an opportunity to reconsider if this is what you want to do in the future. The increased stress of financial downtimes can be detrimental to your health, your relationship with family and friends, and your overall happiness. Take a step back and think about whether small business ownership is for you.

Sources: Christine Janklow, "Why Businesses Fail," *Accounting Today*, September 1, 2009, 10–11; Karen Klein, "How Small Business Owners Can Cope with the Crisis," *BusinessWeek Online*, October 13, 2008, 14; Thomas Houck, "Top 10 Survival Tactics in a Tough Economy," *Rural Telecom*, July-August 2009, 40–42; and Jay Goltz, "Stress Test," *Fortune Small Business*, April 2009, 20.

Additional Considerations

Potential investors will want to know more about you and your business than just the "five 'Cs'." For start-ups, simply having a good idea will not be enough to convince many investors to risk their capital in your business. You will need to show that you are a competent manager with a track record of prior business success. If possible, you should have an informal board of directors made up of people whom you may contact for assistance. Potential members of such a board might include bankers, attorneys, CPAs, and successful business owners.

If yours is a growing or emerging business, you will need to stand ready to provide well-audited financial statements and show a solid record of earnings. It is difficult to attract investors without proven performance and a high likelihood of continued growth and success. The old adage, "You have to have money to make money," is largely true in the area of financing. However, it might be amended to say, "You have to show an ability to make money to attract money."

A common myth suggests that the sheer strength of a business idea can win funding for a venture. In reality, a banker's first question is often "How much money can you put in?" Bankers are not venture capital partners; they will expect you to put in at least 25 percent of total project costs, and perhaps much more if the loan is viewed as a risky one.[5] Remember the ratios we calculated in the last chapter? Your debt/net worth ratio if you are a new businesses should be at least 2 to 1, with the business owner putting up at least 33 percent of the assets needed, according to Wichmann, Abramowicz, and Sparks.[6]

"You will need to show that you are a competent manager with a track record of prior business success."

Basic Financial Vocabulary

Before an entrepreneur can begin looking for sources of funds, she needs to understand the terminology associated with the two basic types of funds, debt and equity.

Forms of Capital: Debt and Equity

Two kinds of funds are potentially available to the entrepreneur: debt and equity. *Debt funds* (also known as *liabilities*) are borrowed from a creditor and, of course, must be repaid. Using debt to finance a business creates **leverage**, which is money you can borrow against the money you already have (see Chapter 8). The goal in using leverage is to put in a little money and get back a lot more. Leverage can enable you to greatly increase the potential returns expected as you invest your equity in the business. Increased leverage also increases risk.

Of course, debt funding can also consume the future cash flows generated by the business and potentially magnify losses. The interest payment on debt becomes a fixed cost that must be paid. Debt creates the risk of your becoming technically insolvent if you cannot make each debt payment on time. Continued nonrepayment of debt will ultimately lead to the bankruptcy of the business. Debt is burdensome, particularly when the economy is in a downturn, which is why some business owners shed it as quickly as possible. Bill Howell of Safe Handling, a transportation and warehouse business in Auburn, Maine, has paid off loans early to prevent collateralization requirements from stifling growth.[7]

Equity funds, by contrast, are supplied by investors in exchange for an ownership position in the business. They need not be repaid. Providers of equity funds forgo the opportunity to receive periodic repayments in hopes of later sharing in the profits of the business. As a result, equity financing does not create a constraint on the cash flows of the business. However, equity providers usually demand a voice in the management of

leverage
The ability to finance an investment through borrowed funds, increasing both the potential for return and the level of risk.

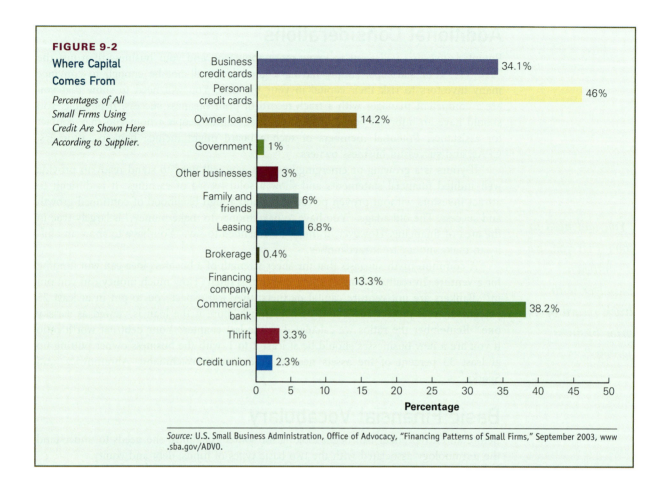

FIGURE 9-2

Where Capital Comes From

Percentages of All Small Firms Using Credit Are Shown Here According to Supplier.

Source: U.S. Small Business Administration, Office of Advocacy, "Financing Patterns of Small Firms," September 2003, www.sba.gov/ADVO.

the business, thereby reducing the business owner's autonomy to run the business as he would like.

It is easy to see that the decision to seek outside funds is both critical and complex. Therefore, a more detailed view of each kind of financing is presented in this chapter. Figure 9.2 contains the results of a survey conducted by the Small Business Administration's (SBA) Office of Advocacy, called the "Survey of Small Business Finance in the United States." In particular, the bar graph shows the sources of capital used by small businesses.

debt financing
The use of borrowed funds to finance a business.

Debt Financing Three important parameters associated with **debt financing** are the amount of principal to be borrowed, the loan's interest rate, and the loan's length of maturity. Together they determine the size and extent of your obligation to the creditor. Until the debt is repaid, the creditor has a legal claim on a portion of the business's cash flows. Creditors can demand payment and, in the most extreme case, force a business into bankruptcy because of overdue payments.

principal
An amount of money borrowed from a lender.

The **principal** of the loan is the original amount of money to be borrowed. Minimizing the size of the loan will reduce your leverage and your financial risk. The pro forma balance sheet estimates the amount of funds needed (see Chapter 8). The amount you need to borrow is the difference between the total of pro forma assets and total owner's equity.

interest rate
The amount of money paid for the use of borrowed funds.

The **interest rate** of the loan determines the "price" of the borrowed funds. In most cases it will be based on the current prime rate of interest. In the past, the *prime rate* was defined as the rate of interest banks charge their "best" customers—those with the lowest risk. More recently, it has developed into a benchmark for determining many other rates of interest. Interest rates for small business loans are normally the prime rate plus some additional percentage points. For example, if the prime rate is 8.5 percent, a bank might offer small business loans at "prime plus four," or 12.5 percent. Additional factors, such as default risk and maturity, will also affect the cost of a loan.

Any interest payment becomes a fixed cost that must be paid. Remember the times interest earned ratio from Chapter 8? The times interest earned ratio calculates how many times you can make your current interest payment. If you miss an interest payment or two, you could be considered in default and the entire loan becomes due. Before you borrow, make sure you can make the interest payment on a timely basis.

The actual rate of interest the borrower will pay on a loan is called the *effective rate of interest*. It is often higher than the stated rate of interest for several reasons. A lender may require a *compensating balance*, meaning that the borrower is required to keep a minimum dollar balance (often as much as 10 percent of the principal) on deposit with the lender. This requirement reduces the amount of funds accessible to the borrower and increases the actual rate of interest because over the life of the loan, the borrower pays the same amount of interest dollars but has fewer funds available.

The frequency with which interest is compounded can also increase the cost of a loan. *Compounding* refers to the intervals at which you pay interest. Lenders may compound interest annually, semiannually, quarterly, monthly, weekly, daily, or even continuously. For example, quarterly compounding involves four compounding periods within a year—one-fourth of the stated interest rate is paid each quarter on the cumulative outstanding balance. The more compounding periods, the higher the effective rate will be. Financial institutions are required to inform borrowers of the effective rate of interest on all loans.

LOANS

"Do you have any other collateral... besides this e-mail from a Nigerian prince?"

© 2005 Randy Glasbergen, http://www.glasbergen.com

Whether a loan has a fixed rate or a variable rate of interest affects its ultimate cost. A **fixed-rate loan** retains the same interest rate for the entire length of time for which the funds are borrowed. With a **variable-rate loan**, the interest rate may fluctuate over time. Typically, the variable rate is tied to a benchmark such as the prime rate or federal funds rate. Every year (normally on the anniversary of the original loan date), the variable interest rate is adjusted according to changes in the benchmark.

fixed-rate loan
A loan whose interest rate remains constant.

variable-rate loan
A loan whose interest rate changes over the life of the loan.

A fixed-rate loan typically has a higher interest rate than the initial rate on a variable-rate loan. Therefore, the cost of a fixed-rate loan is higher in the first year (or longer). But because the variable interest rate could increase each year, it eventually might exceed the rate on the fixed loan by several percentage points. Thus a variable-rate loan represents much more of a gamble than a fixed-rate loan when borrowing for a long period of time.

Your goal is to find the lowest possible effective interest rate, given your current circumstances, by investigating different funding sources. For example, a particular bank may have excess funds available to lend and be willing to offer lower rates than its competitors. A start-up business may want to consider a variable-rate loan to help offset its lower cash flows in the first year of operation.

maturity
The length of time in which a loan must be repaid.

The **maturity** of a loan refers to the length of time for which a borrower obtains the use of the funds. A short-term loan must be repaid within one year, an intermediate-term loan must be repaid within one to ten years, and a long-term loan must be repaid within ten or more years. Typically, the purpose of the loan will determine the length of maturity chosen. For example, you would use a short-term loan to purchase inventory that you expect to sell within one year. Once you sell the inventory, you repay the loan. For the purchase of a building, which presumably will serve the business for decades, a long-term loan is preferable. The maturity of the loan should essentially match the borrower's use of the loan proceeds.

The maturity of the loan also affects its interest rate. Ordinarily, the longer the maturity, the higher the rate of interest. The reason for this is that a lender must be compensated for the opportunity cost of not being able to use those loaned funds in other ways. As a consequence, lenders will add a "premium" to the price that the borrower pays for a longer-maturity loan.

Your goal regarding loan maturity is to obtain as much flexibility as possible. On the one hand, a loan with a shorter maturity will usually have a lower rate of interest but must be repaid quickly, thus affecting cash flow more dramatically. On the other hand, a loan with a longer maturity has a higher rate but gives you more time to repay the loan, resulting in smaller payments and reduced constraints on your current cash flow. Flexibility is created by maximizing the maturity of a loan while retaining the option of repaying the loan sooner than the maturity date, if cash flows allow. Make sure that the lender does not charge a penalty for early repayment.

Consider the principal, effective rate of interest, and maturity very carefully when attempting to obtain debt financing. By ascertaining the proper amount of principal needed, comparing the effective rates of interest at your disposal, and matching the maturity of the loan with the projected availability of cash flows with which to make repayments, you will be able to make the greatest possible use of debt financing.

equity financing
The sale of common stock or the use of retained earnings to provide long-term financing.

Equity Financing As stated earlier, **equity financing** does not have to be repaid. There are no payments to constrain the cash flow of the business. There is no interest to be paid on the funds. Providers of equity capital wind up owning a portion of the business and are generally interested in (1) getting dividends, (2) benefiting from the increased value of the business (and thus their investment in it), and (3) having a voice in the management of the business.

dividends
Payments based on the net profits of the business and made to the providers of equity capital.

Dividends are payments based on the net profits of the business and made to the providers of equity capital. These payments often are made on either a quarterly, a semiannual, or an annual basis. Many small businesses keep net profits in the form of retained earnings to help finance future growth, and dividends are paid only when the business shows profits above the amount necessary to fund projected new development.

Increased value of the business is a natural result of a successful business enterprise. As a successful business grows and prospers, the owners prosper as well. Because the providers of equity capital own a "piece of the action," the value of their investment increases in direct proportion to the increase in the value of the business. The investors are frequently not as concerned about dividends as they are about the business's long-term success. If the business is successful, the equity providers will have the opportunity to sell all or part of their investment for a considerable profit.

A voice in management is an additional consideration for providers of equity capital. The rationale underlying this concept is that because the owners of a business have the most to lose if the business fails, they are entitled to have a say about how their money is used. Not all equity providers are interested in running a business, of course, but many can contribute important expertise along with their capital. They can enhance your business's chances of success.

Other Loan Terminology

Two additional sets of terms that you will often encounter while searching for financing relate to *loan security* and *loan restrictions*. These terms can be of great importance and should be thoroughly understood.

loan security
Assurance to a lender that a loan will be repaid.

Loan Security **Loan security** refers to the borrower's assurance to lenders that loans will be repaid. If the entrepreneur's signature on a loan is not considered sufficient security by a lender, the lender will require another signature to guarantee the loan. Other individuals whose signatures appear on the loan are known as *endorsers*. Endorsers are contingently liable for the notes they sign. Two types of endorsers are comakers and guarantors.

Comakers create a joint liability with the borrower. The lender can collect from either the maker (original borrower) or the comaker. *Guarantors* ensure the repayment of a note by signing a guarantee commitment. Both private and government lenders often require guarantees from officers of corporations to ensure continuity of effective management.

Loan Restrictions Sometimes called *covenants*, loan restrictions spell out what the borrower cannot do (*negative covenants*) or what she must do (*positive covenants*). These restrictions are built into each loan agreement and are generally negotiable—as long as you are aware of them.

Typical negative covenants preclude the borrower from acquiring any additional debt without prior approval from the original lender. Common positive covenants require that the borrower maintain some minimum level of working capital until the loan is repaid, carry some type of insurance while the loan is in effect, or provide periodic financial statements to the lender.

By understanding that lenders will sometimes require the additional assurance of an endorser and will likely create covenants on loan agreements, you can be better prepared to negotiate during the search for financing. Doing your homework and being prepared can improve your chances of successfully obtaining funds.[8]

"Doing your homework and being prepared can improve your chances of successfully obtaining funds."

How Can You Find Capital?

Once you determine how much capital is needed for the start-up or expansion, you are ready to begin looking for capital sources. To prepare for this search, you need to be aware of what these sources will want to know about you and your business before they are willing to entrust their funds to you. You also need to understand the characteristics of each capital source and the process for obtaining funds from it.

Loan Application Process

Typically, to determine creditworthiness, a lending institution will collect relevant information from financial statements supplied by the applicant and by external sources, such as local or regional credit associations, credit interchange bureaus, and the applicant's bank. This procedure is known as *credit scoring*. If the applicant meets or exceeds some minimal score (set by the lender) on key financial and credit characteristics, the institution will be willing to arrange a loan. Today a credit score of 690–700 may be necessary.[9] Most lenders hesitate to make loans to start-up businesses, however, unless either a wealthy friend or a relative will cosign the loan, or unless loan proceeds will be used to purchase assets that could be repossessed and easily resold in case of default.

Sources of Debt Financing

The wide array of credit options available confuses many entrepreneurs. A thorough understanding of the nature and characteristics of these debt sources will help ensure that you are successful in obtaining financing from the most favorable source for you.

The primary source of small-business funding is the local commercial bank.

unsecured loans
A short-term loan for which collateral is not required.

line of credit
An agreement that makes a specific amount of short-term funding available to a business as it is needed.

demand note
A short-term loan that must be repaid (both principal and interest) in a lump sum at maturity.

installment loans
A loan made to a business for the purchase of fixed assets such as equipment and real estate.

balloon notes
A loan that requires the borrower to make small monthly payments (usually enough to cover the interest), with the balance of the loan due at maturity.

Commercial Banks Most people's first response to the question "Where would you borrow money?" is the obvious one: "A bank." Commercial banks are the backbone of the credit market, offering the widest assortment of loans to creditworthy small businesses. Bank loans generally fall into two major categories: short-term loans (for purchasing inventory, overcoming cash flow problems, and meeting monthly expenditures) and long-term loans (for purchasing land, machinery, and buildings, or renovating facilities).

Most short-term loans are **unsecured loans**, meaning that the bank does not require any collateral as long as the entrepreneur has a good credit standing. These loans are often *self-liquidating*, which means that the loan will be repaid directly with the revenues generated from the original purpose of the loan. For example, if an entrepreneur uses a short-term loan to purchase inventory, the loan is repaid as the inventory is sold. Types of short-term loans include lines of credit, demand notes, and floor planning.

A **line of credit** is an agreement between a bank and a business that specifies the amount of unsecured short-term funds the bank will make available to a business. The agreement allows the business to borrow and repay funds up to the maximum amount specified in the agreement. The business pays interest only on the amount of funds actually borrowed but may be required to pay a setup or handling fee. For start-up businesses or businesses where revenue is erratic, lines of credit can make the difference between business success and failure, as the line of credit can augment cash flow. Make sure you apply for the line of credit before you need it, not when you are experiencing cash flow problems.[10]

A **demand note** is a loan made to a small business for a specific period of time, to be repaid in a lump sum at maturity. With this type of loan, the bank reserves the right to demand repayment of the loan at any time. For example, a bank might loan a business $50,000 for one year at 12 percent interest. The business would repay the loan by making one payment of $56,000 ($50,000 principal plus $0.12 \times \$50,000$ interest) at the end of one year. The only reason a bank is likely to demand repayment sooner is if the business appears to be struggling and is potentially unable to repay the loan in full at the end of the specified time period.

Types of long-term bank loans include installment loans, balloon notes, and unsecured term loans. **Installment loans** are made to businesses for the purchase of fixed assets such as equipment and real estate. These loans are to be repaid in periodic payments that include accrued interest and part of the outstanding principal balance. In the case of many fixed assets, the maturity of the loan will equal the usable life of the asset, and the principal amount loaned will range from 65 to 80 percent of the asset's market value. For the purchase of real estate, banks will often allow a repayment schedule of 15 to 30 years and typically lend between 75 and 85 percent of the property's value. In every case, the bank will maintain a security interest in, or lien on, the asset until the loan is fully repaid.

Balloon notes are loans made to businesses in which only small periodic payments are required over the life of the loan, with a large lump-sum payment due at maturity. A typical balloon note requires monthly payments to cover accrued interest, with the entire principal coming due at the end of the loan's term. This scheme allows you more flexibility with your cash flow over the life of the loan. If you are unable to make the final balloon payment, a bank may refinance the loan for a longer period of time, allowing you to continue making monthly payments.

unsecured term loans
A loan made to an established business that has demonstrated a strong overall credit profile.

Unsecured term loans are made to established businesses that have demonstrated a strong overall credit profile. Eligible businesses must show excellent creditworthiness and have an extremely high probability of repayment. These loans are usually made for very specific terms and may come with restrictions on the use of the loan proceeds. For example, a bank might agree to lend a business a sum of money for a three-year period at a given rate of interest. As the business owner, you must then ensure that the funds are used to finance some asset or activity that will generate enough revenue to repay the loan within the three-year time horizon.

Commercial banks remain a primary source of debt financing for small businesses.[11] The type, maturity, and other terms of each loan, however, are uniquely a function of the financial strength or creditworthiness of the borrower.

Commercial Finance Companies Commercial finance companies extend short- and intermediate-term credit to firms that cannot easily obtain credit elsewhere. Because these companies are willing to take a bigger risk than commercial banks, their interest rates are often considerably higher. Commercial finance companies perform a valuable service to small businesses that have yet to establish their creditworthiness. Among the most common types of loans provided by commercial finance companies are floor planning, leasing, and factoring accounts receivable.

floor planning
A type of business loan generally made for "big-ticket" items. The business holds the item in inventory and pays interest, but it is actually owned by the lender until the item is sold.

Floor planning is a special type of loan used particularly for financing high-priced inventory items, such as new automobiles, trucks, recreational vehicles, and boats. A business borrowing money for this purpose is allowed to display the inventory on its premises, but the inventory is actually owned by the bank. When the business sells one of the items, it will use the proceeds of the sale to repay the principal of the loan. The business is generally required to pay interest monthly on each item of inventory purchased with the loan proceeds. Therefore, the longer it takes the business to sell each item, the more the business pays in interest expenses. This is one instance in which the short-term loan is a *secured loan*. That is, the assets purchased with the loan proceeds serve as collateral.

secured loan
A loan that requires collateral as security for the lender.

Manager's Notes

Banker Talk

Even during tougher financial times, banks are still lending money to creditworthy small businesses. Bank of America announced plans to increase small business lending by $4 billion in 2010, but actually increased it by $12.6 billion. While the idea of meeting with a banker can be intimidating to some people, here are some tips to access those needed dollars:

- Don't ask anyone to do something you aren't willing to do yourself. You have to put your own assets on the line to get a business loan.
- Start talking with your banker before you are in dire need. Bankers are naturally conservative because they have to protect their depositors' money.
- Remember cash is king, and examine and be prepared to defend every purchase requiring additional debt. Be prepared to address how the cash flow from the asset will be used to pay off the debt required to purchase the asset.
- Ask about the SBA-guaranteed loan programs. There may be new loans available or guidelines that have been relaxed that now make you eligible.
- Don't surprise your banker. Don't go in on Thursday to say that you can't make your payroll on Friday.

- Have routine meetings with your banker to keep her up to date on how your business is progressing.
- Tell your banker in person when your business is having trouble immediately, and explain how you intend to overcome the problem.
- Review all insurance policies and make sure the coverage you have is adequate. In the same light, avoid insurance you do not need.
- Take time to educate your banker about your business and industry. The better your banker understands your business, the better he can help you.
- Be timely with your payments and any financial information the bank may request from you.
- Give your banker all your business—both your personal accounts and your firm's deposits.
- Keep a positive attitude. A banker asking for more documentation isn't necessarily looking for a reason to turn your loan down. Rather, she needs more information. Bankers look for reasons to say "yes."

Sources: "Banker's Tips for Small-Biz Owners," *DealerNews*, November 2008, 15; Paul Davis, "Holding Pattern for Borrowers," *U.S. Banker*, February 2010, 12; and Jeffrey Moses, "The Most Important Part of a Loan Application," National Federation of Independent Business, June 2004, www.nfib.com/business-resources; and Jeffrey Moses, "Focus on the Plan," National Federation of Independent Business/Business Resources, June 2004, www.nfib.com/business-resources.

Leasing is a contract arrangement whereby a finance company purchases the durable goods needed by a small business and rents them to the small business for a specific period of time. The rent payment includes some amount of interest. Due to current tax laws, this activity is very lucrative for finance companies and often allows entrepreneurs to have the use of state-of-the-art equipment at a fraction of the cost.

factoring
The practice of raising funds for a business through the sale of accounts receivable.

Another important type of loan available from commercial finance companies is accounts receivable *factoring*. Under this arrangement, a small business either sells its accounts receivable to a finance company outright or uses the receivables as collateral for a loan. The purchase price of the receivables (or the amount of the loan) is discounted from the face value of what the business is owed to allow for potential losses (in the form of unpaid accounts) and for the fact that the finance company will not receive full repayment of the loan until sometime in the future.

Typically, the finance company will either purchase the receivables for or will lend the small business somewhere between 55 and 80 percent of the face value of the business's accounts receivable, based on their likelihood of being paid in a timely manner. If a finance company purchases the receivables outright, it will collect payments on them as they come due. If the small business uses its receivables as collateral for a loan, in a process known as *pledging*, as the business collects these accounts due, the proceeds are forwarded to the finance company to repay the loan.

Factoring has historically been viewed as one of the least desirable approaches to financing, but competition from new small and midsized factors is changing that perception. Bryan Bradley, co-founder and designer of Tuleh's, a high-end New York fashion design house, said that he would not even be in business, let alone hosting a runway show for the 2006 Fashion Week, without his factor. When Tuleh makes a sale to an upscale retailer, like Neiman Marcus, the invoice is e-mailed to his factor, Hilldun. The invoice amount is deposited into Tuleh's account minus about 9 percent, providing immediate cash for Bradley to pay for new runway shows or pay his vendors. Factor Hilldun also holds back 20 percent of the receivables in case companies dispute or for some other reason don't pay bills. When payment comes due, Hilldun collects directly from the retailer and sends Bradley the remaining 20 percent minus any adjustments.[12]

policy loans
A loan made to a business by an insurance company, using the business's insurance policy as collateral.

Insurance Companies For some entrepreneurs, life insurance companies have become a principal source of debt financing. The most common type of loan, **policy loans**, are made to entrepreneurs based on the amount of money paid in premiums on an insurance policy that has a cash surrender value. Although each insurance company varies its methods for making these loans, a typical arrangement is for the insurance company to lend up to 95 percent of a policy's cash surrender value.

The collateral for the loan is the cash that the entrepreneur has already paid into the policy. In essence, the insurance company is lending the entrepreneur his own money. Because the default risk is virtually zero (defaulting on the loan merely reduces the cash surrender value of the policy), the rate of interest is often very favorable.

If an entrepreneur has been paying premiums into a whole-life, variable-life, or universal-life policy, it is likely that the option to borrow funds against it will be available. Term insurance policies, however, have no borrowing capacity. One caution about this type of borrowing is that the amount of insurance coverage is usually reduced by the amount of the loan.

Federal Loan Programs Government lending programs exist to stimulate economic activity. The underlying rationale for making these loans is that the borrowers will become profitable and create jobs, which in turn means more tax dollars in the coffers of government agencies providing the funds for the loans. The most active government lender is the Small Business Administration, a federal agency. **SBA loan** programs include the 7(a) loan guaranty program, the Microloan Program, the Small Business Investment Company program, and the 504 loan program. For full descriptions of all SBA loan programs, see www.sba.gov/smallbusinessplanner. Then go to "finance start-up" and the "SBA's role." The majority of these loan funds go to service, retail, and manufacturing businesses (see Figure 9.3).

Guaranteed loans are generally known as the *7(a) program*. Under this program, private lenders—usually commercial banks—make loans to entrepreneurs that are guaranteed up to 85 percent of loans up to $150,000 and up to 75 percent of loans above

SBA loan
A loan made to a small business through a commercial bank, of which a portion is guaranteed by the Small Business Administration.

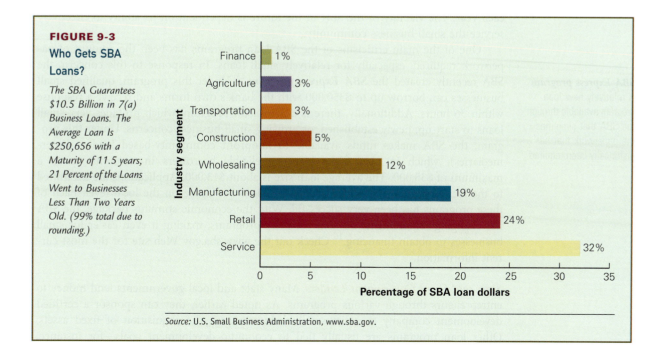

FIGURE 9-3
Who Gets SBA Loans?

The SBA Guarantees $10.5 Billion in 7(a) Business Loans. The Average Loan Is $250,656 with a Maturity of 11.5 years; 21 Percent of the Loans Went to Businesses Less Than Two Years Old. (99% total due to rounding.)

Source: U.S. Small Business Administration, www.sba.gov.

$150,000 by the SBA. This means that the lender's risk exposure is reduced by the amount of the SBA guarantee. The SBA's 7(a) maximum loan amount is $2 million with SBA maximum exposure of $1.5 million.

To be eligible for the 7(a) program, a business must be operated for profit and must fall within the size standards set by the SBA (see Chapter 1). Loans cannot be made to businesses engaged in speculation or real estate rental. Existing businesses must provide, among other things, financial statements for the past three years and financial projections for the next three years. Start-up businesses must provide three years of projected financial statements, a feasible business plan, and proof of adequate investment by the owners (generally about 20 to 30 percent equity).

Successful applicants pay interest rates up to 2.25 percent above the prime rate for loans with maturities of less than seven years and interest rates up to 2.75 percent above the prime rate for loans with maturities of seven years or longer. The borrower must repay the loan in monthly installments, which include both principal and interest. The first payment may be delayed up to six months, and the loans do carry prepayment fees under certain conditions.[13]

certified development company
A nonprofit organization sponsored either by private interests or by state or local governments.

The *504 loan* program provides small businesses with funding for fixed assets when conventional loans are not possible. These funds are distributed through a **certified development company**, which is a nonprofit organization sponsored either by private interests or by state or local governments. In a typical arrangement, a private lender will provide 50 percent of the total value of the loan, the borrower 10 percent, and the certified development company the remaining 40 percent of the necessary funds. Because the 504 portion of the funds—that contributed by the certified development company—is 100 percent guaranteed by the SBA, the private lender's risk exposure is significantly reduced. The maturity for 504 financing is 10 years for equipment purchases and 20 years for real estate.[14]

In addition to the preceding loan programs, the SBA offers loan programs to support small businesses engaged in international trade and rural development, those with women owners, and those with working-capital needs. There is no doubt that the SBA plays a very significant role in providing debt financing for small businesses. However, the agency, like all other federal agencies, is subject to policy changes and budget cuts each year. The viability of the SBA in the future is dependent on its ability to effectively service the small business community.

SBA Express program
A relatively new loan program available through the SBA that simplifies the paperwork that has historically been required.

One of the main criticisms of the SBA loan programs has been the amount of paperwork required, especially for relatively small loans. In response to this concern, the SBA recently created the **SBA Express program**.[15] Under this program, qualified small businesses can borrow up to $350,000 with the bank's own forms and receive a response within 36 hours. Additionally, there is a *Microloan* Program, which provides very small loans to start-up, newly established, or growing small business concerns. Under this program, the SBA makes funds available to nonprofit community-based lenders (intermediaries), which in turn make loans to eligible borrowers in amounts up to a maximum of $35,000. The average loan size is about $13,000. Applications are submitted to the local intermediary, and all credit decisions are made on the local level. Each of these programs has been very successful. With the economic stimulus package, the SBA has changing requirements on some of these programs, making it even easier for small businesses to obtain financing.[16] Check out the www.sba.gov Web site for the most current information.

State and Local Government Lenders Many state and local governments lend money to entrepreneurs through various programs. As noted earlier, they can sponsor a certified development company to assist small businesses with the acquisition of fixed assets. Other loan programs are usually tied to economic development goals—for instance, some loans are made contingent on the number of jobs that will be created by the small business. Most state and local government programs have lower interest rates than conventional loans, often with longer maturities. It is clearly to your advantage to find out if these programs would be available to you.

trade credit
The purchase of goods from suppliers that do not demand payment immediately.

Trade Credit   The last major source of debt financing covered here is the use of **trade credit**, or *accounts payable*. Recall from Chapter 8 that accounts payable are the amounts owed by a business to the creditors that have supplied goods or services to the business. Although start-ups may find it difficult to obtain everything on credit right away, many manufacturers and wholesalers will ship goods at least 30 days before payment is required. This 30-day grace period is essentially a loan to the small business. Because no interest is charged for the first 30 days, the loan is "free." For this reason, you should take advantage of as much trade credit as possible.

What if a Lender Says "No"?

Not every deal gets approved. Not every loan package is accepted. When rejection happens to you, get past the blow to your ego and try to learn what you did wrong. When a lender says, "no," do the following:

- Thank the lender for the time spent reviewing your package. Do not show resentment. Lenders almost always consider applications in a highly professional, objective manner. If you remain professional yourself, you will improve the odds of favorably impressing the lender when you return for future loans. Maintain the relationship.
- Ask what specific information, or lack thereof, counted against you. Federal regulations require a lender to prepare a detailed explanation for its loan rejection. Talk about the points cited, but don't argue—you are trying to learn as much as you possibly can. If you can make the changes suggested, ask when you can reapply.
- Ask the lender for specific, personal recommendations. Straight out ask for any personal advice the lender may have.
- Give the bank a reason to make the loan. Make sure you know exactly what you are asking for and the reason behind the request. Be prepared to tell your story effectively.[17]
- Understand that business loans are generally turned down for one (or more) of four main reasons: a poor credit score, lack of collateral, uncertainty of cash flow, and/or a poorly written business plan.[18]
- Ask whether the bank can rework your application so that it meets the lending criteria. This effort may require substantial changes in your business structure or adding personal collateral.

Sources of Equity Financing

From our discussion of debt financing, you know that lenders will expect entrepreneurs to provide their own funds—equity funds—in the amount of at least 20 percent, and possibly 50 percent or more, before approving a loan. The higher the risk assumed by the lender, the more of your own money you must put into the business. The most common sources of equity financing are personal funds, family and friends, partners, venture capital firms, small business investment companies (SBICs), angels, and various forms of stock offerings.

Personal Funds   Most new businesses are originally financed with their creators' funds. The Department of Commerce estimates that nearly two-thirds of all start-ups are begun without borrowed funds. The first place most entrepreneurs find equity capital is in their personal assets. Cash, savings accounts, and checking accounts are the most obvious

Credit Card Start-up Funding—Really??

Credit cards for financing small business? Your loan officer will say, "Don't use them." Your SCORE (Service Corp of Retired Executives) counselor will say, "Don't even think about it." The Kauffman Foundation states that for every $1,000 increase in credit card debt, the odds that the small business will fail increases by 2.2 percent. These credit cards have increased risk because while the personal credit history of the small business owner is used for the approval process, the credit limit is set higher since it is for business use with no increased collateral required. Today many small business owners are using credit cards as a partial source of funding, but this approach isn't for the faint of heart.

Diana Frerick loved to belt out Whitney Houston songs on karaoke nights. When she tried to turn her passion into a business, however, no one wanted to listen. Frerick used two credit cards to spend $5,000 on a karaoke system and music and started hosting private parties and corporate functions. Three years later, she and a partner opened Karaoke Star Store & Stage, again using her cards to pay for inventory and supplies. Now they employ 14 people and generate revenues of $2 million.

Credit cards are enticing because most offer extremely low introductory rates—3.9 percent, 2.9 percent, even 0 percent—for a limited time. When those introductory rates end, the annual percentage rate charged can jump as high as 22 percent within a matter of months. Think of it this way: If you aren't earning 22 percent on your equity, how can you afford to pay 22 percent for credit? Answer: You can't. Are you anxious to see how bankruptcy court works?

If you choose to finance via credit cards, how do you tell if you are overextended?

- *You are unaware of your bills.* You should know how much you owe and whom you owe it to. Evaluate your credit report and your monthly credit card statement.
- *You are paying the minimum.* Pay off the credit card balances on a regular basis. If you are paying only the minimum payment allowed, it is a sign that you are in over your head.
- *You max out.* If your credit cards are close to or at their limit, you are in debt overload.

If you do choose to use credit cards to finance or cash flow your business, choose wisely; Kiplinger's Personal Finance reports two credit cards that can work effectively for small business owners. The first is the American Express SimplyCash Business Card. This credit card has no fees and offers cash back on certain products purchased, like gas and office supplies. The second credit card is the Plum Card from American Express. With this card, if you pay off your balance early, you get a credit on your next month's statement. Also, if a certain amount of your bill is paid, you can get an extension on the remainder. Clearly all credit cards are not created equally for the small business owner. If you choose to use credit cards for financing, choose carefully and use wisely.

Sources: "Credit Cards with a Head for Business," *Kiplinger's Personal Finance*, October 2009, 70; "The Long View," *Fortune Small Business*, October 2009, 16; Maria Aspan, "Pulling Back in a Big Way in Small-Business Cards," *American Banker*, November 26, 2008, 1–9; Robert Janis, "Small-Business Credit Card Use on the Rise," *Black Enterprise*, April 2007, 48–48; Bobbie Gossage, "Financing with Plastic: A Recipe for Disaster?" *WSJ Startup Journal*, June 2004, www.startupjournal.com.

sources of equity funds. Additional sources are the sale of stocks, bonds, mutual funds, real estate, or other personal investments.

The three Albertos—Perez, Perlman, and Aghion—have created a business opportunity from the fitness trend. Perez created Zumba, a Colombian dance fitness program, by accident. He had forgotten to bring his usual music to a fitness class he was teaching and all he had with him was Latin music. He improvised with the Latin music and new "moves," and a new fitness routine was born. Perez taught lessons and with that money developed a video demo that was sent to a larger company, which then licensed the name and concept and developed home videos and infomercials for Zumba. From this beginning, Zumba has sold hundreds of thousands of videos, developed merchandise, provided instructor certification, and developed training sessions, all from forgotten music.[19]

Family and Friends The National Federation of Independent Business reported a 2010 survey that stated that more than one-third of new businesses are at least partially funded by the family and friends of the entrepreneurs.[20] Family and friends are more willing to risk capital in a venture owned by someone they know than in ventures about which they know little or nothing. This financing is viewed as equity as long as there is no set repayment schedule.

Financing a business with capital from family and friends, however, creates a type of risk not found with other funding sources. If the business is not successful and the funds cannot be repaid, relationships with family and friends can become strained. You should explain the potential risk of failure inherent in the venture before accepting any money from family and friends. The key is to be sure you have a written contract with an investment letter that clearly outlines who approached whom about the funds in question and explains the specific terms of the funding.[21]

"Partners may play an active role in the venture's operation or may choose to be 'silent,' providing funds only in exchange for an equity position."

Partners Acquiring one or more partners is another way to secure equity capital (see Chapter 2). Approximately 10 percent of U.S. businesses are partnerships. Many partnerships are formed to take advantage of diverse skills or attributes that can be contributed to the new business. For example, one person may have the technical skills required to run the business, whereas another person may have the capital to finance it. Together they form a partnership to accomplish a common goal.

Partners may play an active role in the venture's operation or may choose to be "silent," providing funds only in exchange for an equity position. The addition of one or more partners expands not only the amount of equity capital available for the business, but also the ability of the business to borrow funds. This is due to the cumulative creditworthiness of the partners versus that of the entrepreneur alone.

Venture Capital Firms *Venture capital firms* are groups of individuals or companies that invest significant amount of dollars in new or expanding firms. VCs, as they are called, usually expect a higher rate of return, 20%–50%, and expect to have a sizeable ownership position in your business as their return on investment.[22] Of the more than 600 venture capital firms operating in the United States, approximately 500 are private independent firms, about 65 are major corporations, and the rest are affiliated with banks. Obtaining capital from them is not easy.

Most venture capital firms have investment policies that outline their preferences relative to industry, geographic location, investment size, and investment maturity. These firms look for businesses with the potential for rapid growth and high profitability. They provide funds in exchange for an equity position, which they hope to sell off within five to ten years or less.

A recent study showed that the average sum invested by venture capital firms is between $1.5 million and $2 million per business, with an overall range between $23,000 to more than $50 million. An excellent business plan is essential when approaching a venture capital firm, and a referral from a credible source—such as a banker or attorney familiar to the venture capital firm—may also be necessary. It takes an average of six to eight months to receive a potential investment decision. It has been estimated that less than 10 percent of the plans submitted to venture capital firms are ultimately funded.[23]

Venture capital firms rarely invest in retail operations. Instead, they tend to focus on high-technology industries, growth industries, and essential services. Ventures within these fields with strong, experienced management teams have the best chance of being funded. *Pratt's Guide to Venture Capital Success* is a good source of information on this source of financing.

Three engineers, Richard Yemm, Chris Retzler, and Dave Pizer, have created the "Sea Snake," a 180-meter mechanical sea monster that produces electricity when ocean waves hit the giant machine. While developing this new alternative energy source, Yemm sold another invention and used credit cards to work on his entrepreneurial idea. After building a prototype, the team was able to garner financial support from venture capitalists interested in the project. Today, 16 investors are helping to fund the company, Pelamis Wave Power, Ltd., as it further develops and sells this alternative energy technology.[24]

Small Business Investment Companies   *Small business investment companies (SBICs)* are venture capital firms licensed by the SBA to invest in small businesses. SBICs were authorized by Congress in 1958 to provide equity financing to qualified enterprises. In 1969, the SBA, in cooperation with the Department of Commerce, created *minority enterprise small business investment companies (MESBICs)* to provide equity financing to minority entrepreneurs. Any business that is more than 50 percent owned by African Americans, Hispanic Americans, Native Americans, Alaska Natives, or socially and economically disadvantaged Americans is eligible for funding.

SBICs and MESBICs are formed by financial institutions, corporations, or individuals, although a few are publicly owned. These investment companies must be capitalized with at least $500,000 of private funds. Once capitalized, they can receive as much as $4 from the SBA for each $1 in private money invested.

SBICs and MESBICs are excellent sources of both start-up and expansion capital. Like venture capital firms, however, they tend to have investment policies regarding geographic area and industry. There are approximately 300 SBICs and MESBICs currently in operation in the United States. They are listed in the *Directory of Operating Small Business Investment Companies* available from any SBA office.

angel
A lender, usually a successful entrepreneur, who loans money to help new businesses.

Angels   An **angel** is a wealthy, experienced individual who has a desire to assist start-up or emerging businesses, frequently in companies in their communities. Often they provide funding for start-ups that will allow the business to grow to the point where a VC will then pick up the funding. Most angels are self-made entrepreneurs who want to help sustain the system that allowed them to become successful. Usually they are knowledgeable about the market and technology areas in which they invest.

According to a study on business angels, there are more than 250,000 such investors in the United States. A typical angel investment ranges from $20,000 to $50,000, although nearly one-fourth are for more than $50,000. An angel can add much more than money to a business, however. His business know-how and contacts can prove far more valuable to the success of the business than the capital invested.

Several types of angel investors exist. *Corporate angels* are typically former senior managers of *Fortune* 1000 companies. In addition to getting their cash, you may persuade them to fill a management position in your company (they generally do the biggest deals, ranging from $200,000 to $1 million). *Entrepreneurial angels* own and operate their own businesses and are looking for ways to diversify their portfolios. They almost always want a seat on the board, but rarely want a management spot (deals run from $200,000 to $500,000). *Enthusiast angels* generally do smaller deals ($10,000 to $200,000), are older and wealthy, and invest for a hobby. *Professional angels* include doctors, lawyers, accountants, and other professionals. They like to invest in companies that offer products with which they are familiar. They can offer value through their expertise. *Micromanagement angels* are very serious investors. They are typically self-made, wealthy individuals who definitely want to be involved in your company strategy.[25]

When approaching angel investors, some experience and an in-depth knowledge of your business are essential. Since most angels are entrepreneurs themselves, they have "been there" and can spot someone who doesn't know their business inside and out. Be

"Since most angels are entrepreneurs themselves, they have 'been there' and can spot someone who doesn't know their business inside and out."

prepared to answer all questions, including the tough ones, angels will ask, such as why are you purchasing that piece of equipment? Angels will see through "fluff" answers immediately. *Inc.* magazine listed their 2009 guide to angel investors. Here are a few:

- Keiretsu Forum—looking for technology, health care/life sciences, and real estate companies, with a typical investment of $250,000 to $2 million
- Walnut Venture Associates—looking for New England–based businesses involved in IT, software, and Internet apps, with a typical investment of $250,000 to $1 million
- Utah Angels—looking for locally based companies where industry is not important, with a typical investment of $50,000 to $2 million
- Alliance of Angels—looking for high-tech, consumer products and retail businesses with typical investments of $500,000 to $700,000[26]

Finding an angel investor is not easy. The best ways for an entrepreneur to locate one are to maintain business contacts with tax attorneys, bankers, and accountants in the closest metropolitan area and to ask for an introduction. Networking can be key.

Mergers and Acquisitions (M&A)　Merging with a company flush with cash can provide a viable source of capital. Such transactions may trigger many legal, structural, and tax issues, however, that you must then work out with your accountant and lawyer. Deals for small to midsized companies have become increasingly popular as consolidation in technology-based industries occurs.

Stock Offerings　Selling company stock is another route for obtaining equity financing. The entrepreneur must consider this decision very carefully, however. The sale of stock results in the entrepreneur's losing a portion of the ownership of the business. Furthermore, certain state and federal laws govern the way in which stock offerings are made. Private placements and public offerings are two types of stock sales.

Private Placements　A *private placement* involves the sale of stock to a selected group of individuals. This stock cannot be purchased by the general public. Sales may be in any amount, but placements less than $500,000 are subject to fewer government-imposed restrictions and trigger less onerous disclosure requirements than those in excess of $500,000. If the company selling the stock is located and doing business in only one state, and stock is sold only to individuals within that same state, the sale is considered an *intrastate stock sale* subject only to that state's regulations. If the sale involves more than one state, then it is an *interstate stock sale*, and the federal Securities and Exchange Commission's regulations will apply.

What if one partner wants out of a business and the remaining partner or partners don't have the cash for a buyout? *Recapitalization* means rearranging the financial structure of a business—generally by using a combination of debt and third-party investors like private equity firms.

Public Offerings　A *public offering* involves the sale of stock to the general public. These sales always are governed by Securities and Exchange Commission regulations. Complying with these regulations is both costly and time-consuming. For public offerings valued between $400,000 and $1 million, the legal fees, underwriting fees, audits, printing expenses, and other costs can easily exceed 15 percent.

The first time a company offers its stock to the general public is called an ***initial public offering (IPO)***. To be a viable candidate for an IPO, a company must be in good financial health and able to attract an underwriter (typically a stock brokerage firm or investment banker) to help sell the stock offering. In addition, the market conditions must be favorable for selling equity securities.

"Finding an angel investor is not easy. The best ways for an entrepreneur to locate one are to maintain business contacts with tax attorneys, bankers, and accountants in the closest metropolitan area and to ask for an introduction. Networking can be key."

initial public offering (ipo)
The first sale of stock of a business made available to public investors.

ENTREPRENEURIAL SNAPSHOT

© Courtesy of Citi Storage

Brodsky Says ...

Norm Brodsky is a serial entrepreneur who has founded and grown six businesses. His latest venture, CitiStorage, a document-archive business out of Brooklyn, New York, sold for $110 million. He also writes the column "Street Smarts" and is a senior contributing editor for *Inc.*

Over the years with his six businesses, Brodsky has developed what he calls the "knack," a set of guidelines that can be applied to a wide variety of businesses. He attributes these guidelines to lessons he learned as a child, to lessons learned from mentors, and to lessons learned from the school of hard knocks. Here are some of his guidelines for small business owners:

1. Pay attention to the numbers. The only way to truly know how your business is performing is to look at the numbers. Don't wait for the accountant to tell you. Learn enough about the numbers that you understand the story they are telling.

2. Keep the numbers by hand until you understand where they are coming from and what those numbers mean. Software packages are great, but unless you understand the complexities and relationships demonstrated by the numbers, important informa-

tion can be missed. Use paper, pencil, and a calculator, and keep track of the numbers of your business.

3. If short-term liabilities are greater than short-term assets, you are bankrupt. The current ratio is one of those numbers to watch carefully. You must have enough cash on hand to pay your current liabilities as they come due. If you don't, your business won't succeed.

4. Diversify your customer base, especially in the beginning. The bigger the sale to one customer, the greater the risk if that customer does not pay you. Credit checks on customers are important—at least the customers to whom you make big sales.

5. Focus on gross margin, not sales. Gross margin is the profit you make after you pay the direct cost of producing your good or service. All other expenses must come out of gross margin. With a gross margin of 10 percent, you will need $10 of sales for every dollar of overhead just to breakeven.

6. Cash is easy to spend and hard to make. Don't spend cash you do not have, and spend cash only on those assets and expenses that move your company toward being able to sustain its cash flow.

Sources: Norm Brodsky, "Secrets of a $110 Million Man," *Inc.*, October 2008, 77–81; and Norm Brodsky, "It's the Best Way to Spot Problems before They Become Life-Threatening," *Inc.*, January 2008, 63–64.

There are three main reasons companies choose public offerings:

1. When market conditions are favorable, more funds can be raised through public offerings than through other venture capital methods, without imposing the repayment burdens of debt.
2. Having an established public price for the company's stock enhances its image.
3. The owner's wealth can be magnified greatly when owner-held shares are subsequently sold in the market.

One critical caution about public stock offerings is that they require companies to make financial disclosures to the public. If a company fails to live up to its self-reported expectations, shareholders can sue the company, charging that the company withheld or misrepresented important information.

Choosing a Lender or Investor

A key decision facing entrepreneurs is determining which sources of financing to pursue. Your choice will often be limited by the degree to which you meet the requirements of each lending or investing source. If you decide to pursue *debt financing*, you must have the minimum down payment or other capital requirements necessary to secure the loan. Assuming that these requirements can be met, you will have to determine which lending source to approach. Usually the foremost criterion will be finding the lowest cost or interest rate available. However other important lender-selection considerations are:

1. *Size.* The lender should be small enough to consider the entrepreneur an important customer, but large enough to service the entrepreneur's future needs.
2. *Desire.* The lender should exhibit a desire to work with start-up and emerging businesses, rather than considering them too risky.
3. *Approach to problems.* The lender should be supportive of small businesses facing problems, offering constructive advice and financing alternatives.
4. *Industry experience.* The lender should have experience in the entrepreneur's industry, especially with start-up or emerging ventures.

The best guideline may be to seek the lenders with which you feel the most comfortable. A loan relationship can last for a decade or more. Finding a lending source that is pleasant to work with is often as important as finding the lowest cost of debt.

If you decide to pursue *equity financing*, you should consider the fact that close personal relationships can become strained when money is involved. Although the use of funds obtained from family members, friends, or partners is perhaps conceivable, none of these sources may be acceptable or feasible for personal reasons.

Autonomy is another important consideration. Equity financing always requires that you give up a portion of ownership in the venture. If independence is critical to you, then think carefully about the source of equity you pursue.

The most important criterion in choosing investors should be matching what the business needs with what the investors can offer. If the business requires only money, then you should attempt to find a "silent" partner—one who is willing to provide capital without playing an active role in the management of the business. Conversely, if your business needs a particular type of expertise, in addition to money, then you should seek an investor who can provide management advice or other assistance along with needed capital. For example, a new business in a high-tech industry might pursue angel financing from a successful individual who has prospered in that industry.

Entrepreneurial guru Jeffry A. Timmons offers a few more cautions when choosing an investor. Each of the following "sand traps," he says, imposes a responsibility on the entrepreneur:

1. *Strategic circumference.* A fundraising decision can affect future financing choices. Raising equity capital may reduce your freedom to choose additional financing sources in the future, due to the partial loss of ownership control that accompanies equity financing.
2. *Legal circumference.* Financing deals can place unwanted limitations and constraints on the unwary entrepreneur. It is imperative to read and understand the details of each financing document. Competent legal representation is recommended.
3. *Opportunity cost.* Entrepreneurs often overlook the time, effort, and creative energy required to locate and secure financing. A long search can exhaust the entrepreneur's personal funds before the business ever gets off the ground.
4. *Attraction to status and size.* Many entrepreneurs seek financing from the most prestigious and high-profile firms. Often a better fit is found with lesser-known firms that have firsthand experience with the type of business the entrepreneur is starting.
5. *Being too anxious.* If the entrepreneur has a sound business plan, more than one venture capital firm may be interested in investing in it. By accepting the first offer, the entrepreneur could overlook a better deal from another source.[27]

"Although the use of funds obtained from family members, friends, or partners is perhaps conceivable, none of these sources may be acceptable or feasible for personal reasons."

Clearly, choosing a lender or investor takes time and patience. The process is similar to finding a spouse. The relationship that is forged between the entrepreneur and the source of financing can be long-lasting and should be mutually beneficial.

Summary

1. Determine the financing needs of your business.

A straightforward process for determining financing need is to (1) list the assets required for your business to operate effectively and the needed expenses; (2) determine the market value or cost of each asset; (3) identify how much capital you are able to provide; and (4) subtract the total of the owner-provided funds from the total of the assets and expenses required. This figure represents the minimum amount of financing required.

2. Define basic financing terminology.

To procure financing, you must understand the basic financial vocabulary. Each major form of capital (debt and equity) has unique terminology that defines the details underlying financing agreements.

Each form of capital has pros and cons that make it more or less desirable to the entrepreneur under given circumstances.

3. Explain where to look for sources of funding.

The search for capital and the application process can be unsettling as you sort through the various sources of funds. Major sources of debt financing include commercial banks, finance companies, government lenders, and insurance companies. Sources of equity include personal funding sources, partners, venture capital firms, angels, and stock offerings. Finding capital is one of the most important tasks you face in starting and managing a business. A thorough understanding of the issues involved will enhance your chances of finding the best source for your business.

Questions for Review and Discussion

1. Define "initial capital requirements." How can you determine these?
2. What are the five "Cs" of credit, and how do lenders use them?
3. What are the differences between debt funds and equity funds?
4. What kinds of businesses would depend on floor planning?
5. What does "pledging accounts receivable" mean?
6. What are the advantages of borrowing through the SBA?
7. Why do suppliers extend trade credit to other businesses? What are the advantages and disadvantages of using trade credit?
8. How do private placements and public offerings differ?
9. Discuss the types of interest rates that may apply to a loan.
10. What is the difference between a secured loan and an unsecured loan?

Questions for Critical Thinking

1. According to *Inc.* magazine, of the approximately 600,000 companies that started in the year 2000, only about 5,000 received funding from venture capitalists. If just this small percentage actually received venture capital, why do small business magazines print such a disproportionately large number of articles about venture capital?
2. How and why does a small business's capital structure change over time?

What Would You Do?

Finding money to finance your small business can be a real challenge. You might look to the traditional avenues, such as using personal funds, tapping the resources of family and friends, or even relying on partners for financial backing. In the mid-1990s, however, a new approach to finding financing emerged—one that utilizes the networking capability of the Internet. That's what Pam Marrone of AgraQuest, Inc., tapped into when she needed additional financing.

Marrone's Davis, California, company develops and manufactures all-natural pesticides. She needed $ 2.5 million to pay the research, development, and production costs of two pest-control products. Marrone knew how to find money the old-fashioned way. After all, she had raised $300,000 in start-up financing to launch her company. But when she began looking to expand her business's product line, she decided to experiment with a more direct link to potential investors via the Internet.

Marrone chose to list her business idea (at a minimal charge) with Venture Connect, a Web site designed to match investors and entrepreneurs. She also developed her own company home page, which included an extensive business summary and job postings, and promoted it through Yahoo!'s business directory. "This is a potential way to get directly to investors," Marrone said. "The responses have been fast." Marrone was confident that her unique search for financing would pay off, yet she was being just as cautious in her search for financing in this high-tech approach as if she had taken a more traditional approach. After all, we're still talking about money.

Questions

1. What are the advantages and disadvantages of financing via the Internet, as Marrone did?

2. Should Marrone use her Internet financing source exclusively, or should she maintain a relationship with her local bank commercial loan officer? Why or why not?

10
Legal Issues

CHAPTER LEARNING OUTCOMES

After reading this chapter, you should be able to:

1. **Name the laws and regulations that affect small business.**

2. **List and explain the types of bankruptcy.**

3. **Describe the elements of a contract.**

4. **Discuss how to protect intellectual property.**

Zippo lighters have been providing reliable flame for more than 75 years. Unfortunately, up to 50 percent of the simple, iconic lighters sold around the world are counterfeit. Jeff Duke, general counsel for Zippo, says, "It's not rocket science. Anybody involved in light-metal manufacturing could gear up to make this product. We make it better and faster than anybody in the world, but there really isn't anything we can do to stop the counterfeiters from copying it."

What is the big deal, you think? Maybe you've been tempted by a $35 Louis Vuitton purse or $20 Dolce & Gabbana sunglasses. Fakes have cut into Zippo's revenue by about 25 percent, forcing the layoff of 15 percent of its labor force—121 employees. Such is the dilemma faced by many businesses.

The U.S. Department of Commerce reports that U.S. businesses lose an estimated $200 billion annually to the counterfeiting of trademarked and copyrighted products. The International Chamber of Commerce also estimates that counterfeit goods of all kinds account for 6 percent of all world trade—about $600 billion. The electronics industry puts the number of fakes between 5 and 20 percent, costing about $1 billion per year.

A recent study by consulting firm KPMG notes several ways to mitigate

counterfeiting. Among them: use *radio frequency identification (RFID)* and other product-tracking technologies, coordinate with trade groups and business partners to respond to counterfeiting, and partner with and assist police agencies in detecting and busting counterfeiters. Pearl started by changing his packaging to be harder to duplicate, but it only took about six months for the counterfeiters to copy that also.

Imitation may be the sincerest form of flattery, but it's a huge problem for small businesses. Since most small business owners don't have the time, patience, or money to protect themselves, they are more than twice as likely to be victims of counterfeit fraud as big business. In late 2009, the United States appointed its first "IP tsar" to develop a new enforcement strategy. The European Union, United States, and Japan are discussing a new treaty called the Anti-Counterfeiting Trade Agreement (ACTA) to strengthen international controls on counterfeits and piracy.

Sources: "Knock-offs Catch On," *Economist*, March 6, 2010, 81–82; Joe Castaldo, "Counterfeiting Cat-and-Mouse," *Canadian Business*, May 24, 2010, 16; Gay Bryant, "Who's Stealing Your Business," *Fortune Small Business*, May 2008, 68–71; Laura Palotie and Alexandra Zendrain, "Attack of the $35 Gucci Handbag," *Inc.*, April 29, 2008, www.inc.com; Paul Romano, "Prepare Your Counterattack against Counterfeit Parts," *Electronic Design*, June 10, 2010, 3A–5A; and "Counterfeiting, Piracy Persist on a Global Scale," *Industry Week*, June 2010, 17, www.industryweek.com.

Small Business and the Law

"We need laws to ensure competition, enforce contracts, and protect our rights as consumers, workers, and property owners."

Would you like to live in a place with no laws? You could drive as fast as you wanted. You could drink alcohol at any age. You could do whatever you wanted, and, just think, there would be no taxes to pay because there would be no government making up rules and regulations! Although such absolute freedom might sound exciting at first thought, you don't have to picture this scenario for long to realize that it also includes no protection for anyone or any groups—it would be chaos. Orderly, civilized societies are built on laws.

We need laws to ensure fair competition between businesses, to protect the rights of consumers and employees, to protect property, to enforce contracts and agreements, and to permit bankruptcy when things go bad. And we need tax laws to collect the money needed for government to provide these protections. The balance of how much or how little protection we need or we want changes over time. Through elections and open debate, our laws evolve to reflect the needs of and changes in society. But, as an old saying goes, "It's a good thing that we don't get half the government we pay for."

Small business owners face a never-ending job of keeping up with the laws and regulations by which they must abide. One problem is that the wording of many laws and regulations is often baffling and easy to misunderstand. A second problem for small businesses is the enormous amount of paperwork required to generate the many reports and records mandated by regulations. This paperwork imposes time and resource burdens on business owners who are often strapped for both. A third problem is the cost (for administrative and actual expenses) and difficulty in complying with regulations.

Running a small business does not require a law degree, but you do need two things to avoid trouble: a working knowledge of legal basics and a good lawyer. The best time to find a lawyer for your small business is when you are writing your business plan—not when you are already in trouble.

A study by the National Federation of Independent Business (NFIB) titled "Small-Business Problems and Priorities" showed that the top 10 small business problems are split between costs, such as health care, and dealing with government regulations. NFIB Senior Research Fellow Bruce Phillips noted, "Small business owners' most serious problems are politically generated, rather than spawned from free-market competition." Small business owners consider managing the daily burdens of health care costs, taxation, and regulation mandates to be far more difficult than what they do best—running a business. Figure 10.1 shows the top 10 responses from more than 3,500 small business owners to a 2008 survey dealing with cost- and regulation-related issues.

Regulations and the legal environment of small business cover a lot of ground. This chapter will discuss several major areas of business affected by the law: regulations, licenses, bankruptcy, contracts, and protection of intellectual property.

Laws to Promote Fair Business Competition

Competition among businesses lies at the heart of a free enterprise system (see Chapter 1). Healthy competition provides the balance needed to ensure that buyers and sellers are both satisfied. It decreases the need for government intervention in the market.

antitrust laws

Legislation that prohibits firms from combining in a way that would stifle competition within that industry.

Antitrust laws like the Sherman Antitrust Act of 1890 and the Clayton Act of 1914 were written to prevent large businesses from forming *trusts*—large combinations of firms that can dominate an industry and stifle competition, thereby preventing new or small businesses from participating. Under such laws, any agreements or contracts that restrain trade are illegal and unenforceable. The Sherman Antitrust Act and the Clayton Act are two of the best-known antitrust laws and are still widely used in preventing business mergers and acquisitions judged to decrease competition. These laws are worthy of mention here because small businesses benefit from open competitive environments.

The Federal Trade Commission Act of 1914 created the Federal Trade Commission (FTC), the agency that regulates competition, advertising, and pricing in the U.S. economy. The five-member commission has the power to conduct hearings, direct investigations, and issue *cease-and-desist orders*, which prohibit offending companies from unfair or deceptive practices such as *collusion* (acting together to keep prices artificially high). These cease-and-desist orders are enforceable in federal court.

Laws to Protect Consumers

Up until the past few decades, U.S. consumer laws were based on the rule of *caveat emptor*: "Let the buyer beware." Now laws have largely abandoned this precept to offer ever increasing protection for consumers, administered by a wide variety of state and federal agencies. The most common practices that government protects consumers against involve extension of credit, deceptive trade practices, unsafe products, and unfair pricing.

The FTC, for instance, is involved in product-labeling standards; banning hazardous products; ensuring consumer product safety; regulating the content and message of advertising; ensuring truth-in-lending practices, equal credit access to consumers, and fair credit practices; and many other areas. Many laws that are intended to protect consumers fall under the jurisdiction of the FTC, including the Nutrition Labeling and Education Act, the Fair Debt Collection Practices Act, the Truth-in-Lending Act, and the Consumer Product Safety Act, to name but a few. The FTC is an agency of the federal government with broad and deep power when it comes to protecting consumers.

Laws to Protect People in the Workplace

A major thrust of federal employment legislation today is ensuring equal employment opportunity. This goal is based on the belief that an individual should be considered for employment on the basis of her individual merit, without regard to race, color, religion, sex, age, national origin, or disability. This goal dates back to the U.S. Constitution, and it was fortified by passage of the Fourteenth and Fifteenth Amendments in the 1860s. Beginning in the early 1960s, in response to great social change and widespread

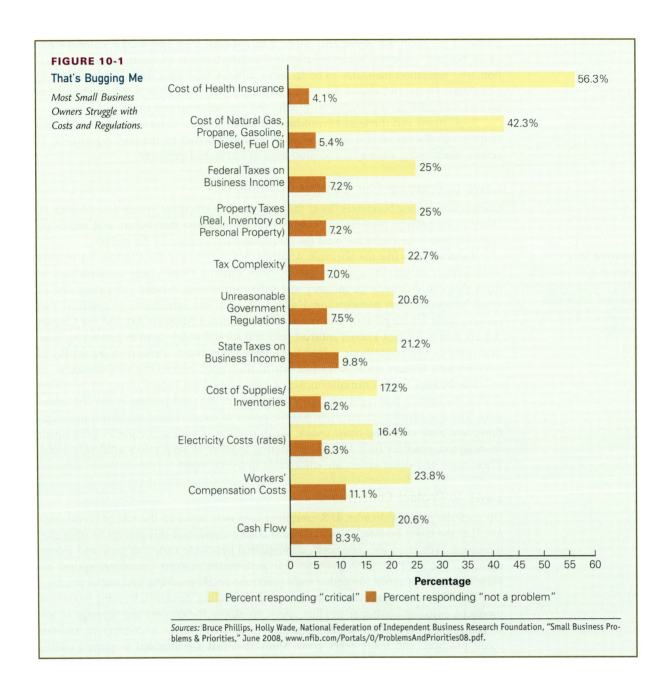

FIGURE 10-1

That's Bugging Me

Most Small Business Owners Struggle with Costs and Regulations.

Cost of Health Insurance — 56.3% / 4.1%
Cost of Natural Gas, Propane, Gasoline, Diesel, Fuel Oil — 42.3% / 5.4%
Federal Taxes on Business Income — 25% / 7.2%
Property Taxes (Real, Inventory or Personal Property) — 25% / 7.2%
Tax Complexity — 22.7% / 7.0%
Unreasonable Government Regulations — 20.6% / 7.5%
State Taxes on Business Income — 21.2% / 9.8%
Cost of Supplies/Inventories — 17.2% / 6.2%
Electricity Costs (rates) — 16.4% / 6.3%
Workers' Compensation Costs — 23.8% / 11.1%
Cash Flow — 20.6% / 8.3%

Percentage

☐ Percent responding "critical"   ■ Percent responding "not a problem"

Sources: Bruce Phillips, Holly Wade, National Federation of Independent Business Research Foundation, "Small Business Problems & Priorities," June 2008, www.nfib.com/Portals/0/ProblemsAndPriorities08.pdf.

unrest, Congress acted to strengthen the legal underpinnings of this belief, passing several comprehensive pieces of legislation, outlined here.

Fair Labor Standards Act   The Fair Labor Standards Act is the primary law, passed in 1938, regulating worker's pay. It sets the minimum wage for all covered employees, overtime pay for nonexempt workers, equal pay for men and women, and rules for child labor.

Five categories of workers are exempt from the minimum wage and overtime pay requirements: executive, administrative, and professional employees; outside salespeople; and people in certain computer-related occupations. Each state also has its own (generally complicated) minimum wage guidelines.

Reality Check

Who Can You Trust?

Unfortunately, some employees turn out to be un-scrupulous individuals. Small business owners have trouble defending themselves against these of-fenders. For example:

- When a sweet elderly lady asked the founder of a small women's clothing manufacturer for a job "at any wage, just to fill up my time," he hired her to clean desks. After exactly 10 days of work, she asked for a leave of absence. Still sentimental, the business owner said, "Give a call when you are ready to come back." The sweet lady didn't call back, but her lawyer did. She had filed a suit against the company claiming that she developed double carpal tun-nel syndrome that prevented her from doing work of any kind—to the tune of $20,000 per wrist! Many months and many legal fees later, the owner ended up settling on the courthouse steps, even though he found out that the ex-employee had lined up her lawyer before she applied at the business.

- A regional law firm hired an applicant who claimed on her résumé that she had a bachelor's degree in management informa-tion systems (MIS) and an MBA. Based on those qualifications, she was hired as information systems director at a $105,000 annual salary. Two years later, the firm dis-covered that the employee had embezzled more than $2 million by creating two ficti-tious suppliers.

- An Alabama bookstore bookkeeper was taking money meant for vendors to pay for personal expenses. Without internal controls, the owner believed her employee—who has since been charged with 25 counts of criminal possession of a forged instrument in the second degree. The bookkeeper had stolen approximately $150,000 over two and a half years.

What can you do if you are a small business owner facing such circumstances? Sometimes not much. As Mark Twain said, "Trust everyone, but make sure you cut the cards."

Sources: Daniel Wolfe, "The Enemy Within," *American Banker*, February 25, 2009, 7; Phaedra Hise, "Employees from Hell," *Fortune Small Business*, March 2007, 18–28; and Natt Reifler, "Employee Theft: What You Don't Know Can Hurt You," *Franchising World*, October 2008, 26–29.

Compliance is regulated by the Equal Employment Opportunity Commission (EEOC). Employers covered by the law must provide, on request, detailed records of compensation, including rates of pay, hours worked, overtime payments, deductions, and other related pay data. In addition, supporting documents, such as wage surveys, job descriptions, job evaluation studies, and collective bargaining agreements, may be requested.

Civil Rights Act of 1964 The Civil Rights Act (CRA) of 1964 prevents discrimination on the basis of sex, race, color, religion, or national origin in any terms, conditions, or pri-vileges of employment. Discrimination on the basis of pregnancy, childbirth, and related medical conditions is also prohibited as a result of a 1978 amendment. Title VII of this legislation applies to all organizations with 15 or more employees working 20 or more weeks per year in commerce or in any industry or activity affecting commerce. As amended, state and local governments, labor unions, employment agencies, and educa-tional institutions are also covered.

Provisions of the act are enforced by the EEOC. Private employers with 100 or more employees are required to annually file Form EEO-1, detailing the makeup of the com-pany's workforce. In addition, all employers are required to keep employment-related documents for at least six months from the time of their creation or, in the case of a personnel action such as a discharge, from the date of the action.

Immigration Reform and Control Act The Immigration Reform and Control Act (IRCA) was passed in 1986 with two intended goals. First, it seeks to discourage illegal immigration into the United States by denying employment to aliens who do not comply with the Immigration and Naturalization Service regulations. It achieves this goal by requiring employers to document worker eligibility. All U.S. employers must complete Form I-9 for new hires, for which the employee must provide documentation proving his identity and work authorization. Permissible documents include a birth certificate, U.S. passport, certificate of U.S. citizenship, certificate of naturalization, unexpired foreign passport, resident alien card, or combination of documents attesting to identity and employment authorization as outlined on Form I-9.[1]

A second goal of the act was to strengthen the national-origin provisions of Title VII of the 1964 CRA by extending coverage to "foreign-sounding" and "foreign-looking" individuals, and to all employers with four or more employees (rather than the "15 or more employees" limit established by the CRA). If found guilty of discrimination under the IRCA, you may be assessed back pay for up to two years and civil fines of up to $2,000 per violation and $10,000 for multiple violations.[2] Enforcement responsibilities were assigned to the Office of the Special Counsel for Immigration-Related Unfair Employment Practices, a division of the Department of Justice.

The ongoing debate and recent demonstrations surrounding immigration reform are being watched closely by politicians, citizens, and businesspeople alike—especially small business owners. In 2010, the Department of Homeland Security increased immigration enforcement through partnerships with state and local law enforcement agencies and expansion of E-Verify. E-Verify is a Web-based system that compares employee information from I-9 forms against federal government databases in order to verify a worker's employment eligibility. Fifteen states have mandated that either government contractors or all employers use E-Verify.[3]

Americans with Disabilities Act   The 1990 Americans with Disabilities Act (ADA) was passed to guarantee individuals with disabilities the right to obtain and hold a job, to travel on public transportation, to enter and use public facilities, and to use telecommunication services. One or more of the act's provisions affects almost all businesses, regardless of size.

If you are a private employer with 15 or more employees (including part-time employees) working 20 or more calendar weeks per year, you are covered by Title I, the employment discrimination provision. As such, you cannot discriminate against qualified disabled individuals with regard to any employment practice or terms, conditions, and privileges of employment. Under the act, a *disabled person* is one who (1) has a physical or mental impairment that substantially limits one or more major life activities, (2) has a physical or mental impairment, or (3) is regarded as having such an impairment. Specifically included within this definition are recovering drug addicts, alcoholics, and individuals who are infected with HIV or who have AIDS.

In turn, a *qualified applicant* is one who (1) meets the necessary prerequisites

Image copyright © Gina Sanders. Used under license from Shutterstock.com

The ADA assures business access to people with all types of disabilities.

for the job, such as education, work experience, or training; and (2) can perform the essential functions of the job with or without *reasonable accommodation*, meaning any modification of the work environment that makes it possible for an individual to enjoy equal employment opportunities without imposing *undue hardship* (defined shortly) on the employer. Once a set of effective accommodations has been identified—which might include restructuring a job, modifying work schedules, providing readers and interpreters, or obtaining and modifying equipment—you are free to select the option that is the least expensive or easiest to provide. Even then, you need make the accommodation only if it does not present an *undue hardship* on the operation of your business, meaning an action that is "excessively costly, extensive, substantial, or disruptive, or that would fundamentally alter the nature or operation of the business."[4] In determining undue hardship, you should consider the nature and cost of the accommodation in relation to your business's size, its financial resources (including available tax credits, as discussed later), the nature and structure of its operation, and the impact of the accommodation on its operation.

In addition to the necessity of making reasonable accommodation for disabled people, you should keep the following points in mind:

- Prior to making a conditional offer of employment, inquiries of others about the applicant's disability, illness, and workers' compensation history are prohibited.
- Required medical or physical examinations are prohibited prior to making a conditional offer of employment. Drug tests may be given at any point in the employment process, however, because they are not considered medical examinations under the law.
- Any selection or performance standards should be job related, be based on a thorough job analysis, and be prepared prior to advertising the position.
- Asking the applicant about the nature, origin, or severity of a known disability is prohibited. You may, however, question the applicant about his ability to perform the essential functions of the job and describe or demonstrate how to perform such functions.
- An employer may not refuse to hire an individual simply because she might or will require accommodation under the act.
- All application materials and processes from the application form to the interview and beyond must be free of references to or inquiries about disabilities.

Under Title III of the ADA, virtually all businesses serving the public must make their facilities and services accessible to the disabled. This may require you to modify your operational policies, practices, and procedures; remove structural barriers; and provide auxiliary aids and services to the disabled. Technical standards for building and site elements, such as parking, ramps, doors, and elevators, have been set forth in the *ADA Accessibility Guidelines for New Construction and Alterations* handbook. The handbook is available from the Office of the Americans with Disabilities Act, U.S. Department of Justice.

Tax incentives are available to aid businesses in complying with the ADA. The Disabled Access Credit allows small businesses to take a tax credit amounting to one-half the cost of eligible access expenditures that are more than $250 but less than $10,500.[5] You may also qualify for tax deductions under the Architectural and Transportation Barrier Removal and Targeted Job Tax Credit provisions. Contact your local IRS or vocational rehabilitation office for additional information.

While the ADA has literally broken down barriers for Americans with disabilities, and most small business owners say they want to comply with the act, many also believe that its requirements are growing vaguer and more onerous. They support the law's aims but find it vaguely written and hard to comply with. A young man with cerebral palsy went out for breakfast at the Blue Plate Café in Memphis. He arrived in a wheelchair, accompanied by a service dog to help him with tasks such as opening doors. The restaurant was crowded, so owner Mike Richmond says he made a decision: Because eight people came with the man and were available to help him, the dog would not be allowed into the dining area. The party then left. Not long afterward, Richmond was served with a lawsuit under the federal Americans with Disabilities Act. To head off a legal battle, he quickly settled. He agreed to pay $3,500 in damages to the man, as well as legal fees and a $1,000 fine. "I was shocked," says Richmond. "But with some of these ADA lawsuits, you don't even know the rules until you get hit."[6]

Civil Rights Act of 1991 Title VII of the Civil Rights Act applies to businesses with more than 15 employees. Some of its provisions are outlined here:

- The act prohibits *race norming*, an illegal activity in which different test standards are set for different groups.
- It provides that, in cases where an otherwise neutral employment practice results in an underrepresentation of minorities (called *disparate impact cases*), employers must show that (1) the practice is job related; (2) the practice is consistent with a *business necessity*, meaning that it exists in the best interests of the firm's employees and the general public; and (3) a less discriminatory practice does not exist.
- In cases of intentional discrimination, the act provides for both compensatory and punitive damages and allows for jury trials.
- It places a cap on the amount of punitive and compensatory damages that can be awarded, depending on company size.

Title VII applies to all employment practices, including help-wanted ads, employee reviews, and daily working conditions.

The Civil Rights Act also added teeth to the EEOC guidelines on *sexual harassment* (see Chapter 3) by providing victims of discrimination, including those subjected to sexual harassment, access to trial by jury, compensatory damages for pain and suffering, and punitive damages if employers are proven to have acted with "malice or reckless indifference."

Title VII applies to a business with 15 or more employees. State and local laws may cover all businesses. Sexual harassment covers behavior that creates a hostile work environment. Examples include the following:

- Unwelcome sexual advances.
- Requests for sexual favors.
- Verbal or physical conduct of a sexual nature.
- Sexually suggestive or offensive personal references about an individual.
- The victim or harasser may be male or female.
- The victim does not have to be of the opposite sex.
- The harasser can be the victim's supervisor, an agent of the employer, a supervisor of another area, a coworker, or a non-employee.
- The victim does not have to be the person harassed but can be anyone affected by the offensive conduct.
- Unlawful sexual harassment may occur without economic injury to or discharge of the victim.[7]

Because they can be held legally responsible not only for their own actions but also for the actions of their managers and employees, small businesses must prepare for potential problems by setting policies and procedures in advance of any complaint. Employees and managers need to be trained, as do subcontractors, because the business can be held liable for their actions as well. A business owner should be ready to investigate any complaint in a timely manner and poised to take appropriate action.

"Title VII applies to all employment practices, including help-wanted ads, employee reviews, and daily working conditions."

Health Care Reform There is no health insurance requirement for business owners with fewer than 50 employees. Firms with 50 workers or more must provide insurance to employees or pay a fine. Part-time employees are counted in the number of employees based on hours and wages, which means 50 part-time workers would be the same as 25 full-time workers.

Starting in 2014, states must create health insurance exchanges (pools) for small businesses and their employees. These marketplaces, or Small Business Health Options Programs (SHOPs), are meant to kick in as the 35 percent tax credit for providing insurance expires. Exchanges will allow small businesses to band together to gain better pricing, more options, and greater bargaining power.[8]

Workers' Compensation Workers' compensation (also known by the shorthand term *workers' comp*) is insurance that provides replacement income and medical expenses to employees who suffer injury, illness, or disease arising out of and in the course of their employment. This is a complex program that varies on a state-by-state basis. Any business with employees must purchase workers' comp either through a state fund or a private insurance company. Premiums are based on two major factors: industry classification and payroll. The number of claims that have been filed by your employees will affect your rates as well. Workers' compensation benefits include medical care to treat the injury, indemnity benefits to pay a fraction (usually two-thirds) of the employee's average weekly wage, and rehabilitation services if the employee has to be retrained for new work. Consequently, the financial ramifications of a claim being filed provide a powerful incentive for small businesses to create a safe workplace. Proper equipment, training in safe procedures, and instruction on how to act in emergencies are critical.

The costs of workers' compensation are now soaring to crisis levels. Nationwide, premiums increased by 50 percent in the first few years of the twenty-first century. Although relief is being sought, small businesses are especially hard hit by this trend because they cannot pass on these costs to their customers. Factors such as increased health care costs of treating claims and fear of terrorism also contribute to the rising premiums.[9]

Unemployment Compensation All employers are required to contribute to an unemployment insurance fund. Employees who have been fired due to cutbacks in the workforce or because of a poor fit with the company are generally entitled to unemployment payments for a set period of time. Employees who are terminated for serious misconduct, such as theft or fraud, or who quit voluntarily are not entitled to benefits. Check with your state unemployment office for details on premiums and requirements in your area.

Occupational Safety and Health Administration (OSHA) Congress passed the Occupational Safety and Health Act (OSHA) of 1970 to "assure, so far as possible, every working man and woman in the nation safe and healthful working conditions and to preserve our human resources."[10] OSHA has set workplace standards covering areas such as the following:

- Exposure to hazardous chemicals
- First aid and medical treatment
- Noise levels
- Protective gear—for example, goggles, respirators, gloves, work shoes, and ear protection
- Fire protection
- Worker training, and workplace temperatures and ventilation[11]

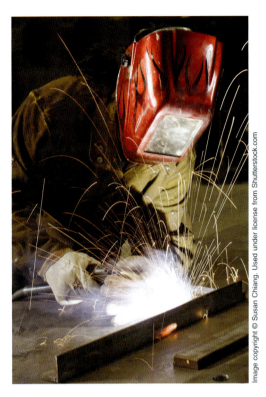

The intent of OSHA is to provide safe working conditions for people in all sizes of business.

OSHA compliance inspections are conducted to investigate a reported accident, injury, or fatality at a worksite; when an employee complaint alleges a violation; or as part of a regular or programmed schedule of inspections. If you, as an employer, are cited for a violation, you may either correct the alleged violation, seek a variance, or appeal the penalty.

OSHA requires most employers with 11 or more employees to keep records of occupational injuries and illnesses. Employers must also post an approved state or federal OSHA poster and any citations, which must be displayed at or near the site of the alleged violation for three days or until corrected, whichever is later.

As a small business owner, you may request information from one of ten regional OSHA offices or ask for a free on-site OSHA-supported consultation through your state's labor or health department. No citations will be issued or penalties proposed during this visit, nor will the name of your firm or any information regarding your firm be given to OSHA. However, you will be expected to correct any serious job safety and health hazards identified as part of the consultation.

Licenses, Restrictions, and Permits

Because requirements for licenses and permits differ at the federal, state, regional, county, and city government levels, presenting a comprehensive list of all of them is not possible here. Nevertheless, we can offer some general guidelines for finding information on regulations at each level.

- Double-check license and permit rules. Check with the appropriate government agency directly—don't rely on real estate agents, sellers, or anyone else's opinion.
- At the federal level, get an employer identification number for federal tax and Social Security withholdings. File Form 2553 if you are forming a corporation. Check with the appropriate agency for your specific type of business. For example, if you are starting a common-carrier trucking company, you should contact the Interstate Commerce Commission.
- At the state level, professionals, such as lawyers, dentists, and architects, need professional licenses. You need to register for a state tax number with the Department of Revenue. You need an employer identification number for state tax withholding. Special licenses are usually needed for selling liquor, food, gasoline, or firearms.
- At the regional level, several counties may form regional agencies that oversee environmental regulations and water usage.
- At the local level, permits and licenses to comply with local and county requirements will vary from place to place. You need answers from the local level—the local chamber of commerce and lawyers are good sources of information. Offices to consult would include the following:

  - City or county clerk
  - City or county treasurer
  - Zoning department
  - Building department

- Health department
- Fire department
- Police department
- Public works department

- If your business involves the sale or preparation of food, you will need not only a permit from a local health department, but also regular inspections. Local health departments may also be involved with environmental concerns, such as asbestos inspections, radon testing, and water purity testing.

Zoning Laws You need to be absolutely sure how a property is zoned before you sign a lease. If it is not zoned properly, you can sign the lease with a contingency clause that the property will be rezoned. You can also apply to the local zoning commission to obtain a *variance*, which allows you to operate without complying with the regulation or without having the regulation be changed.

zoning laws
Local laws that control where and how businesses may operate.

Zoning laws control what a business can sell and where it can operate. They are typically used to control parking, waste disposal, and sign size and placement. You may not even be able to paint the building a certain color due to zoning restrictions. For example, a White Castle hamburger franchise in Overland Park, Kansas, was not allowed to paint the building white because a zoning ordinance prohibited white buildings.

How do zoning laws affect home-based businesses, the fastest-growing segment in business (see Chapter 7)? Technology is making it possible for you to be productive at work from the comfort of your own living room. But are zoning boards comfortable with that idea? Yes, for the most part. Although some zoning ordinances prohibit home businesses, most don't. Restrictions on what you can and can't do on the property are more common. Most zoning laws seek primarily to maintain the residential nature of the surrounding neighborhood.

You should check zoning laws before you start your business, whether or not it is home based. At the zoning department at city hall, find out about not only the written laws but also the attitudes held by administrators, citizens, and the business community. Find out if other home-based businesses are allowed. If you disagree with a zoning ruling, you may be able to appeal to a variance board, the city council, or local commissioners.

Bankruptcy Laws

bankruptcy
A ruling granted by courts to release businesses or individuals from some or all of their debt.

Bankruptcy is a remedy for becoming insolvent. When an individual or a business gets into a financial condition in which there's no other way out, the courts administer the estate for the benefit of the creditors. The Bankruptcy Reform Act of 1978 established eight chapters for businesspeople seeking the protection of bankruptcy. Three of these chapters—Chapters 7, 11, and 13—apply to most small business situations. Bankruptcy can accomplish two different objectives: *liquidation*, after which the business ceases to exist, and *reorganization*, which allows the business owner to file a plan with the court that offers protection from creditors until the debt is satisfied.

Chapter 7 Bankruptcy

Chapter 7 bankruptcy means that the business is liquidated. All of the assets of the business are sold by a trustee appointed by the court. After the sale, the trustee distributes the proceeds to the creditors, who usually receive a percentage of the original debt. If any money is left over, it is divided among shareholders. About three of every four bankruptcy filings take place under Chapter 7.

Declaring bankruptcy does not necessarily leave you penniless and homeless. Most states have provisions that allow individuals to keep the equity in their homes, autos, and some personal property.

Other businesses that declare bankruptcy may provide an opportunity for you. For instance, imagine you are in business and one of your key suppliers goes bankrupt. What are your options? You could try to continue doing business with that firm for as long as possible. You could try to find a new supplier. Or you could use your knowledge of the bankrupt company and industry to your advantage, and buy the supplier at a bargain price, assuming you could operate the failed business more efficiently than the previous management.[12] Other strategic purchases could include buying a financially strapped competitor in an effort to increase your market share, or buying a business that is a customer in an effort to provide an outlet for your products.

The Bankruptcy Abuse Prevention and Consumer Protection Act of 2005 has caused some shifts in bankruptcy responsibilities. Individuals seeking Chapter 7 liquidation face increased responsibilities. While creditors have always had to show documentation of indebtedness—*proof of claim*—the burden is on the debtor to demonstrate that there is no reasonable alternative to the bankruptcy process. The debtor seeking liquidation must now prove an inability to pay his debts as they are due and demonstrate a good-faith attempt to resolve such a crisis without the court's help.

A controversial section in the Bankruptcy Code lies in the creation of a *means test* for eligibility to file under Chapter 7. The Bankruptcy Abuse Prevention and Consumer Protection Act requires a comparison of the debtor's income to the median income in the individual's home state. If the debtor's income is above the median and she is able to pay at least a minimal amount per month to creditors, she is now barred from Chapter 7 filing.[13]

Chapter 11 Bankruptcy

Chapter 11 provides a second chance for a business that is in financial trouble but still has potential for success. This type of bankruptcy can be either voluntary or involuntary. When you seek Chapter 11 protection, you must file a *reorganization plan* with the bankruptcy court. This plan includes a repayment schedule for current creditors (which may be less than 100 percent of the amounts owed) and indicates how the business will operate more profitably in the future. Only about 3 percent of bankruptcy filings take place under Chapter 11.

This reorganization protection keeps creditors from foreclosing on debts during the reorganization period. The business continues to operate under court direction. Both the court and the creditors must approve the plan, which also spells out a specific time period for the reorganization. If the business cannot turn operations (and profits) around, the likelihood of its switching to a Chapter 7 liquidation is great.

"Although much of the negative stigma attached to declaring bankruptcy of any type has decreased, this course of action is still not an 'easy way out.'"

Chapter 13 Bankruptcy

Chapter 13 bankruptcy allows individuals, including small business owners, who owe less than $250,000 in unsecured debts and less than $750,000 in secured debts to pay back creditors over a three- to five-year period. As under Chapter 11, a repayment plan is submitted to a bankruptcy judge, who must approve the conditions of the plan. The plan must show how most types of debts will be repaid in full. Some types of debts can be reduced or even eliminated by the court. About one-fourth of bankruptcies are filed under the provisions of Chapter 13.

Although much of the negative stigma attached to declaring bankruptcy of any type has decreased, this course of action is still not an "easy way out." Bankruptcy stays on your credit report for at least seven years. It is expensive and time-consuming. Chapters 11 and 13 may be better than liquidation, but they are not a solution to all of your problems.

Contract Law for Small Businesses

contract
An agreement between two or more parties that is enforceable by law.

A *contract* is basically a promise that is enforceable by law. Contract law comprises the body of laws that are intended to make sure that the parties entering into a contract comply with the deal and provides remedies to those parties harmed if a contract is broken.

A contract does not have to be in writing to be enforceable. Although it is a good idea to get any important agreement down on paper to help settle future disputes, the only contracts that must be in writing are those that involve one of the following:

- Sale of real estate
- Paying someone else's debt
- More than one year to perform
- Sale of goods valued at $500 or more

Even written contracts do not have to be complicated, formal documents created by a lawyer. Although you may not want to rely on contracts that are too sketchy, a letter or memo that identifies the parties, the subject, and the terms and conditions of the sale can be recognized as a valid contract.

Elements of a Contract

The four basic conditions or elements that a contract must meet to be binding are legality, agreement, consideration, and capacity.

Legality A contract must have a legal purpose. For instance, you can't make a contract that charges an interest rate higher than legal restrictions allow. At the same time, just because a deal is unfair, it is not necessarily illegal. You can't get out of a deal later if you offer to pay $1,500 for a used computer that is worth only $150.

Agreement A valid contract has a legitimate offer and a legitimate acceptance—called a "meeting of the minds." If a customer tells you his traveling circus will pay your print shop $600 to print 200 circus posters and you say, "It's a deal," you have a legally binding contract. In this case, it is an oral contract, which is just as legally binding as a written one.

Consideration Something of value must be exchanged between the parties involved in the contract. Without consideration, the agreement is about a gift, not a contract. In the preceding example, the $600 and the 200 posters are the consideration. If the circus owner picks up the posters, pays you the $600, and says, "Wow, for doing such a great job, come to the circus and I'll give you a free elephant ride," can you legally demand to ride the elephant later? No, you got what you agreed to—the $600—but there was no consideration for the bonus.

Capacity Not everyone has the capacity to legally enter into a contract. Minors and persons who are intoxicated or who have diminished mental ability cannot be bound by contracts. This is an important point to remember when running a small business. For example, if you sell a used car to a person younger than the age of 18, you could end up with a problem. The minor could take the car, run it without oil, smash it into a tree, and then ask you for his money back. You would be legally obligated to return the money because a contract with a minor is not binding.

breach of contract
A violation of one or more terms of a contract by a party involved in the contract.

Contractual Obligations

What can you do if a party with whom you signed a contract doesn't hold up her end of the deal? This scenario is called **breach of contract**, and you have several remedies

Manager's Notes

Legal Answers

Looking for answers to legal questions? Although sometimes no substitute for a flesh-and-blood lawyer exists, they can be expensive, so check out these Internet sites first:

- The mother lode of business-law Web sites is 'Lectric Law Library (lectlaw.com). This site offers true one-stop shopping to answer your small business legal questions. Start with the library tour, where you will find information in thousands of stacks, including the Reference Room, Forms Room, Book Store, Laypeople's Law Lounge, Legal Professional's Lounge, and (most important to you) the Law for Business Lounge.
- Findlaw.com looks like a legal version of Yahoo! with more than 25,000 links. You will be most interested in the Small Business Toolbox (www.small biz.findlaw .com) with sample business plans, step-by-step checklists, downloadable legal forms, and documents.
- FreeAdvice.com uses the slogan "The easy-to-use site for legal information." It's not too catchy, but is fairly accurate. Here you will find information on topics including bankruptcy, business law, employment, intellectual property, tax law, and small claims.
- LegalZoom.com is a comprehensive source of a wide variety of legal documents.
- Allaboutlaw.com offers more than 1,200 downloadable legal forms and documents.
- Nolo.com comes from the publisher of many great self-help guides and books on legal topics. The Web site features downloadable forms and documents, legal software, a legal encyclopedia, a dictionary, and a Q & A section.

available. Usually either money or some specific performance is used to compensate the damaged party. With either remedy, the intent of litigation is to try to put you back to where you were before the agreement was made.

Money awarded by a judge or arbitrator as a remedy for breach of contract is called **compensatory damages**. Go back to the circus poster example. If you were not able to complete the job as agreed and the circus owner had to pay someone else $800 to get the posters printed, you could be sued for $200 for breach of contract (probably in small claims court). Why $200? That amount represents the compensatory damages the circus owner suffered because you couldn't do the job for $600.

In some contract-dispute cases, money alone is insufficient to put a person back to his original state. In these cases, a judge may order a **specific performance** by the damaging party to make sure justice is done—in other words, requiring that party to do exactly what she agreed to do. Specific performance is awarded only if the item involved is unique and not substitutable. In this case, a judge will require the losing party to surrender the item in question.

Consider the case of buying an existing business for which the sales contract includes a *noncompete covenant*, which states that the previous business owner will not start or own a similar business within a specific geographic area for a certain amount of time. If the previous owner breaks the noncompete covenant and starts the same type of business, a single monetary award won't be enough. The judge can issue an *injunction*, which prohibits the previous owner from operating the new business for the duration of the agreement.

---

compensatory damages
Money awarded by the courts to a party of the contract who has suffered a loss due to the actions of another party.

specific performance
A nonmonetary award granted by the courts to a party of the contract who has suffered a loss due to the actions of another party.

injunction
A court order that prohibits certain activities.

Laws to Protect Intellectual Property

intellectual property
Property that is created through the mental skills of a person.

Intellectual property is a broad term that refers to the product of some type of unique human thought. It begins as an idea that could be as simple as a new name or as complex as the invention of a new product. Intellectual property also includes symbols and slogans that describe your business or product and any original expression, whether it takes the form of a collection of words (like a published book), an artistic interpretation (like a recording of a concert performance), or a computer program. These products of human thought have some value in the marketplace. A body of laws determines how, and for how long, a person can capitalize on his idea.

The forms of legal protection for intellectual property that will be discussed in this section are patents, copyrights, and trademarks. Although commonly used, the term *protection* may be misleading when we are discussing intellectual property, because it implies defense, whereas patents, copyrights, and trademarks give the owner more offensive rights than defensive protection. They cannot prevent others from trying to infringe on your registered idea, but they can discourage such attempts by the threat of your taking them to court. Although these court challenges often do not prevail, the possibility that they might prevail reduces attempts to steal your intellectual property. In the United States, this right has been considered so essential a part of the country's economic functioning that it was written into the Constitution.[14]

Patents

patent
A form of protection for intellectual property provided to an inventor for a period of 17 years.

A *patent* gives you the right to exclude someone else (or some other company) from making, using, or selling the property you have created and patented for a period of 17 years. To receive this protection, you have to file for a patent through the Patent Trademark Office (PTO). With a patent application, you must pay both filing fees and maintenance fees. Three maintenance fees must be paid 4, 8, and 12 years after the patent grant, or the patent will expire before 17 years.

Although it is commonly believed that you have to hire a patent attorney to file a patent application, this is not the case. Actually, regulations require the PTO to help individuals who do not use an attorney. Hundreds of patents are granted each year to inventors who navigate the process solo. But just because you can complete the patent process without legal counsel, does that mean you should attempt it? It depends—particularly on factors like your comfort level with processing "red tape." Patent attorneys charge $3,000 to $5,000 to prepare a patent application. How many earth-changing widgets must you sell to cover that kind of overhead? If you are unsure of what the market for your widgets will be, books like *Patent It Yourself* by David Pressman contain all the instructions and forms you need to do it yourself.[15] Doing as much as you can yourself, while checking periodically with an attorney throughout the process, may be a reasonable compromise to offer you both expertise and cost savings.

Three types of patents exist. The most common type is the *utility patent*, which covers inventions that provide a unique or new use or function. If you could come up with a new way to keep shoes on people's feet without using laces, buckles, Velcro fasteners, zippers, or other ways currently used, you would need to file for a utility patent.

Whereas utility patents cover use, *design patents* protect unique or new forms or shapes. If the new shape also changes the function of the object, then you need to apply for a utility patent. If looks alone are different, you need a design patent. For example, if you were to design a ballpoint pen that looked like a fish, but which served no other function than that of a ballpoint pen, you would file for a design patent on your invention.

Reality Check

Protect Your App?

Entrepreneurs are changing some of their thought regarding intellectual property (IP) in the twenty-first century. In the past, companies have treated IP as a asset that must be kept out of the hands of others at all costs, but relaxing that paranoia is becoming less the exception and more the rule.

An interesting, and potentially dangerous, example is seen in the development of free and open-source software (FOSS). FOSS represents an incredible variety of utilities and programs published at no cost for the benefit of all comers. FOSS may be free to use, but may still be licensed. The challenge of creating open-source software and protecting your legal rights comes in writing the FOSS license form. Typical language is: "Nothing other than this License grants you permission to propagate or modify any covered work. These actions infringe copyright if you do not accept this License."

But the bottom line (literally) is that the success of a business is rarely tied to success in protecting IP. Ninety-five percent of patents end up being of absolutely no commercial value. Even in the high-tech industry (where IP is everything), the rule of thumb in protecting patents is … don't bother. According to economics professor Glen Whitman, "The faster the pace of innovation, the less important will be the patent." In other words, superb execution trumps IP protection every time.

Since launching its App Store mobile application marketplace in mid-2008, Apple and a global network of partners have introduced more than 100,000 apps translating to $900 million in application revenue. One of the most successful and earliest application developers is Ilja Laurs, creator of independent GetJar (www.getjar.com). Laurs has 57,000 applications contributed by 350,000 developers yielding 60 million downloads per month—second only to Apple.

Sources: Jason Ankeny, "The App Store That's Never Closed," *Entrepreneur*, February 2010, 22–27; David Wormser, "Open-Source Software: The Value of 'Free,'" *Intellectual Property & Technology Law Journal*, May 2010, 22–26; David H. Freedman, "Relax. Let Your Guard Down," *Inc.*, August 2006, 108–111; and Gabe Fried, "IP: A Reason to Exist," *Mergers & Acquisitions*, June 2010, 42–43.

The third patent type is a *plant patent*. Such a patent covers living plants, such as flowers, trees, or vegetables, that can be grown or otherwise reproduced.

What Can Be Patented? The PTO reviews each application and decides whether to grant a patent on the basis of four tests, which come from the following questions:

- Does the invention fit a statutory class?
- Is the invention useful?
- Is it novel?
- Is it nonobvious?

The invention must fit into one of the five *statutory classes*—which means that you must be able to call it a machine, process, manufacture, chemical composition, or combination of those terms.

The invention must provide some *legal utility*. That is, it must be useful in some way. If the invention has some commercial value, this test shouldn't be difficult to pass. If it doesn't, you will have a hard time building your small business on it. The invention must be possible to build and be workable to be granted a patent. You have to be able to show the examiner that the invention will operate as you say it will.

The invention must be *novel*. It must be different from all other things that have previously been made or described anywhere else in the world (called *prior art*). Meeting this test can be difficult since the definition of *novelty* may be confusing to everyone involved. Three types of novelty that meet this requirement are those created by (1) physical difference, (2) a new combination of existing parts, or (3) the invention of a new use.

The invention must be *nonobvious*. Although this rule is also difficult to understand, it is an important one. It means that the difference between your invention and other developments (or prior art) must not be obvious to someone with common knowledge in that field. The novelty of your invention needs to produce new or unexpected results.

The flowchart in Figure 10.2 can help you visualize the tests your invention must pass to get a patent.

Patent Search Before you file a patent application, you should conduct a *patent search* to save time and money later. You can conduct this search yourself, or you can hire a patent agent or patent attorney to do it for you. You are searching for existing patents for inventions that are or may be similar to yours.

Start by coming up with several keywords that could be used in describing your invention. These keywords will be run through the primary patent reference publication at

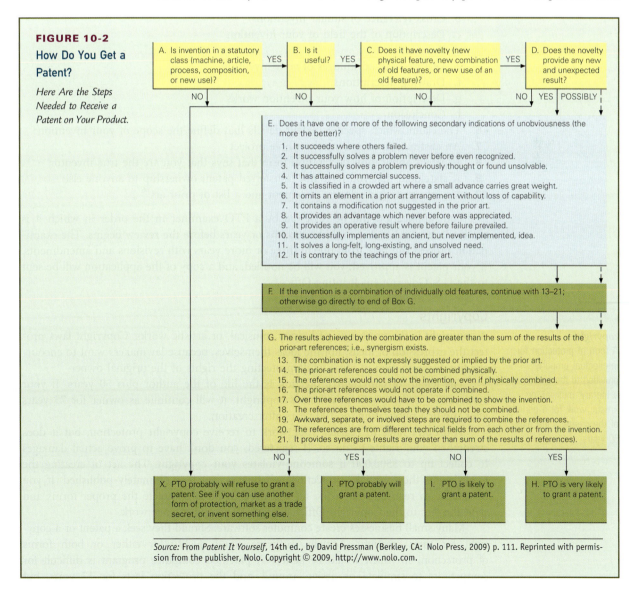

FIGURE 10-2

How Do You Get a Patent?

Here Are the Steps Needed to Receive a Patent on Your Product.

the PTO in Arlington, Virginia, called *Index to the U.S. Patent Classification.* If you can't go to the PTO, you can search a Patent Depository Library. In these libraries, you can use the *Official Gazette of the U.S. Patent and Trademark Office.*

You can also conduct a patent search by subject or by specific patent via the Internet. Such a search is done through the Shadow Patent Office. For more information, visit the PTO's home page at www.uspto.gov.

Patent Application   When submitting your patent application, you should include the following items:

1. Self-addressed, stamped postcard to show receipt of packet
2. Payment of the filing fee
3. Letter of transmittal
4. Drawings of your invention
5. Specifications, including
   a. Title or name of your invention
   b. Cross-reference of similar inventions
   c. Description of the field of your invention
   d. Prior art
   e. Features and advantages of your invention
   f. Drawing descriptions
   g. Description of how your invention works
   h. Conclusion
6. The claim, which specifies patent details that define the scope of your invention
7. An abstract, summarizing the whole project
8. A patent application declaration form that says that you are the true inventor
9. A statement that you have not transferred patent ownership to anyone else
10. An information disclosure statement and a list of prior art[16]

Your application will be reviewed by a PTO examiner in the order in which it is received, meaning that it could be months or years before the review begins. The examination process can take from one to three or more years with revisions and amendments. If your patent is approved, you will be notified, and a copy of the application will be sent to the U.S. Government Printing Office.

Copyrights

copyright

A form of protection for intellectual property provided to the creator of a literary, musical, or artistic work for a period of the creator's life plus 50 years.

A *copyright* is the protection of literary, musical, or artistic works. Copyright laws protect the expression of ideas, not the ideas themselves, because lawmakers want to encourage the dissemination of ideas while protecting the rights of the original owner.

The length of copyright protection is the life of the author plus 50 years. If your corporation is the owner of a book's copyright, it will continue as owner for 75 years after the first publication, or 100 years after creation.

You don't have to register your work to receive copyright protection, but it does strengthen your rights to do so. If registered, you don't have to prove actual damages to collect up to $500,000 if someone violates your copyright. The act of creating the work begins the copyright protection, whether or not it is ultimately published. If you do choose to register your work, all you need to do is complete the proper forms and send the fees to the Copyright Office along with a copy of your work.

Many small businesses create computer software. Should they seek a patent or a copyright for their creation? Actually, software could qualify for either or both forms of protection, so which would be better? A patented computer program is difficult for competitors to simulate or design around, and the protection lasts for 17 years, but consider the disadvantages: Patents can be expensive, require a lot of work to apply for and search, and take several years to obtain. Windows of opportunity open and shut quickly in the software market. Your software may be obsolete before a patent can even be granted.

Copyrighting software is quick and inexpensive but doesn't provide the offensive punch of a patent. You can't copyright what a program does, only the specific way it is written. Thus competing small business programmers need merely to write the program for their software in a different manner to avoid copyright infringement.

What's the answer for "protecting" your software? Frankly, neither patents nor copyrights do a thorough job in this case. Protecting intellectual property for quickly changing industries and global markets is a serious problem that may become more so for small businesses and regulators in the near future.

Trademarks

A **brand** is a name, term, symbol, design, or combination of these elements that clearly identifies and differentiates your products from those of your competitors. A **trademark** is a registered and protected brand. Therefore, all trademarks are brands, but not all brands are trademarks. A trademark can include a graphic as well as a brand name. For example, not only is the Coke name protected, but the style of its script also makes it a trademark.

Your trademark rights remain in effect as long as you continue to use the trademark. This enduring nature offers an advantage over patents or copyrights. Trademarks are useful because they provide brand recognition for your product and are a good way to create an image in your customer's mind.

Because there are more than 1 million trademarks in use in the United States, how do you find one that isn't already taken? As with the patent search, you can either do the *trademark search* yourself or hire someone to do it for you. The problem gets more complicated with the trademark search, though, because a 1989 regulation change makes it possible to reserve a trademark before it is put into use.

brand

A name, term, symbol, design, or combination of these elements that clearly identifies and differentiates your products from those of your competitors.

trademark

A form of protection for intellectual property provided to the owner of a brand name or symbol.

Manager's Notes

Keeping Your Trademark in Shape

When you've got a good thing, you want to keep it. That's why it's important for small business owners to register ideas and products as soon as possible and to monitor for any misuse of their trademarks.

Small business owners must be as vigilant as giants like Coca-Cola, Sony, or Adidas in monitoring for misuse of a registered trademark. But how do you achieve this on-going awareness? Some suggestions follow:

- A press-clipping service can track references to products in articles and advertisements.
- When an infringement is found, send offending parties a letter notifying them of the trademark and informing them to cease and desist using it.
- In extreme instances, legal action must be undertaken to recover proceeds that offenders have received using the trademarked name.

For the past decade, the USPTO has enabled small businesses to file trademarks directly online via the Trademark Electronic Application System or TEAS.

Sources: Lauren Folino, "How to File a Trademark," *Inc.,* February 11, 2010, www.inc.com/guides; Jane Easter Bahls, "The Name Game," *Entrepreneur,* April 2004, 80; and Carl Geffken, "Protecting Your Intellectual Property," *GCI,* January 2004, 22–24.

Several businesses specialize in trademark searches of registered and unregistered marks, including the following: Trademark Service Corporation, 747 Third Avenue, New York, NY 10017, (212) 421-5730; Thompson & Thompson, 500 Victory Road, North Quincy, MA 02171-2126, (800) 692-8833; and Compu-Mark U.S., 1333 F Street NW, Washington, D.C. 20004, (800) 421-7881. You can conduct a search yourself with *The Trademark Register of the U.S.*, which is available in many libraries, or a similar directory. You can file for a trademark with the Patent and Trademark Office, Washington, D.C. 20231 (www.uspto.gov) with an application and a $325 fee. You can also register your trademark in your own state with the secretary of state at your state capitol.

Your trademark is worthless (and actually invalid) if you don't use it. Before your product is registered, use the symbol^{TM}; after it is registered, use®.

Global Protection of Intellectual Property

Global protection of intellectual property has been a contentious issue for a couple of decades. Protection of trademarks, copyrights, and patents has had great difficulty crossing international borders. One of the driving forces in global protection has been the World Intellectual Property Organization (WIPO), which administers some 21 treaties covering intellectual property protection, international filing systems, and trademark classification.[17] WIPO's roots actually stretch back to 1883 (yes, 1883) with the Paris Convention for Protection of Industrial Property and the 1886 Berne Convention for the Protection of Literary and Artistic Works.[18] WIPO is based in Geneva, Switzerland, and currently about 200 member nations depend on and defend its legal protections in the event of documented violations.

In 2004, WIPO launched downloadable software that allows patent applications to be filled out and submitted online. The software is called PCT-SAFE, where PCT stands for Patent Cooperation Treaty. This process could revolutionize patent filing—if applicants trust it. Advantages include faster filing (seconds compared with days), safety (encrypted so it cannot be stolen during delivery), and lower costs (no production of many copies, and no mailing costs).[19]

Summary

1. Name the laws and regulations that affect small business.

Laws and regulations exist to protect competition, consumers, people in the workplace, and intellectual property; to allow bankruptcy; and to establish contracts. Specific laws that owners of small businesses should know include the Fair Labor Standards Act, the Civil Rights Acts of 1964 and 1991, the Immigration Reform and Control Act, the Americans with Disabilities Act, workers' and unemployment compensation, and the Occupational Safety and Health Act.

2. List and explain the types of bankruptcy.

The U.S. Bankruptcy Code is made up of nine chapters, only three of which apply to most small businesses (Chapters 7, 11, and 13). Chapter 7 uses liquidation, meaning that the business ceases to exist in an effort to provide the debtor with a fresh start. Liquidation involves selling all of the business assets and nonexempt personal assets and then distributing the proceeds among creditors. Chapters 11 and 13 allow the business owner to file a reorganization plan with the court that offers protection from creditors until the debt is satisfied.

3. Describe the elements of a contract.

For a contract to be legally binding, it must have a legal purpose. Both parties must come to an agreement including a legitimate offer and a legitimate acceptance of that offer. Consideration, or something of value, must be exchanged. Finally, all parties must have the capacity to enter into a binding contract, meaning that they must not be underage, intoxicated, or of diminished mental ability.

4. Discuss how to protect intellectual property.

Patents, copyrights, and trademarks are legal ways to protect intellectual property. A patent grants an inventor the exclusive right to make, use, and sell an invention for a period of 17 years. A copyright provides legal protection against infringement of an author's literary, musical, or artistic works. Copyrights usually last for the author's life plus 50 years. A trademark is a legally protected name, term, symbol, design, or combination of these elements used to identify products or companies. Trademarks last for as long as they are in use.

Questions for Review and Discussion

1. Are the antitrust laws established in the late 1800s and early 1900s still pertinent in the twenty-first century? Why or why not?
2. How does the Federal Trade Commission protect consumers?
3. What rights does owning a patent protect? How do you get this protection?
4. What tests must an invention pass to receive a patent?
5. What is the difference between a copyright and a trademark? Between a trademark and a brand?
6. Name and explain the four elements that a contract must have to be valid.
7. List and briefly explain the laws that protect people in the workplace.
8. How are liquidation and reorganization used as different approaches to bankruptcy? What chapters of bankruptcy law accomplish these objectives?
9. What licenses are required by the owner of a small business?
10. What risk does an inventor assume when filing for a patent for an invention?

Questions for Critical Thinking

1. Compliance with government regulations is sometimes burdensome for small business owners; what can they (and you) do to change the laws and regulations that influence small business in order to lessen the burden?
2. Think of transactions you have entered into in the past: With whom were you agreeing, what was the agreement about, and what were the terms? When have you had a written contract with someone? When have you had an oral contract? Use several examples to analyze the process of buying a car, accepting a job, and ordering a pizza. What elements of contract law applied in each case?

What Would You Do?

The stories of companies like KFC, Coca-Cola, and McDonald's guarding their recipes for batter, syrup, and hamburger sauce are legendary. Triple-locked safes, binding contractual agreements, spies, and counterspies are all involved. A company's *trade secrets* are worth significant (sometimes staggering) amounts of money. Like any good secret, they are known to only a handful of people.

Many assets, such as chemical formulas or specific designs, are protected by patents. In exchange for the legal protection afforded by a patent, the patent holder must surrender the leverage of secrecy. That's because part of the patent application process involves a full explanation of the process or product. The PTO publishes all patent applications within 18 months of their filing. Protecting a trade secret is complicated by the fact that, unlike patents, copyrights, and trademarks, trade secrets do not fall under federal jurisdiction. They are regulated by individual state laws. Trade secrets must be *proved* to be secret to qualify for protection. At the very minimum, the owner must prove that procedures were in place to protect the information prior to any legal challenge.

Source: Sabra Chartrand, "Patents," *New York Times*, February 5, 2001, C-14.

Questions

1. Imagine that you have developed a unique formula for a soft drink that, upon entering a person's mouth, analyzes the drinker's DNA to determine his favorite flavor, and then the drink instantly realigns its chemical composition to become that flavor. Write a two-page paper describing how you can best protect this trade secret. Will you patent it? Why or why not?

PART 4

Marketing

Chapter 11
Strategy and Research

Chapter 12
Product

Chapter 13
Place

Chapter 14
Price and Promotion

Marketing your small business entails more than just personal selling or writing newspaper ads. Marketing involves every form of customer contact—plus much more. The theme of this book is creating a sustainable competitive advantage. The topics covered in Part 4 will form the basis for many of those advantages. All of them flow from one idea: You must understand how you serve your customers better than your competitors. **Chapter 11** explores small business marketing strategies and marketing research. **Chapter 12** highlights factors related to the products you sell. **Chapter 13** discusses location and layout. **Chapter 14** focuses on pricing and promotion strategies.

11

Strategy and Research

CHAPTER LEARNING OUTCOMES

After reading this chapter, you should be able to:

1. **Explain the importance of marketing to small businesses.**

2. **Describe the process of developing a small business marketing strategy.**

3. **Discuss the purpose of the market research process and the steps involved in putting it into practice.**

C hances are good that if you are reading these words, you have a Facebook page. Your mom, your dog, and the shop where you get your hair cut may have Facebook pages also. In the United States, about 100 million different visitors log on to the site each month.

Understandably, entrepreneurs want to try to communicate their wares to any group so large and active. Ellie Sawits, CEO of Frutels, maker of chocolate candies that treat acne,

© Image Source/Getty Images

© AP Photo/TimesDaily, Jim Hannon

finds Facebook to be an affordable alternative to paying the high pay-per-click fees for acne-related words on Google AdWords. She says, "For me, the economics of Google just don't work."

Since Facebook recently made Bing the default search engine, it can enhance its advertising model even more than with Google AdWords. The ability to search Facebook provides a wealth of psychographic information—attributes relating to personality, values, attitudes, interests, and lifestyles—segmentation variables you will see again in this chapter.

You can extend your advertising to only Facebook users who mention specific words in their profiles or status messages. Howie Goldklang, co-owner of The Establishment hair salon and spa in Milwaukee, will target young women with Facebook pages that mention Justin Timberlake or Lady Gaga.

Tim Kendall, Facebook's director of monetization, says that most advertisers choose to pay based on the number of people who actually see your ad, but you can be charged per person who sees the ad. Twenty bucks will buy a small test ad so you can see which approach is better for your business. Adam Golomb is head of e-commerce at Eat'n Park Hospitality Group, which runs a chain of 76 restaurants out of Pittsburgh. Golumb wanted to bring more eyeballs to the company Facebook page and made an interesting discovery during testing. He found that his restaurant advertising targeting just women worked much better that those targeting both genders. "The click-through rate dropped dramatically when we went out to both," he says.

Goldklang reminds that "it is a social network, so if you put up a traditional ad, you're going to be pushed to the side." He finds that edgy ads work best for his hair salon, which has a target market of younger clientele. His best-performing ad last year stated, "Springtime is here. Time to get waxed."

Of course, Facebook will reject your ad if it is too risqué or lewd. All ads must meet the Facebook Advertising Terms and Conditions and Facebook Advertising Guidelines. Start by checking out www.facebook.com/ads/mistakes.php.

Sources: Jason Del Rey, "Fishing for Friends—Advertising on Facebook," *Inc.*, February 2010, 94–96; Star Hall, "Facebook vs. Google.com," *Entrepreneur*, April 2010, www.entrepreneur.com; and www.facebook.com/ads/mistakes.php.

Small Business Marketing

What do you think of when you hear the term *marketing*? Do you think of selling and advertising? Probably, but marketing is actually much more than just selling or advertising. Marketing involves all the activities needed to get a product from the producer to the ultimate consumer. Management guru Peter Drucker has stated that businesses have two—and only two—basic functions: marketing and innovation. These are the only things a business does that produce results; everything else is really a "cost."[1] This is just as true for the one-person kiosk as it is for the largest corporate giant.

Of course, some selling will always be necessary, but the goal of marketing is to come as close as possible to making selling superfluous.[2] A truly customer-driven company understands what consumers want in a product and provides it so that its products, to a great extent, sell themselves. Of course, this is not easy. To paraphrase President Lyndon Johnson: Doing the right thing is easy; knowing the right thing to do is tough.

Marketing Concept

Many businesses operate today with a customer-driven philosophy. They want to find out what their customers want and then provide that good or service. This philosophy is called the *marketing concept*.

marketing concept
The philosophy of a business in which the wants and needs of customers are determined before goods and services are produced.

Businesses have not always concentrated their efforts on what the market wants. Before the Industrial Revolution and mass production, nearly all a business owner needed to be concerned about was making products. Demand exceeded supply for most goods, like boots, clothing, and saddles. People had to have these products, so about all a business had to do was to make them. This philosophy in which companies concentrate their efforts on the product being made is now called the *production concept* of business.

production concept
The philosophy of a business that concentrates more on the product that the business makes than on customer needs.

After the mid-1800s, when mass production and mass distribution became possible for manufactured products, supply began to exceed demand. Some selling was needed, but the emphasis remained on producing goods. World War II temporarily shifted resources from consumer markets to the military. After the war, when those resources were returned to the consumer market, businesses continued producing at capacity, and many new businesses were started. Managers found that they could no longer wait for consumers to seek them out to sell all they could make. Although these companies still emphasized making products, they now had to convince people to buy *their* products, as opposed to the competition's, which inaugurated the *selling concept* of business.

Early in the 1960s, many businesses began to adopt the marketing concept, which, as just explained, emphasizes finding out what your customers want and need, and then offering products to satisfy those desires. Florence Henderson (yes, the mom from the original TV *Brady Bunch*) admitted that she had a problem—she couldn't send e-mail from her new smartphone. When Tony Hirsch, a business partner, showed her how, she exclaimed, "I want all my friends to be able to do this!" That desire lead to the creation of FloH Club, a telephone-based tech-support service for seniors. For $24.99 a month, members get 24/7 access to help with anything from making an eBay purchase to connecting a printer. Florence has taped infomercials to reach her target market and expects to draw tens of thousands of new members.[3]

relationship marketing
The philosophy of business that concentrates on establishing a long-term buyer-seller relationship for the benefit of both parties.

The business philosophy that broadens the view of the marketing concept is called *relationship marketing*. Here a business owner recognizes the value and profit potential of customer retention; therefore, the guiding emphasis is on developing long-term, mutually satisfying relationships with customers and suppliers.

Of Purple Cows

In your travels you have most likely passed by many cows: black ones, white ones, brown ones, or some combination thereof. Unless you have a specific reason for noticing them, such as being in the cattle business, very few cows probably stand out in your mind. In fact, most people would classify cows as boring. Author Seth Godin makes an analogy between most products that consumers see daily with cows: Consumers see so many products that seem to be alike that they are all boring. But a purple cow? Drive by one of those, even if it is in a field with a whole herd of black, white, or brown cows, and it would get your attention. What products stand out in your mind as different? Krispy Kreme doughnuts? Hard Candy cosmetics? Doing and creating things that are counterintuitive, phenomenal, and exciting are important ingredients to marketing small businesses.[4]

Small businesses can achieve the success that Godin discusses by avoiding the traps of convention and not being afraid to stand out from the crowd by offering unique products and marketing practices. "Purple cows" represent the creation of a competitive advantage or a *unique selling point (USP)*—topics that volumes have been written about. Take a look at Godin's *Purple Cow* for inspiration (you can read it in about an hour).[5]

Marketing Strategies for Small Businesses

marketing strategy
What the marketing efforts of a business are intended to accomplish and how the business will achieve its goals.

Your ***marketing strategy*** should be decided in the early stages of operating your business. It should state *what* you intend to accomplish and *how* you intend to accomplish it. The marketing section of the business plan is a good place for the small business owner to identify marketing strategies. Any potential investor will carefully inspect how you have laid out the marketing action that will drive your business.

A good marketing strategy will help you to be proactive, not reactive, in running your business. You can enhance your marketing plan by making sure that three related bases are covered:

- A single-minded focus on the customer to the exclusion of other stakeholders
- An overly narrow definition of the customer and his or her needs
- A failure to recognize the changed societal context of business that necessitates addressing multiple stakeholders[6]

"A good marketing strategy will help you to be proactive, not reactive, in running your business."

Small businesses in the service industries must pay special attention to marketing. When their service is one that customers could perform themselves, such as lawn mowing, a marketing strategy is critical. It is also often more difficult to differentiate or establish a brand image with services than with tangible products. Can the average car owner tell the difference between automatic transmissions that have been rebuilt by different shops? Probably not. A marketing strategy that communicates the benefits that consumers receive is crucial. However comprehensive or simple your marketing plan, it should include a description of your vision, marketing objectives, sales forecast, target markets, and marketing mix.[7]

Setting Marketing Objectives

Your marketing objectives define the goals of your plans. They can be broken into two groups: marketing-performance objectives and marketing-support objectives.[8] Objectives for *marketing performance* are specific, quantifiable outcomes, such as sales revenue, market share, and profit. For example, an objective of this type for a local insurance agency could be "to increase sales of homeowner's insurance by 10 percent for the next fiscal year." Objectives for *marketing support* are what you must accomplish before your performance objectives can be met, such as educating customers about your products, building awareness, and creating image.

Like any goal you want to accomplish in business, marketing objectives need to be (1) measurable, (2) action-oriented by identifying what needs to be done, and (3) time-specific by targeting a date or time for achievement.

Developing a Sales Forecast

sales forecast
The quantity of products a business plans to sell during a future time period.

Your marketing plan should include a ***sales forecast***, in which you predict your future sales in dollars and in units—in other words, what your "top line" will be. If you are writing a business plan for a start-up business, the sales forecast is one of the most important pieces of information you will gather. Why? Because that "top line" figure becomes the foundation for your pro forma income statements and cash-flow statement. From your projected revenues, you will subtract your expenses and disbursements to see if and when you will make a profit.

Forecasting is difficult, but it will help you establish more accurate goals and objectives. Your sales forecast will affect all sections of your marketing plan, including the choice of appropriate channels of distribution, sales force requirements, advertising and sales promotion budgets, and the effects of price changes.

A faulty sales forecast can do severe damage to a small business. Steve Waterhouse was an understandably excited sales manager when he reported in a budget meeting that one of his sales representatives had secured a $2 million order. Satisfying the order would require the company to invest $100,000 in new tools. The operations manager was not very excited, however, because the purchase order contained a clause allowing the customer to back out. The owner wisely decided to require a deposit for initial supplies before proceeding. After receiving $100,000 from the customer, the company purchased the required tooling. The customer then backed out of the deal. Crisis averted, but a close call nevertheless. What's the moral of the story? Be careful about projections based on "my sales rep says …"[9]

There are two basic ways to forecast sales: build-up methods and break-down methods. With a *build-up method*, you identify as many target markets as possible and predict the sales for each. Then you combine the predictions for the various segments to create a total sales forecast. For example, if you plan to open an ice cream shop, can you estimate how many ice cream cones you will sell in a year? Not very easily or accurately without some research. But you can estimate with some degree of accuracy how much you could sell in one day—especially if you spend several days outside an existing ice cream shop observing how many people go in and out, and roughly how much they are buying. From that daily sales figure, you can project sales for the week, month, and year. Would you expect to sell the same amount per day in April? July? October? January? Probably not, so you would come up with a daily sales projection at different times of the year to allow for seasonal fluctuations.

ENTREPRENEURIAL SNAPSHOT

It Tastes Like What?!

© MANDEL NGAN/AFP/Getty Images/Newscom

"We are the market-share leader in turkey-flavored beverages." What??? Yep, that is what Peter van Stolk, founder of Jones Soda, says about the success of the company's annual holiday novelty pack. During the holiday season, Jones makes soda flavors like Turkey and Gravy, Wild Herb Stuffing, Sweet Potato, and Green Pea. Mmmmmm.

Such flavors were enough to make Diane Sawyer and Joel Siegel gag on *Good Morning America*. Most companies don't go out of their way to make customers sick, but Jones Soda is not your normal company. Jones is known for offbeat marketing strategies—including photos of customers on product labels.

Van Stolk got the idea for the unique flavors while on a road trip from Grand Rapids to Detroit, Michigan, as he was trying to think of ways to boost cold-weather soda sales. It was October 2003, when the diet du jour was low-carbohydrate, so Peter dreamed up the idea of a soda that "tasted" like Thanksgiving dinner. The product line has expanded to zero-calorie soda called Jones Zilch—launching with Vanilla Bean, Black Cherry, and Pomegranate flavors.

If done carefully, a marketing strategy that is offbeat can gain more attention than a traditional strategy, according to Rob Frankel, author of *The Revenge of Brand X: How to Build a Big Time Brand on the Web or Anywhere Else*. Frankel goes on to say that you need to know how tolerant your target market is, tolerance being measured in money. "'Crazy' becomes 'too crazy' when the cash register stops ringing."

Not all of Jones Soda's marketing is outrageous—they also sell yummier flavors like Strawberry Lime, Crushed Melon, and Blue Bubblegum via traditional channels like Target, 7-11, and Kroger. But they do little traditional advertising because van Stolk understands that his niche target market of teens and twenty-somethings responds better to offbeat tactics like music- and photo-sharing Web sites. Since Jones is known for its labels, it created an iPhone app allowing users to be able to order customized soda with user pictures on the label. This type of insight into one's target market is especially important for a small business with fewer marketing dollars to spread around. Jones Soda is a great example of consistency among all marketing variables: target market, product, place, price, and promotion.

Van Stolk recently left Jones Soda in a move he relates to "a bad divorce." As many entrepreneurs do,

he immediately launched another business—this one called Box B (from choices on a sushi menu). Box B creates brands for private label beverages that small independent distributors can own and not lose out when a drink they worked hard to promote moves to a large distributor after becoming successful.

———

Sources: "Jones Fast-tracks Labels," *Beverage Industry*, January 2010, 90; "Zero-calorie Soda," *Beverage Industry*, January 2010, 26; Kenneth Hein, "Soda Entrepreneur Jonesing for a New Opportunity," *Brandweek*, November 30, 2009, 5; Ellen Neuborne, "Gag Marketing," *Inc.*, February 2006, 35–36; and Jeff Cioletti, "An Impish 10-year-old," *Beverage World*, June 2006, 26–27.

With some types of products, of course, it is difficult to estimate daily sales. Then what? You may be able to use a *break-down method*. For this approach, you begin with an estimate of the total market potential for a specific product or an entire industry. This figure is broken down into forecasts of smaller units until you reach an estimate of how large a market you will reach and how many sales you will make. For example, if industry information from a trade association for a product you consider selling shows that 4 percent of a population will be in the market for your product at any given time, how many units and dollars of sales could you realistically generate? Do enough people live in your area, or can you reach enough of the target market for your business to be profitable?

Marketers use many other models in sales forecasting; unfortunately, most don't apply well to small businesses because they depend on historical data. For example, ***time series analysis*** is a forecasting method that uses past sales data to discover whether product sales have increased, decreased, or stayed the same over periods of time. Cyclic, seasonal, and random factor analyses are variations on this model.

Like time series analysis, ***regression analysis*** uses extensive historical sales data to find a relationship between prior sales (the dependent variable) and one or more independent variables, such as income. With regression analysis, the intention is to develop a mathematical formula that describes a relationship between a product's sales and the chosen variable. The best we can hope for is to identify an association, not to find proof or causation. Once a formula is established, you enter all necessary data into it to develop a sales forecast. Of course, because these models of time series and regression analysis depend so heavily on large amounts of historical data, they are useless in forecasting sales for new products.

time series analysis
A forecasting method that uses historical sales data to identify patterns over a period of time.

regression analysis
A forecasting method that predicts future sales by finding a relationship between sales and one or more variables.

Identifying Target Markets

Market segmentation is the process of dividing the total market for a product into identifiable groups, or ***target markets***, with a common want or need that your business can satisfy. These target markets are important to your business because they consist of the people who are more likely to be your customers. They are the people toward whom you should direct your marketing efforts. Identifying and concentrating on target markets can help you avoid falling into the trap of trying to be everything to everyone—you can't do it.[10]

target markets
A group of people who have a common want or need that your business can satisfy, who are able to purchase your product, and who are more likely to buy from your business.

Competitive Advantage
INNOVATION AND SUSTAINABILITY

Sometimes the Best Marketing Strategy Is a Good Defense

We typically associate marketing with aggressive advertising campaigns designed to maximize growth, or open new markets, or gain market share from competitors. Marketing is a powerful offensive weapon—but it can be a valuable defensive tool also. And your business may need a defensive tool, because for every new business or product launched, there is an existing one (maybe yours) that must defend its position.

Greg Sutter, vice president of marketing for Datastream Systems, concentrates more attention on nurturing relationships with existing customers than attending trade shows or working up print advertising. He says, "To defend our position, we don't go wide; we go deep." In short, Datastream spends almost its entire marketing budget playing defense.

Not all customers are equal, though. They can be classified by their value (profitability) and their vulnerability (to competitors). Sutter will work most vigorously to retain customers who are both valuable and vulnerable. Customers who are valuable but not vulnerable are happy with the company, so they will maintain profit margins. Those who are neither valuable nor vulnerable are happy with the company but do not create profit. The business owner should try to make them valuable. An overlooked group are those customers who are vulnerable but not valuable, making them unprofitable and likely to leave. They should be encouraged out the door.

If you are smart in creating a defensive marketing strategy, you can keep competitors away from your turf, or even eliminate them. Some marketing tactics to consider:

- *Leverage your strengths.* If your small business has a hometown advantage over rivals, for example, capitalize on that.
- *Keep rivals guessing.* Moving targets are hard to hit, so innovate and put up barriers like patents and trademarks.
- *Know when to retreat.* Some markets and customers are not worth keeping, so move your resources elsewhere.
- *Make customer satisfaction a priority.* An old saying from ranching, "It doesn't take a good fence to keep in a happy horse," provides an analogy that can be applied to customers.

Sources: John Roberts, "Defensive Marketing," *Harvard Business Review*, November 2005, 150–157; Ellen Neuborne, "Playing Defense," *Inc.*, March 2006, 31–34. For more depth on this topic, read Al Ries and Jack Trout, *Marketing Warfare* (New York: McGraw-Hill, 2005). This updated marketing classic focuses on how to beat the competition by outthinking them, taking powerful examples from ancient military generals to modern guerrilla tactics.

When asked about their target markets, many small business owners will respond, "We don't have specific target markets; we will sell to anyone who comes in the door." Of *course* you will sell to anyone who wants your product, but the point of segmenting target markets is to let the right people know about your product so that more people will want it. A market for your business must have three characteristics:

1. A need that your products can satisfy
2. Enough people to generate profit for your business
3. Possession of, and willingness to spend, enough money to generate profit for your business

segmentation variables
Characteristics or ways to group people that make them more likely to purchase a product.

To identify the most attractive target markets for your business, you should look for characteristics that affect the buying behavior of the people. Does where they live influence whether they buy your product? Does income, gender, age, or lifestyle matter? Do they seek a different benefit from the product than other groups do? These differences, called **segmentation variables**, can be based on geographic, demographic, or psychographic differences, or on differences in benefits received.

"Big companies set their sights on mass markets, but entrepreneurial companies understand that the key to their success lies in satisfying niches."

mass marketing
Treating entire populations of people as potential customers for specific products.

market segmentation
Breaking down populations of people into groups, or target markets.

niche marketing
Segmenting populations of people into smaller target markets.

individualized marketing
Adjusting the marketing mix of a business to treat individual persons as separate target markets.

A small business owner should start (and occasionally revisit) the process of segmenting a market by committing to writing a description of "ideal" customers. For example, for a small accounting firm, that description could be "entrepreneurs in their early thirties to early fifties; owners of retail, service, or manufacturing firms with sales of $500,000 to $3 million." Ideal customer purchasing patterns could include this description: "When they are aware of a business need our accounting firm can solve, they want aggressive and innovative solutions. They don't have time to research solutions themselves." This preference pattern shows that our example accounting firm is segmenting on the basis of benefit received by customers. What makes such customers ideal ones for this firm? They actively want the skills of the professional services offered and are willing and able to pay for them.

Some methods of segmenting a market are more useful for certain businesses than others. For example, if males and females react to the marketing efforts of your business in the same way, then segmenting by gender is not the best way to identify a target market. When segmenting target markets, keep in mind that the reason for grouping people is to predict behavior—especially the behavior of buying from you.

A caveat for the future: Segmenting and targeting may not always be enough. The most common marketing strategy in the 1960s was **mass marketing**, or selling single products to large groups of people. Then, in the 1970s, **market segmentation** was used. Businesses took segmentation a step further in the 1980s with specialized **niche marketing**, which involves concentrating marketing efforts toward smaller target markets. The next step in the evolution of marketing came in the 1990s, with the emergence of **individualized marketing**, or customizing each product to suit the needs of individual customers. These trends in marketing techniques do not mean that businesses need to throw out every technique that has been used in the past. Rather, they indicate that businesses may need to add more tools to their marketing toolbox.

Two factors leading to more individualized marketing are clutter and technology. Clutter in traditional media channels (newspaper, direct mail, television, radio) has reached a point where "shotgun" approaches—the same message directed to no one in particular—do not stand out. Consider that the average American household has access to hundreds of television channels and spends more than 50 hours per week watching them. The American public also has more than 11,500 different magazines from which to choose. Add all the radio stations, catalogs, and direct mail that consumers absorb daily, and you begin to understand how incessantly consumers are bombarded with advertising. An individualized message to segments in need of your product has a better chance of being heard above the noise.

Technology is also allowing us to conduct more individualized marketing by allowing us to track our customers with more precision. Individualized marketing, if taken to an extreme, could mean treating each person as a separate market (offering different products, different advertising, and different channels to each). Although this tactic may not be practical, technology has certainly made it possible.

As "big box" stores get even bigger, the gap between mass markets and niches is actually growing larger as well. Big companies have to concentrate on mass markets to turn a profit. For this reason, large retailers—including supermarkets—are generally reducing the number of brands they stock. If a product is not a top-three brand, it is probably not SKU-worthy. Small businesses, in turn, must concentrate on niches to survive.[11]

A good place for you to start in obtaining specific information about your target market is at the Small Business Administration's home page (www.sba.gov). Here, under the category of Business Development/General Information and Publications, you'll find two files on marketing that are especially worth reading: "Knowing Your Market" and "Marketing Strategies for the Growing Business." Each provides basic background information on marketing topics for small business managers and owners.

When you're ready for more specific information on markets, check out the Census Bureau's Web site (www.census.gov). Here you'll find specific information by state and county regarding business patterns and census information. As you're researching the viability of a target market, you can check for the number and types of businesses already operating and the demographic characteristics of that location's population. The Census Bureau is also fine-tuning its TIGER map service (http://tiger.census.gov), which provides census maps with street-level detail for the entire United States, all 50 states, and all counties in those states; cartographic design; and many other features. However, be aware that this site can be slow in creating the maps because of the large amount of data that must be transmitted.

Understanding Consumer Behavior

Whereas market segmentation and target marketing can tell you *who* might buy your products, it is also essential to your small business marketing efforts to understand consumer behavior—*why* those people buy. Information on consumer behavior comes from several fields, including psychology, sociology, biology, and other professions that try to explain why people do what they do. In determining why people purchase products, we will start with a stimulus-response model of consumer behavior called the *black box model* (see Figure 11.1). This model is based on the work of psychologist Kurt Lewin, who studied how a person's behavior is affected by the interactions of personal influences, such as inner needs, thoughts, and beliefs, and a variety of external environmental forces.

The *black box* is appropriate because it represents what goes on in the customer's mind that remains hidden from businesspeople. We can see the external factors that go in and the responses that come out, but we can't see the internal influences or the decision-making process.

As a small business owner, closeness to your customers is an advantage in understanding the internal influences in customers' minds. Their beliefs, attitudes, values, and motives, as well as their perceptions of your products, are critical to your success. A small business owner needs to be aware of the steps of the mental decision-making process that consumers use in satisfying their needs. We all use them, even if we are not

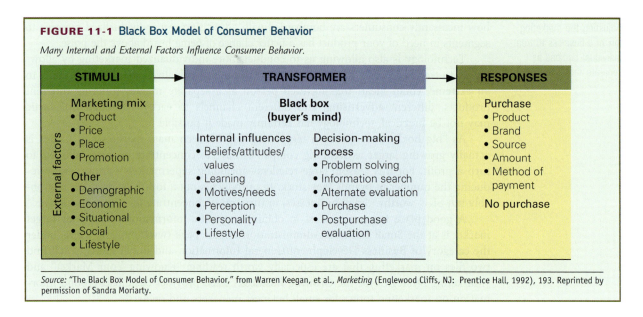

FIGURE 11-1 Black Box Model of Consumer Behavior

Many Internal and External Factors Influence Consumer Behavior.

Source: "The Black Box Model of Consumer Behavior," from Warren Keegan, et al., *Marketing* (Englewood Cliffs, NJ: Prentice Hall, 1992), 193. Reprinted by permission of Sandra Moriarty.

SEO – Search Engine Optimization

Is an Internet marketing strategy essential for your small business? Well, consider how *you* look for information. You search online, right? It's home to some 120 million domains and tens of billions of indexed pages. If you want your site to be on that first page, you need *search-marketing strategies*, including search engine optimization (SEO) and pay-per-click (PPC) advertising. You need to give the search engines what they're looking for to be considered relevant. Then they'll place your site in the top results when people are searching for your product or service.

Here are some key *search engine optimization (SEO)* strategies:

Find the hottest keywords for your market. Determining keywords is the starting point for any search-marketing campaign.

Plug keywords into the right locations in your copy and code. Your Web site is full of hot spots that search engine spiders check regularly for keywords. Put your keywords in the headlines, subheads, and body copy of your Web pages. In your code, use them in anchor text, alt text, title tags, image tags, and meta tags. But use them sparingly: The old strategy of loading up your meta tags with keywords doesn't work anymore—search engines get wise in a hurry and will drop your site immediately for trying to exploit a known ranking element.

Use keywords that relate directly to your content. If you sprinkle keywords like "guaranteed weight loss" through your site that sells shoes, search engines will ignore you. Your keywords will work best if they reflect what your site is about.

Keep the spiders coming back by offering frequent new content. The more fresh, relevant content they find, the higher the search engine spiders are likely to rank your site. Keep all the copy on your pages current, including any changes or updates to your business or products. And archive the newsletters or bulletins on your site. A blog or forum also keeps people heading back for daily updates and discussion.

Do the math. Draw up a list of keywords and phrases that potential customers might search for in looking for your product. Then see how often users search for these terms by plugging each into tools such as www.wordtracker.com or Google Adword's keyword Tool (adwords.google.com/select/keywordtoolexternal). Run your terms through Google to find the number of Web sites returned. Finally, divide the number of indexed pages by the number of daily searches. The lower the result, the more promising the term. Look for a ratio of 500 to 1 or less.

Build a better Web site. How your site is organized, designed, and built will affect its search engine ranking. Search engines have gotten very good at reading domain names, so for example, www.DMCS.com means nothing to a search engine, whereas www.PrivateScubaLessons.com does. Be direct about sprinkling keywords (spider food) throughout, remembering that it must read well to actual people and search engines.

Get the links. Google uses about 200 data points when analyzing your site, but a biggie is whether your site is popular with the in-crowd. If reputable sites link to you, the Google gods smile upon you.

SEO should be at the core of your overall Internet marketing strategy. It's one of the most inexpensive (almost totally free) and effective approaches available. But SEO can be slow.

Sources: "How to Optimize Your Site for Search," *Inc.* July 1, 2010, www.inc.com/magazine; Andrew BE, www.elegantwebsitedesign.com/blog, February 17, 2010; Erin Wienger, "What You Don't Know about SEO," *Entrepreneur*, February 2010, www.entrepreneur.com/article.

conscious of every step. People usually buy products as a solution to some problem or need in their lives, not just for the sake of buying something.

Thus, the first step in the decision-making process that leads to a purchase is *problem recognition*, which occurs when we are motivated to reduce a difference between our current and desired states of affairs. For example, consider a young couple expecting their first child, who realize they do not have a way to record events for future memories. They have recognized a problem. Now they begin the second step in the decision-making process: an *information search*. What products exist that can solve the problem identified in the first step? This search will usually lead consumers to read advertising, magazine articles, and ratings like those found in *Consumer Reports*. They also talk with salespeople, friends, and family members to learn more about products that will satisfy their needs.

These information searches usually turn up several possible solutions, which lead the consumer to the third step: an *evaluation of alternatives*. The parents-to-be need a camera to capture little junior for posterity, but the choices of a digital SLR, a four-thirds camera, a point-and-shoot camera, a small camcorder (like a Flip), a full-scale camcorder, or a smartphone leave them with six alternatives to evaluate. As a small business owner, you enter the customers' decision-making process by being in their **evoked set** of brands or businesses that come to mind when considering a purchase. For example, if you need a pair of shoes, how many businesses that sell shoes come to mind quickly? Those stores are your evoked set for shoes. If your business does not come into customers' minds as a possible solution to their problem, you probably can't sell them too much. The purpose of most advertising (including small business advertising) is to get products into a customer's evoked set.

The most attractive alternative usually leads consumers to the fourth step, which is *purchase*, but many hidden factors can alter this decision. For example, the attitudes of other people can influence the purchase decision. If the prospective parents intended to buy a specific camera and learned that friends had trouble with that model, their decision to purchase would probably change.

Finally, the *postpurchase evaluation* occurs when the consumer uses the product and decides what his level of satisfaction is, which will affect your repeat sales. **Cognitive dissonance**, which, in this context, is the internal conflict we feel after making a decision, is a normal part of the process. If the parents in our example purchased an SLR camera without video capability, you might expect them to later think about the motion and

evoked set
The group of brands or businesses that come to a customer's mind when she thinks of a type of product.

cognitive dissonance
The conflict (i.e., remorse) that buyers feel after making a major purchase.

The consumer decision-making process is a mentally complex one. We process the steps, sometimes subconsciously—even for bagels.

Image copyright © Diego Cervo. Used under license from Shutterstock.com

sound that they could have received from a camcorder. As a small business owner, you try to reduce cognitive dissonance with return policies, warranties, and assurance that the customer made the right choice.

Market Research

market research
The process of gathering information about consumers that will improve marketing efforts.

One of the major advantages that small businesses have over large businesses is close customer contact. Although this closeness can help you maintain your competitive advantage, you will also need a certain amount of ongoing **market research** to stay closely attuned to your market. If you are starting a new business, you will need market research even more.

The American Marketing Association (AMA) defines *market research* as the function that links the consumer, customer, and public to the marketer through information. That information can be used to identify and define marketing opportunities and problems; to generate, refine, and evaluate marketing actions; to monitor marketing performance; and to improve understanding of marketing as a process.

Not all market research conducted by small businesses is formal and intense. Most small business owners want to get information as quickly and as inexpensively as possible. One survey showed that most spend between one and six months and less than $1,000 conducting market research on the last product or service they launched.

Market research can be as simple as trash and peanuts—literally. Owners of small restaurants often inspect outgoing waste to see what customers leave on their plates uneaten. Why? Because customers may order a dish like crayfish and pineapple pizza for the novelty, but if most don't actually eat it, it should be taken off the menu. One creative discount merchant conducted an in-store market research project using peanuts. During a three-day promotion, customers were given all the roasted peanuts in a shell they could eat while in the store. At the end of each day, the empty hulls on the floor provided information about traffic patterns of people moving through the store. Piles of shells in front of displays showed the merchandise that was attracting particular interest.[12]

There is one major factor signaling that small businesses should increase the amount of time and money they spend on market research: changing conditions. Because many markets and demographics change quickly, the businesses that emerge as winners are those that are *proactive* rather than *reactive*. Market research can give you information on what your customers are going to want as opposed to historical data that tell you what they used to want.

"One creative merchant conducted a secret marketing survey by giving his customers roasted peanuts. The piles of empty hulls on the floor showed him how people had moved through the store—and which displays had attracted the most attention."

Some streetwise, down-and-dirty marketing research can be gathered from competitors. No, they will not voluntarily hand anything useful over to you, but you plant yourself in front of a competitor's store for a day or two, and notice how many people walk in. Now, how many walk out with a purchase? Can you get a feel for the average purchase size? This information could be very useful in making your sales projections if you have similar foot traffic.[13]

Small business owners who have been in business for longer than, say, two days have learned two things about market research: They need it, and it's expensive. Fortunately, customer feedback can be a click away. Several online survey tools make it possible for you to more effectively listen to customers and make informed business decisions. David Ambler, a partner in the Phelon Group, a Palo Alto, California, consultancy specializing in building customer relations reminds small business owners that "collecting data is one thing. Acting on it is another thing altogether. If you are unwilling or unable to act on survey data, then the survey is a waste of your customers' time and an unnecessary distraction for your organization."

Zoomerang, *SurveyMonkey*, and *Survey Gizmo* are all online survey tools—and customer touch points, meaning a connection to build relations with your customers. To your customers, your survey invitation, and the actions you take in following up on the survey show them how you value their feedback.[14]

87% OF THE 56% WHO COMPLETED MORE THAN 23% OF THE SURVEY THOUGHT IT WAS A WASTE OF TIME

© Fran Courtesy of www.cartoonstock.com

Market Research Process

The market research process follows five basic steps: identifying the problem, developing a plan, collecting the data, analyzing the data, and drawing conclusions (see Figure 11.2).

Identify the Problem The most difficult and important part of the market research process is the first step—identifying the problem. You must have a clearly stated, concisely worded problem to generate usable information. Many people (novice and experienced researchers alike) have trouble with this step because they confuse problems with symptoms. For example, if you go to a physician complaining of a fever, the physician could prescribe medication that would bring your fever down. That step would not cure you, however, because an infection or other problem is actually causing your fever. Your physician will search until the problem is found and then fix it—not just mask the symptom. Similarly, declining sales in your small business is not just a problem—it is a symptom of another, underlying problem that is its cause. That underlying problem is what you would want to try to uncover with your research. Has the competition increased? Do your salespeople need retraining? Have your customers' tastes changed?

Your marketing "problem" does not always have to be something that is wrong. It could be something that is lacking or something that could be improved. You can use market research not only to solve problems but also to identify opportunities. Whatever your goal, your ability to complete this first step of the research process is important in guiding the rest of your research efforts.

Planning Market Research Market research is often expensive, but a plan for how you will conduct your research project can help keep costs in check. Before you start, you must separate what is "critical to know" from what would be "nice to know." Your next step is to design a way to address the problem or answer the question that you have

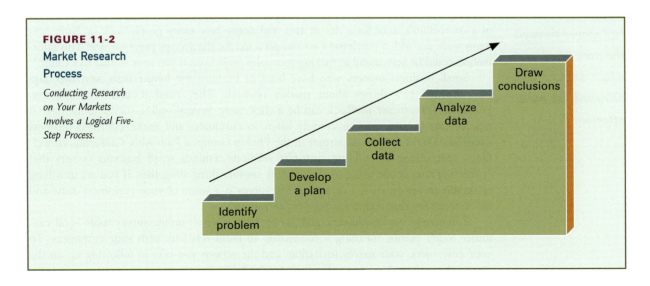

FIGURE 11-2
Market Research Process

Conducting Research on Your Markets Involves a Logical Five-Step Process.

Identify problem → Develop a plan → Collect data → Analyze data → Draw conclusions identified concerning your business. You can do it yourself, and you should keep it as simple as possible.

In planning your market research project, you need to do the following:

- Identify the types of information that you need.
- Identify primary and secondary sources of data.
- Select a sample that represents the population you are studying.
- Select a research method and measurement technique (phone survey, focus group, and so on) to answer your research question.

In conducting market research for your small business, you should choose a method that provides enough reliable data for you to make a decision with confidence. The method you choose must also use your limited time, money, and personnel efficiently.

Collecting Data After you have identified the research problem and laid out a plan, you are ready to gather data. Although it sounds simple, don't get this order reversed. A common research error is to begin the process by gathering data and then trying to figure out what the information means and where to go with it—putting the cart before the horse. Determine what you need, and only then go get it. There are two basic types of data you may seek: secondary and primary.[15]

secondary data
Marketing data that have been gathered, tabulated, and made available by an outside source.

Secondary data are those that already exist, having been gathered for some other purpose. You should check secondary sources first, because they are less expensive than data gathered by conducting your own study. You may be able to solve your problem without an extended primary search.

The good news about secondary data is that the amount of available data is considerable. The bad news is that this mountain of information can prove overwhelming.

A good place to begin your search of secondary data is your local library. Online databases like Lexis-Nexis or ABI-INFORM allow you to enter key terms into the program and immediately receive titles, abstracts, and entire articles from journals and periodicals. The *Government Printing Office Monthly Catalog* contains report references from many government agencies, such as the Department of Commerce and the Small Business Administration (SBA), which may help you. The Department of Commerce also publishes *Selected Publications to Aid Business and Industry*. Check the *Encyclopedia of Associations* for the thousands of trade, professional, technical, and industrial associations that exist. These associations compile information that can be very relevant to your business.

You can get data on your personal computer from online computer services such as Dun & Bradstreet's home page, Yahoo!, or Dow Jones, publisher of the *Wall Street Journal*, which offers Dow Jones News/Retrieval. The latter service can help you scan the newspaper's daily Enterprise column, which is devoted to topics on small business. The SBA provides 24-hour access to information on services it provides, publications, training, trade fairs, and other programs through its electronic bulletin board, *SBA On-line* (www.sba.gov).

Among the best commercial sources of information are research and trade associations. Their information is industry specific and generally available only to association members, but it is thorough and accurate. If you are serious about getting into or being in business, the membership dues for these organizations are worthwhile investments. Check *Encyclopedia of Associations* (Gale Research) and *Business Information Sources* (University of California Press) at your local library to find relevant associations.[16]

Unfortunately, readily available secondary data are not always specific or detailed enough for your purpose, or they may be obsolete. In either case, you will need to gather your own primary data.

primary data
Marketing data that a business collects for its own specific purposes.

"Unfortunately, readily available secondary data are not always specific or detailed enough for your purpose, or they may be obsolete. In either case, you will need to gather your own primary data."

Primary data are qualitative or quantitative data that you collect yourself for your specific purpose. Both qualitative and quantitative data have their advocates and critics, but either can provide valuable information if collected and analyzed correctly.

Qualitative data refer to research findings that cannot be analyzed statistically. Such data are useful if you are looking for open-minded responses to probing questions, not yes-or-no answers.[17] They can be obtained through *personal interviews* or *focus groups* (groups of six to ten people), which provide considerable depth of information from each person. Qualitative data do not lend themselves to statistical analysis, however. Instead, they help you look for trends in answers or obtain specific or detailed responses to your questions.

Quantitative data are structured to analyze and report numbers, so as to help you see relationships between variables and frequency of occurrences. They are useful in providing information on large groups of people. Their less-probing questions yield results that can be analyzed statistically to show causation.

Small businesses that conduct business online (especially business-to-business operations) can obtain marketing research from the search engines that bring customers to their sites. Web reporting packages (such as WebTrends, Hitbox, and Core-Metrics) provide more data than most businesses can use. For example, you can track the exact phrases that are typed into the search bar that led to your site. What types of words are users entering to find your site? What words are misspelled repeatedly? (Hint: You should add the misspelled word to bring the people using it to your Web site.) What supplemental words are users adding into their search queries that you have not identified?[18]

Telephone interviews, *personal interviews*, and *mail surveys* are methods that small businesses commonly use to gather both types of primary data. Because the *questionnaire* is such a popular small business research tool, the following advice is offered to increase its usefulness and enhance response rates.

- Try to make the questionnaire visually attractive and fun to answer. This will help keep it from ending up in the recipient's wastebasket.
- Try to structure possible responses. Instead of asking open-ended questions such as "What do you think of our product?" list answers that focus on specific issues such as reliability, quality, and price for respondents to check off.
- Don't ask for more than most people can remember. Annoying questions, like asking for the number of light bulbs a business uses in a year, can end the response.
- Don't have more than 20 words per question. People lose interest quickly if questions are too long.
- Be as specific and unambiguous as possible.
- Include a cover letter explaining the reason for the questionnaire. Say, "Thank you."
- Include a self-addressed, stamped return envelope to increase the response rate.
- Include a return date. A reasonable deadline will increase the number of responses and will let you know how long to wait before tallying the results.[19]

Other techniques of primary-data collection for small businesses are limited only by your imagination. The automobile license plates of many states show the county where the vehicle is registered. You can get an idea of where your customers live by taking note of the license plates in your parking lot. This information can help you determine where to aim your advertising. You can use the same technique by spending some time in your competitors' parking lots.

Telephone numbers can tell you where customers live, too. You can get them from sales slips, credit slips, or checks.

You would think that greeting card giant Hallmark would have every advantage over a tiny business like Someecards. Hallmark has 14,000 employees—700 of whom are full-time writers and artists. Someecards has been in business for less than two years with a

Image copyright © Dmitriy Shironosov. Used under license from Shutterstock.com

Gathering and analyzing data are important for understanding consumer behavior.

full-time staff of five. The company president also is the chief writer. But when you consider one facet of customer contact, Hallmark has 2,017 followers on Twitter while Someecards scores 1.7 million. Entrepreneurs are much better at tweeting the mood and swagger of their company than large PR departments.[20]

Advertisements that provide coded coupons or phrases in your broadcast advertising that customers can use to get a discount can help you determine the effectiveness and reach of your ads.

Data Analysis Basically, *data analysis* is the process of determining what the responses to your research mean. Once data have been collected, they must be analyzed and translated into usable information. Your first step is to "clean" the data. This effort includes removing all questionnaires and other response forms that are unusable because they are incomplete or unreadable. Depending on the instrument or methodology used to gather data, you may need to code and examine the data to identify trends and develop insights. (An exhaustive description of data analysis is not appropriate for this text. For details of this process, refer to a source such as a market research text.)

For quantitative data, several software programs exist to aid in number crunching and transforming data into charts and graphs to make interpretation easier.

Presenting Data and Making Decisions Market research that does not lead to some type of action is useless. Your research needs to aid you in making management decisions. Should you expand into a new geographic area? Should you change your product line? Should you change your business hours?

Conclusions based on your data analysis may be obvious. Data may fall out in such a way that you can see exactly what you need to do next to address the research problem identified in Step 1.

Market research can provide you with information that will allow you to take proactive steps. This consideration is important because, as a small business owner, deciding what you need to do in the future is much more important than knowing what has happened in the past.

Limitations of Market Research

As important as market research can be for small businesses, it should be used with caution. Market research can provide you with a picture of what people currently know and expect from products or services, but it has limited ability to indicate what people will want in the future. Relying on market research exclusively for your marketing strategy and new product ideas is like driving a car while watching only the rearview mirror.

As noted in Chapter 1, small businesses provide many of the most innovative products that we use. Our economy and consumers depend on a stream of such innovations as fax machines, CD-ROMs, and minivans, but innovation does not come from market research. Peter Drucker notes that although the fax machine was designed and developed by U.S. companies, no U.S. companies began producing these devices for domestic consumption because market research indicated that there would be no demand for such a product.

When asking about a product that does not yet exist, Drucker says your question might go like this (in regard to the not-yet-produced fax machine): "Would you buy a telephone accessory that costs upwards of $1,500 and enables you to send, for one dollar a page, the same letter the post office delivers for 25 cents?" The average consumer would predictably say "no."[21] Hal Sperlich designed the concept of the minivan while he was working for Ford, but when Ford didn't believe a market existed for such a vehicle (based on its historical market research), he switched to Chrysler. Sperlich says, "In ten years of developing the minivan, we never once got a letter from a housewife asking us to invent one." To the skeptics, that proved a market didn't exist.[22]

Although market research works well for fine-tuning concepts for known products, customers don't have the foresight to ask for what they don't know about or don't know they need or want. As one axis of Figure 11.3 shows, there are two types of customer needs: those that customers can tell you about and those that customers have without realizing they have them. How many people were asking for Blu-ray HD video, MP3 players, or GPS units 10 years ago? The other axis of Figure 11.3 shows that there are

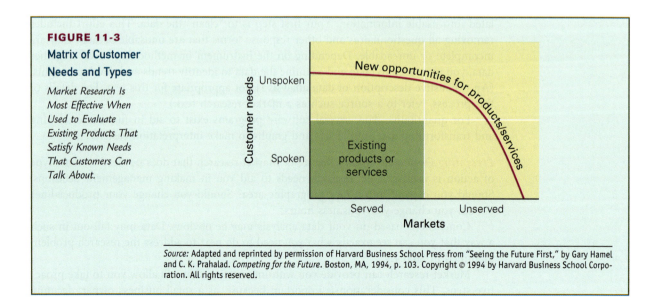

FIGURE 11-3

Matrix of Customer Needs and Types

Market Research Is Most Effective When Used to Evaluate Existing Products That Satisfy Known Needs That Customers Can Talk About.

two types of markets or customers for any given business: those served by the company's existing products and those not yet served—the company's potential customers. Market research can tell us the most about the spoken needs of a served market, but much room for growth can be found by exploring the three other sectors. When you are driving a car, you need to check the rearview mirror occasionally, just as you should check your current and past markets with market research. But the ideal is to concentrate on defining markets rather than reacting to them. An entrepreneur must go beyond what market research can tell.

Summary

1. Explain the importance of marketing to small businesses.

Marketing involves all the points of contact between your small business and your customers. Marketing is how you find out what they want and need; it is how they are treated by you and everyone in your business; it is how you communicate with them through selling and advertising. What could be more important?

2. Describe the process of developing a small business marketing strategy.

Market segmentation is needed because no business can possibly be everything to everyone. Segmenting involves breaking down a population into target markets that have a common want or need that the business can satisfy. Target markets are the focus of a company's marketing efforts.

3. Discuss the purpose of the market research process and the steps involved in putting it into practice.

Market research provides information about the people who are buying the products of a business. Conditions change, and the owner of a business must know about those changes to be proactive and maintain a competitive advantage. The steps of the market research process include problem identification, development of a plan, data collection, data analysis, and drawing conclusions. Market research can provide valuable information regarding people's current tastes, preferences, and expectations. It is useful in fine-tuning products that already exist for markets that are already known. Conversely, it is of limited use for markets that do not exist yet or for needs that customers do not realize they have.

Questions for Review and Discussion

1. Marketing plays a key role in a small business's success. Can a small business succeed without adopting the philosophy underlying the marketing concept? Why or why not?
2. What would happen to a business without a marketing strategy? Why?
3. What determines which type of sales forecast would be appropriate for a small business? Describe how a specific small business would implement the build-up approach.
4. Why is segmenting a niche market so crucial for a small business?
5. We all assume several different roles (parent, student, sibling, athlete, business owner, and so on) at any given time, and those roles affect our behavior as consumers. Describe how your various roles affect your purchases.
6. What is the significance of market research to the small business owner? How is market research defined, and what degree of complexity is necessary in the research plan for it to be valid?
7. Explain the market research process from a small business owner's perspective when he is trying to assess competitive advantage.
8. What types of data should be collected and analyzed to get a clear picture of the market for the good or service being produced?
9. Identify some valuable sources of information for the entrepreneur who is designing a market research plan to analyze competitive advantage.
10. What are some of the limitations of the process of market research? How can the entrepreneur offset these limitations?

Questions for Critical Thinking

1. Segmentation is the process of breaking a population down into smaller groups and marketing to them. Is it possible for a small business to over segment its market? How would that be dangerous?

2. What do you think is the biggest limitation for small businesses conducting market research?

What Would You Do?

The bigger and stronger the competition is, the better a small business's marketing strategy needs to be. That being the case, Amilya Antonetti may need *your* help with a marketing strategy. Antonetti is starting a business to break into the $4.7 billion U.S. laundry detergent market, competing directly with the likes of Procter & Gamble. The niche of the detergent market that she is filling is hypoallergenic cleaning products, because her infant son had health problems aggravated by chemicals in the standard brands. She started her company, called SoapWorks, after conducting market research, primarily from other mothers of infants, and finding that many other families faced similar problems. Her annual advertising budget is limited to $60,000 (about what her huge competitors spend on one 30-second prime-time network TV ad), so she had to find different ways to let people know what SoapWorks would do for them.

Questions

1. If you were in Amilya Antonetti's place starting SoapWorks, what marketing strategy would you use to compete with Procter & Gamble and Clorox? How would you reach your target markets? How and where would you advertise? We talk about the power of word of mouth among our customers—how do you use it to your advantage as a small business marketer?

2. One of the biggest challenges SoapWorks faced was getting its products on the shelves of grocery stores. By 1999, they were in 2,500 stores from California to Florida, and the company had revenues of $5 million. How would you create such market penetration?

Source: D. M. Osborne, "Taking on Procter & Gamble," *Inc.,* October 2000, 66–73.

12
Product

CHAPTER LEARNING OUTCOMES

After reading this chapter, you should be able to:

1. Define the term *marketing mix.*

2. Discuss the different forms a product can take, and identify the five levels of product satisfaction.

3. Explain the importance of purchasing and describe its procedures.

4. Discuss the main concerns in selecting a supplier.

5. Calculate how much inventory you need and when.

6. Describe seven methods of inventory control.

K irk Hawkins and Steen Strand are masters of product design—taking a product that is historically rather technically complex and making it simple, sporty, and elegant. Hawkins and Strand are the co-founders of Icon Aircraft who designed the perfect plane for a new class of aviator—the sport pilot. Hawkins says that "no one has done a ground-up [aircraft] design focused specifically on the consumer recreational sport market."

In 2004, the Federal Aviation Administration changed regulations to create the new Light Sport Aircraft category, which eases the requirement for both pilots and aircraft. ICON Aircraft's sole purpose has been to bring the freedom, fun, and adventure of flying to all who have dreamed of flight. Hawkins and Strand believe that consumer-focused sport aircraft can do for recreational flying what personal watercraft did for boating. Sport licenses can be obtained by about anyone in a couple of weeks training and about $3,500—much less than higher levels of private pilot's licenses.

Hawkins has experience as an engineer who previously worked with Air Force F-16s to American Airlines 767s. Strand invented the Freebord, a skateboard-snowboard hybrid. The pair met

at Stanford University while working on master's degrees in product design (Strand) and engineering (Hawkins). Their sport aircraft are designed not only to deliver an amazing and safe flying experience, but also to inspire us the way great sports cars do. After years of development with some of the world's best aerospace engineers and industrial designers, ICON Aircraft's first of its line of sport planes is the ICON A5. The A5 is a bold yet elegant design that communicates beauty, performance, safety, and, most importantly, fun. They call the A5 a blend of "badass" Apple and BMW product design, powered by engineering from rocket scientists.

The A5 has some very cool, unique features—wings that fold back for hauling on a trailer, is amphibious, a top speed of 120 mph and range of 345 miles, a single rear-mounted engine that runs on either automotive or aviation fuel, and a built-in, full-airplane parachute.

For a new company with a new product, Icon Aircraft is getting a lot of attention; it's been seen in *Iron Man 2* and *Knight and Day*. Hawkins and Strand have been taking orders for two years before their plane comes out of production in late 2010. Even with a lousy economy, the pair are confident that people are going to embrace their different approach. Strand says, "Icon is about recreation, and we really think we can start to change the way people think about recreation." Flying an A5 is like sitting in the front row of the IMAX.

Sources: Jennifer Wang, "Ultimate Flying Machine," *Entrepreneur*, September 2010, 19; Andy Pastor, "Start-up Wants a New Audience to Take to the Air," *Wall Street Journal*, June 22, 2008, B1; Carl Hoffman, "The Ultimate Flying Machine: Sexy as a Sports Car, Portable as a Jet Ski," *Wired*, December 22, 2008; Christopher Sawyer, "Icon A5 Light Sport Aircraft," *ADEP*, January 2009, 14–15; and Bailey Barnhard, "Just for Fun," *Robb Report*, October 1, 2008.

Using Your Marketing Mix

marketing mix
The factors that a business can change in selling products to customers—product, place, price, and promotion.

Marketing involves *all* the activities that occur from the time your product is made until it reaches the consumer. Your **marketing mix** consists of the variables that you can control in bringing your product or service to your target market. Think of them as the tools your small business has available for its use. The marketing mix is also referred to as the *Four Ps*: product, place, price, and promotion. You must offer the right *product* (including goods and services) that your target market wants or needs. *Place* refers to channels of distribution you choose to use, as well as the location and layout of your small business. Your *price* must make your product attractive and still allow you to make a profit. *Promotion* is the means you use to communicate with your target market. This chapter and the following two chapters will cover your use of the marketing mix to build and run your business.

Product: The Heart of the Marketing Mix

product
A tangible good, an intangible service, or a combination of these.

The product is at the heart of your marketing mix. Remember that **product** means tangible goods, intangible services, or a combination of these (see Figure 12.1). Hiring someone to mow your lawn is an example of the service end of the goods-and-services spectrum. In this case, you don't receive a tangible good. An example of a tangible good would be the purchase of a chair that is finished and assembled, but not delivered. Thus, in this case, you don't receive any services. Many businesses offer a combination of goods and services. Restaurants, for instance, provide both goods (food and drink) and services (preparation and delivery).

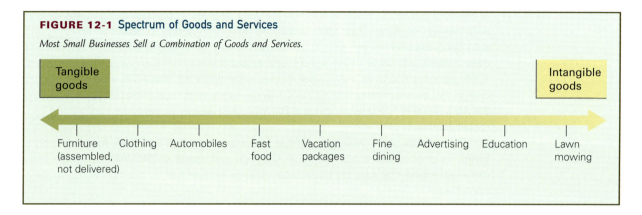

FIGURE 12-1 Spectrum of Goods and Services

Most Small Businesses Sell a Combination of Goods and Services.

Tangible goods

Intangible goods

Furniture (assembled, not delivered) Clothing Automobiles Fast food Vacation packages Fine dining Advertising Education Lawn mowing

When determining your product strategy, it is useful to think about different levels of product satisfaction. Products are the "bundle of satisfaction" that consumers receive in exchange for their money (see Figure 12.2). The most basic level of product satisfaction is its *core benefit*, or the fundamental reason why people buy products. For an automobile, the core benefit is transportation from point A to point B. With a hotel room, the core benefit is a night's sleep. To put this another way, people don't buy drills—they really buy holes.

The next level of product satisfaction is the *generic product*. For an automobile, the generic product is the steel, plastic, and glass. For the hotel, the building, the front desk, and the rooms represent the generic product.

The third level of product satisfaction is the *expected product*, which includes the set of attributes and conditions that consumers assume will be present. U.S. consumers expect comfortable seats, responsive handling, and easy starting from their cars. A hotel guest expects clean sheets, soap, towels, relative quiet, and indoor plumbing.

The *augmented product*, the fourth level of product satisfaction, is all the additional services and benefits that can distinguish your business. For example, night vision built into windshields, satellite-linked navigational systems in autos, and express checkout and health club facilities in hotels are product augmentations. Augmentations represent the sizzle that you sell along with the steak. The problem with product augmentations is that they soon become expected. When you have raised your costs and prices by adding augmentations, you open the door for competitors to come in and offer more of a generic product at a lower price. That's how the Motel 6 franchises became so successful—by offering a plain room for a low price when competitors were adding amenities that raised their cost structure and prices.

The fifth and final level is the *potential product*. It includes product evolutions to come. Not long ago, a DVD-R drive was a potential product for personal computers. It soon became a product augmentation and, very quickly, expected.

Thus the products that you develop and sell in your small business are more than just a combination of tangible features. Always keep in mind which core benefits customers receive from your product, how the actual product satisfies those core needs, and how you can augment your products to make them more appealing.

> *"Always keep in mind which core benefits customers receive from your product, how the actual product satisfies those core needs, and how you can augment your products to make them more appealing."*

Developing New Products

Part of a marketer's job is managing products through the stages of their *life cycle* (see Figure 7.2, page 159). Trends like increased global competition and quickly changing customer needs have shortened product life cycles and increased the need for new products.[1] As a company's current products enter the stages of late maturity and decline,

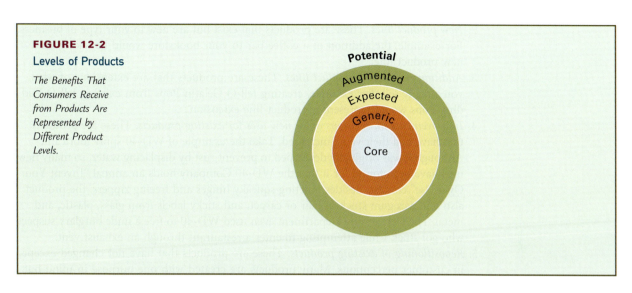

FIGURE 12-2

Levels of Products

The Benefits That Consumers Receive from Products Are Represented by Different Product Levels.

Potential
Augmented
Expected
Generic
Core

they need to be replaced with new ones in demand. What is new? Good question. Marketing consultants Booz, Allen & Hamilton group new products into six categories:

1. *New-to-the-world products.* These are products that have not been seen before, which result in entirely new markets. Ken Fischer developed and patented a marine paint that the U.S. Navy uses to keep its ships free of barnacles. The paint is made from a mixture of epoxy and cayenne pepper. Fischer came up with the idea for the paint after blistering his mouth on a Tabasco-covered deviled egg. He decided that animals would react the same way. He was right.[2]

Companies have economic incentive to develop new products and innovate existing ones because every product moves through its own life cycle.

2. *New product lines.* These are products that exist but are new to your type of business. For example, the addition of a coffee bar to your bookstore would be taking on a new product line.

3. *Additions to existing product lines.* These are products that are extensions of what you already sell. For example, creating Jell-O Gelatin Pops from existing Jell-O Pudding Pops would represent a product-line extension.

4. *Improvements in, revisions of, or new uses for existing products.* These are products that have had their value increased. Take the example of WD-40 spray lubricant. Although it was originally developed to prevent rust by displacing water, so many new uses have been found for it that the WD-40 Company holds an annual "Invent Your Own Use" contest. Besides quieting squeaky hinges and freeing zippers, the product also removes gum stuck in hair or carpet, and sticky labels from glass, plastic, and metal. The Denver Fire Department even used WD-40 to free a nude burglary suspect who got stuck while attempting to enter a restaurant through an exhaust vent.

5. *Repositioning of existing products.* These are products that have not changed except in customer perceptions. Many products are created with one purpose in mind but end up finding success in another arena—including Post-it Notes (originally created to mark pages in the inventor's church choir songbook) and Viagra (originally

ENTREPRENEURIAL SNAPSHOT

© Boston Globe/Bill Brett/Landov

Marketing Kings of Furniture

The mantra for most retailers has been "the customer is king" for many years. Few small retail businesses ignore competitors who take a customer-centric approach to building a wide base of loyal customers. Of course, it sounds more simple than it is to satisfy customers on all the levels shown in Figure 12.2.

Jordan's Furniture, however, is a four-store chain in the Boston area that gets it. Their motto is "There's No Business That's Not Show Business." Brothers Barry and Eliot Tatelman share a magic touch combining shopping and entertainment into what they call "shoppertainment." Each store offers a unique array of interactive, sensory features that can do the impossible of turning furniture shopping into a family event.

At the Natick, Massachusetts, store, the Tatelmans have recreated a Mardi Gras celebration featuring kids' amusement rides, animatronic characters, and refreshment stands lining their version of Bourbon Street. From there, customers can journey through the couch section to take in a movie at the full-size IMAX movie theater located inside the store.

The highlight of the Reading store is the area titled Beantown covering 17,000 square feet and filled with a total of 280,000 pounds of Jelly Belly jellybeans. The 25 million jellybeans are used to construct Boston's Big Dig road construction project, the State House, and a full-sized replica of Fenway Park's "Green Monster," with the Red Sox mascot clutching a New York Yankee. Obviously baseball fans, in the spring of 2007, the brothers promised to give away furniture—every sofa, sectional, dining set, bed, and mattress purchased between March 7 and April 16 if the Sox won the World Series. They took out a $20 million insurance policy in case the Sox came through, and they rooted for the home team so they could give away their wares. (Yes, Boston won that year.)

Barry and Eliot are entrepreneurs who offer more than mattresses—they combine products, service, and fun. Watch the video clip that accompanies this chapter for more of their marketing antics.

Sources: Eli Bortman, "The Jordan's Furniture 'Monster Deal': A Legal Gamble?" *Sport Marketing Quarterly*, Vol. 18, No. 4, 2009, 218–221; Dana French, "Furniture Stores Still King," *Furniture Today*, November 16, 2009, 1, 20; Clint Engel, "Jordan's Scores Big with 'Power Play,'" *Furniture Today*, August 31, 2009, 1, 12; and Janet Groeber, "That's Entertainment," *Display & Design Ideas*, May 2005.

formulated to treat angina—chest pain associated with poor circulation to the heart). Developers at Gore-Tex (makers of waterproof outer clothing and Glide dental floss) tried to expand the use of the company's polytetrafluoroethylene (ePTFE) material to make cables for controlling puppets at Disney theme parks; it didn't work. It turns out, however, that ePTFE lasts five times longer than regular guitar strings. Now Elixir Strings are sold in more than half of all music stores in the United States.[3]

6. *Lower-cost versions of existing products.* These are products that provide value and performance similar to those of existing products but at a lower cost. For example, food stands that sell hamburgers and hot dogs offer products similar to the big-name fast-food franchises but at a lower price, thereby enticing customers with their cost advantage.

Of course, increased risk is associated with the launch of new products. How many new products can you remember seeing on the shelves at the grocery store in the last year? Ten? Fifty? One hundred? Now think of how many of those you chose to adopt. However many you remember, it was surely far less than the 20,000 new food products and 5,000 nonfood items introduced each year.[4] Many of those new products did not survive. Nevertheless, despite the risk, innovation is the key to success. Innovation is part of being proactive in the marketplace.

"Despite the risk, innovation is the key to success."

Inventor's Paradox

At several points in this book, you have been asked to project yourself into a scenario where you have come up with an idea for a new business and decide what you would do at that stage (maybe you are not projecting). Let's take up that discussion again with the following premise: You have developed a new product that fits into one of the six categories cited earlier. What are your options? The best alternative is to start and run your own business based on the new product—that option is the foundation of this whole book. But what other options exist?

Unfortunately, many product innovators believe that they simply need to generate an idea for a new product, service, or process, and Uber-Corporation X will pay them massive amounts of money for this idea. Sorry to disappoint you, but ideas are worth very little in the business world. In fact, most companies strongly discourage inventors from approaching them with ideas. Why? Because they have been approached by hundreds of people who want to cash in on undeveloped ideas. Of course, some people have convinced members of a large corporation that they are serious inventors who have marketable ideas, but lightning has struck in the same place twice, too. Just don't count on it happening.

licensing agreement
An agreement in which the owner of intellectual property grants another person (or another company) permission to produce that product.

If you do gain an audience with a corporate representative at whom you can make a proposal and a presentation, you have a better chance of walking out with a **licensing agreement** than a check. Under a licensing agreement, the owner of intellectual property grants another person (or another company) permission to produce that product. In exchange, the inventor receives royalties, which constitute a percentage (generally 5 percent to 6 percent) of sales. The inventor relinquishes control over what the licensee does with the product. Your chances of getting a licensing agreement are greatly improved if you are already producing the product and have established a track record of sales. Your chances of getting a licensing agreement dwindle if you are seeking a license because you don't have enough money to develop the product yourself.

private-label manufacturing
Producing products under another company's name.

Another alternative for an inventor may be **private-label manufacturing**. For example, Sears does not own a factory in which it builds its Craftsman tools. Instead, the company engages other companies to make the tools to its specifications and puts the Craftsman brand on them. This is where you, the tool inventor, could enter the picture.

Reality Check

The Fairness of Slotting Fees

Did you pick up some of the great flavors of Lee's Ice Cream the last time you were in a grocery store? No? It's great stuff. It must be; the ice cream store in Baltimore has the highest gross sales per square foot of any ice cream stand in America. Sorry, but you couldn't buy it in any grocery store because of slotting fees.

What are slotting fees? They are fees paid by a manufacturer to ensure that a retailer places its products on store shelves. The practice of paying slotting fees has been around for about 20 years, mainly in the grocery business, but it has not been widely publicized. Manufacturers of all types have complained about slotting fees for years, but they keep their complaints to themselves for fear of retailer reprisals. Some companies, such as Pacific Valley Foods of Bellevue, Washington, are going public in saying that slotting destroyed 70 percent of its business.

Large grocery chains justify the practice by saying that the fees offset the expense and risk of putting new products on their shelves in place of proven products, and that they discourage random and poorly researched new products—in short, that they are a tool for improving distribution efficiency. Manufacturers say that slotting discourages product innovation, damages competition, destroys small food processors, and severely restricts product choices for consumers.

With the slim margins of the food industry, the payout period can be stretched up to five to seven years. Large food manufacturers can spread the fees (which can run as high as $50,000 per shop-keeping unit (SKU) per store in a chain) over many existing products, by charging slightly higher prices that go largely unnoticed. Because small producers must include slotting fees in the prices of their new products, they often can't afford to get their foot in the door (or products on the shelf).

One small company recently launched a new kind of meat product and *not counting slotting fees* had to pay a single grocery chain (1) $5,000 per item in warehouse costs, (2) $5,000 per item in quarterly newspaper ads, and (3) $86,000 in free samples. Thus a small manufacturer has put a $100,000 ante in before the product even reaches the store shelves. Even worse, if the product does not sell, the company has to buy it back!

A recent academic study found that slotting fees are used in both the consumer and the durable goods manufacturing industries, though different norms regarding slotting fees exist between product categories. This study evaluated several theoretical approaches regarding slotting fees including the efficiency school of thought, the market power school of thought, and even an approach that slotting fees are simply a new promotional tool from which manufacturers choose when allocating marketing resources.

Are slotting fees a way for grocery stores to shift the financial risk of new grocery products (80 percent of which fail) from the retailer to the manufacturer? Or are they a competition-stifling practice that unfairly punishes the smallest, most innovative companies?

Sources: Oystein Foros and Hans Kind, "Do Slotting Allowances Harm Retail Competition?" *The Scandinavian Journal of Economics*, Spring 2009, 367–384; Robert Innes and Stephen Hamilton, "Vertical Restraints and Horizontal Control, *RAND Journal of Economics*, Spring 2009, 120–143; Benjamin Klein and Joshua Wright, "The Economics of Slotting Contracts," *Journal of Law & Economics*, August 2007, 421–454; P. F. Bone, K. R. France, and R. Russo, "A Multifirm Analysis of Slotting Fees," *Journal of Public Policy & Marketing*, Fall 2006, 224–237; Barry Feig, "Too Clever by Half?" *Frozen Food Age*, January 2003, 20; and Leonard Klie, "Slotting Fees Vary among Products," *Food Logistics*, January/February 2004, 6.

If you have designed a new tool that Sears does not currently have in its product line, you might be able to secure an agreement to produce that tool under the company's brand name. You will get only about one-half of the retail price, but at least you have a sales base from which to begin your operations. A serious downside to this strategy is that you have just one major customer, so your company's fortunes will hang on that firm's willingness to maintain the agreement.

Recall the Chapter 1 discussion of the symbiotic relationship between large and small businesses. Here is another possible connection where each party needs the other:

Similar to private-label manufacturing, you could become an *OEM (original-equipment manufacturer)*, a company that makes component parts or accessories for larger items.[5] For example, your firm might produce circuit boards for computer manufacturers or custom knobs for cabinet makers.

Importance of Product Competitive Advantage

Few would argue that the length of time many products have before they become obsolete has decreased rapidly over the past few years. Factors such as new technologies, increasing numbers of substitute products, quickly changing consumer tastes and preferences, and shifting consumption patterns all play large roles in this rapid phase-out of existing products. Small businesses are more vulnerable to product obsolescence because they typically depend on fewer key products and have fewer resources with which to develop new ones. In addition, the niche markets that small businesses serve can dry up or be lured away by a larger, low-cost competitor. The optimal scenario for these businesses features a steady stream of new products being developed to replace existing ones as they pass through the product life cycle.

Unfortunately, no one actually runs a business that operates within the optimal scenario. Instead, the best you can do is learn from other successful small businesses. A recent study illustrated some fundamental practices of small businesses that succeed in creating and retaining a competitive advantage. Notably, they maintain their focus on specialized products serving niche markets and rely on their existing core competitive advantage to enter new markets. A *sustainable competitive advantage* is based on something that firm does better than others—a *core competency*. To be classified as a core competency, a factor should satisfy three criteria:

1. Be applicable across a range of products.
2. Be difficult for competitors to duplicate.
3. Provide a fundamental and valuable benefit to customers.

> *"A sustainable competitive advantage is based on something that firm does better than others—a core competency."*

Assuming that their core competencies are intact, successful companies share some common characteristics that can be termed *best practices*: They:

- *Leverage existing capabilities*—meaning they understand what they do well, and they use those skills to enter new markets.
- *Enter growth markets*—and thereby avoid cutthroat price competition and zero-sum games.
- *Target niche markets*—because, by definition, niche markets are less crowded with competitors than mass markets, and customers in niche markets are willing to pay premiums for specialized products.
- *Diversify*—so as to spread risk, or, as the cliché goes, they don't put all their eggs in one basket.
- *Add new capabilities*—by building a set of skills, such as technology, marketing, or distribution.
- *Establish strong top management leadership*—which will diversify and take other risks necessary to reposition their organizations when necessary.
- *Have a good workforce*—that is, employees who are skilled, flexible, and self-motivated.
- *Maintain high employee productivity*—and, thus, without adding employees, keep overhead costs low and product output high.
- *Have low overhead*—because they have a lean management structure, and they avoid major new investments in buildings and equipment by adding extra shifts and overtime.[6]

Packaging

If you are selling a packaged consumer product, think of packaging as your last chance to catch customers' attention—kind of like the last five seconds of marketing. Of course, packaging provides more than just a wrapper around your product; it can add value that benefits both you and your customers. Good packaging can make handling or storage more convenient. It can reduce spoilage or damage. Packaging can benefit your customers by making the product more identifiable and therefore easier to find on a crowded shelf.

POM Wonderful is a pricey pomegranate juice that is packaged in a fat, snowman-shaped bottle. Even though customers complain that it feels like it's about to fall out of their hand, they still shell out $4.39 per bottle.[7] Think the company could get that much if the juice was packaged in an aluminum can? Probably not.

Mitchells Luxury ice cream won the innovative packaging award at Grampian Food Forum Awards in England. Rather than using a standard ice cream tub, the firm created a rectangular tub with a perforated label that can be pulled back to access the fork built into the packaging. More important than the award, Mitchells has seen a 36 percent increase in its sales attributed directly to the packaging.[8]

Purchasing for Small Business

Your ability to offer quality goods at competitive prices depends on your purchasing skills. You need to seek the best value—the highest quality for the best price—for the goods, services, and equipment you purchase, because that is exactly what your customers will be expecting when they purchase your products. Price is therefore merely one of many factors to consider. You should also consider the consistency of your suppliers' quality, their reliability in meeting delivery schedules, the payment terms available, product guarantees, merchandising assistance, emergency delivery and return policies, and other factors.

"Your purchasing skills greatly affect your company's profitability, yet price is merely one of many factors you must consider."

Purchasing Guidelines

The following questions provide guidelines for evaluating your small business purchasing and inventory control:

- Are you using the proper sources of supply?
- Are you taking advantage of all purchase discounts?
- How do you determine minimum inventories and reorder points?
- Have you run out of raw materials or finished goods?
- What is the record of your current suppliers for quality, service, and price?
- Are you using minimum quantities or economic ordering quantities?
- What are your inventory holding costs?
- Do you know your optimal average inventory? Does it guide your purchasing policy?
- Could you improve your purchasing to increase profits?
- What is your inventory turnover ratio? How does it compare with the industry average?[9]

To illustrate the importance of purchasing to the profit of your small business, suppose your business spends $500,000 annually, has yearly sales of $1 million, and enjoys a profit margin of 10 percent or $100,000. If you were able to decrease the costs of your purchases by 3 percent, you would save $15,000—increasing your profits by 15 percent. To see the same profit increase through sales revenue, you would have to generate

$150,000 in additional sales, or a 15 percent increase. This means that a 3 percent savings on the cost of purchased items has the same impact on your bottom line as a 15 percent increase in sales.

Purchasing Basics

Whether you're purchasing inexpensive toilet paper for the employee bathroom or expensive components for your manufacturing process, you want to make good purchasing decisions—decisions that will get you the best possible product at the best possible price. To make your decisions wisely, it helps to know how the purchasing process *should* work. Let's look more closely at the steps in the purchasing process.

1. *Recognize, describe, and transmit the need.* If you're the only employee in your business, you'll have to rely on your own knowledge of your work processes to know *what* needs to be ordered and *when*. However, if your small business has other employees, you should train them to alert the person in charge of purchasing (yourself or another person whom you designate) of any needs. You'll probably want to use a *purchase requisition* to standardize this process, a form that lists and describes the materials, supplies, and equipment that are needed. In addition, the purchase requisition should list the quantity needed, the date required, an estimated unit cost, a budget account to be charged, and an authorized signature. This form should also have at least two copies—one for the person who does the purchasing and the other for the person requesting the items.

2. *Investigate and select suppliers and prepare a purchase order.* Once you know what's needed, you can begin to look for the best possible sources for obtaining the desired products. Because elsewhere this text describes the factors you need to examine in selecting a supplier, let's concentrate here on describing the *purchase order*, which is, in most instances, a legal contract document between you and the supplier—so you want to make sure you prepare it carefully.

   Once you've selected a supplier, you should record on a serially numbered purchase order the quantity requirements, price, and delivery and shipping requirements accurately. If you have any quality specifications, they should also be described precisely. If you have any product drawings or other documents that relate to the order, these should be included as well. If you need to inspect sample products before an order is completed, be sure to specify what, when, and how much you want to sample. In other words, include all the data on your purchase order and word it so that it's clear to both you and the supplier what the specifications and expectations are.

   You'll probably want to use a multipart purchase order form so that you and the supplier can keep track of the orders coming in and being fulfilled. In fact, purchasing experts say that *seven* is the minimum number of copies you'd want on a purchase order. Although you may consider this to be extreme, at least make sure that your purchase order form has enough copies so that both you and your supplier can keep track of the order in sufficient detail.

3. *Follow up on the order.* Although the purchase order represents a legal offer to buy, no purchase contract exists until the seller accepts the buyer's offer. The supplier accepts by either filling the order or at the very least notifying the purchaser that the order is being filled. By *following up* on the order by mail, e-mail, fax, or phone call, you can keep on top of its status. If the goods you ordered are critically needed, the follow-up can be doubly important. (For important orders, you'll want to get written verification that your order was accepted.) Besides being a good way to keep on top of your purchasing activities, the follow-up helps you maintain good relations with your suppliers.

"The purchase requisition should list the quantity needed, the date required, an estimated unit cost, a budget account to be charged, and an authorized signature."

4. *Receiving and inspecting the order.* Once the order is received, you should inspect it immediately to confirm that it is correct. The supplier should have enclosed a *packing slip* with the order that you can compare against your copy of the purchase order. You should check for quantity as well as quality of the goods. If someone other than yourself checks orders, you'll probably want to use a *receiving report form* that indicates what's included in the order—quantity and quality. In fact, even if you're the person who checks the order, it would be smart to have some way of noting the condition of the shipment, just in case you need this information in the future. If the order is correct, it's ready to go into inventory or into use. If there's a problem, you should contact the supplier immediately. Let the supplier know what the problem is and follow up with written *documentation* describing the problem. The supplier will let you know the procedure for handling the incorrect order.

5. *Completing the order.* The order isn't complete until you've paid the *invoice*—a bill that should be included with the order or might be sent later by the supplier—and prepared whatever accounting documents you need. Once you've completed this step, the purchasing process is complete.

Although the purchasing process as outlined here may seem burdensome and time consuming, keep in mind that being an effective and efficient purchaser makes an important difference in your small business.[10]

Selecting Suppliers

Whom you buy from can be as important as *what* you buy. At the very least, supplier (or vendor) selection should be based on systematic analysis, not on guesswork or habit. Vendors are an important component of your operation.

Make-or-Buy Decision

A decision you must make in running your small manufacturing business is whether to produce your own parts and components or to buy them from an outside source. This choice is called the **make-or-buy decision**. Much of the decision rests on the availability and quality of suppliers.

The more specialized your needs or the more you need to hide design features, the more likely it is that you will have to make your own parts. But it is generally better to buy standardized parts (such as bolts) and standardized components (such as blower fans) rather than to make them.

The make-or-buy decision is not limited to manufacturing operations or functions. Service and retail businesses need to consider whether to outsource such functions as janitorial or payroll services. You could either use your own personnel for those services or hire another specialized business to produce them for you.

Investigating Potential Suppliers

Because the products you purchase become the products you sell, you want to be sure that you are dealing with the best suppliers available. But how do you do that? Tom Thornbury, CEO of Softub, a hot tub builder in California, asked that very question after his company had been burned by some bad vendors. His answer was to create a *vendor audit team* made up of 10 employees from several areas of the business. The team spends from two hours to two days visiting and investigating the potential supplier.

Such thorough investigation is justified because companies like Softub are viewing their relationship with vendors as a long-term partnership. Since developing the audit team, product defects have dropped, and vendor turnover has been cut in half. To help

make-or-buy decision
The choice of whether to purchase parts and components or to produce them.

the audit team remember everything it wants to look for, Softub developed a checklist (see Figure 12.3).[11] Factors you need to consider in developing your own checklist would include product quality, location, services provided, and credit terms.

A serious question that a small business owner must answer is whether to use one supplier or multiple suppliers. It takes time to investigate and analyze several potential suppliers, so many businesses are working toward building long-term relationships with fewer suppliers and vendors. An advantage for buyer and seller when using a single source comes from a mutual dependence that benefits both companies. Another benefit of using a single source is the savings in paperwork from dealing with only one other business.[12]

An advantage of multiple-source purchasing is the competition between vendors to decrease prices and improve services offered. A lack of this competition can be a disadvantage of single-source purchasing if your one supplier becomes complacent or is unable to provide the goods you need when you need them.

Managing Inventory

Before considering how much inventory is needed, we should investigate the various meanings of the term *inventory*. Depending on the context, there are four common meanings of the term:

inventory
Goods a business owns for the completion of future sales. Also, the act of counting the goods held in stock.

1. The monetary value of goods owned by a business at a given time. "We carry a $500,000 inventory."
2. The number of units on hand at a given time. "We have 1,000 yo-yos in inventory."
3. The process of measuring or counting goods. "We inventory the office supplies every month."
4. The detailed list of goods. "I need to look at the inventory on the computer."

How Much Inventory Do You Need?

Managing inventory is like performing a balancing act. On one side of the scale, you have to keep an adequate supply of goods on hand. You don't want to shut down operations because you ran out of a needed part, and you don't want to lose a sale because customers find an empty shelf where they expected to find a product. On the other side of the scale, inventory represents money sitting idly on the shelf. And to complicate things further, the more you try to decrease the risk of running out of more obscure items, the more you increase the risk that some items will become obsolete.

Retail Business An important factor in considering the inventory needs of many small retail businesses is the time needed to get fresh inventory in and the cost of reordering. If you can replace inventory quickly at a reasonable price, you can hold down your inventory costs by keeping fewer items yourself.

Retailers should be aware of the *80-20 principle*, also called the *Pareto rule*. According to this rule, about 80 percent of the firm's revenue will come from about 20 percent of the inventory. This principle reminds the small retailer to concentrate on the "vital few" rather than on the "trivial many."

"According to the Pareto rule, about 80 percent of the firm's revenue will come from about 20 percent of the inventory."

Service Industry Even service businesses that aren't retail based must consider their inventory needs. For instance, a restaurant needs appropriate food and beverages, cleaning fluids, table service equipment, and miscellaneous supplies, such as menus, toothpicks, cash register tape, and check slips. Financial services firms need adequate supplies of paper, pencils, accounting forms, and other types of office supplies.

FIGURE 12-3 Vendor Audit Checklist

The Checklist That Softub Uses to Analyze Potential Suppliers Can Serve as an Example for Creating Your Own Checklist.

SOFTUB'S MANAGERS POINT OUT THE VIRTUES OF THEIR VENDOR CHECKLIST

"We want to make sure a supplier's sales manager will work with its manufacturing people to meet our needs. When we hit a problem, the sales manager is our liaison. Does he have the influence to change schedules on the production line? Also, the vendor's ability to turn out a quality product is often reflected by the quality-control manager's experience. We want to know all about that."

"We check how busy vendors are in relation to their size. Say they're using only an eighth of a building's footage. Why is it empty? Did they lose business? The ones we'll end up doing business with can answer easily. And if you notice they don't have the proper space, you'll want to know where they keep their material. Will they have to leave it outside in the rain? They might show you a fancy brochure, and you find they're operating out of five garages."

"Once we went into a place where they said they made circuit boards, but they really specialized in making custom boards in very small volumes. We needed someone who could make thousands a month."

"When we get back to the office, we always check with other customers to ask if the supplier delivers on time or has quality problems."

"We don't have the expertise, the manpower, or the time to look into every procedure. If a large company (or the military) has done an audit on the supplier and given it a rating, it gives us a good idea if the supplier has sound systems and procedures in place. Why not let the big company do the work for us?"

Softub
VENDER SURVEY FORM

REPORTED BY: _GARY ANDERSON_

COMPANY NAME: _ANY BOARD CO._   **PROFILE**   DATE: _12-14-93_

ADDRESS
MAIN ST.
ANYTOWN, USA 12345

TELEPHONE: _800-555-5555_
FAX #:
YEARS IN BUSINESS: _14_
NUMBER OF EMPLOYEES: _170_

SQUARE FOOTAGE OF BUILDING(S): _48,000 USA (60,000 IRELAND)_
AGE OF BUILDING(S): _20 YRS_
TYPE OF BUILDING(S): _CONCRETE TILT-UP, OPEN BEAM CEILING AND IN GOOD CONDITION_

PERSONNEL MET
CEO: _JOHN G. DOE_
PRESIDENT: _AS ABOVE_
SALES MANAGER: _JACK B. DOE_
SALES CONTACT: _AS ABOVE_
Q.C. MANAGER: _JANE Q. PUBLIC_
PRODUCTION MANAGER: _JIM Z. SMITH_
OTHERS: _PRODUCT/ACCOUNT SPECIALIST_

BUSINESS PROFILE
ANNUAL SALES IN DOLLARS: _$10 MILLION_
MAIN PRODUCT LINE: _PRINTED CIRCUIT BOARDS_
MINOR PRODUCT LINE: _CABLE ASSEMBLIES_
MAJOR CUSTOMERS: _BENDEX, PACKARD BELL AND GEORGIA PACIFIC._
D & B REQUESTED:

Q.C. DEPARTMENT
EQUIPMENT CALIBRATED: ☑ YES ☐ NO ☐ ATTACHED
CALIBRATION TAGS IN PLACE:
TRAVELERS IN PLACE AT WORK STATIONS: ☑ YES ☐ NO
MILITARY OR ISO RATING: _ISO 9000 U.L. F.C.C. C.S.A. F.D.A. T.U.V. (GERMANY)_ ☑ YES ☐ NO
TOTAL Q.C. EMPLOYEES: _8 + 1 MANAGER_ ☑ YES ☐ NO
GENERAL IMPRESSION: _EXCELLENT, WELL LAID OUT, CALIBRATION EQUIPMENT_
IN GOOD SHAPE, INSPECTION LAB A-1 CONDITION AND
STAFF IS VERY KNOWLEDGEABLE.

PRODUCTION

"Our impression of this supplier was really favorable, and we've learned from it, too. During our audit, we saw illustrated work instructions hanging in front of every station on the line. Each sheet had a checklist of things the operator was supposed to do. We started using similar instructions here. We asked the supplier to send one of its engineers to help us do it."

GOOD FORM

"We always request a Dun & Bradstreet report unless it's a mom-and-pop shop. Our chief financial officer also looks at the report. We want to know if the company owes more than it's worth. If it does, our finance department will call their finance people and ask more detailed questions."

"If the place is messy and dirty, that's an indicator of the kind of service and product you're going to get. But if we see a board with tools hanging there so that when a tool is in use you see a black silhouette, that's a pretty good sign. It means people aren't wasting time looking for things, and they're probably not going to ship us a product with tie wraps in places where they don't belong."

"International ratings are important because we sell our product overseas. If a vendor is already certified to sell in that country, we feel more confident that its product will pass inspection."

"If a vendor is doing preventive maintenance, there are records we can see. If machines are down, it could cost a company hundreds of thousands of dollars a day. Good companies will monitor their machines religiously."

"This company has the resources to make our product. But the 50% capacity would trigger us to check its financials and talk to its management, because it should be a little busier. We'd also ask how many shifts it's running, how many hours a day it's using certain machines, how many people it has now, and how many people it's had there before."

"One big accident and a company can get sued and be out of business. Are first-aid charts posted on the walls? Are people wearing safety glasses? We want to know what a vendor is doing to prevent accidents. It's also a good indication of its management philosophy."

CLEANLINESS: EXCELLENT
ORGANIZED: EXCELLENT
SQ. FOOTAGE: 43,000 APPROX.
CAPACITY PERCENTAGE OF TOTAL PRODUCTION: 50%
SAFETY DEVICES IN PLACE: ☑ GOOD
GENERAL SAFETY CONDITION: ☑ GOOD
GENERAL EMPLOYEE DEMEANOR: ☑ GOOD
EQUIPMENT CONDITION:
REGULAR MAINTENANCE SCHEDULES MAINTAINED:
DOES THE FACTORY APPEAR BUSY?:
IS THE EQUIPMENT RUNNING?:
ARE THERE STOCK PILES OF RAW MATERIAL?:
ARE THERE STOCK PILES OF FURNISHED GOODS?:
IS THE SHIPPING DOCK BUSY?:

☑ YES ☐ NO
☐ AVERAGE ☐ POOR
☐ AVERAGE ☐ POOR
☐ AVERAGE ☐ POOR
☑ YES ☐ NO
☑ YES ☐ NO
☑ YES ☐ NO
☑ YES ☐ NO
☑ YES ☐ NO
☑ YES

SUMMARY

HOW DOES VENDOR INTEND TO MEET OUR REQUIREMENTS?: THEY WILL RAMP UP TO MEET OUR REQUIREMENTS, 3 NEW EMPLOYEES AND 1 NEW FLOW SOLDER MACHINE.

OVERALL IMPRESSION: ☑ EXCELLENT ☐ GOOD ☐ AVERAGE ☐ POOR
SHOULD SOFTUB DO BUSINESS WITH THIS COMPANY?: YES! NOTES: 1) REVIEW D & B WITH FINANCE 2) REVIEW WITH MANAGEMENT AND HAVE THEM VISIT ALSO 3) MAKE FINAL DECISIONS AFTER REFERENCE CHECKS.

VENDOR RATING
PLEASE CIRCLE ONE
1 – SHOULD NOT DO BUSINESS WITH
2 – CAUTION RATING
3 – AVERAGE
4 – GOOD RATING
(5) – WORLD CLASS RATING

WHITE – PURCHASING   CANARY – Q.C.   PINK – OPERATIONS

"The pink copy goes to operations. If the supplier is ISO 9000 certified or doing business with a *Fortune* 500 company, we'll request a copy of its quality manual."

Source: From "The Smart Vendor-Audit Checklist," by Stephanie Gruner, *Inc.*, April 1995, pp. 93–95. Reprinted with permission of Gruner & Jahr USA.

They might even need to have a supply of cash on hand to meet certain customer needs. Security firms need to keep items such as flashlights, mace or pepper spray, whistles or alarms, and, of course, office materials and supplies in their inventories. Auto repair shops must stock tires, batteries, wrenches, engine oil, grease, cleaning supplies, and other items. There are many other types of service businesses not mentioned here. The point is that small service-business managers should pay just as much attention to inventory control as their counterparts in manufacturing and retail.

Manufacturing Business Inventory needs for a small manufacturer are different from those of retailers. Manufacturers' needs are based on production rate, lead time required to get in new stock, and the order amount that delivers the optimal economic quantity. Common techniques of manufacturers include just-in-time (JIT) inventory control and materials requirement planning (MRP), considered later in this chapter.

Costs of Carrying Inventory

There are several obvious and not-so-obvious costs of carrying inventory of any type. Financing is the most apparent cost of inventory. Because inventory is an asset, it must be offset by a liability—the cost of borrowing money or diverting your own cash from other uses. If you can sell merchandise and collect payment before you have to pay the supplier that provided you with the merchandise, you can avoid direct finance costs. Because that usually isn't the case, most inventory has a cash cost to the business.

Reality Check

Money on the Shelf

Inventory represents money stacked on a shelf. Until it is sold, it does not generate cash—in fact, it ties up cash. Many small business owners fail to realize the direct impact that inventory has on cash flow. Lose track of your inventory, and your checkbook balance can hit zero in a hurry. Todd Heim, who owns Future Cure, Inc., of North Olmsted, Ohio, realizes how important inventory control is. Future Cure manufactures automotive paint spray booths. A typical booth contains more than 300 parts (some of which are big and expensive), so Heim has to manage inventory effectively.

Heim installed a state-of-the-art automated financial system that included a component to track inventory in detail. That feature allowed him to cut the inventory the company held in stock by 25 percent in a matter of months. That 25 percent decrease was almost exclusively dead stock, so employees spend less time scrambling and digging to find the parts they need. On top of decreasing inventory, better tracking has led to better stock selection, so parts are on hand when needed. Overnight shipping costs have dropped as well.

Before his automated inventory control, Heim would have a year's supply of some parts on hand and be completely out of others. As you see, inventory control means tracking individual items as well as the total.

If you run a retail business, rather than a manufacturing company like Future Cure, you have to be concerned about shrinkage. Alpha Bay, a Salt Lake City software company created a new Adaptive Integrated Retail System (AIRS) to help you prevent future losses. AIRS is an enterprise retail system that collects and allows users to manage inventory, streamline the supply chain, and analyze sales patterns from your desktop PC. A loss-prevention agent tool helps the user recognize, track, monitor, and report on employee theft, customer theft, administrative errors, and vendor fraud.

Sources: Tucker Marion, "Early-Stage Firms and Delay-Based Inventory Control Using Decision-Making Tableaux," *International Journal of Production Research*, September 2010, 5497–5521; and Leslie Taylor, "Manage Inventory and Prevent Theft—Right from Your Desktop," *Inc.*, January 5, 2007, www.inc.com.

shrinkage
The loss of goods held in inventory due to theft or spoilage.

obsolescence
When products become outdated or fall out of fashion.

holding costs
Expenses related to keeping inventory on hand.

ordering costs
Expenses related to procuring inventory.

Inventory *shrinkage* represents another cost to your business. Shrinkage can come from theft or spoilage. Employee theft and shoplifting by customers result in inventory that you had to pay for that is not available for sale. *Spoilage* is inventory you have purchased that is not fit for sale because of damage or deterioration.

Obsolescence, in which products become outdated or fall out of fashion, produces the same effect as spoilage: unrecoverable inventory costs caused by merchandise you can't sell. Such merchandise is known as *dead stock*. Obsolescence is a problem for a wide variety of businesses, but especially those in which styles, tastes, or technologies change quickly, such as clothing, automobile parts, and computer parts and accessories. You may be able to salvage some money from inventory that is obsolete (or on its way) through price reductions or recycling, but dead stock is still a major cost.

Holding costs are what you incur for keeping extra goods on hand—warehouse building expenses (either purchase and upkeep or rent), added utilities, insurance, and taxes on the building. In addition, there are expenses such as insurance on the value of the inventory and taxes on the inventory. Merchandise that spoils, becomes obsolete, depreciates, or is pilfered is considered part of the holding costs. Finally, you have interest expenses if you borrow money to pay for the goods.

Ordering costs are the expenses you incur in either ordering or producing inventory. Ordering costs tend to be fixed, meaning that they cost about the same no matter what quantity of goods you order. They include all the clerical expenses of preparing purchase orders, processing orders and invoices, analyzing vendors, and receiving and handling incoming products.

If holding costs were your only inventory expense, you would want to order as few items at a time as possible to minimize your cost of holding on to inventory. Ordering one part at a time would cut down on your storage expenses, but think of the cost in time, paper, and people needed to process that many order forms and receive goods one at a time—your total costs would go through the roof. Likewise, if ordering costs were your only inventory expense, you would want to send for as many goods as possible at one time to minimize your costs of ordering. Although your clerical needs would be cut by making out just one order, think of the size of the storage facility you would need and the cash-flow problems created by having all your money tied up in inventory.

In the real world, every business incurs both holding and ordering costs. Striving to maintain a balance between them is part of the difficult job of controlling inventory.

Controlling Inventory

Because inventory is such a significant expense, most businesses look carefully for ways to determine the appropriate levels of control for their inventory. *Inventory control* is the process of establishing and maintaining the supply of goods you need to keep on hand. It is important because inventory represents about 25 percent of a manufacturing firm's capital and as much as 80 percent of a retailer's capital. Many techniques are used to control inventory, with the best choice depending on the type of business and the kind of inventory. Several techniques are described in this section.

Reorder Point and Quantity

inventory cycle
The period of time from the point when inventory is at its highest until it is replenished.

Controlling your inventory begins with determining when you need to restock inventory and how much you need to reorder. These considerations are called the *reorder point* and the *reorder quantity,* respectively. The time period that begins when an item is at its highest desired stocking level, continues as the item is used or sold, and ends when it is replenished is called an **inventory cycle**.

lead time
The period of time from order placement until the goods are received.

Suppose you are a retailer who sells a certain product—Elvis Presley statuettes—with an average weekly demand of 10 units (see Figure 12.4). The **lead time** (time from order placement until delivery) is three weeks. You would need to reorder when inventory drops to 30 Elvises so that you don't completely run out before the ordered items arrive. The reorder quantity would be 100 statuettes, so you would have a 10-week supply of goods on hand at your highest desired stocking level.

Visual Control

Many small businesses operate without a formal or complex inventory control system. If you run a one- or two-person business that sells a relatively narrow selection of items, *visual control* may be the only inventory system you need. Visual inventory control means that you look at the goods you have on hand and reorder when you appear to be running low on items. It depends on your being in the business during most business hours and on your knowing the usage rate and reorder time needed.

Economic Order Quantity

economic order quantity (EOQ)
A traditional method of controlling inventory that minimizes total inventory costs by balancing annual ordering costs with annual holding costs for an item.

Economic order quantity (EOQ) is a traditional method of controlling inventory that minimizes total inventory costs by balancing annual ordering costs with annual holding costs for an item. EOQ balances these two types of costs to minimize your total costs (see Figure 12.5).

Several models exist for the EOQ approach that go beyond the scope of this book, so in practice you simply need to find a model that fits the cost structure of your business and use it. The basic model of EOQ makes three assumptions:

1. You can't take advantage of volume discounts.
2. You can accurately predict annual demand.
3. Your average inventory level is equal to your maximum level minus your minimum level divided by 2.

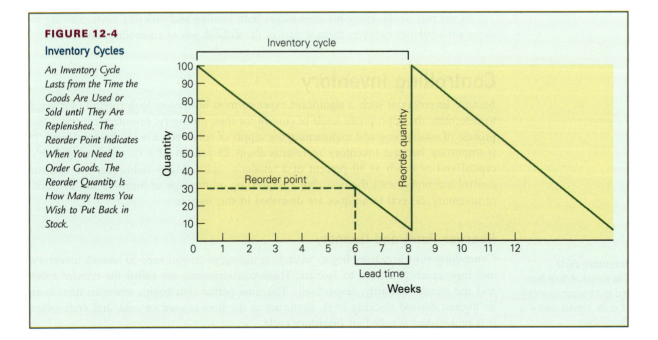

FIGURE 12-4
Inventory Cycles

An Inventory Cycle Lasts from the Time the Goods Are Used or Sold until They Are Replenished. The Reorder Point Indicates When You Need to Order Goods. The Reorder Quantity Is How Many Items You Wish to Put Back in Stock.

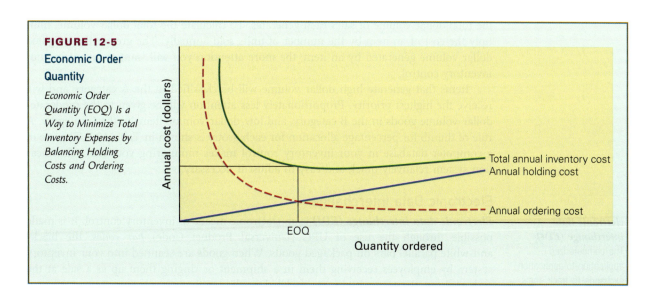

FIGURE 12-5

Economic Order Quantity

Economic Order Quantity (EOQ) Is a Way to Minimize Total Inventory Expenses by Balancing Holding Costs and Ordering Costs.

Annual cost (dollars)

Total annual inventory cost
Annual holding cost
Annual ordering cost

EOQ

Quantity ordered

If your business meets these assumptions, you can use the following formula:

$$EOQ = \sqrt{\frac{2DO}{C}}$$

where

D = annual demand for the product (in units)
O = average ordering cost for the product (in dollars per year)
C = average holding cost for one of the products (in dollars per year)

To illustrate, imagine a sporting goods store that meets the three assumptions stated previously. This store usually sells 12,000 pairs of hiking boots per year. Its ordering costs are $10 per order. The holding costs run $0.96 per pair of boots per year. The EOQ for hiking boots for this store would be 500.

$$EOQ = \sqrt{\frac{2 \times 12,000 \times 10}{0.96}}$$
$$= 500$$

This result tells us that to minimize total inventory costs and balance ordering and holding costs, the sporting goods store would need to order 500 pairs of hiking boots at a time. In selling 12,000 pairs of boots and ordering 500 pairs each time, the store would need to order hiking boots 24 times per year.

$$\text{Orders per year} = \frac{D}{EOQ}$$
$$24 = \frac{12,000}{500}$$

ABC Classification

ABC classification
An inventory control system that classifies items based on the total dollar volume of sales each generates.

In the process of handling many types of goods, some can get misallocated. A reason for misallocation can be that the person in charge of inventory is paying as much attention to an item that costs $5 and is sold twice a year as to items that cost $500 and are sold many times per month. An inventory system that helps to allocate more appropriate time and attention to items is **ABC classification**. This system classifies items based on the total dollar volume of sales each generates. To calculate the total dollar volume, multiply the cost of an item by the number of units sold annually. The greater the weighted dollar volume generated by an item, the more attention you will want to give it in your inventory control.

Items that generate high dollar volume will be classified in the A category and will receive the highest priority. Proportionately less attention will be given to the moderate-dollar-volume goods in the B category, and low-dollar-volume items in the C category. A rule of thumb for percentage allocation for each group is shown in Table 12.1. The use of a computer database in your inventory control makes monitoring your ABC classification system relatively quick and easy to adjust if necessary.

Electronic Data Interchange

electronic data interchange (EDI)
The computerized application-to-application exchange to track items within a business in a standard data format.

perpetual inventory system
An inventory system that indicates how many units of an item are on hand at any given time.

Electronic data interchange (EDI) is an electronic means of inventory control. It is made possible through the use of UPC (Universal Product Code) *bar codes*, the black-and-white parallel bars on packaged goods. When goods are scanned into your inventory system by employees receiving them in a shipment or ringing them up as a sale at the cash register, the transactions are updated in the company's computer inventory program. By using this technology, you can track sales, determine what needs to be ordered, and transmit the inventory data to your suppliers through the same EDI system. EDI is one type of *perpetual inventory system*, which allows you to know how many items you have in stock at any given time.

There are a number of software programs you can use to help you better control your inventory. Peachtree Complete Accounting and Peachtree Accounting (Peachtree Software) are particularly good programs for tracking inventories and accounts receivable. You can also customize these packages to your unique inventory needs. Intuit's Quick-Books Pro is another popular software package that you can use to track inventory. These software packages are relatively inexpensive, ranging from $99 to $199. You might decide to invest a little more in a more extensive software/hardware package called SellWise from CAP Automation (www.capauto.com). This program (list price of about $1,500) handles sales, tracks customers, produces reports, orders, receives, controls inventory, and creates tags (bar codes). This package is particularly good for small retail businesses.

One of the latest software programs is called Big Business (www.bigsoftware.com; the list price is about $350 for a single user or $750 for multiple users on a network version). This program is ideal for many different small business applications because it integrates four critical business functions: sales, marketing, inventory, and finance. Its creators claim that it is perfect for individuals who have limited accounting knowledge. This program may be just the ticket for helping you control your inventory.

Regardless of the specific software that you choose to help you manage your inventory, be sure to select a package that you'll actually *use*. After all, this is one area of your business that you *can* control, so why not be effective and efficient at it?

Major retailers and packaged-goods companies such as Walmart, Ace Hardware, Lowe's, and Target are pushing hard to clean up their product data and change their

TABLE 12-1 ABC Inventory Investment Classification	CLASSIFICATION	PERCENTAGE OF TOTAL INVENTORY INVESTMENT
	A. High dollar volume	60–80
	B. Moderate dollar volume	10–40
	C. Low dollar volume	5–15

inventory processes to make *UCCnet* work. UCCnet is a nonprofit unit of the Uniform Code Council standards organization that seeks to establish a global online registry of product information. Manufacturers and retailers submit their product information and descriptions and share the data with their information technology departments. Then all UCCnet members (currently about 3,500 companies) can easily share consistent product data to drive down supply-chain costs, speed new product launches, maintain more accurate inventory data, and reduce inventory errors.[13]

For the UCCnet system to work, suppliers need to use *radio-frequency identification (RFID)* tags. These RFID tags could eventually make UPC bar codes obsolete. The integrated circuit in each tag sends information about an item via radio waves. Supermarket checkout could be eliminated completely, for example, as RFID scanners detect the items you have selected and deduct their costs from your credit card.[14]

How does RFID affect small business? First, two small companies, Matrics and Zebra Technologies, actually make the tags (remember that symbiotic relationship?). Second, Walmart, the world's largest retailer, has demanded that its top 100 suppliers implement the technology with smaller suppliers to follow.[15] If your small business deals in consumer packaged goods, do you think it won't eventually have to comply with the new standard?

Just-in-Time

An inventory management system based upon the philosophy that well-run manufacturing plants do not require the stockpiling of parts and components is called **just-in-time (JIT)**. The basic idea underlying JIT is to reduce order sizes and to time orders so that goods arrive as close to when they are actually needed as possible. The intent is to minimize a business's dependence on inventory and cut the costs of moving and storing goods. JIT is used more frequently by producers than by retailers.

There are notable differences between a JIT approach and a more traditional approach (which you could think of as "just-in-case"). Table 12.2 highlights some of these differences.[16]

JIT works best in situations that allow accurate forecasting of both demand and production. Because JIT is based on actual rather than projected demand, a small business may have to be in operation for a while before it can take advantage of this system, as a company called Lifeline Systems learned. When Lifeline first began making its

> *"JIT is used more frequently by producers than by retailers."*

just-in-time (JIT)
A Japanese approach to inventory management that aims to reduce order sizes and to time orders so that goods arrive as close to when they are needed as possible.

TABLE 12-2
JIT and Traditional Inventory Comparison

JIT INVENTORY	TRADITIONAL INVENTORY
Small orders and frequent deliveries	Large orders and infrequent deliveries
Single-source supplier for a given part with a long-term contract	Multiple sources of suppliers for the same part with partial or short-term contracts
Suppliers expected to deliver product quality, delivery performance, and price; no rejects acceptable	Suppliers expected to deliver an acceptable level of product quality, delivery performance, and price
Objective of bidding is to secure the highest-quality product through a long-term contract	Objective of bidding is to find the lowest possible price
Less emphasis on paperwork	Requires more time and formal paperwork
Delivery time and quantity can be changed with direct communication	Changes in delivery time and quantity require new purchase orders

voice-activated personal response devices, which allow people to call for help in an emergency, production lead time was 30 days from order to shipment. After the company adopted JIT, total quality management (TQM), and manufacturing resource planning II (MRPII), which will be discussed shortly, that figure decreased to four days. As John Giannetto, corporate manager of materials and purchasing, stated, "What comes in the back door [in parts and materials] is gone four days after it gets here."[17] Keeping in line with JIT philosophies, Lifeline has cut the number of its suppliers from 300 to 75, 85 percent of which offer service and quality at a level that makes inspection unnecessary.

One caveat of JIT is that everyone involved *must* be able to do what they say they can, when they say they can do it. If you are operating with enough inventory to support one day's production, which is common with JIT, a single unexpected event—a trucking strike, a breakdown, or a shortage—can shut down your entire operation. Just-about-in-time or almost-in-time won't cut it.

Materials Requirements Planning

materials requirements planning (MRP)
Inventory control system that depends on computers to coordinate product orders, raw materials in stock, and the sequence of production.

Another new inventory control method for producers is ***materials requirements planning (MRP)***, which depends on computers to coordinate product orders, raw materials in stock, and the sequence of production. A master schedule ensures that goods are available at the time they are needed in the production cycle.

Whereas JIT is a *pull system*, based on the "pull" of actual customer demand, MRP is a *push system*, relying on the "push" of estimated demand. MRP is an inventory management technique that is appropriate when demand for some materials depends on the demand for others. For example, if your business makes customized mountain bikes, and you anticipate sales of 1,000 bikes next month, you know how many components you will need. You need 1,000 frames, 2,000 pedals, 4,000 wheel nuts, and so on. The demand for each of these items depends on the demand for bikes. Rather than keep all of those supplies in stock, as with EOQ, MRP allows you to determine the number of components and subassemblies needed and coordinate their ordering and delivery.

"A master schedule ensures that goods are available at the time they are needed in the production cycle."

A more advanced control system that has evolved from MRP is *manufacturing resource planning II (MRPII)*, which coordinates inventory management with all other functions of a business, such as marketing, accounting, financial planning, cash flow, and engineering. Because it is more complex and expensive, it is used mainly in large businesses. It is worth noting here, however, because techniques and processes used in big business often find their way into small businesses after a period of time.

Summary

1. Define the term *marketing mix.*

The marketing mix consists of the variables that you can control in bringing your product or service to your target market. Also referred to as the *Four Ps*, it includes the *product* (including goods and services) that your target market wants or needs; the *place,* or the channels of distribution you choose to use, as well as the location and layout of your small business; the *price* that makes your product attractive and still allows you to make a profit; and the methods of *promotion* you use to communicate with your target market.

2. Discuss the different forms a product can take, and identify the five levels of product satisfaction.

Products are tangible goods, intangible services, or a combination of these. The five levels of product satisfaction are the core benefit, the generic product, the expected product, the augmented product, and the potential product. The core benefit represents the value a customer gets from a product. The generic product is the simplest components from which a product is made. The expected product represents the characteristics that customers expect to find in a product. The augmented product contains the characteristics of a product that are over and above what customers expect to find. The potential product represents future product augmentations and developments.

3. Explain the importance of purchasing and describe its procedures.

Purchasing is an important part of a small business because the goods or raw materials that you bring into your business become the products you will in turn have available to sell to your customers. A savings gained from the cost of purchased items has a larger effect on your profit level than an increase in sales revenue.

4. Discuss the main concerns in selecting a supplier.

Small manufacturers must first decide whether to make the parts needed in their production or to purchase components from another business. Retailers must decide whether to hire personnel or to outsource needed services. Both of these are examples of the make-or-buy decision. Factors such as product quality, location of supplier, services that suppliers offer, and credit terms available need to be considered when selecting suppliers.

5. Calculate how much inventory you need and when.

If your small business requires inventory, you must maintain a balance between having enough goods on hand to prevent lost sales due to items being out of stock and having inventory dollars lying idle on a shelf. Retailers and manufacturers need to heed the Pareto rule by paying attention to the "vital few" rather than the "trivial many" items in inventory. Shrinkage, obsolescence, holding costs, and ordering costs are factors to be considered in determining the inventory needs of your business.

6. Describe seven methods of inventory control.

To control your inventory, you must begin by determining your reorder point (when you need to reorder) and your reorder quantity (how much you need to reorder). Many small businesses depend on visual control to maintain inventory. Economic order quantity, ABC classification, electronic data interchange, just-in-time, and materials requirements planning are common tools for controlling inventory.

Questions for Review and Discussion

1. What factors should be considered when purchasing for a small business?
2. Explain how the Pareto rule is important to a small business owner.
3. How can shrinkage affect an inventory system?
4. Assume that you are the owner of the sporting goods store used in the example of EOQ inventory control on page 289. You typically sell 14,500 sweatshirts per year. Your ordering costs are $10 per order. Holding costs are $0.60 per sweatshirt per year. What is your EOQ for sweatshirts? How many sweatshirt orders would you place per year?
5. When would an ABC classification inventory system be appropriate?
6. Aside from reducing inventory levels, what does the JIT philosophy promote?
7. What is the difference between a pull system and a push system of inventory control?
8. Consider the make-or-buy decision. Give three examples of situations in which a business should make, rather than buy. Give three examples of situations in which a business should buy, rather than make.

Questions for Critical Thinking

1. Many small businesses are built around one product. What risks does this approach impose? How can small business owners minimize those risks? How can a small business develop new products?
2. Purchasing products or materials is obviously an important part of running a small business. What are the pros and cons of developing a relationship with a single vendor from which to purchase most of your products versus using multiple vendors and not depending on just one other company?

What Would You Do?

Costume Specialists, Inc.

Storybook characters like Madeline, Babar the Elephant, and even Stinky Cheese Man come alive under the watchful eye of Wendy Goldstein of Columbus, Ohio. Her company, Costume Specialists, fashions the complicated costumes for these characters from scratch and sells the creations to book publishers and bookstore chains. Each costume takes about 60 to 80 hours of artistic effort and costs up to $3,000 in materials and labor to produce. Goldstein's business brings in $600,000 annually.

Catch the Wave

Catch the Wave is a marketing information and graphics design firm located in Minneapolis. The company designs Web pages for clients wanting to get on the Internet. Its 20 employees have varied experience in design, advertising, writing, photography, and computer graphics. Prices charged to clients depend on the sophistication and interactivity desired for their Web sites. The popularity of the Internet and World Wide Web has sent the company's annual revenues soaring to $7 million. This figure is expected to continue to rise as more and more clients want to "catch the wave."

Margaritaville Store

Of course, it has to be in Key West! Where else would you expect to find Jimmy Buffett's 400-square-foot shop, Margaritaville Store? And what would you expect to find there except T-shirts and other beach paraphernalia? The first store did so well that Buffett expanded the retail operation and even added a café in New Orleans. Total annual sales revenues for Jimmy Buffett's empire exceed $50 million. That's a lot of CDs, tapes, books, T-shirts, trinkets, and food—even in Margaritaville!

Questions

1. Select one of the companies described and write a short paper (no more than two pages) about the type of inventory control techniques that the business should use. Explain what would be an appropriate number of suppliers for this company and why you chose this number.
2. Effective inventory management also means being ready to cope with problems. Divide into groups based on the companies you selected in Question 1, and discuss how you could design an inventory system that would adapt to "shocks" like the ones described here.

Costume Specialists, Inc.

Your long-time supplier of flexible costume mouthpieces has just been purchased by a Japanese conglomerate that has strict purchasing guidelines and wants you to use EDI.

Catch the Wave

You were hoping it would never happen, but now it has. A computer virus has wiped out all but two of your firm's computers.

Margaritaville Store

Trouble in paradise comes in the form of hurricanes. Even though you've been lucky so far, the last hurricane season came a little too close for comfort.

13
Place

CHAPTER LEARNING OUTCOMES

After reading this chapter, you should be able to:

1. Describe small business distribution and explain how "efficiencies" affect channels of distribution.

2. Explain how the location of your business can provide a competitive advantage.

3. List factors in selecting a state in which to locate your business.

4. List factors in selecting a city in which to locate your business.

5. Discuss the central issues in choosing a particular site within a city.

6. Compare the three basic types of locations.

7. Explain the types of layout you can choose.

8. Present the circumstances under which leasing, buying, or building is an appropriate choice.

So you have a great product or service. Now where do you locate that product and how do you get that product to the right place so the consumer who is the end user can make the purchase? There are a variety of choices when it comes to the location for selling your product. We've all heard the statement: A critical key to the success of your business depends upon location, location, location. With today's technology, there are some new choices as well as more traditional choices when deciding where to locate.

Think—it's two minutes before class and you need caffeine. You run to the closest vending machine—fairly common occurrence, right? Vending machines can provide consumers access to a product 24/7 with no employee costs. Now think pizza, beer, and swimsuits? Not products we ordinarily think of finding in a vending machine. However, with today's technology and a global market, a

consumer can get pizza for $5 with choice of toppings, and you can watch the machine knead dough and bake the pie in about three minutes in Italy, and dispense beer in the Czech Republic and swimsuits in New York, Los Angeles, and Miami right from a vending machine conveniently located with consumer purchases.

A more traditional location is used by East Hampton Edibles, a butter brickle confection business, owned and operated by Anita Zeldin, who sells her caramel, chocolate, and nutty candy at local stores in East Hampton and other upscale settings like Southampton. The Hamptons have become known as a great place for food entrepreneurs due to the higher disposable incomes in this area as well as the more sophisticated palates of the consumers. It is a perfect place to sell a wonderful homemade candy with a recipe known only to Zeldin and her one assistant.

How do you sell 90 percent of a product to American consumers, when you are an Italian company that has been in business for more than 75 years? Vibram has retail stores in the United States that sell its FiveFingers product as well as an online presence located at www.vibramfivefingers.com, where shoppers can go online and buy a pair of these unique shoes. Vibram has produced soles for high-end hiking boots for many years and recently developed Vibram FiveFingers, a "glove for the foot," made popular by Christopher McDougall, a runner who supports running barefoot. These unique-looking shoes are as close as a runner can get to running barefoot and still have on some foot protection.

Where does Water Mill Cupcake Co. sell their "Rosso Velluto" and banana-with-maple frosting cupcakes? This business is located next to the gourmet market Citarella in the Water Mill Shoppes, at Water Mill, NY, a very upscale location for their specialty cupcakes. The owners, Cynthia Formica and Ruth Balletta, said they worked very diligently to be the first cupcake company in the Hamptons with a business in this "sweet" location.

And where does Crane & Co. sell the majority of their product, a high-end writing paper? Eighty percent of its revenue comes from selling paper for printing currency to countries, including the United States. This family business has been around for 210 years and is rumored to have supplied Paul Revere with the first money for the American colonies. This company sells directly to governments, which then use the product to print their money. This specialized product is produced in Berkshire County and used in countries from the United States to China.

This chapter discusses how to get the product or service produced by your small business through distribution channels into locations where the final end user, the consumer, can purchase and use the product.

Sources: Sara Pepitone, "A 210-Year-Old Company's High-Tech Plans," money.cnn.com, August 9, 2010; www.vibramfivefingers.com, retrieved August 17, 2010; Jennifer Alsever, "Barefoot Shoes Try to Outrace the Black Market," money.cnn.com, August 13, 2010; Christina Lewis, "Banker Builds a Candy Business in Bits and Pieces," online.wsy.com, August 14, 2010; and Katrina Brown Hunt, "On Sale Now: Everything," *Travel and Leisure*, September, 2010, 98–99.

Small Business Distribution

In this chapter, we will explore the role of product distribution, business location, and layout of your small business. In marketing terms, these functions are categorized as *place*. Of the *Four Ps* of the marketing mix, place, or *distribution*, is especially significant for your small business because an effective distribution system can make or save a small business as much money as a hot advertising campaign can generate. In fact, distribution is about the last real bastion for cost savings—as techniques for tracking and individualizing promotion improve, as manufacturing becomes more and more efficient, and as employee productivity rises. Your choice of **distribution channel** is especially

distribution channel
The series of intermediaries a product passes through when going from producer to consumer.

direct channel
A distribution channel in which products and services go directly from the producer to the consumer.

indirect channels
A distribution channel in which the products pass through various intermediaries before reaching the consumer.

dual distribution
The use of two or more channels to distribute the same product to the same target market.

important when entering international markets, where you are not likely to have as many options for distribution as in the U.S. market.

In marketing, *distribution* has two meanings: the physical transportation of products from one place to the next, and the relationships between intermediaries who move the products—otherwise called the *channels of distribution*. There are two types of distribution channels: direct and indirect (see Figure 13.1). With a **direct channel**, products and services go directly from the producer to the consumer. Buying sweet potatoes and corn at a farmer's market, or a pair of sandals directly from the artisan who made them, are examples of sales through a direct channel. Other examples are buying seconds and overruns from factory outlets or through catalog sales managed by the manufacturer.

Indirect channels are so called because the products pass through various intermediaries before reaching the consumer. Small businesses that use more than one channel (such as a swimsuit producer selling to an intermediary like a retail chain and directly to consumers via catalog sales) are said to use **dual distribution**.

Intermediaries include agents, brokers, wholesalers, and retailers.

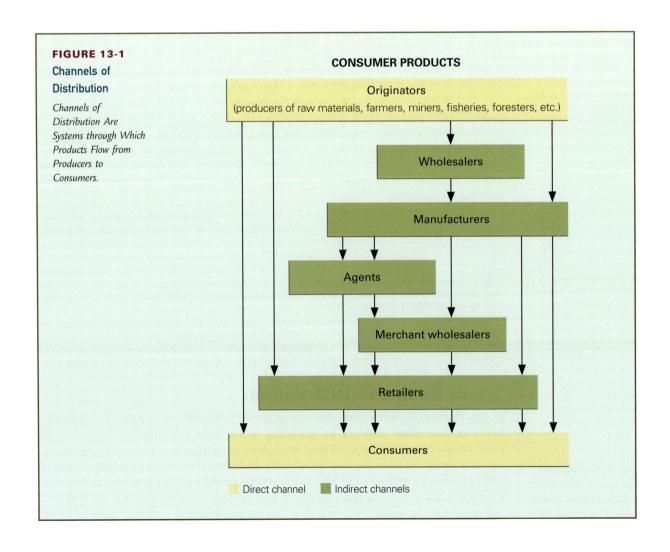

FIGURE 13-1
Channels of Distribution

Channels of Distribution Are Systems through Which Products Flow from Producers to Consumers.

CONSUMER PRODUCTS

Originators
(producers of raw materials, farmers, miners, fisheries, foresters, etc.)

Wholesalers

Manufacturers

Agents

Merchant wholesalers

Retailers

Consumers

Direct channel   ■ Indirect channels

agents
An intermediary who brings buyers and sellers together and facilitates the exchange.

brokers
An intermediary who represents clients who buy or sell specialized goods or seasonal products.

wholesalers
An intermediary who buys products in bulk from producers and resells them to other wholesalers or to retailers.

retailers
An intermediary who sells products to the ultimate consumer.

Agents bring buyers and sellers together and facilitate the exchange. They may be called *manufacturer's agents*, *selling agents*, or *sales representatives*.

Brokers represent clients who buy or sell specialized goods or seasonal products. Neither brokers nor agents take title to the goods sold.

Wholesalers buy products in bulk from producers and then resell them to other wholesalers or to retailers. Wholesalers take title to goods and usually take possession.

Retailers sell products to the ultimate consumer. Retailers take title and possession of the goods they distribute.

The key word for evaluating a channel of distribution is *efficiency*—getting products to target markets in the fastest, least expensive way possible. Did you realize that about three-fourths of the money spent on food goes to distribution?

Does adding intermediaries to the channel of distribution increase the cost of getting the product to the consumer? Or does "doing away with the middleman" always mean savings to consumers? Although the latter has become a marketing cliché, it is not always true. Adding intermediaries can *decrease* the price to the consumer if each intermediary increases the efficiency of the channel. You can do away with the middleman, but you can't replace his function. Someone still has to do the job.

For example, if your business needs half a truckload of supplies every month from your main supplier 400 miles away, should you buy your own truck or have the supplies shipped via a *common carrier* (a trucking company that hauls products for hire)? If that were the only time you needed a truck, of course it would be cheaper to have the supplies shipped, even though it adds an intermediary to your channel of distribution. If you do away with the middleman—in this case, the trucking company—you must replace its function by buying your own truck, paying a driver, maintaining the vehicle, filing paperwork, and so on. The question here is not *whether* the functions of an intermediary are performed; the question is *who* performs them.

You need to be prepared to revise the way you get your products to consumers because the efficiency of channels can change. Currently, the fastest-growing distribution systems involve non-store marketing, including vending machines, telemarketing, and direct mail. Sometimes a break from the industry norm can create a competitive advantage for your business. When Michael Dell started Dell Computer, he eliminated all of the usual intermediaries found in the personal computer market. Dell advertised and sold directly to consumers. This distribution strategy shot Dell Computer into the *Fortune* 500.

Efficiencies in channels of distribution not only allow small businesses to offer goods more efficiently (and therefore more profitably), but also provide opportunities for starting new businesses. If you establish a firm that will increase the efficiency of an existing channel, you are providing a needed service, which is the basis for a good business.

Location for the Long Run

Selecting a location for your business is one of the most important decisions you will make as a small business owner. Although not every business depends on foot traffic for its customers, just about any business can pick a poor location for one reason or another. For example, retail businesses need to be easily accessible to their consumers. A company that produces concrete blocks for construction must be located in an area that frequently uses that type of building material, if it is to keep down transportation costs. Manufacturing businesses need to consider locating near their workers, sources of raw materials, and transportation outlets.

People do not tend to go out of their way to find a business. Although Ralph Waldo Emerson had great literary success when he wrote, "If a man can make a better

ENTREPRENEURIAL SNAPSHOT

Buck Stops in Idaho

© AP Photo/Denis Poroy

Buck Knives is a three-generation family business started by a blacksmith apprentice named Hoyt Buck, who, in 1902, was tired of sharpening hoes and decided that making blades would be more interesting. He experimented for years until he developed a technique for tempering steel that made knife blades so sharp and hard that they would cut bolts. Hoyt and his oldest son, Al, formed H. H. Buck & Son Lifetime Knives in 1947, now Buck Knives. In 1964, Buck introduced the Folding Hunter model, which became the best-selling outdoor knife in America.

Buck grew into a $33 million business with 260 employees making more than a million knives a year under Hoyt's grandson. C. J. Buck Knives was an American legend, but in the late 1990s, it was having some problems also: Profit margins had been gutted by Asian competitors, leaving the company short on cash; energy costs (key in tempering blades) were soaring; and labor costs in Southern California were through the roof. C. J. says, "We were losing money and there was no end in sight."

Energy deregulation in the spring of 2000 sent electricity prices bouncing from 12 cents per kilowatt-hour to 42 cents as speculators tried to manipulate the market. Workers' compensation, labor costs, and taxes were skyrocketing in California. C. J. explains, "Through no fault of what you've done or what you're doing, your workers'-comp premium is going to go from $250,000 a year to $400,000 to $650,000 over a three-year period. That's huge, and it's completely out of your control. You aren't guilty of bad practices, but the cost just goes up and up. Now, that's a scary thing." Something had to give. It occurred to C. J. that that "something" might be the unthinkable—move the company.

"It's a tough decision—especially for family owned companies," he says. "Uprooting a company is a tough,

tough thing to go through. You're uprooting families, uprooting kids." He struggled with the decision until September 11, 2001. Sales plunged to the point that 40 employees had to be laid off and C. J. took a 30 percent pay cut. He realized that moving a company is like having an operation to save your life—you have to move *before* it's too late.

Buck Knives started shopping for new locations, primarily in the Pacific Northwest, using a wish list of cheap electricity, good business climate, low taxes, plentiful labor supply, good transportation connections via highway, rail, and air—and high quality of life—because he was moving people as well a business. In late 2001, Buck executives narrowed the search down to Post Falls, Idaho, population 21,400, and located just outside Coeur d'Alene.

Making the final decisions and preparations for the move was a long and gruelling process. Selling the factory in El Cajon, California; finding just the right site in Post Falls; deciding how many employees to relocate (the final number was 75; 200 were given a year's notice and provided severance and retraining packages); and hundreds of other decisions took time. The groundbreaking ceremony for Buck's new factory happened in June 2004—over a year later than C. J. wanted. The first Buck knife produced in Idaho came off the line in February 2005. It was a Folding Hunter, the original source of Buck fame.

Despite all the hassle factors, the 1,500-mile move was worth it for Buck. C. J. is thrilled with the new surroundings. "It's delivered everything we hoped. Electric bills are roughly 30 percent what they would have been if Buck had stayed in California, workers' comp 10 percent, and labor costs 75 percent." The once-struggling company is now thriving due to the transplant.

Sources: Chris Lydgate, "The Buck Stopped ..." *Inc.,* May 2006, 86–95; Corinne Kator, "Thriving on Lean," *Modern Materials Handling,* February 2007, 33–34; and "Idaho Beckons a Golden State Warrior," *BusinessWeek Online,* November 24, 2003, www.businessweek.com.

mousetrap than his neighbor, though he builds his house in the woods, the world will make a beaten path to his door," it's best not to take his advice literally when selecting a location for your business.

This chapter will follow the building location process from the broadest decisions (selecting a state or region) to the narrowest (designing a layout of your facilities). There are four essential questions you need to ask:

1. What region of the country would be best for your business?
2. What state within that region satisfies your needs?
3. What city within that region will best suit you?
4. What specific site within that city will accommodate your business?

"Selecting a location for your business is one of the most important decisions you will make as a small business owner."

Don't automatically jump to the fourth question. By beginning the site selection process broadly and then narrowing down your choices, you can choose a location that meets the needs of your target market and is near other businesses that are complementary to yours (see Figure 13.2).

To analyze a potential location for your business, you will want to consider the specific needs of your business in conjunction with your personal preferences. First,

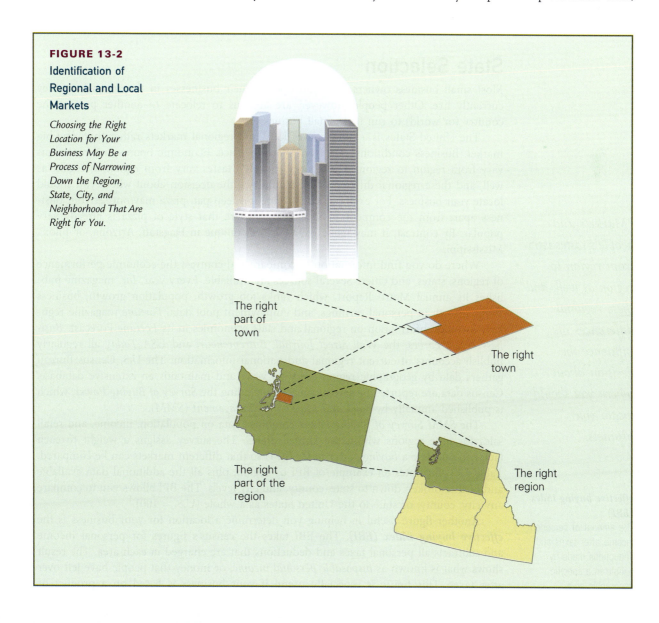

FIGURE 13-2

Identification of Regional and Local Markets

Choosing the Right Location for Your Business May Be a Process of Narrowing Down the Region, State, City, and Neighborhood That Are Right for You.

The right part of town

The right town

The right part of the region

The right region

establish the criteria that are essential to your success. Then list those that are desirable but not mandatory. Examples of criteria include the following:

- Price and availability of land and water
- Quality and quantity of labor pool
- Access to your customers
- Proximity of suppliers
- Access to transportation (air, highway, and rail)
- Location of competition
- Public attitudes toward new businesses
- Laws, regulations, and taxes
- Your personal preference regarding where to live
- Financial incentives provided (tax breaks, bond issues, and guaranteed loans)
- Quality of schools
- Quality of life (crime rate, recreation opportunities, housing, cost of living, and cultural activities)

State Selection

Most small business owners start and operate their businesses in the area where they currently live. Other people, however, are anxious to relocate to another part of the country (or world) to run their small businesses.

The United States is a collection of local and regional markets rather than one big market. Business conditions vary from place to place. Economic booms and recessions vary from region to region. Markets and people's tastes vary from region to region as well, and these regional differences may influence the decision about where you should locate your business. For example, your recipe for deep-pan pizza may not set your business apart from the competition in Chicago, where that style of pizza is already very popular. By contrast, it may make your business unique in Flagstaff, Arizona, or Biloxi, Mississippi.

Where do you find information to compare and contrast the economic performance of regions, states, and cities? Several sources are available. Every year, *Inc.* magazine publishes its annual Metro Report, which ranks job growth, population growth, business starts, growth in personal earnings, and employment pool data. *Fortune* magazine regularly includes information on regional and state economies in its *Fortune* Forecast. *Business Week*, *Forbes*, the *Wall Street Journal*, *Entrepreneur*, and *USA Today* all regularly publish accounts of current regional and national information. The U.S. Census Bureau gathers data by geographic region every 10 years and maintains an extensive database. Census data are reported by several sources, including the *Survey of Buying Power*, which is published annually by *Sales and Marketing Management* (*SMM*).

The *SMM Survey of Buying Power* combines data on population, income, and retail sales for nine regions within the United States. The survey assigns a weight to each factor to calculate a *buying power index (BPI)* so that different markets can be compared. Table 13.1 illustrates an example of BPI by region, plus all the additional data available and further broken down to state, county, and city levels. The BPI allows you to compare any city, county, or state to the United States as a whole (U.S. = 100).[1]

Another figure useful in helping you determine a location for your business is the ***effective buying index (EBI)***. The EBI takes the census's figures for personal income and subtracts all personal taxes and deductions that are charged in each area. The result shows what is known as *disposable personal income*, or money that people have left over after taxes. This figure is especially useful if your business is based on a product or

> "Markets and people's tastes vary from region to region as well, and these regional differences may influence the decision about where you should locate your business."

effective buying index (EBI)
The amount of personal income after taxes and deductions made by people in a specific geographic area.

TABLE 13-1 Regional Summaries of Population, Effective Buying Income, and Retail Sales

2009 TOTALS OF U.S. POPULATION BY AGE GROUP					
REGION	0-17 YEARS	18-24 YEARS	25-34 YEARS	35-49 YEARS	50 & OVER
East North Central	11,248,374	4,550,193	6,041,898	9,880,239	14,799,817
East South Central	4,375,810	1,737,612	2,420,364	3,785,862	5,846,591
Middle Atlantic	9,225,166	3,917,038	5,051,171	8,865,176	13,452,236
Mountain	5,740,588	2,160,057	3,162,001	4,507,693	6,473,624
New England	3,174,393	1,372,719	1,723,155	3,203,410	4,825,037
Pacific	12,481,394	5,024,610	7,063,056	10,833,820	14,560,547
South Atlantic	14,003,644	5,558,689	7,764,007	12,768,667	19,212,865
West North Central	4,903,503	2,026,817	2,612,237	4,163,753	6,522,402
West South Central	9,496,134	3,615,602	5,040,616	7,375,650	10,051,362
TOTAL/United States	74,649,006	29,963,337	40,883,505	65,384,270	95,744,581

2009 TOTALS OF RETAIL SALES ($)			
REGION	TOTAL RETAIL SALES	% OF U.S.	PER HOUSEHOLD RETAIL SALES
East North Central	643,898,123,631	14.01757	35,826
East South Central	268,007,934,547	5.8345	37,204
Middle Atlantic	598,709,875,856	13.03383	39,205
Mountain	360,769,247,520	7.8539	44,481
New England	233,795,854,872	5.0897	41,840
Pacific	760,408,835,390	16.55399	43,986
South Atlantic	918,785,578,255	20.00183	39,938
West North Central	303,457,963,507	6.60624	38,086
West South Central	505,673,307,705	11.00844	39,202
TOTAL/United States	4,593,506,721,283	100	39,837

2009 TOTALS: FOOD & BEVERAGE, FOOD & DRINK, MERCHANDISE, AND FURNITURE ($)			
REGION	FOOD & BEVERAGE	FOOD & DRINK	MERCHANDISE	FURNITURE
East North Central	79,113,630,122	69,160,470,672	88,387,214,740	10,873,682,218
East South Central	28,725,119,108	23,635,093,117	42,555,695,076	5,399,099,177
Middle Atlantic	96,651,904,898	61,114,983,002	57,144,940,357	12,053,354,480
Mountain	44,150,273,091	34,014,414,307	52,158,346,427	8,211,560,474
New England	40,820,792,888	25,453,654,313	19,929,803,587	4,692,404,086
Pacific	113,273,976,037	80,288,818,604	117,418,111,917	16,356,291,694
South Atlantic	121,378,399,719	97,356,200,080	120,635,823,485	22,314,586,965
West North Central	35,128,455,137	28,113,860,165	42,814,803,879	5,198,198,111
West South Central	57,964,001,365	49,445,380,843	74,714,501,801	11,453,146,707
TOTAL/United States	617,206,552,365	468,582,875,103	615,759,241,269	96,552,323,914

(continued)

TABLE 13-1 (continued)

2009 TOTALS: VEHICLES, ACCESSORIES, ELECTRONICS, AND ENTERTAINMENT ($)				
REGION	**VEHICLE**	**ACCESSORIES**	**ELECTRONICS**	**ENTERTAINMENT**
East North Central	91,626,251,511	24,645,042,800	15,007,654,969	12,386,568,773
East South Central	40,268,760,076	10,815,335,037	5,220,128,681	4,121,024,843
Middle Atlantic	79,731,224,252	37,718,017,077	16,186,508,087	12,676,447,021
Mountain	57,669,217,913	13,716,094,549	9,340,854,289	7,537,862,118
New England	31,664,541,478	11,577,377,512	4,956,796,892	4,975,088,953
Pacific	110,628,369,803	37,512,316,780	22,823,748,113	15,933,494,428
South Atlantic	148,077,175,318	44,261,945,672	19,018,238,203	15,962,083,903
West North Central	44,306,576,767	9,709,666,286	6,915,301,560	5,662,751,561
West South Central	89,238,687,680	20,990,443,495	10,805,658,273	9,264,089,578
TOTAL/United States	693,210,804,798	210,946,239,208	110,274,889,067	88,519,411,178

2009 U.S. TOTALS OF EFFECTIVE BUYING INCOME ($)				
	TOTAL EBI	**% OF US**	**PER CAPITA EBI**	**AUG. HH EBI**	**MEDIAN HH EBI**
---	---	---	---	---	---
East North Central	933,944,470,000	14.49325	20,076	51,963	40,735
East South Central	329,590,291,250	5.11469	18,143	45,753	34,837
Middle Atlantic	916,982,757,500	14.23004	22,636	60,047	43,882
Mountain	450,548,887,500	6.99176	20,439	55,550	43,287
New England	353,426,950,000	5.48459	24,717	63,248	47,655
Pacific	1,105,432,255,000	17.15446	22,123	63,945	47,864
South Atlantic	1,276,180,017,500	19.80418	21,518	55,473	41,786
West North Central	406,450,847,500	6.30744	20,093	51,013	40,628
West South Central	671,437,950,000	10.41959	18,872	52,052	39,349
TOTAL/United States	6,443,994,426,250	100.00000	21,016	55,886	42,303

Source: "2009 Survey of Buying Power." *Sales & Marketing Management,* 01637517, Oct/Nov2009, Vol. 161, Issue 5. *Sales & Marketing Management* by Staff. Copyright 2009 by Nielsen Business Media. Reproduced with permission of Nielsen Business Media in the formats Textbook and Other book via Copyright Clearance Center.

service that is more of a luxury than a necessity. You would want to locate a business that sells luxury goods in an area with a high EBI, because a higher average disposable income means that more people in the area are available to buy your goods.

City Selection

To most business owners, what is going on in their own city or state is more important than what is going on in the $14 trillion U.S. economy.[2] The economic condition of a particular city, state, or region is often much different than the national situation. Check out *Entrepreneur* magazine's annual rankings of top U.S. cities for small business. *Inc.* magazine ranks the best large, medium, and small metro areas for small business. Areas and cities seeing the strongest growth recently are those that provide stable housing markets, growing economies, affordable workers, and low crime rates.[3] Look at current issues of these magazines to catch up on the latest trends.

Let's look at the Fort Collins–Loveland metropolitan area of Colorado as an example of the specific demographic information available from the annual *SMM Survey of Buying Power* (see Table 13.2). You can compare population by age groups, retail sales by

TABLE 13-2 Retail Sales by Store Group and EBI to Calculate SCI

RETAIL SALES (IN $000)	FORT COLLINS	CONVERSION FACTOR	SCI	PUEBLO	CONVERSION FACTOR	SCI
Total retail sales	$2,049,038	1.12	83.58	$1,618,533	1.34	119.64
Food	297,362	.16	69.57	274,006	.23	143.75
Eating/drinking places	230,136	.13	86.67	177,150	.15	115.38
General merchandise	312,162	.17	73.91	272,906	.23	135.29
Furniture/ appliances	184,275	.10	166.67	71,467	.06	60.00
Automotive	412,627	.23	100.0	272,686	.23	100.00
Total EBI (in $000)	$1,831,934			$1,209,826		
Buying Power Index	.0508			.0349		

type of store, and percentages of effective buying income to those of other cities that you are also considering for your business location.

If your business is involved in retail or service sales, a technique for comparing different locations based on residents' ability to convert personal income into retail purchases is the *sales conversion index (SCI)*.[4] This index allows small business managers to analyze a market area in relation to a benchmark area with similar income and non-retail spending characteristics. You can even examine specific categories of retail activity. The SCI measures the strength of the retail sector by calculating **inshopping**, which occurs when consumers come from outside the local market area to shop. A city with a weaker retail sector experiences **outshopping**, or consumers' tendency to go outside the community to shop.

inshopping
The effect of more consumers coming into a town to purchase goods than leaving it to buy the same product.

outshopping
The effect of more consumers leaving a town to purchase goods than entering it to buy the same product.

Because it takes only a simple calculation of readily available secondary data, any business can use the SCI. The data can be found in *Sales and Marketing Management's Survey of Buying Power* (refer again to Table 13.2). To make the calculation, you need the following data:

- Total retail sales from the retail trade areas being examined (called the *subject area*)
- Retail sales for an appropriate *benchmark* unit
- Retail sales for the subject and benchmark areas in each of the product categories
- EBI for the subject and benchmark areas (You will recall that EBI is equal to personal income minus personal tax and nontax payments.)

Calculating the SCI takes five steps:

1. Determine the metropolitan area, the city in that metropolitan area, or the county to be examined (the subject area).
2. Establish the benchmark area to use for comparison.
3. Divide retail sales by the EBI for both the trade area and the benchmark area. This provides conversion factors.
4. Divide the subject area's conversion factor by the benchmark area's conversion factor after both are expressed as a percentage of EBI. The figure is the SCI.
5. Calculate the SCI for each of the retail categories from the *Survey of Buying Power*: food, eating and drinking places, general merchandise, automotive, drugs, and furniture, furnishings, and appliances.

An SCI greater than 100 indicates inshopping. The higher the SCI, the more desirable the location is. An SCI less than 100 suggests outshopping. The lower the number, the less desirable the location is. Using the data from Table 13.2, let's calculate the SCIs for Fort Collins, Colorado, and Pueblo, Colorado.

$$\text{Collins conversion factor} = \frac{2,049,038}{1,831,934} = 1.2$$

$$\text{Pueblo conversion factor} = \frac{1,618,533}{1,209,826} = 1.34$$

$$\text{For Collins SCI} = \frac{1.12}{1.34} = .8358 \times 100 = 83.58$$

$$\text{Pueblo SCI} = \frac{1.34}{1.12} = 1,1964 \times 100 = 119.64$$

Because the SCI for Fort Collins is far less than 100, at 83.58, you can conclude that the city experiences substantial outshopping compared with Pueblo. Conversely, Pueblo, with its 119.64 SCI, enjoys considerable inshopping compared with Fort Collins. When Pueblo is used as the benchmark, the only Fort Collins store category that indicates inshopping is "Furniture/appliances," with an SCI of 166.67 (Table 13.2 again). This would be a very interesting piece of information for you to know if you were considering opening a furniture store and were trying to decide in which city to site your business. Calculation of SCI is worth the effort when you consider the importance and permanence of locating your business.

Site Selection

Whereas the total makeup of the U.S. marketplace is diverse and complex, neighborhoods tend to be just the opposite. People are generally more comfortable in areas where people like themselves live. Thus the cliché "opposites attract" doesn't usually hold true in neighborhoods. The reasons for this demographic fact can be a matter of practicality as much as of preference. People of similar income can afford similarly priced houses, which are generally built in the same area. Neighborhoods also tend to contain clusters of similar age groups, religious groups, families, and cultural groups. These factors distinguish one neighborhood from another. They are therefore important to consider in locating your business.

To distinguish different neighborhood types, Nielsen Claritas has three systems to provide detailed demographic and segmentation information: PRIZM, P$YCLE, and ConneXions. These systems provide information on consumer behavior including household affluence, likes, dislikes, lifestyles, purchase preferences, and media preferences based upon 66 segments. Some examples of the segments are Big Fish, Small Pond (older, upper-class college-educated professional without kids); Back Country Folks (over 55, rural lifestyle, median income $33,000); and Park Bench Senior (retired singles with low-key sedentary lifestyles). Want to see what these systems have to say about your ZIP code? Go to www.mybestsegments.com and find out.[5]

Site Questions

Choosing the correct site involves answering many questions about each location being considered. You must find the right kind of site for your business. It must be accessible to your customers and vendors, and it must satisfy all legal requirements and economic needs of your business.

Type of Site

- Is the site located near target markets?
- Is the type of building appropriate for your business?

Manager's Notes

GIS—Improving Decision Making

We have all heard the phrase time and again: location, location, location. Choosing the right place to locate your business is critical to your success. Everything from foot traffic, to turns across lanes of traffic, to parking availability, to other businesses located or not located beside your business can make the difference in your bottom line. So how do you decide where to locate your business or how do you know where to relocate your business if you need additional room to expand?

GIS, geographic information system, is a tool that is providing much needed information on location for business owners. GIS is comprised of both hardware and software as well as methods to acquire, manage, manipulate, display, and analyze spatially referenced information. Differing data sources like aerial maps, demographic information, company databases, and other information can be layered together onto an interactive map, which then can be used to help business owners make location decisions. Maps can graphically demonstrate trends, relationships, and patterns that would be more difficult to notice from a list of numbers. GIS can assist in predicting customer location and behavior, and in determining where market share will grow, all important to increasing revenue.

Insurance companies can use GIS to evaluate risk for both the insured and the company. Logistics can look at channels of distribution, product delivery routes, and schedules. Media can use GIS to target advertising to specific neighborhoods. The GIS team from Pueblo County, Colorado, used GIS to assist a Web-based business with nationwide marketing. They were able to develop strategies that involved television, radio, and direct mail, and then use the zip codes of the customers who were conducting online product searches to find new key words to be used in Google for this business. Not only did these techniques bring in more money, but also the business added more jobs. GIS is changing the way data are used within a business. For more information on GIS, go to www.esri.com and learn of more uses for GIS in your business.

Sources: "Mapping Your Market," *Cabinet Maker*, May 7, 2010; "Driving Directions," *Industrial Engineer*, March 2009; Jessica Tsai, "Here, There and Everywhere," *Customer Relationship Management*, January 2010; "Join the Current Discussion: Retail GIS–Localization, Not just Location," www.esri.com, retrieved August 25, 2010; "Building Local Business," *American City and Country*, September 2009; and Robert Mitchell, "The Grill Jack Dangermond," *ComputerWorld*, July 20/July 27, 2009.

- What is the site's age and condition?
- How large is the trade area?
- Will adjacent businesses complement or compete with your firm?

Accessibility

- How are road patterns and conditions?
- Do any natural or artificial barriers obstruct access to the site?
- Does the site have good visibility?
- Is traffic flow too high or too low?
- Is the entrance or exit to parking convenient?
- Is parking adequate?
- Is the site accessible by mass transit?
- Can vendor deliveries be made easily?

Legal Considerations

- Is the zoning compatible with your firm?
- Does the building meet building codes?
- Will your external signs be compatible with zoning ordinances?
- Can you get any special licenses you will need (such as a liquor license)?

Economic Factors

- How much are occupancy costs?
- Are the amenities worth the cost?
- How much will leasehold improvements and other one-time costs be?

"The volume of automobile and foot traffic, the speed of vehicles, and the presence of turn lanes and parking are factors to consider when choosing a location for a retail or service business."

Traffic Flow

The number of cars and pedestrians passing a site strongly affects its potential for retail sales. If you are a retailer, you need to determine whether the type and amount of traffic are sufficient for your business. Fast-food franchises have precise specifications for number counts of vehicles travelling at specified speeds in each direction as part of their location analysis. State highway departments can usually provide statistics on traffic counts for most public roads.

Type of traffic is important, because you don't receive any particular benefit if the people passing your business are not likely to stop. For example, suppose you are comparing two locations for your upscale jewelry store—one in a central business district and the other in a small shopping center with other specialty stores in an exclusive neighborhood. Total volume of traffic by the central business district location will be higher, but you will enjoy more of the right type of traffic for your store at the small shopping center.

Other businesses in the area will affect the type of traffic. This explains why you often see automobile dealerships clustered together. The synergy created from several similar businesses located together can be very beneficial, with customers coming to a specific area to "shop around" before buying. Your chances of attracting customers in the market for an auto will be much greater in a location with complementary competition than if your location is isolated.

Some key questions to ask as you choose your location are:

- Are you on the correct side of the street for the flow of traffic? How many lanes of traffic must be crossed in order to reach your entrance?
- Do you have sufficient parking all times of the day? Is it easy to get to?
- Do you out-position your closest competitors in this area?
- What does the competition look like that is located by you?
- Is there an anchor store near you? Is your product differentiated from that product?[6]

Going Global

If you are considering expanding your operations into another country, you need information on the location of your foreign project. You can get background information and opinions on foreign locations from magazines and newspapers at your local library. Keep in mind that all local chambers of commerce and economic development groups exist to promote their area, not to criticize it, so view information received from them with a somewhat skeptical eye. The American Management Association and the American Marketing Association (and other organizations) sponsor seminars on opportunities and problems in foreign operations. The U.S. Department of State can be very helpful in telling you about political developments, local customs and differences, and economic issues in specific countries.

In addition to doing your research (and reviewing the information in Chapter 15), it is very important that you get to know the area personally before you establish operations abroad. Visit potential sites, meet with others in business there, and identify possible distribution sources before you consider setting up business in another country.

Finding information on the Internet to help you make intelligent location decisions about global markets is fairly easy. The U.S. government has created Web sites for various government agencies that can provide the small business owner with appropriate information. For instance, the Central Intelligence Agency server (www.cia.gov) provides access to the latest edition of the *CIA World Factbook*, which includes information about every country in the world, with details such as geography, climate, terrain, natural resources, religions, languages, and so forth.

In addition, you might want to access Web sites devoted to specific geographic locations once you've narrowed down your list of potential sites. For instance, you can access information about Vietnam, Latin America, China, the European Union, and Russia and Eastern Europe at the following addresses:

Vietnam: www.vietnamonline.com
Latin America: http://lanic.utexas.edu
China: www.chinesebusinessworld.com
European Union: www.eubusiness.com
Russia: www.einnews.com/russia

"Adventure travel and tourism is a niche market in the travel industry with the locations of the tours literally spread around the world."

How about making the world the location for your business? Adventure travel and tourism is a niche market in the travel industry with the locations of the tours literally spread around the world. This market is growing and ripe for entrepreneurs with 70 percent growth and sales of $52 billion expected in 2010, according to a study conducted by The Adventure Travel Trade Association. These explosive numbers are only from outbound travel from North and South America and Europe. Lauren Hefferon started Ciclismo Classico, a cycling tour company, after a Rotary scholarship took her to Italy. Her company, founded in 1988, was one of the first to specialize in cycling tours of Italy. Her first tour focused on the gorgeous roads of Tuscany and Elba. Mike and Susie Fitzgerald own and operate Frontiers, and were one of the first companies to offer salmon fishing in Iceland as well as photographic safaris to Africa. While this market may not bring in huge sums of money, with operating margins of 9–11 percent, for the small business owners operating in this industry, the additional rewards make it well worthwhile. Oh, the places you can go and the sights you can see, all at the same time you are operating your small business.[7]

Location Types

Service and retail businesses have three basic choices for types of locations: central business districts, shopping centers, and stand-alone locations.

Central Business Districts

The *central business district (CBD)* is usually the oldest section of a city. Although urban blight caused many businesses to desert CBDs in favor of the suburbs, many other CBDs have undergone a *gentrification* process, meaning that old buildings have been restored, or razed and replaced with new offices, retail shops, or housing. This planning and development, such as Denver's Larimer Square and Chicago's Water Tower Place, have created some of the best and most expensive locations for many types of retailers.

The advantages of locating in a CBD are that your customers generally will have access to public transportation; to a variety of images, prices, and services; and to many other

© Kenneth Sponsler/Shutterstock.com

Being located near complementary (or even competing) businesses can be beneficial because target markets are attracted to all.

businesses. The disadvantages can include parking availability, which is usually very tight and expensive; traffic congestion; possibly a high crime rate; older buildings; and sharp disparities between neighborhoods, in which one block can be upscale while the next is rundown.

Shopping Centers

anchor stores

A large retail store that attracts people to shop at malls.

Although concentrated shopping areas have existed for centuries, the last four decades have witnessed the "malling of America." Shopping centers and malls are centrally owned or managed, have balanced store offerings, and have their own parking facilities. ***Anchor stores*** are major department stores that draw people into the shopping center.

Over the last several decades, shoppers have come to demand the convenience of shopping centers. People living in the suburbs want to be able to drive to a location where they can park easily and find a wide variety of goods and services. Shopping centers have also gone through an evolutionary process, tending toward larger centers offering more variety, wider selections, and more entertainment. Have megamalls like the West Edmonton Mall or the Mall of America gone too far in this evolutionary process? Have they reached the point of being "too big"? Ultimately, the consumer market will decide.

Advantages that shopping centers can offer to your business, compared with a CBD, include heavy traffic drawn by the wide variety of products available, closeness to population centers, cooperative planning and cost sharing, access to highways, ample parking, a lower crime rate, and a clean, neat environment.

A disadvantage of locating within a shopping center is the inflexibility of your store hours. If the center is open from 9 a.m. to 10 p.m., you can't open your store from noon until midnight. Your rent is often higher than in an outside location. The central management of the shopping center may restrict the merchandise you sell. Your operations are limited, membership is required in the center's merchant organization, and you face the possibility of having too much competition. Smaller stores may be dominated by anchor stores.

Shopping centers will continue to evolve rapidly. Aging centers are being renovated. As shoppers become more dependent on malls and shopping centers to supply their needs, more service-oriented businesses, such as banks, health clinics, day care centers, and insurance offices, will be located in malls.

Stand-Alone Locations

Drawing in and keeping customers are difficult tasks, especially if you choose a free-standing, or stand-alone, location. With a freestanding location, your business must be the customers' destination point. Therefore, your competitive advantage must be made very clear to them. You must have unique merchandise, large selections, low prices, exceptional service, or special promotions to get them in.

Advantages of stand-alone locations include the freedom to set your own hours and operate the way you choose. You may have no direct competition nearby. More parking may be available, and rent may be lower than what you would pay at a shopping center.

Disadvantages of having your business in a stand-alone location include the loss of synergy that can be created when the right combination of businesses is located together. You have to increase your advertising and promotional spending to get customers in your door. You can't share operating costs with other businesses. You may have to build rather than rent.

If the goods or services that you offer are destination-oriented products (like health clubs, convenience stores, or wholesale clubs), a freestanding location may be the right choice for your business.

Service Locations

With some exceptions, the location decision for service businesses is just as important as it is for businesses selling tangible products. Services tend to be hard to differentiate—that is, to show how one is different from another. People will not go out of their way to visit a specific service business if they think there is very little difference between services, so car washes, video rental stores, dry cleaners, and similar services must be *very* careful about the convenience of their locations. With service businesses that visit the customer (like plumbers, landscapers, and carpet cleaners), location is not critical.

Incubators

"An incubator is an attractive place to start a new small business. It offers support services and such equipment as photocopiers, fax machines, and computers, which young businesses often cannot afford by themselves."

In the early 1980s, government agencies, universities, and private business groups began creating business incubators to help new businesses get started in their area. Today, several hundred incubators operate in the United States, and their number is growing. Approximately 80 percent of business incubator graduates remain in business and they grow 22 times faster than start-ups not using an incubator, according to NBIA.[8] Incubators offer entrepreneurs below-market rent prices, along with services and equipment that are difficult for start-up businesses to provide on their own. They encourage entrepreneurship, which contributes to economic development. Businesses are not allowed to take advantage of these benefits indefinitely, and they must "graduate" to outside locations as they grow.

Choosing an incubator as your starting location can help you through the first months when your new business is at its most fragile. As noted earlier, a major advantage of incubators is that they charge lower-than-market rent. Other benefits follow.

Support Services Incubators typically make copy machines, computers, fax machines, and other equipment available for their tenants to share. These items can improve your productivity as a young business, but they would cost a lot of money if you had to buy them outright. In an incubator, you can have access to such equipment and pay only when and if you use it. Receptionists, secretarial support, and shipping and receiving services are also available on a shared basis, so you don't have to add to your payroll.

Reality Check

Incubation Innovation

Business *incubators* come in two broad varieties: mixed use and sector focused. James Prinster and Steve Kramer needed the expertise of a mixed-use incubator when they set out to create a contract-electronics manufacturing company in Grand Junction, Colorado. They knew the manufacturing side of the business from being employees of such a firm, but they needed help in all other aspects. Starting in 2002 with revenues of $60,000, they quickly grew to $850,000 by 2004. Being located in an incubator was a huge advantage at this time because they could take over more space without moving the business. Finally, they did outgrow the incubator and moved into their own 6,000-square-foot building in Grand Junction.

An interesting variation on the traditional business incubator is emerging: creative incubators, such as the one offered by the Arts Council of New Orleans. This incubator's forte is helping creative start-ups find the right balance between pushing creative boundaries—by producing music, creating jewelry, or launching a theater company—and making smart business decisions with fiscal responsibility.

In addition to typical access to equipment, companies admitted to the Arts Council's Energy Program obtain access to a group health plan, workshops on business topics, fundraising, and board development. Successful performance is expected, exemplified by 5 to 10 percent growth per year at a minimum. According to Chesley Adler, owner of a jewelry design business located in the incubator, bouncing ideas off other businesspeople in the creative incubator has been invaluable.

For information on finding a creative incubator, try these Web sites:

- Acceleratorcorp.com
- the-foundry.com
- launchboxdigital.com
- ycombinator.com
- National Business Incubator Association: www.nbia.org

New ideas inevitably beget new ideas. Incubators are operating at record numbers with some 41,000 start-ups operating in 1,200 incubators in 2010. Survival rate for participants is 87 percent, compared with 44 percent for companies that don't use incubators.

"These incubators are some of the most important things we do, forming the basis of our society. We need to teach people how to be successful entrepreneurs and not cogs in corporate environments," says Dinah Adkins, president and CEO of the National Business Incubation Association.

Sources: Dennis Romero, "A New Take on Incubators," *Entrepreneur*, May 2009, 69–77; Lauren Hatch, "Betting on Incubators to Create Jobs," *Bloomberg Businessweek*, August 16, 2010, 20–22; and Joanne Scillitoe, "The Role of Incubator Interactions in Assisting New Ventures," *Technovation*, March 2010, 155–167.

Professional Assistance Incubators often negotiate reduced rates with needed professionals like accountants and lawyers. They also offer training in cash flow management, marketing practices, obtaining financing, and other areas.

Networking Incubators can put you in contact with other local businesses. A "family" atmosphere often develops between businesses located in incubators because all are at roughly the same stage of development. This atmosphere usually leads to an esprit de corps among tenants.

Financing Incubators often have financial assistance available or access to other funding sources such as revolving loan funds, which can provide loans at lower than market rates.

Layout and Design

After you have selected a site, you need to lay out the interior of your business. If yours is a type of business that customers visit, most of your management decisions will be directed toward getting customers into your business to spend money. No matter what type of business you run, this is where the activity happens. How your location is laid out and designed is important because it affects the image and productivity of your business.

Legal Requirements

The Americans with Disabilities Act (ADA) requires businesses to be accessible to disabled customers and employees, with businesses having more than 14 employees required to accommodate disabled job candidates in hiring. This law affects the way every business operates. Buildings constructed after January 26, 1993, must meet stricter requirements than those built earlier.

Some ADA requirements for customer accommodation include the following:

- Accessible parking must be provided with space for both the vehicle and an access aisle. An accessibility sign must also be located in front of the parking space to identify the parking spot.
- Access ramps must be provided in order to make the entrance accessible with the slope of the ramp not to exceed 1:12.
- Handrails must be provided whenever the ramp slope is more than 1:20 and the vertical rise is greater than six inches.
- Checkout aisles must be at least 36 inches wide.
- Door hardware must be easily grasped like a lever handle.
- Toilet facilities and water fountains must be accessible to people in wheelchairs.
- Self-service shelves, counters, and bars must be accessible to people in wheelchairs and to the visually impaired.[9]

Retail Layouts

The layout of your retail store helps create the image that people have of your business. It is important to display merchandise in an attractive, logical arrangement to maximize your sales and to make shopping as convenient as possible for your customers.

Three types of layouts are commonly used in retail stores in various combinations. The simplest type is the *free-flow layout*, which works well with smaller stores such as boutiques that sell only one type of merchandise (see Figure 13.3). As there is no established traffic pattern, customers are encouraged to browse.

A *grid layout* establishes a geometric grid by placing counters and fixtures at right angles in long rows (see Figure 13.4). It effectively displays a large amount of merchandise with tall shelves and many shelf facings. Supermarkets and drugstores tend to be set up with this layout, because it suits customers who wish to shop the entire store by moving up and down alternate aisles. But if customers can't see over fixtures or if they want only one or two specific items, they may find this layout frustrating.

The *loop layout* has gained popularity since the early 1980s as a tool for increasing retail sales productivity (see Figure 13.5). The loop sets up a major aisle that leads customers from the entrance, through the store, and back to the checkout counter. Customers are led efficiently through the store so as to expose them to the greatest amount of merchandise. At the same time, they retain the freedom to browse or cross-shop. This layout is especially good for businesses that sell a wide variety of merchandise, because customers can be routed quickly from one department of merchandise to another.

free-flow layout
A type of layout used by small retail stores that encourages customers to wander and browse through the store.

grid layout
A type of layout used by retail stores to move customers past merchandise arranged on rows of shelves or fixtures.

loop layout
A type of retail layout with a predominant aisle running through the store that quickly leads customers to their desired department.

Service Layouts

Service businesses that customers visit, such as beauty shops and restaurants, need to be concerned about how their layout affects both their customers' convenience and the business's work flow. The image of these service businesses is just as strongly affected by layout as is the image of retail stores. Speed of service becomes more critical every year. Consider the decreasing amount of time needed for photo finishing—from one week, to two days, to one hour, to while you wait. Layout is critical to maintaining the speed and efficiency of service providers.

FIGURE 13-3

Free-Flow

The Free-Flow Layout Encourages Shoppers to Browse.

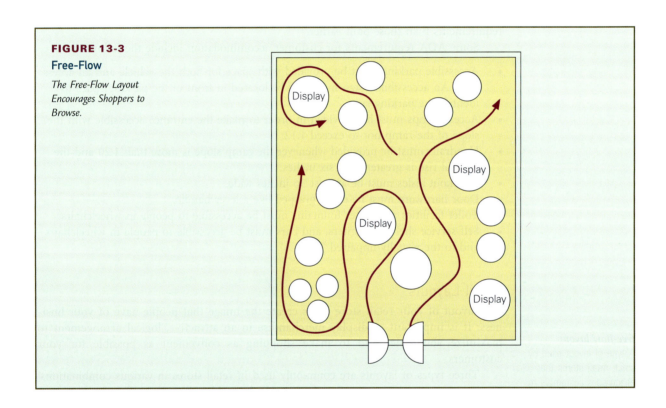

FIGURE 13-4

Grid Layout

The Grid Layout Routes Customers up and down Aisles to Expose Them to a Large Quantity of Merchandise.

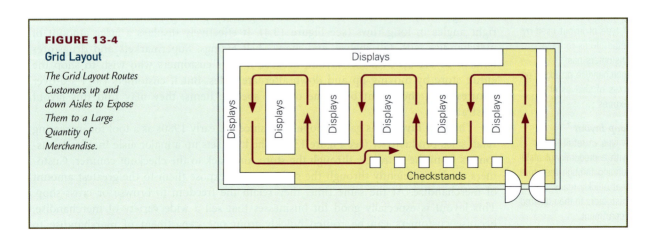

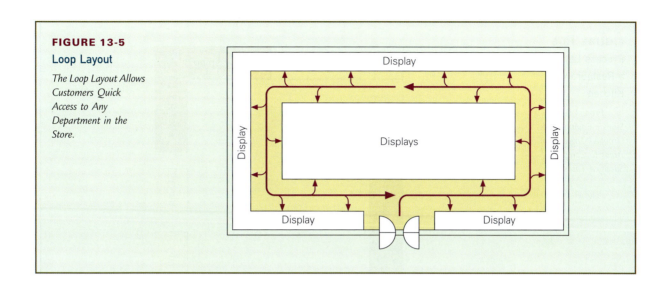

FIGURE 13-5

Loop Layout

The Loop Layout Allows Customers Quick Access to Any Department in the Store.

Manufacturing Layouts

The layout of a manufacturing business is arranged to ensure a smooth flow of work. The specific layout of your plant will depend on the type of product you make, the type of production process you use, the space you have available, and other factors, such as volume of goods and amount of worker interaction needed. There are three basic types of manufacturing layouts, which may be combined as needed.

process layout
A way to arrange a manufacturing business by placing all comparable equipment together in the same area.

Process Layout With the **process layout**, all similar equipment and workers are grouped together so that the goods being produced move around the plant (see Figure 13.6). This layout is common with small manufacturers because of the flexibility it allows. The product being made can be changed quickly. An example of the process layout can be seen in a small machine shop, in which all the grinders would be in one area, all the drills would be in another area, and all the lathes would be in a third area. Restaurant kitchens commonly employ this type of layout as well, with the refrigerators in one place, the ovens in another, and a food preparation area elsewhere.

Another advantage of the process layout is that it minimizes the number of tools or equipment needed. For example, an assembly line (which uses a product layout) might require a company to purchase several grinding machines, one for each point where it is used on the assembly line. With a process layout, by contrast, only one or two grinders need be purchased, and all can be used in one area. Because the machines operate independently, a breakdown in one does not shut down operations.

A disadvantage of the process layout is that when equipment is grouped together, increased handling is needed to move the product from one station to another when more than one task is performed. This effort can require additional employees. Because this layout is more general in nature, producing long runs of the same product would be less efficient than in the product layout.

product layout
A way to arrange a manufacturing business by placing equipment in an assembly line.

Product Layout With a **product layout**, you arrange workers, equipment, and activities needed to produce a single product in a particular sequence of steps (see Figure 13.7). A product layout is best when you are producing many standardized products or using specialized equipment. Auto assembly lines, textile mills, and other continuous-flow assembly lines in which raw material enters one end of the line and finished products exit

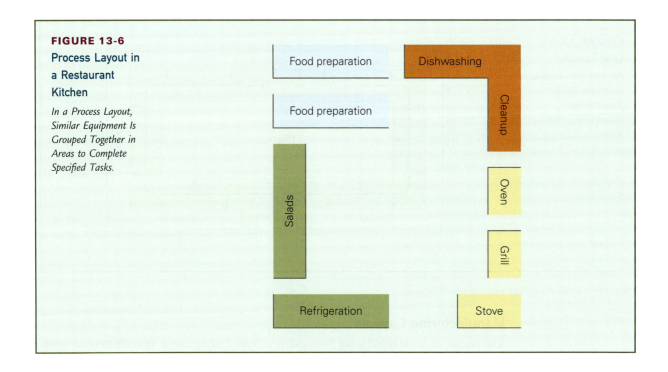

FIGURE 13-6

Process Layout in a Restaurant Kitchen

In a Process Layout, Similar Equipment Is Grouped Together in Areas to Complete Specified Tasks.

Food preparation

Dishwashing

Food preparation

Cleanup

Salads

Oven

Grill

Refrigeration

Stove

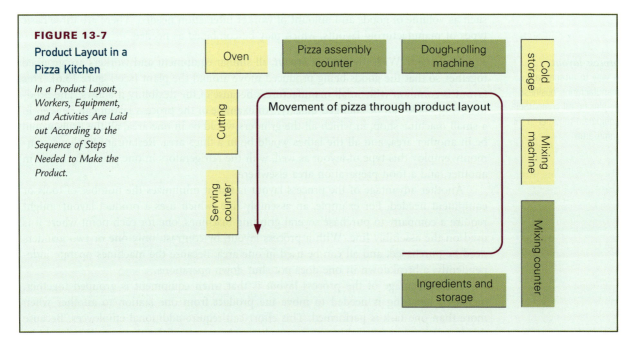

FIGURE 13-7

Product Layout in a Pizza Kitchen

In a Product Layout, Workers, Equipment, and Activities Are Laid out According to the Sequence of Steps Needed to Make the Product.

Oven

Pizza assembly counter

Dough-rolling machine

Cold storage

Cutting

Movement of pizza through product layout

Mixing machine

Serving counter

Mixing counter

Ingredients and storage

the other end are examples of a product layout. Material handling costs can be decreased and tasks can often be mechanically simplified so that skilled labor is not needed.

A restaurant that specializes in a product like bagels, pizzas, or cookies can make use of the product layout by moving through a sequence of steps to prepare the finished product. The kitchen can be arranged to store ingredients and mix the dough at one end of the counter before it is all moved to cold storage. Then batches can be removed and processed through a dough-rolling machine; prepared and mixed with other ingredients; and cooked, cut, and served in an assembly line fashion. The layout works well for making that one product, but what if you want to diversify your menu to offer other food items like hamburgers, French fries, or tacos? You would have to set up separate product lines with new ovens, stoves, and counters for each new product—an expensive way to expand a menu.

A product layout is inflexible because it is costly and difficult to change the product that is being made. It is usually more expensive to set up than a process layout because more specialized machinery is needed. A breakdown anywhere along the line can shut down the entire operation. The specialization needed for a product layout eliminates this option for most small businesses because of cost reasons.

Fixed Layout In a *fixed layout*, the product stays in one spot, and equipment, material, and labor are brought to it as needed for assembly. Types of businesses using this layout include building construction, aircraft and shipbuilding, and other large, immovable product production.

fixed layout
A type of layout for a manufacturing business in which the product stays stationary while workers and equipment are brought to it.

Home Office

Is a home-based business right for you? It is becoming a popular option for business owners. A study based upon U.S. Census data shows that home-based businesses will have "an increasingly significant impact on the U.S. economy."[10] Let's look at some advantages and disadvantages.

© Istockphoto/Xavi Arnau

A home-based business can be a great opportunity for the right person, with the right product, under the right conditions.

Advantages

- *Flexibility in scheduling personal, family, and business obligations.*
- *Low overhead expenses.* You are already paying for the space you live in and utilities.
- *No commute time.* Of course, that walk from the kitchen to the office can seem like a long one if you don't really feel like working.
- *Independence.* You can be your own boss and your own landlord. You have some degree of control over what work you accept and the schedule for doing it.
- *No office distractions.* A lot of time can be wasted in office settings chatting with people who "pop in."

Disadvantages

- *Interruptions.* It's hard for family and friends to understand that you really do have work to do.
- *Isolation.* Much of the social aspect of work can be lost without contact with others. A house can get very quiet and lonely.
- *Credibility.* Although home-based businesses are much more accepted today, being taken seriously as a business can be a challenge. This isn't a hobby, and you are not unemployed.
- *Work space.* Your working area may be cramped and not too private.
- *Zoning issues.* Be sure to check whether it is legal for you to operate a business out of your home.

Michelle Tunno Buelow designs and distributes children's accessories called Bella Tunno from her home in Charlotte, North Carolina. Her business grew from her hobby, which was designing unique accessories like reversible bibs. Her big break came when her products were noticed and included in gift bags given to expectant celebrity mothers at the Golden Globes. Buelow considers herself a home-based business owner with her desk in the corner of her children's playroom. She often works late at night, choosing to spend her days with her children in their home. She was one of Ernst and Young's 2009 Winning Women honorees for most promising businesses. [11]

The approaches to running a home business are as varied as the millions of entrepreneurs who own them. Equipment needs vary almost as much.

You must make sure that it is legal to operate a home-based business where you live. Some communities have adopted tough restrictions, such as not allowing a home office even for work you bring home from your "real" office. More typical concerns involve complying with zoning regulations that govern parking, signage, and types of businesses allowed in residential areas. Check with your local zoning board.

Lease, Buy, or Build?

You have three choices of ownership for your location: leasing a facility, purchasing an existing building, or building your own. In this section, we will discuss the relative advantages of leasing or purchasing your building.

Leasing

A lease is basically a long-term agreement to rent a building, equipment, or other asset. The biggest advantage of leasing is the amount of cash you free up for other purposes. Not only do you avoid a large initial cash outlay through leasing, but you also reduce your risk during the start-up period. Once your business is established, your needs may change. Leasing your business premises can give you the flexibility to move to a bigger, better, or more suitable location in the future.

A disadvantage of a lease is that it may prevent you from altering a building to fit your needs. You also do not have long-term assurance that you can stay in the same location. The owner may decide not to renew your lease at the end of the term or may increase your rent payments. Leased space in shopping centers commonly requires a monthly fee based on square feet of space, plus a percentage of gross sales.

"Review any lease with your lawyer before signing it."

Review any lease with your lawyer before signing it. This advice holds true for any legal document, but with a lease there is a tendency to think, "These forms are pretty much standard," and thus ignore the advice to review them first. Remember who drew up the document—the lessor. Whom do you think the conditions of the lease will favor?

Not you, the lessee. You may need to negotiate the provisions of the lease or *escape clauses*. These items can allow you to terminate the lease if your circumstances change drastically. You will also want to consider the lease's renewal options. Will the lease allow you to remain in the same location at the end of the lease period?

leasehold improvements
Changes that make a property more valuable, such as painting, adding shelves, or installing new lighting.

gross lease
A lease in which the monthly payment made by the tenant remains the same and the landlord pays the operating expenses of the building.

net lease
A lease in which the tenant pays a base monthly rent plus some or all real estate taxes of the building.

net-net lease
A lease in which the tenant pays a base monthly rent plus real estate taxes and insurance on the building.

triple-net lease
A lease in which the tenant pays a base monthly rent plus real estate taxes, insurance, and any other operating expenses incurred for the building.

percentage lease
A lease in which the tenant pays a base monthly rent plus a percentage of their gross revenue.

escalation clause
A lease that varies according to the amount of inflation in the economy.

    Leasehold improvements are important considerations to negotiate. They comprise the improvements you make to the property, such as upgrading lighting or plumbing, installing drop ceilings, building walls, and making other changes to the property. Of course, you cannot take these improvements with you when you leave, so try to negotiate rent payments in exchange for them. These are just a few factors you need to negotiate before signing a lease. Get all agreements in writing.

    The best way to avoid disputes between landlords and tenants is for both parties to understand the lease agreement *before* it is signed. Because a lease will legally bind you for a long period of time, you should have the following questions answered to your satisfaction when you enter the deal:

1. *How long will the lease run?* The length of most leases is negotiable, with 3 to 10 years being typical and even one-year leases written with 10 one-year renewal options. In the past, landlords wanted the lease term to be as long as possible to hold down their vacancy rates. Now, in areas where vacant office space is at a premium, many businesses often want long leases as a hedge against rising prices. For example, in New York City, an office tower may charge $60 per square foot for rent today, whereas the same offices rented for $16 per square foot only five years earlier.

2. *How much is the rent?* Be sure you know the dollar amount per square foot of space that the rent is based on for any location you consider. Find out how much you are paying for different kinds of space—you don't want to pay the same dollar amount for productive office space as you do for space like lobbies, hallways, mechanical areas, and bathrooms.

    There are at least five types of leases, which calculate rent differently, though they are all based on square feet. In a ***gross lease***, the tenant pays a flat monthly amount. The landlord pays all building operating expenses such as taxes, insurance, and repairs. Utility bills may or may not be included. In a ***net lease***, the tenant pays some or all real estate taxes above the base rent. A ***net-net lease*** includes insurance on top of the base rent and taxes. A *net-net-net*, or ***triple-net lease***, requires tenants to pay not only the base rent, taxes, and insurance, but also other operating expenses related to the building, such as repairs and maintenance. A ***percentage lease***, which is common in shopping centers or other buildings that include many different businesses, requires tenants to pay a base rent plus a percentage of gross income.

3. *How much will the rent go up?* To protect against inflation, most landlords include an ***escalation clause*** in leases, which allows them to adjust rent according to the consumer price index (CPI) or some other scale. You should not agree to pay the full CPI increase, especially if you are already paying part of the building operating expenses.

4. *Can you sublease?* There are many reasons why you might not be able to stay in a location for the stated duration of the lease, including, at the extremes, a failure of your business or becoming so successful that you need to move to a larger space. If you must move, can you rent your space to another tenant who meets the same standards the landlord applies to all other tenants?

5. *Can you renew?* Unless a clause is written into your lease that guarantees you the first right to your space at the end of the lease term, the landlord has no legal obligation to continue it. A formula for determining the new rent payment might be included in the renewal clause, or you might pay current market rate.

6. *What happens if your landlord goes broke?* A *recognition,* or *nondisturbance, clause* can protect you from being forced out or into a new lease should the property change ownership.

7. *Who is responsible for insurance?* Landlords should be expected to carry a comprehensive policy on the building that includes casualty insurance on the structure and liability coverage for all public areas such as hallways and elevators. Building owners can require tenants to buy liability and content insurance.

8. *What building services do you get?* Your lease should state the specific services you can expect to receive, including any electricity use limits, cleaning schedules, and heating, ventilation, and air conditioning (HVAC). Note that, unlike residential rents, commercial space does not usually come with 24-hour HVAC service. (Monday through Friday from 8 a.m. to 5 p.m. and Saturday from 8 a.m. to 1 p.m. are normal.) This could produce some hot or cold working conditions if you work at other hours.

9. *Who else can move in?* Clauses can be written into leases that restrict direct competitors, or businesses that are exceptionally noisy or otherwise disruptive to others, from locating in adjoining spaces. Remember that such restrictions can become a problem to you if you need to sublease.

10. *Who pays for improvements?* Construction and remodeling become expensive quickly. Although you are usually allowed to make leasehold improvements, the building owner does not always have to pay for them. Improvements are an area wide open to negotiation in leases—make sure all agreements in this area are in writing.[12]

Before you make a commitment and sign a lease for your small business, you would be well advised to read *Leasing Space for Your Small Business* by Janet Portman and Fred Steingold (published by Nolo Press).

Purchasing

The decision to buy a building can be a difficult one. Ownership increases your upfront expenses and the amount of capital you need. The major expense of purchasing and remodeling can drain already stretched resources from other business needs.

With ownership, you gain the freedom of customizing the property any way you want. You know what your payments will be. At the same time, you are tied down to that location much more if you own rather than rent the property. Tax considerations enter the picture. Although lease payments are deductible business expenses, only depreciation on the building is deductible if you own it. Finally, the value of your investment is subject to the whims of the local real estate market. The value may appreciate or depreciate for reasons that have nothing to do with your own efforts. In the end, the choice comes down to economics and flexibility. Because most entrepreneurs are in business because of what they make or sell, and not in the "brick-and-mortar" business of real estate speculation, a majority will choose leasing.

Building

Building a new facility to meet your own specifications may be necessary if your business has unique needs or if existing facilities are not located where you need them, which may be the case in some high-growth areas.

As with buying an existing property, building a new facility greatly increases your fixed expenses. Will your revenues increase enough to cover these additional expenses? On the plus side, building a new facility may enable you to incorporate new technology or features that will lower your operating costs compared to using an older, existing building. Look at your *total* costs over the long term when making this decision.

Reality Check

Is It Time to Move?

What do you do if your landlord raises your rent or you find a place bigger for less money? What do you do if your landlord won't fix a leaking roof and the resulting water is damaging your product? Or what if you just no longer fit in your current space due to explosive growth? The answer is to move—but where and how? The questions just presented were asked by entrepreneurs who were faced with a moving decision in order to ensure the profitability of their business. So what are some key areas to evaluate when considering moving?

- Make sure you can afford a new space. Rent becomes a fixed cost that must be paid regardless of sales. Check thoroughly the cost of your new space and plot against projected sales.
- Determine the criteria needed to ensure the success of your business. Look at areas like traffic numbers, major highways, and space for future growth, to name a few. Oh, and don't forget availability of customer parking.
- Is the city friendly to your business? Look at areas like the skill level of the available labor pool, taxes, and regulations.

- Are you close to your key people—customers, competitors, suppliers, and employees? Does the move shorten or lengthen distribution channels?
- Where is your competition located? Depending on the business, you may wish to locate close to your competition, like car dealerships, or not, like floral shops.
- What is your opportunity for growth? Does this location provide the basics necessary to encourage and promote the growth of your company not just today but also five years down the road?
- Consider a pop-up for your business, a space that you rent for short time periods. These short-term locations allow you to generate "buzz" about your product but don't tie you down to a long-term location commitment, particularly if you are not sure the location will support the sales levels you need.

Sources: "5 Reasons to Relocate Your Business," nfib.com, retrieved August 21, 2010; Randy Myers, "Why, When and How to Move Your Business," entrepreneur.com, July 30, 2010; "6 Tips for Selecting the Right Company Location," nfib.com, retrieved August 17, 2010; and Sarah Needleman, "Stores That Can't Stay," wsj.com, August 5, 2010.

Summary

1. Describe small business distribution and explain how "efficiencies" affect channels of distribution.

The purpose of a channel of distribution is to get a product from a producer to consumers as quickly and cheaply as possible. Because distribution represents such a large portion of the price of many products, selecting the most efficient channel will help keep costs down.

2. Explain how the location of your business can provide a competitive advantage.

Competitive advantages can be built on many factors. If the location choice of your business makes your product, good, or service more accessible to your customers, to the point where they buy from you rather than other sources, then location is your competitive advantage.

3. List factors in selecting a state in which to locate your business.

In deciding where to locate your business, you should consider the price and availability of land and water, the labor pool from which you can hire employees, accessibility to customers and suppliers, closeness of competition, adequacy of transportation, public attitudes toward new businesses, taxes and regulations, your personal preference about where you want to live, financial incentives offered, and the quality of life available.

4. List factors in selecting a city in which to locate your business.

A city's sales conversion index (SCI) is calculated from *Survey of Buying Power* data to determine the amount of inshopping for a city compared to another benchmark location. Begin by determining a conversion factor for the considered city and the benchmark area by dividing total retail sales by the effective buying income for each place. Then divide the chosen city's conversion factor by the benchmark conversion factor. An SCI greater than 100 indicates inshopping—that is, more people come to that town to buy your type of product than go elsewhere.

5. Discuss the central issues in choosing a particular site within a city.

The most appropriate site for your business is determined by answering specific questions related to matching the needs of your business with the type of site, accessibility, legal considerations, and economic factors.

6. Compare the three basic types of locations.

The three types of locations you may choose are central business districts (CBDs), shopping centers, and stand-alone locations. The CBD for most cities and towns includes the original "downtown" area, so it is usually the oldest urban section. Shopping centers can range from small strip malls that serve the local neighborhood to very large regional malls that draw customers from hundreds of miles. A stand-alone location places your business apart from other businesses.

7. Explain the types of layout you can choose.

For retail businesses, a free-flow layout encourages customers to wander and browse through the store. A grid layout moves customers up and down rows of shelves and fixtures. A loop layout features a wide central aisle that leads customers quickly from one department to another. For manufacturing businesses, a process layout groups all similar equipment and jobs together and provides the flexibility needed by many small manufacturers. A product layout arranges equipment and workers in a specific sequence to produce products in a continuous flow. With a fixed layout, the product being made stays in one place, while equipment, materials, and labor are brought to it.

8. Present the circumstances under which leasing, buying, or building is an appropriate choice.

When deciding whether to lease, buy, or construct a building, you need to consider how long the building will be suitable for your business and whether you can afford to tie up your capital, which could be used for other purposes. Before leasing, you need to carefully examine the terms and conditions of the lease before signing it.

Questions for Review and Discussion

1. How can a small business owner create competitive advantage with a channel of distribution?
2. Why should the small business owner consider the demographics of an area when choosing a location for opening a new business? Name some sources of demographic information that are valuable tools to use in this evaluation.
3. When choosing a location for a new business, what are the most important criteria for the entrepreneur to consider? Explain the connection between type of business and location.
4. Why would a small business flourish in one area of the United States but fail in another region?
5. What is the SCI, and why should the small business owner become familiar with the way it is calculated and the information to be obtained from it?
6. Explain the importance of knowing the legal requirements of an area before attempting to open a small business.
7. What are some considerations that the entrepreneur should take into account if business is to be conducted in a foreign market?
8. What are the three location types and their subcategories? Give an example of a type of small business that would have the greatest chance of succeeding in each location type. State your reason for selecting that particular business type by giving specific advantages.
9. What is the ADA, and how does it affect the small business owner's site layout and design plan?
10. What are the main types of layout plans, and what should the entrepreneur focus on when designing the layout plan for a new business?
11. Compare and contrast the advantages and disadvantages of buying, building, or leasing space for a small business.

Questions for Critical Thinking

1. How can your business location affect customers' image and perception of your business?
2. The old adage "location, location, location" applies as well to cyberspace as it does to brick-and-mortar businesses. How does an Internet-based business influence its "location"? Which of the principles of location discussed in this chapter apply to e-businesses? What other factors do they have to deal with?

What Would You Do?

Jodi has a problem. She has decided to go into business for herself selling used books, videos, music CDs, and DVDs. She lives in a community of about 200,000 in the northeastern part of the United States. No other stores in the area specialize in the used products she will sell. Her community has a large regional shopping center with four anchor stores. Two sites the size she needs (approximately 2,000 square feet) are currently vacant in the mall.

The CBD is thriving, primarily with small, boutique-type stores. The atmosphere is pleasant, with many trees, flower beds, and artistic sculptures lining the streets. The Downtown Business Association does a good job of arranging events like parades and music festivals to draw people to the CBD. One site with 2,500 square feet is available in the CBD.

The community has two primary traffic arteries lined with stand-alone commercial businesses. One stand-alone site is available that has ample parking and a traffic count of approximately 80,000 cars per day passing at 35 mph. This site is the right size, but it is not available to lease; she would have to buy the building. Foot traffic in the mall is the highest, but restrictions and lease payments are by far higher than in the other locations. Not as many people pass by the downtown location, but rent is much cheaper as well.

Questions

1. From the information you have been provided, and considering the advantages and disadvantages of the different types of locations mentioned in this chapter, where would you recommend that Jodi locate? Provide justifications for your recommendation.
2. What additional information would you want to have to make this location decision?

14

Price and Promotion

CHAPTER LEARNING OUTCOMES

After reading this chapter, you should be able to:

1. Identify the three main considerations in setting a price for a product.

2. Explain what breakeven analysis is and why it is important for pricing in a small business.

3. Present examples of customer-oriented and internal-oriented pricing.

4. Explain why and how small businesses extend credit.

5. Describe the advertising, personal selling, public relations, and sales-promotion tools that a small business owner uses to compile a promotional mix.

Pricing and promotion are two critical components to the success of a small business. Let's look at how several entrepreneurs have successfully wrestled with both of these issues.

Zoobie Pets are cuddly toys for preschoolers that are also a pillow and a blanket. Two brothers, Reid and J.C. Smoot, invented Zoobies after watching their younger siblings as they travelled with their stuffed animals, pillows, and blankets. Zoobie Pets wrap all three into one. How did they let the world know about their product? Trade shows were important in getting the word out about the new toy, both domestically and internationally. Magazines, newspapers, and viral marketing were other key components in their promotional mix, as well as bloggers, in disseminating information on this new product. Reid and J.C. chose to sell their product only in the high-end market, using price to emphasize the quality of their Zoobie Pets.

Sayyid Nadimi and his two sons operate a very differing type of business—Social Smoke—a business that focuses on Americans' interest in the Middle Eastern

tradition of hookah smoking. Ali founded Social Smoke while he was a student at the University of Texas in Arlington, and it has become one of the fastest-growing suppliers in the international hookah market. This family business is capitalizing on the increasing interest in hookah lounges, up 400 percent since 1999. Since hookah smoking is a social event, customers coming into a hookah lounge will spend about twice as long as they would in a restaurant. While the customers are there, they will spend up to $16 an hour on shish, plus food and drink. The cost to the business is $2 for the shisha (flavoured herbs, fruits, and/or tobacco mixes smoked in hookah pipes), a significant markup.

The eighth fastest-growing industry hospitable for small businesses currently is niche bakeries. Adriano Lucas opened his bakery, The Best Chocolate Cake in the World, in New York City. Even before the grand opening, Lucas had been mentioned in the *New York Times* and *New York* magazine due to the huge interest by the local press, providing him with much-needed publicity. During their opening weekend, 400 chocolate cakes were purchased.

Kevin VanDeraa is the owner of CupCake, a bakery in Minneapolis. After conducting marketing research, he discovered that his target audience was going to want more than just cupcakes, even though he offers six different categories of them. So he added soups and sandwiches to his product line, as well as serving breakfast all day. In order to even out sales, he realized that soup in the winter and morning coffee year round would allow him a more stable cash flow with which to pay bills.

Promotion can include everything from publicity generated by the press for chocolate cake, to using the Web and trade shows to introduce your product. In the process, paying attention to costs and revenue is also essential. Learn more about both of these areas as you read through this chapter. How will you advertise and price your product in your small business?

Sources: Raven Hill, "How to Write a Bakery Business Plan," inc.com, July 20, 2010; "The Best Industries for Starting a Business Right Now," inc.com, retrieved August 8, 2010; Justin Martin, "Booming Hookah Biz Links China, Iran, Egypt—and Texas," cnnmoney.com, August 26, 2009; Gail Dutton, "Mass Appeal," entrepreneur.com, November 2008.

In the previous chapters, we discussed two of the Four P's of marketing: product and place. In this chapter, we will investigate the third and fourth components of the marketing mix: price and promotion. We will consider why price is one of the most flexible components of a business's marketing mix, factors that must be considered in setting prices, strategies related to pricing, the use of credit in buying and selling, and ways to use the various media in communicating with your customers.

We deal with prices every day. The dollars you exchanged for a cup of coffee on the way to class, the tuition you paid for the semester, and the money you earn from a job all represent a form of price for goods and services.

The Economics of Pricing

Price is the amount of money charged for a product. It represents what the consumer considers the *value* of the product to be worth to them. The value of a product depends on the benefits received compared with the monetary cost. People actually buy benefits—they buy what a product will do for them. If consumers bought on price alone, then no Cadillac convertibles, Denon stereo receivers, or Godiva chocolates would ever be sold, because less expensive substitutes exist. People buy premium products like these because they perceive them to have higher benefits and increased quality that delivers value despite the higher cost. Typical consumers do not want the *cheapest* product available—they want the *best* product for the most reasonable price.

Price differs from the other three components of the marketing mix in that the product, place, and promotion factors all add value to the customer and costs to your business. Pricing lets you recover those costs. Although the "right" price is actually more of a range between what the market will bear and what the product costs, many elements enter into the pricing decision. For example, the image of your business or product influences the price you can charge.

Even though the pricing decision is critical to the success of a business, many small business owners make pricing decisions poorly. Total reliance on "gut feeling" is inappropriate, but so is complete reliance on accounting costs that ignore what is happening in the marketplace—what the competition is doing and what customers demand.

Three important economic factors are involved in how much you can charge for your products: competition, customer demand, and costs. Let's take a closer look at how each of these forces can affect your small business.

Competition

Your competitors will play a big part in determining the success of your pricing strategy. The number of competitors and their proximity to your business influence what you can charge for your products, because the competition represents substitute choices to your customers. The more direct competition your business faces, the less control you have over your prices. Direct competition makes product differentiation necessary, so that you compete on points other than price.

So why will customers come to your store, brand, or product as opposed to the competition? What sets your product apart? The following five areas are good places to start when thinking about what differentiates your product from the competition:

1. *Price.* While you may not be able to compete with the big box stores, you do need to be sensitive to the economic climate. During a recession, consumers are much more careful about how they spend their scarce dollars. What is your competition doing in this arena? What can you do? Maybe you can bundle products, provide quantity discounts, provide frequent shopper rewards, and so forth.
2. *Added value.* How does your product or service add value to the customer. Is your product unique? Do you provide after-sale consultations? Can you provide one-stop shopping for more than one need? Does your price reflect this added value? Are you directly tying the added value to your price?
3. *Convenience.* How convenient are your location and your shopping hours for your customers? If your usual customer is a working mom, then you may need to open earlier in the morning so they can stop by after they have dropped off their children at school before they go to work, or maybe open two evenings a week and the weekends. Check out the lifestyles of your customers and add convenience for them in the shopping process. Convenience is something for which customers will pay.
4. *Trust.* Do you have a family business that has been around for 50 years? If so, then advertise that fact. This is one area where you may be able to beat Walmart and other big box stores, if you have been in the community longer. Local testimonials that attest to not only the quality of the product but also the service that accompanies that product can be useful. Your pricing strategy should then incorporate this strategy. The customer will pay more because your business will be around to take care of them long after the product sale.

5. *Community Member.* Do you participate in your local community? Maybe you sit on the school assessment committee or plant flowers at the local botanical garden. Demonstrate that you are very much a part of the community and plan to be so for a long time, and that you are giving back to the community. Again customers may be willing to pay more for a product when they know you are being a good steward in your community.

These are all factors that can help you to show your customers how your product or service is different from the competition and how your price reflects these areas. Going back to our definition, customers buy benefits. Make sure the benefits your business provides are greater than benefits the competition provides. Include price in this process but be aware that lower prices are not the only factor.[1]

Another factor in evaluating the competition can be the proximity of your competition. The closer the competition is geographically, the more influence it will have on your pricing. For example, if two service stations located across the street from each other had a price difference of 10 cents per gallon of gasoline, to which one would customers go? Conversely, the same price difference between stations located several miles apart may not have as dramatic an impact. Price competition presents a more difficult challenge for all businesses today because customers have more access to information about you and your competitors than you had about your own business even five years ago.[2]

The type of products sold will also have an impact on price competition. If you run a video rental business, then other video rental stores are not your only competition. In reality, your rivals include movie theaters, athletic events, and even the opera. Don't think of yourself as being in the video rental business—think of being in the entertainment business, because you are competing for entertainment dollars. Therefore, you should monitor not only what other video rental places are charging, but also what indirect, or alternative, entertainment services charge.

Today more small businesses are facing stiff competition from large chains like Walmart and Target. Walmart has more than 4,000 stores in the United States alone, employs 1.4 million people, and has 127 million consumers shopping at its stores every week.[3] No wonder small businesses feel intimidated. Can your small business compete? Of course you can. Probably not on price for identical items—the discounters have economy-of-scale advantages from mass purchasing and distribution that can knock a small business out of a head-to-head price war, but there are other areas where small businesses excel, including the ones we discussed earlier: added value, being seen as a good community citizen, flexibility, superior product selection, superior service, and variety to name a few.

Research shows that prices drop anywhere from 1 percent to 3 percent when Walmart enters an area and sales can drop anywhere from 5 percent to 13 percent, depending on the business. However, in one study, sales in eating establishments and home furnishings actually increased by 2 percent to 3 percent when Walmart came to town. The stores most negatively impacted by Walmart were mass-merchandising stores. So how do you compete? According to a study in the *Journal of Marketing Research*, two key factors are important. First, do not locate your business next to Walmart. The closer your business is to this large store, the more you will be negatively impacted. And second, don't carry the same product lines as Walmart. Walmart focuses on national mid-tier large market share products, and due to Walmart's price discounts you may not be able to compete against these brands. However you can compete in both the top-tier and the lower-tier brands. Most small businesses have more tightly defined their market niche, and by offering superior products and service, may still compete quite successfully.

"To survive in an industry dominated by giants, don't compete directly—differentiate. Offer your customers value—the best quality, service, and selection for their money."

Consider how Jayne Palmer took steps to ready her business, Gediman's Appliance, for the new competition when Walmart moved to her area of Bath, Maine. She increased advertising by 30 percent. She added a computer to track her inventory and linked it into General Electric Credit so that she could order directly with better credit terms. She extended the store's hours. She offered more credit to her customers. She built a television viewing room with space for children to play on the floor. Finally, she cut the low-end appliances from her inventory to avoid competing directly with Walmart on those items.

Demand

The second economic factor that affects the price you can charge for your products is *demand*—how much of your product do people want and what price are they willing to pay. Ordinarily as price goes up, people buy less of a product, and as price goes down, people are willing to buy more of a product, an inverse relationship. The ***demand curve*** graphically demonstrates this relationship between price and quantity demanded, and since the relationship is inverse, the demand curve has a downward slope. See Figure 14.1.

Price elasticity is an important factor to take into consideration when discussing pricing. It determines the impact a change of price will have on the quantity of your product you will sell. For some products, like soda pop, if the price goes down, when the product goes on sale, the consumer will buy considerably more of the product. On the other hand, milk is a product that we consume about the same quantity of regardless of the price increasing or decreasing. Price elasticity looks at this relationship between a change in price and the impact on quantity demanded. So if a small business owner has a product that is price sensitive or is elastic in economic terms, if the price is lowered, the consumer will buy more of the product, all other variables held constant. With an elastic product, though, the price should not be lowered, or put on sale, since the consumer will not buy much more of the product even if it is cheaper. You could lose money putting an inelastic product on sale, all other variables being held constant.

If sales rise or fall more than prices rise or fall in percentage terms, demand for your product is price elastic. For example, assume that the demand for your computer

demand curve
The number of units of a product that people would be willing to purchase at different price levels.

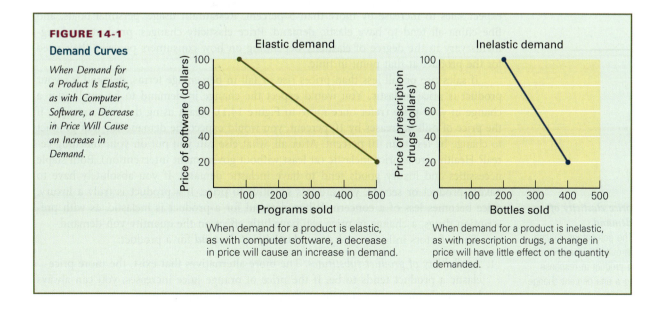

FIGURE 14-1

Demand Curves

When Demand for a Product Is Elastic, as with Computer Software, a Decrease in Price Will Cause an Increase in Demand.

When demand for a product is elastic, as with computer software, a decrease in price will cause an increase in demand.

When demand for a product is inelastic, as with prescription drugs, a change in price will have little effect on the quantity demanded.

Reality Check

Even in a Recession, Don't Give Away the Farm

Many small business owners make the mistake of assuming that in a down economy, the only answer to decreasing sales is to lower price. Not a good idea. Your price should be based upon your pricing strategy, and as such, any change in pricing should be made in order to facilitate accomplishing that strategy, not in response to the economy. Remember, customers buy benefits. Your job becomes, more than ever, to demonstrate to the consumer why they should be willing to pay the price you are asking for those benefits. Build your presentations around the benefits, not the price. A customer price objection just means that the customer does not yet understand how the benefits of the product will outweigh the cost. As the business owner, this is your job. Show them, not just tell them, how the product meets and exceeds their needs.

Another mistake made is to cut store hours and lay off good employees. If your store is not open, you cannot sell. Make sure you carefully evaluate the cost of your labor against potential sales. How many sales do you need in order to pay for that employee being in the store one more hour? And unless you plan to close your doors, hang on to your best employees, remembering that there is more than money you can use to persuade good employees to stay.

If you do offer discounts, do so only for first-time buyers or for one week only. Or better yet, offer free delivery or after-sale consultations, or a discount on their next trip to see you. Rather than lower your price, which can also then damage your product perception, find other ways to lower the cost to the consumer, or add more value for the same price and make sure your customer recognizes the value you are adding. And remember, always treat your customers well. Increasing attention paid to customers and increased attention to detail may not cost you anything but may return large rewards to you. Remember, without customers, your business fails, regardless of the price you are charging.

Sources: "6 Secrets to Achieving Entrepreneurial Success," inc.com, retrieved August 5, 2010; Ryan McCarthy, "Pricing: How Low Can you Really Go?" inc.com, March 1, 2009; Norm Brodsky, "Surviving the Recession," inc.com, March 1, 2009; Grant Cardone, "Get Past the Budget Roadblock," entrepreneur.com, October 29, 2009; and Mark Ritson, "Should You Launch a Fighter Brand?" *Harvard Business Review*, October 2009.

software is elastic (see Figure 14.1 again). If you drop your price by 5 percent, you would expect sales to increase by more than 5 percent. Restaurant usage, personal boats, and fine china all tend to have elastic demand. Price elasticity changes; products and segments vary in the degree of elasticity depending on how consumers perceive their need for the product at that point in time.

If sales rise or fall less than prices rise or fall in percentage terms, demand for your product is price inelastic. You would expect the change in demand to be small after a change in your price (refer once more to Figure 14.1). Again using the milk example, if the price of milk increases by 10 percent, you would expect the demand for that product to change by less than 10 percent. After all, what else can you put on your morning cereal? Health care is price inelastic (at least without government intervention). Both staple necessities and luxury goods tend to have inelastic demand. If you absolutely have to have a product or service, you are less sensitive to price. If a product is truly a luxury, price becomes less of a concern. When demand for a product is inelastic, as with prescription drugs, a change in price will have little effect on the quantity you demand.

Three factors influence the ***price elasticity of demand*** for a product:

1. *Availability of product substitutes.* The more alternatives that exist, the more price elastic a product tends to be. If the price of orange juice increases, you can always have apple juice, pomegranate juice or even tea, making it elastic.

price elasticity of demand

The percentage change in quantity demanded for a product in response to a one percent change in price.

2. *Necessity of the product.* Necessary and luxury goods both tend to be price inelastic.
3. *The share of the purchase to the consumer's total budget.* Salt and toothpicks are inelastic since they represent such a small percentage compared to your overall budget.[4]

The theory of the elasticity of demand is important for small business owners to understand in setting prices. How easily your customers can do without your product or how readily they can use something else in its place will affect what you can charge. Price elasticity can also let you know whether or not putting your product on sale will increase total revenue. Market research can provide price-sensitivity information about your product and should be evaluated for your product and services.

Costs

Earlier we stated that the "right" price is actually a range of possible prices. What your competition charges and what consumers are willing to pay set the ceiling for your price range. Your costs establish the floor for your price range. If you cannot cover your costs and make a profit, you will not stay in business.

Your total costs fall into two general categories: fixed costs and variable costs.

$$\text{Total costs} = \text{Fixed costs} + \text{Variable costs}$$

fixed costs
Costs that do not change with the number of sales made.

variable costs
Costs that change in direct proportion to sales.

Fixed costs remain constant no matter how many goods you sell. In the short run, your fixed costs are the same whether you sell a million units or none at all. Costs such as rent, property taxes, and utilities are fixed. *Variable costs*, in contrast, rise and fall in direct proportion to sales. Sales commissions, materials, and labor tend to be variable costs.

Inc. magazine columnist Norm Brodsky (if you are not reading his monthly feature yet, start now) warns against falling into what he calls the *capacity trap*—that is, accepting a lower price than usual because you have unused capacity. Unused capacity can take the form of an empty warehouse, a truck that is sitting idle, or a machine that is used only occasionally. When the opportunity arises to sell that capacity at a reduced rate, few people would refuse. They think about the money to be made on something that would otherwise go to waste but ignore the problems they create by charging significantly less than the service is worth. Along the way, they ignore the *cost of capital*; we invest in items like trucks and warehouses to make more money from them than if we had bought something else. There are also *opportunity costs*; low-margin sales tend to crowd out high-margin sales. For example, if business is slow in your small job shop and you take on work at half your normal rate to avoid your machinery sitting idle, what happens when a full-pay job comes along? You don't have time to tackle it. Finally, do you think your existing customers won't find out that new customers are paying less than they are or have been for the same product or service? They will—and they will not be amused; they may feel betrayed. Certainly, they will demand the same discount. Bottom line: Don't erode your margins.[5]

"Bottom line: Don't erode your margins."

Breakeven Analysis

breakeven point (BEP)
The point at which total costs equal total revenue and the business neither makes nor loses money.

By using the three cost figures discussed earlier, in a breakeven analysis, you can find the volume of sales you will need to cover your total costs. Your **breakeven point (BEP)** in sales volume is the point at which your total revenue equals total costs. In other words, how much of your product or service do you have to sell in order to cover all your costs? At breakeven, you are not making a profit. However, you are able to pay both your fixed and variable costs. So if your breakeven point is 35 CDs, that number means you must sell 35 CDs just to be able to pay your costs.

Figure 14.2 is an example of a BEP graph. Notice that the fixed-costs line runs horizontally because fixed costs don't change with sales volume. Fixed costs have to be paid regardless of the amount of product sold. Fixed costs are fixed—they do not change. The total-costs line begins where the fixed-costs line meets the *y*-axis of the graph, showing that even if you have sold nothing, you still have costs: your fixed costs. Total costs rise from that point at an angle, as variable costs and sales increase. The area between the total-costs line and the fixed-costs line represents your variable costs. The revenue line represents the number of units you will sell at any given price level—information you can derive from your demand curve. The point at which the revenue line meets the total-costs line is your breakeven point. The area above the BEP between the revenue and total-costs lines shows profit. The area below the BEP between the revenue and total-costs lines represents loss.

The slope and shape of the revenue line for your business will vary depending on your customer demand. The information needed to draw this line can come either from sales history or, if hard data are not available, from your personal best "guesstimate" of how much people will buy. You can also plot other revenue lines based on different selling prices. The revenue line in Figure 14.2 is based on product sales. Let's use the example of compact disks (CDs) selling for $13 each. You can also find your BEP for units with the following formula:

$$\text{BEP (units)} = \frac{\text{Total fixed costs}}{\text{Unit price} - \text{Average variable cost}}$$

where average variable cost equals total variable cost divided by quantity.

Using the data from Figure 14.2, we could calculate the BEP in units for a new CD of Christmas songs from Hatten and His Yodeling Goats. Total fixed costs to produce

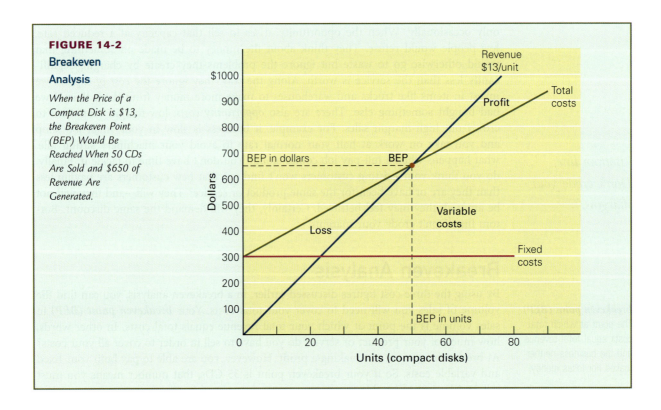

FIGURE 14-2

Breakeven Analysis

When the Price of a Compact Disk is $13, the Breakeven Point (BEP) Would Be Reached When 50 CDs Are Sold and $650 of Revenue Are Generated.

this musical masterpiece are $300. Variable costs run $7 per unit. Charging $13 per CD, we would have to sell 50 CDs to break even on the venture. (Would 50 people pay $13 to hear yodeling goats, or should Hatten keep his day job?)

$$\text{BEP (units)} = \frac{300}{13 - 7} = 50$$

If 50 people will not buy this CD, not only should Hatten keep his day job, he will also have to pay the $300 out of his own pocket since the fixed costs must be paid, even if he does go back to his day job. Fixed costs deserve careful consideration since even if you shut the doors to your business, you will likely still be paying the fixed costs incurred.

To calculate the BEP point in dollars, we need to find the average variable cost of our product. This is done by taking the total variable costs ($350) and dividing by the quantity (50). The following formula is used to calculate the BEP in dollars:

$$\text{BEP (units)} = \frac{\text{Total fixed costs}}{1 - \dfrac{\text{Average variable costs}}{\text{Unit price}}}$$

For our struggling musician's CD, we would find that at $13 per CD, the BEP would be $650.

$$\text{BEP (dollars)} = \frac{300}{1 - \dfrac{7}{3}} = 650$$

Again, unless Hatten feels certain he can sell $650 dollars worth of CDs to cover the fixed costs, he might want to explore another business venture.

What would happen to our BEP in dollars and our BEP in units if we changed the selling price to $20 each or $11 each? At $20 per CD, we would break even at only $400 in sales. At $11 per CD, we would break even at $880. Figure 14.3 illustrates what happens at different price levels.

Breakeven analysis is a useful tool in giving you a guideline for price setting. It can help you see how different volume levels will affect costs and profits. It can also help you to determine the amount of fixed costs you are willing to incur for your business. Let's say you want to open a small lawn-mowing service. You want to purchase a brand-new 2011 truck, trailer, and riding lawn mower. Regardless of whether you mow one lawn or 50 a day, these costs will have to be paid. Using breakeven analysis, you determine that in order to cover your costs, you must mow 50 lawns a day. Now you need to determine if there are 50 lawns to mow and whether you can logistically mow that many every day. If you cannot, then you have some options, like buying a used truck, trailer, and mower in order to reduce the fixed costs. Or you may realize, with the competition available both in providing the service and the price you can charge, a lawn-mowing business is not feasible. Breakeven analysis can be a quick initial check on the financial viability of your business idea.

Another use for breakeven analysis is to tell you how many units you need to sell to earn your desired return. If Hatten and His Yodeling Goats wanted a return of $1,000, how many units would need to be sold?

$$\text{Target return} = \frac{\text{Total fixed cost + Desired profit}}{\text{Unit price} - \text{Average variable cost}}$$

$$\$1,000 \text{ return} = \frac{300 + 1,000}{13 - 7} = 217 \text{ units}$$

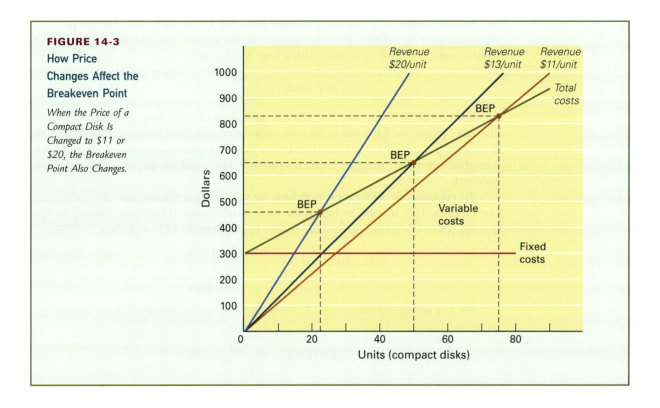

FIGURE 14-3

How Price Changes Affect the Breakeven Point

When the Price of a Compact Disk Is Changed to $11 or $20, the Breakeven Point Also Changes.

When the sales price is $13 per CD, 217 CDs would have to be sold to generate a return of $1,000. Again, based upon your marketing research, what is the likelihood that many CDs can be sold? So now you have options. You can cut your fixed costs, raise your price, or be willing to accept less than the $1,000 return.[6]

Pricing-Setting Techniques

After taking competition, consumer demand, and your costs into consideration, you have made a start toward establishing your "right" price. You have a feel for what the price floor and price ceiling might be, but the price you finally choose will depend on the objectives and strategies you choose to pursue—what you are trying to accomplish in your business.

While one of the most difficult decisions you will make as a small business owner is the price you charge for your product, it is also one of the most critical decisions in the success of your business. Consider the following points when looking at product pricing.

The reason you are in business is to make money, which means you have to sell enough product at a high enough price to more than cover costs. Pricing your product too high can take you out of a market because consumers will not pay that much for your product or your competition will lower their prices. However, pricing your product too low can also cause problems since all costs, both fixed and variable, may not be covered. Consumers can also see low prices as an indication of low quality, to be discussed shortly.

How much will your customers pay? What is the income of your target market? Where does your product fit into their budget? What is your competition doing to lure your customers away?

Where is the market for your product going? Will sales increase? Are substitutes available? What is the likelihood other competitors will show up? Is it a fad item that

"The reason you are in business is to make money, which means you have to sell enough product at a high enough price to more than cover costs."

Reality Check

What Price Is Too Low … or Too High?

Damon Risucci is not a person who backs down from a challenge. When he started his first health club in 1990, he was only 24 and had more experience playing guitar than running a business. Synergy Fitness Clubs has since become a thriving operation, with three upscale New York City locations.

But when it came to raising prices, Risucci turned into the proverbial 97-pound weakling. For more than 10 years he kept his membership fees at $49.99 per month—about half of his competitors' rates—even though he had a rockin' Midtown Manhattan location and escalating rent and utilities. He says, "We thought our prices had to be low. It was almost a core belief."

Finally, after yet another month of reviewing financial statements and talking with staff and customers, Risucci gritted his teeth and did it: He raised monthly fees for new members to $57.99 and personal training sessions by 20 percent. The result? Not a single one of his 9,500 customers even threatened to leave. New customers have continued to join at the same, if not an increased, rate.

Risucci still offers great value, and his business represents another example of people being willing to pay for quality.

At some point, anyone selling anything will hear the objection, "We can't afford your price." How do you respond? Marketing entrepreneur Dann Ilicic, of Wow Branding, says, "We present three price options in our proposals. If they still say we're too expensive, that means we haven't demonstrated the value of what we're doing. Nothing's expensive if it provides you a return greater than the cost." Good observation—problems with price are not usually about price.

Sources: Stephanie Clifford, "Putting the Performance in Sales Performance," *Inc.,* February 2007, 87–95; and Nadine Heintz, "Flexing Your Pricing Muscles," *Inc.,* February 2004, 25–26.

---

won't be around long? What is your goal in pricing? Are you trying to gain market share? Are you conveying a quality product? How much product are you trying to sell? All these questions tie back into what is your pricing goal?[7]

You have surely heard the old joke about the guy who buys 100 watermelons for $100 and sells them in bunches of 10 for $10. When asked how he expects to make money, he replies, "I'll make it up in volume." Okay, so it's not that funny, but you would be amazed how many people think they can grow their businesses merely by pricing their products cheaper than the competition. They assume that low prices will generate enough sales to make up for lower margins.

Setting your prices too low is a dangerous trap to fall into. Take a hypothetical example: You think that some product is too expensive, so you decide to go into business selling that item for less than your competitors. If you sell for less, you have lower profit margins. Lower profit margins, in turn, mean less cash flow. Will you have an adequate cushion if an expense increases? After all, rents go up, utilities raise their rates, and so on. With lower profit margins, you need to cut costs—but where? Will you reduce wages and benefits? If so, will you be able to hire and retain good employees? Will you cut marketing costs? Will customers keep coming in the door, and, if they do, what kind of customers will they be? Low-price shoppers are the most fickle and most likely to switch to the next company that can offer your product for five cents less. Remember, we discussed customers buy benefits. You can add value by more than just lowering price. According to Grant Cardone, "Lowering your price may work temporarily, but it's not a successful formula for growing profits.… When the value of your product exceeds the value of their money, you'll get the sale."[8]

As you see, price can't be everything—but you can't ignore it, either. Instead, you need a bona fide pricing strategy. Pricing strategies fall into two broad categories: customer oriented and internal oriented.

Customer-Oriented Pricing Strategies

Customer-oriented pricing strategies focus on target markets and factors that affect the demand for products. Such strategies include penetration, skimming, and psychological pricing. Both penetration and skimming strategies are based on knowing price elasticity, discussed earlier in this chapter. With an inelastic product, since there are not usually many substitutes, a skimming strategy can be used, setting prices higher. Higher prices can also purposefully be used to bring the customer's attention to specific product advantages. For elastic products that are much more price sensitive, penetration pricing may be a more effective strategy since even a small decrease in price can increase the demand for the product.[9]

Suppose you have the following pricing objectives:

- Increase sales.
- Increase traffic in your store.
- Discourage competitors from entering your market.

penetration pricing
Setting the price of a new product lower than expected to gain fast market share.

To accomplish these objectives and gain rapid market share, **penetration pricing** is the most appropriate strategy. Penetration pricing entails setting prices below what you might expect to encourage customers to initially try your product. This strategy is designed to keep competition from entering the market for your product. Although you make less profit on each unit, the trade-off is to remove the incentive for competition to enter, thereby, it is hoped, helping you build a long-term position in the market.

Suppose that you have a different set of pricing objectives:

- Maximize short- or long-run profit.
- Recover product development costs quickly.

price skimming
Setting the price of a new product higher than expected to recover development costs.

If these are your objectives and you have a truly unique product, a strategy of **price skimming** may be appropriate. Price skimming involves setting your price high when you believe that customers are relatively price insensitive or when there is little competition for consumers to compare prices against. Skimming helps recover high development costs, so businesses with new-to-the-world inventions often use this strategy. It can also encourage consumers to look at your product and see what features differ from your product that are allowing you to charge a higher price. When purposefully used as a strategy, skimming can create a curiosity in your product that causes the consumer to do further research and discover the added benefits. Home electronics, for example, are often introduced using a skimming strategy. Think of the price declines in personal computers, cell phones, and DVDs. These products usually have high development costs, but their unit costs fall as production increases. Of course, consumers have to be willing to pay a premium to be one of the first to own these new products. Skimming is not a long-term strategy. Eventually competition forces prices down.

Finally, suppose you have these pricing objectives:

- Stabilize market prices.
- Establish your company's position in the market.
- Build an image for your business or product.
- Develop a reputation for being fair with suppliers and customers.

psychological pricing
Setting the price of a product in a way that will alter its perception by customers.

prestige pricing
Psychological pricing strategy used with goods whose quality is difficult to determine by inspection or for products about which consumers have little solid information.

odd pricing
Psychological pricing strategy in which goods are priced at, say, $9.99 rather than $10.00 in the belief that the price will seem lower than it really is.

reference pricing
Psychological pricing strategy common in retailing goods for which consumers have an idea of what the price "should be."

price lining
Grouping product prices into ranges, such as low-, medium-, and high-priced items.

markup
The amount added to the cost of a product in setting the final price. It can be based on selling price or on cost.

To accomplish these objectives, you may employ one of the ***psychological pricing*** strategies, which aim to influence the consumer's reaction toward prices of products. Such strategies include prestige pricing, odd pricing, and reference pricing.

People often equate quality with price, a belief that has led to a practice called ***prestige pricing***. Prestige pricing is especially effective with goods whose quality is difficult to determine by inspection or for products that consumers have little solid information about. Products as diverse as jewelry, perfume, beer, and smoke detectors, or the services of law firms, can all be prestige priced.

In an experiment at Harvard Business School, graduate students were given two products, organic lettuce and free-trade coffee. When these two products were priced at an 80 percent premium, the graduate students were able to recall twice as much information about the products and reasons/justifications why 80 percent more could be charged for those products. The students were also much more passionate about and willing to spend more dollars for these products. When products were priced 10 percent higher or over 100 percent higher, the students did not spend the time exploring the product benefits and simply chose their usual product. Pricing can be raised as long as it is neither too high nor too low.[10]

We are more likely to see goods priced at $4.98, $17.89, or $49.95 than at $5.00, $18.00, or $50.00—this is ***odd pricing***. Research has yet to prove a positive effect of odd pricing, but proponents believe that consumers see $99.99 as a better deal than $100.00. Sales of some products seem to benefit from *even pricing* if you are trying to convey the image of quality. For example, pricing a diamond ring at $18,000 gives the appearance of being above squabbling over loose change.

Reference pricing is common in retail goods for which consumers have an idea of what the price "should be" and have a "usual" price for that item in mind. As discussed already, a product's price is supported by the value it generates for the customer; with reference pricing, however, the price can be changed without affecting the value. For example, a 12-pack of Coca-Cola is a commodity well recognized by most shoppers, who have a good idea of what a package of 12 cans of Coke is worth. If the price is dropped, customers are attracted to the product; conversely, if it is raised above that reference point, they are repelled.

If your customers are price sensitive to comparison prices of competing items, you may choose to use ***price lining***. An example of price lining would be a men's clothing store that has ties at three different price points, such as $24.95, $33.95, and $44.95.

Internal-Oriented Pricing Strategies

Pricing strategies that are internal oriented are based on your business's financial needs and costs rather than on the needs or wants of your target markets. If you use these strategies, make sure that you don't price your products out of the marketplace. Remember that consumers don't care what your costs are; they care only about the value they receive. Internal-oriented strategies include cost-plus pricing and target-return pricing.

Cost-Plus Pricing   Probably the most common form of pricing is adding a specified percentage, a fixed fee, or ***markup***, to the cost of the item. Although this type of pricing, called *cost-plus pricing*, has always been common in retailing and wholesaling, manufacturers also use this relatively simple approach. Markup can be based on either *selling price* or *cost*, and it is important to distinguish between the two.

For example, if an item costs $1.00 and the selling price is $1.50, the markup on selling price is 33.3 percent. Fifty cents is one-third of $1.50. However, using the same

Manager's Notes

Customers—Your Key to Sales

- Sales are down, expenses are up, and what do you do next? Focus on your customer. Keep the ones you have and find new ones to purchase the products and services you are providing. And how do you do that?

- Make sure you know your target market. What benefits are most important to this group? Listen to what they are saying, and tailor your product and your sales pitch to meet their needs.

- Create a consumer experience. From the time the customer walks through your door until they exit that same door, ensure they have a pleasant experience. Greet them with a smile. Helpful, friendly, as well as knowledgeable staff can make all the difference. Provide a cup of coffee or a piece of candy at the register. Little things can make a difference.

- Know your competition. Long before a customer ever asks, you should be able to articulate why your business is the better value for the money spent. Make sure you are providing the best value for the hard-earned dollars you are receiving from your customer.

- Work toward long-term relationships. Go into every transaction with the intent of furthering a long-term relationship with this customer. Focus not only on what you can sell them today, but what they will need down the road, not the product that makes you the most money today. Repeat customers are much easier to retain than finding new customers. If you are not sure, ask. Listen to your customers, and ask them what they need. They will tell you and often it may be information you will not get anywhere else. Plus, it goes a long way toward building that long-term relationship. People like to be listened to and have their ideas considered.

- Treat your customers like gold … they are the key to increasing sales.

Sources: Inc. Staff, "10 Ways to Support Your Best Customers," inc.com, August 3, 2010; Sydney Barrows, "Meet—or Exceed—Your Customer's Expectations," entrepreneur.com, June 21, 2010; Elizabeth Wasserman, "How to Find New Customers and Increase Sales," inc.com, December 1, 2009; and John Grossmann, "There's No Such Thing as a Wrong Number," *Inc.*, July/August 2010.

figures, the markup on cost is 50 percent. Fifty cents is one-half of $1.00. Markup based on cost makes your markup appear higher, even though the amounts are exactly the same. Most businesses base markup on selling price.

Effective use of markup depends on your ability to calculate the *profit margin* you need to cover costs. Formulas useful in calculating markup include the following:

$$\text{Selling price} = \text{Cost} + \text{Markup}$$
$$\text{Markup} = \text{Selling price} - \text{Cost}$$
$$\text{Cost} = \text{Selling price} - \text{Markup}$$

Target-Return Pricing If you have accurate information on how many units you will sell and what your fixed and variable costs will be, *target-return pricing* will allow you to set your selling price to produce a given rate of return. To calculate a target-return price, add your fixed costs and the dollar amount you wish to make, divide by the number of units you intend to sell, and then add the variable cost of your product.

$$\text{Target return price} = [(\text{Fixed costs} + \text{Target return}) \div \text{Unit sales}] + \text{Variable cost}$$

As an example, suppose demand for your product is 5,000 units. To meet this demand, you need a target return of $100,000. Your fixed costs are $200,000 and your variable costs run $50 per unit. Using this strategy, your price would be

$$\frac{200,000 + 100,000}{5,000} + 50 = 6 + 50$$
$$= 110 = \text{Your selling price}$$

Creativity in Pricing

The importance of being proactive and creative in running your business is a theme that runs throughout this book. The need for creativity can apply to pricing as well. The key to creativity is breaking out of thought processes that keep you in ruts, such as the cliché "That's not the way it's done in my type of business." To be creative in your pricing, look at techniques and practices of pricing used in different types of businesses and ask yourself, "How can that concept be applied to my business?"

Harvard Business Review offers four suggestions when pricing your product:

- Use Price to Highlight Product Advantages—Offer to add antioxidants to your smoothies for 50 cents extra. You can use this to demonstrate the health benefits of your smoothies, and the addition of an additional health benefit, and increase your price at the same time.
- Overprice to Make Consumers Curious—Let's say you are looking at purchasing a pound of fudge, and as you look at the choices you notice one is $2.00 more expensive. You will probably spend a few moments trying to figure out what is different about this product. Perhaps it is made with organic products. Now, as a consumer, you can decide if that benefit is worthwhile to you. The increased price has encouraged you to ask additional questions.
- Price Your Product in Pieces—This is a great opportunity to demonstrate how each additional feature of your product provides more benefits to the customer. So you can offer the cabinet with a countertop in Formica or granite with a differing price for each. The difference in price allows you to show why the granite countertop, though more expensive, has more benefits.[11]

To begin this process, look at Table 14.1, the Creative Pricing Primer, to take note of how each approach could apply to your business.

Credit Policies

After establishing your pricing practices comes an even more important task: deciding how you will get customers to pay for their purchases. Payment methods include cash, check, or credit.

Obviously, accepting only cash really cuts down on those bad debts. But the trend is toward consumers carrying *less* cash, not more, so a cash-only policy will probably turn off many customers who would like to purchase with another form of payment. Most small businesses accept checks with adequate identification, such as a phone number and driver's license number, in case the bank returns the check for insufficient funds. For bookkeeping purposes, checks are treated the same as cash and actually make bank deposits easier.

The main reasons for your small business to extend credit are to make sales to customers you would not have otherwise reached and to increase the volume and frequency of sales to existing customers.

TABLE 14-1 Creative Pricing Primer

PRICING APPROACH	HOW IT WORKS	EXAMPLES
1. Bundling or unbundling	Sell products or services together as packages or break them apart and price accordingly.	Season tickets; stereo equipment; car rentals charging for air conditioning
2. Time-period pricing	Adjust price up or down during specific times to spur or acknowledge changes in demand.	Off-season travel fares (to build demand); peak-period fees on bank ATMs (to shift demand)
3. Trial pricing	Make it easy and lower the risk for a customer to try out what you sell.	Three-month health club starter memberships; low, nonrefundable "preview fees" on training videos
4. Image pricing	Sometimes the customer wants to pay more, so you price accordingly	Most expensive hotel room in a city; a private-label vitamin's raise in price to increase unit sales by signaling quality to shoppers
5. Accounting-system pricing	Structure price to make it more salable within a business's buying systems.	Bill in phases so no single invoice exceeds an authorization threshold; classify elements so pieces get charged to other line items
6. Value-added price packages	Include free "value-added" services to appeal to bargain shoppers, without lowering price.	A magazine's offering advertisers free merchandising tie-ins when they buy ad space at rate-card prices
7. Pay-one-price	Unlimited use of a service or product, for one set fee.	Amusement parks; office-copier service contracts; salad bars
8. Constant promotional	Although a "regular" price exists, no one ever pays it.	Consumer electronics retailers' pricing always matching "lowest price" in town; always offering one pizza free when customer buys one at regular price
9. Price performance	Amount customers pay is determined by the performance or value they receive.	Money managers' being paid profits; offering a career-transition guide for $80 and allowing buyers to ask for any amount refunded after use
10. Change the standard	Rather than adjust price, adjust the standard to make your price seem different (and better).	A magazine clearinghouse's selling a $20 subscription for "four payments of only $4.99"
11. Shift costs to your customer	Pass on ancillary costs directly to your customer, and do not include those costs in your price.	A consulting firm's charging a fee and then rebilling all mail, phone, and travel costs directly to client
12. Variable pricing tied to a creative variable	Set up a "price per" pricing schedule tied to a related variable.	Children's haircuts at 10 cents per inch of the child's height; marina space billed at $25 per foot for a boat
13. Different names for different price segments	Sell essentially the same product, under different names, to appeal to different price segments.	Separate model numbers or variations of the same TV for discounters, department stores, and electronics stores
14. Captive pricing	Lock in your customer by selling the system cheap, and then profit by selling high-margin consumables.	The classic example: selling razors at cost, with all the margin made on razor blade sales
15. Product-line pricing	Establish a range of price points within your line. Structure the prices to encourage customers to buy your highest-profit product or service.	Luxury-car lines (high-end models enhance prestige of entire line but are priced to encourage sale of more profitable low end)
16. Differential pricing	Charge each customer or each customer segment what each will pay.	In new-car sales, a deal for every buyer; Colorado lift tickets sold locally at a discount, at full price for fly-ins
17. Quality discount	Set up a standard pricing practice, which can be done several ways.	Per-unit discount on all units, as with article reprints; discounts only on the units above a certain level, as with record clubs
18. Fixed, then variable	Institute a "just-to-get-started" charge, followed by a variable charge.	Taxi fares; phone services tied to usage
19. "Don't break that price point!"	Price just below important thresholds for the buyer, to give a perception of lower price.	Charging $499 for a suit; $195,000 instead of $200,000 for a design project

Note: Once you've been creative, make sure you're covered. The most important aspect of any pricing approach is that it be legal and ethical. Check with your legal counsel.

Extending Credit to Your Customers

Should you extend credit to your customers? Good question. Do your competitors? Will your sales increase enough to pay the finance charges? Will sales increase enough to cover the bad debts you will incur? Can you extend credit and still maintain a positive cash flow? Will credit sales smooth out fluctuations in sales volume?

Credit is broken down into two basic categories: trade credit and consumer credit.

trade credit
Credit extended from one business to another.

Trade Credit **Trade credit** refers to sales terms that one business extends to another for purchasing goods. As a small business owner, consider trade credit from both directions—extended to you from vendors and that you may extend to your customers. If you can purchase goods/services and are allowed to take 30, 60, or 90 days to pay for them, you have essentially obtained a loan for those items for that time period. Many new businesses can take advantage of trade credit even when no other form of financing is available. Be warned, however, that habitual late payment or nonpayment may cause your suppliers to cut off your trade credit and place your business on a COD—cash on delivery—basis.

If you extend credit to your business customers, you will need an accounts receivable system to keep cash flowing into your business. A very easy trap that growing new businesses fall into is the thought, "Get the sales now; work on improving profit margins later." This trap is especially serious for service businesses, whose largest expense is labor, which must be paid when the service is provided, not when you the business owner are paid by the customer. Manufacturers also suffer from slow collection due to the long time lag between purchasing raw materials, labor, and inventory and the actual sale of the product. Not collecting your accounts receivable will negatively impact your cash flow and your ability to pay your expenses. If you don't collect on sales, they aren't sales.

"If you don't collect on sales, they aren't sales."

Trade credit can be offered in several forms: extended payment periods and terms, goods offered on consignment, payment not required until goods are sold. Credit lines are popular ways for one business to receive trade credit from another.

consumer credit
Credit extended by retailers to the ultimate customers for the purchase of products or services.

Consumer Credit You have several choices regarding **consumer credit**, which is offered to your ultimate customers rather than to other businesses. You can carry the debt yourself, you can rely on a financial institution such as a bank to loan money to your customers, or you can accept credit cards.

If you wish to carry the debt yourself, you can set up an *open charge account* for customers. Customers take possession of the goods, and you bill them. Invoices are usually sent out monthly. You can encourage early payment by offering cash discounts or punishing late payment with finance charges. Open accounts must be managed carefully. As noted in Chapter 8, open accounts can absolutely kill cash flow and drain the life out of your business.

An *installment account* is frequently offered to customers who are purchasing big-ticket items (such as autos, boats, and appliances). Customers rarely have enough cash to pay up front for such items. With an installment account, they make a down payment and follow with monthly payments on the unpaid balance plus interest for an extended period of time. This type of financing is not quite as dangerous as the open account, because the product typically serves as collateral. Generally, small businesses exist to sell their products, whereas financial institutions are in business to sell money—so let them handle installment loans.

Alternatively, you may extend a *line of credit* to your customers. This system operates like a revolving credit account: You approve credit purchases for each customer up to a certain dollar limit. Lines of credit allow customers to buy goods without going through a new credit check for each purchase. Finance charges are paid on the unpaid balance monthly. Extending lines of credit can reduce the amount of paper in your credit application process, because a new application is not required for each purchase. This type of financing allows you to control the total amount of credit you extend.

To avoid the expense and inconvenience of maintaining your own accounts receivable, you can rely on *credit cards* as your source of consumer credit. Consumers' use of cash and checks is decreasing as a percentage of total consumer spending, whereas the use of credit and debit cards is skyrocketing. According to the Federal Reserve Bank of Boston, 80 percent of consumers currently hold a debit card with 78 percent of consumers owning a credit card.[12] Debit cards are increasing in popularity and have the added benefit that the funds move to your account from the customer's account more quickly. It is estimated that in 2010, 52 percent of all payment-card transactions will be debit card transactions.[13]

A new player in consumer payment is *cell phones* used in place of cash. Customers buying a train ticket, picking up a newspaper, and grabbing a cup of coffee on their way to work just wave their handset and your business has their money. This practice offers a lot more convenience than the consumer fumbling for money and waiting for change, or using plastic and having to tap in numbers or sign a slip of paper. If your target market is between the ages of 18 and 34, you may want to consider taking this type of payment since by 2014, it is estimated the Gen Y consumer will be making 40 percent of all transactions.[14]

Convenience for customers comes at a price for businesses, however. Businesses must pay a percentage of each sale to the credit card company handling the sale. Although card companies offer discount rates for small businesses, transaction and statement fees will increase the amount you pay. The percentage most small businesses pay to credit card companies varies according to the number of transactions made, but most small businesses are charged between 1.5 percent and 5 percent. Besides the percentage fee, each transaction may cost you anywhere between $.25 and $.50 as well as a minimum monthly transaction fee, plus a variety of set-up and other fees.[15] Make sure you understand the fee structure as well as the differing amounts you will be required to pay in order for your customers to use credit cards.

Online Credit Checks For business credit requests, the Yahoo! Web search site lists several merchant credit services that you can access through the Web link capability. Just point your mouse to the one you want to investigate and click. In addition, Dun & Bradstreet provides a free search of millions of U.S. companies. Then, for a nominal fee, you can receive a Business Background Report that lists important credit information about the company you're investigating.

For about $300 per year, you can join the National Association of Credit Management, a membership organization that researches and reports on many small firms that are often overlooked by larger credit agencies. As a member, you can get a comprehensive report on a particular firm from the database, which includes about 6.5 million firms.

Collecting Overdue Accounts

Bill collecting is never fun, but it is critical for small businesses. The longer bills go unpaid, the worse your chances of collecting on the debt (see Figure 14.4).

Begin your collection process by telephone. On large accounts, call a couple of weeks after the receipt has been sent to verify with the customer the invoice is correct. If you don't receive a check after 30 days, call again. Create a sense of urgency that the bill must be paid. Try to get a commitment for a certain amount by a specific day, like $100 by the 25th of the month. That puts the burden on the customer. If the customer

> *"Consumers' use of cash and checks is decreasing as a percentage of total consumer spending, whereas the use of credit and debit cards is skyrocketing."*

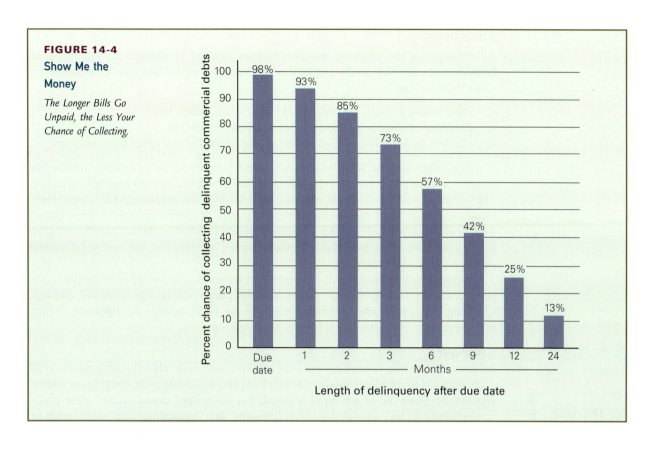

FIGURE 14-4

Show Me the Money

The Longer Bills Go Unpaid, the Less Your Chance of Collecting.

is overdue, do not extend more credit.[16] Fifty-five percent of businesses are calling their customers more often in order to receive payment, while 35 percent have implemented late fees. Twenty-nine percent of respondents are no longer taking orders from late-paying customers.[17] If repeated calls lead you to believe that the customer is playing games, with little intention of paying what she owes, you have five choices: a letter service, an attorney, small claims court, a collection agency, or writing it off. Always remain professional and try to stay on friendly terms. You can say something like "I really busted my tail to get the delivery to you on time. Will you please help us serve other customers by sending a check?"

To facilitate collections, pay attention to your invoices and credit applications. Always print your late-payment service charges on your invoices. Include a venue provision on your invoices if you are selling goods out of state so that any court case concerning the sale will be heard in a court of your choice. State the specific number of days a customer has to notify you of any problems with the shipment.

On your credit application form, ask customers to sign a release that authorizes creditors to disclose relevant information. This step will help you to spot credit problems in advance.

Promotion

The goal of a company's promotional efforts is to communicate with target markets. You have four major tools available when developing your *promotional mix*: advertising, personal selling, public relations, and sales promotions. The weight you choose to give to each of these tools will depend on your type of business.

Advertising

Advertising is a way to bring attention to your product or business by publishing or broadcasting a message to the public through various media. Your choices of media include the following:

- *Print media:* newspapers, magazines, direct mail, Yellow Pages
- *Broadcast media:* radio, television, or computer billboards
- *Outdoor media:* billboards or posters placed on public and other transportation

The habits of your target market will affect your choice of advertising media. For example, if your target market is teenagers, online would be the most appropriate choice. The nature of your product will also help to determine the media selected. Does advertising for your product need to include color, sound, or motion to make it more attractive? The cost of your advertising is another important factor in choosing media vehicles. You should look at the total dollar amount that an ad costs and the cost per thousand people exposed to the message.

Advertising is critical, but it has some real downsides, including slow feedback, expense, difficulty cutting through clutter, and difficulty creating a personalized message. Choosing the appropriate advertising medium for your message is important. Which one should you use? Let's take a look at your options:

"You should look at the total dollar amount that an ad costs and the cost per thousand people exposed to the message."

Newspaper
Advantages: Flexible; timely; covers local markets well; believable (because people read newspapers to get information); relatively inexpensive; can use color, coupons, or inserts.
Limitations: Short life of ad; number of ads per newspaper causes clutter; poor photo reproduction; low pass-along value (meaning that newspapers are rarely read by more than one person).

All television – including cable, syndicated, and spot
Advantages: Reaches large audience; combines sight, sound, and motion; perceived to be prestige medium.
Limitations: High absolute cost; several ads run together increases clutter and decreases impact; short exposure time; ability of consumer to not record the ads with TiVo or mute with regular TV.

Direct mail, social media, and Web technology
Advantages: Can be targeted very specifically; message can be personalized; less space limitations than other media.
Limitations: Perceived as "junk mail"; high relative cost; mailing lists are expensive and often inaccurate.
Shawn Burst founded Dukky, a company that is working to transform direct mail advertising by enabling businesses to track their mailings and create a customer database in the process. It works like this. A company sends out a direct mail piece to its customer base offering them a coupon for a free product. Each piece of direct mail has a PURL, a personal URL for that specific customer. Once the customer receives the direct mailing, in order to receive the coupon for the freebie, the customer must log on to their PURL in order to print the coupon. Before they can print the coupon, they are asked for more information, like e-mail address, birthday, gender, and so forth. Once they collect their coupon, they are given the opportunity to share the offer with their friends through Facebook, Twitter, and so forth. The Dukky dashboard can monitor the entire process and measure the number of customers responding to the original direct mailing. Not only does the coupon bring customers into the store, but also the business now has additional marketing information for the next round of

direct mailing. So far the three entrepreneurs involved with Dukky are quite pleased with their success. Burst projects sales for the current year to be $5 million.[18]

Radio

Advantages: Can be targeted to specific audience; low relative cost; short lead time so ads can be developed quickly.

Limitations: People are often involved with other activities and do not pay full attention to ad; people cannot refer back to ad; competition for best time slots.

Competitive Advantage
INNOVATION AND SUSTAINABILITY

Guppy in a Shark Tank: Small Business, Big Trade Shows

The 1.3 million-square-foot McCormick Place convention center in Chicago can seem like a very large place if you are a small business owner setting up for a trade show. Giant competitors set up booths that dwarf the displays of small businesses. Nevertheless, trade shows can generate big deals for small businesses.

Gregory Perkins uses bright lights, bold and colorful graphics, and 10-foot-tall displays to catch the attention of the 20,000 people attending Book Expo America. Perkins's business, Magic Image, sells African American greeting cards, calendars, and pocket planners. He does about a dozen shows a year, and they generate most of his $500,000 annual sales. At the Book Expo, Perkins caught a big fish of a deal when Target Stores placed a $30,000 order on the spot.

Research shows that trade shows can be more effective at generating sales than direct mail, telemarketing, or other sales strategies—but you have to develop some trade show savvy. To improve your odds of success at trade shows, try the following:

- *Choose the right show.* Trade shows are specialized by industry, market, or product. Size, draw, and cost vary widely. Find shows that offer the right mix of audience, location, industry, and price.
- *Plan ahead.* E-mail, snail-mail a letter or postcard, fax, or phone the customers you want to pitch at the show. Let them know where your booth will be and how to reach you at the hotel. Don't just sit back and wait for people to approach you. Put forethought into your display. If you bought a 10-foot by 10-foot space, re-create that size before you go to the show to ensure that all the products you plan to take will fit and to decide how you want to display them.
- *Get a good spot.* You want a steady flow of foot traffic, so try to get an island location. Your

chances of getting a good spot increase by registering early. You may have to pay a premium to be near the entrance or in a corner.

- *Pool resources with others.* Locating next to businesses with products that complement yours can build synergy. Perkins and five other business owners had their booths adjoin one another to strategically increase the presence of African American products. Each paid for his own space, but the combination made an impressive display for bookstores looking for their products.
- *Use the right stuff.* Your sales tactics at a show should be different than when you are on the floor or on the phone. You have only about 45 seconds to draw someone into your booth. You have to be quick and concise, and use the right buzzwords. Don't concentrate on talking to one customer at the expense of ignoring new people who wander in.
- *Follow up on leads.* Your intent is to turn contacts into sales contracts. Although you may close some deals in the booth, sealing even more will take persistence and patience. Stay in touch via your company newsletters to keep potential customers informed about your business.

Ready for a road trip? The three-day Small Business Expo in Auckland, New Zealand, is designed as a "business-to-business marketplace" for small- and medium-sized businesses, providing all types of business solutions under one roof. Over 7,000 small business owners attend each year.

Sources: Sarah Needleman, "Exhibitions Game," *Wall Street Journal*, May 11, 2009, R7; "Is Small Beautiful or Is Big Better," *Management Today*, November 2009, 64–68; Maggie Overfelt, "Gotham Inc.," *Fortune Small Business*, November 2009, 66; and Kate Meere, "Largest Event Ever Held for Small Business," *Chartered Accountants Journal*, November 2005, 16–17.

Magazine

Advantages: Target markets can be selected geographically and demographically; long life because magazines are often passed along; high-quality reproduction.

Limitations: Long lead time needed in purchasing ad; no guarantee of placement within magazine; higher relative cost than other print media.

Outdoor

Advantages: High, repeated exposure; low cost; little competition.

Limitations: Limited amount of message due to exposure time to ad; little selectivity of target market.

Yellow Pages

Advantages: People viewing ad are likely to be interested buyers; relatively inexpensive; effectiveness of ad easy to measure.

Limitations: All of your competitors are listed in the same place; easy to ignore small ads; may need to be listed in several sections.

The Yellow Pages is still an important piece of the small business promotional mix, Usage for this medium has been approximately 13 billion looks for print and 4 billion for online. Yellow Pages still provides a 65:1 average return on investment, according to Scott Klein, CEO of Verizon Yellow Pages. While still important, the Yellow Pages have evolved. Some new features include: pay per click or pay per call; ATT411, a texting service where customers can inquire about deals or coupons; and call-tracking numbers that are unique numbers assigned to advertising that can literally be used to determine how many people are responding to an ad.[19]

Internet

Advantages: Good selectivity of target markets; inexpensive.

Limitations: Often negative reaction to advertising on computer networks; uncertainty of number of people reached.

Miscellaneous[20]

Known as *unmeasured media advertising,* miscellaneous advertising includes things like catalogs, ads on bus stop benches, and signage at sport fields. Many small businesses determine how much to spend on advertising by allocating a percentage of their total sales revenues. This percentage varies considerably by type of business (see Table 14.2).

Advertising Objectives Different types of advertisements help to accomplish different objectives. You may be trying to do any of the following:

- *Inform* your audience of the existence of your business, your competitive advantage, or product features and benefits.
- *Persuade* people to take an immediate action—such as buying your product.
- *Remind* people that your business or product still exists. Get them to remember what they received from your business in the past so that it remains in their evoked set.
- *Change the perception* of your business rather than trying to sell specific products. Generally called *institutional advertising*, advertising with this objective aims to build goodwill rather than to make an immediate sale.

"Creating effective advertisements is both a science and an art."

It is a challenge to achieve these broad objectives with your advertising. Creating effective advertisements is both a science and an art. Originality, humor, and excitement can make your ad break through the clutter of other media, but, at the same time, these traits can obscure the real message of your ad. Communicating your message clearly

TABLE 14-2 Advertising Costs by Different Types of Businesses	INDUSTRY	AD DOLLARS AS % OF OPERATING INCOME
	New and Used Car Dealers	1.1%
	Furniture and Home Furnishing Stores	4.1%
	Electronics and Appliance Stores	2.1%
	Hardware Stores	.5%
	Food and Beverage Retail Stores	0.7%
	Beer, Wine, and Liquor Stores	0.5%
	Non-store Retailers	2.9%
	Software Publishers	5.5%
	Commercial Banking	0.3%
	Advertising and Related Services	3.2%
	Food Services and Drinking Places	2.4%
	Motor Vehicle Manufacturers	1.6%
	Breweries	7.3%
	Soft Drink Companies	7.8%

Source: *Almanac of Business and Industrial Financial Ratios* (2009) by Leo Troy. Copyright 2010 by Aspen Publishers, Inc. Reproduced with permission of Aspen Publishers, Inc. in the formats Textbook and Other book via Copyright Clearance Center.

while catching the viewer's attention is a tough balance to achieve. Consider these common strategies, all of which you might choose to achieve your advertising objectives:

- *Testimonials.* Use an authority or a personal testimony from a celebrity to present your message. Athletes and movie stars attract attention, but their public images can change rapidly and must remain consistent with that of your business.
- *Humor.* Humor can grab the viewer's attention, but be careful who bears the brunt of the joke or you could offend some group and generate negative publicity for your business. Advertising history is also full of some very funny ads that did not generate a single dollar of additional revenue.
- *Sensual or sexual messages.* According to the cliché, "Sex sells." Sex is certainly used in a lot of ads, but research shows that it is not an effective way to get a message across. As with humor, using sex to attract attention is worthless if it doesn't translate into sales.
- *Comparative messages.* Naming competitors in your advertising is legal and quite common. It can be a very powerful way to position your product in customers' minds against another known entity—although it also gives your competitor free exposure.
- *Slice-of-life messages.* These messages may use a popular song or a brief scene from life to position your product. Music is a great way to transport people mentally back to another time in their life. Nostalgia can help create a brand identity for your product.
- *Fantasy messages.* These messages present an idealistic self-image of the buyer. What you are trying to do is link a product with a desirable person or situation. Certainly, this is what almost every beer or soft-drink commercial attempts—the message is "Drink this liquid and you will be beautiful, popular, and desirable." Right.

How do you tell if your advertising works? A common complaint among advertisers runs along this line: "I know that half of my advertising dollars are wasted, I just don't know which half." Measuring the effectiveness of your advertising is difficult. Is the cost of producing and running the ad justified by increased sales and profit? A few techniques might help you find out.

- *Response tracking.* Coded or dated coupons can let you compare different media, such as the redemption rate for coupons in newspapers compared with flyers handed out on the street.
- *Split ads.* Code two different ads, different media, or broadcast times to see which produces a greater response.
- *In-store opinions.* Ask in-store customers where they heard about your business, what they think, what you are doing right, and why they buy from you rather than from a competitor.
- *Telephone surveys.* Make random phone calls with numbers gleaned from customer files. Ask customers whether they have seen your advertising and what they think of it.
- *Statement questionnaires.* Drop a brief questionnaire in the monthly bills you send out to ask customers if they are satisfied with the product or service and how they found out about it.

Advertising Development Most small business owners plan their own advertising programs, which is usually more appropriate for them than hiring a professional producer. Even if you choose to use an advertising agency, you should still take active control of your advertising campaign. Remember, you cannot afford to buy a solution to every problem you will face. This is true with your advertising. Spending money will not automatically get you better advertising. As Paul Hawkin has said, "The major problem affecting businesses, large or small, is a lack of *imagination*, not a lack of capital."[21] Don't let money replace creativity.

A common problem among self-produced advertisements is that business owners try to cram too much into them. Their reasoning is "This space costs a lot of money, so I am going to use every minuscule part of it." The result is usually an ad that is busy, unattractive, and uninteresting. Simplicity should be the rule here. White space draws the reader's attention. The same principle applies to package design: It doesn't have to tell the consumer everything. Susan Gunelius suggests you employ the Red Pen Rule. Once you have your final copy completed, take out a red pen and delete approximately 30 percent of the words. Clear and concise messages appeal to the customer better and will be remembered longer. With 30 percent of the copy gone, you now have your message crystal clear and ready to be delivered.[22]

Even though self-produced ads are appropriate for many small businesses, owners should at least investigate the options and promotions that outside professional advertising services make available.

> *"Clear and concise messages appeal to the customer better and will be remembered longer."*

Advertising Agencies To mount an effective campaign, you may want to consider consulting an advertising agency. These businesses can help you by conducting preliminary studies, developing an advertising plan, creating advertisements, selecting the appropriate media, evaluating the effectiveness of the advertising, and conducting ad follow-up.

A small agency that specializes in and understands your type of business may be a better choice for a small business than a large agency. Ask your friends and colleagues for recommendations, and get samples of the agency's work before signing a contract. Remember that fees are often negotiable, so the agency's fees may be flexible.

Media Agencies You can create your own advertising and hire a media buyer to coordinate the purchase of print space or broadcast time for your ads. Why would you choose to use a media buyer? If you have identified your specific target market, a media buyer can help coordinate your media mix to reach that market. Suppose you have designed a new line of blue jeans targeted to urban females from 13 to 17 years old. A media buyer can tell you in which magazine, on which radio station, or on which television show to advertise.

Art and Graphic Design Services If you design your own ads and write your own copy but lack the artistic skills needed to produce the final piece of art or film, an art service can handle this task for you. Like the art director in an advertising agency, this service needs to work closely with the person writing your copy to coordinate the message.

Other Sources Radio and television studios, newspapers, and magazines with which you contract to run your advertising can also produce ads for you. Their services generally cost less than those of an advertising agency.

Personal Selling

Personal selling involves a personal presentation by a salesperson for the purpose of making sales and building relationships with customers. There are many products not large enough, complex enough, or differentiated enough to warrant personal selling, but for those products that do, this technique is the best way to close the deal. Through personal selling, you are trying to accomplish three things: identify customer needs, match those needs with your products, and show the customers the match between their need and your product.

Cost is the biggest drawback to personal selling. When you calculate what it costs for a salesperson to contact each prospect, you see that this strategy is much more expensive than the cost per person for advertising. Another drawback is that salespeople have gained a poor reputation because of the high-pressure tactics and questionable ethics a few of them employ. The biggest advantage of using personal selling is the

"Personal selling, though costly, can be closely tailored to customer needs—making it an effective way to close a sale."

A good salesperson can show customers how they can solve a problem through the purchase of a product or service.

flexibility of the presentation that becomes possible. A trained salesperson can tailor a presentation to the prospect around three aspects of the product:

Features: What the product is
Advantages: Why the product is better than alternatives
Benefits: What the product will do for the customer

Customer expectations are rising. A good product at a fair price, offered by a well-trained sales staff, backed by a responsive customer service department, is just the starting point in a competitive marketplace. For your business to stand out, its products need to be tailored to the particular needs of your customers. Fortunately, technology is helping to supercharge your sales performance. For example, many salespeople dread making cold calls, partly because they don't know much about the prospective customer they are about to call. You could Google the prospects, but that's not enough. Services such as Before the Call automatically scour Internet sites like Hoover's and Factiva as well as their own proprietary database for new articles. Before the Call can be incorporated with your sales systems like Salesforce.com and Oracle OnDemand to keep customer databases up-to-date and full of current information.[23] Such services could provide just the bit of information your salesperson needs to spark conversation.

The personal-selling process involves seven steps:

1. *Pre-approach.* Before meeting with the prospective customer, a salesperson must acquire knowledge about the product and perhaps about the customer and his business.
2. *Approach.* Upon first meeting the customer, the salesperson tries to establish a rapport with her. People seldom buy from someone they don't trust, so a successful salesperson must first earn a customer's trust.
3. *Questioning.* To find out what is important to the customer, the salesperson will try to identify his needs as early in the process as possible.
4. *Demonstration.* The salesperson shows how the product will solve the customer's problem and meet her needs.
5. *Handling objections.* An effective salesperson will listen to what the customer is really saying. An objection shows that the customer is interested but needs more information. Would you raise objections to a salesperson if you were not really interested in a product? No, you would probably just walk away.
6. *Closing the deal.* When he senses that the customer is ready to buy, the salesperson should ask for the sale. Many sales are lost when a customer is ready to buy, but the salesperson continues to sell.
7. *Suggestion selling and follow-up.* An effective technique is *suggestion selling*, or recommending products that are complementary to those just sold. *Follow-up* with a phone call after the sale will build rapport and work toward creating a long-term relationship with the customer.

Public Relations

Public relations (PR) involves promotional activities designed to build and sustain goodwill between a business and its customers, employees, suppliers, investors, government agencies, and the general public. **Publicity** is an aspect of PR consisting of any message about your company communicated through the mass media that you do not have to pay for. Generally, PR works by generating publicity.

PR involves a variety of communication formats, including company publications such as newsletters, annual reports, and bulletins; public speaking; lobbying; and the mass media. Each format can have an appropriate use and benefit for your company's marketing effort. Table 14.3 shows some PR activities, their target audience, and their effects on your business.

publicity
An aspect of public relations consisting of any message about your company communicated through the mass media that you do not pay for.

Small businesses benefit by the publicity generated from teams they sponsor appearing in the sports page of a local newspaper.

© Jupiterimages

A welcome change in the PR business has been firms that charge by pay-for-placement rather than retainer deals. PayPerClip is just such a firm based in Califon, New Jersey, that can help remove some of the mystery from PR bills. PayPerClip would receive $400 for a brief airing on a small market TV news show, $2,000 for a sizable story in a small trade magazine, and $8,900 for a full feature in the *Wall Street Journal*.[24]

Sales Promotions

Any activity that stimulates sales and is not strictly advertising or personal selling is called a *sales promotion*. Special in-store displays, free samples, contests, trade show booths, and the distribution of coupons, premiums, and rebates are examples of sales promotions. These activities enhance but do not replace your advertising or personal selling efforts. They are most effective when used in intervals, because customer response decreases over time as customers become familiar with the promotions.

Ratchet Effect Advertising and personal selling are used on a continuous basis, whereas sales promotions are intermittent. A strategy that combines all three can produce a *ratchet effect* on sales (see Figure 14.5). Advertising is used to increase customer interest, whereas personal selling is used to increase sales. Sales promotions at the point of purchase are usually employed to increase sales over a short period of time.

The Business Card An important image builder that is often overlooked and taken for granted is a 3.5-inch by 2-inch paper rectangle—the business card. If done correctly and

TABLE 14-3 Relationship between Marketing and Public Relations	TARGET	PR ACTIVITIES	BENEFITS TO MARKETING
	Customers	Press releases	Increase name awareness
		Event sponsorship	Increase credibility
	Employees	Newsletters	Improve communications
		Social activities	Decrease absenteeism and product defects
			Increase morale
	Suppliers	Articles in trade publications	Improve image
		Promotional incentives	Improve delivery schedule
	General public	News releases	Attract better employees
		Plant tours	Improve image to customers
		Support for community activities	Improve local relations
	Government	Lobbying	Favorable legislation
		Direct mail Personal calls	Less regulation

FIGURE 14-5

Short-Term
Ratchet Effect of
Sales Promotion

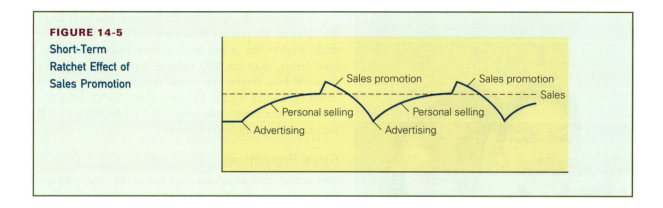

creatively, a business card not only provides information about your small business but also becomes hand-to-hand advertising. Neil Hair states, "A really cool business card can put a smile on someone's face, and it allows people to associate a good experience with your business."[25]

A tactic to differentiate your business card from the competition to is to think outside the rectangle. Kevin Mitnick, founder of Mitnick Security Consulting in Henderson, Nevada, hands out an aluminium card featuring twist-off lock-picking tools. Matcards .com has their business information seared into a real piece of beef jerky. And Moo .com, a hip printer, uses a MiniCard that can also be used as a display for your digital photos. If you choose the more traditional route, make sure you use a good-quality paper, since the quality and feel of your cards can say as much as what you have printed on them. For as little as $69 for 250 cards, that's cheap advertising.[26]

Don't make the common mistake of trying to include everything there is to know about your business on the card. You don't have to include *every* phone, fax, and cell number the business owns. You do, however, need to include your Web site, because it provides a wealth of business information (doesn't it?), and, of course, your e-mail address.

Promotional Mix

In deciding how to combine each of your four tools into a promotional mix, you need to consider when each type of promotion may be appropriate. Advertising reaches so many people that it is good for creating awareness, but its power to stimulate action decreases quickly. Personal selling, by contrast, is the most effective tool for building customer desire for the product and prompting customers to take action. Because it requires one-on-one contact, however, it is less useful in creating awareness. Sales promotions are most effective with customers who are already interested in the product, but who may need prompting to make the purchase. Public relations builds awareness, but results in few immediate sales.

Summary

1. Identify the three main considerations in setting a price for a product.

The economic factors that have the largest influence on pricing are the prices charged by competitors, the amount of customer demand for your product, and the costs incurred in producing, purchasing, and selling your products.

2. Explain what breakeven analysis is and why it is important for pricing in a small business.

Breakeven analysis ensures that your prices are set above total costs, allowing you to make a profit. It is also useful in estimating the needed demand for a product at different price levels. Finally, breakeven analysis shows how many units need to be sold to generate a target dollar return.

3. **Present examples of customer-oriented and internal-oriented pricing.**

   Customer-oriented price strategies, such as penetration pricing, skimming, and psychological pricing, focus on the wants and needs of your target customers and the number of units of your product they will buy. Internal-oriented pricing involves setting your prices according to the financial needs of your business, with less regard for customer reaction.

4. **Explain why and how small businesses extend credit.**

   Small businesses extend credit to their customers to realize sales that would not have been made without credit, and to increase the volume and frequency of sales to existing customers. Credit is extended through open charge accounts, installment accounts, lines of credit, and acceptance of credit cards.

5. **Describe the advertising, personal selling, public relations, and sales-promotion tools that a small business owner uses to compile a promotional mix.**

   A promotional mix is the combination of advertising, personal selling, sales promotions, and public relations that best communicates the message of a small business to its customers.

Questions for Review and Discussion

1. What strategies should be considered if a small business is setting prices for a product that is to be exported? How do these strategies differ from those used in a domestic market?
2. What advantages and disadvantages are involved for a small business offering sales on credit?
3. As the owner of a small, hometown drugstore, how would you prepare for a Walmart being built in your area?
4. What can happen if the price of a product does not fit with the three other Ps of the marketing mix?
5. Should a small business owner's judgment be used to determine prices if so many mathematical techniques have been developed for that purpose?
6. Discuss the importance of remaining professional and friendly when trying to collect an unpaid bill.
7. What factors should be considered when a small business owner decides to advertise?
8. Discuss the personality traits that a good salesperson should have. What traits would detract from the personal-selling process?
9. Explain the ratchet effect on sales.
10. How would promotional mix decisions change for a small business that is expanding into a foreign market?

Questions for Critical Thinking

1. Much of the self-produced small business advertising is weak. Think of an example of a local small business that uses especially effective advertising. Why is it successful at communicating with its target market when so many are not?
2. Of the pricing techniques described in this chapter, which one do you think is most commonly used by small businesses? Why?

What Would You Do?

Developing an effective marketing strategy can be tough. Without one, however, a small business will be fighting for survival. Read through the following two examples and answer the questions at the end.

DAPAT Pharmaceuticals

DAPAT is a small manufacturer of external analgesics (pain relievers) based in Nashville, Tennessee. Its main product, called Dr.'s Cream, faced this marketing challenge: In competition with much larger makers of over-the-counter remedies (such as Ben Gay), it had to find some ways to attract customers despite having only a small advertising budget.

Macromedia, Inc

Macromedia is also in a highly competitive field—software publishing. The company makes graphic arts software tools for graphic designers, CD-ROM developers, and people who need to make "flashy" presentations. Macromedia's products are full of technical "bells and whistles," but are they enough to compete effectively? Creating computerized dancing mice could be cool, but technology alone won't sell the product.

Questions

1. Working in teams of no more than three, choose one of the two examples to work on. Develop an outline for a comprehensive marketing strategy for the company and its product. Be specific in defining the product, place, price, and promotion aspects.

2. Once your team has developed its marketing strategy, find another team in the class that has worked on the same example. Take turns presenting your information to each other.

PART 5

Management

In this section we will bring together all the phases of running your own business. Visualize yourself making the decisions needed to make it all happen as you read these chapters. Are there opportunities for your business in other countries? Many small businesses find that there are possibilities. Foreign sales can be an excellent way to generate growth, and **Chapter 15** explores those possibilities. **Chapter 16** explains professionally managing your business through the various stages of growth it will experience. **Chapter 17** looks at managing your most valuable resource—people. **Chapter 18** covers the management of service and manufacturing operations.

15

The Global Environment

CHAPTER LEARNING OUTCOMES

After reading this chapter, you should be able to:

1. List factors to consider when preparing an international business plan.

2. Name five ways for small businesses to conduct international trade.

3. Analyze the advantages and disadvantages of exporting for small businesses.

4. Discuss factors to consider when importing products and materials.

5. Explain how small businesses can manage their finances in international trade.

6. Articulate the cultural and economic challenges of international small business activity.

What do mud from the Dead Sea, instant coffee, plastic containers called roti keepers, and Chinese hutongs have in common? International business opportunities. For many business owners today, growth lies not in the domestic markets where their business resides but in markets outside their home country. Look at the following four cases to see some examples of businesses growing sales as they promote their products internationally.

Tupperware is a U.S. company that grew popular in the 1940s with a unique selling strategy: Tupperware parties. These parties were used by homemakers to introduce their friends and families to the plastic food storage containers that reside in many American homes yet today. Tupperware has now taken their product to India. The goal of 100,000 Indian women selling Tupperware, everything from the roti keeper (round bread containers) to the masala box (used for spices), has allowed this company to become the leading seller of kitchenware in India. With growth in the Indian market, Tupperware has grown at a compounded rate of 30 percent since 1996, something they probably could not have done selling only in the U.S. market.

Bobby Zhang opened Templeside Hutong Guest House, a hutong hotel, in 2006 after leaving both the investment banking industry and studying in Australia. Hutongs

are Beijing's only single-lot homes and have been a part of Chinese culture for 600 years. Today as many as 82 percent of these icons have been destroyed in order to make room for high-rise apartments built to fulfill the need for adequate housing. Zhang has created a step back in time. And though the Chinese take the hutong and the way of life it represents for granted, foreigners are anxious to explore this piece of Chinese culture. In 2007, Zhang received the Best Hostel in China award and as such has opened another guesthouse in a neighboring hutong to serve the international travellers visiting Beijing.

Nestlé is taking to the water with a 90-foot barge called Nestlé Até Você a Bordo (Nestlé Takes You Onboard) destined for an 18-day journey through the Amazon River in Brazil. Realizing they were missing an international market, Nestlé decided to take their product to the customer, particularly in an area where the 800,000 population might never travel and discover the Nestlé product line. Even though Nestlé is the world's largest food company, they realize that to grow in a global market, they will need to look at marketing and selling their products in new ways. So on the barge, products are available in small, low-priced packages and feature such favorites as Leche Ideal (powdered milk), Maggi (soups and seasonings), and the ever-popular Nescafé, the world's leading instant coffee.

In 1988, Ziva Gilad watched as female tourists scooped mud from the Dead Sea, bottled it, and took it home. The high mineral concentration found in the Dead Sea creates a compound that women were using to hydrate their skin and slow the aging process, and foreign tourists provided Gilad with the idea of selling the mud and salt crystals already bottled. This business was so successful they made nearly $1 million in revenue the first year alone. However, since Israel has only 7 million people, her company, Ahava, realized that if they wanted to grow they had to sell their products internationally. Twenty years later, Ahava (Hebrew for love), sells its lotions, exfoliators, and masks in more than 30 countries including the department store Nordstrom in the United States. They have very successfully positioned their Dead Sea product line as a prestige brand in an international market. Ahava has successfully turned the mud and salt of the Dead Sea into a cosmetic empire.

As you can see from the just-discussed businesses, selling your product internationally can create opportunities that will not occur if you stay within your own borders. However, as you read through this chapter, you will also see that growing your business internationally is not for everyone and for every business.

Sources: Michal Lev-Ram, "Turning Dead Sea Mud into Money," www.cnnmoney.com, December 10, 2009; Marc Gunther, "The World's New Economic Landscape," *Fortune*, July 26, 2010; Joanne Yao, "Beijing's Hutongs: Preserving History through Business," www.entrepreneur.com, August 14, 2008; and Ashish Singh and Satish Shanker, "Tupperware Parties Help Reshape India's Kitchens," www.businessweek.com, July 13, 2010.

Preparing to Go International

When most people think of international business, they envision large, multinational corporations with operations all over the globe. A common conclusion is that small- and medium-sized businesses are at a disadvantage in terms of their ability to compete internationally. Actually, research shows that the size of a business is not a barrier to entry into international markets; it merely limits the number of markets you can serve.[1] Having improper strategies, negative attitudes toward expansion abroad, or lack of experience may keep businesses out of the international game, but size does not have to be a factor. In fact, the same competitive advantages—your unique skills, talents, and products—that have made your business successful in local markets may create the same advantage in foreign markets.

Growth of Small Business

International trade and the global market are a critical component of today's businesses. With the technology that is ever present, you can connect around the world not only easily but also inexpensively. While a current trend, trade is certainly not a new trend. Think of Marco Polo, the Silk Routes of Asia, or the Nile River in ancient Egypt. Trade has been important not only in moving goods and services but also in sharing knowledge and culture. Exporting is essential to the economic health of the United States. In May 2010, United States exports alone equalled $152.3 billion dollars. That is a lot of capital goods, industrial supplies, and business and technical services for one month.[2] And when looking at the companies that are engaged in exporting, according to the U.S. Census, those companies with less than 100 employees account for 91 percent of the companies that are exporting goods and services.[3] Seventy-seven percent of U.S. exporters to China are small businesses.[4] For many businesses today, going global is a reality (see Figure 15.1).[5]

International Business Plan

To navigate these shifting international tides, you will, of course, need a business plan. As we discussed in Chapter 4, a solid business plan is behind most successful small businesses.

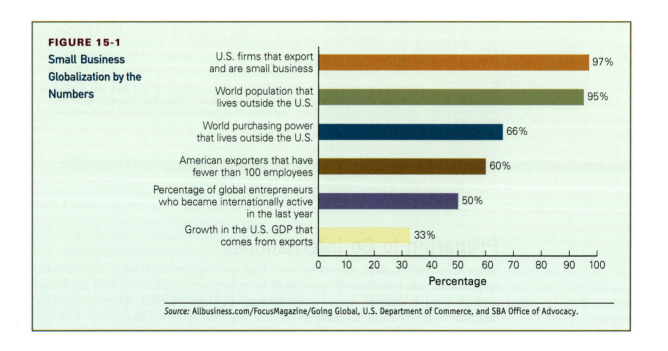

FIGURE 15-1
Small Business Globalization by the Numbers

Category	Percentage
U.S. firms that export and are small business	97%
World population that lives outside the U.S.	95%
World purchasing power that lives outside the U.S.	66%
American exporters that have fewer than 100 employees	60%
Percentage of global entrepreneurs who became internationally active in the last year	50%
Growth in the U.S. GDP that comes from exports	33%

Source: Allbusiness.com/FocusMagazine/Going Global, U.S. Department of Commerce, and SBA Office of Advocacy.

What do you need in an *international business plan*? Begin with everything that is included in a domestic plan. You have to have a unique product, a market (or preferably multiple markets) for your product, the managerial skills to take advantage of the opportunity you have identified, and the financial capability to do the deal. In addition to the business-plan content and analysis described in Chapter 4, the following information, at a minimum, is necessary to help you analyze your ability to go international and chart the best course to follow. Note that with any business plan, a balance between information and analysis is needed. The following list identifies areas and questions you should be able to answer as you consider taking your business outside the United States.

- Are you committed and are you willing to commit the resources that will be needed to enter the international market?
- Do you have an international marketing plan with specific strategies detailed?
- Do you understand the culture and the customer needs where you plan to sell your product?
- Do you have the production capacity to produce the additional amount of product needed and the ability to make any needed changes?
- How will you transport your product to the location and what will be the cost?
- Do you have the financial resources and cash necessary to not only get started but carry you through until your product is generating cash flow in the new location?[6]
- One expert recommends that an international business plan should include both market entrance and exit approaches because markets that are difficult to leave can drain export sales profits.[7]

"Note that with any business plan, a balance between information and analysis is needed."

Take the Global Test

Taking your small business across national borders can be a good move. You've heard stories of others striking gold just over the horizon—but it's not easy. Your chances of building competitive advantage and therefore being successful in international business are good if you can pass this 10-part test.

1. *The "good reason" test.* If exporting is not part of your core business strategy, don't bother going international. A one-shot deal, even a big one, may not be worth the trouble. Software company Blue Pumpkin, which has operated internationally since its beginning in 1996, is an example of a company with a "good reason" for going global. Because Blue Pumpkin provides customer-service software to many *Fortune* 1000 firms that want to use it all over the world, it has to be global.

2. *Do you have the right stuff to pull this off?* To be taken seriously by foreign buyers, your business needs a certain degree of success at home. Depending on your industry, this level of achievement could be measured by market share, technical expertise, or brand awareness. In selling fishing lures, for example, brand awareness is key, so Kendall Banks makes sure that T-shirts for his Silver Buddy lures cover the BassMasters trade show in New Orleans for the benefit of foreign buyers.

3. *Can you identify a market?* Every country provides different sets of problems and customers. Forget about trying to enter more than one at a time. Randy Reichenbach has trouble competing in the Middle East against a competitor from Trieste, Italy, selling reconditioned surgery tables. Randy's U.S.-made tables are top of the line; the Italian models are great, too, but the strong euro makes their prices higher. Good news for Randy as the currency exchange rates tip the price advantage in his favor.

4. *Are you flexible?* With few exceptions, product modifications will need to be made. Carroll Mixon's Kelley Manufacturing makes digger shaker inverters for planting peanuts in Georgia (United States). South Africa uses different row spacing that required product changes. Mixon had to determine whether the expense of modifying his product for export was worth it. Such modifications can be, if they are part of the overall strategy (see number 1 in this list).

5. *Can you find a good distributor?* Getting your products into the hands of end users in other countries is especially challenging for small businesses. Export managers and foreign distributors can prove very helpful in preparing you for the twists and turns in reaching markets, but they may also change the perception of your product.

6. *Can you cope with all the complexity?* Jim Hunt, president of Kabobs, makes frozen hors d'oeuvres for ritzy hotels. He says that "every shipment to Canada requires 40 pieces of paper, and you have to save all paperwork for at least three years." Another complexity is dealing with differing standards: If one of his appetizers is, say, 25 percent chicken, does it fall under Canada's chicken import quota? You get the idea.

7. *Can you brave the, shall we say, nonlegal barriers?* Roger Berkeley wanted his textiles from Weave Corporation to reach buyers in Italy. The problem is that Americans were banned from the annual trade show in Como, Italy. Berkeley fought through the problem by laying out his goods at a nearby villa and picking customers up directly at the trade show to drive them to his goods. Someone, he alleges, got his drivers arrested. That was enough, so he now focuses on a friendlier show in Belgium.

8. *Are you willing to extend credit or deal with currency turmoil?* Sure, you would prefer to be paid up front and in U.S. dollars, but that option is not always available. You are more likely to receive a bankable letter of credit, which slows your ever-critical cash flow. Then you face the volatility of currency exchange rates. Weave Corporation saw its sales plunge with the decline in value of the euro relative to the U.S. dollar because European rivals then had a price advantage.

9. *Are you ready to run a much different kind of company?* Exporting will inevitably change your company—and your life. Changes may be as simple as going in to the office at 4 a.m. for a foreign conference call because of time-zone differences.

10. *Do the rewards outweigh the costs?* This will be a personal decision that depends on what you want to get from the business, and your answer to this question may change from time to time. Many small business owners involved in international trade sometimes ask themselves, "What have I gotten myself into this time?" At other times, when sales are growing through the roof, you may feel like you're on top of the world.[8]

"To be taken seriously by foreign buyers, your business needs a certain degree of success at home."

If you conclude from your planning and testing that you should proceed with your expansion into other countries, you have five basic choices: exporting, importing, licensing your product, establishing a joint venture, or setting up operations in the other country. Each of these options represents an increased level of commitment on your part, so let's look at your options in that order.

Establishing Business in Another Country

The vast majority of small business activity in the international market will be conducted via importing and exporting. Still, for the experienced, visionary, and adventurous businessperson, other options exist that represent an even greater commitment to global trade. Small businesses can license their products or services, form joint ventures or strategic alliances, or even set up their own operations to conduct business in other countries.

Exporting

exporting
Selling goods or services in a foreign country.

The primary mechanism for small businesses to engage in international business is *exporting*, or sending the products they make to another country. Because of the importance of this option for establishing business in another country, we will cover direct and indirect exporting in more detail later in this chapter.

Importing

Many small business owners recognize not only that markets for their products exist in other countries, but also that their domestic markets can be served by bringing in products from other countries via importing. Importing represents such a viable option for small business that we will discuss it in more detail later in this chapter.

International Licensing

licensing
The agreement that allows one business to sell the rights to use a business process or product to another business in a foreign country.

As an exporter, you can stop exporting anytime you wish. However, other forms of international business represent a larger commitment on your part. The next level of commitment above exporting in international business is *licensing*. As a licenser you are contractually obligated to another business for a period of time.

Licensing offers a way to enter foreign markets by assigning the rights to your patents, trademarks, copyrights, processes, or products to another company in exchange for a fee or royalty. The two biggest advantages of licensing are speed of entry and cost. You can enter a foreign market quickly without investing virtually any capital. Licensing is similar to franchising domestically. Licensing agreements are generally written to endure for a specified period of time. A disadvantage of this approach is that your licensee may become your competitor after the agreement expires if the licensee continues to use your licensed process without paying you for it.

International Joint Ventures and Strategic Alliances

joint venture
An agreement in which two businesses form a temporary partnership to produce a product or service in a market that neither could satisfy alone.

A foreign *joint venture* is a partnership between your business and a business in another country. As with any partnership, choosing the right partner is critical to the success of the venture. Joint ventures can provide several advantages, including economies of scale, the ability to produce products less expensively, and help through the maze of local culture, business practices, and legal requirements.

Partnerships of *any* type can be difficult (see Chapter 2). Joint ventures and alliances are often costly failures. A study by McKinsey and Company found that only half of partnerships and alliances produced a return above the cost of capital.[9] Despite the difficulties, joint ventures and strategic alliances are and will be needed to be competitive globally. Finding a local partner is the only way to enter some countries.

Following are some important questions to address in assessing whether a joint venture is right for your business:

1. What resources do you need to successfully produce your product, and what is the best source for these resources, including labor?
2. Are you looking at the international component of your business as a long-term strategy or a short-term strategy? If you are planning on getting in and out in a short time frame, a joint venture is probably not your best option.
3. What are the goals of your partner in the joint venture? Do their goals for their company align with your goals for your company?
4. What are the business practices of the country in which the joint venture will be located? Are those practices compatible with the business practices of your company?
5. How and who will evaluate the performance of the joint venture?

6. Who will ultimately manage the joint venture? Has an effective organizational chart been drawn and agreed upon?

7. How will disagreements be resolved? Who ultimately will make a final call in the event you cannot agree?

8. How will the joint venture be dissolved, if necessary or when needed? This is an important question to resolve long before the answer is needed.[10]

strategic alliances
A partnership between two businesses (often in different countries) that is more informal than a joint venture.

Strategic alliances are somewhat similar to joint ventures; however, in the past usually they were used to outsource less important pieces of the supply chain. The focus was on service-level agreements that stated what each partner would provide and how the performance would be measured. The majority of the effort went into the service agreement. Today, strategic alliances may provide an essential piece of the competitive advantage of your company and as such need careful planning—and attention. Evaluating what your objectives are for the alliance, how joint wins will be measured, how performance will be assessed, and how new initiatives can be developed can be key to the success for a strategic alliance. Lorraine Segil, of the Lared Group, specializes in establishing strategic alliances, helping to match small organizations with large ones through a chain of contacts in the United States, Europe, and Australia. The match is often made with a large, well-established company abroad that needs fresh ideas and products. Because many entrepreneurial firms have just such assets, but only limited capital, the result is often a profitable alliance for both.

Competitive Advantage
INNOVATION AND SUSTAINABILITY

Outsourcing—Key Factors for Success

Even small businesses today are realizing the benefits of outsourcing. A more flexible cost structure, an increased skill base, lower costs, and an ability to focus time and talents on core business competencies are all benefits of outsourcing for businesses of all sizes. Increases in technology and a more hungry supply of outsources due to the economic downturn have made outsourcing viable for large and small businesses alike. Here are some tips for ensuring that outsourcing is a successful venture for you:

- An emphasis on communication with the supplier. Make sure your supplier knows what you need and why. Too much information is seldom a cause of an unsuccessful outsourcing venture.
- Maintain an appropriate staff to assist with the outsourcing. Too many people overseeing the outsourcing makes life difficult for the outsourcing company. Too few employees overseeing the outsourcing may leave you open to products and services that do not meet your quality standards.

- Think virtualization for your company. As you enlist the services of other companies, strategically plan how all the parts work together to successfully execute the needs of your business. This must be planned. It will not "just happen."
- Profitability may increase due to access to an increased skill base. Outsourcing allows your small business access to experts that range from IT to HR. This knowledge base can be beneficial to the bottom line of your business.
- Implement processes to be used in outsourcing. Include in those processes key employees who will help work through the transition needed for this type of change.
- Plan for the transition. Successful outsourcing does not occur overnight. Training and investing in the transfer of knowledge are critical to the long-term success of the business.

Sources: Manish Vora, "Best Practices in Business Process Outsourcing," *Financial Executive,* June 2010; Karl Funders, "Open to Outsourcing," *Computer Weekly,* December 2, 2008; and Ed van den Berg, "Outsourcing for SMEs," *Credit Management,* June 2009.

© Image Source/Getty Images

Direct Investment

Once you have established your international operations, you may choose to set up a permanent location in another country. Opening an office, factory, or store in a foreign land is the highest level of international commitment you can make. Of course, you are making a significant financial investment that costs you money, but what other risks are involved with direct investment? Think about what might happen if you set up operations in a country experiencing political instability. What if a new political regime takes power? Will you be allowed to operate as you did before? Will you even be allowed to keep the assets you have invested in there? Perhaps not, on either count. Here are some points to consider before you decide upon direct investment:

- Can you legally emigrate or obtain the appropriate documentation to either reside in the country or visit regularly? Obtaining the necessary visas is not always easy and varies from country to country, as does the time frame for which you can stay. Corey Kidd, who owns Intuitive Automata, a robotics health care start-up in Hong Kong, found that getting the initial visa was easier than the process of yearly renewal that is required. You do not want to get your business up and going only to find out you have to leave the country.

- Choose the country you are going to do business in carefully. China, India, Brazil, Russia, and Africa can be fairly difficult places to start a business. Hong Kong, Singapore, and Japan are much easier, according to Larry Harding, an international business services firm founder. Laws, rules, and regulations may vary dramatically. In the United States, we assume the police force is there to serve and protect. In other places, this is not the case. We also assume uninterrupted supplies of basics like water and electricity. Again, depending upon the location, this may not be the case. Danny Wong, a Shanghai-based custom dress shirt company, knows that Internet access in China is restricted, so using the Internet as an advertising medium must be modified in order to be effective in this location.

- Go visit before you open your business in a new location—and spend more than a couple of days. Experience the location, the culture, and the way of doing business firsthand before you make a decision. Knowing the local language is a huge benefit. Seeing where you will be selling your product and understanding the location on more than the surface level can be extraordinarily helpful in making decisions.

- Understand local business practices including employee norms. In the United States, working an 80-hour work week through the weekend may be expected during rush times or particular seasons. In contrast, in France, for example, employees do not view overtime as a positive, and governmental regulations limit the amount of time employees can actually work. Also consider the employee turnover rate. If employees move jobs frequently, your product quality and efficiency may be seriously compromised.

- Find a reputable and competent financial advisor who understands not only the local laws, taxes, and regulatory requirements but also the U.S. equivalents. Elizabeth Helsley, who owns and operates Global Luxe in Mexico, hires an accountant and legal services for much less than in the United States. She also pays much less in corporate taxes, 40 percent less in fact. If you continue to operate your business in the United States as well, you now will likely be paying taxes in two countries. Make sure you know or have hired someone who can successfully navigate the maze of governmental requirements in all locations in which you do business.[11]

For all the previous reasons, small businesses rarely start out their global experience with direct investment. Exporting, licensing, or joint ventures are much more common vehicles.

ENTREPRENEURIAL SNAPSHOT

Tony and Maureen Wheeler

© AP Photo/Chiang Ying-ying

In 1973, Tony and Maureen Wheeler went on their honeymoon. And the trip wasn't simply a weekend at Niagara Falls. Tony had just received his master's degree from the London Business School, and Ford Motor Company had just offered him a job, but he deferred accepting for a year. The couple took a year-long trip to try to get the wanderlust out of their systems before "settling down." They bought a very used Austin minivan for $150 and still had $1,400 in savings. They drove across Europe and the Middle East to Afghanistan. There they sold the Austin and continued across Asia via train, bus, rickshaw, and boat, eventually ending up in Sydney, Australia, after spending a mere $6 per day. On this trip they kept a journal. Tony noted specific details. Maureen mused romantically. Their 96-page travel notebook became the foundation of a travel guide empire called Lonely Planet.

When they returned to Australia flat broke, they were surprised to find people they knew asking them repeatedly, "How did you do that?" So they wrote a travel guide entitled *Asia on the Cheap* to tell adventurous, unconventional people just that—how they did it. They set up a tiny office in Melbourne, where they returned from far-flung expeditions to compile their notes in another book. Since the 1970s, the Wheelers have compiled more than 400 guides touching every continent.

Like most small businesses starting out, Lonely Planet kept its overhead to a minimum. Maureen organized layouts and set the type herself. Tony packed shipping cartons and wrote. They both did it all. Their traveling and their business were done on a shoestring, which became the competitive advantage of their guides. People wanted to learn how to travel on the cheap and were willing to pay for it. The Wheelers loved to travel and write about their experiences. *South-East Asia on a Shoestring*, which sold 15,000 copies at $1.95 each, was followed by more shoestring guides for Hong Kong, Australia, Nepal, and Africa. The

Wheelers thought they were over their heads with the India guide, because it was twice the length (700 pages) and twice the price ($10) of their other products, but it sold more than 100,000 copies in its first edition.

Tony recalls that in the early days most of their books were about Asia, and a lot of their business was done in Asia. He remembers one Asian distributor who hated to pay for the books he imported via the more traditional methods. "'So much paperwork and bureaucracy, so many bribes to be paid,' he'd complain. 'It's much better I just pay you in cash anytime you're in the country.' So the invoices would mount up for a year or so, and then one day, in some back-street cafe, large rolls of greenbacks would be counted out across the table, and I'd stuff them into every available pocket."

In 1980, the Wheelers decided to get serious about their international business after the birth of their first child. They opened an office in Oakland, California, and one in London six years later. Lonely Planet was turning into a real business, gradually expanding its staff to 12 people.

Today, Lonely Planet has gone high tech. Lonelyplanet.com supports the guidebooks with message boards, author blogs, Q&A columns, and medical advice. The Web site receives over 650,000 hits per day and has developed a reputation as one of the best travel sites around.

World events continue to conspire against the travel industry, but Lonely Planet forges ahead. Tony Wheeler says, "In the short term there's still the terrorist/SARS/Iraq madness impact to overcome, but in the longer term we're going to get back to the same old problems: not killing the golden goose by too much ill-planned tourism."

Although their company has certainly changed over its 30-plus years, the Wheelers' mission has not changed—getting unique information to travelers as quickly and accurately as possible. They love books as a way to carry around information but are receptive to the idea of changing formats. Maureen says that whatever way travelers learn about new places, the Wheelers hope it will be from Lonely Planet.

Sources: Tony Wheeler, "The Way We Were," *Publishers Weekly,* March 12, 2007, 66; Joanna Doonar, "It's Not Such a Lonely Planet," *Brand Strategy,* January 2004, 25–25; Maggie Overfelt, "Wanderpreneurs," *Fortune Small Business,* April 21, 2000, fsb.com; "Roughing It," *Fortune Technology Guide,* Summer 2000, 257; Michael Schuman, "The Not-So-Lonely Planet," *Forbes,* May 22, 1995, 104–108; and Cade Metz, "How They Built It," *PC Magazine,* February 8, 2000, 147.

Exporting

Exporting is defined as selling in another country the goods or services that you offer domestically. It is the most common way for small businesses to operate in other countries. Of all the ways to conduct business internationally that we are considering in this chapter, exporting provides the lowest levels of risk and investment, increasing your chances of being profitable. The Small Business Administration (SBA) has identified both advantages and disadvantages of exporting. Advantages include the following:

- Increased total sales and profits
- Access to a share of the global market where two-thirds of the world's purchasing power resides
- Reduced dependence on your existing markets
- Enhanced domestic competitiveness
- Opportunity to exploit your technology and know-how in places where they are needed
- Realization of the sales potential of existing products and extension of the product life cycle
- Stabilization of seasonal market fluctuations
- Opportunity to sell excess production capacity[12]

Disadvantages to exporting revolve around the additional responsibilities and obligations your business may incur. You may be required to do the following:

- Develop new promotional material suitable for foreign customers
- Forgo short-term profits in the interest of long-term gains
- Incur added administrative costs—the paperwork will increase
- Allocate funds and personnel for travel
- Wait longer for payments than with your domestic accounts
- Modify your product or packaging
- Acquire additional financing
- Obtain special export licenses

Only you can decide whether the disadvantages of global expansion outweigh the advantages. The timing of entering a foreign market may not be right, or you may be short on the cash needed to fund the expansion at this point. In any event, no hard-and-fast rules govern international expansion.

If you decide that exporting is right for your business, you have two methods that you can use: indirect exporting and direct exporting. Whether you choose to use intermediaries is the primary difference between the two.

Indirect Exporting

The simplest and perhaps most cost-effective way for a small business to export is to hire an export service company to market products abroad. This method minimizes the financial and personnel resources needed to promote international sales. Using an intermediary reduces your risks and can help you learn the exporting process. Even if you start using indirect exporting, you may choose to set up an international sales staff once you develop the capital and expertise.

Of course, the fee charged by an export service company will reduce your profit margin, but the increased sales should offset this disadvantage. A more dangerous disadvantage is that you lose control by operating through an intermediary. Your company name and image are in the hands of this intermediary. Finally, the price the ultimate consumer pays may be increased by using intermediaries. You should negotiate what all costs, fees, and the final price will be up front in the contract.

"Of all the ways to conduct business internationally that we are considering in this chapter, exporting provides the lowest levels of risk and investment, increasing your chances of being profitable."

Reality Check

China—Here We Come ... or Not

The Chinese market has been seen as a place of lower-cost production. With a growing economy of 8.7 percent in 2009 and an increase in retail sales of 15.5 percent, China as a market for goods and services is seen as increasingly viable. And its people are also increasingly wealthier, able to purchase a wide variety of goods and services. Before you move your business to China tomorrow, here a few things to consider:

- Do your preparatory homework. Due to the increased focus on China, there is also more information available today. Use that information to your advantage as you develop a strategic plan that includes China.
- Get the appropriate documentation in place before you begin. Since rules and regulations vary, you may need to deal directly with the local authority to ensure you are meeting the requirements of that location.
- Hire the right people. While someone who speaks Chinese will be helpful, management is more than just speaking the language. Your management team must all understand and implement your company mission, values, and ethical standards.
- Prices and currency are going up. As the yuan appreciates against the dollar, China's low-cost advantage may disappear. If you do not understand the role of exchange rates on your company, hire someone who does.
- Network based upon trust. Guanxi is more than just making connections. This concept involves establishing a trusted network that is stable over time, which takes time. Invest in relationships.
- Clearly understand who owns your business and the rules and regulations that apply. The rules of the game are different in China, and understanding those rules becomes critical to the success of your business. If you are caught breaking a rule, the government may very well make an example of you.

While China is an exciting new market, working internationally in China requires a strategic process in order to be successful.

Sources: Shaun Rein, "How Not to Run a Business in China,"www.business week.com, June 25, 2010; Courtney Rubin, "In China, the Cost of Doing Business Rises," www.inc.com, June 8, 2010; Diana Ransom, "In Focus: Setting Up Shops in China," www.smsmallbiz.com, March 1, 2010; and Issie Lapowsky, "10 Steps to Starting a Business in China," www.inc.com, July 12, 2010.

There are several kinds of intermediaries for you to consider. Agents and brokers, export management companies (EMCs), export trade companies (ETCs), and piggyback exporting are all domestic-based intermediaries. Foreign-based intermediaries include foreign distributors and foreign agents.

Agents and Brokers Both agents and brokers will put your company in touch with foreign buyers. They set up the deal, but they don't buy the products from you. They can also provide consultation on shipping, packaging, and documentation.

Export Management Companies Export management companies (EMCs) provide a much broader range of services than agents or brokers, but they still do not take title to your goods, although it is becoming more common for an EMC to do so. Instead, EMCs act as your own export department, conducting marketing research, arranging financing and distribution channels, attending trade shows, handling logistics, and advising on the legal and compliance issues involved with foreign trade. These intermediaries will even use your company letterhead in all correspondence and provide customer support after a sale. EMCs are a good option for small businesses new to international trade.

Approximately 600 EMCs operate in the United States, each representing an average of 10 suppliers. For example, Transcon Trading Company, of Irmo, South Carolina, has made sales in more than 70 countries. Although it deals in animal health products most of the time, it also represents a company that makes go-carts and a firm that makes bug zappers. Transcon works comfortably in any region, thanks to the people on its staff, who speak 10 different languages.[13]

Export Trade Companies *Export trade companies (ETCs)* perform many of the same functions as EMCs, and, in addition, generally take title to your goods and pay you directly. ETCs operate individually but may also join together to form cooperative groups of companies selling similar products. There is little risk for you, the small business owner, under this arrangement.

Piggyback Exporting If you can find another company that is already exporting, you may be able to make a *piggyback arrangement*, thereby taking advantage of the international connections the other company has already established. If your products do not directly compete with the other company's products, it may simply add your product line to its own.

Foreign-Based Distributors and Agents Using a distributor or an agent that is based in the foreign country rather than one that is based in the United States can provide the advantage of cultural and local knowledge that you may not be able to get elsewhere.

The SBA 2010 Small Business Exporter of the Year, Daniel Nanigian, President of Nanmac Corporation, developed an export strategy that included foreign markets, particularly China. Part of the strategy for China involved partnering with distributors and in-country sales representatives, as well as using a localized Chinese Web site to market his product, temperature sensors. His company doubled its revenue from 2008–2009 and is on target to hit international sales of $1.7 million this year.[14]

George Grumbles, president of Universal Data Systems, has been exporting electronic equipment for more than 25 years. He believes in building groups of local distributors in his foreign markets. Grumbles says, "You have to work through nationals [residents of the foreign country]. If you send U.S. folks into a foreign country, you

Shipping products overseas in containers makes transportation more efficient and, therefore, cheaper.

have to expect it will take a couple of years for them to find their way around. Instead, you should find people who are embedded in the local economy."[15]

Foreign agents do the same jobs overseas that manufacturer's representatives do in the United States. They work on commission within their sales region of specific countries. Local laws and customs vary greatly between countries, so you must be clear on what you can expect an agent to do legally. Some countries go to extremes in protecting their citizens from foreign companies. Make sure your agreement specifies whether or not the agent/distributor has the legal authority to make commitments on behalf of your company.

Foreign distributors may sell on a commission basis or buy your goods directly. You and the distributor should work together to produce your marketing materials because translating your packaging and promotional material into another language can be a problem.

Direct Exporting

With direct exporting, you do not use intermediaries, as opposed to indirect exporting. If you choose to use direct exporting as your method of selling your products in other lands, you have more control over the exporting process, greater potential profit, and direct contact with your customers. A point you must remember when considering any channel of distribution is that you can do away with the intermediary, but *someone* has to perform this function. If you choose not to use an intermediary for your exporting, then *you* have to perform those duties. You have to choose the target countries, arrange the most efficient channel of distribution, and market your product in the foreign country. Direct exporting is therefore riskier, more expensive, requires more resources, and is more difficult than indirect exporting. Because you pay less in service fees or commissions, however, your potential profit could be greater.

In direct exporting, one approach could entail the use of sales representatives who sell your products and other (noncompeting) products on a commission basis. You may choose to use a distributor or to sell directly to the final consumer.

Selling your product in other countries can be a logical extension of your domestic business. Many business executives say that exporting is essentially no different from expanding into a new market in your own country. Of course, operating in other countries can create unique challenges, but taking care of "the basics" will help you meet those challenges. First you have to perform market research to determine who will buy your product and where those buyers are located. Then you have to determine your channels of distribution and your prices.

Identifying Potential Export Markets

Successful marketing depends on your knowledge of the people and places with which you are dealing. In addition to the marketing research you would ordinarily conduct locally, marketing research in the international sector needs to include the following activities.

Find Countries with Attractive, Penetrable Markets Sometimes the largest trading partners of the United States may not be the best countries for you or your products. For example, Harden Wiedemann, of Assurance Medical, a provider of alcohol- and drug-testing services, was surfing around the Internet one day when he stumbled on information about growing alcohol-related problems in Argentina. A little more investigation revealed a sizable opportunity for his company.

Most small businesses begin their search for market information with U.S. government sources. Go to www.export.gov to find market research to learn your product's

> *"You and the distributor should work together to produce your marketing materials because translating your packaging and promotional material into another language can be a problem."*

potential in a given market, the best prospects for success, and the market's business practices before you export. From the home page you can access Market Research, by Industry, Trade Data and Analysis as well as information on International Sales, Finance and Logistics.

The SBA provides current market information to small businesses on foreign markets where their products are being bought and sold, and on which countries represent the largest markets. At www.sba.gov, you can find full-text versions of *SBA Take Your Business Global* and even online courses like *Global Enterprise: A Primer on Exporting.*

Canada, China, and Mexico top the list of importers of products made in the United States (see Figure 15.2). More detailed information on foreign markets for small businesses is available through sources like the *CIA World Factbook* (see Figure 15.3).

Define Export Markets That Match Your Product After you have identified potential countries, you must find out if a need exists there that you can satisfy. Ask yourself these questions:

- How does the quality of products in the foreign country compare with that of your products?
- Will your prices be competitive, keeping in mind the additional costs involved?
- Can you segment customers?
- Are there political risks in the country you are considering?
- Will your products, packaging, and advertising need any modifications?
- Will tariffs or nontariff barriers (restrictions or quotas) prevent your entry into the market?

The Department of Commerce and the SBA produce various publications and reports to help provide this information. The Department of State gathers information on

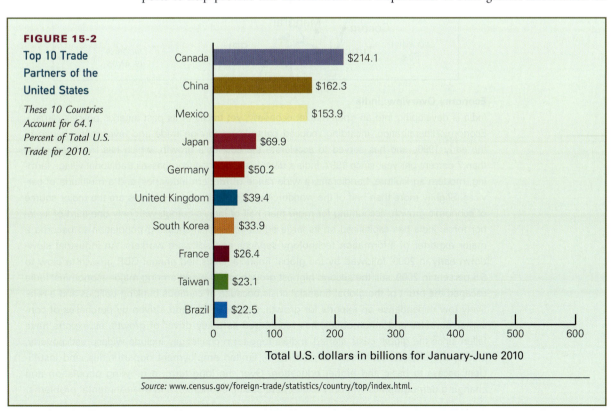

FIGURE 15-2

Top 10 Trade Partners of the United States

These 10 Countries Account for 64.1 Percent of Total U.S. Trade for 2010.

Country	Total U.S. dollars in billions for January-June 2010
Canada	$214.1
China	$162.3
Mexico	$153.9
Japan	$69.9
Germany	$50.2
United Kingdom	$39.4
South Korea	$33.9
France	$26.4
Taiwan	$23.1
Brazil	$22.5

Total U.S. dollars in billions for January-June 2010

Source: www.census.gov/foreign-trade/statistics/country/top/index.html.

FIGURE 15-3

India at a Glance

For Information about a Rapidly Growing U.S. Trade Partner, Go to India's Listing in the CIA World Factbook. (https://www.cia.gov/ library/publications/ the-world-factbook/ geos/in.html).

Economy Overview: India

India is developing into an open-market economy, yet traces of its past autarkic policies remain. Economic liberalization, including reduced controls on foreign trade and investment, began in the early 1990s and has served to accelerate the country's growth, which has averaged more than 7 percent per year since 1997. India's diverse economy encompasses traditional village farming, modern agriculture, handicrafts, a wide range of modern industries, and a multitude of services. Slightly more than half of the workforce is in agriculture, but services are the major source of economic growth, accounting for more than half of India's output, with only one-third of its labor force. India has capitalized on its large educated English-speaking population to become a major exporter of information technology services and software workers. An industrial slowdown early in 2008, followed by the global financial crisis, led annual GDP growth to slow to 6.5 percent in 2009, still the second-highest growth in the world among major economies. India escaped the brunt of the global financial crisis because of cautious banking policies and a relatively low dependence on exports for growth. Domestic demand, driven by purchases of consumer durables and automobiles, has reemerged as a key driver of growth, as exports have fallen since the global crisis started. India's long-term challenges include widespread poverty, inadequate physical and social infrastructure, limited employment opportunities, and insufficient access to basic and higher education. Over the long term, a growing population and changing demographics will only exacerbate social, economic, and environmental problems.

foreign markets through consulates and embassies. Foreign affiliates of the U.S. Chamber of Commerce, called American Chambers of Commerce (AmChams), also collect and disseminate information.

Some additional steps to consider to make your exporting experience more successful and consequently more profitable are as follows:

• Choose and commit at least one person in your organization to work on your strategy for exporting, and then be willing and able to commit the additional personnel and monetary resources that will be needed.
• Instead of selling to the world, choose one or two locations and focus on those countries. Canada may be a great first choice due to the similarities with the United States.
• Ensure that you can secure the additional financing that will be necessary. Not having the necessary cash flow available will make it difficult to be successful. The SBA has several programs that can assist small businesses desiring to export their products.[16]

Importing

When your small business is importing rather than exporting, the major focus of your activities shifts from supplying to sourcing. You need to identify markets making products for which you see a domestic demand.

Factors to consider when choosing a foreign supplier include its reliability in having products available for you, the consistency of product or service quality, and the delivery time needed to get products to you. A bank subsidiary office and the embassy of the supplier's home country are sources for this information.

As an importer, you must comply with the regulations and trade barriers of both the foreign country and the United States. You must make sure that your product can legally cross national borders. For example, cigars made in Cuba cannot be imported into the United States because of an embargo against that country. The United States also has established import quotas that limit the amount of products such as steel and beef that can be brought into this country. Such quotas are intended to protect domestic industries and jobs, although their results are not completely positive. Trade restrictions remain a topic of political discussion, and the debate will likely continue for years. You should try to stay as current as possible on trade and tariff regulations if you are involved in global trade.

"As an importer, you must comply with the regulations and trade barriers of both the foreign country and the United States."

Anthony Raissen knew from personal experience that he needed a product that could cleanse his breath, especially after eating the spicy foods that he loved. He found that gum, mints, candies, and other breath aids didn't do the job. These products tended to mask the bad breath as opposed to eliminating it. The same problem is faced by many people. During a trip to his native South Africa, Raissen was introduced to a group of chemists who had developed a formula of parsley-seed oil and sunflower oil that worked like magic on the bad-breath problem. Raissen bought the rights to the formula and returned to the United States to form BreathAsure, of Calabasas, California. Selling this product, Raissen's company has achieved annual sales revenues of nearly $18 million. In fact, responding to consumer demand, the company released Pure Breath, a version of the original BreathAsure product designed for dogs and cats—another obvious target market for this imported formula.[17]

Financial Mechanisms for Going International

Once you decide to enter the international trade game, you face challenges such as how to finance your expansion, how to pay your debts and get paid, and where to find information and assistance.

International Finance

Selling overseas is only half the challenge; the other half is finding the money to fill the order and dealing with currency fluctuations. Working capital may be needed for your new transaction level. Options for additional sources of capital include conventional financing, venture capital from investor groups, and prepayment or down payments from overseas buyers. To start looking for export financing, contact the Export-Import Bank (Ex-Im Bank) or the SBA.

The Ex-Im Bank is an independent federal agency that assumes credit and country risks not covered by private sector lenders. Approximately 85 percent of its transactions impact small businesses through programs like working capital guarantees, export credit insurance and loan guarantees, or direct loans. The export credit insurance program covers your business in the event your foreign buyer does not pay you, which then allows you, the U.S. business, to provide better credit terms to your export customers. To get information on the Ex-Im Bank's lending and insurance programs, visit its Web site (www.exim.gov).

The SBA has several financial services for exporters, including an international trade loan program for short-term financing and the 7(a) business loan guarantee program for medium-term working capital and long-term fixed-asset financing. The SBA's financing programs can be found at www.sba.gov.

"Keeping current on the exchange rates and forecasted moves in the exchange rates is important when dealing with international business."

Currency fluctuations can impact your bottom line quickly, both importing and exporting. A competitive advantage based upon price through lower input costs like materials or labor can be erased as the currency of the country with which you are doing business moves against the U.S. dollar. Keeping current on the exchange rates and forecasted moves in the exchange rates is important when dealing with international business. If one currency appreciates, the other currency must depreciate so a change can be positive for you as you export and negative for the business next door who is importing from that same country. China is a great case in point. From 2005–2008, the yuan appreciated 21 percent against the dollar. China's less expensive prices in everything from wages to materials vanished, forcing some companies to move from China to other countries where the currency gap was more favorable. This same change has also been a positive for U.S. businesses who export to China. David and Goliath, Inc., an apparel company in Clearwater, Florida, produces its clothing in the United States and sells its products in 15 stores worldwide. While they have no stores in China, their online business from China is significant and the appreciating yuan will lower the cost of this clothing for Chinese consumers. Make sure you understand the impact currency fluctuations will have on your business and plan accordingly.[18]

Managing International Accounts

A problem for most small businesses is getting paid. Small businesses rarely have the financial resources to carry excessive accounts receivable, which can be amplified by selling in other countries. Brian Burt is the chief finance officer for Hardwoods of Michigan, a flooring supply company out of Clinton, Michigan. He feels the biggest issue in exporting is the risk involved, which includes both not getting paid at all and also the time it takes to get paid. In the flooring industry in the United States, it takes about a month to collect on accounts. For international customers he says it can take 70 to 90 days, a huge difference for small businesses who are often short on cash.[19] In the United States, the average number of days needed to collect accounts receivable is 42. That's quite a long time for a small business to have money outstanding, but the international branch of the National Association of Credit Management says that some countries average much longer waits. For example, you can expect to wait more than 120 days for payment from customers from Greece, Albania, and Lithuania. Companies from many less developed countries may take even longer to pay their bills.

Your primary financial concern as a global operator should be to ensure that you get paid in full and on time. Keep in mind that your foreign buyers will be concerned about receiving products that meet their specifications on time. Thus terms of payment must be agreed upon in advance in a way that satisfies both parties.

The primary methods of paying for international transactions are described next, presented in order from most secure for the exporter to least secure (see Figure 15.4).

Payment in Advance Requiring clients to pay in advance provides the least risk to you, but unless you have an extremely specialized product, the buyer can probably get a better deal from someone else. Still, it is reasonable to negotiate partial payment or progress payments.

Letter of Credit A letter of credit is an internationally recognized instrument issued by a bank on behalf of its client, the purchaser. It is a guarantee that the bank will pay the seller if the conditions specified are fulfilled and one of the safest payment methods.

Documentary Collection (Drafts) Drafts are documents that require the buyer to pay the seller the face amount either when the product arrives (called a *sight draft*) or at a specified time in the future (called a *time draft*). Because title does not pass until the draft is paid, both parties are protected. Drafts involve a certain amount of risk but are cheaper for the purchaser than letters of credit.

Consignment Selling on consignment means that you advance your product to an intermediary, who then tries to sell it to the final user. If you sell on consignment, you don't get paid until the intermediary sells the product. Consignment is risky because there is no way of knowing when, if ever, the goods will be sold.

Open Account Although commonly used in selling products in the United States, delivering goods before payment is required is very risky for international sales. If the creditworthiness of the buyers or the political and economic stability of their country is questionable, you stand to lose your entire investment, possibly without recourse.

Countertrade and Barter

countertrade
The completion of a business deal without the use of money as a means of exchange. Barter is a common form of countertrade.

A problem encountered in trading with many economically emerging countries (such as many Eastern European and former Soviet countries) is that their currency is virtually worthless outside their borders. A solution to this problem may be **countertrade**. Although countertrade takes several forms, it is basically substituting a product for money as part of the transaction. Although countertrade is rarely a long-term solution, it may be a tool to make deals that could not be reached otherwise.[20]

The most common form of countertrade that small businesses can use is *barter*. This type of trading has existed throughout history. Some creativity may be needed to find a business that has complementary needs. PepsiCo arranged creative trades within the former

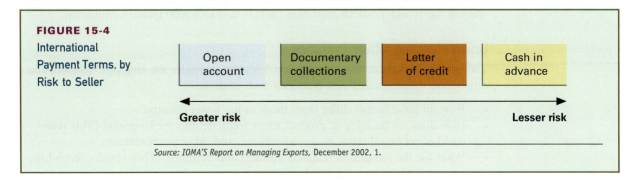

FIGURE 15-4
International Payment Terms, by Risk to Seller

| Open account | Documentary collections | Letter of credit | Cash in advance |

Greater risk ← → Lesser risk

Source: *IOMA'S Report on Managing Exports,* December 2002, 1.

Soviet Union by trading soft drinks for vodka, which was worth much more on the open market than the ruble and was much easier to sell. You may make deals just as creatively.

The key to making money in countertrade is to have somewhere to sell the goods you receive in trade. Swapping your product for something you can't sell later is no bargain. The golden rule of countertrade is this: *Do not quote prices until the countertrade situation is clearly understood.*

Information Assistance

Where can you go on the Internet for help in going global?

- *U.S. Census Bureau* (www.census.gov). Great site for international trade statistics, export classification assistance, and profiles of exporting companies.
- *U.S. Department of Commerce* (www.doc.gov). One-stop shop for useful statistics on business, trade, and the world economic picture.
- *STAT-USA/Internet* (www.stat-usa.gov). This site is a single point of access to authoritative business, trade, and economic information from across the federal government.
- *U.S. Small Business Administration* (www.sba.gov). You've been sent here before, but this time you will find information on export assistance in the "Expanding" section.
- *International Logistics* (www.export.gov/logistics/index.asp). The U.S. government's international logistics homepage.
- *Currency Conversion Calculator* (www.oanda.com).
- *Foreign Incentives* (www.export.gov). One-stop site for info on trade leads, commercial specialist, marketing research, and advocacy.
- *Tradenet's Export Advisor* (link through www.sba.gov). Another one-stop shop for exporting. A joint venture with the SBA, Department of Commerce, and other agencies. Its credo is "No business is too small to go global."
- Also see these sites:

  - American Association of Exporters and Importers (www.aaei.org)
  - Federation of International Trade Associations (www.fita.org)
  - International Chamber of Commerce (www.iccwbo.org)
  - International Federation of Customs Brokers Association (www.ifcba.org)
  - International Organization for Standardization (www.iso.org)

The International Challenge

Success for many small businesses will depend increasingly on some degree of sales to markets in other countries. International business presents quite a few challenges, but, then, most entrepreneurs thrive on challenge. There are no hard-and-fast rules for going global, and space does not permit coverage of every situation you may face, but some issues you need to be aware of are cultural differences, global trading regions (especially NAFTA), the effect of the World Trade Organization (WTO), and ISO 9000 quality certification.

Understanding Other Cultures

The most important cultural factors you'll want to consider are language, religion, education, and social systems. Ask questions such as these:

- How do these factors differ from those in my home country?
- How does my business or product name translate into the language? (This issue could affect brand-name usage, advertising, and other promotions.)
- What are the recognized religious holidays and customs? (They could affect when, where, and how you conduct business.)

"The most important cultural factors you'll want to consider are language, religion, education, and social systems."

- What is the average educational level of your potential customers? (It could influence the type of employee training needed or packaging and advertising decisions.)
- What are the accepted and practiced social rituals, customs, and behaviors? (They could influence many different business decisions.)

And just where can you find this information? First, numerous books and other publications describe cultural customs and the differences among countries. A trip to your local library can uncover a wealth of sources. You could also contact international business professors or foreign-language professors at a local college. These individuals are typically highly knowledgeable about cultural factors or, at the very least, can point you toward other sources of such information. If you know someone who has visited or lived in the country you're investigating, most certainly talk to that person. Such first-hand knowledge is invaluable. Another source of information would be the U.S. Department of Commerce, which has a number of programs and services for companies interested in doing business in other countries.

When marketing your product globally, you must think and act globally. This means that you need to be sensitive to cultural beliefs that vary from country to country. Every culture has different accepted norms and ways of doing business. Not understanding and not following these norms can lead to embarrassment for you at best, and completely blowing your deal at worst. *Insha'llah* is an Islamic phrase that translates as "God willing." *Mañana* is a Latin American phrase that means "later." *Hakuna matata* is an African phrase that translates as "no worries." In the United States, those phrases seem relatively harmless and would often be used lightly. In the countries mentioned, those phrases have a deeper meaning. The phrases may indicate there is no point in worrying about an inventory deadline, for example, since if the deadline is supposed to be met, it will happen regardless of personal initiative or action. Consequently, precautions or emphasis that Westerners would employ to meet the deadline would not be seen as nearly so important. Or take, for example, holidays. In the West, the week between Christmas and New Year's Day is typically a slower time. In Islamic countries, Ramadan lasts for 30 days based upon the lunar calendar, so the date varies from year to year. For that 30-day period, work will either slow or in some instances stop.[21]

Training the employees you send overseas can help them adjust to cultural differences so that they can perform their jobs better. Do not assume that just because your employee is successful in the United States, he or she will automatically be able to deal with an international assignment. The *Harvard Business Review* suggests that intellectual, psychological, and social capital broken down into these nine attributes are important to assess to ensure your employee (or you, for that matter), will succeed in a global environment:

- Global business knowledge—How does your industry work, not only in the United States but also around the world?
- Cognitive complexity—Can you deal with multiple moving parts and still move forward in decision making?
- Cosmopolitan outlook—Do you enjoy other parts of the world, the different cultures, food, music, people, and so forth?
- Diversity—Do you like to try new experiences, meet new people, and travel to new places?
- Adventure—Can you handle uncertainty and the unknown?
- Self-assurance—Are you self-confident, and able to deal with new situations?
- Intercultural empathy—Can you connect with people from other cultures?
- Interpersonal impact—Can you bring together a variety of viewpoints?
- Diplomacy—Can you successfully navigate through both the verbal and nonverbal issues in communicating with a diverse group of people?[22]

Some employees will exhibit more of these traits than others. Choose carefully when deciding who will represent you and your business in a foreign country.

Customs like gift giving are important to understand. Gifts from business partners are expected in some cultures, but they are considered offensive in others. Should you present the gift on the first meeting or afterward? In public or private? To whom? What kind of gift is appropriate? In Japan, gifts are exchanged to symbolize the depth and strength of a business relationship.[23] When dealing with a Japanese business, the first meeting is the appropriate time to exchange gifts; if you are presented with a gift, you are expected to respond with one in return. By contrast, gifts are rarely exchanged in Germany, Belgium, and the United Kingdom.

Exchanging business cards is no big deal, right? Wrong. Taking someone's card and immediately putting it in your pocket is considered very rude in Japan. After the bow, you should take the card with both hands, carefully look at the card, observe the title and organization, acknowledge with a nod, and make a relevant comment or ask a question. In presenting the card, you should use both hands and hold it so the other person can read it. If English is not the primary language, you should have the information printed in the recipient's native language on the reverse side. Never put the card in your back pocket or write on the business card. Showing respect for the business card is seen as demonstrative of the respect you have for the person who gave you the card.[24]

Language is another obvious problem. You are not expected to speak another language like a local, but making an attempt to learn some of the language can be a sign of good faith. Most trade specialists recommend that you employ a professional translator for written communication and always have one available when you travel for face-to-face meetings. It may cost a few hundred dollars per hour, but as Jeff Barger, president of CTS (Corporate Translation Services), says, "Look at the marketing dollars you spent to win a customer—are you going to skimp when you finally sit down with him?"[25] In

© Fcarucci/Shutterstock.com

While not all training may be as fun as costumed dancing, immersion into another culture is a great learning experience.

addition to hiring an interpreter, don't rely on your memories of seventh-grade Spanish class—get documents professionally translated. Get free price quotes on translation services at www.buyerzone.com.[26]

And just because you speak the same language, do not assume words hold the same meaning. In the United States, to "table a motion" means you are no longer going to discuss the item. In the United Kingdom, "to table a motion" means to place the item on the agenda. Creating a glossary of commonly used terms and phrases at the beginning of the meeting can help to avoid communication misunderstandings.[27]

Trade experts at Moran, Stahl & Boyer International, an international consulting firm, say that culture has two components: surface culture (fads, styles, food, and holidays) and deep culture (norms, attitudes, values, and beliefs). According to the tip-of-the-iceberg concept, only 10 to 15 percent of a region's culture is visible (see Figure 15.5).[28] This means you must look below the surface to identify forces that truly drive a culture.

As you can see, the cultural aspects of international business are very complicated and confusing, but their importance cannot be overstated. Doing your homework can prevent serious mistakes.

Pat McGovern states that when a small business ventures abroad, the CEO needs to be the point person, traveling frequently and acting boldly and enthusiastically. McGovern has the experience to back up what he says; in the 40 years since the start of his business, IDG, he has averaged four months of travel per year launching technology publications, events, and research from Antarctica to Zimbabwe.

Being the point person opening new territory is not an easy job. When McGovern first went to Changsha, capital of the Hunan province, business associates took him to a restaurant where the waiter decapitated a snake and poured its blood in everyone's glass. People in his party told him that toasting with the blood would make him a member of the "Hunan Mafia." McGovern says, "Fortunately, I have an iron stomach (I've also eaten monkey brains and scorpion), so I downed the stuff." It pays to be in the inner circle, as many of his Chinese business leaders today are from Hunan.[29]

> *"Just because you speak the same language, do not assume words hold the same meaning."*

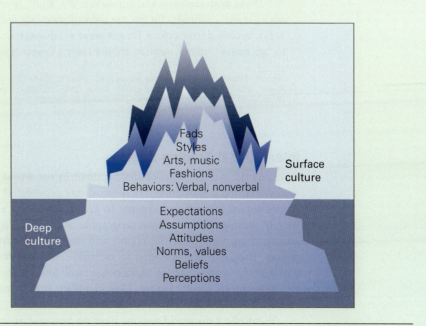

FIGURE 15-5

The Cultural Iceberg

Many Important Cultural Factors Are Not Easily Seen.

Fads
Styles
Arts, music
Fashions
Behaviors: Verbal, nonverbal

Surface culture

Deep culture

Expectations
Assumptions
Attitudes
Norms, values
Beliefs
Perceptions

Source: Kevin Walsh, "How to Negotiate European Style," *Journal of European Business*, July/August 1993, 45–47.

Manager's Notes

International Trading Regions

Since World War II, a major development in the world economy has been the creation of regional trade groupings. That trend has accelerated in recent years. A trade region is established through agreements to create economic and political ties among nations usually located within a close geographic area. These agreements reduce trade barriers among countries within the region and standardize barriers with countries outside the region. They also are intended to increase competition within them, so that inefficient nationalized companies or monopolies will lose their protective walls and be forced to come up to speed. Figure 15.6 identifies major trading regions and the member countries.

What effect do world regions have on you and your small business? The passage of the North American Free Trade Agreement (NAFTA) was intended to open markets and

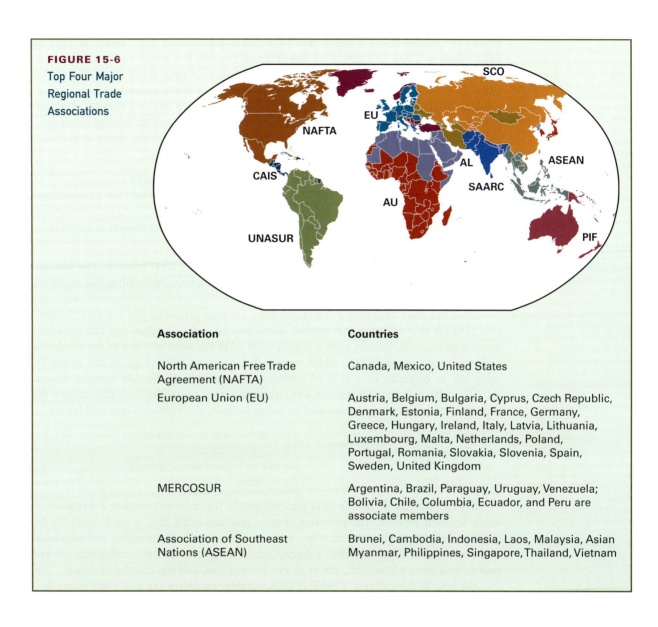

FIGURE 15-6

Top Four Major Regional Trade Associations

Association	Countries
North American Free Trade Agreement (NAFTA)	Canada, Mexico, United States
European Union (EU)	Austria, Belgium, Bulgaria, Cyprus, Czech Republic, Denmark, Estonia, Finland, France, Germany, Greece, Hungary, Ireland, Italy, Latvia, Lithuania, Luxembourg, Malta, Netherlands, Poland, Portugal, Romania, Slovakia, Slovenia, Spain, Sweden, United Kingdom
MERCOSUR	Argentina, Brazil, Paraguay, Uruguay, Venezuela; Bolivia, Chile, Columbia, Ecuador, and Peru are associate members
Association of Southeast Nations (ASEAN)	Brunei, Cambodia, Indonesia, Laos, Malaysia, Asian Myanmar, Philippines, Singapore, Thailand, Vietnam

to reduce barriers for U.S. companies to send their products to Mexico and Canada. Regional agreements may also change your strategy for dealing with businesses in those countries. For example, because the European Union (EU) has higher tariffs and barriers for products coming from countries outside the region than for products that come from within, it might make sense to establish operations in an EU country if you intend to do a lot of business there. Then you can sell in any of the 27 member nations under reduced barriers.

North American Free Trade Agreement In 1993, Congress passed the North American Free Trade Agreement (NAFTA), which joined Canada, Mexico, and the United States into a free-trade area. One of the primary goals of NAFTA is to ultimately eliminate tariffs and nontariff barriers between the United States, Canada, and Mexico on nearly all qualifying goods. NAFTA links 444 million people producing $17 trillion dollars worth of goods and services, making it the largest free-trade area in the world. Overall, trade among the United States, Canada, and Mexico has grown from $297 billion in 1993 to $883 billion in 2006, an increase of 198 percent.[30]

A key word here is *qualifying*. Products will qualify for tariff elimination if they *originate*, as defined in Article 401 of NAFTA, in one of the three countries. For example, products that are made in Japan and are shipped through Mexico cannot enter the United States under preferential NAFTA duty rates. So you need to determine whether your products are originating goods. There are four primary ways for goods to qualify:

1. Goods wholly obtained or produced in a NAFTA country
2. Goods made up entirely of components and materials that qualify
3. Goods that are specifically cited in an article of the agreement (very few products are cited)
4. Goods that are covered under specific rules of origin for that product, as listed in NAFTA Annex 401 (the most common way to qualify)[31]

Your products need to be assigned a *harmonized system (HS)* number. The harmonized system classifies products so that their chapter, heading, and subheading numbers are identical for all three countries.

Once you have determined the HS number for your products, you can find the specific NAFTA rule of origin that applies. Some specific rules of origin will call for additional requirements. Usually such a requirement takes the form of a test of the product's *regional value content (RVC)*, which means that a certain percentage of the product's value has to originate in a NAFTA country. For example, if the rule specifies that a good must have at least 65 percent RVC, then you need to demonstrate that at least 65 percent of the good's value originated in either Canada, the United States, or Mexico.

Chapter 95	Toys, games, and sports requisites
Heading 95.04	Table or parlor games
Subheading 9504.20	Articles for billiards and accessories
Tariff item 9504.20.21	Billiard tables

If your products do qualify as originating goods, you need to complete a *certificate of origin* for each product. The importer of your products must have a valid certificate to claim preferential tariff treatment. The certificate of origin shows the names and addresses of the importer and the exporter, a description of the goods, the HS number, the preference criteria (how it qualified), the producer, the net cost, and the country of origin.

For help in determining a product's HS number, exporters can visit the Census Bureau's Foreign Trade Web site (www.census.gov) or the NAFTA Web site (www.ustr.gov). The Department of Commerce home page has several helpful links (www.commerce.gov). To learn about NAFTA rules of origin and other important provisions, exporters should go to www.export.gov, where the NAFTA rules of origin for documenting the origin and the certificate of origin can be found. Information videos are available on this site to assist you in completing the appropriate paperwork. Obtain a copy of the NAFTA agreement online (www.tech.mit.edu/Bulletins/nafta.html) or from the U.S. Government Printing Office (202-783-3238). U.S. Customs has several links including Basic Importing and Exporting, which has many useful publications that can be downloaded at www.cbp.gov. The Trade Information Center (TIC) is a convenient first stop for new exporters, offering information on the export process, and it is integrated into the www.export.gov Web site.

World Trade Organization The first global tariff agreement began in 1947 with the General Agreement on Tariffs and Trade (GATT). This agreement, which originally included the United States and 22 other countries, has grown to include 153 member countries that represent more than 90 percent of world trade. Since GATT's inception, it has gone through eight "rounds" of negotiations or meeting sites. The latest series of negotiations, called the Uruguay Round, lasted from 1986 until 1994. One of its provisions was to create a successor to GATT, called the World Trade Organization (WTO). Created in 1995, the WTO promotes international trade through a "level playing field for all" as well as a legal and institutional framework for settling disputes.[32]

ISO 9000

Quality isn't a concern just among American managers within their own businesses; it is also an international issue. The International Standards Organization (ISO), based in Europe, has established 18,000 international quality standards for manufacturers' *methods* of product development. These ISO standards are intended to minimize the need for on-site visits by vendors to verify that their suppliers are taking the proper steps to ensure quality production. *ISO 9000 certification* relates to quality standards of production, not to the quality of the product itself. *ISO 14000 standards* relate to environmental issues.[33]

The process of getting your business ISO certified is time-consuming, complex, and expensive. The procedure works like this: After you document all the steps of your operations that ensure the quality of goods and services, an auditing firm visits your company to conduct a process audit and a financial audit to determine whether you pass. Two follow-up audits per year are required to maintain certification.

Why would a small business bother? Partners and Napier, an ad agency in Rochester, New York, is not the usual type of company that pursues ISO 9000 certifications. However, upon the request of one of their clients, Kodak, the business was certified. Certification took six months and about $20,000.. Each step of the ad assignment was documented, from developing the brief to sharing the finished product with the client. During this process, what Partners and Napier found were some major inefficiencies that once resolved allowed them to go from spending eight weeks on a job to three weeks. They were able to save their client approximately 40 percent and increase their billings by 300 percent in the last five years. The ISO 9000 certification was a win-win for both the client and this business.[34]

Currently, large businesses and divisions of major corporations are the ones getting ISO certified, but small manufacturers are quickly following suit. Free information packets are available from the American Society for Quality (www.asq.org.) or the American National Standards Institute (www.ansi.org). Of course, you can also go right to the source (www.iso.org) to find a wealth of information on ISO standards, principles, and forms—even business plans for public review. We will revisit the topic of ISO 9000 in more depth in Chapter 18.

Summary

1. List factors to consider when preparing an international business plan.

In addition to everything included in your domestic business plan, your international business plan should specify your preferred method for entering foreign markets, markets that represent the best opportunities for your business, projected costs and revenues, any contacts you have in overseas partnerships or foreign investment, and any legal requirements or restrictions you must consider.

2. Name five ways for small businesses to conduct international trade.

The five methods for small businesses to conduct international business are exporting, importing, licensing, joint ventures, and direct investment.

3. Analyze the advantages and disadvantages of exporting for small businesses.

The advantages of exporting are that it offers you a way to increase sales and profits, increase your market share, reduce your dependence on existing markets, increase your competitiveness in domestic markets, satisfy a demand for your products abroad, extend your product's life cycle, stabilize seasonal sales fluctuations, sell excess production capacity, and learn about foreign competition.

The disadvantages of exporting are the expense of changing your products and promotional material, the increased costs that cut into short-term profits, added administrative and travel costs, time needed to receive payment (which may be longer than for domestic accounts), the need for additional financing, and the increased paperwork involved.

Small business owners have a choice of two approaches to exporting: indirect and direct. Indirect exporting involves the use of intermediaries such as agents and brokers, export management companies, export trade companies, piggyback exporting, and foreign-based distributors and agents. With direct exporting, the small business owner makes all contacts and handles the logistics and paperwork of exporting alone.

4. Discuss factors to consider when importing products and materials.

The focus of a small business in regard to importing is on finding international sources of products to satisfy its domestic customers. The small business owner must consider the reliability of the foreign supplier, the consistency of the product quality, and the additional time that will be needed to ship products from another country.

5. Explain how small businesses can manage their finances in international trade.

In managing your finances for international trade, you must plan how to raise additional funds and how to get paid. Funding can come from your current commercial bank, from the Ex-Im Bank, or with assistance from the SBA. Methods for payment include payment in advance, by letters of credit, by draft, on consignment, and by open account.

6. Articulate the cultural and economic challenges of international small business activity.

Challenges you will face when going global include learning and adapting to cultural differences, dealing with provisions of trade regions and agreements like NAFTA and GATT, and ensuring the quality of your products to customers who are not familiar with you or your business, through compliance with international standards such as ISO 9000.

Questions for Review and Discussion

1. Discuss the difference between and the advantages and disadvantages of indirect and direct exporting.
2. What is the advantage of a strategic alliance over direct investment when entering a foreign market?
3. What information should a small business owner gather before deciding to export products?
4. Why is finding financial assistance for international expansion more difficult than finding such help for domestic expansion?
5. Why would a small business choose to license its products in other countries?
6. Choose three foreign markets and find out what the customs and courtesies for greetings are in those countries (possibly using the Internet as a source).
7. Imagine that you own a small manufacturing business. Identify the product that you produce and a foreign market that appears to represent an opportunity. What is one country that would pose a bigger risk?
8. Name a form of countertrade and indicate when it would be an appropriate strategy.
9. Discuss the differences and similarities between domestic- and foreign-based intermediaries.
10. What does the Ex-Im Bank do for potential exporters? For importers?

Questions for Critical Thinking

1. Now that the Internet has opened up international trade, especially for small businesses, what effect do you think it will have on trade standards for selling goods abroad? Do you expect an increase in nontariff barriers?
2. Which countries are riskier markets for small businesses to enter? Why? Where would you find information regarding political stability, financial risks, and cultural differences?

What Would You Do?

Refer to the Entrepreneurial Snapshot on Lonely Planet. The Wheelers built their business by describing travel in many countries around the globe. In the process, they created a Web site (www.lonelyplanet.com) that offers an incredible wealth of information for entrepreneurs. Choose a country that you believe has potential to be a market for the small business you wish to own. Working in teams of two, use Lonely Planet online to become "experts" on this country. Use all of the site's resources, such as Worldguide, Theme Guides, The Thorn Tree, and The Scoop. Once you have gathered this valuable information on Iceland, Singapore, or anywhere in between, prepare a two-page executive summary on the opportunities you find for your chosen country. Present your findings to your class.

16

Small Business Management

CHAPTER LEARNING OUTCOMES

After reading this chapter, you should be able to:

1. Describe the functions and activities involved in managing a small business.

2. Explain the stages of small business growth and their consequences for managing your business.

3. Discuss the significance of leadership and motivation in regard to employees of small business.

4. Discuss time and stress management as they relate to small business.

S o what do small business owners do with the hours in the day? After all, it is their own business so they are the masters of their own time and activities, correct? Let's look at four small business owners and the tasks they regularly perform. You might be surprised at the variety of activities required every day. Small business owners, literally, must do it all.

Caroline Geishecker owns, operates, and manages Chatham Coffee Company Deli and Variety in North Chatham, Massachusetts. Her day begins with baking bagels and

other bread items at 5:30 every morning. After the breakfast rush, she must then forecast the number of sandwiches needed for lunch, check inventory, and then place orders for food supplies that will be needed. She also stocks shelves, washes dishes, makes trips to the warehouse, sends e-mails to her legislative representatives, and reviews the financial reports at the end of every day. It is early to bed so she can get up early the next morning and do it all over again.

Chris Jordan is the owner of Atlanta Insurance Live, located in Atlanta, Georgia. He makes sales calls, deals with customer service issues, answers phones, utilizes his social networking resources, and plans his schedule, using differing days as focal points for each activity. Calling on customers, while an important job, can take hours of time and is a task he time manages wisely. Some days he works on business planning, and on others on the financial side of his business—both very important management tasks.

Mike Mitternight owns Factory Service Agency, Inc., in Metairie, Louisiana, a commercial heating and air-conditioning small business. He sees his first task of the day as compiling a critical to-do list with tasks to delegate to others, since he realizes he cannot do it all. Once the day is underway, he is back at his desk, designing equipment, working on new proposals and quotes, calling on suppliers, and then networking with everyone from his CPA to the local economic development board. He must also be on call all day to answer employee questions, solve supplier problems, and deal with the inevitable equipment and machinery challenges.

Sue Berk owns and operates Sue Berk Designs based in Dallas, Texas. Her business features baby blankets, wooden frames, and intricately painted ceramic crosses that she envisions, designs, and creates In the beginning of her business, she hand painted all the crosses herself, drawing upon her creativity and perseverance. Her business became so successful that she was forced to outsource the creating of her products since she no longer could keep up the demand. Now not only is she dealing with issues in the United States but also, since she outsourced to China, she has had to plan, forecast product demand, and implement quality control in order to ensure the integrity of her product. She believes her ability to plan has been critical to the success of her business.

As you can see from the previous examples, running your own business requires a myriad of managerial skills that are used every day in a variety of ways. Small business owners seldom have the luxury of focusing on any one task until completed. They must be the proverbial jack-of-all trades. As you read through this chapter, you will learn how small business managers manage their businesses successfully through the functions of management: planning, organizing, leading, and controlling.

Sources: "A Day in the Life of a Small-Business Owner," *MyBusiness*, www.nfib.com, retrieved June 29, 2010; Marla Tabaka, "Six-Figure Solopreneurs: The Common Link," www.inc.com, retrieved June 29, 2010; and Peter Vanden Bos, "How to Run a One-Person Business," www.inc.com, June 21, 2010.

Managing Small Business

Businesses of every size must be managed or they will cease to exist. Although there are many similarities between managing a large business and managing a small one, significant differences also exist. Managing a small business is a complex job. You have to perform many activities well without the resources available to your large competitors. The expectations of customers, associates, and employees are increasing to the point where small businesses can rarely survive without understanding the tools and practices of professional management. In this chapter, we will investigate the processes of managing a growing business, of leading people, and of facing the concerns of a small business owner.

Four Functions of Management

management

The process of planning, organizing, leading, and controlling resources in order to achieve the goals of an organization.

The major functions of **management** are generally accepted to be *planning*, *organizing*, *leading*, and *controlling*. To some extent, a manager performs these functions whether he is in charge of a large or a small operation, a for-profit or a nonprofit organization, or a retail, service, or manufacturing business.

These four functions are *continuous* and *interrelated* (see Figure 16.1). In other words, managers do each of them all the time. You don't have the luxury of getting out of bed in the morning and saying, "I think I am going to just organize today." Rather, you will have to do some planning, some organizing, a lot of leading, and some controlling every day.

These four functions are interrelated in that their achievement occurs as part of a progressive cycle. Planning begins the process, as the manager determines what to do. Organizing involves assembling the resources (financial, human, and material) needed to accomplish the plan. Leading is the process of getting the most output possible from those resources. Controlling is comparing what was initially planned with what was actually accomplished. If a deviation exists between what was planned and what was done, which is almost always the case, a new plan is needed, and the cycle begins again.

What Managers Do

Management is getting things done through people. When running a small business, you will have to spend a certain amount of time performing the actual duties and daily tasks of the business—probably more during the early stages in the life of the business and less later. You must decide where to strike a balance between doing and managing. This doesn't mean that managers don't "do" anything. Rather, it means that the time that you spend on the daily tasks, like selling or writing new software or cleaning machinery, is time when you are not managing. Those tasks have to be done, and the small business owner is usually the one who has to do them, but managing a business is more than a collection of tasks.

First-time managers and business owners often think of management as doing the job they have previously done, only with more power and control. Rather, to use the analogy of a master chef, a novice business owner or manager must move from being

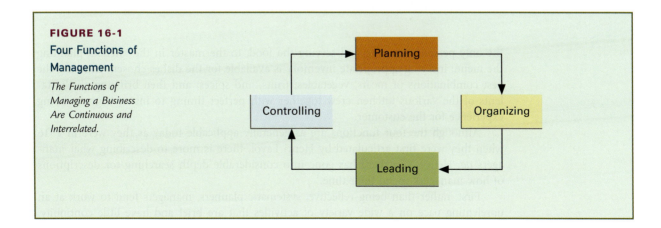

FIGURE 16-1

Four Functions of Management

The Functions of Managing a Business Are Continuous and Interrelated.

Planning

Organizing

Leading

Controlling

Manager's Notes

Help Me, Help Me, Help Me

Managing a small business can be tough and lonely. Where can a small business owner go on the Internet to get help? Is there anywhere an entrepreneur can gain insight into the daily nitty-gritty of running a business? Or, a place to chat with others about difficult situations?

Several small business portals have sprung up to go past advice and offer real online service. Portals are gateways to a wealth of resources.

- allbusiness.com. At this self-described one-stop resource for growing businesses, you will find the following topics: Business Advice, Professional Journals, Business Bloggers, Forms & Agreements, Tools & Services, and Industry Centers.
- bizjournals.com. Bizjournals is the online media division of American City Business Journals, the nation's largest publisher of metropolitan business newspapers. Characterized among the "Best of the Web" by *Forbes* magazine, bizjournals' archives contain 1.25 million business news articles published since 1996. Bizjournals' sites have more than 4 million unique monthly visitors.
- startupjournal.com. From the publishers of the *Wall Street Journal*, it's not just for big businesses anymore. Good small business portal.
- www.toolkit.cch.com. CCH Business Owner's Toolkit. Good portal for start-ups, less so for existing businesses. Good information on marketing, taxes, incorporation, financing, and employees—all the stuff you need for starting a business.
- Workz.com. Good, comprehensive site for running an online business—from accepting credit cards to creating banner ads. Over 1,000 articles, templates, and tools targeted specifically for small businesses are available.
- inc.com. *Inc.* magazine is one of the best small business magazines going—and their Web site is packed with useful info and full-text article archives.
- money.cnn.com/magazines/fsb/. *Fortune Small Business* magazine combines the credibility that *Fortune* has created over decades of business journalism and focuses on practical applications for running your own business.
- fastcompany.com. *Fast Company* magazine combines two things in each issue: cutting-edge cool and depth of coverage. Good combo.
- money.cnn.com/magazines/business2. *Business 2.0* magazine provides a lot of information on leveraging technology for your small business. Good e-commerce, Web design, and tech strategy.
- businessweek.com/smallbiz. We normally associate *Business Week* magazine with big business and the economy, but their online section has great small business tactics.

the only person preparing and serving the food, to the master in the kitchen, planning the menu; insuring appropriate inventory is available for the dishes chosen; choosing the best combinations of meats, vegetables, fruits, and spices; and then bringing all the talents of the various kitchen crew together with perfect timing to insure a great dining experience for the customer.

Although the four functions are as generally applicable today as they were in 1916 when they were first articulated by Henri Fayol, there is more to describing what managers *do*. Henry Mintzberg has gone into considerable depth searching for descriptions of how managers spend their time.[1]

First, rather than being reflective, systematic planners, managers tend to work at an unrelenting pace on a wide variety of activities that are brief and have little continuity.

The front-line managers in Mintzberg's study averaged 583 activities per eight-hour day—one activity every 48 seconds. Half of CEOs' activities lasted less than nine minutes, and only 10 percent took longer than an hour.

Second, rather than managers having no regular duties to perform, Mintzberg found that managers spend a lot of time on regular duties, such as performing rituals and ceremonies, negotiating, and dealing with the external environment. They receive visitors, take care of customers, and preside at holiday parties and other rituals and ceremonies that are part of their job, whether the business is large or small.

Third, even though management is often viewed as a technological science, information processing and decision making remain locked in the manager's brain. Managers are people who depend on judgment and intuition more than on technology. Computers are important for the business's specialized work, but managers still greatly depend on word-of-mouth information to support almost all of their decisions. A manager's job is complex, difficult, and as much an art as a science.

Mintzberg suggests several important roles that a manager needs to fulfill so as to plan, organize, lead, and control successfully:

- Resource allocator role: Decides how resources are to be used
- Monitor role: Determines if quality control standards have been met
- Leader role: Determines the direction of the company
- Entrepreneur role: Keeps fresh new ideas and innovations flowing into the company
- Negotiator role: Continuously goes to bat for the resources needed for the success of the company[2]

As a manager, you must use your resources *efficiently* and *effectively*. The difference is more than an exercise in semantics. *Effectiveness* means achieving your stated goals. Having a helicopter fly you everywhere you go (across town to meetings, to the grocery store, to a ball game) is an effective way to travel. You get where you intend to go. But, of course, with the reality of limited resources, effectiveness cannot be your only goal. You need *efficiency*, too—making the best use of your resources to accomplish your goals. In running a small business, you have to get the job done, but you have to contain costs as well. Wasting your limited resources—for instance, on helicopter rides—even though you achieve your goals, will lead to bankruptcy just as fast as if you were not making sales. A small business manager must balance effectiveness and efficiency to be competitive.

Jerry Murrell opened a hamburger and french fry business with his five sons in 1986 in Virginia. In 2002, they began selling franchises and today have 570 stores across the United States and Canada with sales of $483 million in 2009. In order to compete in this saturated market, Jerry chose to focus on quality control. The potatoes for the fries come from Idaho, their hamburger is never frozen, the buns are baked fresh daily and toasted on a grill, and their burgers are made to order. Due to the focus on quality, Jerry was reluctant to begin franchising his business, but his sons were insistent. In order to maintain the quality that is important to this business, they have two third-party audits in each store each week. One crew checks on customer service, and the other crew checks on kitchen safety. In this way, *Five Guys Burgers and Fries* has been able to grow successfully and still maintain the quality that gave their business its success in the beginning.[3]

Small Business Growth

Growth is a natural, and usually desirable, consequence of being in business. Growth of your business can take several forms, albeit not necessarily all at once. You may see evidence of it in revenues, total sales, number of customers, number of employees, products offered, and facilities needed. It is something to be expected and planned for as your business evolves, but it should not be an end in itself. Bigger is not necessarily better. A sunflower is not better than a violet. And growth brings changes that may not always be positive ones.

As your business makes upward progress, you will experience "growing pains" just as people do as they move through childhood, adolescence, and adulthood. Signals of growing pains can be jobs that are not delivered on time, costs that continue to rise, the need to borrow additional money, increased reliance on partners or employees, and increased risk taking. Breakdowns in customer service and product quality can soon follow if growth is not managed appropriately.[4] Managing growth is difficult in small business because of the transitions needed as your business passes from one stage to another.

Your Growing Firm

When a business grows in size by increasing its number of employees and its volume of sales, the way it is managed must also change. As it evolves from a bare-bones start-up to an expanded, mature firm, it may pass through roughly five stages.[5] Naturally, not all small businesses are the same size at start-up, nor do they all seek to achieve the same level of growth in maturity. Even so, these five stages provide a way to understand the changing needs of your business.

In the first, or *existence* stage, the owner runs the business alone (see Figure 16.2). Although not every business begins with one individual running (and being) the entire business, it is not uncommon. In fact, technology is making the solo type of business much more common than ever before. Online networks have allowed the creation of electronic cottage industries out of people's homes. Thus, although some people intentionally keep their businesses at the solo size, it also represents the first stage of growth. In fact there is even a new word to describe these business owners, solopreneurs.[6]

A business reaching the second stage, *survival*, has demonstrated that it has a viable idea; at this point, the key problem shifts from mere existence to generation of cash flow. Now the entrepreneur is no longer responsible for just her own efforts. She may need to hire employees if the business is to move forward. Hilda Kernc owns and operates a Lebanese food production company, Deleez Appetizers, in the Chicago area. This cuisine, which focuses on vegetarian dishes, has increased in demand to the point where she is working 20 hours a day. Due to the popularity of the dishes, Hilda is looking at renting a larger facility and hiring her first employee. "It will kill me if I am going to work like this," she stated. However, hiring employees is expensive, particularly when looking at not only wages but also the hidden costs that must be addressed. Hilda has discovered that while hiring employees is expensive, so is working 24 hours a day every day.[7]

When the business grows to the point where employees operate within several departments, the entrepreneur must either become a professional manager or hire managerial expertise. In this third stage, *success*, the owner accepts a degree of disengagement as a level of supervision is added—employees to lead departments or divisions. Care must be taken that these supervisors understand the culture of the business they are joining and will work toward building it. At this point, the entrepreneur is performing less of the daily production personally and may not be in direct contact with part of the company's efforts. He must turn loose more of the "doing" and assume more of the "managing." Giving up control in this way can be difficult, but delegation of authority and responsibility is something an entrepreneur must do to enable the business to grow. Well-written job descriptions can prove helpful in not only hiring the right people in this stage but also insuring that tasks are completed as needed.[8]

FIGURE 16-2 Stages of Business Growth

Businesses Tend to Evolve through Five Stages as They Grow from Single-Person Firms to Full-Fledged Businesses.

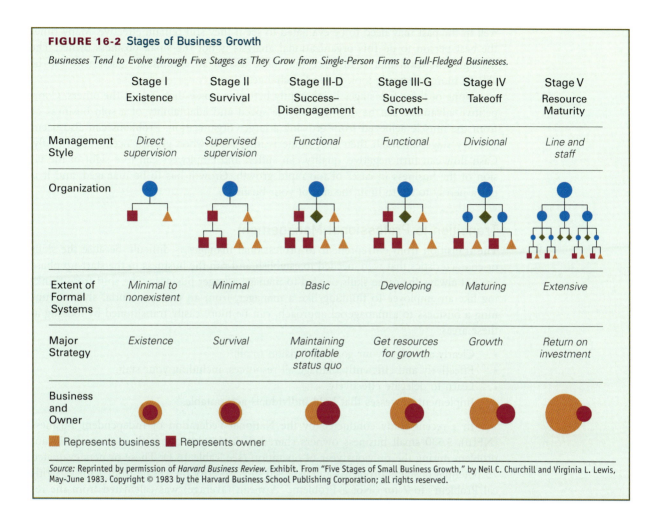

	Stage I Existence	Stage II Survival	Stage III-D Success– Disengagement	Stage III-G Success– Growth	Stage IV Takeoff	Stage V Resource Maturity
Management Style	Direct supervision	Supervised supervision	Functional	Functional	Divisional	Line and staff
Extent of Formal Systems	Minimal to nonexistent	Minimal	Basic	Developing	Maturing	Extensive
Major Strategy	Existence	Survival	Maintaining profitable status quo	Get resources for growth	Growth	Return on investment

■ Represents business   ■ Represents owner

In the fourth stage, *takeoff,* the business has grown to include multiple departments managed by numerous supervisors. As in the preceding stages, the owner remains the "head honcho," but now her responsibilities are more conceptual than technical in nature. In other words, rather than focusing on daily operations—making and selling the product or service—she will more intensely focus on managing the bigger picture—through long-range planning and overseeing supervisors, for instance. The business now needs someone to establish policies, handbooks, job descriptions, training, and budgets, and the owner will assume those executive duties. In this stage the entrepreneur must go through the difficult metamorphosis of becoming a professional manager, hire someone else to run the business and step out of the way, or sell the firm. The key problems in this stage are how to grow rapidly and how to finance that growth.

In the fifth stage, *resource maturity,* the company has arrived. The greatest concerns at this point are to consolidate and control the finances generated by rapid growth and to professionalize the organization. By this stage, the owner and the business are separate entities, both financially and operationally. The child the entrepreneur bore has grown up, moved out, and taken on a full life of its own. At this stage, it may be time for the organization to take a long, hard look at itself. Strategies and processes that have worked well in the past may need to be evaluated to see if they still remain effective. Many times the best person to do this organizational analysis is not the small business owner. The management team that is in place may have less of an emotional attachment and be able to more effectively look at needed changes.

None of these five stages is inherently better or worse than any of the others. Competitive advantage can be drawn from the speed and adaptability of a solo business or from the muscle achieved from growing a larger organization. Problems can also occur at every stage, although their magnitude is intensified when growth occurs too rapidly. Cash flow can turn negative, quality can suffer, and employees can lose sight of the vision of the business in cases of too rapid growth. Growth has to be managed, and it is not a heresy to try to limit the size of your business.

Transition to Professional Management

The transition from entrepreneur to professional manager is difficult, because the skills or characteristics that were needed to establish and run the business in the start-up phase are not always the same skills needed to manage a larger business. The shift from thinking like an employee to thinking like a manager, from an entrepreneurial style of running a business to a managerial approach, can be more easily transitioned by looking at these areas:

- Clearly articulate your goals and vision to all.
- Effectively and efficiently manage all resources, including your staff.
- Learn to delegate effectively.
- Implement processes that hold individuals accountable.[9]

In a recent study conducted by the National Federation of Independent Business (NFIB), 3,530 small business owners shared their insights about their most significant problem during the previous year of operation (see Table 16.1). These owners evaluated 75 potential business problems and assessed their severity on a scale from 1 for a "Critical Problem" to 7 for "Not a Problem." A mean (average) was calculated from the responses for each problem.

Certain attributes distinguish professionally managed small businesses and can facilitate the process of transitioning from a solopreneur to a larger business. In order to make this transition, small business owners need to stop "running the show" to "managing the show." To achieve that goal, look at the following:

- Develop an effective infrastructure—this is a must if the small business owner wants to retain control but not have to constantly micromanage every decision.
- Plan and manage growth—the biggest challenge here for the small business owner may be in the realization of how his role has now changed.
- Protecting the small business owner's time—the challenge again may be for the owner to stop doing things that he has always done. Delegation becomes key.[10]

"Just as you needed a plan to start this deal, so you need a plan to finish it. An exit strategy must be well planned."

The Next Step: An Exit Strategy

To every thing there is a season. There comes a time that every business must end. Unfortunately for many entrepreneurs, the arrival of this time means that the business could not sustain itself or them any longer and must cease to exist for that unhappy reason. But for many others, the business appears capable of continuing indefinitely. Then the question becomes, how long will *you* last? How will you and the business part ways?

Just as you needed a plan to start this deal, so you need a plan to finish it. An exit strategy must be well planned. Not only can the process take a long time, but also there

TABLE 16-1 Measures of Small Business Problem Importance

PROBLEM	RANK	MEAN	STANDARD DEVIATION	PERCENT "CRITICAL"	PERCENT "NOT A PROBLEM"	2004 RANK
Cost of Health Insurance	1	1.93	1.50	56.3	4.1	1
Cost of Natural Gas, Propane, Gasoline, Diesel, Fuel Oil Federal Taxes on Business	2	2.41	1.72	42.3	5.4	4
Income Property Taxes	3	3.00	1.81	25.0	7.2	5
(Real, Inventory or Personal Property)	4	3.08	1.85	25.0	7.3	6
Tax Complexity/Unreason-able Government	5	3.13	1.81	22.7	7.0	new
Regulations State Taxes on Business	6	3.25	1.83	20.6	7.5	9
Income	7	3.26	1.90	21.2	9.8	8
Cost of Supplies/Inventories	8	3.26	1.72	17.2	6.2	14
Electricity Costs (Rates)	9	3.27	1.72	16.4	6.3	10
Workers' Compensation Costs	10	3.28	1.97	23.8	11.1	3
Cash Flow	11	3.37	1.88	20.6	8.3	7
Locating Qualified Workers	12	3.42	1.99	20.7	12.0	11
Cost and Availability of Liability Insurance	13	3.44	1.90	18.8	9.5	2
Poor Earnings (Profits)	14	3.60	1.90	17.3	8.8	12
Frequent Changes in Federal Tax Laws and Rules	15	3.61	1.82	14.9	8.8	15
Fixed Costs Too High	16	3.61	1.77	13.3	8.2	20
Finding and Keeping Skilled Employees	17	3.70	2.04	17.6	14.4	(modified) 28
Federal Paperwork	18	3.70	1.83	12.3	10.1	18
FICA (Social Security Taxes)	19	3.71	1.83	12.9	10.7	13
Projecting Future Sales Changes	20	3.75	1.68	8.9	8.8	25

Source: From Bruce D. Phillips and Holly Wade, "Small Business Problems and Priorities," NFIB Research Foundation/Wells Fargo, June 2008, www.nfib.com/page/research-foundation.

can be negative ramifications for your business if you do not plan the exit as carefully as you planned the start-up. Here are some tips to consider as you plan how you will end your business.

- Recognize when it is time to exit. Maybe the zest for the business is eluding you on a daily basis, maybe your mentor is suggesting it is time to quit, or maybe market conditions are changing. Pay attention to the small signs that may indicate it is time to exit.

- Watch out for your employees. You may be leaving; however, your employees are probably planning on staying. Selling the business and changing management will cause uncertainty in their work lives that can cause additional employee stress.
- Make sure you have the right people in place as you leave. The management team you leave behind will be the people who take the business to the next level in the future. As much as possible, ensure that the people leading the charge will have the skills and resources needed to succeed.
- Follow your instincts. Look at the numbers, review the forecasts, analyze performance appraisals, but then pay attention to what you feel in your gut.[11]

You have three broad choices, with many themes and variations upon each: You can sell, merge, or close. None of the three is especially easy, but whether or not you have a strategy, you will exit sooner or later.

Consider these exit options:

- *Sell to a financial buyer*—someone like you who wants to buy and run a business.
- *Sell to a strategic buyer*—a company that wants to expand into your industry or a company in a similar business. Perhaps a competitor wants to buy more market share. Such a buyer is more likely to pay market value, currently four to six times EBITDA, as well as understand the intricacies of the business. Unless you want to continue to run the business after the sale, train your successor beforehand.[12]
- *Sell to a key employee or group of key employees.* This kind of deal is similar to selling to an individual buyer, but employee-buyers tend to be more intimately familiar with what they are purchasing. They will drive the price down, however, because they feel they deserve a lower price due to their years of service.
- *Sell to all employees via an employee stock ownership plan (ESOP).* This strategy is a great option for the seller if the business has a key group of motivated employees. You are much more likely to receive market price or even a premium because the ESOP will be based on a formal business valuation by a professional.
- *Take the company public.* This step takes a tremendous commitment, both physically and financially, to comply with all elements of the Securities Exchange Commission (SEC) requirements. This option will often lead to loss of control over the company as management is faced with quarterly earnings numbers that must meet estimates in order to maintain the stock price of the company.
- *Create a family succession.* This tactic is a popular, highly desired option. But the question must always be asked, "Are my family members up to it, and which family member do I choose?" Managing expectations as well as developing transitional training opportunities like internships can be key to the success of this approach. Twenty-five percent of a group of small business owners surveyed stated they would look outside their family rather than at family succession.[13]
- *Undertake a planned liquidation.* This approach would involve running the business until the day you're done, then you sell the assets. It takes a lot of planning and patience, and can be an emotional roller coaster.

Next comes *valuation*, in which the company's worth is in the eye of the beholder. There are as many ways to value a business as there are businesses, but the three most common are the *market approach* (what others have paid for comparable businesses), the *asset-based approach* (essentially the cost to re-create the operating assets of the business), and the *income approach* (how much a buyer could make from the business; see Chapter 6).

Business valuation is a complex topic. A great resource on this subject—the Annual Valuation Guide—can be found at www.inc.com/valuation. In addition, the following Web sites offer useful information:

- *www.conference-board.org.* The Conference Board collects and publishes information on the U.S. economy.
- *www.bizcomps.com.* This fee-based site offers small business transaction sales data contained in databases organized by state. The databases are updated annually with each region's sales data over the past 10 years.
- *www.dnb.com.* The Dun & Bradstreet Business Information Report (fee-based) provides detailed company data.
- *www.corporateinformation.com.* This site will search company names to bring up links to related Web sites for those businesses.
- *www.nacva.com.* This site is operated by the National Association of Certified Valuation Analysts.

© Nick Kim. Courtesy of http://www.cartoonstock.com

Leadership in Action

Small businesses need managers who are also leaders, because building an organization requires every employee to contribute to productivity and efficiently use every resource. Owners of small businesses must be very visible leaders because they work closely with their people. Porter Keadle Moore, an Atlanta-based accounting firm, has found the importance of the leadership in the success of their organization. Consultants in analyzing this business state that not only is "corporate culture … incredibly strongly linked to a leader's personality," but also "the chief motivator for change in an entrepreneur-led company is the leadership."[14]

Jim Kouzes, president of Tom Peters Group/ Learning Systems, says that the foundation of small business leadership is *credibility*. He sums up his concept with one sentence: "If people don't believe in the messenger, they won't believe in the message."[15] How do you build credibility? Kouzes prescribes an acronym—DWWSWWD (Do What We Say We Will Do).

A lot of literature on management is devoted to an ongoing debate over management versus leadership. The debate began with a now famous statement from Warren Bennis: "American businesses are overmanaged and underled."[16] Managers are more likely to be reactive, focusing on current information and making decisions based upon necessity. Leaders are much more active, shaping ideas and providing the vision for the organization. Managers establish processes, enable compromise, and limit choices within the context of organizational objectives. Leaders develop new approaches to problems, motivate followers to engage in the vision, and avoid routine, day-to-day tasks.[17] Is one more important than the other? Not really, because running a small business takes a combination of *both* qualities. Vision without analysis produces chaos, and orderliness without passion produces rigid complacency. **Leadership** is the inspirational part of the many things a manager must do through directing and influencing team members— along with an amount of planning, directing, and controlling. Can one person be both? Of course it is possible, but not a combination regularly found. Upon occasion, you may find a leader who can manage as well as that someone "who can handle everything that comes along and has the uncanny ability to see the future while working for today."[18]

leadership
The process of directing and influencing the actions of members within a group.

Is leadership changing? The following are some of the leadership trends for 2010 according to BusinessWeek Online:

- An eye on the future—Leaders must develop strong forward-thinking strategic skills in order for their businesses to remain competitive.
- Practicing social responsibility—Leaders are finding out that positive corporate involvement can increase the success of their business.
- Attracting younger workers—Leaders realize developing leaders is a process that must be continuously implemented.
- Maintaining a broader view—Leaders realize the global economy and marketplace present new opportunities and challenges.[19]

Where do small businesses find the next generation of leaders? Andy Medley and Scott Hill, owners of Indianapolis-based holding company CIK Enterprises, with 80 employees, grow their own. They run a manager's book group that meets weekly to discuss the theories of Jim Collins, Jack Stack, and other business thinkers. They call the program The Incubator. Managers nominate candidates based on enthusiasm, drive, and smarts. Only 10 percent of employees can participate at any given time. Those that come through to be future leaders will thrive, having been embued with an understanding of the company culture. Hill states that "even if they don't want to do management, they'll come through saying, 'Hey, I learned a lot,' and they'll be better able to help in any way they can."[20]

Leadership Attributes

Numerous studies have been conducted in the area of leadership, using a variety of approaches. One of the major approaches to looking at leadership is to study the attributes

© Digital Vision/Jupiter Images

Small business owners communicate their vision in formalized and informal ways.

Reality Check

Leadership Tips

So your small business needs you to not only be able to successfully manage, market, finance, and produce your product, but also lead? What are some key components necessary to lead your small business forward? On top of all your other tasks, how can you work in the now and also plan for the future? Here are some ideas.

- Leaders must develop a vision for the future, often with little data to fall back on. Maintaining the competitive advantage over time is essential to the success of the business and involves moving into new territory.
- Leaders must be prepared to fail. Not every idea, product, or new strategy will work. You must be able to pick yourself up, dust yourself off, and get back to work.
- Leaders must be fair. Employees want to know the process is equal for everyone and to be able to see and understand that process.

- Leaders need to demonstrate a certain amount of vulnerability. You cannot do it all well. Find key people who supplement and strengthen your areas of weakness.
- Leaders must develop a safe environment in which to make mistakes. If you want new ideas, new products, or new processes, employees must have the freedom to fail.
- Leaders get rid of the "bad" as soon as possible. Bad permeates the organization quickly. If it is bad, get rid of it whether it is a bad product, a bad supplier, or a bad employee.
- Leaders check frequently to see how others view their leadership capabilities. It is easy to have a jaundiced view of your leadership capabilities. Make sure you have at least one or two people who can accurately assess you and your leadership abilities and make appropriate suggestions when needed.

Sources: Robert Sutton, "12 Things Good Bosses Believe," *Harvard Business Review*, May 28, 2010; C. K. Prahalad, "The Responsible Manager," *Harvard Business Review*, January/February 2010; and Patrick Lencioni, "The Most Important Leadership Trait You Shun," wsj.com, June 22, 2010.

---

that business leaders need in order to be successful, called the Trait Approach to leadership. Following are some of the traits found in most leaders.

Defining the Vision Having a mental picture of where the company is going not only today but also tomorrow, a vision, will always be an important part of leadership. Moreover, a good leader is able to describe that vision to others so that everyone is headed in the same direction and buys into the vision. A person with a vision that can't be put into action is a dreamer, not a leader.

Communication Ability Constant communication is needed for a leader, not only to find out what is going on but also to let others know about the vision and the plans to implement the vision. The ability to communicate clearly with all groups of people ranks as one of the most important attributes a leader must possess.

Self-confidence and dependability Leaders must believe in themselves and their ability to accomplish their vision. Leaders must demonstrate day in and day out their commitment and perseverance in pursuing the vision.

Adaptability Leaders must be able to roll with the punches and take advantage of the opportunities presented. Resources, including people, must frequently be rearranged in order for the vision to be accomplished.

Commitment Loyalty to one's company is more precarious in today's climate of economic uncertainty. With this being the case, it is more important than ever that leaders

Manager's Notes

Entrepreneurial Evolution

Contrary to much of what management literature and many consultants say, there is more than one right way to run a new entrepreneurial business. The key is to recognize your style and match your strategy to your business goals.

You can be a successful business owner as a *Classic* manager—involved in every aspect and every decision of the business. You may be reluctant to admit you are a Classic for fear of receiving criticism for not delegating (not seen as politically correct). Actually, this is a very legitimate way to run your business. The biggest problem with this style is not the lack of delegation, but acting like a Classic while deluding yourself into thinking you is using a team approach. Delegating is fine, and not delegating is fine—but don't *pretend* to delegate, because then no one will be happy.

You can run your business as a *Coordinator*—operating without a single employee and farming out everything from accounting, to sales, to manufacturing. Do what you enjoy or what you do well, and subcontract out the rest.

Your style may be that of an *Entrepreneur + Employee Team*—you, plus a team of employees. This style gives you both control and the ability to grow. Authority can be delegated to key employees, but you retain final control.

What we as a society define as a business leader changes over time. In the 1950s, the so-called corporate man ruled, thinking "inside the box" was rewarded, and mavericks were disdained. Business leaders in the 1990s swung toward entrepreneurs, people who stood apart from the crowd because of their creativity. In the twenty-first century, a diversity of people, backgrounds, and styles epitomize leadership. Management in this century poses challenges that have not been seen in the past. To deal with them, a blend of male and female traits is needed—both intuition and focus on bottom line, both people skills and analytical strengths.

Still, some things don't change. Some leadership traits apply no matter what decade you live in: You have to set standards and live up to them, you need to innovate, and you need to execute. What is your leadership style? Take a quiz at www.entrepreneur.com/quiz/leaderstyle to find out.

Sources: Carol Tice, "Building the 21st Century Leader," *Entrepreneur,* February 2007, 64–69; Rieva Lesonsky, "Entrepreneur Evolution," *Entrepreneur,* February 2007, 10; and Ronald E. Merrill and Henry D. Sedgwick, *The New Venture Handbook,* 2nd ed. (New York: AMACOM, 1993).

be seen as caring about the business and the employees. Passion for what is good for both the business and the workers can't be faked.

Creative Ability Good leadership involves creating something that didn't exist before. A tolerance for ambiguity and risk taking is important as something different and new is created.

Ability to Follow Through Leaders must make tough decisions, often based upon incomplete information with no guarantee of success. A leader needs a certain amount of toughness to make unpopular decisions or to stand against the majority when necessary in order to accomplish the vision.

Ability to Take Action Small business leaders must realize that without action, all of the foregoing attributes are mere academic rhetoric. Leaders must also be able to make decisions, frequently with less-than-perfect information, and manage and set priorities on a daily basis as they persuade and motivate others to participate in accomplishing the vision. Leadership attributes need to be practiced consistently to be effective. The subject of leadership is easy to talk about, but a challenge to demonstrate.[21]

Negotiation

The art of negotiation occurs continuously while running your small business, from the time the idea pops into your head until the day you harvest it. *Negotiation* can be defined as the communication process in which two or more people come together to seek mutual agreement about an issue. Negotiation can involve obtaining a certain action from someone, achieving approval from someone, or simply getting someone to agree with you. When you are raising money, hiring employees, shopping for suppliers, or signing contracts, you are negotiating. Whenever two or more people get together to exchange information for the purpose of changing their relationship in some way, they are negotiating. From merging onto the freeway in rush-hour traffic, to scheduling an appointment with a client, to deciding which television program to watch with your family, negotiation is involved.[22]

Every negotiation ends with one of four possible outcomes:

- *Lose-lose.* Neither party achieves his needs or wants.
- *Win-lose.* One counterpart loses and the other wins.
- *Win-win.* The needs and goals of both parties are met, so they both walk away with a positive feeling and a willingness to negotiate with each other again.
- *No deal.* Neither party wins or loses since they agree at this time they cannot meet each other's needs and goals. This approach leaves the door open for negotiating at a later date since a win-lose or lose-lose did not occur.[23]

Negotiation is so important to businesses of all sizes that we can see the free enterprise system at work by considering the sheer number of books written on the subject. *Getting to Yes* has sold over 3.5 million copies since it was first published in 1981. *The Power of Nice*, *The Negotiation Tool Kit*, *The Art and Science of Negotiation*, *You Can Negotiate Anything*, *Negotiating Rationally*, and *The Art of the Deal* are other popular examples. Virtually every one of these books includes some simplistic examples, such as the Parable of the Orange, which goes like this: Two people each want an orange and agree finally to split the fruit in half. But it turns out that one side simply wanted the juice, and the other side wanted the rind. If only they had worked together to solve the problem, each side could have received what it wanted. Okay, so such simplistic solutions don't often turn up in the world of business. Nevertheless, there are some great pieces of advice in these tomes. Here's a sampling of some of the best:

"The goal should be win-win. If you wish to negotiate with this party again, both sides have to walk away feeling good about the outcome."

- The goal should be win-win. If you wish to negotiate with this party again, both sides have to walk away feeling good about the outcome.
- Stay rationally focused on the issue being negotiated.
- Exhaustive preparation is more important than aggressive argument. The party with the most information often wins. You can never be overprepared in negotiating.
- Think through your alternatives. The more options you believe you have, the better your negotiating position.
- Know your BATNA, the best alternative to a negotiated agreement. Compare all outcomes to the BATNA you have developed before negotiations began.
- Spend less time talking and more time listening and asking good questions. The more you understand the other party, the better alternatives you can propose.
- Sometimes silence is your best response.
- Use one strong argument and repeat as needed. Do not dilute a strong argument with a weaker argument.

- Let the other side make the first offer. If you're underestimating yourself, you might make a needlessly weak opening move. You frequently have more power than you realize.
- Create a vision. How will this agreement benefit both parties?
- Don't walk into negotiations with a fallback position. If you are willing to compromise before you begin, you need to reevaluate your goals and alternatives.[24]

Delegation

delegation

Granting authority and responsibility for a specific task to another member of an organization; empowerment to accomplish a task effectively.

By ***delegation*** of authority and responsibility, a manager gives employees the power to make many decisions that she would otherwise have to make, thereby giving her time to concentrate on more important matters. Delegation *empowers* employees, meaning that it increases their involvement in their work. Also, by holding employees more accountable for their actions, delegation allows managers to maximize the efforts and talents of everyone in the company.

Many small business owners are either unwilling or unable to delegate for several reasons. For entrepreneurs who have started a business, giving up control is difficult. Owners often know the business more thoroughly than anyone else and feel as if they *have* to make all the decisions so as to protect the business.[25] They may feel that subordinates are unwilling or unable to accept responsibility. In reality, this attitude may become a self-fulfilling prophecy. If employees' attempts to take responsibility or to show initiative are squelched too often, they will either stop trying to show initiative or will leave the business.

Some small business owners simply misunderstand the meaning of management. They believe the only way to get the job done right is to do it themselves. That is a commendable attitude, but it can be counterproductive to being an effective manager, which, by definition, is someone who needs to get things done through other people.

Delegation is not the same as abdication. Nor is empowering people the same as instituting a pure democracy, where you simply count votes and the majority rules. In using delegation and empowerment, an effective leader is trying to encourage participation and take advantage of shared knowledge so that everyone can contribute. Of course, consensus can't always be reached, so sometimes the leader has to make a decision and go with it.

Some tips to help you delegate effectively:

- Understand the task and the results that are needed. Make sure needed authority as well as resources are provided.
- Choose the person carefully. Make sure the person has the needed skill set to successfully accomplish the task.
- Check on the progress of the delegated task before the completion date. See if additional information or resources are needed, and provide necessary feedback.
- Provided recognition and appropriate rewards when the task is successfully completed.[26]

Motivating Employees

motivation

The forces that act on or within a person that cause the person to behave in a specific manner.

The word *motivation* comes from the Latin *movere*, which means "to move." For our purposes, ***motivation*** is the reason an individual takes an action in satisfying some need. It answers the question of why people behave the way they do.

Motivation Theories Some people say that one person cannot motivate another, that one can merely create an environment for self-motivation. Whether this is the case or not, as a small business manager, you will be interested in motivating your employees to accomplish the goals of the company. Many theories on motivation exist, and a thorough examination of each is not appropriate for this book, but you can obtain more information on the subject from texts on principles of management or organizational behavior. Here we will summarize two of the most well-known and accepted theories.

One of the best known is *Maslow's hierarchy of needs*. Psychologist Abraham Maslow stated that people have in common a set of universal needs occurring in order of importance. The lowest-level needs are *physiological* (food, water, air, sleep, sex, and so on). *Safety and security* needs are the next level, followed by *social* needs, *esteem* needs, and then the highest-level needs for *self-actualization*.

As a small business owner, you should be aware of the fact that your employees will not always manifest these needs in the same order. People will be at different levels of needs at different times—sometimes simultaneously—so a variety of ways to motivate their behavior is needed. For example, the use of money to motivate is often misunderstood, especially in terms of Maslow's hierarchy. Money is generally seen as providing for basic physiological needs and not being important to the higher-level needs. In fact, money is actually a motivator because it buys the time and resources needed for self-actualization. Social needs and esteem needs may be fulfilled through social events at the workplace or recognition from the manager and be more effective motivators than money, depending upon the person.[27]

The biggest contribution of Maslow's theory to motivating employees is its recognition that people have needs that "pop up" and continue to require attention until they are satisfied. If a lower-level need pops up for an employee, he will not be able to concentrate on a higher-level need until the lower-level need is fulfilled. For example, if an employee receives a phone call from a school nurse informing him that his second-grade child had an accident and broke her arm on the playground, a safety need has popped up. This employee will probably not be very productive on the job until he can be sure the situation is under control, either by going to the school in person or by making other arrangements. Any effort to interfere with his handling of this need will create frustration and antagonism, which will undermine your employee's motivation and damage his attitude toward work.[28]

Another important motivational theory is *Herzberg's motivation-hygiene theory*. This theory is important to the small business owner because it recognizes that the factors producing job *satisfaction* are not the same as the factors that motivate employees to excel. Herzberg called things that cause people to feel good about their job *motivators* and things that people expect on the job *hygiene factors*. Since hygiene factors on the job are expected (such as safe working conditions or reasonable pay), the presence of these factors may create contentment among employees but not necessarily motivate them to excel (see Figure 16.3). To truly motivate your employees, motivational factors such as recognition, advancement, or job enrichment may be needed.[29]

Look at the factors listed in Figure 16.3 that cause satisfaction on the job: achievement, recognition, the work itself, and responsibility. These provide intrinsic rewards to people. The practical application of Herzberg's theory gives a small business manager some direction in keeping employees satisfied on the job. Satisfaction may not translate directly into motivation, but it is a significant component in keeping employees on the job.

Motivation Techniques A key to motivating the employees of your small business is to know what is important to them. For instance, if you provide a motivational reward that they do not want, it is a kind of inadvertent punishment. Say you promise a "sweet year-end bonus" for the top performer for the month of December. You will probably set up healthy competition that increases morale and achievement. But if your sweet bonus

> *"The biggest contribution of Maslow's theory to motivating employees is its recognition that people have needs that 'pop up' and continue to require attention until they are satisfied."*

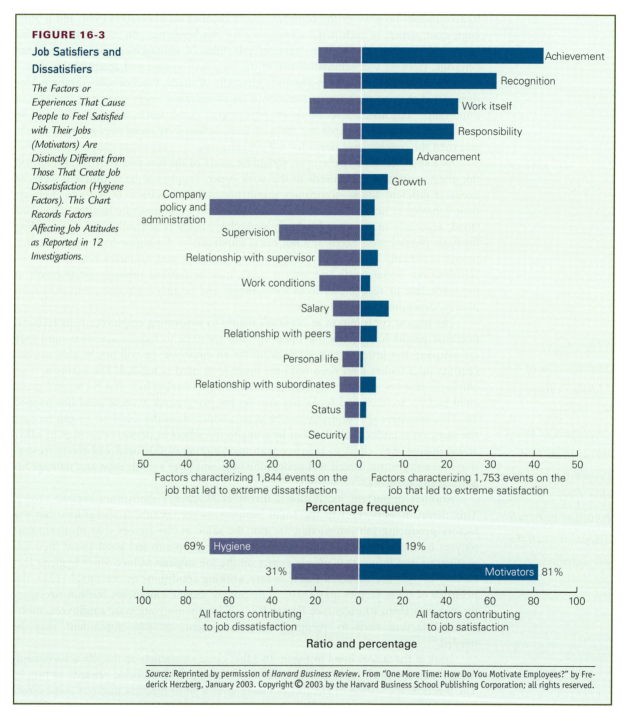

FIGURE 16-3

Job Satisfiers and Dissatisfiers

The Factors or Experiences That Cause People to Feel Satisfied with Their Jobs (Motivators) Are Distinctly Different from Those That Create Job Dissatisfaction (Hygiene Factors). This Chart Records Factors Affecting Job Attitudes as Reported in 12 Investigations.

Factors characterizing 1,844 events on the job that led to extreme dissatisfaction

Factors characterizing 1,753 events on the job that led to extreme satisfaction

Percentage frequency

69% Hygiene   19%

31%   Motivators 81%

All factors contributing to job dissatisfaction

All factors contributing to job satisfaction

Ratio and percentage

turns out to be a fruitcake—and your employees don't care for fruitcake—don't expect your next incentive to be motivational.

Bill Mork is the owner of Modern of Marshfield, a furniture maker located in Marshfield, Wisconsin. Mork followed the popular advice of using recognition instead of cash to reward participants in his new employee-suggestion program. From the suggestions received, Mork and other managers picked a "colleague of the month," who was awarded with a special parking space and a big handshake in front of all the gathered employees.

The number of suggestions that came in as a result of the new program was underwhelming. One winner pleaded not to be chosen again, to avoid embarrassment and being called a "brown nose" by coworkers. As a result, Mork changed the whole program and added cash bonuses at each step. For any cost-saving suggestion made by an employee that was implemented by the company, the employee was given a bonus worth 10 percent of the estimated savings. An additional 10 percent of the savings was added to a fund to be split among all suggestion makers at the end of the year. Anyone who had contributed a suggestion was eligible for prize drawings, whether or not the suggestion was implemented. The "colleague of the month" is now chosen by previous winners rather than by managers.

Employees have taken a very different attitude toward the program since bonus checks were added.[30] Modern's sales have almost doubled. Each year Mork pays out $10,000 in rewards for about 1,200 suggestions submitted by 100 employees. Although that may sound like a lot of money, Mork estimates the savings generated by the suggestions to be five times that amount. This example suggests an answer to that long-asked management question, does money motivate? Apparently, at a very visceral level, *yes*!

Motivation Myths So many motivation theories have been put forth that some misconceptions have resulted:

- *All employees need external motivation.* Some employees have such a strong internal drive that external techniques will not increase their motivation—though they still need your support, backing, and guidance.
- *Some employees don't need any motivation.* Motivation is the force that prompts every action—we all have to have motivation; it just comes from different sources.
- *Attempts to motivate always increase performance and productivity.* If our attempts to motivate involve incentives that employees do not desire, they can decrease performance. And some incentives can increase happiness and morale without producing an increase in productivity.
- *Money always motivates people.* Base salary is generally not a long-term motivator. A person who receives a raise may temporarily work harder but will soon rationalize, "I'm *still* getting paid less than I'm worth," and return to her previous level of productivity.
- *Intrinsic rewards provide more motivation than money.* As seen in the Bill Mork example, money—as a one-time bonus—*does* motivate at a visceral level.
- *Fear is the best motivator.* Workers who are afraid of a boss will work hard in the boss's presence, but may not have the business's best interests in mind. The best workers will also be looking for another job—so fear may drive out the very people the business needs the most.
- *Satisfied workers are always productive.* Happy people do not necessarily produce more. The goal of employee motivation is not to create a country club or amusement park atmosphere. Rather, the goal is to get everyone in the company to maximize his efforts so as to increase contributions (and earnings).
- *This generation of workers is less motivated than the last.* Most generations hold this attitude toward the following generation. While members of the so-called X generation have been mislabeled as "slackers," they have already produced notable entrepreneurs, including many who have been used as examples throughout this book.

Can You Motivate without Using Money?

Money is not the only motivator. Employees value the recognition of their accomplishments and the contributions they make to the business. Here are some ideas on nonmonetary methods to use in recognizing and consequently motivating employees. And not one will negatively impact the company's profitability.

- Allow employees to be flexible in the hours that they work. A longer lunch or coming into work 30 minutes later, while usually not a problem for the company, can be very beneficial to the employee trying to balance family issues with work—and the cost is nothing.
- Give a handwritten thank you note. Take the time to write a short, yet specific, thank you to an employee who has gone above and beyond.
- Give a pass for a day off. Let employees earn extra days off to use as they like, spending time with their family or participating in a favorite activity.
- Celebrate employee birthdays. Make a birthday cake and have cake and coffee on the employee's birthday, or provide a birthday breakfast or lunch.
- Provide reserved parking to the employee of the week. Have a special parking spot for the honored employee, with appropriate recognition of the honor.
- Say, "Thank you." Too often we all forget the power of these two magical words. A simple, yet heartfelt, thank you for a job well done can be very motivating to employees.[31]

Reality Check

Motivate More with Less

Many small businesses, from specialty coffee shops to CPA firms, are dependent on hourly employees for the operation of the business and contact with customers. Think about what is expected of these employees, who are making only $7 to $8 per hour. They are expected to spend eight hours per day providing quick, friendly, and superior service to every customer. They are expected to be diligent and honest, and to sacrifice their personal time (often with little or no notice) to cover a shift they were not scheduled for. The bottom line is that business owners expect their hourly employees to be as motivated about their businesses as they are. It is no surprise that a recent survey of 500 small and mid-sized business owners showed that retaining and motivating workers are their biggest challenges. More than 48 percent of respondents placed this concern at the top of their problem list.

In response, many small business owners are creating "work/life" policies to sustain a competitive advantage in hiring employees. Work/life issues can include on-site child care, time-off policies, flex-time, job sharing, and personal days. The problem is

this: How do you afford to offer such perks on limited revenues and razor-thin margins? The answer comes from the same source as many other solutions—creativity. For example:

- Graham Weston, 42, co-founder and CEO of Rackspace Managed Hosting, which hosts Web applications for other firms from San Antonio, hands top performers the keys to one of his cars, a BMW M3 convertible, for a week. Weston says, "If you gave somebody a $200 bonus, it wouldn't mean very much. When someone gets to drive my car for a week, they never forget it."
- David Williams, CEO of Merkle, a database-marketing agency in Lanham, Maryland, with $114 million in annual sales, pays for his 851 employees to take classes during *business* hours on subjects ranging from computer programming to public speaking.
- Richard Caturano, president of Boston accounting firm Vitale Caturano, offers workers free gourmet dinners and Saturday lunches during the busy season, and a concierge service for errands, such as picking up dry cleaning.

Sources: Elaine Pofeldt, "Better Bosses," *Fortune Small Business,* October 2006, 90–93; and Tom Macon, "Motivating the Troops," *Specialty Coffee Retailer,* March 1999, 10–11.

Employee Theft

Can you spot a thief in your business as easily as you can in the cartoons (you know, the guy with beady eyes, slick black hair, and droopy moustache)? Of course you can't. But employee theft accounts for 1 to 2 percent of gross sales each year according to the U.S. Chamber of Commerce. And small businesses are especially vulnerable because they have fewer defenses.

Fraud and other employee abuse cost employers more than $400 billion per year. The U.S. Chamber of Commerce estimates that 30 percent of business failures are related to employee theft. And 33 percent of employees admit to stealing products or money from their employers in the last three years.[32] So what is a small business owner to do?

- Get a good small business insurance policy covering outside theft, employee theft, and/or computer fraud.
- Screen out potential problem employees at the hiring stage by administering a standardized test that indicates level of integrity, and conduct background checks before hiring.
- Create a culture of honesty with a written code of ethics and conduct. Instruct employees in how to spot problems and what to do about them (tell you).
- Set an example. Do not send a mixed signal by taking money out of the register for personal use or using the business credit card for personal purchases. Employees pay attention to your behavior.
- Minimize the amount of cash on hand, and put excess cash in a safe.
- Never schedule an employee to work alone.
- Let everyone know that you look at every deposit and every check. Make sure that you get monthly bank statements delivered to your desk unopened.
- The most important point for small business: Divide up financial tasks. The person who keeps the books should not be the same person who keeps the money.
- Implement a zero tolerance policy. If an employee is stealing from the company, be prepared to implement the policy quickly and effectively.

Special Management Concerns: Time and Stress Management

Beyond the standard functions of management lie many other duties and responsibilities. Besides running your business, you also have personal, family, and social activities. You must be a good manager of time and be able to keep stress at acceptable levels.

Time Management

"You can't store, hoard, or buy time—so you had better use it wisely!"

As noted earlier, management is the *effective* and *efficient* use of resources. Most of us in business focus on our money: How much do I need? Where can I get it? We take the risking of our money seriously. But what is the most important component to making that money? What is a small business owner's most precious and most limited resource that can't be replaced? Time.[33] No one seems to have enough of it, yet everyone has the same amount—24 hours per day, 168 hours per week, or 8,760 hours per year. You can't store it, rent it, hoard it, sell it, or buy any more of it. So you had better use it wisely.

Few of us use time as effectively or as efficiently as possible. The key to effective time management for a small business owner is establishing priorities, investing time in what is important in life—and in the business. Thus time management is a goal-oriented

Competitive Advantage
INNOVATION AND SUSTAINABILITY

More Hours in Your Day

As a small business owner, you may very well find there are never enough hours in the day. Between customer relations, employee questions and challenges, forecasting sales, ordering inventory, advertising your newest product line, and balancing the cash drawer, the hours of the day run out long before the tasks. Try some of the following time management tips to help increase your productivity as you use your time more wisely. Time is truly the most precious resource you have to invest into yourself and your small business.

- Develop a plan—What would your perfect day look like? Take some time and determine your ideal day and week. Before you can make changes or implement a plan, you have to know what it is you want.
- Set aside days for specific tasks—Mondays could become planning days, Fridays days to focus on finance. Too often we jump from activity to activity and lose precious time as we are forced to majorly shift gears.
- Schedule "you" time—If you have a big project that needs your focused attention, schedule it into your appointments and then treat it as an appointment that needs to occur.

- Forget multitasking—Few of us multitask well. Important projects, jobs, conversations, and so forth need our undivided attention. Set aside the necessary time to concentrate on one task thoroughly.
- Delegate—Not all tasks must be accomplished by you. With which employees can you begin to share some of your many duties?
- Switch gears if procrastinating—If there is a job you are avoiding, rather than continuously trying to get that job done and spinning your wheels, go accomplish another task and return to this one later.
- Manage interruptions—A constant barrage of interruptions can steal huge quantities of time. Not only are you taking time to address the interruption, but also you must then reengage with the task you were working on. Have an escape phrase that allows you to get back to the project on which you were working.

Sources: Meryl Evans, "12 Ways to Find More Time," webworkerdaily.com, retrieved June 26, 2010; and Jay Joelle, "Maximize Your Time," *American Salesman*, April 2010.

© Image Source/Getty Images

activity. It requires that you prioritize what needs to be accomplished in any given day. Following are some indications that you are having problems with time management:

- You are frequently late for or forget meetings and appointments.
- You are consistently behind in responsibilities.
- You don't have enough time for basics—eating, sleeping, and family.
- You are constantly working and still miss deadlines.
- You are often fatigued, both mentally and physically.

How can you improve your effectiveness in using your time? A good starting point is to conduct a *time audit*. A time audit makes as much sense as conducting a financial audit, yet few small business managers can account for their minutes as precisely as they can their dollars. Why? They don't have time to conduct a time audit!

Begin your time audit by keeping a log to record your activities. Break days down into 15-minute intervals and keep track of what you do for about two weeks. When the log is complete, you can analyze how you have spent your time. Did you accomplish your most urgent needs? Which activities were a waste of time and could be eliminated? In the end, the time audit should help you prioritize activities and set daily goals.

After you conduct your time audit, use these tips to your advantage:

- *Make a to-do list.* Write down and rank by importance what you want to accomplish each day. Make sure the most important activities receive top priority. The return you receive will be many times greater than the small amount of time you invest in this exercise.
- *Eliminate time wasters.* Combine similar tasks and eliminate unnecessary ones. Pay special attention to time spent in meetings.
- *Remember Parkinson's law.* "Work expands to fill the time available." If you schedule too much time to accomplish something, you'll probably set a pace to take that amount of time.
- *Schedule time for special projects and activities.* Other people can put appointments on your calendar; you can do the same, ensuring important tasks will get completed.
- *Know when you are most productive.* We all have a daily cycle. Some of us are "morning people." Some are "night owls." Schedule your work so that you handle your most demanding problems when you are at your best.

How late is late? Every culture has its own concept of time. In an experiment at California State University, Fresno, 200 students were surveyed in California and Brazil about their definition of "early" and "late." American students believed they were "late" for a lunch date when they made a friend wait for 19 minutes, compared with 34 minutes for the Brazilians. Does this finding mean anything to your small business? Yes, groups form "temporary cultures" that can be used to influence their attitude toward time.[34] Since perceptions of lateness vary, you need to clarify exactly what time employees are expected to be at work, to be back from lunch, and to show up for meetings.

Stress Management

stress
Emotional states that occur in response to demands, which may come from internal or external sources.

One of the most ambiguous words in the English language is **stress**. There are almost as many interpretations of this term as there are people who use it, but technically, the stress response is actually the unconscious preparation to fight or flee that a person experiences when faced with a demand. Common usage leads us to think of stress as a negative thing, as if it were something to be avoided, yet there is a positive side to stress. Positive stress (called eustress) stimulates us to face challenges, motivates us to achieve, enhances our performance, increases efficiency, and adds excitement to life, as when you are anticipating a wedding or vacation. It produces favorable chemicals in our body—endorphins, serotonin, and dopamine—and is necessary for life and health. But the negative side of stress, called **distress**, entails unfavorable psychological, physical, or behavioral consequences, and this is the stress that we must learn to manage. It is also the stress managers need to be aware of when dealing with employees since this type of stress can decrease productivity, negatively impact customer relations, and increase absenteeism.[35]

distress
The negative consequences and components of stress.

For a situation to create distress for a person, two conditions are necessary: Its outcome must be uncertain, and it must be a matter of importance to the person. Another way to look at distress is as a mismatch that has occurred between the requirements to complete a task successfully and the resources that are available. Stress over time can lead to burnout, which, in turn, can decrease productivity dramatically.[36] Very few (if any) small businesses are "sure things" guaranteed to produce the outcome that the owner desires. Because small businesses are almost always the sole means of support for their owners, saying that they are extremely important to the owners is not an understatement. Therefore, both conditions causing distress exist in running a small business.

Other sources of stress that small business owners encounter include role conflict, task overload, and role ambiguity. *Role conflict* exists when we are faced with a situation that presents divergent role expectations. For example, a two-day business trip to meet with a potential client could help you land a large new account and prove very profitable for your business. But suppose taking the trip would cause you to miss your second grader's school play. The result is role conflict. The desire to attend both the meeting and the play—to be both a focused entrepreneur and a loving parent—creates a stressful internal conflict.

Task overload is another source of stress for a small business owner. More is expected of you than time permits—a common scenario in a small business. Unfinished work can be a sign of overload. In a business climate that calls for leaner organizations, work can pile up and more work be taken on before existing jobs are finished. Unfinished work creates tension and uneasiness. If the pattern of taking on more and more continues, eventually an accumulation of unfinished work produces stress and decreases performance.

Role ambiguity occurs when you are not entirely sure what you should do in a situation. Owning a small business generally means that you don't have anyone to consult when problems arise and that you will have to make decisions on a wide variety of topics. Some people have a higher tolerance or preference for ambiguity than others, but it still produces stress.

Stress is cumulative—it builds up. Sales declining at the business, a key employee being unhappy, a child having discipline problems, and the transmission going kaput in the family car all can combine to form a lot of stress. Individual stressors that could be handled by themselves may combine and become overwhelming.

Stress cannot, and should not, be eliminated from everyday life, but it must be managed. There are three basic responses to stress: avoid the situation causing the stress, alter the situation so it no longer causes stress, or accept the situation. Realistically for the small business owner, avoiding the business or altering the business may not be practical solutions. Acceptance of the situation and making positive changes over how we personally manage the stress may be the only true alternative. General recommendations for controlling your stress level include the following.

"Stress cannot, and should not, be eliminated from everyday life, but it must be managed."

Preventive Stress Management

- Attempt to modify, reduce, or eliminate the source of distress. Any changes you can make in your schedule or role as business owner can help prevent distress from building to a dangerous level.
- Maintain a positive outlook. Optimism can pay big rewards when addressing stressful situations.
- Prioritize tasks and ensure there is a balance between the task that needs to be completed and the resources available. If not, you may need to rearrange resources.[37]

Relaxation Techniques

A few minutes of concentrated relaxation will prevent a build-up of distress. Practice a five-step relaxation exercise:

- First, sit in a comfortable position in a quiet location. Loosen any tight clothing.
- Second, close your eyes and assume a passive, peaceful attitude.
- Third, relax your muscles as much as possible—beginning with your feet and continuing to your head—and keep them relaxed.
- Fourth, slowly breathe through your nose and develop a quiet rhythm of breathing. After each exhale, quietly say "one" to yourself.
- Fifth, continue relaxing muscles and concentrate on breathing for 10 to 20 minutes. Open your eyes occasionally to check the time. It will take practice for you to learn to ignore distracting thoughts during relaxation, but soon this exercise can help you reduce stress.

Social Support Systems

Working in an environment that provides social and emotional support can help us deal with distress. Relationships within the workplace, family, church, and clubs provide emotional backing, information, modeling, and feedback.

Take Care of Your Health Exercise! A person's physical condition affects his response in stressful situations. Aerobically fit people have more efficient cardiovascular systems and better nervous system interaction, which allow them to deal with and recover from stressful events more quickly.

Eat a balanced diet with plenty of water, fruits, and vegetables.

Get enough rest. Sleeping in front of the television, catnapping, or sleeping for less than four to six hours a night does not provide the body the regenerative time it requires to be able to address the demands of the day.

If (once you own your own business) you find yourself struggling with any of the varied topics in this chapter, from motivating employees to battling stress, and cannot win the struggle alone, you may want to consider a fast-growing trend in small business—hiring a business coach. The practice is not unusual; managers have sought outside counsel ever since Machiavelli first advised a young prince. The number of business coaches has grown from 2,000 in 1996 to over 10,000 in 2007.[38]

Summary

1. Describe the functions and activities involved in managing a small business.

Managers plan, organize, lead, and control. To accomplish these functions, they perform many activities, such as developing relationships, negotiating, motivating, resolving conflicts, establishing information networks, making decisions, and continually learning.

2. Explain the stages of small business growth and their consequences for managing your business.

In the earliest stage of many businesses' life, the entrepreneur acts alone. Many entrepreneurs even prefer to keep their businesses as one-person organizations. In the second growth stage, employees are added, so the entrepreneur often acts as a coach in getting work accomplished through other people. In stage 3, a new layer of supervision is added, so the entrepreneur does not directly control all the people or activities of the business. In the fourth stage, takeoff, the business has grown to include multiple departments managed by numerous supervisors. By the fifth stage, the owner and the business are separate entities, both financially and operationally.

3. Discuss the significance of leadership and motivation in regard to employees of small business.

Leadership means inspiring other people to accomplish what needs to be done. Leadership is part of a manager's job of providing the vision, passion, and creativity needed for the business to succeed.

Because management is getting things done through people, a small business manager must be able to motivate employees. The manager must therefore understand employees' behavior and recognize what is important to them. Maslow's and Herzberg's theories provide small business managers with frameworks for understanding motivation.

4. Discuss time and stress management as they relate to small business.

Besides running your business, you must be a good manager of time and be able to keep stress at acceptable levels.

Questions for Review and Discussion

1. Give examples of efficiency and effectiveness in managing your everyday life.
2. Discuss some of the skills or characteristics that are needed by a manager in the start-up phase of a business, and explain how they differ from the skills or characteristics needed later to manage a larger, established firm.
3. Study the management styles mentioned in the Manager's Notebook, "Entrepreneurial Evolution." Which one best describes you? Explain. Do you recognize a different style in managers you have worked for in the past?
4. What is motivation? Can managers really motivate employees?

5. Which exit strategy discussed in the chapter would you consider ideal? What would a downside of that strategy be?

6. Are you a good manager of time in your personal life? How will this affect your ability to manage your time as a business owner?

7. Give examples of stress, eustress, and distress.

8. How can the owner of a small business apply Maslow's hierarchy of needs to working with employees?

9. What are positive and negative aspects of delegation?

10. As a business owner, in which of the leadership attributes discussed in the text are you the weakest? How could you help yourself improve in this area? How could others help you? What is your strongest leadership skill?

Questions for Critical Thinking

1. Review the five stages of business growth. Which of these five would you aspire to for your own business? Be prepared to justify your answer.

2. Refer to the chapter opening story. List two differing activities in which each manager engages.

What Would You Do?

Ten years ago, Linda Turner was in an exercise class and saw a pregnant woman struggling through her routine. After class, Turner asked the woman if she knew of any products that would help her be more comfortable. Because none existed, she began developing a prototype of the BellyBra—a support device designed for women in their third trimester. The BellyBra has tank-top shoulder straps and fits snugly all the way down below the wearer's enlarged stomach area. Turner experimented with different fabrics, including white lace and CoolMax fabric that pulls heat away from the body.

The BellyBra prototypes tested well with consumers, but because Turner was a stay-at-home mom, she was not able to build a company at that time. She licensed the product to a company called Basic Comfort and became the firm's first employee. As the success of the BellyBra increased, Turner eventually left on friendly terms to go out on her own. She sold 1,000 units in her first year and 10,000 units in her second year. Some growth rate! She has now expanded her focus from obstetricians and gynecologists to selling on her Internet site (www.bellybra.com).

_____

Sources: Cynthia Griffin, "It's a Bra!," *Entrepreneur*, April 2001, 29 (4), 44. Rachel Zimmerman, "Stay-at-Home Moms Get Entrepreneurial," Career Journal @ Wall Street Journal, October 25, 2004, www.careerjournal.com; and www.bellybra.com/meetlindainventorofthebellybra.htm.

Questions

1. Linda Turner will face different challenges as her company progresses through the five stages of growth described in this chapter. Describe how you believe her business would change in each stage.

2. Business growth that occurs too quickly can present some significant problems and challenges compared with a business that grows at a slow, steady pace (of course, zero growth or decline makes for a whole new set of problems). Describe the challenges of hypergrowth that Turner could face, and explain how she should respond as a small business owner.

17

Human Resource Management

CHAPTER LEARNING OUTCOMES

After reading this chapter, you should be able to:

1. Discuss the importance of hiring the right employees.

2. Describe the job-analysis process and the function of job descriptions and job specifications.

3. Evaluate the advantages and disadvantages of the six major sources of employee recruitment.

4. Describe the four tools commonly used in employee selection.

5. Discuss the need for employee training and name the seven methods of providing this training.

6. Explain the two components of a compensation plan and the variable elements of a benefits system.

7. Profile an effective sequence for disciplining and terminating employees.

H iring employees becomes one of the most important and frequently difficult tasks of the small business owner. For some, turning some of the decision-making ability over to an employee can cause extreme anxiety. However, not having a "second in command," and employees who can help move the

business forward, can also create its own set of challenges. Hiring good employees is critical to the success of the small business. Sandy Hansen, AgVenture Feed & Seed, Inc., in Watkins, Minnesota, discovered this difficult lesson when her husband, the owner, died after running the business singlehandedly for 20 years. The company almost failed while she and others tried to "learn information only he knew."

Jay Steinfeld of Blinds.com spends time each day debating whether or not to hire more employees. His company is an in-house call center that sells blinds and, more importantly, fixes customer problems when customers call in with questions about how their blinds function. To complicate the task, Blinds.com also handles phone calls for Sears and 11 other retailers, so the amount of knowledge employees must possess in order to effectively assist customers is daunting. Employees are critical to the success of this business. However, managing payroll costs is also imperative to the success of the business. Furthermore, management is also aware of the damage to employee morale if too many employees are hired and then must be laid off due to decreasing sales. Having the right number of good employees is no small task for this business.

The Amish are some of the most successful entrepreneurs in the United States with the lowest small business failure rates, 2.6 percent to 10 percent. With the average five-year survival rate of small business in the United States at 50 percent, what does this group of entrepreneurs do differently to so dramatically increase their rate of success? Donald Kraybill, who has researched these entrepreneurs, believes the success rate lies in their culture and in their qualities of hard work and their ability to cooperate successfully. Employees become critical in providing customers with a quality product and courteous and competent service.

As can be seen from these small businesses, hiring the right employees can make or break your business. In this chapter, you will learn more about the process of hiring as well as tools to use in choosing the right employee for your small business.

Sources: Geoff Williams, "Why Amish Businesses Don't Fail," CNNMoney.com, May 4, 2010; Nick Leiber, "For Small Businesses, the Big Decision Is Hiring," *Bloomberg Businessweek*, June 21, 2010; and Sarah Needleman, "Control Freak No More: Picking No. 2," wsj.com, June 10, 2010.

Hiring the Right Employees

Are human resource management (HRM) issues important to small businesses? Can small business owners afford the time and cost of developing formal recruitment, selection, training, and benefits programs? Perhaps the more appropriate question is whether small business owners can afford *not* to spend the time and money on such programs? In today's marketplace, one of the most valuable resources as well as a competitive advantage is the employees of the business.

One of the most important decisions a small business owner makes is the hiring of the first and then successive employees. Not only do employees cause an increase in costs, but also hiring a bad employee can negatively impact the business. Particularly in a service business, a bad hire could cause the business to fail.[1] Estimates about the costs of employee turnover range between 25 percent and 300 percent of the employee annual salary, depending upon the job. Using a 30 percent estimate, if you are paying your employee $30,000, the cost of replacing that one employee could be at a minimum $9,000.[2] Using data from the NOBSCOT Corporation, employee turnover rates vary depending upon the industry. NOBSCOT reports the employee turnover rates for the construction industry to be as high as 28 percent, accommodation and food services to be 56 percent, and leisure and hospitality to be

Manager's Notes

Finding the Right One

Hiring the right employee is no easy task. Hiring the wrong employee could cost you your business. So in the midst of producing your product, ordering inventory, stocking the shelves, developing your marketing campaign, controlling costs and formulating your strategic plan, small business owners must also carefully hire one of their most valuable business assets—employees. Following are some tips to facilitate that process.

- *Check out the attitude.* New employees can be taught appropriate skills and "how to" a variety of tasks. Changing a less-than-positive attitude likely isn't possible. Make sure their attitude fits your business culture.
- *Check for intensity.* How hard is the employee willing to work? Let them know your expectations up front. Better they know now and you don't hire than to find out later they only want to work a 20-hour week.
- *Check for product passion.* Does the potential employee know what you sell? Do they use the product? Do they think that product is the best? That level of enthusiasm is difficult to develop. Check to see if it is present from day one.
- *Check for great skills and abilities.* Too often managers hire people with the same level of skills or less. Hire better than you to move your business forward and into the future.
- *Check for the fit.* Does the potential employee fit within your organization? Everything from the way this employee deals with customers to their work ethic needs to fit within the culture of your organization. "More than 50 percent of your decision to hire should be based on fit," according to Paul Spiegelman.
- *Check for communication ability.* The line of communication need to remain open between you and the potential hire. Make sure you check the communication fit during the interview process.

Sources: Paul Spiegelman, "Weeding the Employer Garden," Entrepreneur .com, October 21, 2009; Guy Kawasaki, "Lessons in Recruiting," Entrepreneur.com, December 2008; and Bill Bartmann, "Hire Great Employees," Entrepreneur.com, April 1, 2010.

> *"Small business owners need to realize that their most valuable assets walk out the door each day at closing time."*

52 percent. On the other hand, turnover in educational services was reported at 13 percent and natural resources and mining at 17 percent.[3] If your business employs 10 people at an average wage of $30,000, and your turnover rate is a record low of 10 percent, you are still spending $30,000 a year just from employees leaving your business.

As alarming as these figures are, they do not include other potential costs, such as defending against charges of discrimination, the loss of customer satisfaction, low employee morale, and wrongful-discharge suits. Once you find people to hire, you must find ways to retain and motivate them, which costs money. These costs may also increase as you implement more employee incentive and benefit plans.

All told, the costs and risks associated with HRM issues are too great for any company to ignore. Small business owners need to realize that their most valuable assets walk out the door each day at closing time.

Job Analysis

The recruitment process involves attracting talented individuals to your company. To achieve this goal, you must be able to (1) define the positions to be filled and (2) state the qualifications needed to perform them successfully. This endeavour requires that you conduct a job analysis, prepare a job description, identify a list of job specifications, and identify alternative sources of employees. While this list may seem long, time spent defining the job, describing the job, and determining the needed employee abilities is time well spent. Since the goal is to hire employees who fit the organization and who will stay, the following steps become critical in order to effectively hire.[4]

job analysis
The process of gathering all the information about a particular job, including a job description and the job specifications.

The *job analysis* indicates what is done on the job, how it is done, who does it, and to what degree. It is the foundation on which all other HR activities are based and, if necessary, defended in court. Although no single job-analysis technique has been endorsed by the courts or the Equal Employment Opportunity Commission (EEOC), both entities urge—and in some cases require—that the information from a job analysis be used to ensure equal employment opportunity.

The first step in completing the job analysis is to gain the support and cooperation of employees, because they often know best what the job involves. The next step is to choose the jobs that should be analyzed. Generally, the amount of time and money you have available, and the importance of the particular job to the company's overall success, will determine the order and the number of jobs you will analyze.

Step three involves identifying the job-analysis technique or techniques you will use to obtain information about each job. Although numerous techniques exist, for reasons of cost, ease of use, and time savings, the most commonly used technique is the questionnaire. Questionnaires typically seek to gather the following information: identification facts about the job, skill requirements, job responsibilities, effort demanded, and working conditions. Once you have analyzed your jobs, you are ready to prepare the job description and job specifications.

Job Description

job description
A written description of a nonmanagement position that covers the title, duties, and responsibilities involved for the job.

A *job description* identifies the duties, tasks, and responsibilities of the position. Although a standard format for the job description (often termed the position description) does not exist, it is generally agreed that each job description should include the following elements:

- *Job identification.* The job title, location or department within the company, and date of origin should be included in this introductory section. This section might also include the job code, salary range, pay classification, and analyst's name.
- *Job summary.* This summary should outline the jobholder's responsibilities, the scope of her authority, and superiors to whom she is to report.
- *List of essential duties.* Although this list may contain both essential and nonessential duties, the Americans with Disabilities Act (ADA) requires that each be clearly identified, because employment decisions may be based only on the essential components of the job (see Chapter 10). The duties should be listed in order of importance with the most important duties first. Any duty that will represent at least 5 percent of an employee's time should be included.[5]
- *Task statement.* Task statements detail the logical steps or activities needed to complete the overall duties. These statements should focus on the outcomes or results rather than on the manner in which they are performed. For example, a loading-dock worker might "move 50-pound boxes from the unloading dock to the warehouse" rather than "lift and carry 50-pound boxes from the unloading dock to the warehouse." Task statements help to identify the knowledge, skills, abilities, and educational levels needed to perform the job and help to establish performance

standards for the position. In addition, these statements are valuable in complying with various federal and state employment provisions.

General working conditions, travel requirements, equipment and tools used, and other job-related data may also be included in the job description. To preserve your status as an at-will employer, which gives you the right to discharge an employee for any reason (discussed further later on in this chapter), you may add a general-duty clause, such as "and other duties as assigned" or "representative tasks and duties," to indicate that your list is not comprehensive. This also assists employers when employees do not perform a task because "It's not in my job description." Figure 17.1 shows an example of a typical job (position) description.

Job Specifications

job specifications

The identification of the knowledge, skills, abilities, and other characteristics an employee would need to perform the job.

The ***job specifications*** indicate the skills, abilities, knowledge, experience, and other personal requirements a worker needs to successfully perform the job. In writing the specifications, take care to ensure that the stated requirements are truly necessary for successful performance of the job. For example, in some cases, stating that a college degree is a requirement for a given job may be difficult, if not impossible, to prove if questioned by an EEOC representative. For this reason, you may wish to add a qualifier, such as "or equivalent," and always limit the specifications to those that are truly job related and necessary. Job specifications are often integrated into the job description, as shown in Figure 17.1.

Under Title VII and other anti-discrimination laws, you may not discriminate based upon gender, religion, race, color, or national origin. In order to choose only people from one of the protected groups listed, the employer must demonstrate specific job requirements that only this group possesses, termed bona fide occupational qualifications or BFOQs—for example, a director of a theatre can only consider females for a role requiring an actress.[6]

Employee Recruitment

You may recruit employees from a variety of sources, each of which has advantages and disadvantages. The six major sources are help-wanted ads, employment agencies, Internet job sites, executive recruiters (headhunters), employee referrals, and relatives or friends.

Advertising for Employees

Help-wanted ads in newspapers, trade publications, or storefronts generate a large number of responses, but generally the quality of applicants is not equal to that generated by other sources. Nevertheless, ads reach a wider, more diverse audience than other techniques, which may be needed to ensure equal opportunity representation or an adequate supply of employees with unique or specialized skills.

Employment Agencies

Located in all states and most large cities, government-funded employment agencies focus primarily on assisting blue- or pink-collar employees, so they may not always offer the candidates you want. On the positive side, they allow you to obtain screened applicants at no cost. On the negative side, the quality of applicants may not be equal to that generated by some other sources. Private employment agencies can be useful in helping you find more skilled employees. Fees for professional and management jobs are usually paid by you, the employer.

FIGURE 17-1 Sample Job Description

Job Title: Marketing Researcher

Department: Marketing

Reports To: Marketing Manager

Status: Non-Exempt

Summary: Employee is responsible for monitoring market conditions in local, regional, and national areas to determine sales potential for company's products and services.

Essential Duties and Responsibilities: All of the following, plus other duties as assigned. Employee will:

- Conduct marketing research and analyze data on customer demographics, preferences, and buying habits for the purpose of making intelligent marketing decisions.
- Prepare reports of marketing research conclusions, illustrating data graphically and explaining findings in written copy.
- Monitor internal and external environments including financial, technological, competitive, regulatory, and demographic factors so that market opportunities may be capitalized upon.
- Measure customer and employee satisfaction.
- Coordinate research to implement the organization's Integrated Marketing Communications (IMC) including print, broadcast, and online messages.
- Forecast and track marketing and sales trends.
- Measure effectiveness of marketing strategies and individual campaigns.
- Gather data on competitors and analyze price, sales, and distribution comparisons.
- Establish effective controls and corrective action needed to achieve marketing goals within designated budgets.
- Prepare monthly marketing activity reports.

Supervisory Responsibilities: None. Marketing Researcher is an autonomous staff position with no direct subordinates.

Qualifications: Requirements listed below represent the knowledge, skills, and/or abilities required to perform the job satisfactorily. Reasonable accommodations may be made to enable individuals with disabilities to perform the essential functions.

- *Education and/or Experience*—Bachelor's degree (BA, BS, or BBA) or equivalent required, Master's degree (MBA) preferred; or six years related experience and/or training; or equivalent combination of education and experience.
- *Language Skills*—Fluency in the English language with ability to read and analyze financial reports, legal documents, and industry trade journals. Ability to effectively communicate with customers, regulatory agencies, or members of the business community. Ability to effectively present information to top management, public groups, and/or boards of directors.
- *Mathematical Skills*—Knowledge of arithmetic, algebra, geometry, calculus, statistics and their applications. Ability to perform statistical operations such as frequency distribution, test reliability and validity, analysis of variance (ANOVA), correlation techniques, and factor analysis—and analyze using SPSS statistical software.
- *Analysis Ability*—Ability to define problems, collect data, establish facts, and draw valid conclusions.
- *Physical Demands*—Employee is regularly required to sit for extended periods of time. The employee is occasionally required to stand, walk, and lift up to twenty-five pounds. Reasonable accommodations may be made to enable individuals with disabilities to perform required duties.

Source: Adapted from www.jobdescriptions.com.

Internet Job Sites

Online job-posting sites like Monster.com, Yahoo!'s HotJobs.com, ajb.dni.us (Department of Labor), and Careerbuilder.com provide access to millions of potential employees. Prices to list jobs vary by geographic location, industry, and the package you select. Many trade associations today have job listings on their Web sites. Check out weddles.com for some industry examples. Another great place to list jobs can be your company Web site.[7]

Reality Check

Working with Gen Yers

For this age group of employees, born between approximately 1980 and 2000, the Internet has always existed, Google has been used to research everything from movie tickets to directions, and cell phones have been a constant companion. This age group has grown up with technology, prefers to work in teams, and is ardent about social responsibility. They are also one of the best-educated group of employees in the workforce today. They also have differing requirements to successfully fit within your business. Here are some tips on understanding and motivating your Generation Y employees:

- They multitask—they have grown up texting, listening to their iPod, and working on the computer while carrying on a conversation. They do not understand completing one task before moving on to another.

- They thrive on competition—they have competed under pressure to excel at everything from sports to hobbies to academics. They are willing to work hard to succeed and to win.
- They want to contribute—they need to understand where their job fits in the big picture and how their contributions help the organization succeed. Show them and tell them frequently how they are positively contributing to the company's vision.
- They like praise—they have grown up with positive reinforcement and will expect that to continue in the workplace. They need to feel appreciated.
- They want a career—they expect to succeed and rise quickly in the organization, and a career plan will not only help them progress, but also is a great tool to retain this group of employees.

Sources: Jan Ferri-Reed, "The Key to Engaging Millennials," *Journal for Quality and Participation,* April 2010; "5 Things You Should Know about Gen-Y Hires," nfib.com, retrieved July 17, 2010; and David Port and Sara Wilson, "Your Employee Handbook," Entrepreneur.com, June 2009.

Executive Recruiters (Headhunters)

Executive recruiting, or so-called headhunting firms, can be useful for small businesses looking for a key management person or two. Governmental employment agencies are much less expensive when looking for candidates for the manual-labor or other lower-level positions. Headhunting firms search confidentially for people who are currently employed and usually not actively seeking another job. Their services can be expensive. However, the process and results can be tailored specifically to your business.

Employee Referrals

Because your employees know the skills and talents needed to work in your company as well as the culture of your company, they can be a good source for finding people to fill slots. This inside-track approach to recruiting is not very costly and can generate qualified, highly motivated employees as long as your current employee morale is high and your workforce is somewhat large and diversified. On the downside, exclusive use of this source may perpetuate minority underrepresentation or create employee cliques. Moreover, in cases where the referral is not hired or does not work out, the referring employee may become resentful.

Scott Glatstein relies on the referral approach almost exclusively in his $2.5 million consulting firm, Imperatives. Glatstein says that the number one benefit of this approach is hiring a better quality employee who becomes productive quicker and has superior skills. He says, "People aren't going to recommend people who [will] make them look bad in the eyes of their employers."[8]

Relatives and Friends

The advantage of hiring relatives or friends is that you generally know beforehand of their abilities, expertise, and personalities. At the same time, no approach is more laden with long-term repercussions. The effects of a poor decision may be felt long after the desk has been cleared and the nameplate changed. According to Peter Drucker,

- Family members working in the business must be at least as able and hardworking as any unrelated employee.
- Family-managed businesses, except perhaps for the very smallest ones, increasingly need to staff key positions with nonfamily professionals.
- No matter how many family members are in a company's management, no matter how effective they are, one top job must be filled by a nonrelative.
- Before the situation becomes acute, the issue of management succession should be entrusted to someone who is neither part of the family nor part of the business.[9]

Other Sources

Job fairs, trade association meetings, and specialized Internet sites run by professional organizations (accountants, environmental specialists, and so on) can be good sources of potential employees. Finally, don't forget the simple things, such as putting a "help wanted" sign in the window or a notice on the employee bulletin board.

Obviously, hiring employees in a foreign location presents special challenges. Unless you have a lot of firsthand knowledge about or experience in the country where you'll be hiring employees, you'd be wise to get assistance and advice from local experts. That's what Eli E. Hertz, founder of Hertz Computer Corporation in New York, did. When Hertz wanted to expand into Israel, he purchased a small distributor there to handle his computer equipment. Because of the nature of the business, potential employees needed technological as well as cultural understanding. Hertz felt that this approach was the best option for him in expanding into this market.[10]

Joel Spolsky, of Fog Creek Software, wants to hire the best of the best software developers. He knows that the top 1 percent can easily be 10 times more productive than the average developer in inventing new products, save months of work by creating shortcuts, and, when there are no shortcuts, plow through coding problems "like a monster truck at a tea party." He has had success recruiting talent while they are still in college by hiring interns (paid interns, at $750/week, plus free housing, free lunch, free subway passes, relocation expenses, and various other benefits). More than half of Fog Creek's developers started as interns, then were recruited for full-time work.[11]

Hiring decisions should not be made in haste. An incorrect decision can be costly to you and your business. A Saratoga Institute survey reports that the cost of filling a position averages around $5,000 and can run as high as $12,000. This number does not include the time it takes to get the new employee acclimated and productive in your business. According to this survey, the average time to fill a position was 52 days.[12] Hiring is an expensive process with many long-term consequences. Almost without exception, you are better off holding out for the best employee, rather than filling a position quickly. Keep the following factors in mind when trying to hire the best.

"Almost without exception, you are better off holding out for the best employee, rather than filling a position quickly."

- Keep your focus on hiring the best. Don't settle for second best.
- Have a current written job description. Do not just use the last one written because it is convenient.
- Use a written rating system so that you don't forget about attributes of early candidates. This is also important if you have to defend your employee choice.
- "Overqualified" is better than "underqualified."
- A person with a long history of self-employment will, in all probability, return to self-employment as soon as possible. Hire this person as a consultant if you need her skills.

- Test specific skills and industry knowledge. You want to observe the candidate performing the work to be done (as closely as it can be duplicated) during testing.
- Check the candidate's background and all references thoroughly. While this many take time, it will pay off.
- Keep a written record of all terms of employment.

Selecting Employees

Once you have a pool of applicants from which to choose, you should match the applicants with the job requirements outlined in your job description and specifications. Four commonly used tools for selecting employees are the application form, the résumé, the selection interview, and testing.

Application Forms and Résumés

Application forms and résumés contain essentially the same information. Both contain the candidate's name, address, telephone number, education, work experience, and activities. The difference between them is that applications are forms prepared by your company and the first formal contact the prospective employee has with your company. Résumés are personal profiles prepared by job candidates to highlight specific skills. Both have the following four purposes:

1. To provide a record of the applicant's desire to obtain the position
2. To provide a profile of the applicant to be used during the interview
3. To provide a basic personnel record for the applicant who becomes an employee
4. To serve as a means of measuring the effectiveness of the selection process

The application form need not be complex or long to achieve these objectives. It must, however, ask enough of the right questions to enable you to differentiate applicants on the basis of their knowledge, skills, and ability to perform the job. In addition, the application form should provide the names of potential references and obtain the applicant's permission for you to contact each reference to discuss qualifications and prior job performance. Finally, it should include a notice that you are an at-will employer (discussed further later on in this chapter) and may therefore discharge an employee for cause or no cause and that any misinformation provided on the application form is grounds for immediate dismissal.

A caveat on résumés: They are sometimes the best fiction written, so view them with some degree of skepticism. You want to believe what people tell you, but check out all the facts, and contact previous employers.

Time and money constraints will prevent you from interviewing every candidate. Applications and résumés give you a screening tool to decide who to bring in for the next stage of the selection process—the interview.

Interviewing

Considered by many employers to be the most critical step in the selection process, the personal interview gives you a chance to learn more about the applicants; to resolve any conflicts or fill in any gaps in the information they provided; and to confirm or reject your initial impressions of them, drawn from the application or résumé. The interview also gives you a chance to explain the job and company to the applicant. Always remember that you are selling your company to the potential employee as well as determining his suitability to join your company. If the applicant is a good fit, you want her to join your firm. But even if you don't hire this applicant, the image you create may well lead to another suitable person through a word-of-mouth referral.

Manager's Notes

Don't Even Ask!

In order to meet EEOC and other government guidelines, questions allowed during interviews must be job related and only job related. This is not the time to chitchat and discuss hobbies, families, and weekend activities. You are limited to information concerning how the person would handle the job and provide value to the company. In the back of your mind, a great mantra to repeatedly chant during an interview is "it must be job related, it must be job related." To avoid discrimination allegations, do NOT ask questions like these:

- How long have you been disabled? (You *can* ask if they can perform essential job tasks.)
- Do you have children or plan to have children in the near future?
- What was your maiden name?
- To which church do you belong, and how often do you attend?
- Have you ever been arrested? (You *can* ask whether the applicant has ever been convicted of a felony.)
- Do you own your own home, and how long have you lived there? Who lives with you at this address?
- How frequently and in what quantity do you drink alcohol? (You *can* ask if they use illegal drugs.)
- Do you have any religious obligations that would prevent you from working any day of the week or on any holidays?
- Can you make child care arrangements in order to work at night or on the weekends?
- What language do you most frequently speak?
- Do you have any kind of disability that would require reasonable accommodation?
- To which social clubs and organizations do you belong?
- Are you in a financially stable position personally?
- What is your weight?
- Have you ever filed a workers' compensation claim?
- What are the names and addresses of two relatives?

Sources: "The Interview Process: How to Select the 'Right' Person," sba.gov, retrieved July 16, 2010; "Interview Tips: Keeping It Legal," Inc.com, July 11, 2005; and Tyler Paetkau, "Surviving the Interview Minefield," Entrepreneur.com, retrieved July 18, 2010.

To conduct an effective interview, you should do the following.

Be Prepared Start by thoroughly reviewing the job description and job specifications. You must know what your needs are before you can find a person to fulfill them. Next, review the candidate's application form. Look for strengths and weaknesses, areas of conflict, and questions left unanswered or vaguely worded. Time spent during the interview should be used to dig deeper, not just review information already contained on the résumé or in the cover letter.

Set the Stage for the Interview Arrange to hold the interview at a time and location demonstrating its importance. Begin the interview on time. The location should provide

Hiring an employee is a big commitment for a small business, so interviewing is critical.

privacy and comfort, and present the right image of your company. It should allow you to talk without interruptions. Taking telephone calls, answering employee questions, or working on another task while conducting the interview does little to ease the fears of the applicant and simply does not facilitate good communication or present a good image.

Use a Structured Interview Format Develop a set of questions to ask each candidate so that you can compare their responses. The job description and specifications should be the source of the majority of your questions and the questions must be job related. Such a format will allow you to collect a great deal of information quickly, systematically cover all areas of concern, and more easily compare candidates on the basis of similar information. If interviewing several candidates, take notes on the answers provided by the candidates, so that you can remember and make comparisons later.

Use a Variety of Questioning Techniques Although closed-ended questions are appropriate when looking for a commitment or for verifying information, they are very limiting. Consequently, you should use open-ended or probing questions that are related to the job. For example, rather than asking, "Have you ever dealt with an upset customer?" which can be answered with a yes or a no, instead ask, "How would you handle a customer who is upset with the quality of the product that was purchased from our store?" Open-ended, probing questions encourage the applicant to talk, providing you with a wealth of information and insight into the applicant's ability to communicate effectively.

No Matter the Type of Question, Make Sure That It Is Job Related The EEOC requires that all job-interview questions be nondiscriminatory in nature. In other words, they must be devoid of references to race, color, religion, sex, national origin, or disability, and they must be job related. You should be able to relate each interview question to one or more of the items in your job description or job specifications and to show how the information obtained from the questions will be used to differentiate candidates.

Keep Good Records, Including Notes from the Interview The EEOC construes any selection device as a test, and if a test results in underrepresentation of a protected group, it must be validated. Therefore, if the interview results in underrepresentation, the interview process must be validated. In the case of most small business owners, the problem is not one of questionable behavior or wrongdoing within this area, but rather one of inadequate documentation. You must be able to show that your decision to hire or not to hire was based on a sound business reason or practice as proven by your interview notes.

Testing

Employee testing has long been used by U.S. businesspeople to screen applicants. For the most part, prior to the 1971 Supreme Court decision in *Griggs v. Duke Power Co.*, employers were fairly free to do as they pleased in this matter.[13] Today, however, employers must be able to prove that their tests and other selection criteria are valid predictors of job performance. This can be done, according to the Supreme Court and the EEOC, through statistical or job-content analyses.

For small business owners, the process of statistically validating a test is generally far too time-consuming and expensive. Therefore, short of eliminating all tests, two options remain: purchasing preprinted tests from commercial vendors that have conducted the necessary standardization studies to ensure test reliability (although ultimate liability still rests with the employer) or using content-based tests. Although it is not an absolute defense, you are more likely to be able to prove a test's validity if the test is a sample or measure of the actual work to be performed on the job. For example, if a clerk's job involves counting back change to customers, then asking an applicant to count back change as a test is probably content valid and its use is therefore permitted.

Regardless of the type of test used, rarely should you use the results of a single test or indicator as the sole reason for hiring or not hiring an applicant. In addition, all test results should be kept strictly confidential and in a file other than the employee's personnel file. If you are unsure about a using a test, consult a lawyer who specializes in hiring law. Commonly used tests include the following.

Achievement, Aptitude, and Personality Tests These types of tests are given to measure specific skills a person has attained as a result of his experiences or education. These tests are easy and inexpensive to administer and score. Proving validity and job-relatedness, however, is another matter. Therefore, you should have a very compelling, business-related reason to justify their use during the selection process.

Performance (Ability) Tests Performance tests are administered to assess the applicant's ability to perform the job. The tests provide direct, observable evidence of performance. They are also easily administered, relate directly to the job, and are relatively inexpensive to conduct. Validity is generally not an overriding issue with performance testing. For a person with a disability, reasonable accommodations must be made during the test.[14]

Physical Examinations Often considered the last step in the screening process, physical examinations are given to discover any physical or medical limitations that might prevent the applicant from performing the duties of the job.

The ADA states that physical examinations can be given only after a conditional offer of employment and only if they are administered to all applicants in the particular job category.[15] In addition, you cannot disqualify individuals as a result of such examinations unless the findings show that the person would pose a "direct threat" to the health and safety of others.[16] All medical findings must be kept separately from general personnel files and be made available only to selected company personnel on a need-to-know basis.

Drug Tests   Organizations are increasingly using drug tests to screen applicants, and with good reason. According to the American Council for Drug Education, employees that use drugs on the job are

- "Ten times more likely to miss work
- 3.6 times more likely to be involved in on-the-job accidents—and 5 times more likely to hurt themselves or another in the process
- 33% less productive"[17]

Although tests for illegal use of drugs are not considered tests under the ADA and are therefore not subject to its regulations, many state legislatures have imposed conditions under which drug tests may be administered, samples tested, and results used. Generally, to justify the cost and privacy concerns caused by these tests, you must be able to demonstrate a strong need for safety within your workplace or services.

Honesty Tests   The 1988 Employee Polygraph Protection Act essentially outlawed the use of voice stress analyzers and other devices in most business situations. As a result, employers have increasingly relied on paper-and-pencil honesty tests. So far, these tests remain suspect in terms of their validity, and the courts have yet to rule decisively on their use. Several congressional committees are also looking into restricting or outlawing their use as a pre-employment tool. Unless you have an overriding reason for employing this kind of test—for example, the employee will have ready access to merchandise or money—the use of an honesty test is not recommended without proper legal advice. Court rulings on honesty testing do vary from state to state.

Which Tests to Use?   There are thousands of employee evaluations for you to choose from, but which one(s) should you use? Following are some of the most extensively validated, most respected instruments for cognitive ability and personality:

1. Watson-Glaser Critical Thinking Appraisal. This widely used cognitive test measures problem-solving skills, creativity, and other factors with 40 difficult questions ($10 to $20 per test).
2. Wesman Personnel Classification. This cognitive exam uses a combination of verbal and numerical questions to evaluate employees for decision-making roles ($7 to $15 per test).
3. Multidimensional Aptitude Battery II. This 303-question test of general mental ability, developed in 1998, is administered in 100 minutes. It measures ability to reason, plan, and solve problems ($190 for 25 tests).
4. Wonderlic Personnel Test. This classic test, developed in 1937, is probably most familiar to those who follow the NFL draft, as the football league administers it to college recruits. It takes only 12 minutes and is most appropriate for entry-level to midlevel jobs ($10 per test).
5. NEO Personality Inventory-Revised. This personality test measures respondents on five scales: neuroticism, extroversion, openness to experience, agreeableness, and conscientiousness ($245 for 25 tests).
6. 16PF. This personality test targeted for leadership positions includes 185 items measuring 16 personality factors ($8 to $30 per test).
7. Hogan Personality Inventory. This personality test consists of true-false questions that measure seven personality scales, such as ambition and prudence. This test has

been around for about three decades, so responses can be compared to those of people actually doing most jobs in the United States ($25 to $175 depending on the amount of detail in the report).[18]

Temporary Employees and Professional Employer Organizations (PEOs)

Today many small business owners are recognizing the benefits of hiring temporary employees. In the past, agencies such as Kelly Services and Manpower, Inc., were generally called upon only when someone in the company went on vacation or demand suddenly exceeded capacity. Although these are still the most popular reasons for using temporary services, other motivations include the need to fill new or highly specialized positions, to ensure a full workforce during periods of labor shortages, and to take advantage of the growing pool of workers who like the flexibility and challenge of working for multiple employers.

The employment costs of temporary employees are often lower than those associated with permanent or full-time employees. The employment agency generally takes care of all federal and state reporting and record-keeping requirements, thereby lowering the company's overhead costs. In addition, training and other costs, such as workers' compensation, unemployment insurance, and fringe benefits, are paid by the agency rather than by the company. Finally, once the job has been completed in the case of seasonal demands, temporary workers can be laid off quickly and with fewer concerns for wrongful-discharge claims.

A relatively recent and growing trend in HR are employee-leasing firms called professional employer organizations (PEOs). The PEO becomes the legal employer, providing the business with HR professionals who will handle employee benefits, health care plans, tax laws, and the ever-increasing amount of new law and regulation compliance. The PEO assumes the responsibility for payroll, taxes, worker's compensation, unemployment claims, and any other employee perks that may be provided. According to a 2007 Human Capital Management trends survey, the services that businesses cite as most beneficial from a PEO are payroll processing (30 percent), employee assistance programs (28 percent), and background screening (27 percent). From the businesses perspective, the benefits are seen as freeing up internal staff (18 percent), streamlining operations (17 percent), and access to industry expertise (14 percent). Another survey, the HR Outsourcing Buyer Pulse, found that businesses were looking for the following from a PEO: cost reduction, external skills and knowledge, process improvements, and the ability to focus on more strategic activates.[19]

The handling of benefit packages, especially health insurance, is usually what makes outsourcing the HR function attractive to small businesses. Because employees are part of a larger group with an employee leasing company than they would be with a small business, they can obtain insurance coverage that is otherwise unavailable or prohibitively expensive. For the small business owner, the cost savings associated with not providing benefits and other HR functions may outweigh the associated fees.

Despite the cost savings, many business owners are understandably reluctant to turn over responsibility of their most important assets—employees—to an outside company, so cost is seldom the only factor in this decision. PEOs may be a viable alternative for your small business if you can pick the right company. Make sure the company you choose is ESAC (Employer Services Assurance Corporation) accredited. PEOs who receive this accreditation have met ethical, financial, and operational standards, and must continue to do so to remain accredited. You can get assistance in choosing a PEO company from the National Association of Professional Employer Organizations (napeo.org).

Placing and Training Employees

You have hired your new employee—now what? ***Employee orientation*** is the process of introducing the new person to your business, to the current employees, and to your company culture, your way of doing things. The first few days and sometimes weeks on the job are critical for both employee success and productivity, and can be the difference between someone staying and leaving the organization. After the time, effort, and dollars spent getting to this point, you do not want to lose a good hire.

Orientation can be formal or informal, but regardless of the method used, there should be a process by which new employees are welcomed into the business. This can also be a critical component later in the event of a wrongful discharge claim. According to Caruth, Caruth, and Haden in Industrial Management, there are five general purposes that should be accomplished during orientation:

1. Introduce the company. Talk about the history, the founders, the organization as a whole, and, more importantly, the culture. The roots of a company are important in helping a new hire to become grounded.
2. Get the employee excited about working for you. Make sure they receive a positive impression of the company, its employees, its products, and its services.
3. Provide mechanisms to help the new employee adjust to this new environment. Think back to your first day on a new job and all the information you did not know. Little things like how to use the phone system to the time for breaks to how to log in to the computer system can be overwhelming. Finding a senior employee to assist in mentoring a new hire can be helpful. Just make sure there is a "fit" between the two and that the new hire feels comfortable going to the established employee with questions.
4. Define job expectations. Make sure the new employee knows what she is expected to do. It is hard to hit the target if the target is unknown. Spend some time discussing procedures and expected outcomes.
5. Discuss employee policies and benefits. Here is where your HR person can be very helpful, assisting the employee with these types of questions.[20]

When an employee reports to work for the first time, she has many needs, some of which are more immediately pressing than others. For example, the fear of not being at the right place at the right time, or of saying the wrong thing to the wrong person, generally far outweighs concerns over fringe benefits or the company's plan for future growth. Consequently, the order of the orientation presentation should be directed toward fulfilling the most pressing needs first.

If you as the small business owner are not conducting the orientation, ensure that the person in your organization who is doing it understands the importance and the process you expect. Employee turnover is expensive and retaining good employees begins on day one with an effective orientation to your business. Spend some time developing processes by which to start your new employees off right.

William Brodbeck, president and CEO of Brodbeck Enterprises of Platteville, Wisconsin, preaches the importance of employee training and orientation for reducing employee turnover and thus being able to keep service levels high. His company owns and operates eight supermarkets, for which a highly systematic training program is in effect for new hires. The company's basic training and orientation session is 6.5 hours long. Cashiers receive another 38.5 to 40 hours of training on top of the basic training, deli employees get another 33 hours, and seafood workers receive an additional 47.5 hours of training. Brodbeck feels strongly that his company's commitment to training and orientation makes a difference in the customer service his supermarkets provide.[21]

Employee Training and Development

employee training
A planned effort to teach employees more about their job so as to improve their performance and motivation.

Often overlooked by managers is the use of *employee training* and *development* as a motivating tool. Training involves increasing the employee's knowledge and skills to meet a specific job or company objectives. It is usually task and short-term oriented. Development, by comparison, is more forward looking, providing the employee with the knowledge, skills, and abilities needed to accept a new and more-challenging job assignment within the company.

employee development
A planned effort to provide employees with the knowledge, skills, and abilities needed to accept new and more challenging job assignments within the company.

A trained workforce can give your business a competitive advantage that, once gained, is not easily duplicated by competitors. That advantage can be maintained and enhanced through an ongoing training-and-development program. Such a program helps prevent boredom and, consequently, increases retention rates for qualified personnel. Not only are turnover costs reduced, but also, over a period of time, the overall level of employee morale is raised. Finally, training and development assure your firm a place in tomorrow's competitive environment. New employee skills and abilities will inevitably be required as the business expands into new product lines, acquires new technologies, and strives to maintain or reach a higher level of customer service.

Ways to Train

Depending on the objectives of your training program, several techniques are available. The seven most common methods are on-the-job training (OJT), lecture, conferences, programmed learning, role-playing, job rotation, and correspondence courses.

On-the-Job Training Everyone from the mail clerk to the company president experiences on-the-job training (OJT) from the time he joins a company. This type of training entails learning the job while you are doing it. OJT is effective, but the small business owner should try to ensure that it is not the only type of training provided. The most familiar types of OJT are coaching and mentoring, in which a new employee works with an experienced employee or supervisor. This practice not only instructs new employees on how to operate equipment, but also ideally builds a bond between the employee, her mentor, and the business.

In order to be effective, OJT should encompass the following steps:

- Prepare the new employee for the training. What information is important to know before the employee even begins?

  - Outline the task to be completed. Go over the steps and the processes to be used in successfully completing the job. Make sure the new employee knows where to get any required resources.
  - Demonstrate the task. Break down the process into manageable steps the new employee can easily follow.
  - Watch the new employee perform the task. After you have told and shown the new employee, watch to see if he understood your previous directions.
  - Provide feedback. Once the employee demonstrates the task, let him know he did a good job or provide more information in order to help improve his process. Observing and providing feedback are critical steps in OJT. [22]

Image copyright © Lisa F. Young. Used under license from Shutterstock.com

Every level of employee experiences some type of on-the-job training.

Manager's Notes

Sixty-Second Guide to Hiring the Right Employee

Hiring new employees can be one of the most important decisions a small business owner makes as the impact on the business, other employees, the product or service line, and customers can be major. It can also be an exciting time as you search for a new person to bring new "blood" to your business. Here is a 60-second guideline to help you hire the right employee for your business.

0:60 Define the job and duties.
Each position should have a written job description detailing specific responsibilities, performance and evaluation criteria, relationships with other functions within the business, and so forth. The more specific you are in this step, the more successful you will be in finding just the right person. Make sure each time you hire, you update the position and its requirements.

0:51 Define the knowledge, skills, and abilities needed to do the job.
Carefully evaluate the knowledge, skills, and abilities needed to fulfill the job. Requiring more or less can eliminate qualified people from the pool. Differentiate between skills that are essential and ones that would be nice to see. Don't get in a hurry to hire and settle for second best. If the fit is not there, wait.

0:38 Let people know you are looking.
Ask your network for referrals. Place a help-wanted sign in your window. Trade associations are another great place to spread the word. And don't forget customers, suppliers, and current employees as resources.

0:30 Make the compensation fair.
Look at industry ads and scan the help-wanted ads. Don't eliminate good people because your pay is far from the market price. On the other hand, don't pay too much.

0:18 Ask the right questions during the interview.
With a well-written job description in hand, interview questions should come easily. Remember to keep all questions job related. Beware of hiring people just like you, called the halo effect. Choose the person that best fits the job, not the one you personally like best. Prescreen by phone when possible. And bring in others to help evaluate potential hires. Sometimes they will see things you have missed.

0:09 Check references.
This is a step that can get skipped or even ignored, if you happen to really like the potential new hire. References who provide less-than-glowing recommendations or who are vague on information provided are red flags. Reevalute your hiring decision if and when this happens.

0:03 Retain the employees you hire.
Orientation, training, and developmental opportunities are important to get the new hire "off on the right foot." Have a formal process in place to help new employees learn the ropes of your business. After you have spent this amount of time and money, you do not want to lose a good employee because you dropped the last ball in the hiring process.

Sources: "60-Second Guide to Hiring the Right People," SCORE Association, nfib.com, retrieved July 17, 2010; Joan Lloyd, "Tips to Avoid Costly Hiring Mistakes," *Receivables Report*, February 2010; and "Hiring Right Remains a Challenge: Here's How to Overcome the Odds," *Business Credit*, September/October 2009.

Lecture Lecturing involves one or more individuals communicating instructions or ideas to others. The technique is often used because of its low cost, the speed with which information can be covered, and the large number of individuals who can be accommodated in each session. Employee participation is limited, however, and no allowance is made for individual employee differences.

Conferences Also termed group discussions, the conference technique is similar to the lecture method, except that employees are actively involved in the learning. Although this technique produces more ideas than lecturing does, it takes more time, and only a limited number of participants can participate.

Programmed Learning Programmed learning or instruction is achieved through use of a computer or printed text. The employee receives immediate feedback and learns at her own speed. This method works well for almost any type of training. However, outside materials must generally be purchased, and the learner must be self-directed and motivated for this technique to be effective.

Role-Playing In the role-playing method, employees take on new roles within the company, acting out the situation as realistically as possible. If the sessions are videotaped, playing back the tapes allows for employee feedback and group discussions. Some employees find the technique threatening, and not all business situations lend themselves to this type of training.

Job Rotation Job rotation allows employees to move from one job to another within the company. In addition to ensuring that employees have a variety of job skills and knowledge, the technique provides management with trained replacements in the event that one employee becomes ill or leaves the company. On the downside, job rotation does not generally provide in-depth, specialized training.

Correspondence Courses, Internet Classes, and Webinars These techniques are especially useful for updating current knowledge and acquiring new information. Generally sponsored by a professional association or university, these techniques allow for specialized training without the employee having to leave work to attend. Accommodations will need to be provided if the training is to occur during work hours, but travel costs are significantly reduced using these methods. Webinars on a variety of topics are becoming more readily available and can be a great way to update skills or provide information on recent industry changes. With these techniques, the employee must be motivated to learn, and course costs may be high.

Compensating Employees

"Wages and incentives—including health care and other benefits—are necessary to keep employees alive, healthy, and motivated."

Employees expect to be paid a fair and equitable wage. Determining what is fair and equitable is a challenging and ongoing task that involves primarily two components: wages and benefits. The U.S. Bureau of Labor Statistics reported that for March 2009, employees, on average, made $29.39 an hour. Of that amount, $20.49 was wages and $8.90 was benefits. Of the $8.90 in benefits, 7.8 percent went to Medicare, Unemployment, and Worker's Compensation; 8.6 percent went to life, health, and disability insurance; 7.15 percent went to paid leave; and 4.5 percent went to retirement and other savings.[23]

Determining Wage Rates

Based on the Fair Labor Standards Act (FLSA), employees are classified as either exempt or nonexempt. Exempt employees are not covered by the major provisions of the FLSA, which specifies minimum wage, overtime pay, child labor laws, and equal-pay-for-equal-work regulations. Most exempt employees are paid on a straight salary basis. Nonexempt employees, however, must be paid a minimum wage set by Congress (or your state government, if higher). These payments may take the form of hourly wages, salary, piecework rates, or commissions.

Hourly Wages Most organizations pay their nonexempt employees an hourly wage (a set rate of pay for each hour worked). Exempt employees are not paid on an hourly basis but rather a straight salary.

All-Salaried Employees Some organizations are moving to an all-salaried workforce. These companies pay both exempt and nonexempt employees a salary (a fixed sum of money). Although still subject to FLSA provisions, this type of compensation plan removes the perceived inequity between the two "classes" of employees and fosters a greater esprit de corps.

Piecework Rates Unlike salaried or hourly wage rates, the piecework rate is a pay-for-performance plan. Under a piecework rate, the employer pays an employee a set amount for each unit he produces. Some employers pay, as an incentive, a premium for units produced above a predetermined level of production. For example, an employee might receive $2 per unit for the first 40 units produced and $2.25 for any units above 40. Other plans might pay a straight rate for all units—say, $2.15—once the standard output quota of 40 units has been surpassed.

Commissions Commissions represent another type of pay-for-performance approach. Some jobs, especially those in sales, are not easily measured in terms of units produced. Under a straight commission plan, the employee's wages can be based solely on her sales volume. Because employees often cannot control all of the external variables that affect sales, employers are increasingly paying these workers on a base-salary-plus-commission basis. Employees tend to favor this combination approach in which they are provided with a degree of income security during slow sales periods.

Still other employers are allowing their employees to "draw" against future commissions. This means that an employee may receive an advance from the employer during a slow sales period and repay the advance (draw) out of commissions earned during the remainder of the pay period or, in some cases, future pay periods. Such draws are particularly effective if sales fluctuate from month to month or from quarter to quarter.

Jim Lippie, CEO of consulting firm Thrive Networks of Concord, Massachusetts, paid salespeople via commission, but wanted to foster more teamwork. He considered switching them to salaries, but was concerned about decreasing motivation. Lippie then created a quarterly commissions pool shared equally by the six salespeople. Approximately one-third of their total compensation is tied to the performance of the whole sales team, and the rest is salary. Lippie says, "We've become much better at sharing information while spreading around both incentives and the risks."[24]

Incentive-Pay Programs

bonus
A one-time reward provided to an employee for exceeding a performance standard.

An incentive-pay program is a reward system that ties performance to compensation. Two common types of incentive-pay programs involve the awarding of bonuses and profit-sharing programs. *Bonuses* are generally doled out on a one-time basis to reward employees for their high performance. They may be given to either an individual employee or a group of employees. Bonuses are frequently awarded when an employee meets objectives set for attendance, production, sales, cost savings, quality, or performance.

To be an effective motivator, a bonus must be tied to a specific measure of performance. The reason for which the bonus is being awarded must be communicated to employees at the time they are informed that they will receive it. The bonus should be paid separately from the employee's regular paycheck to reinforce its effect. In this way, the bonus is less likely to be viewed by employees as an extension of their regular salary and something to which they are automatically entitled.

profit-sharing plan
A plan in which employees receive additional compensation based on the profitability of the entire business.

Under most **profit-sharing plans**, employers make the same percentage of salary contributions to each worker's account on a semiannual or annual basis. The percentage of contributions varies according to the amount of profits earned, making the system highly flexible. Most employers believe these plans serve to motivate workers by giving them a sense of partnership with the employer. Profit-sharing plans are a mainstay of many small business owners' compensation plans. David Haynes is the CEO of Skyline Construction in San Francisco, a construction company that focuses on green building. The company uses a 100 percent employee stock ownership program. Haynes states, "Great pride takes over knowing you are responsible for what happens here, not just the CEO … It creates tremendous peer pressure to perform on all levels.[25]

ENTREPRENEURIAL SNAPSHOT

Cooking up a Cause

© Trae Patton/NBC/NBCU Photo Bank/AP Images

One of Miami's hottest chefs, Lorena Garcia, was born, raised, and graduated from law school in Venezuela. She credits family gatherings spent entertaining family and friends as her career inspiration. "Bringing loved ones together to enjoy wonderful food—it's natural—it is something that has always fulfilled me," she says.

In 2005, Garcia started an ambitious venture named Elements. Tierra [Earth] featured an eclectic blend of Latin- and Asian-inspired dishes in the heart of Miami's design district. In addition to Tierra, Garcia opened Agua (Water), a convenience store; Fuego (Fire), a catering business; and Aire (Air), an office headquarters of sorts for Garcia's marketing.

Lately, Garcia has also lent her talent to a bigger cause—the health and social problems caused by childhood obesity. Since 2004, Garcia, 37, has conducted free cooking workshops for children in southern Florida. "I love kids and I love cooking, so I put these passions together," she says. Garcia created Big Chef, Little Chef, a nonprofit organization that teaches children 8 to 12 years old how to give their favorite treats a nutritious twist. She was inspired to start Big Chef, Little Chef by her nephews and nieces, who, like many kids, were eating fattening prepackaged meals. "I want kids to know about nutrition and make food they can be proud of and will love to eat. Getting them involved in preparing their own meals and having a great time doing it is the first step in getting them to make dietary changes."

Garcia's charismatic personality and contagious enthusiasm for great food have caught the attention of many and landed her in front of the camera. She hosted several nationally syndicated shows on the Gems and Mun2 television networks. Garcia is currently the host of *El Arte del Buen Gusto*, one of the highest-rated shows on MGM's "Casa Club TV," airing in both the United States and Latin America. She also appears weekly on Telemundo's nationally syndicated morning show *Cada Dia con Maria Antonieta*. Garcia has also caught the eye of companies like Nestlé and Splenda. Nestle tapped the chef to host the nationally syndicated segment *Cocinando con Nestlé*, and she is the spokeswoman for SPLENDA® No Calorie Sweetener.

Sources: Andrea C. Poe, "Nutritious Meals Cook Up an Idea," *Entrepreneur Magazine*, August 2007, 91; Idy Fernandez, "Earthly Delights," *Hispanic Magazine Online*, February 2006, http://www.hispaniconline.com/magazine/2006/february/la_buena_vida/spice.html; and "Big Chef, Little Chef," http://cheflorenagarcia.com/bclc.html.

Benefits

benefit
Part of an employee's compensation in addition to wages and salaries.

An employee ***benefit*** consists of any supplement to wages and salaries. Health and life insurance, paid vacation time, pension and education plans, and discounts on company products are examples. The cost of offering and administering benefits has increased greatly in recent decades—up from 25.5 percent of total payroll in 1961 to about 38 percent today. Often employees do not realize the market value and high cost of the benefits they receive.

According to the *2010 Employee Job Satisfaction* survey report, job security was number one on the list of very important contributors to job satisfaction, and benefits was number two. The opportunity to use skills and abilities, the work itself, and the organization's financial stability preceded compensation in the list of the top six contributors to employee satisfaction. Health care remains the most important benefit, with paid time off second on the list. Sixty-five percent of the respondents felt health care benefits were very important, and yet only 38 percent said they were satisfied with the health care benefits provided to them by their employers compared to 54 percent of respondents who were very satisfied with their paid time off.[26]

As an employer, you are required by law to do the following:

- Provide time off for employees to vote, serve on a jury, and perform military service.
- Meet all workers' compensation requirements.
- Withhold Social Security retirement and disability, as well as Medicare and Medicaid, and pay the employer's percentage.
- Pay state and federal unemployment taxes, thus providing benefits for unemployed workers.
- Contribute to state short-term disability programs in states where such programs exist.
- Comply with the Federal Family and Medical Leave Act (FMLA) if your business has 50 or more employees. Check the requirements for your state. Some businesses with less than 50 employees may need to comply if state regulations so dictate.[27]

While you may need to in a competitive job market, you are not required to provide the following:

- Retirement plans
- Health plans (except in Hawaii)
- Dental or vision plans
- Life insurance plans
- Educational assistance
- Child care
- Discounts on products or services
- Paid vacations, holidays, or sick leave[28]

With an increasing discontent and call for a new mix of benefits, the challenge for small business owners is to provide a mix of benefits that is both affordable for the employer and motivational for employees.

Flexible Benefit Packages With the diversity in today's workforce, one benefit package seldom fits all. Since all employees do not have the same needs, a flexible-benefit package, or cafeteria plan, allows each employee to select the benefits that best suit his financial and lifestyle needs. Employees generally favor such plans due to their flexibility and pretax benefits

Increasingly, flexible-benefit packages not only provide employees with a menu of benefits from which to choose, but also include choices between taxable and nontaxable benefits. Under the latter, IRS-approved plans, employees are allowed to purchase benefits with pretax dollars. In this way, they can reduce their taxable income while at the same time increasing their benefit options.

The advantages of flexible plans are not realized without additional costs. As the number and mix of benefits increase, so do administrative costs associated with activities such as record keeping, communications with employees, and compliance with government regulations. A second, but no less important, concern is that employees may select the wrong mix or types of benefits. Often employees do not worry about their benefits until they are actually needed, generally in response to a major illness or accident. Yet the law does not allow benefit choices to be changed during the plan year, so employees often find that their benefit options do not match their immediate needs.

Health Insurance The impact of the Affordable Health Care for America Act has yet to be fully realized. Many of the provisions will not go into effect until 2014. However, small business owners do now have a differing mandated requirement to provide health care for their employees. According to the Council of Economic Advisors, 99 percent of companies with over 200 employees offered health insurance in 2008 compared to only 49 percent of firms with three to nine workers—thus, the impetus for this bill.

One of the provisions in the bill is for the establishment at the state level of SHOP exchanges, Small Business Health Options Program. These exchanges will allow small businesses to join pools in order to obtain lower premiums and to help in administering the health care programs. If a SHOP is not available in your state, the federal government is obligated to provide an alternative.

The details of the act differ based upon the number of employees in your small business. For example, if your state has an established SHOP and your business has 10 or fewer employees who make less than $25,000, your business will be eligible for a tax credit equal to 35 percent of the cost of the premiums.

However, since this act is in the beginning stages of implementation, changes may occur during the next few years. For more information and to keep current on developments, the Small Business Administration (SBA) has created a guide for small business owners. You can find this guide on the front page of the SBA Web site located at www.sba.gov.[29]

In an attempt to hold down the growing costs of health insurance, many small business owners are joining cooperative health maintenance organizations (HMOs) or preferred provider organizations (PPOs). Under an HMO system, a firm signs a contract with an approved HMO that agrees to provide health and medical services to its employees. In return for the exclusive right to care for the firm's employees, the HMO offers its services at an adjusted rate. Unfortunately, employees often object to these plans because they are restricted to using the health care specialists employed or approved by the HMO.

To overcome this objection, some companies are switching to PPOs. With a PPO, a firm or group of firms negotiates with doctors and hospitals to provide certain health care services for a favorable price. In turn, member firms encourage their employees, through higher reimbursement payments, to use these "preferred" providers. Employees tend to favor PPOs because they can use the doctor of their choice.

Retirement Plans To assist employees in saving for their retirement needs, employers provide them with retirement, or pension, plans. Such plans present employees with an accumulated amount of money when they reach a set retirement age or when they are unable to continue working due to a disability. Retirement plans rate high on the list of benefits employees desire. According to a survey by the Transamerica Center for Retirement Studies, 47 percent of respondents said they would prefer minimum pay and better retirement benefits compared to more pay and less retirement benefits. And 58 percent said they would leave their current job for a similar position if the retirement benefits of the new job were better.[30] Four common retirement options described here are individual retirement accounts, simplified employee pension plans, 401(k) plans, and Keogh plans; another, less common, option is the 412(i) plan.

- *Individual Retirement Accounts.* Individual retirement accounts (IRAs) allow employees to make tax-exempt contributions to a retirement account.
- *Simplified Employee Pension Plans.* A simplified employee pension (SEP) plan is similar to an IRA but is available only to people who are self-employed or who work for small businesses that do not have a retirement plan.
- *401(k) Plans.* Named after Section 401(k) of the 1978 Revenue Act, 401(k) plans allow small businesses to establish payroll reduction plans that are more flexible and have greater tax advantages than IRAs. As was true of the foregoing plans, the amount deferred and any accumulated investment earnings are excluded from current income and are taxed only when finally distributed (usually when the worker retires).
- The relatively unknown *412(i)* plan (named for a section of IRS code) is designed for small business owners with 20 or fewer employees planning to retire within 10 years. It is a defined-benefit plan that allows you to accumulate significant retirement assets in a short period of time.
- A 412(i) is ideal for small business owners in their peak earning years who have saved less for retirement than they would like. Contributions are based on age and income and can be as high as $350,000 per year. In general, the older you are, the more you can contribute. The plan is fully insured, which means it is funded with a combination of life insurance and annuities, or annuities alone.
- Another recent option for small business owners is a PEO-MEP, Multiple Employer Plan. A PEO can also provide retirement assistance in combination with the other HR functions mentioned previously. The PEO establishes the retirement plan, sponsors the plan, and administers the plan for businesses that have opted in. This allows the business to utilize the expertise of the PEO, alleviates the personnel costs of retirement planning at the business level, and reduces costs since the MEP is sponsored by the PEO.[31]

For a review of retirement plans, see Table 17.1.

Child Care and Elder Care As the number of dual-income families continues to increase and the concern over family values grows, more and more employees are looking to their employers for help in managing what is often called the work–family balance. For example, in a recent survey conducted by Hewitt Associates, 98 percent of major U.S. employers offered some form of child care assistance. This assistance ranged from child care on site at the place of employment, to resource and referral programs, to backup child care, to flexible work schedules, to flexible spending accounts that allow workers to set aside a portion of their pretax earnings to pay for child care costs. Employers that offer child care assistance generally do so for one or more of the following reasons: to accommodate employee requests, thereby increasing employee morale; to retain high-performing employees; to improve recruiting efforts; to reduce employee absenteeism and tardiness; and to increase employee productivity. A useful component of child care assistance is flexibility, since "one size fits all" frequently does not work in the child care arena.[32]

Another major consideration for today's employers is employees who are caring for aging parents. It is estimated that over 60 percent of the 34 million people providing elder care are employed. The costs to business of employees providing this care through absen-

TABLE 17-1 Retirement Plan Preview

	ELIGIBILITY	FUNDING RESPONSIBILITY	ANNUAL CONTRIBUTIONS PER PARTICIPANT	VESTING OF CONTRIBUTIONS	ADMINISTRATIVE RESPONSIBILITIES
Simple IRA	Businesses with 100 or fewer employees that maintain any other retirement plan do not currently maintain any other retirement plan	Funded by employee salary reduction contributions and employer contributions	3% employer match; employee contributions to maximum of $11,500 or $14,000 if older than 50	Immediate	No employer tax filings
SEP-IRA	Any self-employed individual, business owner, or individual who earns any self-employed income	Employer contributions only	Up to 20% of your net self-employment income or 25% of your salary if you are employed by your own corporation, to maximum of $49,000	Immediate	Form 5498 and IRS testing
401(k)	Any business; employees who have worked at least 1,000 hours in the past year	Primarily employee salary-reduction contributions and optional employer contributions	For employees, limit is up to $16,500 per employee or $22,000 if older than 50. Employer can match up to 25% of employee's compensation	Determined by employer	Form 5500 and special IRS testing to ensure plan does not discriminate in favor of highly compensated employees
Defined-Benefit Plan	Any self-employed individual, business owner, or individual who earns any self-employed income	Generally employer contributions only	Maximum annual retirement benefit of $170,000 or 100% of 3-year average compensation	May offer vesting schedules	Form 5500

Sources: "Small Business Retirement Plans," *Entrepreneur* magazine online, August 2007, www.entrepreneur.com/humanresources/compensationandbenefits/article79282.html; Rosalind Resnick, "A Better Plan for Not Working," *Entrepreneur*, June 2010; and "The Benefits of Individual 401(k) Plans," *The Tax Adviser*, December 2009.

teeism, unpaid leave, and other work challenges amount to approximately $34 billion a year. Furthermore, this employer challenge will only increase as not only workers but also the parents of these workers grow older.[33]

Employers who respond to these work-family balance issues frequently see an increase in not only productivity but also employee loyalty.

Other Benefit Information Benefit plans are expensive but can be helpful in retaining your good employees. Health care and retirement are two benefits that rank high on the priority list of employees. According to the Bureau of Labor Statistics, employers paid

Competitive Advantage
INNOVATION AND SUSTAINABILITY

Perks That Small Businesses Can Afford

Salary is not the only incentive that cannot only motivate employees but also retain good employees. Other benefits or perks as they are sometimes called, can also encourage motivation and increase productivity among your staff. Consider the following perks offered by these small businesses:

- PreEmptive Solutions, which is a Cleveland, Ohio, software development company, sponsors Microbrew Fridays, replete with Guitar Hero.
- Adrienne Lenhoff Wise has a marketing communications firm in Southfield, Michigan, where she provides a fully stocked kitchen at work for employees, along with bonus accounts for items like oil changes and manicures.
- Steve Channon, vice president of Mongoose Atlantic, Inc., provides nonvacation days off, free lunches, and flexible work hours.

- McGraw Wentworth, a company providing group benefits, offers laundry delivery and pickup to employees.
- Akraya, an IT staffing company, pays for professional cleaners to go to employee's homes and do housework.
- Azavea, a mapping software company, allows employees to spend up to 10 percent of their time on their own research projects.
- LoadSpring Solutions, an enterprise software company, provides employees up to $5,000 if they travel abroad on their vacations.
- Patagonia, an outdoor apparel company, gives employees two weeks of full-paid leave to work for their favourite green nonprofit.

Sources: "10 Perks We Love," inc.com, retrieved July 18, 2010; "5 Small Business Employee Perks That the Big Guys Can't Match," nfib.com, retrieved July 17, 2010; and Francis Kizner, "Secrets of Superstar Employers," Entrepreneur.com, March 6, 2008.

© Image Source/Getty Images

$1.92 per hour for employee health care costs. For every hour work, $.96 cents paid was for retirement benefit costs. Employers paid on average 81 percent of the total health care coverage for single coverage and 71 percent of the cost for family coverage for their employees.[34] Figure 17.2 summarizes the types of benefits that employees of small private establishments have access to and the percentages that participate.

Note that under the Uniformed Services Employment and Reemployment Rights Act of 1994, an employer, regardless of the size of the business, is required to reemploy Reservists, Guard members, and other employees who have been away on active military service for periods of five years or less. Employers are not required to pay employees for their service while on military leave, but they are required to provide health care and other benefits to the employee and dependents, depending upon the circumstances. For more information, go to www.esgr.org and check out the Frequently Asked Questions section.[35]

When Problems Arise: Employee Discipline and Termination

Despite your best efforts at maintaining harmony in the workplace, sometimes problems may arise. When they do, you need policies established for discipline or dismissal of employees.

Disciplinary Measures

Discipline involves taking timely and appropriate action to change the performance of an employee or group of employees. The purpose of discipline is to ensure that company rules and regulations are consistently followed for the well-being of both the company and its employees. A fair and just disciplinary procedure should be based on four components: the employee handbook, performance appraisal, progressive approach, and appeal process.

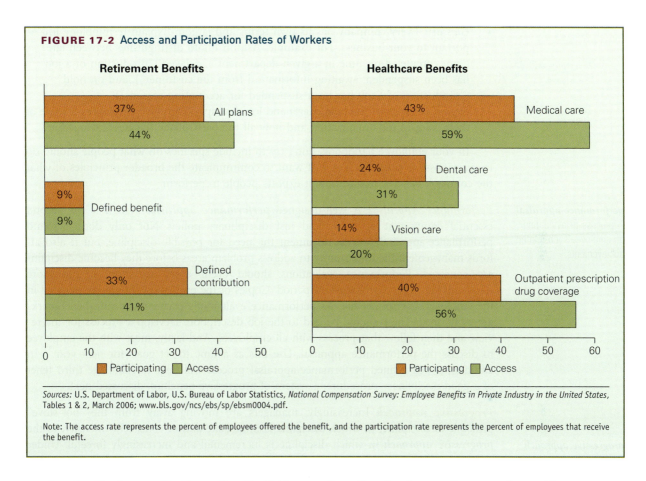

FIGURE 17-2 Access and Participation Rates of Workers

Retirement Benefits

- All plans: Participating 37%, Access 44%
- Defined benefit: Participating 9%, Access 9%
- Defined contribution: Participating 33%, Access 41%

Healthcare Benefits

- Medical care: Participating 43%, Access 59%
- Dental care: Participating 24%, Access 31%
- Vision care: Participating 14%, Access 20%
- Outpatient prescription drug coverage: Participating 40%, Access 56%

Legend: ■ Participating ■ Access

Sources: U.S. Department of Labor, U.S. Bureau of Labor Statistics, *National Compensation Survey: Employee Benefits in Private Industry in the United States,* Tables 1 & 2, March 2006; www.bls.gov/ncs/ebs/sp/ebsm0004.pdf.

Note: The access rate represents the percent of employees offered the benefit, and the participation rate represents the percent of employees that receive the benefit.

employee handbook
Written rules and regulations informing employees of their rights and responsibilities in the employment relationship.

Employee Handbook The **employee handbook**, or policy manual, provides a comprehensive set of rules and regulations to inform employees of their rights and responsibilities in the employment relationship. To be effective, the rules and regulations must be up-to-date, easily understood, and, most importantly, communicated to employees. An effective way to achieve this latter goal is to go over the employee handbook during employee orientation and have employees sign a statement acknowledging its receipt.

Following are suggestions for what to include in your employee handbook:

- *The disclaimer.* Every employee handbook should have a disclaimer (it's a good idea to include it at the beginning and the end) specifying that the handbook is not a contract of employment. Without such a notice, a fired employee might attempt to sue you for breach of contract. Lawyer Robert Nobile recommends including a disclaimer such as the following: "This handbook is not a contract, express or implied, guaranteeing employment for any specific duration. Although we hope that your employment relationship with us will be long term, either you or the company may terminate this relationship at any time, for any reason, with or without cause or notice."[36]
- *Employment policies.* Describe work hours, regular and overtime pay, performance reviews, vacations and holidays, equal employment opportunities, and other items that affect employment.
- *Benefits.* Relate insurance plans, disability plans, workers' compensation, retirement programs, and tuition reimbursement.
- *Employee conduct.* Explain your expectations on everything you classify as important, from personal hygiene to dress codes to employee development.

- *Glossary.* Every company has its own terms and jargon. Explain terminology important to your business. For example, Ashton Photo distinguishes between late ("not completed on time in a given department"), delayed ("production of a job has been suspended, awaiting information from the customer"), and on hold ("production of a job has been suspended for accounting reasons").
- *Organization chart.* Include charts and job descriptions to give employees a sense of their place in the organization and how all the parts of the business fit together.

In your employee handbook, don't try to include specifics on what people should do in every possible situation. You just want to communicate the broader principles of what the company believes in and how it expects people to perform.

performance appraisal
A process of evaluating an employee's job-related achievements.

Performance Appraisal A well-designed ***performance appraisal*** system is the second essential component of a fair and just disciplinary policy. Not only does a sound performance-appraisal process document the need for possible discipline, but it also affords management the opportunity to address problem areas before they become disciplinary concerns. Performance evaluations should occur every six months, and more frequently during the probationary period. Copies of the evaluation should be included in the employee's personnel file. As performance evaluations occur, make sure benchmarks are established. These should be tied to the job description. Develop a process for the review and then follow that process with all employees. And lastly, meet with the employee to discuss the performance appraisal. Use this as a time to set goals for next year.[37] In addition, a well-defined performance-appraisal process will help to fulfill the third tenet of a good disciplinary procedure: a system of progressive penalties, discussed next.

progressive approach
Discipline that is applied to employees in appropriately incremental and increasingly forceful measures.

Progressive Approach Increasingly, managers are moving away from the "hot-stove" principle of discipline, in which discipline is immediate and of consistent intensity, to the ***progressive approach*** in which discipline is incremental and increasingly forceful. Under most progressive systems, managers first issue an oral (informal) reprimand, then a written warning (formal notice), followed by suspension, and finally discharge. Arbitrators and the courts generally favor progressive discipline over that of the hot-stove approach, except in cases of gross misconduct, such as theft or assault, when immediate discharge is warranted. Note that a record of any disciplinary action should be placed in the employee's file even if the reprimand is verbal. A written record is essential if termination occurs and to ensure that the discipline is in accordance with a union contract, if one exists. Write out what happened, what was said by both parties, and when it happened as soon as practical—after all, memories fade. The written notice should have three components: (1) specifically what was unacceptable in the employee's performance, (2) what the expected performance is, and (3) what the consequences are of not making the required changes.[38] Steps for a progressive disciplinary approach include the following:

- Determine whether discipline is needed. Is the problem an isolated incident or part of an ongoing pattern?
- Have clear goals to discuss with the employee. You should discuss the problem in specific terms. Indirect comments will not make your point clear. You must also state what you expect the employee to do. If the employee has no idea about your expectations after discussing a performance problem with you, she is likely to repeat past performance.
- Talk about the problem in private. Public reprimand is embarrassing both for the employee and for everyone who witnesses it. If you chastise an employee in public, you will lose trust and respect not only from that individual but also from those who observe the act.

- Keep your cool. A calm approach will keep a performance discussion more objective and prevent distraction by irrelevant problems.
- Watch the timing of the meeting. If the problem is not obvious and you schedule the meeting far in advance, the employee will spend time worrying about what is wrong. Conversely, if the problem is obvious, the meeting should be scheduled to give the employee plenty of time to prepare.
- Prepare opening remarks. Performance meetings will be more effective if you are confident in your opening remarks. Think them out in advance and rehearse them.
- Get to the point. Beating around the bush with small talk does more to increase the employee's anxiety level than to reduce it.
- Allow two-way communication. Make sure the disciplinary meeting is a discussion, not a lecture. You can get to the heart of the problem only if the employee is allowed to speak. Your intent is to arrive at a solution to a problem, not to scold the employee.
- Establish a follow-up plan. You and your employee need to agree to a follow-up plan to establish a time frame within which the employee's performance is to improve.
- End on a positive note. Highlight the employee's positive points so that he will leave the meeting with a belief that you want him to succeed in the future.[39]

appeal process
A formal procedure allowing employees to seek review of a disciplinary measure at a higher level of management.

Appeal Process The final component of an effective disciplinary program is an ***appeal process***. The most common appeal process in nonunion companies relies on an open-door policy, a procedure whereby employees seek a review of the disciplinary decision at the next level of management. For such a process to be effective, it must involve a thorough and truly objective review of the facts of the case by an executive of higher rank than the supervisor who applied the discipline. Open-door policies are appropriate for companies with many employees and levels of management. In the majority of small businesses, however, the only level of management is you—the owner. In that case, if an employee feels unjustly treated and is not satisfied with your decision, her only recourse is through the courts.

Dismissing Employees

Because dismissing an employee is the most extreme step of discipline you can exercise, it must be taken with care. Your legitimate reasons for dismissing an employee may include unsatisfactory performance of the job or changing requirements of the job that make the employee unqualified.

at-will doctrine
Essentially means an employee hired for an indefinite period may be discharged for any or no reason, cause or no cause, unless specifically prohibited by law.

When it comes to discharging an employee, what you can and cannot do will be influenced to a large degree by two considerations. First, the decision to discharge an employee must be based on a job-related reason or reasons, not on race, color, religion, sex, age, national origin, or disability. Second, your ability to legally discharge an employee and the manner in which you may do so will be highly dependent on your at-will status. Under the ***at-will doctrine***, unless an employment contract is signed, an employer has great leeway in discharging an employee, in that she has the right to discharge the employee for a good reason, a bad reason, or no reason at all. Within the past decade, however, the courts and some state legislatures have imposed one or more of the following restrictions on at-will employers. Check the laws of your state to find which apply to your business. And remember that an employee cannot be fired for union-related activities, even if a union does not exist in the company.

Implied Contract An employer may be restricted in discharging an employee if an implied contract exists as a result of written statements in the company's employment application, employment ads, employee handbook, or other company documents. Verbal statements by company representatives to employees may also erode an employer's at-will status, as may an employee's record of long-term employment with the firm.

Reality Check

We Need to Talk …

Firing employees is never a pleasant duty, and few managers handle the process well. That's because, whatever the facts of the dismissal, most managers feel bad about letting someone go. Ironically, expressing feelings of remorse can be cruel, because it gives the employee false hope. Instead, the best way to deal with the termination is to make it a quick, unambiguous act. Spell out exactly why you are letting the employee go, state clearly that the decision is final, and explain the details of the company's notice policy or severance. Then ask the employee to leave by the end of the week if possible (so that his presence won't demoralize the rest of the staff) and to sign a letter of acknowledgment, which will make it more difficult for him to reopen the discussion—or to sue. Above all, resist any attempts to turn the discussion into an argument.

Icebreaker. I'm sorry to have to give you some bad news: Your job here is being terminated. If for economic reasons: I think you'll find the terms of the severance quite generous. I have also prepared a letter of reference, which I'll give you at the end of this meeting.

Fired for Poor Performance. Please understand that this decision is final. You haven't made any real progress with the problems we discussed at your last two performance reviews. I'm sure you'll be able to put your skills to better use in a different position. If you'll sign this letter that says you understand our discussion, we can put this matter behind us.

Laid off for Economic Reasons. Unfortunately, this decision is final. Please understand that it's purely an economic move and no reflection on your performance. I'll be happy to make that clear to any new employers you interview with. If you'll just sign this letter outlining what I've just said, we can get this unhappy business over with.

Gets Angry. You've got some nerve getting rid of me this way. This company might not be in such a mess if it didn't treat its employees so shabbily.

Gets Defensive. You're singling me out. I've performed as well as anyone else—better, in fact, considering the new accounts I just landed.

Gets Personal. How could do this to me? We're friends. You've come over to my house for dinner. Isn't there something you can do?

Absorb Anger. I'm sorry to hear that you feel that way. Everyone here, including me, wanted to see your position work out. Unfortunately, it hasn't. Why don't you take a few minutes to look over this letter and then sign it?

Deflect Defense. As I've said, this is purely an economic decision. You were simply the last one hired. Or: Your skill in lining up new clients doesn't make up for your consistent problems with our existing accounts.

Deflect Guilt. I feel bad about this, but it is strictly a business decision. My personal feelings don't count. As your friend, I'll do everything I can to help you land another job. For now, though, I need you to take a look at this letter and then sign it.

Demands More Severance. I'm not going to sign anything until we talk about this severance package. It isn't nearly enough, considering how long I've worked here.

Threatens Legal Action. I'm not going to sign anything until I speak to my lawyer. I think there are some issues that I need to get some legal advice on.

Asks for Another Chance. Isn't there something I can do to reverse this decision? I need this job. I promise my work will improve. Please give me another chance.

End Discussion. You're welcome to discuss the severance offer with someone higher up, although I have to warn you that they're the ones who set the terms. Or: Of course. You have every right to speak with your attorney first. I'll hold on to the check and the paperwork until I hear from you. Or: I'm terribly sorry, but the decision really is final. [Stand up.] Good luck in the future.

Sources: Lifescripts: What to Say to Get What You Want in Life's Toughest Situations, Completely Revised and Updated (9780471631019/0471631019) by Stephen M. Pollan and Mark Levine. Flowchart on page 237. Reproduced with permission of John Wiley & Sons. Excerpted from *Lifescripts* by Stephen M. Pollan and Mark Levine, Copyright © 1996. Reprinted by permission of the Stuart Krichevsky Literary Agency, Inc.

Good Faith and Fair Dealing The good faith and fair dealing exception holds that the employer must have acted fairly and in good faith in discharging the employee. For example, an employee cannot be fired simply because he is about to become vested in the company's pension plan.

Public Policy Exception Under the public policy exception, employers cannot discharge workers for exercising a statutory right, such as filing a workers' compensation claim, or performing public service, such as serving on a jury. Nor can an employee be fired for refusing to break the law or engaging in conduct that is against his or her beliefs— for example, refusing to falsify an employer's records to cover up possible misconduct on the part of the company.

Proving Just Cause In the event that a terminated employee seeks legal redress by filing a lawsuit against your business, whether or not you have acted in a manner consistent with the at-will principle will be decided by a judge. In all cases, you should be able to provide evidence of just cause for the dismissal, which generally implies due process and reasonability on your part. You are likely to have just cause if you can do the following:

- Cite the specific work-rule violation and show that the employee had prior knowledge of the rule and the consequences of violating it.
- Show that the work rule was necessary for the efficient and safe operation of the company and was therefore a business necessity.
- Prove that you conducted a thorough and objective investigation of the violation and, in the process, afforded the employee the opportunity to present his side of the story.
- Document that the employee was given the opportunity to improve or modify her performance (except in cases of gross misconduct or insubordination, when it is unnecessary).
- Show that there was sufficient evidence or proof of guilt to justify the actions taken.
- Show that you treated the employee in a manner consistent with past practices.
- Demonstrate that the disciplinary actions taken were fair and reasonable in view of the employee's work history.
- Document that the disciplinary action was reviewed by an independent party either within or outside the company prior to being implemented.

Summary

1. Discuss the importance of hiring the right employees.

Some of the most valuable resources and competitive advantages a small business has are its employees. There are too many costs and risks involved in HR issues not to pay attention to them.

2. Describe the job-analysis process and the function of job descriptions and job specifications.

Job analysis is the process of determining the duties and skills involved in a job and the kind of person who should be hired to do it. A job description is part of the job analysis; it lists the duties, responsibilities, and reporting relationships of a job. Job specifications are another part of the job analysis; they

identify the education, skills, and personality that a person needs to have to be right for a job.

3. Evaluate the advantages and disadvantages of the six major sources of employee recruitment.

Help-wanted advertising reaches numerous potential applicants, but many of them will not be right for the job you are trying to fill. Employment agencies prescreen applicants so that you do not have to deal with as many people. The agencies run by the government are usually appropriate only for positions requiring lower-level skills. Private employment agencies and executive recruiters (headhunters) offer more expensive services but can help you find people with higher-level skills. Internet job sites offer limited resources, for a fee. Employee referrals are effective because your current employees know the skills and talents needed, but hiring in this manner can create cliques and build resentment if the new hire does not work out. Moreover, it can lead to underrepresentation of protected groups. Hiring friends and relatives gives you the advantage of knowing their abilities and expertise, but personal relationships can become strained on the job.

4. Describe the four tools commonly used in employee selection.

In the selection process, you narrow the applicant pool generated by recruitment by trying to match the needs of your business with the skills of each person. Application forms and résumés, interviews, and testing are the most common tools of selection.

5. Discuss the need for employee training and name the seven methods of providing this training.

To become a better, more productive worker, every employee needs to have his knowledge and skills enhanced through orientation and training. On-the-job training; lectures; conferences; programmed learning; role-playing; job rotation; and correspondence courses, Internet classes, and webinars are seven common techniques.

6. Explain the two components of a compensation plan and the variable elements of a benefits system.

Employees can be compensated for their efforts with hourly wages, with straight salary, or on the basis of piecework or commission plans. Incentive-pay programs offer a way to motivate and reward employees above their base pay by paying bonuses or profit-sharing amounts. Common benefits included as part of a compensation package are flexible-benefit plans, health insurance, pension plans, and child care accounts. The most common pension plans adopted by small businesses are individual retirement accounts (IRAs), simplified employee pension (SEP) plans, 401(k) plans, and defined contribution plans.

7. Profile an effective sequence for disciplining and terminating employees.

The progressive disciplinary system, favored by many managers today, begins with an oral reprimand, followed by a written warning, then suspension without pay, and, finally, termination from the company.

Questions for Review and Discussion

1. What is the difference between a job analysis and a job description?
2. When would you, as a small business owner, prefer to receive a résumé than an application form?
3. How is the use of temporary employees different from employee leasing? What are the advantages and disadvantages of each?
4. What are the differences between hard and soft issues during a job orientation? Is one more important than the other?
5. List the advantages of a flexible-benefit package to employees and to the employer.
6. Explain the four components of an effective disciplinary system.
7. Define "at-will" employment status.
8. Discuss three key pieces of legislation that are used to prevent job discrimination.
9. What factors influence the type and amount of employee benefits that a small business can offer?
10. Review the section on training new employees. Give examples of types of jobs that would best lend themselves to each training method.

Questions for Critical Thinking

1. As a young entrepreneur, you may soon be in the position of hiring one or more of your college friends in your own business. What are the advantages of hiring your friends? What are the potential pitfalls?

2. Hiring an employee is a big step for a small business. How can you make a wise hiring decision if so many limitations are put on the interview questions you can legally ask?

What Would You Do?

Todd owns and manages a T-shirt shop in a small resort town. He has two full-time employees who have been with the business for more than three years. He also employs as many as five part-time employees, depending on the tourist season. They help him keep the shop open from 10:00 a.m. to 9:00 p.m. seven days a week. Todd opens the shop every day but typically has his employees close. Whoever closes the store follows a checklist of closing procedures, including ringing out the cash register, filling out the bank deposit, and putting the daily receipts in the safe, with $300 kept in a separate cash bag for the next day's opening cash on hand. As with many businesses, the cash drawer is often off by a small amount, but usually no more than a couple of dollars.

One day Todd opened the store and found that the cash drawer was short $35 for the previous day. Todd called a meeting that afternoon and told all seven employees that they would each have to chip in $5 to cover the shortage and that any time there was a shortage, they would have to split the reimbursement. Todd walked out of the room. The seven employees sat in disbelief.

Questions

1. Is Todd within his legal rights to take this action? If his actions are legal, what are some possible consequences?
2. How would you have handled the situation if you were Todd?

18

Managing Operations

CHAPTER LEARNING OUTCOMES

After reading this chapter, you should be able to:

1. List the elements of an operating system.

2. Describe how manufacturers and service providers use operations management.

3. Explain how to measure productivity.

4. Recount the methods of scheduling operations.

5. Discuss the role of quality in operations management.

6. Identify the three ways to control operations.

T hink water, rocketing toward the sky. Think fire, blazing in the water. Think lights, illuminating the water. Think color, infusing the water. Think music, beckoning the water to dance. Think nothing short of—spectacular. This is why Mark Fuller, founder and CEO of WET, Water Entertainment Technologies, a *feature creator* as he likes to be called, is cited as one of FastCompany's 100 Most Creative People in

Business in 2010 and one of the Top 10 in the Design Industry for 2010. WET, a company based in Sun Valley, has produced some of the most spectacular water fountain projects in the world. One of the latest fountains contains 1,500 water jets, 1,000 fog jets, and water streams that blast 500 feet in the air, all artfully and skilfully choreographed to music located in a 32-acre manmade lake at the foot of the world's tallest building, the Burj Khalifa in Dubai. And this is just one of his many creations. Las Vegas, Nevada, houses some of his best known, including the *Fountains of Bellagio* as well as the Las Vegas *CityCenter*.

The story of WET and Mark Fuller is an interesting one, beginning as a teenager when he built his own version of the Disney Jungle Cruise in his backyard, replete with underwater lights. He studied civil engineering in college and also built theatrical sets, combining his love of theatre and engineering. After completing his master's degree from Stanford in mechanical engineering, he applied for a job with Disney. Disney definitely wanted to hire him after looking at the laminar fountain he had built, but did not know which position he fit. He became an "Imagineer," one of the group of people responsible for dreaming up new ideas for the parks. While still at Disney he started WET in 1983 in his garage, and like many small businesses, the company went through some difficult financial times, maxing out 13 credit cards attempting to stay afloat. Fuller's big break came in 1995, when Steve Wynn was creating the Bellagio. One of Wynn's employees had seen the fountains that Fuller had created at Disney and told Wynn about them. After Fuller made a trip to Vegas to meet with Wynn, the *Fountains of Bellagio* were conceived.

The engineering underlying the WET fountains is remarkable. Fuller invented water cannons that use compressed air to shoot water into the air, called shooters. The shooters range from NanoShooters that have a range of six feet to XtreamShooters that can shoot water 500 feet into the air. The water can move so fast it literally breaks the sound barrier. He also invented new types of nozzles that he calls oarsmen, which have a broad range of motion that are attached to underwater robotic arms that move forward and back and twirl. Today all the component parts are made in house. Nothing is outsourced, which Fuller believes gives WET a "competitive advantage" since the company can make changes quickly and efficiently as is needed on the dynamic projects they create. The Fountains of Bellagio have 1,000 independently programmed nozzles, 5,000 lights, 200 speakers, and 33 technicians who keep the show running. Since the water is shot into the air through compressed air instead of big pumps, it requires only about 20 percent of the energy that big pumps use. The water is pumped from wells that were originally drilled to irrigate a golf course on that site, using much less water than if the golf course were still located there.

WET is a great example of the operations system. They have taken natural inputs that most of us take for granted—water, fire, color, and music—and transformed them into a remarkable phenomenon. John Seabrook says Fuller is the "fountain architect who gave water a voice." The output is a glorious show guaranteed to wow the viewer. Control systems are in place for the complicated process to ensure that each and every nozzle and shooter is functioning appropriately. The feedback comes not only from the computerized system running the shows but also from the applause of the crowds demonstrating their enjoyment. Mark Fuller and WET entice us to look at water with an entirely new perspective, transforming the usual into something spectacular.

Sources: Marty Sklar, "Mark Fuller of WET," 16th Annual Thea Awards, February 3, 2010; "Top 10 by Industry," *FastCompany*, March 2010; John Seabrook, "Water Music," *The New Yorker*, January 11, 2010; Edie Cohen, "Shooting for the Stars," *Interior Design*, June 2010; "The 100 Most Creative People in Business," *FastCompany*, June 2010; E. C. Gladstone, "How WET's Water Features Give Gravitas to the Vegas Strip," *Las Vegas Weekly*, March 17, 2010; and Darrell Satzman, "A Gushing Combination of Engineering, Showbiz," *Sunday Los Angeles Times,* March 14, 2010.

This chapter focuses on *operations management*, sometimes referred to as *OM*, and the processes associated with it. The function of operations management has evolved over the last few decades from a narrow view of production, inventory, and industrial management into a broader concept that includes services. Indeed, the management of production and operations is critical to all small businesses, not just those involved in manufacturing. Every business performs an operations function—the processes and procedures of converting labor, materials, money, and other resources into finished products or services available for consumer consumption.

Elements of an Operating System

Operations management systems contain five basic elements: inputs, transformation processes, outputs, control systems, and feedback. These elements must be brought together and coordinated into a system to produce the product or service—the reason for the business to exist.

Inputs

inputs
All the resources that go into a business.

The **inputs** in an operations management system include all physical and intangible resources that come into a business. Raw materials are necessary as the things that will become transformed in a business. A company that makes in-line skates, for instance, must have polymers, plastics, and metals. Skills and knowledge of the people within the organization are other inputs. The in-line skate manufacturer needs trained workers that know how to fabricate the product. A management consulting firm, for example, needs people with special expertise who will provide recommendations for clients. For WET, the business featured at the beginning of this chapter, creativity and innovation become critical inputs to produce the product of the business. Money, information, and energy are resources all needed in varying degrees. Inputs are important to the quality of the finished product of the business. Remember the computer cliché "Garbage in—garbage out"? The idea holds true for operations management, too: You can't produce high-quality outputs from inferior inputs.

Transformation Processes

transformation processes
What a business does to add value to inputs in converting them to outputs.

Once we have identified the inputs of a business, we can look at the processes that are used to transform them into finished products. **Transformation processes** are the active practices—including concepts, procedures, and technologies—that are implemented to produce outputs. Dry cleaners, for instance, take soiled clothing (inputs) and use chemicals, equipment, and know-how to transform them into clean clothing (the outputs of the business). WET takes water, fire, music, and color, along with vast amounts of creativity and technology, and transforms something we all use every day, water, into a totally new entertainment experience.

Outputs

outputs
The tangible or intangible products that a business produces.

Outputs, the result of the transformation processes, are what your business produces. Outputs can be tangible, such as a CD, or intangible, such as a doctor's diagnosis, or the entertainment experience of watching the *Fountains of Bellagio*.

© Fuse/JupiterImages

Every business utilizes inputs, takes them through some transformation, and creates multiple outputs.

control systems
The means to monitor input, transformation, and output so as to identify problems.

Since a business's *social responsibility*, or obligations to the community, has become as serious a matter as product-liability and other lawsuits, we need to consider *all* the outputs a business produces—not just the beneficial or intended ones. When we look at the big picture of the transformation process, we see that employee accidents, consumer injuries, pollution, and waste are also outputs.

Control Systems

Control systems provide the means to monitor and correct problems or deviations when they occur in the operating system. Controls are integrated into all three stages of production—input, transformation, and output (see Figure 18.1). An example of a control system would be the use of electronic monitors in a manufacturing process to tell a machine operator that the product is not being made within the allowed size tolerance. In service companies, employee behavior is part of the transformation process to be controlled. A bank manager, for instance, might hire people to pose as new bank customers and then report back to the manager on the quality of service they received from tellers or loan officers. Control systems ensure the quality of the product or service the customer expects occurs every time, like eating a Big Mac or a Krispy Kreme doughnut. The customer expects the same product and service with each purchase, regardless of location.

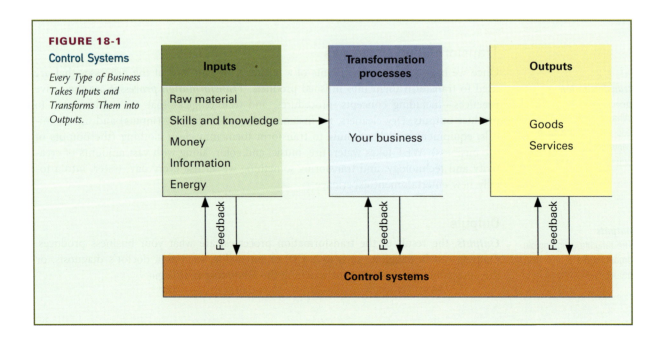

FIGURE 18-1
Control Systems

Every Type of Business Takes Inputs and Transforms Them into Outputs.

Inputs	**Transformation processes**	**Outputs**
Raw material		
Skills and knowledge		Goods
Money	Your business	Services
Information		
Energy		

Feedback · Feedback · Feedback

Control systems

Feedback

feedback
Communication tools to connect control systems to the processes of a business.

Feedback is the information that a manager receives in monitoring the operation system. It can be verbal, written, electronic, or observational. Feedback is the necessary communication that links a control system to the inputs, transformation, and outputs. Once feedback is received, the cycle begins again since the transformation process is a continuous process, with any needed changes taking place throughout the process.

Types of Operations Management

Production broadly describes what businesses of all types do in creating goods and services. Computer hardware and software companies, health care providers, and farmers are all involved in production. Manufacturing is just one type of production, making goods as opposed to providing services or extracting natural resources. One of your highest priorities as a manager is to ensure that *productivity*—which is the measure of production, or output per worker—remains high. It is important to measure productivity so as to control the amount of resources used to produce outputs.

productivity
The measure of outputs according to the inputs needed to produce them; a way to determine the efficiency of a business.

Operations Management for Manufacturing Businesses

Manufacturing in the United States plays a key role in our economy, accounting for approximately 11 percent of GDP and one out of six private sector jobs. The United States is the world's largest manufacturing economy, producing 21 percent of global manufactured products, followed by Japan at 13 percent and China at 12 percent. U.S. manufacturers are the most productive workers in the world, in fact twice as productive as the workers in the next 10 leading manufacturing economies.[1] Manufacturing businesses can be classified by the way they make goods and by the time spent on making them. Goods can be made from analytic or synthetic systems, using either continuous or intermittent processes.

analytic systems
Manufacturing system that reduces inputs into component parts so as to extract products.

Analytic systems reduce inputs into component parts so as to extract products. For example, automobile-salvage businesses buy vehicles from insurance companies or individuals to dismantle them for parts or scrap iron to sell. *Synthetic systems*, by contrast, combine inputs to create a finished product or change it into a different product. Thus, restaurants take vegetables, fruits, grains, meats, seafood, music, lighting, furniture, paintings, and a variety of human talents to create and serve meals.

synthetic systems
Manufacturing system that combines inputs to create a finished product or change it into a different product.

Production by a *continuous process* is accomplished over long periods of time. Production of the same or very similar products goes on uninterrupted for days, months, or years. Microbreweries and wine makers are examples of small businesses that produce goods via a continuous process.

continuous process
A production process that operates for long periods of time without interruption.

Production runs that use an *intermittent process* involve short cycles and frequent stops to change products. Small businesses using intermittent processes are also called *job shops*. Custom printing shops and custom jewelry makers are examples.

intermittent process
A production process that operates in short cycles so that it can change products.

Can small businesses compete in a manufacturing sector long associated with gigantic factories? Yes, primarily because automation makes flexible production possible. Computers assist small manufacturers in determining raw material needs, scheduling production runs, and designing new products. Automation allows the retooling of production machines in seconds, rather than hours or days, so that shorter batches can be produced profitably. Machines can be programmed to perform many combinations of individual jobs and functions, rather than just one. With the help of computers, products and processes can be designed at the same time, rather than designing a product and then figuring out a way to make it.

Many small businesses are benefiting from the number of large businesses that are examining what they do best, determining that manufacturing is not their strongest suit, and farming out production to smaller specialty firms. For example, your new Dell computer did not come from a Dell computer factory—none exists. Dell concentrates on marketing, buying computer components from different companies, and assembling them in a warehouse.[2] This type of flexible contract production opens up many opportunities for entrepreneurs.

Manufacturing is already evolving past flexible production, however, to **mass customization**, which can provide tailor-made products with almost the efficiency of mass production, and thus a lower cost, plus the needs of the customer will be more specifically fulfilled. The advent of computer-aided manufacturing systems has allowed this new technology to change the method of producing products.[3] As an example of mass customization, suppose a customer in need of a new business suit steps into a kiosk-like device, where an optical scanner measures his body. As soon as he chooses a fabric and style, the order is beamed to the plant, where lasers cut the material and machines sew it together. The suit could be ready and shipped directly to the customer in a matter of days.[4] Or, a company may need a customized machined tool. With eMachine Shop.com, a customer can upload a design, select the material from which the tool is to be made, and then in as little as 48 hours the completed tool is delivered to the business. Some companies, as an added benefit to mass customization, allow customers to watch the whole production process through a webcam.[5]

Operations Management for Service Businesses

As pointed out earlier, service providers need and use operations management just as much as product manufacturers do. Both types of businesses take inputs and produce outputs through some type of transformation process. However, operations processes differ from one product and service to another, and some overlap. For example, manufacturers often offer repair services. Restaurants offer food products as well as services.

Traditionally, all service businesses were seen as intermittent-process businesses, because standardization didn't seem possible for businesses such as hair salons, accounting firms, and auto service centers. Today, in an effort to increase productivity, some service businesses are adopting continuous processes. For example, Merry Maids house cleaners, Jiffy Lube auto service, Fantastic Sam's family hair-cutting salons, and even chains of dentists located in malls are all using manufacturing techniques of continuous production. A notable difference between service and manufacturing operations is the amount of customer contact involved. Many services, such as hair salons, require the customer to be present for the operation to be performed, that is, service and delivery of the service occur at the same time. This makes the quality of the service of paramount importance. And many times this comes back to one of the most important inputs of a business, employees.[6]

Consider the examples of product and service operations systems in Table 18.1.

What Is Productivity?

According to Chapter 16, as a manager, you are involved in planning, organizing, leading, and controlling. But how do you tell if and when you are reaching the goals that you have set? You can measure your success by assessing your *productivity*, the measure of output per hour worked which is labor productivity, the most common productivity measure.[7] Or, from another perspective, it is the amount of output produced compared to the amount of inputs used. Productivity can be described numerically as the ratio of inputs used to outputs produced. The higher the ratio, the more efficient is your operating system. You should constantly look for ways to increase outputs while keeping inputs constant or to keep outputs constant while decreasing inputs, both of which will increase

TABLE 18-1 Product and Service Operations Systems	INPUTS	TRANSFORMATION	OUTPUTS	FEEDBACK
Restaurant				
	Food	Cooking	Meals	Leftovers
	Hungry people	Serving	Satisfied people	Complaints
	Equipment			
	Labor			
Factory				
	Machinery	Welding	Finished products	Defects
	Skilled labor	Painting	Services	Returns
	Raw material	Forming	Waste products	Market share
	Engineering	Transporting		Complaints
	Management			
	Buildings			

"Increasing the productivity of labor revolves around investing in capital, improving technology, and making sure workers have appropriate and better skill levels."

your productivity. In a market that becomes more competitive daily, increasing productivity is key to profitability. The company that can do more with less is the company that succeeds.[8] Increasing the productivity of labor revolves around investing in capital, improving technology, and making sure workers have appropriate and better skill levels.

Ways to Measure Manufacturing Productivity

Productivity can be measured for your entire business or for a specific portion of it. Because many inputs go into your business, the input you choose determines the productivity you are measuring. The goal becomes to produce the optimal amount of output and to minimize costs in the process. Total productivity can be determined by dividing total outputs by total inputs:

Total productivity = Outputs/Labor + Capital + Raw materials + All other inputs

A variety of factors can go into lowering the productivity of your business, literally producing less output or using more resources to produce the same amount of outputs:

- Older technology, tools, or out-of-date processes can decrease the amount of output produced, increasing the costs of production. This in turn decreases your profitability.
- Lack of key materials or suppliers for the materials can stop production if the needed resources are not available.
- Lack of employees with the appropriate skills or employees who are not proficient in those skills can slow or even stop production in some instances.[9]
- Not enough dollars to provide the needed resources. Money is also a necessary input, and too little can make all the other resources also unavailable or not available in the quantities needed.

If your software company sold $500,000 worth of software and used $100,000 in resources, your total productivity ratio would be 5. But you may not always want to consider all of your inputs every time. For example, because materials may account for as much as 90 percent of operating costs in businesses that use little labor, materials productivity would be an important ratio to track.

$$\text{Materials productivity} = \text{Outputs/Materials}$$

If 4,000 pounds of sugar are used to produce 1,000 pounds of candy, the materials productivity is 1,000 divided by 4,000, or 0.25, which becomes a base figure for comparing increases or decreases in productivity. Stated simply, you can increase the productivity of your business by increasing outputs, decreasing inputs, or a combination of both. Most productivity improvements come from changing processes used by your business, from your employees accomplishing more, or from technology that speeds production.

Productivity ratios can be used to measure the efficiency of a new process. Suppose that you run a furniture shop with a productivity ratio of 1:

$$\text{Output/Input} = \text{Number of tables/Hours} = 100/100 = 1$$

You have invented a new process that will save 20 percent on your labor costs. Now you can still produce the same number of tables (100) but take only 80 hours to produce them. Your new productivity ratio is 1.25:

$$\text{New productivity ratio} = 100/80 = 1.25$$

Unfortunately, your new process ends up increasing defects in the tables. To correct these defects, you have to increase labor hours to 120. Your productivity ratio is now 0.833:

$$\text{Corrected productivity ratio} = 100/120 = 0.833$$

Your corrected productivity ratio shows that it is back to the drawing board for your new process.

Ways to Measure Service Productivity

The importance of the service industries in the United States has grown over the last three decades. Approximately 80 percent of the U.S. workforce is employed in the service sector.

Productivity in service-related businesses has not grown as rapidly as productivity in manufacturing businesses because service businesses are more labor intensive and less standardization occurs. For example, you do not want your doctor giving you the same health care plan as he gives to your grandmother. Service-related businesses also usually require time spent one-on-one with or for the client-customer, often again without the benefit of standardization. So factories can substitute machines for people and increase output. Can service businesses do the same?

Actually, to some degree they can. Rick Smolan, president of Wildfire Communications, has developed an electronic device that can totally automate telephone communications. By blending computer, telephone, and voice-recognition technology, Wildfire receives and directs calls wherever you are, takes messages, and maintains your calendar and schedule—and does it all by responding to your voice. Smolan and others who are always on the phone but rarely in an office use Wildfire instead of a personal secretary. "Secretarial work is just not good use of a human being," according to Smolan.[10]

Providing quality service has its own unique set of challenges. The service and delivery of the service often occur at the same time. There is no opportunity to "remake" the product if it does not turn out "right." Say you are getting a haircut. The service and delivery are simultaneous, and if the hairdresser makes a mistake, there is no opportunity to pull the product and go back and remake it. The skill level of employees and the consistency of that skill level become critical in offering quality services.

Besides technological innovation, another key to enhancing productivity in a service business is making sure your employees are comfortable and free from work-related health issues. *Ergonomics* studies the fit between people and machines. "The human body is simply not designed to sit. Yet between 70 percent to 75 percent of today's

"Ergonomics is the key to worker productivity. Make sure that there is a healthy fit between people and equipment."

ergonomics
The study of the interaction between people and machinery.

workforce is sitting and working on computers," says corporate ergonomist Rajendra Paul.[11] Lighting levels, furniture size and height, and the location of computers and telephones are important factors to consider when designing your workstations. Given the myriad physical differences and varying employee needs, you may need to consider chairs with adjustable armrests and footrests, keyboards and mouse pads that adjust to the correct height and angle, and nonglare monitor screens.

The Department of Labor and Industries in Washington estimates that 1 out of 13 truck drivers will have an injury related to musculoskeletal problems from overexertion, falling, and being struck by the truck or cargo. These injuries, in addition to the lost work hours from these employees, are $30,000 per claim. In order to address some of the ergonomic issues for truck drivers, steps, tilting steering wheels, and adjustable pedals are being used. Proper training is also key.[12]

Management style is another key factor in improving the quality and quantity of service workers' output. At Mountain Shadows, Inc., in Escondido, California, owner H. Douglas Cook knew that keeping his employees' productivity high meant that he had to stay out of the way and let his employees do their jobs. Cook has a special interest in Mountain Shadows, a residential facility for the developmentally disabled, because not only is he its owner, but his son Brian is also a resident there. The facility's 105 residents range in age from 7 to 63, and almost all of them use wheelchairs. Mountain Shadows is, by necessity, a highly labor-intensive operation. Yet Cook doesn't interfere with the 170 employees. Instead, he has introduced an open management style that recognizes the importance of the employees. By doing so, he has dramatically reduced employee turnover, which in turn has increased his workers' efficiency.[13]

A recent development in the area of workplace ergonomics is to create a work team whose purpose is to assess and evaluate ergonomic issues in the workplace. With the increasing number of baby boomers in the workplace, productivity, employee morale, competitiveness, and financial costs make work-related health issues too large to be ignored. When developing this team, make sure you include the employees who are doing the tasks being evaluated. After all, they know the job better than anyone and often have ideas on how to improve their work stations, whether it is in an office or on the factory floor.[14]

What about Scheduling Operations?

Scheduling is a basic operations management activity for both manufacturing and service businesses that involves the timing of production. The purpose of scheduling is to put your plans into motion by describing what each worker has to do.

Scheduling is necessary to maximize levels of efficiency and customer service. For example, if a beauty shop schedules one haircut every 30 minutes, although each could actually be done in 20 minutes with no decrease in quality, the operator could be working one-third more efficiently. Three haircuts could be produced per hour rather than two. In contrast, a shop that schedules too much work cannot complete jobs on time, resulting in poor customer service and probably losing future business from customers who become aggravated by having to wait for their appointments. If you can schedule the exact amount of resources needed in order to meet your customer demand at a given time, you will optimize your resources and increase profitability.

forward scheduling
Scheduling in which materials and resources are allocated for production when a job order comes in.

Scheduling Methods

Most business operations use forward scheduling, backward scheduling, or a combination of the two methods. With ***forward scheduling***, materials and resources are allocated for production when a job order comes in. Any type of custom production in which the product changes or in which demand is unknown in advance needs forward scheduling.

Competitive Advantage
INNOVATION AND SUSTAINABILITY

So How Do I Increase Productivity?

Productivity growth has been positive since the Bureau of Labor Statistics began measuring this indicator, in 1947. Since 1995, the increase in productivity has been attributed to investments in capital and technology improvements. While the overall productivity trend has been upward, productivity often decreases during a recession. Since the majority of the businesses in the United States are service oriented, the quality of the service provided to customers becomes key. In fact, the quality of your service can become your competitive advantage. Here are tips on how to increase productivity and produce more with less.

- Continuously improve the quality of the service you provide since service can be a key.
- Kevin Ryan founder of Alley Corp, a group of Internet start-ups, believes the key to productivity is to hire great people. He is personally involved every day in the interviewing of potential employees.
- Garrett Camp, founder of StumbleUpon, a Web service, has a wiki page for every person with whom he needs to interact regularly. For him this is more productive than e-mail.
- Barbara Corcoran, a panelist on Shark Tank, looks at prioritizing her to-do list as entrées, side dishes, and desserts. Entrées are important items that need to occur now, while desserts are nice to have but not necessary to the success of the business.

- Rocio Romero's namesake company manufactures prefab homes. She found her key to productivity was moving her business to her home once she had twins. The offices—except hers, on the first floor—are on the third floor, and her living quarters are on the second floor, allowing her quick and easy access to both her family and her business.
- Jordan Zimmerman, founder of Zimmerman Advertising, believes a key to productivity is to keep in touch with clients. He talks to each client CEO every day to discuss strategy. He also believes keeping in good physical shape and sleeping when you are tired are important productivity tools.
- Caterina Fake has a new start-up, Hunch, which takes user input and makes recommendations about all sorts of subjects. She follows the two pizza rule: Any team should be small enough that two pizzas would be sufficient for a lunch break.

Today, more than ever, productivity is key to the success of your business. How can you increase your productivity?

Sources: Leigh Buchanan, "The United States of Productivity," *Inc.*, March 2010; Michael Chernousov, Susan Fleck, and John Glaser, "Productivity Trends in Business Cycles: A Visual Essay," *Monthly Labor Review*, June 2009; and Erhan Mergen and William Stevenson, "Can't Fix Service Quality: Read This," *Total Quality Management*, June 2009.

backward scheduling
Scheduling that involves arranging production activities around the due date for the product.

Backward scheduling involves arranging production activities around the due date for the product. You take the date on which the finished product must be delivered, then schedule in reverse order all material procurement and work to be done.

Henry L. Gantt devised a simple bar graph for scheduling work in any kind of operation. Developed in 1913, it still bears his name: the *Gantt chart*. This chart can be used to track the progress of work as a product makes its way through various departments (see Figure 18.2). It allows you to see the time required for each step and the current status of a job.

Routing

routing
Information showing the steps required to produce a product.

Scheduling involves routing, sequencing, and dispatching the product through successive stages of production. *Routing* shows the detailed breakdown of information explaining how your product or service will be produced. *Routing sheets* are the paper copies, and *routing files* are the electronic versions of this information. Needed information could include tooling specifications and setups, the number of workers or operators needed, the sequence in which steps are to be taken, and the control tests to be performed.

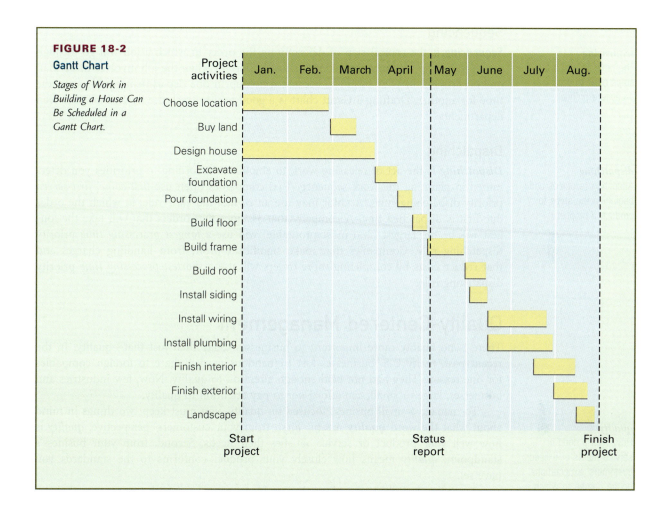

FIGURE 18-2

Gantt Chart

Stages of Work in Building a House Can Be Scheduled in a Gantt Chart.

Project activities: Jan. | Feb. | March | April | May | June | July | Aug.

- Choose location
- Buy land
- Design house
- Excavate foundation
- Pour foundation
- Build floor
- Build frame
- Build roof
- Install siding
- Install wiring
- Install plumbing
- Finish interior
- Finish exterior
- Landscape

Start project — Status report — Finish project

Reality Check

How Good Is Good Enough?

If 99.9 percent accuracy were good enough ...

- The Internal Revenue Service would lose 2 million documents per year.
- *Webster's Third International Dictionary of the English Language* would have 315 misspelled words.
- 12 newborn babies would go home with the wrong parents daily.
- 107 medical procedures would be performed incorrectly every day.

- 114,500 pairs of new shoes would be mismatched each year.
- 2,488,200 books would be printed each year with no words.
- Telephone companies would send 1,314 calls to the wrong number each minute.
- 5,517,200 cases of soft drinks would be made every year with no fizz.
- Two airplanes would crash at Chicago's O'Hare International Airport every day.

Sequencing

sequencing
The order in which the steps need to occur to produce a product.

Sequencing is the critical step of determining the order in which a job will go through your production system. Sequencing is most important when the job involves more than one department of your business, because a holdup in one department could cause idle time for another. Drafting a Gantt chart is a good way to track the flow of jobs between departments.

Dispatching

dispatching
Allocating resources and beginning the steps to produce a product.

Dispatching is the act of releasing work to employees according to priorities you determined in planning the work sequence. Taxi companies often use *first-come, first-served* priority dispatching rules. A tailor may use an *earliest due date* rule, in which the order due first is dispatched first. A company that assumes that orders that will take the longest will be the largest (and most profitable) will use a *longest processing time* priority dispatching rule. Companies that make significant profit from handling charges and that reduce costs by completing more orders will use a *shortest processing time* priority dispatching rule.

Quality-Centered Management

There is no quality more important to businesses today than just that—quality. In the recent past, many U.S. businesses lost tremendous market share to foreign companies for one reason: They had not paid enough attention to quality. Now, few industries and businesses, large or small, can afford *not* to pay attention to quality.

quality
How well a good or service meets or exceeds customers' expectations, or the degree to which a product conforms to established tolerance standards.

To manage a small business focused on quality, you must keep two things in mind about what the word **quality** means. First, from your customers' perspective, *quality* is how well your product or service satisfies their needs. Second, from your business's standpoint, *quality* means how closely your product conforms to the standards you have set.

According to Bill Eureka, all quality problems are related back to processes that did not work correctly. Or, conversely, all process hang-ups will result in quality issues. Consequently, he feels that analyzing the processes of your business is time well spent and will assist in increasing the quality of your business. He suggests the following steps to ensure quality processes.

- Develop clear guidelines on output requirements, and then communicate those requirements to all employees.
- Rather than correct problems, prevent problems, which is usually much less expensive.
- Implement control features for each step so a problem is identified and corrected early in the process.[15]

Six Sigma in Small Business

defect rate
The number of goods produced that are outside the company's boundaries of acceptable quality.

tolerance range
The boundaries a manager sets in determining the acceptable quality of a product.

Six sigma is a methodology that emphasizes improving business processes in order to continuously meet and exceed customer expectations. Frequently, companies measure the quality of a product by tracking the **defect rate**. A defect rate is the number of goods produced that were out of the company's accepted **tolerance range**—the boundaries of acceptable quality. But how good is good enough? Is 99 out of 100 good enough? With a 1 percent defect rate, consider this: The U.S. Postal Service would lose more than 18,000 pieces of mail per hour!

six sigma
The tolerance range in which only 3.4 defects per million are allowed.

"Perfection is not possible, but companies need to strive for it—that is, for zero defects."

Perfection is not possible, but companies need to strive for it—that is, for zero defects. **Six sigma** is the term that has come to signify the quality movement, not just in manufacturing but also throughout entire organizations where businesses are committed to looking at problems by extensively analyzing data and then ensuring end goals are met. Solving the underlying problem is central to six sigma. In statistical terminology, *sigma* denotes the *standard deviation* of a set of data. It indicates how all data points in a distribution vary from the mean (average) value. Table 18.2 shows different sigma levels and their corresponding defects per million.[16]

With a normal distribution, 99.73 percent of all the data points fall within three standard deviations (three sigma) of the mean—pretty good, but that is just for one stage of the production process. Products that have to go through hundreds or thousands of stages could still come out with defects.

If you choose six-sigma defects as your production goal, you will have 99.99966 percent of your products within your specification limits—only 3.4 defects per million! Even if your product has to go through 100 different stages, the defect rate will still be only 3,390 defects per million.

The concept of six sigma is not limited to producing goods in your small business. You can also apply it to customer satisfaction in your service business. Consider a company with 1,000 customers and 10 employees (or stages) that can affect customer satisfaction. The difference between three sigma (499 dissatisfied) and four sigma (60 dissatisfied) is 439 dissatisfied customers. That represents 44 percent of your entire customer base![17]

Let's take a closer look at the basic components of a six-sigma quality program and the activities and tools needed.

Basic Components The basic components of a six-sigma program include the actual improvement process and quality measurement. The actual improvement process involves the following steps:

1. Define products and services by describing the actual products or services that are provided to customers.
2. Identify customer requirements for products or services by stating them in measurable terms.
3. Compare products with requirements by identifying gaps between what the customer expects and what she is actually receiving.
4. Describe the process by providing explicit details.
5. Improve the process by simplification and mistake proofing.
6. Measure quality and productivity by establishing baseline values and then tracking improvement.

TABLE 18-2 Sigma Levels and Defect Rates	SIGMA LEVEL	DEFECTS PER MILLION
	3.0	66,810.0
	3.5	22,750.0
	4.0	6,750.0
	4.5	1,350.0
	5.0	233.0
	5.5	32.0
	6.0	3.4

Since six sigma is data driven, it requires the collection of appropriate and meaningful data, the analyzing of the data, the understanding of the data, and then necessary action is taken. This requires accessible and understandable data and someone who understands the process as well as the data. Green belts and Black belts as they pertain to six sigma are individuals who have been trained in the area of statistics in order to analyze the data appropriately. Green belts have been trained on the basic techniques, while Black belts have an advanced level of statistical training.[18]

Two types of statistical analysis are used in six sigma, descriptive statistics and inferential statistics. Descriptive statistics is a useful tool for summarizing the data collected, usually including the use of measures of central tendency, the mean, median, and mode, and variance and standard deviation and distribution charts. Inferential statistics is the process of looking at a sample and then using statistical analysis to interpret results to your whole population of customers based upon that sample, and usually looking for relationships. Statistical tools used in this area include probability; *analysis of variance (ANOVA)*, which is used to identify where in the process this variation occurs (by location, person, or process step); and *regression analysis*, which is used to determine the magnitude of the effect these factors have on the process and to identify potential causes of variation.

One of the challenges of six sigma is implementation. There is no one way to implement six sigma in your business. There are no handy six steps you can check off. Many times the success or failure lies in the implementation of six sigma and the commitment and resources needed in order for successful implementation, particularly since it is a process, not a one-time project. In order for six sigma to be effective, it is a process that can take years, not days, to successfully implement.[19]

Quality Activities and Tools The quality activities encompass ongoing management processes that businesses need to practice in a six-sigma program. They include participative management, short-cycle manufacturing, designing for manufacturing benchmarking, statistical process control (SPC), and supplier qualification. The improvement tools and analytical techniques include flowcharts (schematic representations of an algorithm or a process), Pareto charts (charts used to graphically summarize and display the relative importance of the differences between groups of data), histograms (the graphical versions of tables that show what proportion of cases fall into each of several or many specified categories), cause-and-effect diagrams (diagrams, also known as fishbone diagrams because of their shape, that show causes of certain events), and experimental designs (the designs of all information-gathering exercises where variation is present, whether under the full control of the experimenter or not).

The speed at which e-business is conducted fits like a glove with six-sigma principles, because these principles are aimed at enabling businesses to deliver just what customers need when they want it.

Small businesses that would like to achieve six-sigma status must work diligently to reduce the incidence of defects. Those that do will find six sigma to be not just a strange phrase, but also the means toward achieving the ultimate goals of improved manufacturing and increased customer satisfaction.[20]

Quality Circles

A popular technique for improving quality relies on **quality circles**, which seek to involve everyone within the organization in decisions that affect the business. Small groups of employees meet regularly to discuss, analyze, and recommend solutions to problems in their area, after they receive training in problem solving, statistical techniques, and organizational behavior.

> *"In order for six sigma to be effective, it is a process that can take years, not days, to successfully implement."*

quality circles
The use of small groups of employees to analyze products and processes in an effort to improve quality.

Manager's Notes

Six Sigma Online

www.6-sigma.com This site, created by the Six Sigma Academy, offers a good look within the academy and training provided. Start with a click on "What Is Six Sigma?" A wealth of information on training and the six-sigma philosophy is provided. "News and Reviews" reveals which companies have implemented the process and describes how it has affected their operations.

www.isixsigma.com This site provides information on how to implement quality strategies into your business. Clicking on "Methodologies" will take you to a variety of papers describing differing quality methodologies.

www.sixsigma.de Start with the site-map link at the top of the page, where you will find an outline of site topics. It is easy to navigate from there. You may be interested in the detailed boundary conditions with graphics of six sigma.

www.thequalityportal.com Here you will find a wide range of quality-related items, including plenty of information on six sigma. Click on "Six Sigma" for a description of what this concept is, why it is important, when to use it, how to use it, and what a six-sigma Black belt is.

www.sixsigmaonline.org Looking for six-sigma certification? This site offers online certifications—with Yellow, Green, and Black belts to boot. Six-sigma training encourages individuals to stop what they are doing, examine how well they have done it, and then implement improvements to iron out defects.

How Do You Control Operations?

The issue of quality affects the entire production process, so controls need to be built in at every stage. *Feedforward quality control* applies to your company's inputs. *Concurrent quality control* involves monitoring your transformation processes. *Feedback quality control* means inspecting your outputs. Each will be discussed here.

Feedforward Quality Control

feedforward quality control
Quality control applied to a company's inputs.

Control of quality begins by screening out inputs that are not good enough. **Feedforward quality control** depends strongly on the *total quality management (TQM)* principles stating that every employee is a quality inspector and is responsible for building better, long-term relationships with suppliers. When you have a long-term relationship with suppliers, they can help you achieve higher quality standards by continuously improving their products. Teamwork with your employees and cooperation with suppliers are keys to feedforward control.

Concurrent Quality Control

concurrent quality control
Quality control applied to work in progress.

ISO 9000
The set of standards that certifies that a business is using processes and principles to ensure the production of quality products.

Concurrent quality control involves monitoring the quality of your work in progress. To facilitate this type of monitoring, many small businesses are realizing the value of the international quality standards known as **ISO 9000** (pronounced ICE-oh 9000), discussed also in Chapter 15. The purpose of the ISO 9000 standards is to document, implement, and demonstrate the quality assurance systems used by companies that supply goods and services internationally.[21]

Reality Check

Six Sigma: Beyond Manufacturing

In the past, six sigma was seen as primarily a tool to be used in the manufacturing industry to achieve defect reductions in the production process. Quality was increased through the process of eliminating products that did not conform to the production standards. Today businesses other than manufacturing are realizing the benefits of six sigma. Kaj Ahlmann was working for General Electric (GE) when he decided to follow his dream—buy some land and establish a vineyard. A key component to his ranch and vineyard was the concept of quality. As a veteran of GE, Ahlmann had used six sigma principles throughout his GE career and realized those same principles would work for his ranch and winery. Thus, The Six Sigma Ranch and Winery was created with a focus on quality and consistency. Ahlmann realized the key piece of six sigma was determining what the customer wanted in the product. Once that was determined, using statistical controls to achieve those goals could be accomplished. Ahlmann used his math degree, his experiences at GE, and wine-making classes to grow his small business in the direction he felt was important. The business uses the DMAIC—define, measure, analyze, improve, and control—during all steps of the wine-

making process from the time the vines are planted until the customer is enjoying the product. For Ahlmann, using six sigma for quality control for his ranch and winery was a natural progression.

Some other nonmanufacturing businesses that have employed six sigma and seen results because of its use are as follows:

- An insurance company that found costs were skyrocketing due to the number of steps involved in the claims process. Using six sigma, the steps were reduced, generating greater efficiencies and cost savings.
- A retailer who found that little things, like the paperwork that employees were required to fill out for customer price matching and online ordering, were actually costing the business lots of dollars and not improving service.
- A call center that found that by redesigning its system, employees could handle customer calls on the first call, which increased both customer satisfaction and reduced costs.

Six sigma is not just for manufacturers anymore.

Sources: Peter Guarraia, Gib Carey, Alistair Corbett, and Klaus Neuhaus, "Six Sigma—At Your Service," *Business Strategy Review,* Summer 2009; Erick Jones, Mahour Parast, and Stephanie Adams, "A Framework for Effective Six Sigma Implementation," *Total Quality Management & Business Excellence,* April 2010; and Monica Elliott, "A Quality Vintage," *Industrial Engineer,* June 2010.

ISO standards do not address the quality of your specific products. Rather, compliance with them shows your customers (whether consumers or other businesses) how you test your products, how your employees are trained, how you keep records, and how you fix defects. ISO standards are more like generally accepted accounting principles (GAAP) than they are a spinoff of TQM.[22] Certification in the United States comes from the American National Standards Institute, 11 West 42nd Street, New York, NY 10035 (212-642-4900).

ISO 9000:2000 series was implemented to further promote quality assurance, quality management systems, continuous improvement, and business excellence. ISO 9000:2000 series has four main areas of improvement compared to the ISO:1994 series. Top management must not only be committed to the process but also serve as role models for the business. Processes must become the focus. The customer is key, and as such, customer satisfaction must be monitored. The setting of goals and improvements is a continuous process. Companies that were certified to the previous ISO 9000:1994 series need to revamp and evaluate where the current gaps are before applying to the ISO 9000:2000 series.

American Saw of East Longmeadow, Massachusetts, an 800-employee, family-owned business, was the first in its industry to receive ISO certification. Tim Berry, quality control manager, believes that because the company took the steps necessary to become certified, its product defects have decreased, communication has improved, and workplace accidents have been reduced.[23] What's more, meeting the standards will ease entry into foreign markets and cut costs. Unfortunately, the up-front costs of certification can be high for small businesses. American Saw, for example, laid out $60,000 for outside consultants and registrars.

Richard Thompson, of Caterpillar, states, "Today, having ISO 9000 is a competitive advantage. Tomorrow, it will be the ante to the global poker game."[24] Small businesses may find themselves between the proverbial rock and a hard place relating to certification and costs if the larger companies that buy their products require certification before they will purchase from the small business. Some suggestions for dealing with costs follow:

- *Negotiate consultation prices.* Different consultants and registrars charge different amounts. Consultation prices are on the way down, so shop around. Always make sure that the consultant you select is familiar with your particular industry.
- *Request customer subsidies.* If the company you are selling to is pushing its suppliers for certification, it may help you become certified. A primary customer of Griffith Rubber Mills, of Portland, Oregon, paid the entire certification bill because it needed the technology.
- *Look for consultant alternatives.* A local college may be able to help set up an ISO networking group.
- *Consider your need for full certification.* You may be able to save money if it is more important to your suppliers for your business to meet ISO standards than to have full certification.

statistical process control (SPC)
The use of statistical analysis to determine the probability of a variation in product being random or a problem.

An important tool for monitoring the quality of a product while it is being produced (concurrent control) is **statistical process control (SPC)**, the process of gathering, plotting, and analyzing data to isolate problems in a specified sample of products. Using SPC, you can determine the probability of a deviation being a simple, random, unimportant variation or a sign of a problem in your production process that must be corrected.

For example, if you are producing titanium bars that need to be 1 inch in diameter, not every single bar will measure *exactly* 1 inch. You need to calculate the probability that various deviations will occur by chance alone or because of some problem. If a sample bar measures 1.01 inches, you wouldn't be too concerned, because that amount of variation occurs by chance once in every 100 products. But if a sample bar measures 1.05 inches, a variation that occurs by chance only once in 10,000 products, you know a problem needs correction in your production process. See the *control chart* in Figure 18.3 for this example. A control chart consists of the following:

- Points representing averages of measurements of a quality characteristic in samples taken from the process and shown over a period of time
- A center line, drawn at the process mean
- Upper and lower control limits (called *natural process limits*) that indicate the threshold at which the process output is considered statistically unlikely

benchmarking
The process of comparing key points within your business with comparable points in another external entity.

Another powerful tool for concurrent control is **benchmarking**, which allows the comparisons necessary for measurement. To identify or measure a competitive advantage for your small business, you must have a comparison base. Your products, services, and practices—almost anything related to your business that can be measured—can be benchmarked. Where can you find benchmark information? First, visit your local library reference section to find *RMA Annual Statement Studies*. RMA is second to none for providing small business industry averages. In addition, industry groups and trade associations often publish industry averages in journals, magazines, and newsletters.

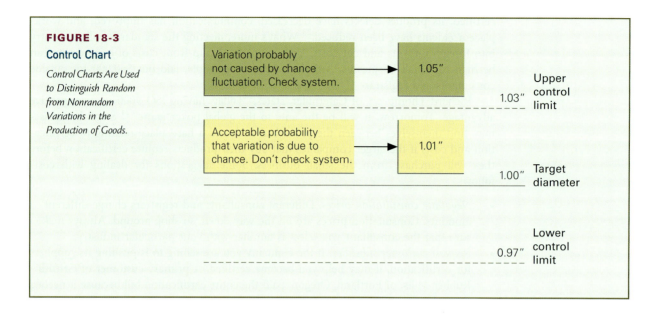

FIGURE 18-3

Control Chart

Control Charts Are Used to Distinguish Random from Nonrandom Variations in the Production of Goods.

Variation probably not caused by chance fluctuation. Check system. → 1.05″

1.03″ — Upper control limit

Acceptable probability that variation is due to chance. Don't check system. → 1.01″

1.00″ — Target diameter

0.97″ — Lower control limit

Benchmarking can be used to improve every facet of your business. Some examples follow:

Production Process

- Methodology
- Equipment needs
- Assembly time
- Inspection
- Parts availability
- Facility needs
- Personnel needs
- Quality control
- Cost considerations
- Returns and repairs

Customer Service

- Goods and services availability
- Warranties and guarantees
- Cost considerations
- Returns, repair, and replacement
- Feedback mechanisms (surveys, toll-free numbers, etc.)

Feedback Quality Control

feedback quality control

Inspecting and testing products after they are produced.

Inspecting and testing products after they are produced is called ***feedback quality control***. Quality control inspectors may be used to check products. Rejected products will be discarded, reworked, or recycled.

A problem with many types of product inspection is that the product can no longer be used because it has to be cut up, taken apart, or disassembled to test and measure it. However, nondestructive testing of several metal and plastic parts is being perfected by using laser ultrasound and other electromagnetic and acoustic-based methods.[25]

What is the fate of manufacturing in the United States? Prior to the 2001 recession, manufacturing jobs had remained stable at around 18 million workers. That number slipped to 16 million after 2001 and in 2009 reached 12 million. However, even though employment has decreased, output has not, with the price of U.S. manufactured goods falling by 3 percent between 1995 and 2008. International competition has kept prices low and productivity has increased, fueled by research and development, factory automation, and increases in technology. Harry Moser, chairman emeritus of GF AgiCharmilles, stated, "We can't reshore products that are low quality, rely on cheap labor, or have no regulatory or safety issues. But if you need high quality, a short pipeline that can handle volatile demand that fluctuates month to month, or a reduced carbon footprint, we're [i.e., the U.S. is] competitive."[26]

Summary

1. List the elements of an operating system.

In developing a system for producing your product or service, your business takes inputs such as raw materials, skills, money, information, and energy, and transforms them in some way to add value to product outputs. You need to receive feedback at every stage to control the process.

2. Describe how manufacturers and service providers use operations management.

Operating systems used by manufacturers are either analytic (systems that take inputs and reduce them into component parts to produce outputs) or synthetic (systems that combine inputs in producing outputs). The processes that manufacturers use are either continuous or intermittent. A continuous process produces the same good without interruption for a long period of time. An intermittent process is stopped with some frequency to change the products being made. Service businesses also take inputs and produce outputs through some transformation process. Most have used intermittent processes, but some have adopted continuous processes in an effort to increase productivity.

3. Explain how to measure productivity.

The ratio of inputs used to produce outputs is called *productivity*. Productivity measures the efficiency of your entire business or any part of it. It can be improved by changing processes used by your business, by getting your employees to accomplish more, or by using some type of technology that speeds produc-

tion. To calculate productivity, simply divide outputs by inputs.

4. Recount the methods of scheduling operations.

Scheduling involves planning what work will need to be done and determining what resources you will need to produce your product or service. Forward scheduling is accomplished by having resources available and ready as customer orders come in. Backward scheduling is used when you plan a job around the date when the project must be done. Gantt charts are a useful backward-scheduling tool.

5. Discuss the role of quality in operations management.

A company's tolerance range denotes the boundaries of acceptable quality. The defect rate indicates the number of products made that fall outside the tolerance range. Six sigma establishes a tolerance range of only 3.4 defects per million products produced. Statistical process control (SPC) is a procedure used to determine the probability of a deviation being a simple, random, unimportant variation or a sign of a problem in your production process that must be corrected.

6. Identify the three ways to control operations.

Controlling operations enables you to measure what is being accomplished in your business. Feedforward quality control applies to your company's inputs. Concurrent quality control involves monitoring your transformation processes. Feedback quality control relies on inspecting your outputs.

Questions for Review and Discussion

1. Discuss the elements of an operations management system. What would happen if the control system were not included? The feedback?
2. What is the difference between flexible production and mass customization?
3. Define *productivity*.
4. How can ergonomics be tied to productivity?
5. Explain the difference between forward and backward scheduling.
6. Define *six sigma* both technically and as used as a business standard.
7. What types of small businesses would benefit from having ISO 9000 certification?
8. Give examples of products that would be suited to each of the dispatching rules.

Questions for Critical Thinking

1. This chapter concentrated on both productivity and quality. In running your small manufacturing business, can you increase both, or aren't they mutually exclusive?

2. You have read about ISO 9000 certification in both Chapter 15 and this chapter. Bearing in mind that such certification is both time-consuming and expensive, describe what type of small business should pursue it.

What Would You Do?

Reread the chapter-opening vignette about WET. This vignette provides a lot of information about the company's products and processes. Find related articles about the company and visit its Web site (www.wet design.com).

Questions

1. Using Figure 18.1 and Table 18.1 as models, describe your college's inputs, transformation process, outputs, feedback, and control systems.

2. How would you apply six-sigma principles to making education?

Appendix: Cases

Chapter 1 Case

Small Business Lessons from the Movies

Movies are magical. They take us to new places, they spark our imagination, and they entertain us. Lessons from movies are open to interpretation that may differ from what the filmmaker ever intended. Spielberg and Lucas may have never intended to teach people how to run businesses, but let's step back, open our minds, and consider what we have seen that may solve problems in business. With some thought, we can come up with stories of communication, branding, ethics, customer service, and leadership applicable to starting and running a small business.

Here's some examples to get you started. Popcorn please …

It's a Wonderful Life (1946) OK, so we equate this one with Christmas, but consider the lesson of leading by example that Capra shows. It comes down to a confrontation between two businesspeople—Mr. Potter (Lionel Barrymore) wants to turn Bedford Falls into Pottersville, while George Bailey (James Stewart) puts his customers, employees, and family interest first by taking personal responsibility.

The Godfather I and II (1972, 1974) Not the most savory of mission statements, but these movies are about family business. There are lessons about loyalty and consequences. Many quotes are still used often in the business world—"go to the mattresses…," "I'm gonna make him an offer he can't refuse," "My father taught me many things … keep your friends close, but your enemies closer."

Jerry Maquire (1996) After being jettisoned from a large firm, the title character (Tom Cruise) becomes a reluctant entrepreneur that brilliantly captures the manic-depressive roller-coaster ride of starting a business. With one employee and one client, Maquire literally has all his eggs in one basket to show that fewer clients and more personal attention are a good business strategy.

Wall Street (1987) This study of values compares and contrasts the differences between a father and a son. The small business lesson can be that "there are no short cuts" in life or business. Just because you can visualize where you want to be does not mean that you can get there without paying dues.

A League of Their Own (1992) Just the tagline for the movie sets it up with a small business lesson: "To achieve the incredible you have to attempt the impossible." Memorable quotes include "There's no crying in baseball," and "Of course this is hard." No matter how it appears—*every* business is hard. Don't complain.

Hustle & Flow (2005) Once again, the viewer needs to look past some seedy images on screen to see that you can be successful no matter where you come from. Small business lessons abound including the following: (1) You are in charge of your business, (2) relationships are powerful, and (3) marketing pays.

Tucker: The Man and His Dream (1988) I, your author, admit personal bias on this one—I believe this is the *best business* movie *ever!* The best part is that the whole story is true. It's about an inventor who sets out to revolutionize the auto industry during WWII. It's got it all—business started in a barn, naysayers, faithful followers, time-crunched prototypes, creative technology advances, giant corporate adversaries, and failure. If you are in a class on small business/entrepreneurship—watch this one.

You get the idea by now and yes, some of these were made before most students were born, but they are available as rentals. Some other contenders to consider include:

Apollo 13 (1995)
The Bridge on the River Kwai (1957)
Dead Poets Society (1989)
Elizabeth (1998)
Glengarry Glen Ross (1992)
Norma Rae (1979)
One Flew over the Cuckoo's Nest (1975)
Twelve Angry Men (1957)
Twelve O'Clock High (1949)

Sources: Lori Grant "The 10 Best Business Movies," www.smartlemming.com/2009/05/the-10-best-business-movies, May 21, 2009; Mike Hofman "Everything I Know about Leadership, I Learned from the Movies," *Inc.*, March 2000, 58–70; Leigh Buchanan, "Cinema for the Enterprising," *Inc.*, February 2007, 75–77. For more on this topic, see a new book by Coupe and Sansolo titled *The Big Picture: Essential Business Lessons from the Movies* (2010) from Brigantine Media.

Questions

1. What are your personal screen inspirations? What lessons do these or other movies provide in running a small business?
2. In addition to the movies cited in this case, think of other titles for business lessons such as *Risky Business*, *Pirates of Silicon Valley*, and *Office Space*. What lessons do they provide?
3. What movies portray leaders who think creatively, who keep their heads, who manage communication, and, as for failure, well, that's just not an option (a line from *Apollo 13*)?
4. Bearing in mind that the intent of movies is artistic, rather than educational, what movie lessons do you think illustrate the opposite of what a manager should do or say?

Chapter 2 Case

Blind Date—Crazy

About the only thing harder than finding a date is choosing which Web site to meet him or her on. David Evans, online dating industry consultant, says there are over 2,000 online dating sites in the United States alone. The field wasn't quite that crowded when Harvard mathematician friends Chris Coyne, Christian Rudder, Sam Yagan, and Max Krohn founded OkCupid in 2004—but they still had to figure out how to get noticed.

In previous ventures, *free* had been the operative word for OkCupid CEO Yagan. In the late 1990s, the team forever altered the market for student cheat sheets, then dominated by the iconic black-and-yellow CliffsNotes booklets, with SparkNotes, a free Web-based copycat they later sold to Barnes & Noble. After that, they disrupted the music business, creating the file-sharing tool eDonkey. Before the company was litigated out of existence by a record-industry lawsuit, it boasted the world's most popular file-sharing software, bigger even than Napster.

Could *free* work in the industry of online dating? The growing market was, and still is, dominated by two large competitors: Match.com with 20 million users and $350 million revenue and eHarmony at 20 million users and $250 million revenue. Yagan figured he could inflict serious damage on the industry by using the same strategy they employed with SparkNotes. "Take an existing business," he explains, "reduce the revenue that industry produces by offering a free product, and then claim the remaining revenue for yourself."

Yagan and crew spent three years building the site, had raised nearly $7 million, but they were not gaining traction. Being free to join, they needed a massive audience to generate advertising dollars. After two years of growth, traffic was flatlining while competitors were growing rapidly. By early 2007, Yagan realized his window of opportunity was closing. He needed to jump-start his company or face a slow death.

Yagan figured the magic numbers needed were 8 million users and 2 million regular daters, roughly eight times his current traffic. And upping the pressure, new free dating sites were popping up and beating Yagan at his own game. PlentyofFish.com, a fast-growing Canadian site founded in 2003, surpassed OkCupid, attracting nearly 1.5 million unique viewers a month in the United States by early 2008. The online world constantly changing didn't help their business model—people were turning to social networking sites as de facto dating services.

OkCupid could try fighting back with an ambitious advertising campaign, but where? "Any place you might advertise to attract daters, someone's already there," he says. "You might think Times Square. But JDate's there. You might think Google, but Match is willing to spend well over $50 per subscription." A quirky dating site like OkCupid seemed like a perfect fit for a guerrilla marketing campaign. They spent $10,000 in a test to distribute 10,000 red roses in Boston, but gained few users. "It was a flop."

A possible opportunity opened in May 2010 when Facebook founder Mark Zuckerberg announced that outside software developers could build programs, called widgets, that would operate within his company's wildly popular social network. But the problem with operating inside Facebook was the serious constraint on OkCupid's ability to sell advertising. Furthermore, he worried that OkCupid risked being seen as just another widget maker in a crowded marketplace.

The OkCupid team could see potential—10 percent of U.S. newly married couples met online—but promotional options seemed exhausted. Then Yagan remembered a wacky idea he and Coyne had once tossed around: a dating site with "a blind-date button." What had been little more than a running joke suddenly seemed like a competitive advantage. They named their idea Crazy Blind Date (CBD). CBD would not be for everyone, but for social, outgoing, and adventurous twentysomethings it could be fun. Since all blind dates would be local, they could launch in selected cities such as Austin, Boston, New York City, and San Francisco. Potential daters would get verified by providing phone and e-mail contact info pulled from OkCupid profiles. Participants select the day of the week, the times available to meet up, and neighborhood on Google maps. Then they provide a freeform description of ideal date, age range, and gender of date. Finally, daters select the usual body type, ethnicities, religion, and so forth, and hit the "CBD" button.

At best, the novelty of instantaneous, face-to-face blind dates might catch on among users inundated with e-mails, phone calls, and instant messages; at worst, it might at least generate buzz for OkCupid.

_____

Sources: Max Chafkin, *Inc.*, May 1, 2008, 54–56; Kira Bindrim, "Crafting Online Dates That Resonate," *Crain's New York Business*, May 3, 2010, 12; "Connecting Up," *The Economist*, March 28, 2009; Jenna Wortham, "Looking for a Date?" *New York Times*, February 13, 2010, B1; and "A Picture Pulls 1,000 Mates," *Irish Times*, February 22, 1010, 17.

Questions

1. We read in this chapter that entrepreneurs try to build competitive advantages for their businesses by being unique. How will these partners know if their CBD idea will make OkCupid stand out, or just creepy?
2. Put yourself in the position of Yagan and Coyne. What should these partners do next?

Chapter 3 Case

Not Easy Being Indie

Tough time to be in the retail music business. That wasn't always the case as chains such as Sam Goody's and Tower Records competed side by side with thousands of independent record stores. Back in the day, one of the best independents was Millennium Music in Charleston, South Carolina—perennially winning awards for best CD store and best store staff. But things change.

Millennium Music owner Kent Wagner had done everything possible to fight the changing tide brought on by the rise of digital music: At the apex of the business, Wagner owed seven stores, but for seven straight years, Millennium had suffered double-digit revenue declines. "We always thought of ourselves as a community center, a meeting place," says Wagner. "We knew the industry was in decline, but we thought we were different."

It turned out Millennium wasn't different. And Wagner and his business partner, Clayton Woodson, soon faced a stark choice: fold up the business completely and walk away, or attempt to transform it into something entirely different. The once-hot business had but one glowing ember left: a small but growing online trading business that allowed customers to exchange used CDs, DVDs, and books for electronics—iPods and the like. Millennium was able to make money by reselling the used merchandise on Amazon, eBay, and other sites.

Millennium was launched by Wagner in 1994 with the focus of creating a thinking person's music store. Their competitive advantage was based on an inventory of hard-to-find records with large classical and jazz sections and stellar customer service. Millennium would make music connoisseurship friendly and accessible.

In the early years, that philosophy worked well, and revenue grew some 20 percent annually. At its peak, Millennium generated sales of about $10 million annually. Live bands played regularly, Millennium hosted a live-jazz happy hour, and they held book readings. Wagner opened a restaurant and a bar and expanded to book sales and DVD rentals.

But the seismic industry shifts that put Sam Goody's, Tower Records, and many others out of business started catching up to Millennium. As the years rolled by, the losses mounted. Wagner's empire was hemorrhaging, and he was soon ready to try anything. In 2006, he turned for help to his marketing director, Clayton Woodson, whose eclectic background included making furniture, teaching first grade at a charter school in New York, and teaching acrobatic yoga. "Clayton tends to see looking at the abyss as a growing experience," says Wagner. "I'm the opposite."

That glowing ember of Millennium's business— the used-CD section—gave Woodson an idea. Customers often came in hoping to exchange their old CDs for store credit. What if Millennium could formalize the process to entice additional customers by offering to trade iPods for used CDs? In the summer of 2005, he persuaded Wagner to give the idea a try. Woodson soon had another insight: Buying a used CD online was actually cheaper than buying an MP3 album through iTunes. If Millennium moved its iPod trading program online, it could collect discs from across the globe, profitably resell them online, and still undercut iTunes's prices.

Millennium launched FeedYourPlayer.com in 2006. Traffic soared from a few hundred visitors per week to more than 15,000. New customers were soon mailing in more than 6,000 items a week. By 2007, the online exchange brought in $400,000 of Millennium's $1.7 million revenue.

FeedYourPlayer's performance was heading in the exact opposite direction of Millennium's lone remaining store. In its last full year of operation, the store lost nearly $1 million. In September 2007, Wagner called a company meeting with his 50 or so remaining employees. He delivered the news that many had already foreseen. The retail business was dying. The future was online. The store would remain open, but resources would be put toward building FeedYourPlayer.

Employees were still upset even if they had seen the changes coming. Millennium's music buyer quit when he realized the emphasis would be peddling used CDs rather than fresh releases. Wagner understood his employees' anguish. He says, "staff members were accustomed to being tastemakers." Wagner felt the confliction himself. He clung to the hope that the huge changes might save the store. "When you spend so much of your energy fighting against the blindingly obvious," says Wagner, "you can lose your focus on the big picture."

Sources: Ryan McCarthy, "An Indie Record Store Fights for Survival," *Inc.*, June, 2009; Ed Christman, "NARM Roundup," *Billboard*, May 24, 2008, 15; Kelsey Abbott, "New Ways to Make Money off Recycling," www.thestreet.com, August 6, 2008; Patrick Sharbaugh, "Best Store for New CD's, Used CD's, and Staff," *Charleston City Paper*, March 7, 2007; and www.abundatrade.com/aboutus.

Questions

1. Using the strategic planning process discussed in this chapter, what was the core problem to be solved by Millennium? What were *all* of their potential alternative solutions to that problem?
2. Apply Porter's Five Forces Model to this case.
3. What would you have done if you were in Wagner and Woodson's place at this decision point?

Chapter 4 Case

Memory by Music

Blake Harrison was a good student in high school, but he struggled to memorize facts for tests. He had no problem knowing all the lyrics to his favorite rap songs, but when it came to academics, forget it—literally. It was then that he realized that if a rapper hip-hopped things like vocabulary words, students like him would score better on the SAT exam.

Harrison earned a degree in English from the University of Pennsylvania and headed to San Francisco where he met Alex Rappaport. Rappaport had graduated from Tufts with a degree in music and was trying to break into the business by writing tracks for indie films and TV commercials. One evening, Harrison told his friend about his idea for using hip-hop to help students. Rappaport said, "let's do it." They wrote and recorded two songs that together defined 80 SAT vocabulary words, using lyrics like: "They don't say the word *think*, they say *ratiocinate*/ They don't render *repeat*, they say *recapitulate*." They sent demos to various educational publishers and knew they were on to something when study guide publisher SparkNotes commissioned two songs and showcased both songs as free, streamable MP3s on its Web site. Harrison and Rappaport invested their life savings into their new company, Flocabulary. They launched a Web site and began selling a self-published hip-hop guide to the SAT.

For two years, the pair hustled to make their start-up work, but sales were hard to close and they were nearly out of money. In the spring of 2007, Harrison and Rappaport were working the International Reading Conference in Toronto. They were desperate to close some deals.

"Wanna hear about how to teach history through hip-hop?" they beckoned across the aisles. An attendee wandered over, and Harrison and Rappaport cued up "Let Freedom Ring," one of their fact-filled rap songs, an ode to Martin Luther King Jr.'s "I Have a Dream" speech. The educator listened intently to their pitch. He picked up a copy of their book, *Hip Hop U.S. History*, and flipped through the pages, nodding his head in approval. Then it happened again. "You kids have a million-dollar idea here," the man told them. And then he walked away. It seemed like they always walked away.

Educators walking away from their product just didn't make sense. Most of the teachers and administrators they talked to seemed genuinely interested in their product. Time after time, they would listen to the pitch and rave about the concept—but more often than not would leave the booth with just one $18 book, or worse, an earful of praise. Harrison wondered, if Flocabulary's idea was so great and the materials so impressive, *why weren't people*

buying? The two friends wondered if they were cut out to run a business at all.

In April 2006, *Flocabulary: The Hip-Hop Approach to SAT Vocabulary* hit bookshelves worldwide thanks to a deal with Cider Mill Press, a novelty book publisher in Kennebunkport, Maine. "I thought that with our design sensibilities and publishing experience, we could really make this a commercially viable product," says John Whalen, founder of Cider Mill. The best part: Cider Mill worked with Sterling Publishers, the distribution arm of Barnes & Noble, which meant Flocabulary's books would find space in bookstores nationwide. *The Hip Hop Approach to SAT Vocabulary* sold 10,000 copies in its first year and has since been reprinted five times. And Flocabulary received a slew of attention from media outlets, such as CNN, DailyCandy, MTV, and NPR—even historian Howard Zinn offered praise.

So Flocabulary guides began to sell due to distribution outlets, but the partners decided that students taking the SAT or shopping at Barnes & Noble were not the ones who could benefit from their approach the most. They decided to transform Flocabulary into an actual publishing business. They raised about $50,000 from friends and family and began visiting schools and attending education conferences. But just as when they first started, educators were a tough sell. "Teachers would say, 'This is so cool; my kids will love this!' but would buy just one book," Rappaport recalls.

They decided to participate in a program at Columbia Business School that pairs new business owners with MBA students who analyze business plans and offer advice. Harrison and Rappaport didn't claim to be experts in business. But the analysis from the Columbia students stunned them: Not one of them thought Flocabulary should continue self-publishing or pursue the school market. Instead, they urged Flocabulary to find a new publisher. After conducting extensive research, the students warned that Harrison and Rappaport were in way over their heads. Nearly every school district works differently, and selling to schools requires an immense amount of paperwork, they warned. One student concluded his critique: "If you do this, you're going to die."

Those words stung Harrison and Rappaport. Six months later they could still hear them as they sat in the Flocabulary booth at the Toronto trade show. Most of their initial $50,000 investment was gone. Perhaps, they thought, the students were right. Perhaps it was time to give up.

Sources: Lauren Bans, "How to Reinvent a Failing Start-up," *Inc.*, May 5, 2009, 62–65; www.wikipedia.og/wiki/flocabulary; Jana Winter, "Flocabulary Is the Hip-hop Way to Educate," *The Arizona Republic*, April 13, 2006, www.azcentral.com; and www.focabulary.com/bios.

Questions

1. If you were in Rappaport and Harrison's situation, how would you change your business plan for the future?
2. Is Flocabulary's problem (a) the wrong target market, (b) a bad product, (c) too few products, or (d) something else? What are their alternative solutions to their problem?

Chapter 5 Case

Extreme Garage Makeover

Marc Shuman tries to solve a problem common to most every homeowner—getting to their cars without tripping over tools and toys or hurdling barbecue grills and bikes. "Garages can be a lot more than just a place to dump junk," says Shuman.

Shuman's solution to the war on clutter is a "garage organizational system" consisting of patented slotted wall panels and an array of modular attachable cabinets, shelves, bike racks, and workbenches—all styled in the same light-gray steel and plastic and bearing the yellow GarageTek logo.

Marc describes himself as a "neat freak" and devised an early version of the slotted wall panel while running his family's store-fixture manufacturing company on Long Island. He and a partner adapted the panels and tested them out on his mother-in-law's two-car garage, which was packed with 30 years' worth of junk. "The transformation was just staggering," he says.

Selling the panels at home-improvement stores such as Home Depot and Lowe's was tempting, but eventually Shuman decided to build a garage-makeover business. He could envision GarageTek experts going to customers' homes, designing and installing organization systems—complete with shelves, cabinets, bike racks, and workbenches. Custom work justifies a premium price so margins would be higher. No one sold such garage systems, but it would not be difficult to copy the idea so Shuman needed to be the first in the market and get big fast. Franchising seemed like the best way to do both.

Shuman placed an ad in the *Wall Street Journal* soliciting franchisees. The phone started ringing. His attorney advised him to choose carefully, but Shuman's first-mover advantage could be lost quickly so

he approved anyone that met minimal standards. Franchisees invested between $200,000 and $250,000 up front, including a $50,000 licensing fee, and pay 6 percent of gross sales as an annual royalty, plus another 4 percent for advertising. He believed that should have been enough to purchase supplies, buy newspaper ads, and turn a profit within 18 months. Franchisees received three days of basic training and a manual written by Shuman. "If they had the money and a strong sales and marketing background, we felt they were qualified," Shuman says.

All went smoothly—at first. In the first half of 2001, GarageTek franchises opened in Connecticut, New Jersey, and New York. By 2003, 57 franchises had sprung up in 33 states, and annual revenue at the corporate office was on track to top $12 million. In the summer of 2003, Shuman detected 15 franchisees who were struggling. One franchisee in California begged Shuman to send executives out west to train his staff. Another complained that GarageTek's suggested marketing method—ads in local newspapers—was ineffective, costing as much as $500 per lead. Desperate for help, Shuman enlisted iFranchise Group, a consulting firm in Homewood, Illinois, to help him develop a strategy. Top managers began benchmarking successful franchisees for tactics that worked best. Franchisees wondered where their royalty and franchise fees were going.

GarageTek's target market is owners of houses worth an average of $350,000 or more, or roughly the top 20 percent of the nation's 50 million houses with garages. The company's average sale (including design, components, and installation) is $4,500.

About three-quarters of GarageTek's franchisees were doing well. But, of course that means that 25 percent were losing money or barely breaking even. Complaints from disgruntled franchisees were pouring in. Shuman and crew were struggling to create operational systems that would help the unprofitable franchises get back on track, but they were losing ground. The picture painted by financial statements made Shuman start to think about closing the failing locations and get it over with.

Shuman and his managers knew they needed more data before making major decisions, so they compiled a spreadsheet with information on every GarageTek franchise, including the size and demographics of each territory, overhead costs, pricing models, management assessments, and the amount of capital being invested by owners. Two trends became apparent: The failing franchises were either underfunded or being run by non-owner managers hired by hands-off investors.

Shuman knew he bore some of the blame approving marginal franchisees in the first place and that GarageTek training and support had not been first rate. At the same time, the struggling franchisees were at fault too. Shuman, who had a reputation for being a tough boss, was torn. He, his management team, and the consultant from iFranchise all wanted to close the doors of struggling locations.

But legally, pulling franchise agreements could get messy. GarageTek's contract clearly stated that the franchisor could shut down franchises that failed to meet specific sales goals. But Shuman's attorney warned that could cause more problems. "I envisioned a bloodbath," Shuman says.

Sources: Stephanie Clifford, "Case Study: Hooked On Expansion," *Inc.,* March 2006, 44–50; Patricia Mertz Esswein, "Extreme Makeover: Garage," *Kiplinger's Personal Finance,* July 2005; Patrick J. Sauer, "Garage Makeover," *Inc.,* July 2007, 7; and Joseph Rosenbloom, "Space Man," *Inc.,* May 2002.

Questions

1. What problems such as lawsuits, reputation, and public image would GarageTek face if they closed failing franchises?
2. Is shuttering the failed franchises the right move for Shuman? What are his other options?

Chapter 6 Case

Is Buying Two Businesses Better Than One?

Fred Schwarzer is a venture capitalist in Palo Alto, California, who was looking at a different kind of deal than VCs normally do. Schwarzer had been watching two different start-ups for months. Both had recently been jilted by investors, both were on the verge of collapse, and both were biotech companies. Schwarzer believed he had the solution to both men's problems—combine the two companies to make an attractive investment for his firm, Charter Life Sciences. But negotiating a merger between companies on opposite sides of the globe wouldn't be easy.

On one side of the globe, in Singapore, was Joe Santangelo. It was August 2008 when he had been working hard to find a new partnership for SingVax, his vaccine-development start-up—a move he had hoped would provide the resources his venture so dearly needed. But when Santangelo met with one of his investors that day, he learned that the deal was vaporizing. Due diligence had turned up some troubling facts about the would-be partner. Santangelo would have no choice but to close SingVax. Only five months ago another potential partnership had fallen through, leaving the company with little cash and a board with little patience.

On the other side of the globe, Dan Stinchcomb's vaccine-development company, Inviragen, sat in Fort Collins, Colorado, equally left at the altar. Stinchcomb had learned that a venture capital firm was not able to raise the last pool of money needed to join a syndicate of investors he had put together to fund clinical trials. Without that pool of money, progress on Inviragen's dengue fever vaccine would stall. Without passing clinical trials, his vaccine could never cure anyone. Stinchcomb thought he could raise the money in 12 months, but 24 months had now passed.

Stinchcomb had made his first pitch for Inviragen to Schwarzer back in 2005. Schwarzer listened carefully as Stinchcomb described his plan to license dengue fever research from the Centers for Disease Control and Prevention and use it to develop a vaccine for a disease that infects more than 70 million people each year. Even though Schwarzer was impressed, he saw funding challenges due to (1) a difficult economic environment, (2) general bias against early-stage companies, and (3) "a huge percentage of U.S. investors had no interest in vaccines for emerging economies."

Rejection is part of the fundraising game, so Stinchcomb and his cofounder, Jorge Osorio, were not deterred. Osorio is a professor of veterinary medicine at the University of Wisconsin–Madison. He grew up in Colombia, where dengue fever is endemic. The pair lined up $250,000 in angel funding and some grants from the National Institutes of Health. That money funded initial animal trials of Inviragen's vaccine that showed promising results.

Santangelo was working on a vaccine for hand, foot, and mouth disease, or HFMD—a sometimes fatal childhood illness with annual outbreaks across Asia. By mid-2008, SingVax's vaccine was ready for clinical trials. Unfortunately, Bio*One Capital, Santangelo's primary backer, would make a second investment in SingVax only if the company brought on another investor, but one was not to be found. Survival and growth via a merger seemed the best way to attract capital from the United States or Europe, but so far that had also failed.

Both company's CEOs knew each other and their respective products—they had even briefly discussed working together but had reached no consensus. Now, Schwarzer was urging Stinchcomb to give SingVax another look.

Partners Stinchcomb and Osorio flew to Singapore in October 2008 for two days of intense discussions with Santangelo and his investors. By the end of the second day, Stinchcomb, Osorio, and Santangelo felt confident that a union was the answer to both companies' problems. SingVax had expertise that Inviragen lacked in scaling up lab production. And Inviragen's dengue fever vaccine had a larger potential market than SingVax's HFMD vaccine. Still, there were myriad details (or factors bigger than details) to work through. Who would run the company? What name would they use? How would they prioritize development of current and new products?

As you read in this chapter, the biggest sticking point was the question of each company's relative valuation going into the merger. Although Inviragen had received no VC investment, Schwarzer insisted that the two firms be valued equally because complex valuation negotiations would kill the deal. Santangelo, for his part, had shareholders to report to. Persuading SingVax's board to accept the equal valuation—and to provide funds to cover costs during the months it was expected to take to hammer out the details of the union—would not be easy. "All of us left not knowing whether this would be possible," Santangelo says.

Sources: Malika Zouhali-Worrall, "Case Study: Attempting a Global Merger," *Inc.*, May 2010, 68–72; "Inviragen Risky, SingVax Less: They Marry in Vaccine Heaven," www.allbusiness.com, May 30, 2010; and "Inviragen Merges with SingVax and Completes $15 Million Series A Financing," Singapore Economic Development Board, October 6, 2009, www.sebd.com/edb/sg.

Questions

1. The CEOs lived on different continents and barely knew each other. Could they make a deal work?
2. What do you believe the biggest barriers to this two-way business purchase would be?
3. What would you recommend to overcome those barriers?

The Price of Admissions

When Luke Skurman was a high school senior, he read all he could find about potential colleges, but he wanted more. "There just wasn't enough good, honest information for me to feel confident about where I was going to spend the next four years of my life. I didn't really know whom to talk to. The whole process felt like a giant crapshoot," he says. "In all my research, there were only two ways to get the information I wanted. The first was by physically visiting the campus and seeing if things were really how the brochures described them, but this was quite expensive and not always feasible. The second was the missing ingredient: the students. Talking to real students who actually attended the schools that I was interested in gave me the information that I needed so badly." He was happy with his eventual choice of Carnegie Mellon, but still wondered...

During his junior year, Skurman did a business class project with partner Joey Rahimi about a company prospectus to gather school information from students across the country and publish it online. Their aspirations for an online business somehow morphed into print editions.

With the ink still wet on their business diplomas, Skurman and Rahimi put their business plan into motion with two other former classmates by launching College Prowler. Their "by students, for students" approach has been popular from the start as undergrads give firsthand accounts of campus life. Student authors distribute surveys to their peers, who rate their school on a variety of criteria—including academics, dorms, and food, as well as Greek life, the drug scene, and (of course) the hotness of the girls and guys.

Tom Russell, publisher of the *Princeton Review*, says that "one of the reasons Zagat guides are so popular is that people want to read about other people's experiences at restaurants. It's no different in this category, students want to hear from other students."

The team received assistance from a former professor who gave them a bit of office space in a nearby biotech incubator, and two angel investors invested $5,000 each in exchange for 2 percent of the company. By September 2002, College Prowler had produced guides to nine schools and was ready to debut its products at the National Association for College Admission Counseling trade show in Salt Lake City. Skurman and his colleagues chatted up guidance counselors and admissions officers and nailed down their first two orders. "We made $240," Skurman says, "but we felt like we had validated our idea."

The trade show helped College Prowler begin attracting coverage in *Publishers Weekly*, the *New York Times*, and the *Washington Post*, and on CNN, all of which responded to the guides' honesty and irreverence. "Alcohol seems to be the drug of choice for most students and just about everyone knows that guy who sits in his room and smokes pot all day," according to the guide to Carnegie Mellon. "We at the University of Arizona are not 'everyday people.' We are beautiful and hot," a U of A student wrote. More good news followed. A new investor, Glen Meakem, now the cofounder of Meakem Becker Venture Capital in Sewickley, Pennsylvania, put $500,000 into the company in August 2004. The country's largest book wholesaler, Ingram, agreed to distribute College Prowler's guides, which helped get them into major bookstore chains like Barnes & Noble and Borders. Revenue hit about $500,000 in 2005. Soon, the company was publishing guidebooks for 220 colleges.

Skurman was pleased and concerned at the same time. He reviewed the list of the reasons he had started College Prowler. First, he wanted to create great content about colleges and universities. He also sought to help as many people as possible make the right college choices. Finally, he wanted College Prowler to be financially successful. Looking over the list, Skurman came to a bitter conclusion: He had succeeded at the first goal but failed at the other two.

A sobering realization hit: Skurman did the math and concluded that even if he could get 1,000 retail stores to carry a rack of 60 books at $14.95 apiece—an all but impossible goal—College Prowler's revenue potential was still less than $1 million. To generate more revenue, they began selling ads on the books' inside covers and on the company's Web site. Wachovia signed on as an advertiser, with a six-figure deal that included book and Web banner ads, plus sponsorship of an online scholarship contest. Skurman decided to experiment with a subscription model. They digitized 50,000 pages of College Prowler's content on more than 250 schools and, in March 2007, offered it online for $39.95 per year. The site mimicked the format of the books, with student-generated ratings for a variety of campus experiences.

The company generaed a small profit in 2007, but revenue stuck just under $1 million, and Skurman began to second-guess the strategy. He knew he had to do something. The marketplace for college information was changing. Universities were beefing up their Web sites. Most concerning was a new competitor called Unigo that had launched a free student-generated site. Skurman was preparing to renew College Prowler's contract with Wachovia in June 2008, but the bank announced massive losses and layoffs. It continued to advertise, but the deal was scaled back. Now Skurman was really worried.

College Prowler had created great content, but in an age of social media and so much free information online, the question was getting people to pay for it. Skurman began to think that maybe he should stop trying altogether and begin giving it away. He had been toying with the idea since attending the 2008 National Association for College Admission Counseling (NACAC) conference. Strolling around the show, Skurman took a close look at the exhibitors and was surprised at how many of them were in the business of selling sales leads—that is, information about prospective students—to colleges. His contact at Wachovia, in fact, later told him that qualified leads were the single most valuable element of the bank's relationship with College Prowler. Skurman wondered if lead generation could be a primary income stream.

Such a radical strategy shift would be risky, but did they really have a choice? Lead generation had some serious competitors such as College Board, which sells the names of students who take the SAT to colleges. Meakem, who had invested another $500,000 in College Prowler at the end of 2005 and now serves as chairman, encouraged the shift, but was it the right thing to do?

Sources: Donna Fenn, "Finding the Right Price for a Hot Product," *Inc.*, October 2009, 54–57; Lucinda Dyer, "Cramming for Tests, Trolling for Schools," *Publishers Weekly*, March 22, 2010, 43–45; Ron Hogan, "The Price of Admissions," *Publishers Weekly*, September 1, 2005, 19–24; Geoff Gloeckler, "Campus Life: A User's Guide," *Business Week Online*, September 15, 2009, 13; Nicole Torres, "Projecting Success," *Entrepreneur*, July 2005, 14–15.

Questions

1. What are the advantages and disadvantages of giving content away?
2. What if the new strategy didn't work and the content was now free?
3. What would you advise Skurman to do and still have a viable company?

Chapter 8 Case

To Tea or Not to Tea?

Jill Portman and Gary Shinner associate tea with romance, relaxation, digestion, and profit. When shopping for wedding rings in Chicago in 1990, a jeweler served them an aromatic oolong. After marriage, Portman enjoyed rooibos tea when she was pregnant to help with digestion. Tea was such an integral part of their lives that the pair founded Mighty Leaf Tea in 2000.

Mighty Leaf fills a niche market in high-end hotels, restaurants, and specialty-food shops with organic tea bags made from corn starch holding 2.5 grams of tea, flowers, herbs, dried fruit, and sometimes cacao ribs. Pretty packaging and names like Green Tea Tropical or Organic Breakfast also helped. But in early 2007, the pair was considering a bold move—moving into the mass market by selling in supermarkets.

Major player Lipton Tea had just introduced an upscale whole-leaf line in thousands of grocery stores. Shinner and Portman wondered whether Mighty Leaf should follow suit, a move that would be very expensive and time consuming just to get onto grocery shelves, let alone stay there—and with no guarantees. Everyone in the company had worked hard to create the ultra-luxury image it enjoyed in specialty markets. The young company was at a crossroads—go big or continue on the path it had started on.

The question had sparked heated debate within the company. Some employees thought rapid expansion through supermarket sales would be a great idea; another faction intensely believed such a move would risk seriously diluting the brand. "I'm really going to fight this, and I'll win," Charlie Woodruff, sales director for the eastern U.S. and a strong opponent of the supermarket strategy, often told his colleagues. Shinner and Portman were seeking a consensus.

Mighty Leaf's gourmet approach to tea was perfect and perfectly timed for America's growing foodies who were infatuated with experimentation. The organic flavors and biodegradable pouches endeared it to green-conscious consumers. Before long, Mighty Leaf was everywhere affluent consumers could be found—in Ritz-Carlton and Mandarin Oriental hotels, and at the cafés inside Nordstrom and Neiman Marcus stores. "You could no longer throw a paper tea bag in front of people and expect them to accept it" in a high-end setting, says Portman. And it didn't hurt that medical research was showing that tea, rich in antioxidants, was a healthier choice than coffee. Mighty Leaf's sales more than tripled in the four years ending in 2006, reaching $13.5 million. It was late that year that Shinner and Portman began discussing a strategy to move into the mass market.

Shinner and Portman were keeping an eye on Lipton, but hardly panicking. They believed that Lipton's arrival would raise the profile of whole-leaf tea, ultimately making more people aware of the benefits and expanding demand for all in the market. Supermarket chains showed they were willing to allocate valuable shelf space to this emerging niche by stocking Lipton's Pyramid brands. Shinner and Portman estimated that the move into supermarkets could double the company's sales within a few years.

Of course, there were risks. Moving into supermarkets would require a rapid increase in production. The company would need to source a whole bunch more tea leaves from suppliers in India and up production of pouches at its factory in North Africa. They would have to hire a whole new national sales staff with success in selling to big chains. That sales force would have to set up countless tastings and demonstrations in stores because consumers would have to be educated about tea and why they should shell out over $8 for a box of 15 bags.

These in-store promotions, including coupons and discounts, would cost about $1.2 million, enough to require bringing in outside investors for the first time. Even then, Mighty Leaf would cost at least twice what Lipton was charging for its premium Pyramid brand. "It's one thing to get into a supermarket, especially in a crowded category," Shinner says. "But it's even more difficult to stay there and thrive."

The supermarket move would jeopardize the company's reputation as a premium brand. Though Mighty Leaf's comparatively higher prices in supermarkets might turn off cost-conscious shoppers, its mere presence in mass chains threatened to alienate the company's upscale fans. Woodruff, the eastern U.S. sales director since 2003, argued that seeing Mighty Leaf on the supermarket shelf would be deeply offensive to his most coveted accounts—the elite hotels and restaurants that had helped build the brand. How special would tea be at the Waldorf if a customer could also get it at Kroger?

Still, Shinner and Portman saw supermarkets differently. As consumers' tastes had evolved, the pair believed, the big chains had been forced to keep pace and were adding gourmet and natural products in droves. The result was that Whole Foods shoppers were making regular stops at Safeway or Publix for the sake of convenience or price. Prestige products had the chance to penetrate both channels and become what Portman likes to call *masstige*.

Sales reps were eager to access new selling channels, so most were fired up for the supermarket strategy. They lobbied Woodruff with a steady flow of e-mails and phone calls. But he was still unconvinced. His East Coast sales had trailed the more developed West Coast markets for a couple of years. "I felt there were more customers I could get on board, more places I could wow, before I became a supermarket brand," he says.

Sources: Andrew Park, "Mighty Leaf Is a Darling of Upscale Restaurants and Natural-Food Stores, *Inc.*, January 2009, 54–60; Elizabeth Fuhrman, "Tea Supports Cultural Heritage," *Beverage Industry*, March 2009, 82; and Dorothy Pomerantz, "Tea Party," *Forbes*, November 17, 2008, 60–62.

Questions

1. What financial risks would Mighty Leaf take by pursuing a supermarket strategy?
2. How could they moderate cash flow problems?
3. What would you recommend Mighty Leaf do? Be sure to justify your recommendation.

Chapter 9 Case

When the Bank Cuts the Cord

Kevin Semcken was wandering the aisles and browsing the booths at a technology conference in Denver in 2004. At the time, he was the head of HealthTek Ventures, a venture capital firm in Evergreen, Colorado. Semcken came across a two-person start-up company named Able Planet with a promising idea—headphones embedded with a magnetic coil to enhance sound quality—but a lousy business. Since Semcken only has partial hearing in his left ear, he was intrigued. He was hardly ever able to hear high-frequency sounds like those produced by cymbals. The guys at the Able Planet booth gave him two headsets—one with the coil and one without—while he listened to Dean Martin's "You're Nobody 'Til Somebody Loves You." "When I switched to the Able Planet headphones, I could hear the cymbals," says Semcken. "I was instantly a fan."

Being a venture capitalist, Semcken believed in the product so much he not only invested in Able Planet but also he eventually took over as CEO and chairman. In 2006, Able Planet's LINX headphones won an award for innovation at the Consumer Electronics Show. Soon, the calls began pouring in. By 2008, revenue had jumped more than 1,000 percent, to $2 million.

In the first week of January 2009, Semcken got a call that every small business owner dreads. The loan officer for the bank Able Planet used was changing the terms of the $2.5 million line of credit it provided to Semcken's Wheat Ridge, Colorado-based audio-equipment business. Under the new terms, the bank would no longer provide funding for the cost of raw materials and manufacturing. Able Planet had been a customer of that bank for almost three years and had never missed a payment. And though Able Planet was not yet generating a positive cash flow, Kevin was understandably stunned. Without those funds, he would have no way to pay for inventory demanded by retailers such as Walmart and Costco. "They waited until the last minute and dropped it on us," Semcken says.

Up until the moment of that phone call, Able Planet's business plan had been fairly simple. The company used the bank line of credit to fund the manufacturing of Linx Audio headphones with a price range of $24 to $299 a pair. For more than a year, Semcken had been using some of the funds generated by the headphones to produce more of them and some of it to develop a promising new technology.

The promising new technology was called Sound Fit, which would expand his product line beyond headphones— like hearing aids and Bluetooth devices. Sound Fit is a listening device designed to fit snugly in the opening of the ear canal, eliminating nearly all ambient noise. Semcken got the idea for Sound Fit from a previous investment in a company developing a balloon-like stent that expanded and contracted to prevent debris from blocking small arteries during heart surgery. Semcken thought something similar could work for the ear. He urged Able Planet's audiologists to create an inflatable disk that could conform to the size of an individual's ear canal. Such a device wouldn't fall out during jogging or other activities like earbuds. They wouldn't rest awkwardly against the ear like Bluetooth devices. And Sound Fit would not require a costly fitting procedure like hearing aids.

Semcken had secured nondisclosure agreements from 30 potential customers for Sound Fit who were interested in seeing more. But before Semcken could move forward with any of these negotiations, he needed funds to create production-quality prototypes, as well as operating cash for the headphone business.

After Semcken finished the phone conversation with his banker, he did what all good business owners facing a problem do: identify all his alternatives. A common funding source for manufacturers is known as a factor. A factor loans against or purchases accounts receivables, but they charge very high interest rates. He could shop for a less risk-averse bank. The company also had more than 20 angel investors who had recently kicked in $1.4 million. But that money was gone. What were the chances those investors would be willing to pitch in more so soon? Previously, Sound Fit's potential customers might have been willing to fund the development of prototypes in exchange for a sweeter deal in the event that the technology panned out. Five companies seemed particularly hot on the product, but in a recession, none wanted any extra risk.

The timing of the bad bank news was especially unfortunate. High school and college graduation season was coming soon—one of the busiest times of the year. Following this, there would be back-to-school sales and then Christmas, which account for some 60 percent of annual sales. No money to fund production in January meant no significant revenue for almost the entire year.

Semcken sat down with two of Able Planet's board members, Rob Cascella and Steve Parker, both investors in the business. They advised Semcken to put Sound Fit on hold and redouble his efforts on Linx Audio. "When you're at the point where you're not generating operating cash flow," says Cascella, "you have to worry about today or you're not even going to be there in three years."

But Semcken wanted to continue negotiating with all 30 of Sound Fit's prospects. "The way you get a partner committed is out of fear they're going to lose it," he says. He was open to pushing Linx harder, but if he couldn't finance production of the headphones for existing customers, then expanding the line and finding new accounts would be out of the question. When he told Cascella and Parker that he wanted to ask Able Planet's other angel investors for a loan, they gave him the go-ahead. His offer: For every $100,000 loan they guaranteed, investors would get warrants for 30,000 shares at $3 apiece. Within three days, Semcken had a dozen takers. A representative at U.S. Bank, where Semcken kept his personal account, offered to make the loans, but only up to a certain amount. Semcken was hoping to raise some $1.5 million this way.

Trying to cover all his financial bases, Semcken had been scrambling to find a replacement for the company's $2.5 million line of credit. He traveled around the country to meet with 15 banks—but none were yet stepping up.

Sources: Nitasha Tiku, "When Your Bank Stops Lending," *Inc.*, July 2009, 58–61; and Christopher Schweitzer and Kevin Semcken, "Everyday Listening," *Audiologists*, March 2, 2010, www.audiology.advanceweb.com; Jay Palmer, "Technology Trader: Gadget of the Week: Phoning It In," *Barron's*, August 4, 2008; Christopher Schweitzer, "Mind the Porta! The Effect of Severe Microphone Inlet Occlusion," *Hearing Review*, June 2008, www.hearingreview.com; and Christopher Schweitzer and Desmond Smith, "From Horsepower to Hearpower," *Hearing Review*, July 2009, www.hearingreview.com.

Questions

1. Kevin Semcken identified some possible alternative solutions to his financing problem. Did he come up with all possible alternatives, or can you think of more?
2. Do you agree with board member Rob Cascella, who told Kevin to concentrate on producing headphones and put off the Sound Fit for later … or do you agree with Kevin, who sees Sound Fit as the future of Able Planet? Defend your choice.
3. As a small business consultant, what would you advise Kevin Semcken do to guide Able Planet through its financial storm?

Chapter 10 Case

To Sue or Not to Sue

Jonathan Hoffman got an unpleasant surprise in the spring of 2003. An employee had seen books and flash cards in a local Target that looked suspiciously like those made by his company, School Zone Publishing. Unfortunately, his employee was correct. The composition, fonts, language, and concepts screamed copycat. He turned a book over and it all made sense—the competing publisher was Dogs in Hats.

Peter Alfini started Dogs in Hats just two months before, after resigning as School Zone's vice president of national sales and marketing. As if to pour salt in Hoffman's wounds, Alfini had taken two former School Zone designers with him to Dogs in Hats. Now the competing workbooks and flash cards were beside Hoffman's on the shelves of School Zone's largest customer. Target accounted for about 10 percent of School Zone's sales.

Alfini claims that all of Dogs in Hats products came from his own ideas and resources. He had worked in educational publishing for more than a decade before joining School Zone. But Hoffman could not believe that Alfini had used what he learned at School Zone from product design and marketing to equipment and contacts to launch Dogs in Hats. Hoffman was infuriated.

Hoffman called an emergency meeting of his executive team—which includes his mother, Joan, the company's president and co-founder, and his sister, Jennifer Dexter, the vice president of design and development—and his attorney. They analyzed Alfini's products spread across the table. In one example, a School Zone alphabet flash card featured a drawing of a blond girl in pigtails with green bows and a yellow shirt collar and with a blue capital G on the card's flip side. A Dogs in Hats alphabet flash card was nearly identical, except for the girl's hair color, which was brown. They all reached the same conclusion: School Zone's intellectual property had been stolen. The executive team had little choice but to take Dogs in Hats to court.

Summer sales data confirmed Hoffman's worst fears. School Zone revenue fell by 23 percent over one six-week period, when Dogs in Hats products were side by side at Target. Hoffman became a man obsessed with preparing the legal case against Alfini. When he suspected one of his salespeople of passing company information to Alfini, he didn't know who he could trust. In contrast to his normal management style, he limited access to the copy room and banned employees from the office on weekends and after hours. But he was doing what he had to do.

In August 2003, School Zone filed a complaint in federal district court in western Michigan listing 84 allegations against Dogs in Hats. Hoffman was seeking payment for damages and attorneys' fees. Furthermore, he was demanding that Alfini destroy all materials that infringed on School Zone's copyrighted and trademarked material. In Dogs in Hats' response to the complaint, Alfini denied most of the allegations, conceding only that he had hired former employees of School Zone and had re-entered School Zone's property after resigning.

The extensive discovery process lasted for more than two years. School Zone had spent close to $200,000 on legal filings and attorneys' fees. Joan Hoffman and Dexter were begging Hoffman to drop the case. But Jonathan was haunted by the thought of what his father would have done. Hoffman's father Jim started School Zone in 1979 and had passed away a few months before the Alfini affair began. "Jim Hoffman would have fire in his eyes," his son believed. The company's attorneys had warned that if School Zone did not defend its marks now, it would be increasingly more difficult to do so in the future. So Hoffman wouldn't drop the case.

In March 2005, a judge magistrate sent the parties into mediation. Neither side should have been surprised; western Michigan courts regularly seek alternative means of resolving disputes over litigation. But Hoffman now faced a dilemma: whether to compromise via mediation and put an end to the case or to hold out for a shot at total victory in court.

_____

Sources: Lora Kolodny, "Jonathan Hoffman Was Sure a Former Staffer Had Stolen His Company's Ideas," *Inc.*, September 2005, 55–56; Patrick Sauer "Talk about Some Bad Hires," *Inc.*, March 2008, 74; Karyn Peterson "A Smart Start," *Playthings*, November 2007, 12; and Troy Dreier "Educational Software," *PC Magazine*, September 6, 2005, 149–184.

Questions

1. Hoffman's gut told him to litigate aggressively. But do you think that was a smart move?
2. Should he settle? Or should he press his case before a judge?
3. Put yourself in Hoffman's place. What would you do?

Chapter 11 Case

Specialize or Diversify?

Dimension One Spas was founded by Bob Hallam in 1977 and has grown to become one of the world's leading manufacturers of hot tubs and aquatic fitness systems. The company was first established as a chain of retail hot tub stores. But because Bob and wife Linda Hallam received requests from their retail customers that were not being fulfilled by hot tub makers at the time, the husband-wife team refocused Dimension One into a manufacturing business. The company grew to 450 distributors in 35 countries with international sales comprising 35 percent of the company's business. Before the economy unravelled, 2007 annual sales hit a peak of $57 million.

But one morning in November 2009, Hallam had a lot on his mind as he strode through the lobby. The business news was bad. The housing market was in full collapse. Dealers were struggling to secure financing for their spa purchases, and few consumers seemed interested in shelling out $15,000 to $25,000 for what suddenly seemed like the most discretionary of items. For only the second time in its history, the company's annual sales were shrinking.

Hallam called a companywide meeting to confront the crisis head-on. "There's been a fundamental shift in the industry," he began. The company's sales were plummeting, he said. If Dimension One ever hoped to grow again, it would need to quickly move in a whole new direction. But how? Making what? Hot tubs were all that Hallam knew.

Sales were tumbling—2010 revenue was expected to drop to just $28 million—and Hallam knew he had to act. Doing nothing would condemn his company to mediocrity or worse. Hallam considered the option of selling the business. In fact, a buyer had approached him a year earlier. At the time, Hallam considered the offer too low and turned it down. Another option was to lay off employees, continue focusing on hot tubs, and try to rehire when and if the market rebounded.

Just surviving was not good enough, though; Hallam wanted to thrive. What could the company do to reinvent itself? Could they produce products for other industries? He liked to think of his company as a kind of idea lab in the world of plastics and thermoforming, the process of heating plastic in order to mold it. The factory was now operating only four days a week, so Hallam looked for something to fill his excess capacity.

It was not the first time Hallam diversified his product lines. Two years earlier, Hallam realized that many of his dealers were loading up with competitors' low-end spa products. So Dimension One launched a new line of colorful, portable, and lower-cost plug-in tubs under the brand Spa Berry. A group of the company's more creative staff members brainstormed business opportunities outside the hot tub market—including urinals and horse trailers.

When the economy tanked, Hallam realized product tweaking wasn't enough—they needed radical change. "He told us if we wanted to be a big company again, hot tubs alone won't get us there," James Hedgecock, the company's 32-year-old director of business development, recalls Hallam saying at the November meeting. "We would have to get some other things going."

A bad fall turned into a worse winter. "We sold nothing in November and December," Hallam says. "Literally nothing." Hallam closed the factory for four weeks. He cut his pay 50 percent and his top executives' pay 5 percent. A series of layoffs brought Dimension One's employee count to 175 from a high of 400 a few years earlier. "It's tough to swallow, because they're all like family" says Hallam. He had to do something … but what?

Sources: Jason Del Rey, "A Hot-Tub Maker Hits Hard Times," *Inc.*, November 2009, 68–72; "The Science behind the Soak," April 16, 2009, via www.d1spas.com; "2008 Most Admired CEO Awards," *San Diego Business Journal*, January 16, 2009, via www.d1spas.com; and www.d1spas.com/founders-bio.

Questions

1. Should Hallam come up with some new products or continue to concentrate on hot tubs?
2. If new products are the answer, what should they be?
3. What are your recommendations to revive Dimension One?

Chapter 12 Case

Healthy Grub for Man's Best Friend

Some small businesses gain instant fans, often because their products or services strike a nerve to customers or generate buzz. But getting those customers to become loyal fanatics can be a challenge.

Marco Giannini's natural dog treat company, Dogswell, had seen annual sales of items such as Happy Hips and Mellow Mut grow from zero to $17 million in five years. With that kind of loyalty, he wanted to take Dogswell into the much bigger market for natural pet food.

Marco was fresh out of business school and had experience starting one company, a natural beverage company called Clear Day, had gone bust in 2003. Giannini had overspent on an unproven concept—forcing him to fold the business, give up his apartment, and sack out on his father's couch. That was where he decided to launch Dogswell later that year. The idea was to create healthy dog treats enhanced with supplements to help fight conditions such as arthritis and hip dysplasia—something Giannini's childhood dog, Emily, had suffered from.

Giannini attributes the success of Dogswell to the "no frills" attitude of the product packaging. "It's about simplicity. It's a simple product line with easy-to-read ingredients. We make everything easier for the customer, even the product names. The Breathies are for a dog's breath. The Hippies are for a dog's hips—it's very self-explanatory and that's what people appreciate."

Dogswell had seen more than 100 percent growth each year since its launch in 2004. The company had 21 employees, 60 varieties of treats, and revenue of $17 million. So all was well, but Giannini felt he had outgrown the dog treats niche. "I wanted to become a household name, and I figured, food was the way to get us there," he says. Many of Dogswell's customers had the same idea: For years, they had sent the company's Los Angeles offices e-mails asking when Dogswell was going to introduce a line of dog food.

In the spring of 2008, Giannini decided the timing was right and he had enough cash on hand to take the plunge. He hired food scientists who worked on recipes for kibble, and after settling on one that seemed right, he contracted with a food manufacturer. He sent the kibble to a testing facility to stage a series of canine "focus groups." The result: Dogs preferred Dogswell kibble 15 to 1 over the leading natural-food brand. "That's what made us press the Go button," Giannini says. Meanwhile, his sales team hit the dog parks and retail stores to quiz people about packaging.

With product developed, Giannini had to figure out how to launch it. Obviously, he couldn't personally drive his product to customers, as he had in 2003. Dogswell was a national brand now, with successful accounts at retailers such as Whole Foods and Target. He would need national distribution and a full-blown marketing plan immediately.

Dogswell bought a warehouse on the East Coast and hired 15 employees, most of them in sales. Finally, in September, Dogswell shipped its first bags of Happy Hips kibble to about 1,000 stores nationwide. To entice customers, the company offered coupons for a free $10.99 bag of kibble with every purchase of a 15-ounce bag of treats, which retails for $16 to $20.

It didn't take long for the rollout strategy to begin straining at the seams. Salespeople complained that their take-home pay wasn't what they had been promised. Credit memos from stores looking for their rebates from those free $10.99 bags of food were starting to pile up. "I felt like I was losing control of the company," Giannini says. "I felt like I was losing control of everything."

Upping the ante even more, Dogswell was scheduled to have its first board meeting with its brand-new private equity investors in March. The investors knew that the dog-food rollout had been troubled. Soon, they were going to want to know how Giannini intended to fix things. He had three months to come up with a plan.

Regrettably, Giannini wasn't around much to deal with these problems. He and Berenice Officer, Dogswell's chief financial officer, were busy making the rounds of private equity firms, in a drive to raise capital to finance the company's brand-building efforts. At least things had been going well on the funding front—especially with TSG Consumer Partners in San Francisco. Most private equity investors had grown cautious, but TSG was continuing to invest and liked Dogswell's track record of rapid growth. By late November, TSG appeared close to signing a deal.

The fact that Dogswell's numbers were slipping wasn't immediately apparent to either party. "They asked for updates, but it was hard to detect what was different," says Officer. Indeed, Dogswell closed a deal with TSG on December 31.

But when Giannini and Officer sat down a few days later with the fourth-quarter results, the damage was clear. They had less than three months to stop the food line from siphoning off the profits from the next quarter. And they had to figure out what they were going to tell their new investors at TSG.

Sources: Nitasha Tiku, "Lining Up Investors for a Turnaround," *Inc.*, December 2009, 56–63; Raymund Flandez, "Entrepreneurs Strive to Turn Buzz into Loyalty," *Wall Street Journal*, July 21, 2009, B4; Alexa Hyland, "He's Making Pet Food the Natural Way," *Los Angeles Business Journal*, November 17, 2008, 1; "Healthy Choice," *Pet Business*, September 2008, 146; and Nichole Torres, "Young Millionaires," *Entrepreneur*, September 2008, 63.

Questions

1. Dogswell's marketing plans were ambitious, but were not working. What is their primary problem?
2. Would money from the new investors solve the problem? What other options do they have?
3. What do you recommend Giannini do to save the company?

Chapter 13 Case

Big-Box or Specialty Shop?

Lance Fried is an electrical engineer who loves to design new products. He and a buddy were watching surfers and scenery at the beach near his home in Del Mar, California, when the buddy dropped his 20 Gig iPod into a cooler full of water and ice. The trashed iPod gave Fried an idea—to make an MP3 player that would work underwater.

Fried spent months tinkering with his invention, a waterproof MP3 player designed specifically for athletes who need tunes while surfing, swimming, waterskiing, or snowboarding. Like most all entrepreneurs, Fried had invested his personal savings but he had also somehow convinced half a dozen friends to work for him for free (pretty smooth).

By August 2004, Fried finished a working prototype. It was lightweight (40 grams), with a 40-hour battery and lots of memory (for 2004). The headphones wrap tightly around ears, and all of it is waterproofed using a proprietary technology. He projected to sell the units for $180.

It was then that Fried brought Greg Houlgate into the story. Houlgate was a friend who served on Freestyle's board and had worked as a sales strategist for a number of large sporting goods companies, including Callaway Golf. Houlgate showed the player to some of his contacts in the big-box retail world. "I've never had such a quick and positive response on any consumer electronics," he says.

Lance was amazed when Houlgate told him that major retailers—including Best Buy and Bass Pro Sporting Goods—wanted to put his gadget on their shelves side-by-side with players by giants like Apple and Sony. Fried knew that such a deal with just a single big chain could be worth an instant million dollars in revenue.

But the idea also scared him. Distribution via mass retailers had never been part of the San Diego start-up's plan. Instead, the idea always had been to start small, selling through specialty shops. A big-box strategy meant a whole new business plan—one that would involve mass production and a potentially huge up-front investment. Oh yeah, and retailers wanted the players in time for the holiday shopping season, which was just four months away.

How, or should, Freestyle capitalize on that interest? Fried quickly convened a meeting of his three-man board at Jimmy O's, a local ocean-view hangout. Houlgate presented the good news to the third partner, Mike Brower. "Mass distribution gets your name out fast and gives you an instant hit," Houlgate said. "Your vendors really start to take you seriously." That wasn't the only advantage. With mainstream retailers on board, it would be easier to attract investors. That part appealed to Fried, who was ready for money to come into rather than out of his own bank account.

But Brower, CFO of the popular sunglasses company Spy Optic, was not jumping on board. His experience working at sporting goods companies had always been to start small, get an influential niche group to love you, and go for bigger distribution deals only after that groundwork had been laid. How would Freestyle get its key customer groups—surfers and snowboarders—into big, unhip retail outlets like Best Buy and Bass Pro? And what would Freestyle have to give for the privilege of a good position on big-box shelves? "They'll make you a commodity if you don't know how to negotiate, asking for discounts that just kill your margins," Brower said.

Ramping up production would be no small feat also. It would require a significant capital investment. How could Freestyle find that kind of money? Would the company's manufacturing partners be able to maintain quality if orders suddenly spiked? How would the company get more attention than competing MP3 player brands manufactured by corporate giants and backed by multimillion-dollar marketing campaigns?

Fried had to make a huge decision—fast. The action sports retail trade show—where independent retailers go to test and order new gear to sell at their surf, dive, skate, and snowboard shops for the holiday season—was just weeks away. Making a big splash at the show had always been part of Freestyle's plan. If Fried signed on for a big-box deal, that plan would have to change.

Sources: From Lora Kolodny, "Case Study," *Inc.*, April 2005, 44–45; Brandi Stewart, "As Easy as MP3," *Fortune Small Business*, September 2007, 96; Darren Dahl, "Outside the Big Box," *Inc.*, April 2007, 54; and Reed Albergotti, "For the Half Pipe," *Wall Street Journal*, December 22, 2007, W7.

Questions

1. Can Fried really say "no" to the big-box retailers? Why or why not?
2. What do you think Lance should do?

Chapter 14 Case

The Price Is … Wrong?

Change can be hard … and when you start messing with people's music, well watch out. In this case, customers of eMusic were a little upset by a rise in subscription rates—as much as 100 percent for some subscribers. But there was a bigger source of outrage.

eMusic was founded in 1998 as *the* download site for the best place to discover independent artists—those not affiliated with major record labels. But eMusic had just signed a deal with the opposite of small independent labels, Sony BMG. The deal promised to add a million new songs by artists like Bruce Springsteen, Michael Jackson, and Bob Dylan, to the site. But many long-time users saw the addition of mainstream artists as a betrayal of the cool, alternative space eMusic was supposed to be.

CEO Danny Stein expected "the very unpleasant probability that we'd get some hate mail from very impassioned users." Still, reading e-mail that began with "Stupid" and got nastier was a little unnerving. Stein was convinced that the Sony deal was a good one, both for users and for the company. He also knew that prices had to go up. But they could have done a better job of explaining the changes to eMusic's core audience. Now Stein felt like a fireman with serious fires he had to extinguish.

Pricing had always been a contentious issue at eMusic. Stein and his partners purchased the service from Vivendi in 2003. One of the first things they did was to abandon the site's initial price structure of $9.99 a month for unlimited downloads. Instead, they offered customers a menu of monthly subscription plans. Current subscribers complained, but the new monthly rates were about a fourth of the price at iTunes—about 25 cents per track compared to 99 cents. By 2007, the number of eMusic subscribers grew to some 400,000.

Customers were generally happy to pay less per tune, but as the laws of supply and demand explain, many of the record labels supplying the site with songs were not. For indie artists, eMusic was a great outlet, with an audience of passionate music fans eager to discover new talent. But lower prices for users meant lower payments for the labels and their artists, sometimes less than 15 cents a track. Indeed, in 2007, several prominent labels, including Drag City and Tzadik, pulled their catalogs from the site, citing the low payments.

The only way Stein could prevent even more labels from bailing was to raise prices for subscribers. But eMusic couldn't get away with another price hike without including a value added in return. He brought together his executive team and some eMusic subscribers for a series of focus groups. The feedback trend pointed in one direction: broaden the eMusic catalog. Since eMusic was already connected with all the independent labels, Stein says, "It was pretty obvious that in order to take a big swing, we needed to start working with the major labels."

Joining forces with a major label once would have seemed unthinkable, but the world of digital music was changing fast. eMusic was unique for online music sites—at least legit ones—songs were sold in unencrypted MP3 format. MP3 means that once you buy a song, it was yours to burn it to as many CDs or listen to it on as many different players as you wanted. On iTunes, by contrast, music files were sold with digital rights management, or DRM, protection limiting how and where they could be used. Such protections were added at the insistence of the major labels, which were struggling to discourage piracy online.

Stein's conversations with the major labels could never get past the stubborn DRM issue as early as 2003. But by 2008, all four of the major labels—EMI, Warner, Universal, and Sony BMG—had agreed to make at least some of their catalogs available in an unrestricted format. And Sony was open to putting its back catalog (songs older than two years) of one million songs on eMusic.

Stein knew that eMusic could bring on a major label, but should they? Their core identity was being the Web's top independent music store. But he was sure that most customers cared more about an artist's music than which record label it was on and happy to pay more for access to more music. Too many potential customers were leaving the site because they didn't recognize any artists.

A bigger problem was eMusic customers who joined before 2003. Their subscription plans had been grandfathered through subsequent price changes. These tens of thousands of people were now paying legacy prices that were far lower than those paid by newer customers, dragging down revenue. Was it time to finally get them up to date? "We knew this was the area where we were susceptible to taking the biggest criticisms," Stein says. Was there any way to soften the blow? Stein wasn't so sure. "At some point," he says, "we just had to take our medicine."

Sources: Adam Bluestein, "Coping with Fury at a Price Hike," *Inc.*, March 2010, 54–58; Cortney Harding, "Major Problem?" *Billboard*, June 13, 2009, 11; Eamonn Forde, "Major Changes," *Music Week*, May 13, 2009, 18; Antony Bruno, "6 Questions with David Pakman," *Billboard*, July 26, 2009, 10; and www.emusic.com/about.

Questions

1. Danny Stein faces several problems with eMusic, some with conflicting ends. What problems do you see?
2. What possible alternative solutions exist to the problems identified in question 1? Consider the impact of each alternative on other areas of the business.
3. What recommendation(s) do you make for Stein?

Chapter 15 Case

Employees Fight to Save the Farm

Hamakua Springs Country Farms, located on the slopes of Mauna Kea on the Big Island of Hawaii, is run by three generations of the Ha family.

Richard Ha is president of Hamakua Springs, concentrating on researching and experimenting with new products. Richard's farming experience goes way back. When he finished college with an accounting degree, his father asked him to come run his 40-acre chicken farm at Waiakea Uka. Richard decided to grow bananas on part of his father's farm, and he talked grocery stores into saving him banana boxes. He traded chicken manure to other farmers for banana plants.

That was 30 years ago, and that banana business took off and evolved into Hamakua Springs Country Farms, a 600-acre banana and vegetable farm. Although Richard is its president, Hamakua Springs truly is a family business. "The family members all have a vote, and I have three-quarters of a vote," he laughs.

Richard Ha tends not to take himself too seriously, calling his eco-farming blog "Ha Ha Ha!" But earlier this year, Ha was not smiling. He made the difficult decision to shut down the banana-growing operation, a move that would leave 400 acres unplanted. His costs were soaring—banana prices were flat or declining, and there seemed to be no end in sight.

On the first Friday in April, Ha delivered the bad news to his nine full-time banana pickers. But on Monday morning, Ha was surprised to find that seven of the workers had shown up to discuss keeping the farm going. His crew members had a fairly sophisticated plan: plant a less labor-intensive variety of banana that would require less land and could be grown closer to the packing facilities. That would do away with the need to hire additional workers at harvest time. Ha was tempted. The last thing Ha wanted to do was close down his farm and fire his trusted full-time workers. But all of his business instincts were telling him that was what needed to be done.

Bananas are the most popular fruit in the world and the fourth most important crop on the planet after rice, wheat, and corn. Consequently, banana production operates on a gigantic industrial scale with five huge companies controlling 80 percent of the global trade between them.

In Hawaii, most pineapples and sugar cane are sold to consumers off the island. The mainland United States gets bananas from Central America, so Ha primarily sold to the island market. He eventually became one of the state's more successful farmers, responsible for as much as a third of Hawaii's bananas. He was among the first in the state to develop the market for apple bananas, a small, extra-sweet variety that carries a premium price. Hamakua Springs is also one of only a few banana farms to receive an "Eco-OK" certification from the Rainforest Alliance, an influential environmental group. Ha was diversifying operations into other crops—including tomatoes, lettuce, and Japanese cucumbers—that he grew hydroponically.

Cheap imports from Central America increasingly flooded Hawaiian markets, forcing a number of banana farms in the state to close, including Ha's largest competitor. Independent banana producers all over were struggling; in the Westward Islands in the Caribbean, 20,000 out of 25,000 banana farmers went out of production between 1992 and 2010. The prices of fertilizer and energy, always higher on Hawaii than on the mainland, were climbing every day, taking a bigger and bigger bite out of profits. Because of the constant refrigeration needed to control the ripening of green bananas, Ha's utility bills recently hit $15,000 per month.

Ha's biggest concern, as with many small businesses, was finding good workers. "Our yields were suffering, because we were struggling to keep a stable work force," says Ha, who figured it was only a matter of time before the farm started losing money. For months, he had wrestled with the idea of closing down the banana farm. Ha carefully calculated his operational costs and profitability on weekly spreadsheets that showed a gradual downward trend line for profits. Finally, in early April, he discussed closing down with the rest of his family, who all agreed that time was running out. "We were doing OK," says Ha. "But I thought it would be better to shut it down rather than lose money and be forced to shut down later."

Ha was shocked that his full-time pickers made their case—he figured they would go for unemployment or hunt for other jobs. Picking bananas is about as tough as manual labor gets. A banana picker carefully notches away at a banana bunch with a razor-sharp machete. He then positions himself below the bunch so that, with the final notch, it falls on his shoulders. He then carries his bundle over to a nearby trailer. In a typical day, a worker might handle 100 bunches, or more than 10,000 pounds, of bananas.

There may be easier ways to make $12 an hour, but the job at Ha's farm provided full health benefits and lots of free fruits and vegetables. "It's hard work, but it's good work," says Eric Garcia, who's been picking bananas for Ha for five years and was among those lobbying to save the jobs. "You get to work out in the fresh air, mostly by yourself. I said let's do whatever it takes to keep it going."

Other full-time blue-collar jobs with benefits and decent pay were rare. The only other work at similar pay is in hotels and restaurants. But most of those jobs were located on the other side of the island. For Ha's pickers, that would mean a three-hour round-trip commute by car and hundreds of dollars per month in gasoline.

When the workers showed up that Monday morning, they huddled with Ha for several hours. Together they penciled out a plan that would eliminate the 100 acres of apple bananas, which yield less per acre than regular bananas and are more difficult to pick. A second step would be to move the remaining banana plantings much closer to the packinghouse and chiller room to reduce the workload and speed up turnaround. The workers argued that they could run the operation with a much smaller workforce and get nearly 10 percent more output per acre. The higher productivity would be sufficient to return the banana operation to healthy profitability.

Ha listened to the plan closely. Under normal circumstances, he wouldn't consider such an idea. But he saw some factors changing that might work to his farm's advantage. Ha knew that energy savings from a hydroelectric generator he planned to install along a stream on his property would offset increasing oil prices. At the same time, the surge in oil prices was hurting importers far more than it was hurting him. Importers were paying shipping companies a 30 percent or higher fuel surcharge on containers coming to the islands. The weakness in the dollar had further pushed up prices for Central American bananas.

Considering these factors, Ha and his family saw that a sustained period of higher prices for imported bananas and decreased costs could give them the profit margin cushion they needed, and might make the workers' proposal tenable. "For the first time in recent memory, banana prices did not fall steeply during the summer," says Ha. "That made us think something had changed."

Sources: Alex Salkever, "How Richard Ha's Workers Saved His Company," *Inc.,* August 1, 2008, 54; Michael McCarthy, "Why Are Bananas So Cheap, and What Does It Mean for Producers?" *The Independent* (London), October 6, 2009, 34; "Banana Wars," *The Grocer,* May 29, 2010, 44; "Banana Glut Is Bad News for Growers," *Northern Territory News* (Australia), and June 16, 2010, 34; www.hamakuasprings.com/about.

Questions

1. Put yourself in Ha's situation, and analyze the pros and cons of his workers' proposition.
2. Since Hawaii is so isolated and Ha sells bananas locally, why is he affected by international competitors?
3. What would you recommend the family running Hamakua Springs Country Farms do?

Chapter 16 Case

Family Matters

Accurate Perforating Co. punches holes in sheet metal—LOTS of holes. The company, founded in 1940, perforated 40 million pounds of sheet metal annually (and, we assume, accurately) for industrial and architectural purposes.

Accurate's president Larry Cohen had a meeting scheduled with his bankers at the Chicago headquarters of Cole Taylor Bank, but he was not looking forward to it. The Chicago-based metal company owned by Cohen's family had run out of operating capital. Cole Taylor had loaned Accurate $1.5 million two years earlier. In that dreaded meeting, the bank gave Cohen two choices: liquidate the business or find a new lender. Cohen was shocked by the ultimatum. "They were basically going to put us out of business," he says.

For decades, Cohen and his father, Ralph (the company founder), had focused on one thing: putting as many holes in as many sheets of metal as possible. They bought the metal from steel mills in the Chicago region, punched holes in it, and sold it in bulk to distributors, which then sold it to metal workshops. There the metal was fabricated and finished—that is, cut, folded to specification, and painted—and sold to manufacturers of products like speaker grilles and ceiling tiles. "We were really just selling tonnage," Cohen says. "We stayed away from sophisticated products, and as a result we wound up in a very competitive situation where the only thing we were selling was price."

Accurate's business model became increasingly unsustainable due to a worldwide glut of steel forcing prices down. The costs of manufacturing steel climbed while its prices stayed flat, shrinking once-healthy profit margins. Most competitors found more profitable niches in fabricating, finishing, and selling metal directly to manufacturers, but Accurate survived through militant budgeting. "If we couldn't pay cash, we didn't do it," recalls Cohen, who was unwilling to invest in the equipment required to become a fabricator. While times were so difficult, employees built perforating machines from scratch—repairing them only when absolutely necessary—and used outmoded manufacturing processes developed by the Cohen family way back in the 1940s. Annual revenue stayed between $10 million and $15 million for more than two decades. Accurate was decades behind the competition in terms of both technology and business strategy.

Aaron Kamins was the only member of the family's younger generation working at the company. Kamins was the 36-year-old nephew of Cohen who took over day-to-day operations as general manager in 2001. Even though decades behind competition in both technology and business strategy, Kamins says, "There was a culture here that resisted change. Everyone was comfortable with what they were doing. We were making a living and that was that." Kamins, who had worked on Accurate's factory floor since graduating from college, hoped to steer the company in a new direction. In 2002, with Cohen's approval, he borrowed $1.5 million from Cole Taylor Bank to purchase Semrow Perforated & Expanded Metals, a business in Des Plaines, Illinois, that produced and sold fabricated products. He hired two of the company's top executives, Mike Beck and Mike Zarnott, to oversee the division, along with 10 of Semrow's 40 factory workers.

Selling fabricated metal directly to manufacturers generated $1.5 million, but Beck, Accurate's director of new product development and engineering, and Zarnott, the company's director of sales and marketing, had bigger aspirations. They begged Kamins to break from the 1960s-type marketing. Kamins refused, being worried about diverting too much time and money away from the core commodity business, and Cohen agreed. "Everything I said about marketing Aaron thought was rubbish," says Zarnott, who struggled with a marketing budget of $15,000 a year—split between Yellow Page ads and a listing in the Thomas Registry. Beck and Zarnott were not amused.

Spring of 2003 was a downturn period for Accurate. The Iraqi invasion made customers skittish. Orders fell by 50 percent. The bank "strongly recommended" that the company hire Stonegate Group, a turnaround firm in Deerfield, Illinois. Their primary recommendation was to renegotiate payment schedules with vendors. Meanwhile, Cohen liquidated half a million dollars in personal real estate to pay overdue bills. To cut costs, the company laid off 13 of its 85 employees.

Even with Stonegate's stellar advice, Accurate lost more than $500,000 in 2003. Then came the meeting with Cole Taylor that December; the bank agreed to give Cohen a few weeks to devise a plan. He immediately began looking for a new lender but was able to borrow an additional $400,000 in loans from friends—just enough to purchase three months' worth of steel. That meant that the company had 90 days to make some serious decisions about Accurate's future.

Liquidation seemed too dramatic because Cohen believed that Accurate could thrive with the right business model. Another alternative was to continue cutting costs and hope for a rebound in steel prices—a strong possibility due to growing demand from China. Beck and Zarnott's idea of scaling back the commodity business to focus on selling finished metal seemed like the smartest long-term strategy. But that alternative would take huge amounts of time and money to perfect the new manufacturing process, retrain factory workers, cultivate new clients, and revamp Accurate's nuts-and-bolts image —time and money they didn't have.

Cohen wrestled with the most difficult question: Should he replace his nephew with a more seasoned executive? Kamins had little formal business training. Was he the person to lead a turnaround? "I worried that we would just continue repeating all the mistakes that we had made," Cohen says. An outsider would offer a fresh perspective, but hiring a CEO would be expensive and time-consuming. Cohen felt like the owner of a baseball team with a losing manager. "I didn't know if a new guy would do a better job," he says. "I just knew the old guy wasn't doing a good job."

What do you think? Does Aaron Kamins deserve one last chance to save the company?

_____

Sources: From Max Chafkin, "Case Study," *Inc.,* June 2006, 58–60; www .accurateperforating.com; Allison Enright, "Not Just Metal with Holes," *Marketing News,* June 15, 2007, 7; and Patrick Sauer, "Family Ties," *Inc.,* August 2007, 18.

Questions

1. Put yourself in Larry Cohen's position. What would you see as your most immediate problem? What are your long-term problems?
2. Would you keep Aaron Kamins as CEO? Why or why not? If you fire him, who would do the job?
3. What do you recommend Cohen do to save Accurate Perforating?

Chapter 17 Case

Lost in Translation

Claudia Mirza and Azam Mirza spotted a trend—the growth of the non-English-speaking population in the United States, increasing the need for translators and interpreters. So they proceeded to start a translation business, with big ambitions. For a while, Akorbi Language Consulting thrived. They broke the $1 million annual revenue mark in just two years, bolstered by translation jobs for corporate clients such as Southwest Airlines and Aetna. But that was their revenue plateau. They spent the next three years feeling pretty dejected. Marketing and revenue dollars were headed in opposite directions—the more they spent on sales and marketing, the more their business seemed to shrink. The Mirzas were on the verge of the entrepreneurial unthinkable: bringing in an outsider as CEO. "Just because I own the business doesn't mean I am the best person to lead the company," says Claudia. "Are we the right people to run it, or should we let someone else take the reins?" Azam wondered.

You can surely understand the reasons for their thoughts of self-doubt—they have marketable skills, the global translation market is worth billions of dollars, but their business plan is not becoming business reality. Indeed, the Mirzas feared that getting to the next level of growth and profitability may be something they could not do on their own.

Hiring an outsider to manage her business would be especially tough for Claudia. She was always a self-starter, launching her first business, a copy center and translation service, to put herself through business school in her native Colombia. That business supported not only her as a student but also two full-time employees—translating study guides for college students. After graduating, she moved to the United States for a telecom job. After growing up in India, Azam had been an IT consultant at Ernst & Young before becoming a freelance IT worker. The pair dreamed of starting a business together. "We are skeptical about working in an environment where our life and livelihood are decided by someone else," said Azam.

Soon after the couple got married in 2002, they also joined her language skills with his technical talents to create software that would make it easy for corporate customers to automate high-volume routine translations. Their software would allow corporate clients to reduce their reliance on human translators.

Claudia began lining up pro bono work for some high-profile clients, such as the Dallas Arboretum and the Greater Dallas Hispanic Chamber of Commerce. Savings from previous careers financed the launch. Azam handled sales and project management, while Claudia oversaw translations.

Akorbi Language Consulting targeted large companies willing to spend several thousand dollars per translation contract. By November 2002, through word of mouth, they won their first paid project: translating brochures into Spanish for 3M. Workload and number of employees grew so that at least three translators worked on each job—including brief memos, billboards, or hefty insurance guides—to get the subtleties just right. Azam also helped companies find freelance IT talent.

Akorbi's staff grew to eight full-timers in Dallas; a dozen in Buenos Aires and Medellín, Colombia; and five tech developers in India, as well as a network of hundreds of freelance translators who pitched in on big jobs. The company had 33 language clients and nine IT customers. Revenue jumped from $20,000 to $1.2 million. Spanish translations accounted for about half the business, with Chinese a strong second.

Akorbi developed a reputation for its attention to cultural nuances and reliability. For example, a slogan for Dallas Area Rapid Transit, "Dump the Pump," was rendered into lyrical, rhyming Spanish by Akorbi: "Keep your wallet safe and say goodbye to the gas station" is the English rendering.

It turned out that demand for translation business was far greater than it was for IT, partly because of intense international IT competition. The Mirzas decided to cut IT staffing and concentrate on translations. This move freed Azam to use his tech skills to push so-called localization services, an offshoot of the translation business that helps companies adapt their Web sites and software to foreign markets.

But the proverbial next level was elusive. After two years under its new plan, Akorbi's language customers had increased to 56, but revenue had dipped to $904,000, even though the sales staff had increased from three to five people, with each employee making some 50 cold calls a day. Over $200,000 was spent on marketing in 2006 and 2007, including about 1,000 mailers sent out each week. Profits had been slightly in the black since 2005, but the Mirzas were not pleased with the small return received for all the time, energy, and money they had invested. Akorbi had received positive PR in many major publications, including *U.S. News and World Report*, *Dallas Morning News*, *Dallas Business Journal*, *Latina Style*, *Hispanic Trends*, *Al Día*, and *Forbes*, but that had not translated into profit. Something needed to be done, but what?

The Mirzas decided to get company-wide input to answer that question. They shut down the company for a day in October 2007 to bring together their Dallas employees and their top-producing Latin American translators in a rented conference room. International employees connected via teleconference for a marathon strategy session. The Mirzas started with a presentation that analyzed Akorbi and the translation market. But the day was also intended to boost morale. The staff took notes and threw out suggestions. The Mirzas decided to reconsider their pricing, which some staff members viewed as too low, and increase online presence. They also discussed opening a Washington, D.C., office to be in a better position to bid for government contracts. Says Maria Clara Buzzini, translation services manager, "The meeting helped us understand the big picture."

The strategy meeting was useful, but the Mirzas are still frustrated by lack of growth. "I'm tired of seeing the same million [revenue] number," says Claudia. She says 99 percent of Akorbi's customers return, but the company just can't seem to gain ground. "We want to know what we should be doing that we are not doing right," says Azam.

To help them answer that question, they say, they are on the verge of hiring a top-level outsider with more perspective and experience. That could be a CEO or a sales executive. Either way, says Claudia, "I know I need someone aggressive who can keep my company on its toes." But the Mirzas have yet to post a job opening because of worries about the risks of handing over their labor of love to another person. As Claudia is quick to point out, "At the end of the day, we are liable for what happens to this business."

Sources: Renuka Rayasam, "They Aimed High, but Now Their Translation Business Is Stuck," *Inc.*, October 2008, 67–70; "Claudia Mirza, Microentrepreneur of the Year," November 6, 2007, www.acciontexas.org; and www.akorbi.com/press-center.

Questions

1. Could a new CEO do better?
2. Would you recommend the Mirzas hire their own boss? What would that new job description include?
3. If hiring a CEO is not the answer, what should they do to get their business to the next level?

Back in the Saddle

When Tom Pastorius opened Penn Brewery in 1986, he had modest goals—brew real German beer and serve it in a real German beer hall environment as the first craft brewery in Pennsylvania. Twenty-two years later, he was ready to step away. Pastorius had turned 65 when he retired from Penn Brewery, the company he had founded, then sold his majority interest in, then worked for as president. Tom's wife, Mary Beth, was fine with the idea of retirement. The couple had had a great run building the local Pittsburgh microbrewery and restaurant. But the time had come to kick back a bit and enjoy life.

It didn't take long before Tom started to feel bored. He was also frustrated watching what the new owners were doing with his company—and he still owned 20 percent of it. He was nostalgic for the early days, when he and Mary Beth worked endless hours to get the brewery up and running. In the spring of 2009, the new owners offered to sell him back his brewery for a small fraction of what they had paid him. Tom was thrilled.

The problem would be persuading Mary Beth. He knew she would be against jumping back into the brewery business. The couple had run the brewery together for 17 years, but she still felt pangs of guilt at the memory of her two young sons sleeping on a couch in the brewery office before she would carry them to the car in their pajamas. No way would she go back to the brewery. Tom put off the talk as long as he could. Then, in July 2009, he broached the topic: "There is this opportunity to buy back the brewery." Mary Beth was not amused, stating, "You are nuts." A few more times Tom brought up the subject again, but Mary Beth would just walk away.

The Pastorius family had built a successful microbrew production business, with Penn Pilsner being their flagship brand, making 15,000 barrels a year with $3.5 million in sales. Over the years, Penn Dark, Penn Weizen, Penn Oktoberfest, and other labels under their brand had racked up 14 medals at the Great American Beer Festival.

In 2003, they sold a majority equity position of the business to Birchmere Capital, a Pittsburgh private equity fund. Tom retained a 20 percent stake and stayed on as president for five years. The proceeds allowed the couple to pay off their home mortgage, pay for their two sons to go to private colleges, and still have plenty left over for retirement.

But Tom had been miserable working for the new owners. "I am not a good employee," he says. "I'm a solo act." Tom agreed with the new owners' strategy of turning Penn Brewery into a regional player. What he didn't like was the way they went about it. He fought over details such as installing a cooling system that he argued was too big for the operation. He unsuccessfully lobbied against a $120,000 billboard campaign. "We couldn't make enough beer to pay for it," he says. Sales went up, but expenses went up even more.

Tom couldn't take anymore when the new owners announced that they would outsource manufacturing to The Lion Brewery in Wilkes-Barre, Pennsylvania, laying off 8 of the 10 brewery employees. The many Penn Pilsner fans were just as upset as Tom. "For beer people in Pittsburgh, Penn Pilsner was the Holy Grail," says Paul Cosentino, leader of the Boilermaker Jazz Band, which often played at the brewery's restaurant. "If it was no longer made here and it didn't taste the same, why should we buy it?" Tom winced at the headlines in 2008 and 2009. Sales were dwindling. Birchmere closed the restaurant and sold off much of the brewing equipment. "It was so hard to sit back and watch this place sink," says Tom.

In 2009, Birchmere put the brewery up for sale. Tom started working on his business plan, beginning with a risk-benefit analysis. On the downside, the brewery was almost $1 million in debt. He would have to absorb the loss. The brand was tarnished. And he wasn't exactly young, but he still had plenty of experience and energy. He would much rather be making beer in Pittsburgh than playing golf in Florida. If he didn't rebuild the business, then the value of his 20 percent stake would be zero. With his reputation, he knew he could bring the lustre back to

Penn Pilsner if he returned production to the Victorian-era redbrick building.

Mary Beth seemed determined to talk Tom out of buying back the brewery—and her opinion certainly mattered. For 17 years she had developed the traditional German menu, selling potato pancakes and bratwurst. The couple debated all through the summer of 2009, with their two grown sons eventually weighing in. "They ganged up on me," Mary Beth said. "They were proud of the brewery. It had been part of their childhood. They wanted to save it." But Tom Jr. says he also sympathized with his mother. "She knew it was a slippery slope," he says. Mary Beth had already launched a new business of her own, restoring historic buildings. She felt liberated

away from the brewery. "It is the baby who never grows up," she says.

———

Sources: Cristina Rouvalis, "Case Study: When a Married Couple Disagree," *Inc.,* July, 2010, 70–74; Tim Schooley, "Penn Brewery Rolling Out Bottled Beer Again," *Pittsburgh Business Times,* July 23, 2010, via www.pennbrew.com; Bob Batz, "Founder Leads Group to Buy Back Brewery," *Pittsburgh Post-Gazette,* November 24, 2009, via www.pennbrew.com; and Rick Stouffer, "Penn Brewery Founder Ready to Have His Last Call," *Pittsburgh Tribune-Review,* May 24, 2008, via www.pennbrew.com.

Questions

1. What alternatives does the Pastorius family have to resolve their conflict?
2. What operations management principles would apply to running a microbrewery?
3. What would your recommendation be to Tom and Mary Beth?

Notes

Chapter 1

1. Small Business Administration, Office of Advocacy, "Firm Size Data," March 2010, www.sba.gov/advo.
2. Small Business Administration, Advocacy Small Business Statistics and Research "FAQs," March 2010.
3. Small Business Administration, Office of Advocacy, "Small Business Economic Indicators," June 2006, www.sba.gov/advo.
4. Small Business Administration, Office of Advocacy, "Frequently Asked Questions," June 2006, www.sba.gov/advo.
5. Small Business Administration, "Guide to SBA's Definition of Small Business," September 28, 2006, www.sba.gov/size/indexguide.html.
6. Small Business Administration, Office of Advocacy, "Small Business Economic Indicators," January 2010.
7. www.hoover.com, March 22, 2010.
8. John A. Byrne, "How Entrepreneurs Are Reshaping the Economy and What Big Companies Can Learn," *Business Week,* Enterprise Edition, October 1993, 12–18.
9. Laura D'Andrea Tyson, "Outsourcing: Who's Safe Anymore?" *Business Week,* February 23, 2004, 26.
10. Randall W. Forsyth, "Happy Anniversary for Finance, Not Small Business," *Barron's*, March 10, 2010.
11. Small Business Administration, Office of Advocacy, "Frequently Asked Questions," November 3, 2006, www.sba.gov/advo.
12. *Statistical Abstract of the United States* (Washington, DC: U.S. Government Printing Office, 2010), 494–495.
13. Small Business Administration, Office of Advocacy, "Frequently Asked Questions," March 23, 2010, www.sba.gov/advo.
14. Judith Cone, "Teaching Entrepreneurship in Colleges and Universities: How (and Why) a New Academic Field Is Being Built," January 2010, Kauffman Foundation, www.kauffman.org/entrepreneurship/teaching.
15. Small Business Administration, Office of Advocacy, *The Small Business Economy: A Report to the President* (Washington, DC: U.S. Government Printing Office, 2009).
16. Lauren Folino, "Fast Earners: Cool College Start-Ups 2010," *Inc.,* March 2010, 88.
17. Nichole L. Torres, "Leader of the Pack," *Entrepreneur*, March 2006.
18. Small Business Profile: United States, December 2006, www.sba.gov/advo.
19. Ying Lowery, "Dynamics of Minority-Owned Employer Establishments, 1997–2001," *Small Business Research Summary No. 251,* February 2005.
20. Ying Lowery, "Women in Business: A Demographic Review of Women's Business Ownership," *Small Business Research Summary No. 280,* August 2006.
21. Amy Choi, "How Minority-Owned Businesses Can Catch a Break," *BusinessWeekOnline*, December 7, 2009, 24.
22. Faye Rice, "How to Make Diversity Pay," *Fortune,* 8 August 1994, 79–86.
23. J. A. Schumpeter, *Capitalism, Socialism, and Democracy* (New York: Harper & Row, 1943).
24. Joshua S. Gans, David H. Hsu, and Scott Stern, "When Does Start-Up Innovation Spur the Gale of Creative Destruction?" *RAND Journal of Economics,* Winter 2002, 571–586.
25. "Report Examines Small Business Innovative Activity," *The Small Business Advocate,* December 1993, 10.
26. "Small Serial Innovators: The Small Firm Contribution to Technical Change," February 27, 2003, www.sba.gov/advo.
27. Dun & Bradstreet Corporation, Business Failure Record, as reported in "Business Failures by Industry: 1990 to 1998,"

Statistical Abstract of the United States (Washington, DC: U.S. Government Printing Office, 2001), 561.

28. Andrew L. Zacharakis, G. Dale Meyer, and Julio DeCastro, "Differing Perceptions of New Venture Failure: A Matched Exploratory Study of Venture Capitalists and Entrepreneurs," *Journal of Small Business Management,* July 1999, 1–14.

29. "Avoiding the Pitfalls," *Wall Street Journal Report on Small Business,* May 22, 1995, R1.

30. Richard Monk, "Why Small Businesses Fail," *CMA Management,* July/August 2000, 12–13; Udayan Gupta, "How Much?" *Wall Street Journal,* May 22, 1995, R7; and Stephanie N. Mehta, "Small Talk: An Interview with Wendell E. Dunn," *Wall Street Journal,* May 22, 1995.

31. Jack Welch and Suzy Welch, "The Danger of Doing Nothing," *Business Week,* July 10, 2006.

32. John Case, "The Wonderland Economy," *The State of Small Business,* March 16, 1995, 29.

33. James Aley, "Debunking the Failure Fallacy," *Fortune,* September 6, 1993, 21.

34. Brian Headd, "Redefining Business Success: Distinguishing between Closure and Failure," *Small Business Economics,* vol. 21, 2003, 51.

35. "Marriages and Divorces Number and Rate by State: 1990–2007," Statistical Abstract of the United States, 129th ed. 94.

36. Steven Burd, "Graduation Rates and Student Mobility," *Chronicle of Higher Education,* April 2, 2004, A22.

37. "Fish out of Water," *Economist,* October 31, 2009, 78.

Chapter 2

1. Robert Hisrich, "Entrepreneurship/Intrapreneurship," *American Psychologist,* February 1990, 209.

2. P. VanderWerf and C. Brush, "Toward Agreement on the Focus of Entrepreneurship Research: Progress without Definition," *Proceedings of the National Academy of Management Conference,* Washington, DC, 1989.

3. Denis Gregoire, Martin Noel, Richard Dery, and Jean-Pierre Bechard, "Is There Conceptual Convergence in Entrepreneurship Research? A Co-Citation Analysis of Frontiers of Entrepreneurship Research, 1981–2004," *Entrepreneurship Theory and Practice,* May 2006, 333–372.

4. Carol Moore, "Understanding Entrepreneurial Behavior: A Definition and Model," in *Academy of Management Best Paper Proceedings*, edited by J. A. Pearce II and R. B. Robinson, Jr., 46th Annual Meeting of the Academy of Management, Chicago, 1989, 66–70. See also William Bygrave, "The Entrepreneurial Paradigm (I): A Philosophical Look at Its Research Methodologies," *Entrepreneurship: Theory and Practice,* Fall 1989, 7–25; and William Bygrave and Charles Hofer, "Theorizing about Entrepreneurship," *Entrepreneurship: Theory and Practice,* Winter 1991, 13–22.

5. A. Shapiro and L. Sokol, "The Social Dimensions of Entrepreneurship," in *Encyclopedia of Entrepreneurship,* edited by J. A. Kent, D. L. Sexton, and K. H. Vesper (Englewood Cliffs, NJ: Prentice-Hall, 1992).

6. J. A. Schumpeter, *History of Economic Analysis* (New York: Oxford University Press, 1934).

7. William Gartner, "'Who Is an Entrepreneur?' Is the Wrong Question," *Entrepreneurship: Theory and Practice,* Summer 1989, 47. See also J. W. Carland, F. Hoy, W. R. Boulton, and J. A. C. Carland, "Differentiating Entrepreneurs from Small Business Owners: A Conceptualization," *Academy of Management Review*, 1984, 354–359; William Gartner, "What Are We Talking about When We Talk about Entre-

preneurship?" *Journal of Business Venturing,* 1990, 15–28.

8. Steven Covey, *The Seven Habits of Highly Effective People* (New York: Simon & Schuster, 1989), 95.

9. Peter Drucker, *Innovation and Entrepreneurship: Practice and Principles* (New York: Harper & Row, 1985).

10. Jess McCuan, "It's Good to Be King," *Inc.,* December 2003, 32.

11. Sanjay Goel and Ranjan Karri, "Entrepreneurs, Effectual Logic, and Over-Trust," *Entrepreneurship Theory and Practice,* July 2006, 480.

12. Jon Goodman, "What Makes an Entrepreneur?" *Inc.,* October 1994, 29.

13. David C. McClelland, *The Achieving Society* (New York: Van Nostrand Reinhold, 1961). See also David C. McClelland, "Achievement Motivation Can Be Developed," *Harvard Business Review,* November/December 1965; David Miron and David McClelland, "The Impact of Achievement Motivation Training on Small Business," *California Management Review,* Summer 1979, 13–28.

14. Robert Brochhaus and Pamela S. Horwitz, "The Psychology of the Entrepreneur," in *The Art and Science of Entrepreneurship,* edited by Donald Sexton and Raymond W. Smilor (Cambridge, MA: Ballinger, 1986), 25–48.

15. T. S. Hatten, "Student Entrepreneurial Characteristics and Attitude Change toward Entrepreneurship as Affected by Participation in an SBI Program," *Journal of Education for Business,* March/April 1995, 224–228.

16. Michael O'Neal, "Just What Is an Entrepreneur?" *Business Week* (Enterprise Edition), 1993, 104–112.

17. NFIB Foundation/American Express Travel, *A Small Business Primer,* (2003).

18. Jerome Katz, "The Institution and Infrastructure of Entrepreneurship,"

Entrepreneurship: Theory and Practice, Spring 1991, 85–102.

19. Judith Cone, "Teaching Entrepreneurship in Colleges and Universities: How (and Why) a New Academic Field Is Being Built," January 2010, Kauffman Foundation, www.kauffman.org /entrepreneurship/teaching.

20. "Best Schools for Entrepreneurs— Top 25 Undergrad Programs – 2009" April 1, 2010, *Entrepreneur.com.*

21. Fred Steingold, *Legal Guide for Starting and Running a Small Business,* 11th ed. (Berkeley, CA: Nolo Press, 2009).

22. James W. Reynolds and Steven Frost, "Uniform LLP Amendments Make Welcome Changes to Revised Uniform Partnership Act," *Journal of Limited Liability Companies,* Spring 1997, 189; James Hopson and Patricia Hopson, "Helping Clients Choose the Legal Form for a Small Business," *The Practical Accountant,* October 1990, 67–84.

23. Steingold.

24. "Legal Structure and Registration," *The Colorado Business Resource Guide* (Denver, CO: SBA and Colorado Office of Economic Development and International Trade, 2001). www.coloradosbdc .org, 15.

25. Thomas Stemmy, "Business Structure Basics," *Entrepreneur,* June 2010, www.entrepreneur .com/startingabusiness/startup basics

26. Society of Nonprofit Organizations "Setting Up a Nonprofit Organization," June 2010, www .snpo.org/resources/startup.php.

Chapter 3

1. For a more complete discussion of corporate social responsibility, see R. Griffin, *Management,* 10th ed. (Mason, OH: South-Western/ Cengage Learning, 2011). See also, Archer Carroll, "The Pyramid of Corporate Social Responsibility: Toward the Moral Management of Organizational Stakeholders," *Business Horizons,* July/August 1991, 39–48; and Richard Rodewald, "The Corporate Social Responsibility Debate: Unanswered Questions about the Consequences of Moral Reform," *American Business Law Journal,* Fall 1987, 443–466.

2. Gopal Kanji and Parvesh Chopra, "Corporate Social Responsibility in a Global Economy, *Total Quality Management,* February 2010, 119–143.

3. Milton Friedman and Rose Friedman *Free to Choose* (New York: Harcourt Brace Jovanovich, 1980); Milton Friedman, *Capitalism and Freedom* (Chicago: University of Chicago Press, 1963), 133.

4. "Social Responsibility: 'Fundamentally Subversive'?" interview with Milton Friedman, August 15, 1006, www.businessweek.com. Online Extra.

5. Milton Zall, "Small Business and the EEOC: An Overview," *Fleet Equipment,* March 2000, BIZM4.

6. Jack Gordon, "Rethinking Diversity," *Training,* January 1992, 23.

7. Cait Murphy, "Keeping Small Business Off the Street," *Fortune Small Business,* November 2003, 18.

8. Ken Rankin, "SEC Seeks to Ease Section 404 Burden," *Accounting Today,* November 27, 2006, 1, 33.

9. Mary-Kathryn Zachary, "Another Blonde, Another Situation, Another Outcome," *Supervision,* November 2003, 21.

10. 29 CFR 1604.11(a).

11. Jan Bohren, "Six Myths of Sexual Harassment," *Management Review,* May 1993, 61–63.

12. Ellyn Spragins, Maggie Overfelt, and Julie Sloane, "Dangerous Liaisons," *Fortune Small Business,* February 2004, 62.

13. Ibid.

14. Stuart Dawson, John Breen, and Lata Satyen, "The Ethical Outlook of Micro Business Operators," *Journal of Small Business Management,* October 2002, 302–313.

15. Jeannine Reilly, "Charitable Works Sells at a Number of Firms," *Arizona Daily Star,* September 11, 2000, 16.

16. "Social Capitalists," *Fast Company,* April 2010, www.fast company.com.

17. Anne Murphy, "The Seven (Almost) Deadly Sins of High-Minded Entrepreneurs," *Inc.,* July 1994, 47–51.

18. Steve Bates, "Survey: Business Ethics Improved during Recession," November 24, 2009, www.shrm.org.

19. Ferrell and Fraedrich, 10.

20. Josh Spiro, "How to Write a Code of Ethics for Business," *Inc.,* February 24, 2010, www.inc.com.

21. Heledd Jenkins, "A 'Business Opportunity' Model of Corporate Social Resopnsibility for Small- and Meduim-sized Entreprises," *Business Ethics: A European Review,* January 2009, 21–36.

22. Karen Klein, "A Push for 'Ethical Innovation,'" *BusinessWeek Online,* February 3, 2010, 12.

23. George Manning and Kent Curtis, *Ethics at Work: Fire in a Dark World* (Cincinnati: South-Western Publishing) 77.

24. David H. Freeman, "The Technoethics Trap," *Inc.,* March 2006, 69–70.

25. Scott Baca and Erin Nickerson, "Ethical Problems, Conflicts, and Beliefs of Small Business Professionals," *Journal of Business Ethics,* November 2000, 15–24.

26. Richard Kaleba, "Strategic Planning: Getting from Here to There," *Healthcare Financial Management,* November 2006, 74–78.

27. Charles Toftoy and Joydeep Chatterjee, "Mission Statements and Small Business," *Business Strategy Review,* November 2004, 41–44.

28. Tom Peters, *Thriving on Chaos* (New York: Knopf, 1988).

29. Robert Linnman and John Stanton, "Mining for Niches," *Business Horizons,* May/June 1992, 43–51.

30. Fran Tarkenton and Joseph Boyett, "Taking Care of Business," *Entrepreneur,* February 1990, 18–23.

31. Anil Gupta, "Business-Unit Strategy: Managing the Single Business," in *The Portable MBA in Strategy,* edited by Liam Fahey and Robert Randall (New York: Wiley, 1994), 84–107.

32. Michael Porter, "Know Your Place," *Inc.,* September 1991, 90–95.

33. David Cravens and Shannon Shipp, "Market-Driven Strategies for Competitive Advantage," *Business Horizons,* January/February 1991, 90–95.

34. Porter, op cit.

35. Robert Hartley, *Marketing Mistakes,* 9th ed. (New York: Wiley, 2004), 2.

36. Brad Stone and Leslie Cauley, "For Apple, Expectations Run High," *The New York Times,* March 29, 2010, B1.

37. David Menzies, "The Museum of Mortal Marketing Mistakes," *Marketing,* April 23, 2001, 9.

38. O. C. Ferrell and Michail Hartline, *Marketing Strategy,* 5th ed (Mason, Ohio: Cengage, 2011).

39. Fred Amofa Yamoah, "Sources of Competitive Advantage: Differential and Catalytic Dimensions," *Journal of American Academy of Business,* March 2004, 223–227.

40. Michael Porter, *Competitive Advantage: Creating and Sustaining Superior Performance* (New York: Free Press, 1985).

41. Jenny McCune, "In the Shadow of Wal-Mart," *Management Review,* December 1994, 10–16.

42. Stephanie Clifford, "It's 2006! Whatchagonna Do About It?— You Can't Out Wal-Mart Wal-Mart," *Inc.,* January 2006, 84.

43. Aodheen O'Donnell, Audrey Gilmore, David Carson, and Darryl Cummins, "Competitive Advantage in Small to Medium-Sized Enterprises," *Journal of Strategic Marketing,* October 2002, 205–223.

44. Oren Harari, "The Secret Competitive Advantage," *Management Review,* January 1994, 45–47.

45. M. A. Lyles, J. S. Baird, J. B. Orris, and D. E. Kuratko, "Formalized Planning in Small Business Increasing Strategic Choices," *Journal of Small Business Management,* April 1993, 38–50.

46. Ferrell and Hartline, op cit.

Chapter 4

1. William A. Sahlman, *How to Write a Great Business Plan* (Cambridge, MA: Harvard Business School Press, 2008).

2. Norm Brodsky and Bo Burlingham, *The Knack: How Street-Smart Entrepreneurs Learn to Handle Whatever Comes Up* (Boston, MA: Portfolio Hardcover, 2008).

3. Mark Henrichs, "Do You Really Need a Business Plan?" *Entrepreneur,* March 2008, 104.

4. Nicole Gull, "Plan B (and C and D and …)," *Inc.,* March 2004, 40.

5. Rosalind Resnick, "Are Business Plans a Waste of Time?" *Wall Street Journal,* www.wsj.com, March 24, 2010.

6. Andrea Cooper, "Serial Starter," *Entrepreneur,* April 2008, 28.

7. *Guidelines for Entrepreneurs,* pamphlet, Colorado Small Business Development Center.

8. Michael V. Copeland, "How to Make Your Business Plan the Perfect Pitch," *Business 2.0,* September 2005, 88.

9. Kayte Vanscoy, "Unconventional Wisdom," *Smart Business for the New Economy,* October 2000, 78–88.

10. William Sahlman, "How to Write a Great Business Plan," *Harvard Business Review,* July/August 1997, 101.

11. Nicole Gull, "Plan B (and C and D …)," *Inc.,* March 2004, 40.

12. Ralph Alterowitz and Jon Zonderman, "Financing Your New or Growing Business," *Entrepreneur Mentor Series* (Irvine, CA: Entrepreneur Press, 2002), 113.

13. Guy Kawasaki, *The Art of the Start* (Boston, MA: Portfolio Hardcover, 2004), 188; Scott Clark, "Great Business Plan Is Key to Raising Venture Capital," *Portland Business Journal,* March 31, 2000, 36; and Dee Power and Brian Hill, "Six Critical Business Plan Mistakes," *Business Horizons,* July/August 2003, 83.

Chapter 5

1. Thomas Dicke, *Franchising in America: The Development of a Business Method,* 1840–1990 (Chapel Hill, NC: University of North Carolina Press, 1992), 13.

2. PricewaterhouseCoopers, "2010 Franchise Business Economic Outlook," study for the International Franchise Association Educational Foundation, 2009, www.franchise.org/edufound/researchef.asp.

3. "Franchise How-to Guide," www.entrepreneur.com/franzone/guide, accessed May 2010.

4. www.franchisehandbook.com.

5. U.S. Department of Commerce.

6. Andrew Caffey, "Hey, Get a Clue!" *Entrepreneur,* January 2004, 112–118.

7. Mark Seibert, "How to Franchise Your Business," *Entrepreneur,* May 2010, www.entrepreneur.com.

8. Ibid.

9. David Kaufmann, "The Big Bang," *Entrepreneur,* January 2004, 86.

10. Ibid.

11. International Franchise Association "Key Legal Questions to Ask," www.franchise.org, accessed May 2010.

12. "Best in Show," *Business Franchise,* May 2010, 15–16.

13. Thomas Dambrine, "Less Is More," *Franchising World,* April 2004, 14.

14. Derek Sankey, "U.S. Franchisors Eye Canada for Growth, First Stage of International Expansion Strategies, *The Gazette* (Montreal), November 17, 2009, B6.

15. June Wang Zhiqiong, Mingxia Zhu, and Andrew Terry, "The Development of Franchising in China," *Journal of Marketing Channels,* 2008, 167–184.

Chapter 6

1. Ed Pendarvis, "What to Consider Before Buying a Business," *Entrepreneur*, August 1, 2008, www.entrepreneur.com/startingabusiness/startupbasics.
2. Bill Broocke, "Buy—Don't Start—Your Own Business," *Entrepreneur Magazine Online*, March 22, 2004, www.entrepreneur.com/your_business.
3. Darren Dahl, "How to Find a Business to Buy," *Inc.*, March 11, 2009, www.inc.com.
4. "How to Buy a Business," *Entrepreneur* Starting a Business series, www.entrepreneur.com/startingabusiness/startupbasics/article/79638.html.
5. Ryan McCarthy, "Valuation Guide 2009—A Buyer's Market," *Inc.*, June 2009, 82–90.
6. Peter McFarlane and Deborah Gold, "Do the Due," *CAmagazine*, August 2003, 37–42.
7. "For Business Buyers and Sellers: A Guide," http://www.businessesforsale.com/us, accessed May 28, 2010.
8. Dalia Fahmy, "Deal Jitters?" *Inc.*, October 2005, 48.
9. Bill Broocke, "Buy—Don't Start—Your Own Business," *Entrepreneur Magazine Online,* March 22, 2004, www.entrepreneur.com/your_business.
10. RMA Annual Statement Studies (Philadelphia: Robert Morris Associates).
11. Ryan McCarthy, "Valuation Guide 2009 – A Buyer's Market," *Inc.*, June 2009, 82–90.
12. Fred Steingold, *Legal Guide for Starting and Running a Small Business,* 11th ed. (Berkeley, CA: Nolo Press, 2009), 9–17.
13. John Johansen, "How to Buy or Sell a Business," *Small Business Administration Management Aid, No. 2.029* (Washington, DC: U.S. Small Business Administration, Office of Business Development).
14. Lola Sim, "What Is It Worth?" *CAmagazine*, April 2010, 39–41.
15. Ryan McCarthy, "Valuation Guide 2009 – A Buyer's Market," *Inc.*, June 2009, 82–90.
16. Danielle Fugazy, "Throwing Darts," *Mergers & Acquisitions: The Dealmakers Journal*, November 2009, 42–61.
17. Darren Dahl, "How to Close the Deal When Buying a Business, *Inc.*, March 11, 2009, www.inc.com/guides/buy_biz.
18. Family Firm Institute, "Family Business in the U.S.," www.ffi.org.
19. David Port, "The Family Business: Making Sure Both Stay Intact," *Entrepreneur*, March 24, 2010, www.entrepreneur.com/management/familybusiness.
20. Christine Lagorio, "How to Run a Family Business," *Inc.*, March 5, 2010, www.inc.com/guides/running-family-business.
21. Ibid.
22. Matthew Fogel, "A More Perfect Business," *Inc.,* August 2003, 44.
23. Jason Kwiatkowski, "Six Essential Elements of an Effective Exit," *CMA Management,* April 2010, 16–17.
24. Christine Lagorio, "How to Run a Family Business," *Inc.*, March 5, 2010, www.inc.com/guides/running-family-business.
25. David Bork, "If Family Members Ask for a Job," *Nation's Business*, April 1992, 50–52.

Chapter 7

1. John Tozzi, "Revisiting the Face of 'Necessity Entrepreneurship," *Bloomberg Businessweek*, March 9, 2010, www.businessweek.com.
2. "The State of Small Business Report," *The Small Business Success Index*, August 2009, www.growsmartbusiness.com.
3. "The Ultimate Business Tune-Up," *Inc.*, February 2009, 70–77.
4. "E-Stats," U.S. Census Bureau, May 27, 2010, www.census.gov/estats.
5. Nada Hashmi and Jean Pierre Nshimyimana, "From Campus to Commerce," *Fast Company,* April 2010, 51–56.
6. Amy Choi, "Entrepreneurs Who Thrive on Risky Business," *Bloomberg Businessweek*, December 4, 2009, www.businessweek.com.
7. Max Chafkin, "The Case, and the Plan, for the Virtual Company," *Inc.*, April 2010, 62–73.
8. Jason Daley, "The Entrepreneur Economy," *Entrepreneur,* December 2009, 53–57.
9. American Association of Home-Based Businesses, www.aahbb.com.
10. "Homepreneurs: A Vital Economic Force," *The Small Business Success Index,* October 2009, www.growsmartbusiness.com.
11. Maya Payne Smart, "There's No Place Like Home," *Black Enterprise,* February 2009, 79–81.
12. David Bangs and Linda Pinson, *The Real World Entrepreneur Field Guide* (Chicago: Upstart Publishing, 1999), 474.
13. John Tozzi, "The Rise of the Homepreneur," *Bloomberg Businessweek*, October 23, 2009, www.businessweek.com.
14. "Homepreneurs: A Vital Economic Force," *The Small Business Success Index*, October 2009, www.growsmartbusiness.com.
15. Sari Crevin, "How to Grow a $1 Million Side Biz," *Women-Entrepreneur*, May 17, 2010, www.womenentrepreneur.com.
16. All data on *Inc.* 500 companies come from *Inc. Special Issue*, September 2009.
17. Jason Snell, "Test Driving the iPad," *Macworld*, June 2010; Diane Goldner, "Ahead of the Curve," *The Wall Street Journal Small Business Edition,* May 22, 1995, R16.
18. John Case, "Why 20 Million of You Can't Be Wrong," *Inc.,* April 2004, 102.
19. "The State of Small Business Report," *The Small Business Success Index,* January 2010, www.growsmartbusiness.com.
20. David Kopcso, Robert Ronstady, and William Rybolt, "The Corridor Principle: Independent

Entrepreneurs versus Corporate Entrepreneurs," in *Frontiers of Entrepreneurship Research* (Wellesley, MA: Babson College, 1987), 259–271.

21. Tim Blumerntritt, "Does Small and Mature Have to Mean Dull? Defying the Ho-Hum at SMEs," *Journal of Business Strategy*, 25(1), 2004, 27–33.

22. Phaedra Hise, "Where Great Business Ideas Come From," *Inc.*, September 1993, 59–60.

23. Neil A. Martin, "Invincible Spirit," *Success,* October 1994, 24.

24. Michael Treacy and Fred Wiesema, "How Market Leaders Keep Their Edge," *Fortune,* February 6, 1995, 88–98.

25. David Freedman, "The Secret of Their Success," *Inc.*, April 2010, 92–93.

Chapter 8

1. David Wallace, "Sarbanes-Oxley Sets Standard for Small Companies," *Rural Telecommunications*, March/April 2004, 68–73.

2. "Bye, Bye, SOX?", *Information Management*, Vol. 44, Issue 2, March/April 2010, p. 11. Sarbanes-Oxley Section 404 A Guide for Small Business, retrieved from www.sec.gov, May 30, 2010.

3. Karen Klein, "Where Accounting Isn't a Dirty Word," *Business Week Online*, July 30, 2002, www.businessweek.com.

4. Carly Bohach, "CPAs Get Credit Flowing to Cash-Starved SMBs," *Accounting Today*, December 14, 2009, 30.

5. Kathy Yakal, "Do You Need Accounting Software?" *PC Magazine*, March 2009, 1.

6. "Making Sense of Your Dollars," *Home Office Computing*, November 1993, 79–88.

7. Allen Beck, "The Cash Method for Small Business," *Tax Advisor*, October 2002, 623.

8. For an overview of FASB, see Craig Schneider, "Who Rules Accounting?" *CFO*, August 2003, 34–40.

9. Rick Telberg, "Mom and Pop Shops," *Journal of Accountancy*, July 2003, 49.

10. Lyn Fraser and Aileen Ormiston, *Understanding Financial Statements*, 9th ed (Upper Saddle River, NJ: Prentice Hall, 2010).

11. Jay Finegan, "Corporate Cost Cutters," *Inc.*, August 1995, 28.

12. C. J. Prince, "Catch Your Cash," *Entrepreneur*, June 2004, 57.

13. Antoinette Alexander, "CPA Firms Answer SOS Calls from Small Biz Clients," *Accounting Today*, December 14, 2009, 26–29.

14. New York Society of CPAs, "10 Ways to Improve Small Business Cash Flow," *Journal of Accountancy*, March 2000, 14.

15. Daniel Akst, "The Survival of the Fittest," *Fortune Small Business*, February 2002, 77.

16. Richard Flynn, "Keep Cash Flowing with Trade Terms," *Progressive Grocer*, March 2010, 50.

Chapter 9

1. Gar Thompson, "Factoring the Opportunities," *Equities*, Winter 2009, 40–41.

2. Ed Van den Berg, "Outsourcing for SMEs," *Credit Management*, June 2009, 24–25.

3. Amanda Watt, "The Money-Go-Round," *NZ Business*, October 1, 2009, 58.

4. Henry Wichmann, Kenneth Abramowics, and Charles Sparks, "SBA Helps Businesses Think Big," *Strategic Finance*, October 2008, 45–49.

5. Crystal Detamore-Rodman, "Truth and Consequences," *Entrepreneur's Be Your Own Boss,* October 2003.

6. Wichmann, Abramowics, and Sparks.

7. Crystal Detamore-Rodman, "The Burden of Borrowing," *Entrepreneur*, April 2003, 53.

8. "Impress Loan Officers," *Entrepreneur*, June 2009, 24.

9. Carol Tice, "Can Your Business Still Land a Loan?" *Entrepreneur*, August 2009, 62.

10. Deborah Cohen, "A Line or a Loan?" *ABA Journal*, November 2009, 24.

11. "How Will a Credit Crunch Affect Small Business Finance?" *FRBSF Economic Newsletter*, March 6, 2009, number 2009-09.

12. Catherine Curan, "Factoring Gets a Face-lift," *Inc.*, February 2006, 38–40.

13. www.sba.gov.

14. www.sba.gov/financing.

15. www.sba.gov.

16. Emily Flitter, "SBA Widens 504 Loan Program," *American Banker*, June 25, 2009.

17. "How to Court a Banker," *Entrepreneur*, February 2010, 47.

18. Jeffrey Moses, "Five Steps to Take When a Lender Says No," National Federation of Independent Business, May 27, 2003, www.nfib.com.

19. "How to Ask Family and Friends to Invest," NFIB.com, retrieved June 6, 2010.

20. Issie Lapowsky, "Zumba Turns Dancers into Entrepreneurs," *Inc.*, May 26, 2010, www.inc.com /articles/2010/05/zumba-fitness -entrepreneurs.html.

21. "Angels: A Funding Source for Firms with Limited Revenue," National Federation of Independent Business, April 22, 2003, www.nfib.com.

22. "Venture Capital," Entrepreneur .com, retrieved June 6, 2010.

23. Marc Ashton, "Suck It Up!" *Finweek*, May 2010, 45.

24. Jeremy Lovell, "In the Land of the Loch Ness Monster, 'Sea Snake' Prepares to Ride the Waves," *Scientific American*, June 3, 2010, www.scientificamerican.com /article.cfm?id=sea-snake-prepares -to-ride-waves.

25. Dalia Fahmy, "Want Power and Money?" *Inc.*, April 2006, 44–46.

26. Kasey Wehrum, "Angel Investing 2009," *Inc.*, January/February 2009, 83–89.

27. Jeffry A. Timmons and Stephen Spinelli, *New Venture Creation*, 7th ed. (Homewood, IL: Irwin, 2009).

Chapter 10

1. 8 USC 1324 (a).
2. 8 USC 1324 (B) (g) (2) (B) (iv) (I)–(III).
3. NFIB Small Business Legal Center "2010 Immigration Update" and "Rule Mandating E-Verify for Federal Contractors Now in Effect," www.nfib.com. Accessed June 22, 2010.
4. "Does Small Biz Want Immigration Reform?" *Business Week Online,* May 10, 2006, 4.
5. Ibid., 19–20.
6. Justin Martin and Matthew Phan, "Why the Disabilities Act Exasperates Entrepreneurs," *Fortune Small Business,* May 2005, 52–54.
7. "Federal Employment Law Handbook: Indispensable Guide to Small Business," NFIB Legal Foundation, June 2010, www.nfib .com.
8. Carolyn Brown, "Healthcare Reform Affects Small Business Owners," *Black Enterprise,* June 2010, 88.
9. "Are Your WC Policies Ready for the Next Decade?" *Safety Compliance Letter,* March 1, 2010, 7.
10. 29 USC 651 (b).
11. Fred Steingold, *Legal Guide for Starting and Running a Small Business,* 7th ed. (Berkeley, CA: Nolo, 2003), 15/30.
12. Alan Zeiger, "Bankruptcy Can Also Mean Smart Investment," *Management Review,* May 1992, 36–39.
13. Rozane DeLaurell and Robert Rouse, "The Bankruptcy Reform Act of 2005: A New Landscape," *The CPA Journal,* November 2006, 36–39.
14. "Constitution of the United States of America," Article I, Section 8, in Daniel J. Boorstin, *An American Primer* (Chicago: University of Chicago Press, 1966), 94.
15. David Pressman, *Patent It Yourself,* 14th ed. (Berkeley, CA: Nolo Press, 2009).
16. Ibid.
17. Gabe Fried, "IP: A Reason to Exist," *Mergers & Acquisitions,* June 2010, 42–43.
18. Tim Studt, "Protecting Your Intellectual Property," *R&D Magazine,* April 2004, 22.
19. James Nurton, "WIPO Launches Online Filing Option for PCT," *Managing Intellectual Property,* March 2004, 59.

Chapter 11

1. Peter Drucker, *People and Performance: The Best of Peter Drucker on Management* (New York: Harper's College Press, 1977), 90.
2. Ibid., 91.
3. Jennifer Wang, "*Entrepreneur's* Annual 100 Brilliant Ideas—Reboot, Sonny," *Entrepreneur,* June 2010, 68.
4. Sean Moffitt, "In Pursuit of Purple Cows," *Marketing,* May 17, 2004, 25.
5. Seth Godin, *Purple Cow: Transform Your Business by Being Remarkable* (New York: Portfolio, 2002).
6. N. Craig Smith, Minette Drumwright, and Mary Gentile, "The New Marketing Myopia," *Journal of Public Policy and Marketing,* 29(1), Spring 2010, 4–11.
7. Holly O'Neill, "Back-to-Basics Best for Small Companies," *Marketing News,* March 27, 2000, 12.
8. Kevin Clancy and Peter Krieg, "Getting a Grip," *Marketing Management,* Spring 2010, 19–23.
9. Michele Marchetti, "Advanced Planning," *Sales and Marketing Management,* May 2004, 16.
10. Sally Dibb and Lyndon Simkin, "Implementation Rules to Bridge the Theory/Practice Divide in Market Segmentation," *Journal of Marketing Management,* 25(3-4), 2009, 375–396.
11. J. Ford Laumer Jr., James Harris, and Hugh Guffey Jr., "Learning about Your Market," *Management Aid No. 4.019,* Small Business Administration Management Assistance Office.
12. Ibid.
13. *Inc.* Guidebook "How To: Keep Tabs on the Competition," *Inc.,* April 2010, 53–56.
14. *Inc.* Guidebook "How To: Use Online Tools for Customer Surveys," *Inc.,* July 2010, www.inc .com/guides/2010/07/how-to-use -online-tools-for-customer-surveys .html.
15. "60-Second Guide to Conducting Market Research," *Entrepreneur .com,* accessed August 1, 2010.
16. *Inc.* Guidebook "How To: Know Your Customer Better," *Inc.,* September 2009, 65–68.
17. American Marketing Association, www.marketingpower.com.
18. Ron Belanger, "Using Search Engine Marketing as Market Research Tool," *B to B,* March 8, 2004, 20.
19. U.S. Small Business Administration, www.sba.gov/starting _business/marketing/research.html.
20. Robert Kiara, "For Smaller, Independent Brands, How Tweet It Is," *MediaWeek,* February 8, 2010, 4–5.
21. Oren Harrari, "The Tarpit of Marketing Research," *Management Review,* March 1994, 42–44.
22. Gary Hamel and C. K. Prahalad, "Seeing the Future First," *Fortune,* September 5, 1994, 70.

Chapter 12

1. Tucker Marion and Rifat Sipahi, "Early-Stage Firms and Delay-Based Inventory Control Using Decision-Making Tableaux," *International Journal of Production Research,* September 2010, 5497–5521.
2. Mark Malyszko, "Foul-Weather Gear: Strategies for Facing the Storm," *Accounting Today,* December 14, 2009, 31.
3. Danielle Sacks, "The Gore-Tex of Guitar Strings," *Fast Company,* December 2003, 46.
4. Benjamin Klein and Joshua Wright, "The Economics of Slotting Contracts," *Journal of Law & Economics,* August 2007, 421–454.

5. Mahesh Gupta, Chahal Hardeep, and Ramji Sharma, "Improving the Weakest Link: A TOC-Based Framework for Small Business," *Total Quality Management*, August 2010, 863–883.

6. Christopher J. Sandvig and Lori Coakley, "Best Practices in Small Firm Diversification," *Business Horizons,* May/June 1998, 33–40.

7. Kenneth Hein and Michael Applebaum, "Get a Grip … Packaging Dept.," *Brandweek,* May 17, 2004, 50.

8. "Ice Cream Collaboration Comes Up Trumps," *Printing World,* April 29, 2004, 24–25.

9. C. J. Prince, "Balancing Act," *Entrepreneur*, July 2007, 48.

10. "Stay in Control," *Wearable's,* June 2009, 24.

11. Stephanie Gruner, "The Smart Vendor-Audit Checklist," *Inc.,* April 1995, 93–95.

12. Herrian Wong, "Buy Low, Pile High," *Fortune Small Business,* September 2008, 83.

13. Deborah Moss, "Guitar Hero," *Fortune Small Business,* May 2009, 86–87.

14. Zahir Irni, Angappa Gunaesekaran, and Yogesh Dwivedi, "Radio Frequency Identification (RFID) Research Trends and Framework," *International Journal of Production Research*, May 2010, 2485–2511.

15. Miguel Bustillo, "Wal-Mart Tadio Tags to Track Clothing," *Wall Street Journal*, July 23, 2010, A1, A14.

16. Robert Kaplan, "Linking Strategy to Operations," *Journal of Accountancy*, October 2008, 80–84.

17. M. Gupta and D. Snyder, "Comparing TOC with MRP and JIT: A Literature Review." *International Journal of Production Research*, July 2009, 3705–3739.

Chapter 13

1. "2009 Survey of Buying Power," *Sales and Marketing Management,* October/November 2009.

2. "Full Release and Tables," bea.gov, retrieved August 15, 2010.

3. Jason Del Rey, "Top Small Business Cities and a Twitter Challenge," inc.com, October 19, 2009.

4. Gary Brockway and W. Blynn Mangold, "The Sales Conversion Index: A Method for Analyzing Small Business Market Opportunities," *Journal of Small Business Management,* April 1988, 38–48.

5. "Market Segments Explained," www.mybestsegments.com, retrieved August 16, 2010.

6. Peter Vanden Bos, "How to Choose the Right Location," inc.com, May 24, 2010.

7. Alaina Abbott, "When the World Is Your Office," entrepreneur.com, August 27, 2010.

8. "How a Business Incubator Can Help Your Startup," nifb.com, retrieved August 17, 2010.

9. "Americans with Disabilities Act ADA Guide for Small Businesses," U.S. Small Business Administration Office of Entrepreneurial Development and the U.S. Department of Justice Civil Rights Division, www.ada.gov, retrieved August 21, 2010.

10. Tamara Schweitzer, "How to Make a Million in Your Pajamas," inc.com, January 8, 2010.

11. Lois Goodell, "How to Evaluate Your Office Leasing Strategy," inc.com, June 23, 2010; "How to Get a Good Deal," inc.com, May 1, 2009; and "Leasing Checklist," sba.gov, retrieved August 25, 2010.

12. Ibid.

Chapter 14

1. Kim Gordon, "5 Ways to Outshine the Competition," entrepreneur.com, June 15, 2010.

2. Geoffrey Colvin, "Pricing Power Ain't What It Used to Be," *Fortune,* September 15, 2003, 52.

3. Kusum Ailawadi, Jie Zhang, Aradhna Krishna, and Michael Kruger, "When Walmart Enters: How Incumbent Retailers React and How This Affects Their Sales Outcomes," *Journal of Marketing Research*, August 2010.

4. William Baumol and Alan Blinder, *Microconomics: Principles & Policy*, (Mason, OH: Cengage Learning, 2009), 7–116.

5. Norm Brodsky, "The Capacity Trap II," *Inc.,* December 2003, 55–57.

6. Catriona Knapp, "What Does It Mean to Really Breakeven?" *NZ Business*, May 2010.

7. Elizabeth Wasserman, "How to Price Your Products," inc.com, February 1, 2010.

8. Grant Cardone, "Get Past the Budget Roadblock," entrepreneur.com, October 29, 2009.

9. Marco Bertini and Luc Wathieu, "How to Stop Customers from Fixating on Price," *Harvard Business Review*, May 2010.

10. Ibid.

11. Ibid.

12. "The Survey of Consumer Payment Choice," Federal Reserve Bank of Boston, www.creditcards.com, retrieved August 7, 2010.

13. "Debit or Credit: Which Card to Use?" *Consumer Reports*, July 2010.

14. Will Wade and Steve Bills, "An 'IN' with Generation Y," *American Banker*, October 29, 2009.

15. "Credit Card Transaction Fees for Small Businesses," smallbusiness.yahoo.com, retrieved August 7, 2010.

16. Gwen Moran, "How to Get Paid," entrepreneur.com, July 16, 2010.

17. "Cash Management," *Controller's Report*, July 2010.

18. Jason Meyers, "The Future Has Been Delivered to Your Mailbox," entrepreneur.com, June 21, 2010.

19. Hayli Morrison, "Not Your Father's Phone Book," entrepreneur.com, February 16, 2010.

20. "Ad-Spending Totals by Medium," *Advertising Age*, June 23, 2008.

21. Paul Hawkin, *Growing a Business* (New York: Simon & Schuster, 1987), 33.

22. Susan Gunelius, "The Red Pen Rule for Marketing Copy," entrepreneur.com, August 4, 2010.
23. Alex Salkever, "We're Now in the Era of Sales 2.0," *Inc.,* December 2006, 110–115.
24. Stephanie Clifford, "Goodbye Retainers," *Inc.,* October 2006, 35–38.
25. Jennifer Wang, "Smoke the Competition," *Entrepreneur,* February 2010.
26. Heather Kelly, "Customize Your Calling Cards," *Macworld,* April 2009.

Chapter 15

1. Johnathan Calof, "The Impact of Size on Internationalization," *Journal of Small Business Management,* October 1993, 60–69.
2. "May 2010 Trade Gap Is $42.3 Billion," www.bea.gov, retrieved July 30, 2010.
3. "A Profile of U.S. Exporting Companies, 2007–2008," *U.S. Census Bureau News,* April 13, 2010.
4. "Small & Medium-Sized Exporting Companies: Statistical Overview, 2008," www.trade.gov, retrieved July 30, 2010.
5. "Take Your Business Global," www.sba.gov, retrieved July 30, 2010.
6. "Export Questionnaire," www.export.gov, Retrieved July 30, 2010.
7. "How to Take Your Company Global," www.entrepreneur.com, December 11, 2003.
8. Kenneth Kale, "Going Global?" *Fortune Small Business,* March 2001, 98–103.
9. Robert Kaplan, David Norton, and Bjarne Rugelsjoen, "Managing Alliances with the Balanced Scorecard," *Harvard Business Review,* January/February 2010.
10. Paul Beamish and Nathaniel Lupton, "Managing Joint Ventures," *Academy of Management Perspectives,* May 2009.
11. Michelle Goodman, "Becoming an Entrepreneurial Expat," www.entrepreneur.com, July 14, 2010.

12. "Take Your Business Global: A Small Business Guide to Exporting," www.sba.gov, retrieved July 31, 2010.
13. Gene Goudy "Ex-Im Bank," *Business Credit,* November/December 2003, 48–50.
14. "SBA 2010 Small Business Exporter of the Year," www.sba.gov, retrieved July 30, 2010.
15. Clark Cassell, *The World Is Your Market: The Export Guide for Small Business* (Washington, DC: Braddock Communications, 1990) 25.
16. Diana Ransom, "6 Ways to Ease Exporting," www.entrepreneur.com, February 10, 2010.
17. Small Business Administration, *Breaking into the Trade Game: A Small Business Guide to Exporting,* 3rd ed. (2006), www.sba.gov/international, 86.
18. Emily Maltby, "China Currency Impacts Entrepreneurs", www.wsj.com, May 24, 2010.
19. Diana Ransom, "Obama's Math: More Exports Equals More Jobs," www.smartmoney.com, February 4, 2010.
20. "Understand and Heed Cultural Differences," *Business America,* September 1992, 30–31.
21. Gail Dutton, "Everything Starts with Culture," *World Trade,* December 2009.
22. Mansour Javidan, Mary Teagarden, and David Bowen, "Managing Yourself Making It Overseas," *Harvard Business Review,* April 2010.
23. Mie-Yun Lee, "Decipher Tricky Documents with a Translation Service," *Entrepreneur,* January 28, 2002.
24. "Etiquette," *Japan Country Review,* 2010.
25. Kevin Walsh, "How to Negotiate European-Style," *Journal of European Business,* July/August 1993, 45–47.
26. Ellen Neuborne, "Bridging the Cultural Gap," *Sales and Marketing Management,* July 2003, 22.
27. Matthew Hill, "Better Understanding? Better Business,"

Engineering and Technology, October 10, 2009.
28. Pat McGovern, "How to Be a Local, Anywhere," *Inc.,* April 2007, 113–114.
29. Ibid., 114.
30. "North American Free Trade Agreement (NAFTA)," www.ustr.gov/trade-agreements, retrieved August 1, 2010.
31. Leslie Brokaw, "ISO 9000: Making the Grade," *Inc.,* June 1993, 98–99.
32. "The WTO," www.wto.org, retrieved August 1, 2010.
33. "About ISO," www.iso.org, retrieved August 1, 2010.
34. Linda Tischler, "Partners in Time," *Fast Company,* March 2010.

Chapter 16

1. Henry Mintzberg, "The Manager's Job: Folklore and Fact," *Harvard Business Review,* March/April 1990, 163–176.
2. James Clawson, *Level Three Leadership,* (Upper Saddle River, NJ: Prentice-Hall/Pearson, 2009), 452–453.
3. Liz Welch, "How I Did It: Jerry Murrell, Five Guys Burgers and Fries," Inc.com, April 1, 2010.
4. Joel Spolsky, "Does Slow Growth Equal Slow Death?" Inc.com, November 1, 2009.
5. Neil C. Churchill and Virginia Lewis, "The Five Stages of Small Business Growth," *Harvard Business Review,* May/June 1983, 30–50.
6. Marla Tabaka, "Six Figure Solopreneurs: The Common Link," Inc.com, June 22, 2010.
7. Catherine Clifford, "Why a $14/Hour Employee Costs $20," CNNMoney.com, March 26, 2010.
8. Mark Henricks, "Charting Your Business Timeline," *Entrepreneur,* July 28, 2009.
9. Jonathan Goldhill, "Take 9 Steps to Teach Managers to Think Like Owners," Landscapemanagement.net, October 2009.
10. John Tozzi, "Are You Losing Control of Your Business?" *BusinessWeek Online,* February 19, 2008.

11. "10 Tips for Planning Your Exit," Inc.com, June 23, 2010.

12. Norm Brodsky, "Norm Brodsky on Exit Strategies," Inc.com, April 1, 2010.

13. Rick Johnson, "Family Succession—The Final Challenge," *Supply House Times*, January 2010.

14. Jason Daley, "Creating a Culture of Excellence," Entrepreneur.com, March 2010.

15. Genevieve Capowski, "Anatomy of a Leader: Where Are the Leaders of Tomorrow?" *Management Review*, March 1994, 10–17.

16. Warren Bennis, "Why Leaders Can't Lead," *Training and Development Journal*, April 1989, 35–39.

17. "Leading vs. Managing," sba.gov, retrieved July 2, 2010.

18. Joshua Brown, "Leadership vs Management," *Supply House Times*, January 2010.

19. "Leadership Trends for 2010," BusinessWeek Online, February 17, 2010.

20. Peter Barron Stark and Jane Flaherty, "How to Negotiate," *Training and Development*, June 2004, 52–55.

21. James Clawson, *Level Three Leadership*, (Upper Saddle River, NJ: Prentice Hall/Pearson, 2009).

22. Michael Donaldson, *Negotiating for Dummies* (Hoboken, NJ: Wiley and Sons Publishing, 2007).

23. Steve Thurlow, "Making the Most of the Win-Win Window," *Engineering and Technology*, May 23, 2009.

24. Sam Wilson, "Think like a Negotiator," *Entrepreneur*, May 2009.

25. "How to Build Your Management Team," Inc.com, April 1, 2010.

26. Wayne Turk, "Effective Delegation," *Defense AT&L*, September/October 2009.

27. Hank Darlington, "Motivation Can Make You Better," *Supply House Times*, September 2009.

28. Michael Cronin, "Motivation the Old Fashioned Way," *Inc.*, November 1994, 134.

29. Elizabeth Cudney, "Ask the Expert," *Industrial Engineer*, February 2009.

30. Norm Brodsky, "The Most Important Resource," *Inc.*, February 2006, 61–62.

31. "25 Ways to Reward Employees without Spending a Dime," HRWorld.com, July 13, 2010.

32. J. Tol Broome, Jr., "Avoiding the Inside Job," *Playthings*, March 2010.

33. Daniel Finley, "Master Time," *Advisor Today*, January 2010.

34. Alison Stein Wellner, "The Time Trap," *Inc.*, June 2004, 42.

35. Judith Ross, "Monitor and Manage Your Stress Level for Top Performance," *Harvard Management Update*, April 2009.

36. Jonathon Halbesleben, "Addressing Stress and Beating Burnout," *Healthcare Executive*, March/April 2010.

37. Bonnie Miller, "Hard Times," *Public Management*, April 2010.

38. Mark Henricks, "Put Me In!" *Entrepreneur*, June 2007, 85–86.

Chapter 17

1. Karen Klein, "When to Make Your First Hire," BusinessWeek Online, December 17, 2008.

2. Reece, Brandt and Howie, *Effective Human Relations: Interpersonal and Organizational Applications*, 11th Edition (Mason, OH: South-Western/Cengage Learning, 2011).

3. Retention Management and Metrics, NOBSCOT Corporation, September 2005–August 2006, retrieved, July 15, 2010.

4. Christine Lagorio, "How to Write a Job Description," Inc.com, April 1, 2010.

5. "Writing Effective Job Descriptions," sba.gov, retrieved July 15, 2010.

6. "Title VII of the Civil Rights Act of 1964," eeoc.gov, retrieved July 16, 2010.

7. "How to Find and Hire Good People," Inc.com, May 1, 2008.

8. Mark Hendricks, "You Know Who?" *Entrepreneur*, May 2007, 89–90.

9. Peter F. Drucker, "How to Save the Family Business," *Wall Street Journal*, August 19, 1994, A10.

10. Amy Barrett, "It's a Small (Business) World," *Business Week*, April 17, 1995, 96–101.

11. Joel Spolsky, "There's a Better Way to Find and Hire the Very Best Employees," *Inc.*, May 2007, 81–82.

12. Joan Lloyd, "Tips to Avoid Costly Mistakes," *The Receivables Report*, February 2010.

13. Griggs v. Duke Power Company, 401 U.S. 424 (1971).

14. Bridget Styers and Kenneth Shultz, "Perceived Reasonableness of Employment Testing Accommodations for Person with Disabilities," *Public Personnel Management*, Fall 2009.

15. John S. O'Connor and Carlene Warner, "How to Develop Physical Capacity Standards," *Personnel Journal New Product News Supplement*, May 1996, 8, 10.

16. Ibid.

17. "Keeping Employees Drug-Free," *EHST Today*, November 2009.

18. Jess Blumberg and Stephanie Clifford, "The Science of Hiring—Choose Your Weapon," *Inc.*, August 2006, 90–98.

19. Louis Basso and Barry Shorten, "Growing PEO Industry Continues to Raise Its Standards," *The CPA Journal*, October 2009.

20. Donald Caruth, Gail Caruth, and Stephanie Haden, "Getting off to a Good Start," *Industrial Management*, March 2010.

21. Frank Hammel, "Tackling Turnover," *Supermarket Business*, October 1995, 103–108.

22. Bruno Neal, "Stop Following Joe Around," *T+D*, January 2010.

23. "Employer Costs for Employee Compensation," Bureau of Labor Statistics Economic News Release, June 19, 2009.

24. "Ask Inc.," *Inc.*, June 2006, 61.

25. Francine Kizner, "Secrets of Superstar Employers," Entrepreneur.com, March 06, 2008.

26. Rebecca Hastings, "Job Security and Benefits Most Valued by Employees," shrm.org, June 28, 2010.

27. "EBRI Databook on Employee Benefits," EBRI.org, retrieved July 18, 2010.

28. "The Basics of Employee Benefits," *Entrepreneur Magazine Online*, 2007, www.entrepreneur.com/humanresources/compensationandbenefits/article80158.html.

29. Christine Lagorio, "How to Make Health Care Reform Work for Your Business," Inc.com, April 21, 2010.

30. Burton Goldfield, "A Cost-Effective Retirement Benefits Package," Entrepreneur.com, April 27, 2010.

31. "The Basics of Employee Benefits," Entrepreneur.com, retrieved July 19, 2010.

32. Fran Durekas, "Companies and Their Employees Realize Value through Employee-Sponsored Child Care Benefits," *Employee Benefit Plan Review*, October 2009.

33. "Employers' Rising Stake in Elder Care," *HR Magazine*, December 2009.

34. "Program Perspectives on Health Benefits," U.S. Bureau of Labor Statistics, October 2008; "Program Perspectives on Retirement Benefits," U.S. Bureau of Labor Statistics, March 2009.

35. "Frequently Asked Questions," Uniformed Services Employment and Reemployment Rights Act of 1994, esgr.org, retrieved July 19, 2010.

36. Josh Spiro, "How to Write a Warning Letter for Employee Conduct," Inc.com, May 5, 2010.

37. "Essentials of an Employee Handbook," How-To section, www.allbusiness.com.

38. "How to Conduct Annual Employee Reviews," Inc.com, December 1, 2008.

39. Material adapted from D. Day, "Training 101: Help for Discipline Dodgers," *Training and Development,* May 1993, 19–22.

Chapter 18

1. "Facts about Manufacturing, Did You Know ..." National Association of Manufacturers, www.nam.org, retrieved July 24, 2010.

2. Shawn Tully, "You'll Never Guess Who Really Makes ..." *Fortune*, October 3, 1994, 124–128.

3. Chia-Chi Chang and Hui-Yun Chen, "I Want Products My Own Way, But Which Way?" *Cyber Psychology and Behavior*, February 2009.

4. Otis Port, "Custom-Made, Direct from the Planet," *Business Week, 21st-Century Capitalism Edition*, November 18, 1994, 158–159.

5. Jean Thilmany, "Democratization of Manufacturing," *Mechanical Engineering*, April 2009.

6. Erhan Mergen and William Stevenson, "Can't Fix Service Quality? Read This," *Total Quality Management*, June 2009.

7. Michael Chernousov, Susan Fleck, and John Glaser, "Productivity Trends in Business Cycles: A Visual Essay," *Monthly Labor Review*, June 2009.

8. "A Common Sense Look at Productivity," www.nfib.com, retrieved June 29, 2010.

9. Andrew Okely, "Managing the Downturn: Now Is the Time for Excellence in Operations," *Engineering and Mining Journal*, March 2009.

10. Dan Gutman, "Always in Touch," *Success*, March 1995, 54.

11. "Office Ergonomics: Not the Same as in a Plant," *Industry Week*, December 5, 1994, 37.

12. Tom Kelley, "Ergonomics Health and Wealth," *Beverage World*, October 2009.

13. Michael Barrier, "You Have a Purpose in Life," *Nation's Business*, September 1995, 13–14.

14. Benjamin Harris, "How to Build a Successful, Sustainable Ergonomic Team," *EHS Today*, July 2010.

15. Bill Eureka, "The Process of Quality," *Material Handling Management*, May 2010.

16. Gwen Fontenot, Alicia Gresham, and Ravi Behara, "Using Six Sigma to Measure and Improve Customer Service," Proceedings of 1994 National Small Business Consulting Conference, San Antonio Small Business Institute Director's Association, San Antonio, 1994, 298–304.

17. Ibid., 303.

18. Karman Moosa and Ali Sajid, "Critical Analysis of Six Sigma Implementation," *Total Quality Management*, July 2010.

19. Katerina Gotzamani, "Results of an Empirical Investigation on the Anticipated Improvement Areas of the ISO 9000:2000 Standard," *Total Quality Management*, June 2010.

20. John Welch, "Timeless Principles," *Executive Excellence*, February 2001, 3–4; Fred R. McFadden, "Six-Sigma Quality Programs," *Quality Progress*, June 1993, 37–42; Gwen Fontenot, Ravi Behara, and Alicia Gresham, "Six Sigma in Customer Satisfaction," *Quality Progress*, December 1994, 73–76; Jim Carbone and Thomas Pearson, "Measure for Six Sigma Success," February 2001, 36–40.

21. *Breaking into the Trade Game: A Small Business Guide to Exporting* (Washington, D.C.: U.S. Small Business Administration, 1994), 94.

22. Ronald Henkoff, "The Hot New Seal of Quality," *Fortune*, June 28, 1993, 116–117.

23. Michael Barrier and Amy Zuckerman, "Quality Standards the World Agrees On," *Nation's Business*, May 1994, 71–72.

24. Henkoff, "The Hot New Seal," 116.

25. Steven Ashley, "Nondestructive Evaluation with Laser Ultrasound," *Mechanical Engineering*, October 1994, 63–66.

26. Alan Brown, "Manufacturing at the Crossroads," *Mechanical Engineering*, June 2010.

Index